S0-DQW-578

BEHAVIORAL INSIGHTS FOR SUPERVISION

BEHAVIORAL INSIGHTS FOR SUPERVISION

Ralph W. Reber
Supervisor, Training and Development
Champion Papers
Pasadena, Texas

Gloria E. Terry
Training and Education Coordinator
Memorial Hospital System,
Houston, Texas

PRENTICE-HALL, INC., Englewood Cliffs, New Jersey

Library of Congress Cataloging in Publication Data

Reber, Ralph W
Behavioral insights for supervision.

Includes bibliographical references.
1. Psychology, Industrial. 2. Supervision of employees. I. Terry, Gloria E. joint author. II. Title. [DNLM: 1. Behavior. 2. Psychology, Industrial. T58 R291b 1974]
HF5548.8.R38 658.3'02 73-19662
ISBN 0-13-073163-3

Printed in the United States of America

10 9 8 7 6 5

Prentice-Hall International, Inc., *London*
Prentice-Hall of Australia, Pty. Ltd., *Sydney*
Prentice-Hall of Canada, Ltd., *Toronto*
Prentice-Hall of India Private Limited, *New Delhi*
Prentice-Hall of Japan, Inc., *Tokyo*

CONTENTS

PREFACE

Today's management and most of our society accept the fact that many, if not most, of our problems exist because *people* are involved in every activity. Whereas our past concern was with obtaining and maintaining the machines of our technological age, we are now faced with coping with the human element—that which we have either ignored or have attempted to mold to fit the demands of our ever-increasing mechanistic world. Consequently, in the most lavish retail shopping center, the contemporary skyscraper office, the modern hospital, and the sophisticated space-age industry are found perplexing situations; productivity is down, absenteeism and turnover rates are up, and supervisors are bemoaning that "people just don't want to work like they used to." Dealing with "people problems" consumes more and more of management's time.

Educational institutions and company training programs share the responsibility of helping managers and potential managers develop their skills for effectively managing people. Attempting to meet this responsibility, this volume provides the background information necessary to understanding the behavior of individuals and groups at work. Inasmuch as there are few rules that explain the actions of people, this book presents material as basic ideas and concepts that the supervisor can use within the framework of his abilities and the characteristics of his organization and its people. Short "how-to" lists and supervisory rules are avoided. Rather, a combination of textual material explaining the basic concepts of human behavior under varying circumstances, carefully selected articles containing "must know" information, and realistic cases that provide an opportunity to explore supervisory problems and strengthen decision-making are provided. It is hoped that the experience gained in reading, discussing, and analyzing these materials will bring about real understanding of oneself, employees, the job itself, and the influence of the supervisor in maintaining a productive work climate.

Working in a community college located just outside the nation's sixth largest city, surrounded by one of the world's largest industrial complexes, and being a scant ten miles from the Manned Spacecraft Center offers a unique experience. Both day and night classes boast an array of students seeking ways to better their supervisory performance or hoping to enter the supervisory portals—managers of multi-million dollar industrial plants, department managers of retail stores, eighteen-year-old management hopefuls, small business managers, and blocks of middle-management and supervisory personnel from space-oriented industries—all sharing a common goal: a desire to be more effective in their jobs. Trying to help these students of varying backgrounds meet their objective provided the authors with many memorable experiences.

Foremost among our problems was finding materials that could be easily understood, yet lead to understanding of behavioral concepts and the application of these concepts to real world situations. Never being quite successful in finding the combination of exactly what we wanted, we proceeded to develop our own materials—first a few cases, exercises, and articles. With encouragement and appreciation from our students and our publisher's representative, Weldon Rackley, we started on what was to become the long road to this publication.

In writing this book, one objective remained uppermost in our efforts: No matter how complex the concept may be, explain it in such a way that understanding and useful application are possible. We believe the result of this goal to be a not-too-lengthy book written in easy-to-read, down-to-earth language. Examples of practical application of the concepts presented are sprinkled liberally throughout the text. Our second objective has been the complete involvement of the student in the learning process. The cases are examples of real problems faced by real supervisors. These cases, along with role-playing exercises and discussion questions, provide the participation opportunities essential to emotional and intellectual acceptance of behavioral concepts.

In selecting readings for the text, two main criteria were used: (1) the reading selection must contain essential information; and (2) it must be readable. Experience in using the reading selections has shown that, in addition to meeting these criteria, they are also quite successful in stimulating individual thinking and group discussion.

The materials have been used with students representing different levels of management and a wide variety of businesses and industries—both in the college classroom and in in-house business training programs. From these students have come the most useful suggestions for writing and content changes, stimulating case information, and the encouragement to finish this work. We are proud to express our sincere appreciation to them.

The infinite patience of our Prentice-Hall editor, Cary Baker, will, we hope, be rewarded. Certainly, we also appreciate the generosity of the authors of articles and journal editors who have given us permission to include various readings and exercises in this volume.

Special appreciation is given to the Bureau of Business Practice, 24 Rope Ferry Road, Waterford, Connecticut 06385, whose material and cartoons are used extensively throughout this text.

R.W.R
G.E.T.

BEHAVIORAL INSIGHTS FOR SUPERVISION

1

UTILIZING HUMAN RESOURCES—TODAY'S SUPERVISORY CHALLENGE

"If my supervisors knew half as much about the people they supervise as they do about machinery, processes, and products, we could double our rate of production." The speaker was the superintendent of a large metal fabricating plant. His statement points out an interesting fact: We have progressed more in adapting ourselves to our machines than to each other.

We have amply demonstrated in this country an ability to cope with scientific and technological problems of immense difficulty. Vast amounts of knowledge have been acquired in such areas as space technology, nuclear energy, and medicine. Our mastery of machinery has been proven repeatedly; yet we have not made comparable progress in learning about human behavior.

What happens when there is a malfunction in the office copier, a computer, a drill press, or a lathe? As a rule, the supervisor gets together with his employees or the appropriate maintenance personnel, studies the problem, has it corrected, and gets things under way again. But should anything go wrong with an employee—or worse, with a group of employees—many supervisors don't know where to begin to find out the cause of the problem. They are poorly equipped to deal with the human problems existing in their organization.

Yet despite the dynamic changes going on in the business and industrial scene, the basic responsibility of today's supervisor remains the same. **The supervisor's fundamental responsibility in any organization is to get work done through people.** In order to reach required objectives effectively, he coordinates the activities of others rather than performing operations himself. **He is dependent on people for the particular results he wants.**

People are an organization's most valuable resource. Which is costlier to replace—people or machines? Assume, for instance, that you're the manager of a multimillion-dollar plant with thousands of employees. Which would be more difficult to replace, the plant or the organization? Should you have a highly skilled worker who has been trained to use intricate tools, which could you replace in less time and at smaller cost—the employee or his tools?

The efficiency of an organization depends more on the human being than on any other resource. In the final analysis, machines and all other resources of an organization produce nothing without the human element to activate and control them.

Why, then, is there often an apparent difficulty in understanding and dealing with the human elements of supervision? In addition to being the most *important* resource, the human being is by far the most *complex* resource utilized by an organization. The supervisor is faced with different problems in dealing with people than in dealing with other resources. Unlike machinery and materials, the human resource is not standardized and does not respond to the use of impersonal formulas and techniques. Human beings vary in intelligence, attitudes, emotions, needs, and skills—all of which determine, to a greater extent than we sometimes realize, the quality of their performance on the job. Possibly because the subject seems so complex, many supervisors simply choose to ignore the problem, preferring instead to concentrate on inanimate objects—machines, facts, or figures—while letting people take care of themselves. (Unfortunately, they seldom do!)

The problem often seems to be particularly acute among individuals with scientific or technical backgrounds and training who are moved from technical jobs to supervisory or managerial positions requiring that they work with groups of people. Their experience has usually placed a premium on precision, predictability, and control. Conditioned by the predictability of the laws of the physical sciences, the technically oriented person may expect the people in his work group to act in a similar rational, predictable fashion. This expectation can often lead to an explosive situation; people do not act like machines, and they seldom appreciate being treated as such.

THE BEHAVIORAL APPROACH TO SUPERVISION

In getting things done through people, the supervisor must understand and influence the behavior of these people, both as individuals and as members of groups. **Just as we must study a machine before we can know how to operate and maintain it, we have to study the employee as a human being before we can hope to get him to cooperate, work willingly, and maintain a high performance level.** To do this effectively requires at least an elementary knowledge of human behavior.

As our society and employees acquire higher levels of education, more affluence, and different attitudes and values, the need for understanding human behavior and approaches for solving human problems within organizations has become greater than ever before. Fortunately, increasing efforts and successes have been made in unlocking the mysteries of people at work in organizations. A growing body of knowledge—resting on the principle that **where**

people work together as groups in order to accomplish objectives, people should understand people—is available to assist the supervisor in developing good relations with subordinates and in getting the most from them. This body of knowledge has drawn heavily on the disciplines of *psychology, sociology,* and *anthropology,* collectively known as the *behavioral sciences.* Although the relationships among people at work cannot be the exclusive sphere of any one of these sciences, psychology—the study of human behavior—has probably played the biggest role in influencing management thought.

Both the quantity and quality of research findings in the field have been steadily improving through the years, and the newest concepts represent a considerable spin-off from the appealingly simple notions on which the pioneers of the behavioral management school originally concentrated. A common thread running throughout a large majority of behavioral science research findings seems to be: "You are not utilizing human resources at their full capacity. You are appealing to lower-level needs to motivate employees, rather than higher social and psychological needs. You have designed jobs to take advantage of only the minimum performance human beings are capable of."

This research has necessarily upset and torn down many traditional and cherished notions about the direction and motivation of people and has developed new approaches that offer considerable promise for the fulfillment of both individual and organizational goals. As is the case with many new ideas and changing methods, these findings have frequently been resisted or ignored by those who could profit the most from them—namely, managers. After all, American enterprise has enjoyed tremendous success through the years using the older methods of management, and "you can't quarrel with success!"

Recently, however, there has been a renewed interest in human behavior and motivation, sparked by the fact that the traditional concepts about the management of people are simply not working in all situations as they once did. Thus, management personnel are increasingly interested in the discoveries of behavioral science that can be applied to the task of improving productivity and profit in their organizations.[1]

Unfortunately, we are presently dealing with an *inexact science*—if indeed, as many argue, it can even be referred to as a science. The known elements of human behavior in organizations are only a small portion of what is yet to be learned. No one has been able to define and apply very basic principles of human behavior comparable to the precise relationships of the physical sciences. Certainly we know a great deal about human behavior, but the application of our knowledge is less direct and far more difficult to understand.

The probability appears to be high that much more knowledge will become available and management of the future will possess more factual

[1] Saul W. Gellerman, "Business Discovers Behavioral Science," *Guidelines for Better Management, Vol. II.* (Houston: Hydrocarbon Processing/Gulf Publishing Company, 1969), pp. 142-144.

information for coping with human problems. Yet we can't wait for the perfecting of behavioral management science before attempting to apply it. It may well be another hundred years (if ever) before we have reliable knowledge of precisely what causes people's behavior. In the meantime, supervisors must supervise. Just as a physician must treat a cancer patient to the best of his present ability without waiting for complete scientific understanding, so should a supervisor take advantage of what is currently known about human behavior. Although our knowledge admittedly may be inexact and incomplete, enough is known to make examination of the subject quite fruitful. As John P. Grier said, "Just because a problem is large is no excuse for not applying intelligence to it!"

FUNDAMENTAL SKILLS OF MANAGEMENT

Supervision, as a subject for study, should not concern itself exclusively with human behavior, as this topic constitutes only a part (although an integral part) of the total field, just as algebra is merely a part of the total field of mathematics. In other words, skill in dealing with human behavior is not the only responsibility a supervisor has, nor is it the only knowledge he needs.

In Reading Selection 1, Robert Katz indicates that a successful manager at any level in an organization must exhibit three distinct yet related skills in carrying out his job effectively: (1) *technical skill,* (2) *human skill,* and (3) *conceptual skill.* Katz suggests that the relative importance of these three skills varies with the level of management; a rough approximation of this relationship is shown in Figure 1-1.

FIGURE 1-1. Relative Importance of Skills at Different Management Levels

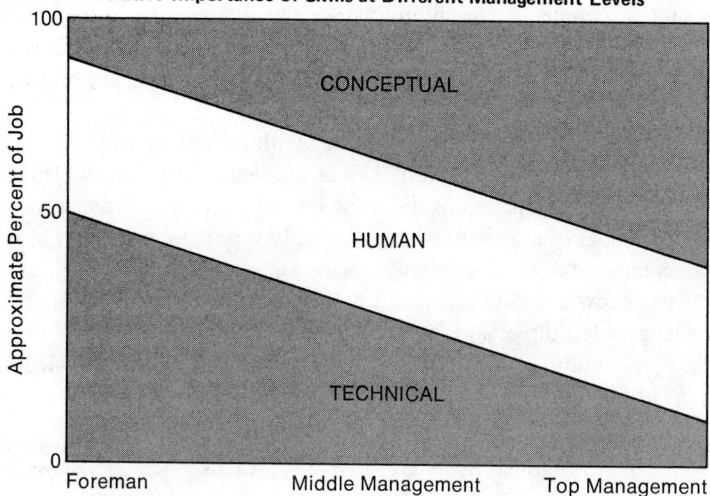

Technical skill refers to a person's proficiency in, and understanding of, the specific techniques, processes, methods, and procedures required in carrying out a particular job. The skills of accountants, computer programmers, engineers, typists, nurses, scientists, and mechanics are examples.

Human skill is the ability to interact effectively with people. It includes the ability to motivate and influence others toward achieving stated goals, to win cooperation and develop an effective work team, to communicate intelligibly, and to gain acceptance of change.

Conceptual skill enables a manager to visualize the organization as an integrated whole, recognizing how a change in any one part affects all the other parts. For example, a top-level manager of a manufacturing firm must sense the total interrelationships of such diverse functions as engineering, production, sales, advertising, finance, and personnel. Of course, this process also extends to viewing the organization within the external environments that it is influenced by and, in turn, influences—the *social, economic,* and *governmental environments.*

In summary, technical skill is basically concerned with *things,* while human skill deals with *people,* and conceptual skill deals with *ideas.*

Technical skill is obviously the most important skill at the operative level. However, as shown in Figure 1-1, as a person is promoted above the operative level and given leadership responsibilities, the need for this skill becomes proportionately less. Why? Because he can depend on his *subordinates'* technical skills. (Remember that a supervisor gets work done through others.) At higher levels of management, technical skill is often almost nonexistent.

Human skill, in contrast, seems to be a basic requirement for managers at *any* organizational level. However, it would appear to be most important at lower and middle levels where the number of direct contacts with subordinates is usually greatest.

As he moves up the organizational hierarchy, the manager's need for conceptual skill increases rapidly. He must increasingly deal with long-range planning decisions that are outside the realm of any particular group within the company; such decisions must take into account the *overall* relationships between various other groups, both within and outside the organization.

Although we certainly cannot discount the importance of either technical knowledge and proficiency or an ability to see the organization as a whole, this book is devoted to the analysis and development of human skills—those involved in getting work done through others. Success in this area appears to be the most difficult challenge today's supervisor faces.

THE UNIQUE ROLE OF THE SUPERVISOR

Supervisory functions, of course, occur at all management levels in an organization. Therefore, much, if not all, of what we will discuss in the following chapters is also applicable to individuals in higher management positions. However, this book is primarily focused on the increasingly important role of the first-line supervisor in an organization.

As the first level of management above the rank-and-file operative worker, the first-line supervisor occupies a unique and strategic position in the hierarchy of management. His importance to both the success of the company's management and to the satisfaction of his workers is frequently understated. The first-line supervisor is responsible for directly supervising the largest portion of an organization's work force. As both management's representative at the point of immediate contact with workers and the worker's point of contact with management, he is a vital link in the organization's downward and upward flow of communication. All the policies and plans of top management flow through the supervisor to be implemented by the employees who work under his direction.

The supervisor's high number of contacts with employees in his work group and his effect on the satisfaction they derive from their jobs makes him a key individual in the lives of the people who work for him. They look to him as a source of information, guidance, counsel, decisions, approval, and so on. To the rank-and-file worker, the supervisor is "management."

Occupying the unique position as the only member of the management team who primarily supervises *nonmanagement* personnel, the supervisor is faced with pressures and problems different from other levels of management. For example, he usually has minimal voice in top-management decision-making and has little control over the organizational climate in which he must function. Not infrequently he is used as a scapegoat for a top management that doesn't manage efficiently! Often he may feel like a sitting duck for unions that whittle away at his power in the work group. The union may, in fact, be more influential in hiring, making promotions, increasing salaries, and firing than he is.

"What a day! A problem a minute—what's next?"

Often referred to as the "man-in-the-middle," he is constantly confronted by pressures from two groups—his subordinates and higher management. To be accepted and respected by both groups, the supervisor must be a *member* of both groups, dividing his attention and loyalty between them. Each group has its own set of expectations concerning the supervisor's role; frequently these expectations are in conflict. Management usually expects the supervisor to put priority on higher production, lower costs, and exacting schedules. Subordinates, on the other hand, expect the supervisor to be understanding of their work problems, fair, helpful, and friendly and to represent them in their dealings with higher management. Each group expects the supervisor to be loyal to it—to "be on its side." Needless to say, living up to both sets of expectations is seldom an easy task, but it is one to which the supervisor must become accustomed. When the goals and expectations of subordinates and management are in direct conflict, it is usually up to the supervisor to work out a fair compromise.

THE SUPERVISOR'S CHANGING ENVIRONMENT

The supervisor of today and tomorrow will be increasingly confronted by an environment of change and complexity. Change is creating new kinds of problems that challenge the human skills of even the best of supervisors and compel them to take advantage of the newer concepts of management.

The Changing Values of Today's Work Force

Many segments of our society are experiencing a transition from traditional values and attitudes, which is especially noticeable in the youth of the work force. Today's general trend against "the establishment" is marked by growing opposition to the authority of traditional institutions and values. Young people are less inclined to defer automatically to their elders simply because they are more experienced. With the lessening acceptance of the status quo by this generation, there seems to be an almost constant state of dissatisfaction with what *is,* relative to what *could be.* The degree of idealism expressed by youth is unmatched by that of any previous generation.

If the supervisor is to lead this new breed of employee effectively, he must recognize the presence of such changes and deal with them on a rational basis, regardless of whether he personally views the changes in values and attitudes as good or bad. Already, more than 50 per cent of our population is under 25, and the U. S. Bureau of Labor Statistics has predicted that by 1975 there will be a 30 per cent increase in the 15 to 24 age group and a 40 per cent increase in the 25 to 35 bracket. Clearly, the elders of our tribe are becoming outnumbered![2]

[2]Eugene Koprowski, "The Generation Gap, From Both Sides Now," *Management of Personnel Quarterly,* Winter, 1969.

Increased Mobility and Independence of the Work Force

Simple reward-and-punishment systems that were hallmarks of earlier concepts of motivation were largely based on the fact that employees could not easily switch jobs. Because workers feared losing their jobs, the threat of dismissal could always be used to move them to action; even after the Depression years were over, this fear persisted.

Not so today. Because alternative employment opportunities are more readily available, today's worker is relatively more mobile and independent than the typical worker of only a generation ago. Having never experienced a real depression, younger workers are more likely to view losing a job as a temporary inconvenience than as a tragedy. Security is almost taken for granted by many.[3]

Desire for Meaningful Work

The youth of the work force are also entering their first jobs with a much higher level of educational attainment than any previous generation. The days of the elementary-school dropout are about over. Typically, the more education a worker has, the less satisfied he is with routine, unchallenging work. The boredom tolerance of today's young workers is usually quite low. They want and expect meaningful work. Seldom looking for the routine, "safe" jobs that prior generations were often attracted to, they expect to be more involved in responsible work as soon as possible. They actively seek more participation in decisions affecting them—to help control their work, not to be controlled by it. They expect their supervisors to recognize and utilize whatever skills, talents, and knowledge they have to offer. Fulfilling these expectations is often a large order for the supervisor, to say the least. In lieu of such meaningful work, however, young workers seem quite willing to "job hop" until they find a place that offers more satisfying opportunities.[4]

Adjusting to a Changing Environment

Such additional changes as the justified demands of racial minorities and women for equal employment opportunities, hard-core employment programs, increasing government action in all sectors of business, and the revitalized power of labor unions—not to mention the technological advances that must be kept up with—add still more complexity to the supervisor's task, leaving him little time

[3]R. Douglas Brynildsen and T. A. Wickes, "Agents of Change," *Automation,* October, 1970, pp. 36-40.

[4]Koprowski, *loc. cit.*

for complacency. Given this dynamic state of affairs, today's supervisor is required to know much more about how to get things done through people than ever before.

Adjusting to this changing environment is not always easy, particularly since it involves for many supervisors an entirely new philosophy of managing people. For instance, it is increasingly evident that a supervisor can no longer simply "make" his subordinates perform in a desired manner. In the past, authoritarian means—threats of job loss, demotion, wage reduction, verbal abuse, and so on—may have been quite effective in forcing people to work harder. Most current behavioral research, however, indicates that strict reliance on autocratic supervision and various forms of negative motivation have little relevance in today's work environment. The supervisor currently must rely heavily on the *voluntary cooperation* of his employees to accomplish the goals of his work group. Power alone can no longer generate the initiative and resourcefulness needed for such cooperation.[5]

REQUIREMENTS FOR THE DEVELOPMENT OF HUMAN SKILLS

Many qualities and attitudes contribute to the improvement of a supervisor's effectiveness in interpersonal relationships with his employees. Although it would be difficult to make a complete list of such qualities and attitudes, we can easily single out five that the supervisor definitely needs to cultivate: *empathy, self-awareness, acceptance of individual differences, perceptual awareness,* and *an employee orientation.* Their importance will become increasingly apparent as we examine the various topics of the following chapters.

Empathy

Empathy, perhaps the key requirement for the development of effective human skills, can be defined as **the ability to project oneself imaginatively into the thoughts, feelings, and probable reactions of another person while maintaining an objective viewpoint**. Put a bit more simply, it is the capacity to put yourself in the shoes of the other person and look at things from his point of view.

Note that empathy does not imply *agreement* with another's feelings; it does imply *respect* for those feelings. Nor is empathy a case of asking, "What would I do if I were in your position?"; any one of us would bring quite different attitudes and experiences to a particular position. We are truly empathic only when we can sense how the other person feels and reacts to a given situation.

[5]Robert C. Miljus, "Effective Leadership and the Motivation of Human Resources," *Personnel Journal,* January, 1970, pp. 36-40.

It is also necessary to make a clear distinction between empathy and *sympathy*, for the two are quite different. In sympathy, you come to feel the same way as the one for whom you sympathize; you allow yourself to become emotionally involved. If you empathize, however, you know how the other person feels, but you don't allow these feelings to determine your own. Empathy requires an *objective attitude* toward the behavior of another. The viewpoint needed by the supervisor is similar to that of a physician. A good physician understands his patient's feelings and needs—that is, he is empathic. But his emotional involvement with the patient must be limited if he is to make an objective diagnosis.[6]

Empathy requires the development of an instinctive awareness of what people want and need. Most truly successful salesmen exhibit this talent. Empathy enables them to intuitively sense the prospect's *true*—as opposed to *stated*—needs. They then can direct their sales presentations to demonstrating how their product can satisfy these needs.

In practice, the ability to empathize well is largely a result of sincere and continued effort by the supervisor. It is seldom easy, especially when you are attempting to understand the attitudes and needs of someone who has a completely different background from your own, as is often the case in relationships with subordinates. Yet, improvement in this ability should be a continuing goal of every supervisor. If the supervisor is to effectively motivate and communicate with his subordinates, this capacity to project himself into another person's position is indispensable; it is a foundation for working more effectively with people. Armed with a full understanding of the worker's feelings, the supervisor's decisions and actions are invariably more effective.

Self-Awareness

Along with empathy, a prerequisite for increasing your effectiveness in dealing with people (a primary objective of this book) is *a basic awareness of yourself as an individual.* Developing this awareness necessitates a serious examination of your own personality and behavior patterns, often an initially painful process when it results in recognition of the need to change.

Knowledge of the particular impact you have on the behavior of others is of utmost importance in your job as a supervisor. You should know your own inclinations toward, say, taking action hastily, being brusque with employees who don't understand your instructions the first time, and so on. Only through an awareness of your own particular prejudices, values, weaknesses, habits, and

[6]William H. Newman, Charles E. Summer, and E. Kirby Warren, *The Process of Management* (second edition; Englewood Cliffs, New Jersey: Prentice-Hall, Inc., 1967), pp. 587-588.

the impression you make on others can you begin to make any changes in your attitudes and behavior that would be beneficial to you and your work group.

Acceptance of Individual Differences

As a supervisor, your job would be much easier if all your subordinates had the same ability, personality, interests, intelligence, and needs. All you would need would be a magic formula applicable to every individual in your work group. Minimal human skill would be needed, and the long-sought "1-2-3 approach" for dealing with employees would be a practical reality.

The sad truth is, though, that there are no "sure-fire" formulas or "tried-and-true" techniques for dealing with people. Each individual employee is a unique personality, having been exposed in his lifetime to different people, things, situations, and learning experiences that make him different from every other person in the world.

Therefore, the supervisor must try to understand and work with the distinct personalities and behavior patterns of each of his subordinates. This, of course, reinforces the desirability of knowing each employee individually and attempting to understand his unique attitudes, values, aspirations, habits, fears, frustrations, and so on. Only through understanding these factors can the supervisor deal with the *variable*—not the fixed—responses of each individual.

Nevertheless, while it is true that all people differ from one another, there are also many things that we all have in common. For example, as we shall see in Chapter 2, there are general needs to which the supervisor can appeal in his motivational efforts and many effective ways of dealing with subordinates in groups.

Perceptual Awareness

Closely related to our acceptance of individual differences, but worthy of separate mention, is the topic of *perception.* By perception we simply mean the way each individual views his world. It should be obvious to anyone who reflects on the matter that **no two people perceive the same event or situation in exactly the same way.** Each person will perceive the event based on his own needs, his expectations, his interests, and his background and previous experiences. In this sense, then, each of us does not react to the world as it is but as we *interpret* it; in other words, it is our "mental image" that counts, not objective reality. That a person sees and interprets everything through his own "rose-colored glasses" is a well known (and quite true!) cliché.

As a simple example of perceptual differences, let us consider the common house cat, Felix Domesticus. To an old maid, the cat may be perceived as a sorry substitute for the suitor that eluded her; to a bird-lover, the cat is a menace to the world; to the householder, he may be a walking mousetrap. To another cat, he is a fellow creature. To the dog, the cat is something to be chased and eradicated. To a mouse, the cat is a monster to be feared. Each has a different perception of the cat that determines his reactions.[7]

In the same way, a job requiring overtime for your department may be perceived quite differently by various people. The salesman may view it as a way of impressing his customers with prompt service; you, the supervisor, may see it as a drain on your overtime budget; your employees may perceive it as extra money on payday or as an imposition that interferes with a bowling game that evening.

As we shall fully discuss in Chapter 7, awareness of perceptual differences is particularly important in all attempts at communication. What one person may consider a simple to-the-point statement or action may be interpreted by another in a completely different light. For example, there is the old story of a supervisor who told one of his production employees, "How about cleaning up this mess around here?" A couple of hours later, the supervisor found the employee just returning to the job he had previously been working on, that of preparing a component that was a rush order for a special customer. His machine and the entire area surrounding it, however, were spotlessly shining. Upon asking the man why the job was not completed on schedule, the employee replied, "I've been cleaning up like you said. See, I've cleaned the entire machine." The supervisor was slightly aghast. The mess he had referred to was only a small oil spill on the floor, an obvious safety hazard. He had, of course, meant for the man to wipe up the spill and return to his work. Who was to blame in this situation—the employee or the supervisor? Each interpreted the statement in his own way and *assumed* that the other person understood it as he did.

Again—at the risk of being repetitious—no two people will perceive the same event in exactly the same way; employees will react to the supervisor, the organization, and their jobs according to their individual perceptions. Awareness and acceptance of this fundamental fact of life can go a long way toward alleviating potential conflicts and misunderstandings and helping the supervisor more easily influence and understand human behavior.

An Employee Orientation

It was once commonly believed that by giving constant close attention to production activities, results of high quantity and quality would naturally follow. Contrary to this belief, there is consistent evidence that *employee-oriented* supervisors generally achieve somewhat higher production than their solely *productivity-oriented* counterparts.

[7] John Douglas, George A. Field, and Lawrence X. Tarpey, *Human Behavior in Marketing* (Columbus, Ohio: Charles E. Merrill Books, Inc., 1967), pp. 24-25.

What is an employee-oriented supervisor? He is one who expects a good deal from his employees but is also considerate of them as human beings and concerned about developing them on the job and helping them with their problems. He is personally interested in his people, viewing them as worthwhile individuals deserving of his attention. He views responsibility and initiative as things that must be developed rather than commanded.

Note that there is not an inherent dichotomy between an employee orientation and high levels of production. An employee-oriented supervisor is not unconcerned about production; certainly, a supervisor must produce or else he ceases to be a supervisor. In fact, the most successful supervisors seem to be those who combine both orientations, giving more emphasis to employee orientation.

Why can an employee orientation usually achieve better results? From what we have already discussed in this chapter, the answer should be apparent. Although we must recognize that production of either goods or services and their resultant profits are our primary objectives and necessary for the survival of any type of organization, these objectives are attained principally through human endeavor and cooperation. Employees achieve the productivity. As a supervisor, you can achieve your particular goals only through your employees. If they are not motivated to produce, production won't occur.[8]

Thus, **our goal should be sustained, superior productivity from satisfied, motivated employees.** High job satisfaction and better job performance usually go hand in hand, just as low output, frequent mistakes, accidents, grievances, high turnover, and absenteeism are factors often related to low job satisfaction.

MUTUALITY OF INTERESTS

Running throughout our discussions in the following chapters is this general premise: **As we help satisfy an employee's personal goals, he will be more ready to cooperate in achieving the company's goals.** Put another way, our objective is to integrate people into a work environment in such a way that the goals of both the organization and its individual members can be successfully realized. Through close cooperation, the individual and the organization can shape each other in order that both may achieve their objectives. Under such an ideal condition, the individual and the company may realize a *mutuality of interests;* in other words, the employee prospers as the organization becomes more productive and efficient; and, in turn, the organization gains higher performance as the individual's respective needs are reasonably satisfied.

Obviously, this is a far from easy goal to accomplish, and it is doubtful that a supervisor acting *alone* can completely achieve such a climate in his

[8]Keith Davis, *Human Relations at Work* (third edition; New York: McGraw-Hill Book Company, 1967), pp. 107-108.

particular work group. There must be an *overall* atmosphere of mutual trust, respect, and confidence among all levels of management and all subordinates. Nevertheless, the authors view such an environment as a very worthwhile goal for any organization to constantly strive for. It is especially worthwhile when one considers that, if employees' goals and objectives are in conflict with those of the organization, conflicts, friction, and frustrations are likely to result.

The general philosophy expressed in this book assumes that the individual employee is the most important unit in any organization. Therefore, only to the extent that his particular economic, social, and psychological needs are reasonably satisfied is the organization able to make the best use of its human resources.

NO "COOKBOOK APPROACH" TO SUPERVISION

Many supervisors would undoubtedly like a collection of simple, concise, proven rules that they might use in effectively dealing with their subordinates, thus providing an appropriate solution to any problem. But, contrary to the advice of hundreds of "how-to-do-it" human relations books and the prescriptions of many "quick-and-easy" seminars, such a set of rules unfortunately does not exist, and probably never will. Because every person and every situation is different, there can seldom be any common cure-alls that can be applied to ensure high motivation and morale.

We mention this not to discourage you, but to emphasize again that human beings are a most complex phenomenon and that there is simply no one method or collection of methods that will solve all problems in dealing with them. Within wide limits, virtually all sorts of supervisory methods and techniques are successful in certain situations and unsuccessful in others. Therefore, no "cookbook approach" to human behavior problems will be offered in this book. To do so would be naive and frustrating to you as a supervisor when you discover that such universal panaceas aren't always successful.

We have tried to stress throughout the book that there are no simple "off-the-shelf" formulas that a supervisor can apply without first carefully diagnosing the particular situation and its problems as they exist at a specific point in time. An approach that works extremely well in one situation may not work or may be less effective in a different situation, even though the problems may appear to be very similar. **A unique supervisor who deals with unique subordinates in a unique set of circumstances must usually seek unique solutions.**[9]

So, as you examine the material in the following chapters, keep in mind that many of the concepts presented are at best general rules. As with all generalizations, there are always exceptions!

[9] Aaron Q. Sartain and Alton W. Baker, *The Supervisor and His Job* (second edition; New York: McGraw-Hill Book Company, 1972), pp. 153-155.

IN PERSPECTIVE—
THE NATURE AND NURTURE OF HUMAN RESOURCES

With the rapid expansion of technology in recent years—larger factories, more elaborate machines, automation, more complex processes—the fact that any business, service, or industrial organization is composed first and foremost of people has frequently been obscured. With the problem obscure no longer, a new awareness and philosophy of management has been slowly emerging. Its basis is the recognition that people with the ability to think and plan are far more valuable assets than any machines or materials can ever be.

People, we reiterate, are the chief resources of a supervisor, the primary raw material with which he works. The efficiency with which any organization can be operated depends to a considerable extent on how effectively its human resources can be utilized and developed. Consequently, it is becoming more and more necessary that every supervisor become thoroughly acquainted with the basic factors and forces influencing and causing human behavior. Unless you, the supervisor, have insight and knowledge about *why* your employees behave as they do—very often in ways that seem irrational or unreasonable—their behavior will doubtless make little sense to you. Furthermore, your not knowing why can cost your organization time and money.

A successful supervisor might well be viewed as a "human relations engineer," one who has a high degree of skill in diagnosing complex human problems and applying his knowledge of human behavior and understanding of his people to arrive at a solution. Development of this skill requires study in several areas.

Certainly, the supervisor must understand the fundamental concepts of *motivation.* He also needs an awareness of the problems involved in the planning and implementation of *change* within his organization. Perhaps no human skill is more important (and less understood) than *communication,* the passing of information and understanding from one person to another; thus, the supervisor must recognize the factors that promote and prevent effective communication within his work group and the organization. And, last, he should understand the behavior of both *formal and informal groups,* the influence they have on their members and their impact on the organization as a whole. Helping you to develop insight and understanding in each of these areas is the goal of the ensuing chapters.

You, as a supervisor, cannot influence an employee you do not understand. Thus, study of the determinants of human behavior can surely help you. Studying human behavior is essentially like studying anything else; it requires constant curiosity and interest in the subject. The observation of people's behavior has always been an interesting pastime. Only in relatively recent years, however, has the serious study of human behavior become imperative in leading employees with a minimum of friction and a maximum of cooperation.

Reading Selection 1

*SKILLS OF AN EFFECTIVE ADMINISTRATOR**

Robert L. Katz

Although the selection and training of good administrators is widely recognized as one of American industry's most pressing problems, there is surprisingly little agreement among executives or educators on what makes a good administrator. The executive development programs of some of the nation's leading corporations and colleges reflect a tremendous variation in objectives.

At the root of this difference is industry's search for the traits or attributes which will objectively identify the "ideal executive" who is equipped to cope effectively with any problem in any organization. As one observer of American industry recently noted:

The assumption that there is an executive type is widely accepted, either openly or implicitly. Yet any executive presumably knows that a company needs all kinds of managers for different levels of jobs. The qualities most needed by a shop superintendent are likely to be quite opposed to those needed by a coordinating vice president of manufacturing. The literature of executive development is loaded with efforts to define the qualities needed by executives, and by themselves these sound quite rational. Few, for instance, would dispute the fact that a top manager needs good judgment, the ability to make decisions, the ability to win respect of others, and all the other well-worn phrases any management man could mention. But one has only to look at the successful managers in any company to see how enormously their particular qualities vary from any ideal list of executive virtues.[1]

Yet this quest for the executive stereotype has become so intense that many companies, in concentrating on certain specific traits or qualities, stand in danger of losing sight of their real concern: *what a man can accomplish.*

It is the purpose of this article to suggest what may be a more useful approach to the selection and development of administrators. This approach is based not on what good executives *are* (their innate traits and characteristics), but rather on what they *do* (the

*Reprinted with the permission of *Harvard Business Review,* Vol. 33, No. 1 (January-February, 1955), pp. 33-42.

[1]Perrin Stryker, "The Growing Pains of Executive Development," *Advanced Management* (August, 1954), p. 15.

kinds of skills which they exhibit in carrying out their jobs effectively). As used here, a *skill* implies an ability which can be developed, not necessarily inborn, and which is manifested in performance, not merely in potential. So the principal criterion of skillfulness must be effective action under varying conditions.

This approach suggests that effective administration rests on *three basic developable skills* which obviate the need for identifying specific traits and which may provide a useful way of looking at and understanding the administrative process. This approach is the outgrowth of firsthand observation of executives at work coupled with study of current field research in administration.

In the sections which follow, an attempt will be made to define and demonstrate what these three skills are; to suggest that the relative importance of the three skills varies with the level of administrative responsibility; to present some of the implications of this variation for selection, training, and promotion of executives; and to propose ways of developing these skills.

THREE-SKILL APPROACH

It is assumed here that an administrator is one who (a) directs the activities of other persons and (b) undertakes the responsibility for achieving certain objectives through these efforts. Within this definition, successful administration appears to rest on three basic skills, which we will call *technical, human, and conceptual.* It would be unrealistic to assert that these skills are not interrelated, yet there may be real merit in examining each one separately, and in developing them independently.

Technical Skill

As used here, technical skill implies an understanding of, and proficiency in, a specific kind of activity, particularly one involving methods, processes, procedures, or techniques. It is relatively easy for us to visualize the technical skill of the surgeon, the musician, the accountant, or the engineer when each is performing his own special function. Technical skill involves specialized knowledge, analytical ability within that specialty, and facility in the use of the tools and techniques of the specific discipline.

Of the three skills described in this article, technical skill is perhaps the most familiar because it is the most concrete, and because, in our age of specialization, it is the skill required of the greatest number of people. Most of our vocational and on-the-job training programs are largely concerned with developing this specialized technical skill.

Human Skill

As used here, human skill is the executive's ability to work effectively as a group member and to build cooperative effort within the team he leads. As *technical* skill is primarily concerned with working with "things" (processes or physical objects), so *human* skill is primarily concerned with working with people. This skill is demonstrated in the way the individual perceives (and recognizes the perceptions of) his superiors, equals, and subordinates, and in the way he behaves subsequently.

The person with highly developed human skill is aware of his own attitudes, assumptions, and beliefs about other individuals and groups; he is able to see the usefulness and limitations of these feelings. By accepting the existence of viewpoints, perceptions, and beliefs which are different from his own, he is skillful in understanding what others really mean by their words and behavior. He is equally skillful in communicating to others, in their own contexts, what he means by *his* behavior.

Such a person works to create an atmosphere of approval and security in which subordinates feel free to express themselves without fear of censure or ridicule, by encouraging them to participate in the planning and carrying out of those things which directly affect them. He is sufficiently sensitive to the needs and motivations of others in his organization so that he can judge the possible reactions to, and outcomes of, various courses of action he may undertake. Having this sensitivity, he is able and willing to *act* in a way which takes these perceptions by others into account.

Real skill in working with others must become a natural, continuous activity, since it involves sensitivity not only at times of decision making but also in the day-by-day behavior of the individual. Human skill cannot be a "sometime thing." Techniques cannot be randomly applied, nor can personality traits be put on or removed like an overcoat. Because everything which an executive says and does (or leaves unsaid or undone) has an effect on his associates, his true self will, in time, show through. Thus, to be effective, this skill must be naturally developed and unconsciously, as well as consistently, demonstrated in the individual's every action. It must become an integral part of his whole being.

Because human skill is so vital a part of everything the administrator does, examples of inadequate human skill are easier to describe than are highly skillful performances. Perhaps consideration of an actual situation would serve to clarify what is involved:

When a new conveyor unit was installed in a shoe factory where workers had previously been free to determine their own work rate, the production manager asked the industrial engineer who had designed the conveyor to serve as foreman, even though a qualified foreman was available. The engineer, who reported directly to the production manager, objected, but under pressure he agreed to take the job "until a suitable foreman could be found," even though this was a job of lower status than his present one. Then the following conversation took place:

Production Manager: "I've had a lot of experience with conveyors. I want you to keep this conveyor going at all times except for rest periods, and I want it going at top speed. Get these people thinking in terms of 2 pairs of shoes a minute, 70 dozen pairs a day, 350 dozen pairs a week. They are all experienced operators on their individual jobs, and it's just a matter of getting them to do their jobs in a little different way. I want you to make that base rate of 250 dozen pair a week work!" [Base rate was established at slightly under 75% of the maximum capacity. This base rate was 50% higher than under the old system.]

Engineer: "If I'm going to be foreman of the conveyor unit, I want to do things my way. I've worked on conveyors, and I don't agree with you on first getting people used to a conveyor going at top speed. These people have never seen a conveyor. You'll scare them. I'd like to run the conveyor at one-third speed for a couple of weeks and then gradually increase the speed.

"I think we should discuss setting the base rate [production quota before incentive bonus] on a daily basis instead of a weekly basis. [Workers had previously been paid on a daily straight piecework basis.]

"I'd also suggest setting a daily base rate at 45 or even 40 dozen pair. You have to set a base rate low enough for them to make. Once they know they can make the base rate, they will go after the bonus."

Production Manager: "You do it your way on the speed; but remember it's the results that count. On the base rate, I'm not discussing it with you; I'm telling you to make the 250 dozen pair a week work. I don't want a daily base rate."[2]

Here is a situation in which the production manager was so preoccupied with getting the physical output that he did not pay attention to the people through whom that output had to be achieved. Notice, first, that he made the engineer who designed the unit serve as foreman, apparently hoping to force the engineer to justify his design by producing the maximum output. However, the production manager was oblivious to (a) the way the engineer perceived this appointment, as a demotion, and (b) the need for the engineer to be able to control the variables if he was to be held responsible for output. Instead the production manager imposed a production standard and refused any changes in the work situation.

Moreover, although this was a radically new situation for the operators, the production manager expected them to produce immediately at well above their previous output—even though the operators had an unfamiliar production system to cope with, the operators had never worked together as a team before, the operators and their new foreman had never worked together before, and the foreman was not in agreement with the production goals or standards. By ignoring all these human factors, the production manager not only placed the engineer in an extremely difficult operating situation but also, by refusing to allow the engineer to "run his own show," discouraged the very assumption of responsibility he had hoped for in making the appointment.

Under these circumstances, it is easy to understand how the relationship between these two men rapidly deteriorated, and how production, after two months' operation, was at only 125 dozen pairs per week (just 75% of what it had been under the old system.)

Conceptual Skill

As used here, conceptual skill involves the ability to see the enterprise as a whole; it includes recognizing how the various functions of the organization depend on one another, and how changes in any one part affect all the others; and it extends to visualizing the relationship of the individual business to the industry, the community, and the political, social, and economic forces of the nation as a whole. Recognizing these relationships and perceiving the significant elements in any situation, the administrator should then be able to act in a way which advances the over-all welfare of the total organization.

Hence, the success of any decision depends on the conceptual skill of the people who make the decision and

[2]From a mimeographed case in the files of the Harvard Business School; copyrighted by the President and Fellows of Harvard College.

those who put it into action. When, for example, an important change in marketing policy is made, it is critical that the effects on production, control, finance, research, and the people involved be considered. And it remains critical right down to the last executive who must implement the new policy. If each executive recognizes the over-all relationships and significance of the change, he is almost certain to be more effective in administering it. Consequently the chances for succeeding are greatly increased.

Not only does the effective coordination of the various parts of the business depend on the conceptual skill of the administrators involved, but so also does the whole future direction and tone of the organization. The attitudes of a top executive color the whole character of the organization's response and determine the "corporate personality" which distinguishes one company's ways of doing business from another's. These attitudes are a reflection of the administrator's conceptual skill (referred to by some as his "creative ability")—the way he perceives and responds to the direction in which the business should grow, company objectives and policies, and stockholders' and employees' interests.

Conceptual skill, as defined above, is what Chester I. Bernard, former president of the New Jersey Bell Telephone Company, implies when he says: ". . . the essential aspect of the [executive] process is the sensing of the organization as a whole and the total situation relevant to it."[3] Examples of inadequate conceptual skill are all around us. Here is one instance:

In a large manufacturing company which had a long tradition of job-shop type operations, primary responsibility for production control had been left to the foremen and other lower-level supervisors. "Village" type operations with small working groups and informal organizations were the rule. A heavy influx of orders following World War II tripled the normal production requirements and severely taxed the whole manufacturing organization. At this point, a new production manager was brought in from outside the company, and he established a wide range of controls and formalized the entire operating structure.

As long as the boom demand lasted, the employees made every effort to conform with the new procedures and environment. But when demand subsided to prewar levels, serious labor relations problems developed, friction was high among department heads, and the company found itself saddled with a heavy indirect labor cost. Management sought to reinstate its old procedures; it fired the production manager and attempted to give greater authority to the foreman once again. However, during the four years of formalized control, the foremen had grown away from their old practices, many had left the company, and adequate replacements had not been developed. Without strong foreman leadership, the traditional job-shop operations proved costly and inefficient.

In this instance, when the new production controls and formalized organizations were introduced, management did not foresee the consequences of this action in the event of a future contraction of business. Later, when conditions changed and it was necessary to pare down operations, management was again unable to recognize the implications of its action and reverted to the old procedures, which, under existing circumstances, were no longer appropriate. This compounded *conceptual* inadequacy

[3] *Functions of the Executive* (Cambridge: Harvard University Press, 1948), p. 235.

left the company at a serious competitive disadvantage.

Because a company's over-all success is dependent on its executives' conceptual skill in establishing and carrying out policy decisions, this skill is the unifying, coordinating ingredient of the administrative process, and of undeniable over-all importance.

RELATIVE IMPORTANCE

We may notice that, in a very real sense, conceptual skill embodies consideration of both the technical and human aspects of the organization. Yet the concept of *skill,* as an ability to translate knowledge into action, should enable one to distinguish between the three skills of performing the technical activities (technical skill), understanding and motivating individuals and groups (human skill), and coordinating and integrating all the activities and interests of the organization toward a common objective (conceptual skill).

This separation of effective administration into three basic skills is useful primarily for purposes of analysis. In practice, these skills are so closely interrelated that it is difficult to determine where one ends and another begins. However, just because the skills are inter-related does not imply that we cannot get some value from looking at them separately, or by varying their emphasis. In playing golf the action of the hands, wrists, hips, shoulders, arms, and head are all interrelated; yet in improving one's swing it is often valuable to work on one of these elements separately. Also, under different playing conditions the relative importance of these elements varies. Similarly, although all three are of importance at every level of administration, the technical, human, and conceptual skills of the administrator vary in relative importance at different levels of responsibility.

At Lower Levels

Technical skill is responsible for many of the great advances of modern industry. It is indispensable to efficient operation. Yet it has greatest importance at the lower levels of administration. As the administrator moves further and further from the actual physical operation, this need for technical skill becomes less important, provided he has skilled subordinates and can help them solve their own problems. At the top, technical skill may be almost nonexistent, and the executive may still be able to perform effectively if his human and conceptual skills are highly developed.

We are all familiar with those "professional managers" who are becoming the prototypes of our modern executive world. These men shift with great ease, and with no apparent loss in effectiveness, from one industry to another. Their human and conceptual skills seem to make up for their unfamiliarity with the new job's technical aspects.

At Every Level

Human skill, the ability to work with others, is essential to effective administration at every level. One recent research study has shown that human skill is of paramount importance at the foreman level, pointing out that the chief function of the foreman as an administrator is to attain collaboration of people in the work group.[4] Another study reinforces this finding and extends it to the middle-management

[4] A. Zaleznik, *Foreman Training in a Growing Enterprise* (Boston: Division of Research, Harvard Business School, 1951).

group, adding that the administrator should be primarily concerned with facilitating communication in the organization.[5] And still another study, concerned primarily with top management, underscores the need for self-awareness and sensitivity to human relationships by executives at that level.[6] These findings would tend to indicate that human skill is of great importance at every administrative level, but notice the difference in emphasis.

Human skill seems to be most important at lower levels, where the number of direct contacts between administrators and subordinates is greatest. As we go higher and higher in the administrative echelons, the number and frequency of these personal contacts decrease, and the need for human skill becomes proportionately, although probably not absolutely, less. At the same time, conceptual skill becomes increasingly more important with the need for policy decisions and broad-scale action. The human skill of dealing with individuals then becomes subordinate to the conceptual skill of integrating group interests and activities into a coordinated whole.

In fact, a recent research study by Professor Chris Argyris of Yale University has given us the example of an extremely effective plant manager who, although possessing little human skill as defined here, was nonetheless very successful:

This manager, the head of a largely autonomous division, made his supervisors, through the effects of his strong personality and the "pressure" he applied, highly dependent on him for most of their "rewards, penalties, authority, perpetuation, communication, and identification."

As a result, the supervisors spent much of their time competing with one another for the manager's favor. They told him only the things they thought he wanted to hear, and spent much time trying to find out his desires. They depended on him to set their objectives and to show them how to reach them. Because the manager was inconsistent and unpredictable in his behavior, the supervisors were insecure and continually engaged in interdepartmental squabbles which they tried to keep hidden from the manager.

Clearly, human skill as defined here, was lacking. Yet, by the evaluation of his superiors and by his results in increasing efficiency and raising profits and morale, this manager was exceedingly effective. Professor Argyris suggests that employees in modern industrial organizations tend to have a "built-in" sense of dependence on superiors which capable and alert men can turn to advantage.[7]

In the context of the three-skill approach, it seems that this manager was able to capitalize on this dependence because he recognized the interrelationships of all the activities under his control, identified himself with the organization, and sublimated the individual interests of his subordinates to *his* (the organization's) interest, set his goals realistically, and showed his subordinates how to reach these goals. This would seem to be an excellent example of a situation in which strong conceptual skill more than compensated for a lack of human skill.

[5]Harriet O. Ronken and Paul R. Lawrence, *Administering Changes* (Boston: Division of Research, Harvard Business School, 1952).

[6]Edmund P. Learned, David H. Ulrich, and Donald R. Booz, *Executive Action* (Boston: Division of Research, Harvard Business School, 1950).

[7]*Executive Leadership* (New York: Harper & Brothers, 1953); see also "Leadership Pattern in the Plant," HBR (January-February, 1953), p. 63.

At the Top Level

Conceptual skill, as indicated in the preceding sections, becomes increasingly critical in more responsible executive positions where its effects are maximized and most easily observed. In fact, recent research findings lead to the conclusion that at the top level of administration this conceptual skill becomes the most important ability of all. As Herman W. Steinkraus, president of Bridgeport Brass Company, said:

"One of the most important lessons which I learned on this job [the presidency] is the importance of coordinating the various departments into an effective team, and, secondly, to recognize the shifting emphasis from time to time of the relative importance of various departments to the business."[8]

It would appear, then, that at lower levels of administrative responsibility, the principal need is for technical and human skills. At higher levels, technical skill becomes relatively less important while the need for conceptual skill increases rapidly. At the top level of an organization, conceptual skill becomes the most important skill of all for successful administration. A chief executive may lack technical or human skills and still be effective if he has subordinates who have strong abilities in these directions. But if his conceptual skill is weak, the success of the whole organization may be jeopardized.

IMPLICATIONS FOR ACTION

This three-skill approach implies that significant benefits may result from redefining the objectives of executive development programs, from reconsidering the placement of executives in organizations, and from revising procedures for testing and selecting prospective executives.

Executive Development

Many executive development programs may be failing to achieve satisfactory results because of their inability to foster the growth of these administrative skills. Programs which concentrate on the mere imparting of information or the cultivation of a specific trait would seem to be largely unproductive in enhancing the administrative skills of candidates.

A strictly informative program was described to me recently by an officer and director of a large corporation who had been responsible for the executive development activities of his company, as follows:

"What we try to do is to get our promising young men together with some of our senior executives in regular meetings each month. Then we give the young fellows a chance to ask questions to let them find out about the company's history and how and why we've done things in the past."

It was not surprising that neither the senior executives nor the young men felt this program was improving their administrative abilities.

The futility of pursuing specific traits becomes apparent when we consider the responses of an administrator in a number of different situations. In coping with these varied conditions, he may appear to demonstrate one trait in one instance—e.g., dominance when dealing with subordinates—and the directly opposite trait under another set of circumstances—e.g., submissiveness when dealing with superiors. Yet

[8]"What Should a President Do?" *Dun's Review* (August, 1951, p. 21.

in each instance he may be acting appropriately to achieve the best results. Which, then, can we identify as a desirable characteristic? Here is a further example of this dilemma:

"A Pacific Coast sales manager had a reputation for decisiveness and positive action. Yet when he was required to name an assistant to understudy his job from among several well-qualified subordinates, he deliberately avoided making a decision. His associates were quick to observe what appeared to be obvious indecisiveness.

But after several months had passed, it became clear that the sales manager had very unobtrusively been giving the various salesmen opportunities to demonstrate their attitudes and feelings. As a result, he was able to identify strong sentiments for one man whose subsequent promotion was enthusiastically accepted by the entire group."

In this instance, the sales manager's skillful performance was improperly interpreted as "indecisiveness." Their concern with irrelevant traits led his associates to overlook the adequacy of his performance. Would it not have been more appropriate to conclude that his human skill in working with others enabled him to adapt effectively to the requirements of a new situation?

Cases such as these would indicate that it is more useful to judge an administrator on the results of his performance than on his apparent traits. Skills are easier to identify than are traits and are less likely to be misinterpreted. Furthermore, skills offer a more directly applicable frame of reference for executive development, since any improvement in an administrator's skills must necessarily result in more effective performance.

Still another danger in many existing executive development programs lies in the unqualified enthusiasm with which some companies and colleges have embraced courses in "human relations." There would seem to be two inherent pitfalls here: (1) Human relations courses might only be imparting information or specific techniques, rather than developing the individual's human skill. (2) Even if individual development does take place, some companies, by placing all of their emphasis on human skill, may be completely overlooking the training requirements for top positions. They may run the risk of producing men with highly developed human skill who lack the conceptual ability to be effective top-level administrators.

It would appear important, then, that the training of a candidate for an administrative position be directed at the development of those skills which are most needed at the level of responsibility for which he is being considered.

Executive Placement

This three-skill concept suggests immediate possibilities for the creating of management teams of individuals with complementary skills. For example, one medium-size midwestern distributing organization has as president a man of unusual conceptual ability but extremely limited human skill. However, he has two vice presidents with exceptional human skill. These three men make up an executive committee which has been outstandingly successful, the skills of each member making up for deficiencies of the others. Perhaps the plan of two-man complementary conference leadership proposed by Robert F. Bales, in which the one leader maintains "task leadership" while the other provides "social leadership," might also be an example in point.[9]

Executive Selection

In trying to predetermine a prospective candidate's abilities on a job, much use is being made these days of various kinds of testing devices. Executives are being tested for everything from "decisiveness" to "conformity." These tests, as a recent article in *Fortune* points out, have achieved some highly questionable results when applied to performance on the job.[10] Would it not be much more productive to be concerned with skills of doing rather than with a number of traits which do not guarantee performance?

This three-skill approach makes trait testing unnecessary and substitutes for it procedures which examine a man's ability to cope with the actual problems and situations he will find on his job. These procedures, which indicate what a man can *do* in specific situations, are the same for selection and for measuring development. They will be described in the section on developing executive skills which follows.

This approach suggests that executives should *not* be chosen on the basis of their apparent possession of a number of behavior characteristics or traits, but on the basis of their possession of the requisite skills for the specific level of responsibility involved.

DEVELOPING THE SKILLS

For years many people have contended that leadership ability is inherent in certain chosen individuals. We talk of "born leaders," "born executives," "born salesmen." It is undoubtedly true that certain people, naturally or innately, possess greater aptitude or ability in certain skills. But research in psychology and physiology would also indicate, first, that those having strong aptitudes and abilities can improve their skill through practice and training, and, secondly, that even those lacking the natural ability can improve their performance and effectiveness.

The *skill* conception of administration suggests that we may hope to improve our administrative effectiveness and to develop better administrators for the future. This skill conception implies *learning by doing.* Different people learn in different ways, but skills are developed through practice and through relating learning to one's own personal experience and background. If well done, training in these basic administrative skills should develop executive abilities more surely and more rapidly than through unorganized experience. What, then, are some of the ways in which this training can be conducted?

Technical Skill

Development of technical skill has received great attention for many years by industry and educational institutions alike, and much progress has been made. Sound grounding in the principles, structures, and processes of the individual specialty, coupled with actual practice and experience during which the individual is watched and helped by a superior, appear to be most effective. In view of the vast

[9] "In Conference," HBR (March-April, 1954), p. 44.

[10] William H. Whyte, Jr., "The Fallacies of 'Personality' Testing," *Fortune* (September, 1954), p. 117.

amount of work which has been done in training people in the technical skills, it would seem unnecessary in this article to suggest more.

Human Skill

Human skill, however, has been much less understood, and only recently has systematic progress been made in developing it. Many different approaches to the development of human skill are being pursued by various universities and professional men today. These are rooted in such disciplines as psychology, sociology, and anthropology.

Some of these approaches find their application in "applied psychology," "human engineering," and a host of other manifestations requiring technical specialists to help the businessman with his human problems. As a practical matter, however, the executive must develop his own human skill, rather than lean on the advice of others. To be effective, he must develop his own personal point of view toward human activity, so that he will (a) recognize the feelings and sentiments which he brings to a situation; (b) have an attitude about his own experiences which will enable him to re-evaluate and learn from them; (c) develop ability in understanding what others by their actions and words (explicit or implicit) are trying to communicate to him; and (d) develop ability in successfully communicating his ideas and attitudes to others.[11]

This human skill can be developed by some individuals without formalized training. Others can be individually aided by their immediate superiors as an integral part of the "coaching" process to be described later. This aid depends for effectiveness, obviously, on the extent to which the superior possesses the human skill.

For larger groups, the use of case problems coupled with impromptu role playing can be very effective. This training can be established on a formal or informal basis, but it requires a skilled instructor and organized sequence of activities.[12] It affords as good an approximation to reality as can be provided on a continuing classroom basis and offers an opportunity for critical reflection not often found in actual practice. An important part of the procedure is the self-examination of the trainee's own concepts and values, which may enable him to develop more useful attitudes about himself and about others. With the change in attitude, hopefully, there may also come some active skill in dealing with human problems.

Human skill has also been tested in the classroom, within reasonable limits, by a series of analyses of detailed accounts of actual situations involving administrative action, together with a number of role-playing opportunities in which the individual is required to carry out the details of the action he has proposed. In this way an individual's understanding of the total situation and his own personal ability to do something about it can be evaluated.

On the job, there should be frequent opportunities for a superior to observe an individual's ability to work effectively with others. These may appear to be highly subjective evaluations and to depend for validity on the human skill of the rater. But does not every promotion, in the last analysis, depend on someone's subjective judgment? And should this subjecti-

[11]For a further discussion of this point, see F. J. Roethlisberger, "Training Supervisors in Human Relations," HBR (September, 1951), p. 47.

[12]See, for example, A. Winn, "Training in Administration and Human Relations," *Personnel* (September, 1953), p. 139; see also, Kenneth R. Andrews, "Executive Training by the Case Method," HBR (September, 1951), p. 58.

vity be berated, or should we make a greater effort to develop people within our organizations with the human skill to make such judgments effectively?

Conceptual Skill

Conceptual skill, like human skill, has not been very widely understood. A number of methods have been tried to aid in developing this ability, with varying success. Some of the best results have always been achieved through the "coaching" of subordinates by superiors.[13] This is no new idea. It implies that one of the key responsibilities of the executive is to help his subordinates to develop their administrative potentials. One way a superior can help "coach" his subordinate is by assigning a particular responsibility, and then responding with searching questions or opinions, rather than giving answers, whenever the subordinate seeks help. When Benjamin F. Fairless, now chairman of the board of the United States Steel Corporation, was president of the corporation, he described his coaching activities as follows:

"When one of my vice presidents or the head of one of our operating companies comes to me for instructions, I generally counter by asking him questions. First thing I know, he has told me how to solve the problem himself."[14]

Obviously, this is an ideal and wholly natural procedure for administrative training, and applies to the development of technical and human skill, as well as to that of conceptual skill. However, its success must necessarily rest on the abilities and willingness of the superior to help the subordinate.

Another excellent way to develop conceptual skill is through trading jobs, that is, by moving promising young men through different functions of the business but at the same level of responsibility. This gives the man the chance literally to "be in the other fellow's shoes."

Other possibilities include: special assignments, particularly the kind which involve inter-departmental problems; and management boards, such as the McCormick Multiple Management plan, in which junior executives serve as advisers to top management on policy matters.

For larger groups, the kind of case-problems course described above, only using cases involving broad management policy and inter-departmental coordination, may be useful. Courses of this kind, often called "General Management" or "Business Policy," are becoming increasingly prevalent.

In the classroom, conceptual skill has also been evaluated with reasonable effectiveness by presenting a series of detailed descriptions of specific complex situations. In these the individual being tested is asked to set forth a course of action which responds to the underlying forces operating in each situation and which considers the implications of this action on the various functions and parts of the organization and its total environment.

On the job, the alert supervisor should find frequent opportunities to observe the extent to which the individual is able to relate himself and his job to the other functions and operations of the company.

Like human skill, conceptual skill, too, must become a natural part

[13] For a more complete development of the concept of "coaching," see Myles L. Mace, *The Growth and Development of Executives* (Boston: Division of Research, Harvard Business School, 1950).

[14] "What Should a President Do?" *Dun's Review* (July, 1951), p. 14.

of the executive's makeup. Different methods may be indicated for developing different people, by virtue of their backgrounds, attitudes, and experience. But in every case that method should be chosen which will enable the executive to develop his own personal skill in visualizing the enterprise as a whole and in coordinating and integrating its various parts.

CONCLUSION

The purpose of this article has been to show that effective administration depends on three basic personal skills, which have been called *technical, human,* and *conceptual.* The administrator needs: (a) sufficient technical skill to accomplish the mechanics of the particular job for which he is responsible; (b) sufficient human skill in working with others to be an effective group member and to be able to build cooperative effort within the team he leads; (c) sufficient conceptual skill to recognize the interrelationships of the various factors involved in his situation, which will lead him to take that action which achieves the maximum good for the total organization.

The relative importance of these three skills seems to vary with the level of administrative responsibility. At lower levels, the major need is for technical and human skills. At higher levels, the administrator's effectiveness depends largely on human and conceptual skills. At the top, conceptual skill becomes the most important of all for successful administration.

This three-skill approach emphasizes that good administrators are not necessarily born; they may be developed. It transcends the need to identify specific traits in an effort to provide a more useful way of looking at the administrative process. By helping to identify the skills most needed at various levels of responsibility, it may prove useful in the selection, training, and promotion of executives.

QUESTIONS FOR REVIEW AND DISCUSSION

1. a. "The major problems facing supervision today are 'people problems'." Do you agree? Explain.
   b. What part of an average day do *you* spend dealing with "people problems"? What seem to be the bases for most of these problems?
2. A high rate of turnover is obviously expensive to a company. Specifically, estimate what it would cost your company to replace you.
3. "There isn't all that much to learning how to supervise. It basically involves knowledge that everyone—if he's half-way intelligent—already has. It's just a matter of using common sense and 'doing what comes naturally.' Getting along with your subordinates is nothing more than practicing the Golden Rule." Evaluate these comments.
4. Think of a particular individual you regard as an outstanding supervisor. List the characteristics you feel are responsible for his success. Can these characteristics be *developed* by someone who does not possess them? Explain.
5. Picture yourself 10 years from now, or 10 years ago. What do you believe would be (or would have been) your response to an announcement that your department was being abolished? Why might your responses at another time be different from your current response to such an announcement?

6. How does a higher level of education influence the expectations of an individual?
7. a. Name and explain the three skills needed for effective administration as outlined by Robert Katz.
   b. Discuss the relative need for each of these skills at various levels of management.
   c. Katz's classic article, "Skills of an Effective Administrator," was published in 1955. Do you feel that the ideas and concepts discussed are still applicable in business and industry today? Explain.
8. a. What specific methods would you suggest for developing each of the three skills—*technical, human,* and *conceptual*—in supervisors?
   b. Through a series of promotions, a once outstanding department head has now become an incompetent company vice-president. What fundamental skill is he probably lacking? How might he have acquired this skill?
9. a. In *Reading Selection 1,* Katz implies that the need for human skill decreases as one progresses up the management hierarchy. Do you agree or disagree? Explain.
   b. Is the same type of human skill required in dealing with managerial personnel as is needed by the first-line supervisor?
10. Name and briefly discuss the five requirements for the development of human skills.
11. a. How does *empathy* differ from *sympathy*?
    b. What do you foresee as the major problem in effectively practicing empathy?
    c. Cite a recent example in which you feel that you effectively used empathy in dealing with another person.
12. What differences exist among the members of this class? Do these differences result in different opinions and viewpoints? Why?
13. a. Why is it that no two people perceive the same situation in the same way?
    b. Based on your own experiences, recall a problem that occurred because of perceptual differences. Could the incident have been avoided? How?
14. "A supervisor should be employee-oriented so that he is able better to please the subordinate and therefore make him happier." Do you agree? Explain.
15. "I can't help it if his son is having trouble in school," remarks a supervisor about one of his subordinates. "He can leave his personal problems at home; he has a job to do here and I intend to see that he does it." How would you respond to this comment? What skills may be needed to resolve a potential conflict?
16. Explain the concept of "mutuality of interests."

SUGGESTED ADDITIONAL READINGS

Davis, Keith. "Can Business Afford to Ignore Social Responsibilities?" *California Management Review,* Spring, 1960.

McMurry, Robert N. "Empathy: Management's Greatest Need," *Human Relations in Management,* S. G. Huneryager and I. L. Heckmann, editors. Second edition. Cincinnati: South-Western Publishing Company, 1967. Pp. 722-738.

Miljus, Robert C. "Effective Leadership and the Motivation of Human Resources," *Personnel Journal,* January, 1970, pp. 36-40.

Singer, Henry A. "The Impact of Human Resources on Business," *Business Horizons,* April, 1969, pp. 53-58.

Zalkind, Sheldon S., and Timothy W. Costello. "Perception: Implications for Administration," *Readings in Managerial Psychology,* Harold J. Leavitt and Louis R. Pondey, editors. Chicago: University of Chicago Press, 1964. Pp. 32-47.

2

MOTIVATION—
THE "WHY" OF HUMAN BEHAVIOR

Year after year, business costs keep mounting. Wages and fringe benefits continue their upward climb. Vacations grow longer and work days shorter. At the same time, management at all levels finds itself in an unending search for new ways to get the most out of each payroll dollar and to obtain maximum employee cooperation in achieving the company's objectives; means are constantly sought for increasing productivity and reducing errors, poor work, waste, turnover, absenteeism, and other costly problems. And yet, it is widely recognized that in the majority of cases employees are still not motivated to perform at a level anywhere near that of which they are capable.

At one time, it was thought that the only way to get extra effort out of an employee was to pay him more or to reward him with additional fringe benefits. If that didn't work, there was always the threat of dismissal.

Now, management is finding that neither more money nor more fringe benefits automatically leads to more productivity. Neither does the threat of firing; barring any long-term economic recession, it simply isn't that difficult for almost anyone to find another job if he so chooses.

Hence, more and more companies are realizing that the motivation of employees isn't the simple matter they once viewed it as; in reality, human motivation is a very complicated subject, deserving much more attention and study than has been given it in the past.

Essentially, the study of motivation is concerned with the "why" of human behavior. Why do people behave as they do? Why do some workers devote all their energy to their jobs, while others are satisfied with what appears to be only a half-hearted effort? Why does one worker enjoying performing a job while another loathes it?

The answer to all these questions can be at least partially explained in one word: *motivation.*

A supervisor must understand why people are motivated to behave as they do. Only then can he make the types of decisions that will encourage his subordinates to direct their efforts toward helping to achieve the company's goals.

WHAT IS MOTIVATION?

There are a great number of individual theories on the subject of human motivation—often seemingly as many as there have been psychologists! This does not mean that nothing concrete is known about the subject, but rather that there is more than one interpretation of it.

While there is not universal agreement on the makeup of the complex process of motivation, one of the concepts that has traditionally been found useful in understanding it is that of *human needs.*

Psychologists tell us that all human behavior, whether on a conscious or unconscious level, is caused by a person's *need structure.* Thus, a person is motivated to do something because of what he needs and wants.

Or, put another way, **all human behavior is motivated or caused, in that it is directed toward the satisfaction of the individual's physiological or psychological needs.**

We can define motivation in its simplest form as **goal-seeking behavior.** Such goal-seeking behavior revolves around the desire for need satisfaction. This process is presented in Figure 2-1. An unsatisfied need causes a state of *tension* which is uncomfortable to the individual.[1] Action is then taken to reduce, eliminate, or divert the tension state. The need for food, for example, produces a tension state that we call hunger. A goal to be sought (depending on your tastes and degree of affluence) might be a steak dinner. Action would be taken to seek this goal; and if the action were successful, the tension would be removed and the need, at least temporarily, fulfilled.

FIGURE 2-1. Motivation as Goal-seeking Behavior

NEEDS ⟶ ACTION ⟶ GOALS
(Tension) (Tension Release)

The Hierarchy of Human Needs

If we accept the premise that behavior is goal-directed toward need satisfaction, it seems obvious that a superivsor has but two choices if his motivational efforts are to be successful: (1) he can create felt needs within the employee or (2) he can offer a means for satisfying needs already within the employee. Either way, it is essential to have a basic understanding of the fundamental needs of man.

[1] The dictionary defines a *need* as a condition requiring supply or relief; it is a lack of something desirable or useful. It is also a feeling of inadequacy; it is the restlessness that results from dissatisfaction with the present state of affairs. It is desiring what you do not have; it is the conviction that you are not enjoying maximum personal satisfaction.

For this, we turn to psychologist Abraham Maslow, who has supplied what many consider to be the core theory of human motivation. Maslow suggested that all of us are subject to a *hierarchy of needs.* This simply means that we all share certain fundamental needs that can be ranked in the sequence in which they normally occur. This hierarchy is pictured in Figure 2-2.

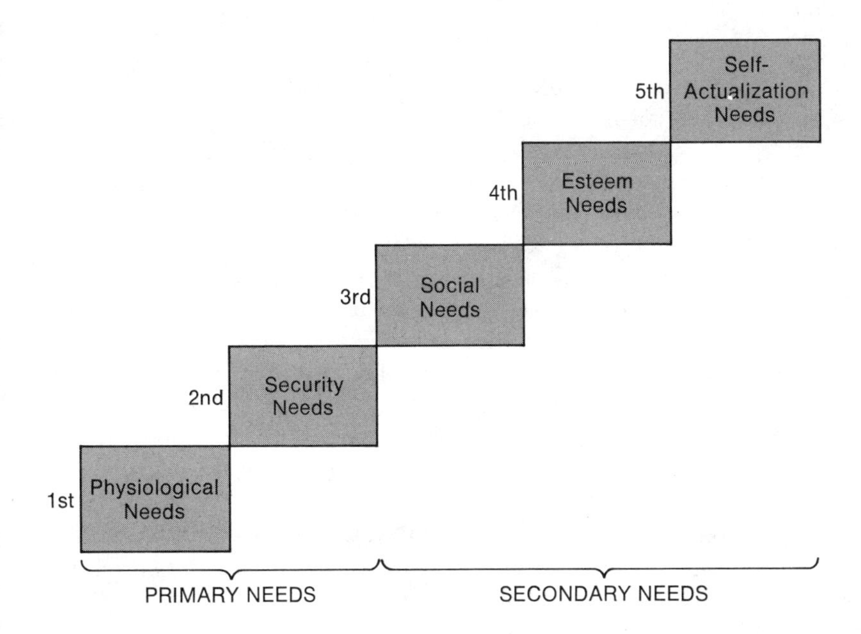

According to Maslow, individuals tend to satisfy their needs in the order of priority shown in the hierarchy. Thus, needs in the first two categories are usually met first; these are often called the *primary* needs. Needs in the remaining three categories are *secondary* needs; they are satisfied after the primary needs are met.

Although the need hierarchy does not give us a complete understanding of human behavior or the means to motivate people, it is a helpful starting point in understanding ourselves and those with whom we work.

Physiological needs. First in the Maslow hierarchy of needs are those basic physiological drives that man requires for survival and subsistence, including the need for food, drink, rest, air to breathe, shelter, and satisfactory temperatures.

Little conscious thought is typically given to these needs unless something jeopardizes their satisfaction. For example, if you haven't eaten in a week, you will be totally motivated by the need for food. "Man lives for bread alone when there is no bread." Your needs for social status, sex, or recognition are inoperative when your stomach has been empty for a while. But when you eat regularly, hunger ceases to be an important motivator of your behavior.

In the work situation, these physical needs are primarily satisfied by salaries and other economic benefits supplied by management and, to an extent, by the physical conditions of the job—for example, adequate lighting and ventilation, restrooms, drinking fountains, rest periods, and other physical facilities needed to satisfy these primary drives. However, because most companies do a reasonably good job of taking care of these needs, satisfying them is no longer a prime motivating factor, as it once was.

Security needs. Security needs have both *physical* and *economic* dimensions, with the latter being more significant to management. Although concerned with physical safety, the avoidance of pain, and the seeking of comfort, they can best be seen on the job in attempts to ensure job security and to move toward greater financial support. The desire to fulfill these needs might best be considered as seeking "peace of mind."

Once his physiological needs have been satisfied, the individual wants to feel that they are secure and will continue to be satisfied in the foreseeable future; in other words, having taken care of his physiological needs today, he wants a guarantee for tomorrow. The employee specifically seeks protection against the loss of his job and earnings, whether because of illness, accident, old age, arbitrary firing, or other reasons. Security needs are reflected on the job by such things as pension plans, group medical and hospital plans, and all types of job security, especially seniority.

Security, of course, is a relative thing. To one person it may mean the ability to maintain a house with fifteen rooms, five servants, and a yacht. To another, it may simply mean some assurance that he will be able to pay the rent next month. But to all, there must be a sense of continuing ability to provide the necessities of life.

Social needs. When your physiological and security needs are reasonably satisfied, social needs become important motivators of your behavior; they are the needs that are satisfied through relationships with other people.

Man is a social animal. His social needs include such motives as the need to belong, the need for love and affection, and the need for approval and acceptance by his peers. He wants to be a participant in activities with others, to be a part of things. He wants to identify with a group or groups.

Close friendships, informal work groups, clique formation, and the desire to feel "in" or to be a part of the company reflect social needs on the job.

Management in many cases becomes apprehensive about this natural tendency of workers to group together, fearing that informal work groups represent a threat to the organization. On the contrary, any attempts to prevent informal groups from forming usually result in frustration on the part of workers, leading to uncooperativeness and even aggression. Indeed, many studies confirm that cohesive, tightly-knit work groups are the most productive.

It is often argued that these needs are (and should be) met mostly outside the job situation. However, if one third to one half of man's waking hours are spent in the work environment, is it not reasonable to expect that at least *some* of a man's social needs should be met at work? This view seems especially reasonable in our affluent society in which most people's physiological and security needs are satisfied in large degree.

Esteem needs. Above the social needs on the hierarchy are the needs for self-esteem: the desire for prestige, status, recognition, self-confidence, appreciation, and the respect of one's co-workers.

On the job, sincere praise for a job well done or a pat on the back in the presence of other workers are small but important ways of satisfying these needs for the worker. They can also be seen in the worker's desire to have the respect of his supervisor both as a person and as a valued contributor to the organization's goals.

These needs are of great significance to management because, unlike the three previously listed needs on the hierarchy, they are often difficult to satisfy in the typical business or industrial organization. Our emphasis on job specialization and mass production often offers little opportunity to provide increased self-esteem or status to the rank-and-file employee.

Self-actualization needs. These needs (also commonly referred to as *self-fulfillment* and *self-realization* needs) reflect our desire to actually achieve that personal development that we are capable of attaining. As Maslow said, "What a man *can* be, he *must* be."[2]

At the workplace, self-actualization becomes a need to work toward or to reach a job level consistent with the employee's skills, abilities, and aptitudes. Thus, the *work itself* can become a source of gratification, especially if the work includes responsibility, achievement, creativity, challenge, and personal growth. Nonetheless, the jobs of many employees (if not most) do not provide this kind of satisfaction, and many would argue that for some jobs it may be unreasonable to expect that they ever will. In this case, the employee must seek to fulfill his higher-level needs off the job, if at all.

Self-actualization is seldom a dominant motivator of behavior because so many people (especially those at the lower levels of the organizational "pecking order") are still attempting to satisfy their social and esteem needs; however, it influences the behavior of nearly everyone. It is usually a constant motivator, as most people will never fully satisfy it.

Much of the discussion in Chapter 3 and in other parts of the book will be aimed at possible ways that these needs (along with the esteem needs) can be better satisfied on the job.

[2]A. H. Maslow, "A Theory of Human Motivation," *Human Relations in Management,* S. G. Huneryager and I. L. Heckmann, editors (Second edition; Cincinnati: South-Western Publishing Company, 1967), p. 343.

"I'd like a little appreciation—that's what!"

Premises of the Hierarchy

Maslow's theory of human motivation sets forth two fundamental premises that have important implications for the supervisor:

1. *Man's needs are arranged in a hierarchy of importance.* Saying that needs are hierarchical simply means that man is a continually "wanting animal"; as a person has one need satisfied, he will look up to the next higher order of needs. Conversely, **the higher needs do not become important as motivators until the lower-order needs are relatively well satisfied.**

If needs lower on the hierarchy are not satisfied, the person never gets around to doing much about the needs higher on the hierarchy. For example, if a worker's wage level is too low to satisfy his basic physiological and security needs, his behavior will be continually dominated by his lower-level needs. It is unlikely that he would respond to incentives designed to satisfy social, esteem, or self-actualization needs. However, once he has achieved a better standard of living, his thoughts will turn to the higher-level needs.

Or, if lower-level needs that have been previously satisfied suddenly face loss of satisfaction, pursuit of higher need fulfillment will cease and attention will again be focused on the lower needs. Anyone who has suddenly become unemployed will vouch for this!

2. *Satisfied needs are no longer motivating.* Perhaps the most important point to remember is that employees are actively motivated by what they are seeking, not by what they already have. As lower-level needs are reasonably satisfied, they become less of a motivational force in a person's behavior. According to Maslow, a need does not have to be completely satisfied before the next need emerges. If, for example, a worker's physiological and security needs (*primary* needs) are 75 per cent satisfied and his social, esteem, and self-actualization needs (*secondary* needs) are satisfied 30, 20, and 5 per cent,

respectively, his behavior will be aimed primarily in the direction of satisfying the higher-level needs. The physiological and security needs would take a subordinate role.

An individual is motivated primarily by the next level of unsatisfied needs in the hierarchy. Thus, in a sense, satisfied needs disappear. The supervisor must look to those needs that are relatively unsatisfied if he wishes to influence the behavior of his employees.

Changing Motivational Emphasis

At one time, management viewed the individual employee as an "economic man" who regarded his job solely as a means of satisfying his material wants. More recently, with a little help from Maslow and other psychologists, we have come to see that man seeks to satisfy other than his purely economic needs.

The role of money. Many supervisors, however, still believe that a worker's motivation can be bought; regardless of the problem, they feel that it can be solved by more money or the threat of less money. The authors have often heard supervisors declaring that "money is still the best motivator."

Certainly money *is* important. As we have previously mentioned, an employee's lower-order needs are primarily satisfied through the wages and other economic benefits derived from his job. The money that he earns purchases satisfactions for his physiological and security needs. In many cases, money can also purchase material goods that the person perceives as necessary to satisfy higher-level needs such as belonging, esteem, and status. For example, one might buy an expensive foreign sports car if he feels that it is necessary to his being accepted by his social group. However, the individual does not satisfy his higher-level needs *on the job* through this type of behavior.

In either case, **money itself is not a motivator**. It is more correctly viewed as a means to need satisfaction; money is seldom an end in itself. For example, money is the means to buy food and shelter that will satisfy the physiological needs.

Emphasis on secondary needs. Although no one discounts the importance of money, it is seldom enough to keep employees motivated in today's affluence. Employees today seek to satisfy needs other than their economic needs.

For most of our country's employed workers, the primary needs (physiological and security) are reasonably satisfied. Based on the previous premise that a satisfied need no longer motivates, we can conclude that as an employee's primary needs are satisfied, the incentives needed for motivation must be designed to appeal to his secondary needs (social, esteem, and self-actualization). This fact is regularly ignored in the conventional approaches to motivation.

Thus, the fact that management has provided satisfaction of the primary needs has shifted the motivational emphasis to the secondary needs. There must be opportunities at work to satisfy these higher needs. The failure of many supervisors to realize this is the reason why employees are often dissatisfied even though their wages and working conditions are quite good. When their higher-level needs go unsatisfied, employees will often make insistent demands for more money. Such a reaction does not, however, indicate an attempt to further satisfy lower-level needs; rather money becomes increasingly important for buying the material goods that may provide limited satisfaction of the higher-level needs that are not being satisfied on the job.

Behavior Is Multi-Motivated

Analysis of an individual's behavior would be simple if we could ascribe it to one basic need alone. Needs rarely influence behavior individually, however. Rather, they usually work in combination with each other. Thus, any specific behavior tends to be determined by several of the basic needs simultaneously rather than by only one. For example, the act of eating may be motivated partially by the social needs and the esteem needs (in the case of dining at a gourmet restaurant). As another illustration, sexual behavior in our society is usually multi-motivated. It reflects satisfaction of simple physiological drives as well as aspirations for such needs as belonging, love, esteem, status, and achievement. As we have already seen, earning wages often helps satisfy many of the secondary needs as well as the primary needs.

Thus, we must view Maslow's five-way classification as being somewhat artificial; in reality, the needs are intertwined within the whole man. However, even though the division between the needs is not sharp, it is still usually possible to find one dominant need that is influencing a person's behavior at any one moment. Therefore, their separation for purposes of analysis is still quite useful.

The Influence of Aspiration Levels

You may argue that some people do not seem to exhibit some of the *secondary* needs at all. As an extreme example, how do you explain the hermit who seeks no social contacts and appears to have little or no need for esteem or self-actualization?

Level of aspiration is probably a major determinant in this case and is directly related to the individual's *expectations of success* in goal achievement. Repeated failures (goal blockages) normally deflate one's self-image of competence and achievement and lead to a downward adjustment of aspirations. By the same token, a sequence of successes tends to reinforce the individual's image of his competence and ability to achieve, thereby raising his level of aspiration.

Thus, the potency of a secondary need depends to a great extent on whether the person expects to be successful in meeting that need. An employee, for instance, may have little desire to join the management ranks because he says to himself, "I know I'll never make it"; his fear of failure keeps his level of aspiration low so that he will not run the risk of failure.

To understand an employee's need structure, then, we not only have to identify his needs and know how well each is already being met, but we also need to take into account how much more satisfaction of each need a man really expects to attain, i.e., his level of aspiration.[3]

DETERMINING EMPLOYEES' INDIVIDUAL NEEDS

Understanding a theory such as Maslow's need-hierarchy by itself does not solve a supervisor's motivation problems. **The supervisor's most difficult task is to judge where his subordinates stand on the need hierarchy and then provide appropriate incentives to satisfy them.** Although it is valuable to know something about human needs in a general sense, it is even more important to know the personal needs of each of your subordinates.

Obviously, a supervisor must know a great deal about his employees before he can use the "hierarchical ordering" to his advantage. First, he must understand them as individuals. Motivation is personal; it occurs *within the individual.* As such, the incentives that appeal to one employee may be less than successful with another.

Motivation Must be Inferred From Behavior

Understanding the motivation of employees is first complicated by the fact that it cannot be directly observed, but must be *inferred* from the individual's behavior. We can measure presumed *indicators* of motivation, but not motivation itself.

The measurable indicators of motivation are based on observation of employee action: what a worker does and how he behaves. These actions can be expressed in such things as productivity, quality, turnover, grievances, promptness, absenteeism, waste prevention, high interest in the work, and so forth. For example, if we observe Jack Smith producing considerably more than any of his co-workers, we would probably infer that Jack is motivated; however, we did not directly measure his motivation.

[3]William H. Newman, Charles E. Summer, and E. Kirby Warren, *The Process of Management* (Second edition; Englewood Cliffs, New Jersey: Prentice-Hall, Inc., 1967), p. 198.

This approach, of course, often paves the way for errors of interpretation as we attempt to explain the cause of behavior from the behavior itself.

Differences in Individual Needs

Further compounding the difficult task of judging where each subordinate stands on the need hierarchy is the fact that individuals require *varying degrees* of satisfaction of each need. For example, one individual may feel reasonably secure if he knows that he will have his job for the next month; another may become quite anxious if he feels that his job might be abolished at the end of five years. Likewise, some people require little attention and affection; others seek constant reassurance of their acceptability. Thus, although the need hierarchy in particular cultures and subcultures tends to be similar, **the required degree of need fulfillment varies with individuals** due to differences in interests, attitudes, aptitudes, and past experiences. In addition, the urgency of each need may be vastly greater or smaller within the same individual at different times.

Therefore, a supervisor cannot assume that a single approach can be used to motivate all employees toward the accomplishment of the organization's goals. The supervisor must come up with an incentive that is meaningful to the individual employee.

How does the supervisor find out what the needs of each individual employee are? The answer is not a simple one.

It would be relatively easy if we could just ask a person what his needs are and rely on his answer. Unfortunately, the answers would seldom be reliable, as people themselves are often not very clear about their own needs and desires. In the case of the secondary needs, their motivations are often unconscious. For example, a dissatisfied worker may attribute his dissatisfaction to his wages, only to find later that a salary raise hasn't really satisfied him at all.

There must be considerable *rapport* between the supervisor and the employee; this takes time, personal involvement, and, above all, *empathy* on the part of the supervisor. Observations of the employee and his work record, informal talks with him, performance ratings, comments from others, and watching for the employee's responses to a variety of work assignments and incentives should provide the supervisor with a reasonable evaluation of the employee's needs. Knowing these needs, he can then proceed to try satisfying them in the job environment.

The Influence of Perception

As was discussed earlier, human behavior is goal-seeking or directed rather than being random or illogical. It is important to realize that no form of behavior is irrational or illogical *to the individual,* even though it may seem so to others who do not understand why he behaves the way he does.

People behave in ways that make sense *to them,* based on their perception and understanding of the circumstances in which they find themselves at that point in time; they behave the way they do simply because they believe that they will be better off because of the behavior.

Take the case of the welfare recipient who drives a new Cadillac. You and I may be convinced that this is irrational behavior, declaring that this person doesn't need a Cadillac. We'll never convince the welfare recipient of this, however, because to him the car is fulfilling definite needs, most likely needs for esteem and status. The person is not motivated by what you or I think he ought to need and want, but by what he himself needs and wants. In this sense, then, **all behavior is rational.**

The important topic of *perception* is treated in other parts of the book. Suffice it to say at this point that **the process of motivation always operates within the framework of the individual's perception of the situation.** The manner in which the individual perceives or interprets the situation is just as important as what the situation really is in the motivation of his behavior. Perhaps this partially explains why the rank-and-file employee typically sees his world as far different from that of his superiors.

Do Supervisors Really Know the Needs of Their Employees?

There have been countless studies of what workers want and need. Let us sum up one such typical study:

Three thousand employees were asked two questions:

1. What do you want most from your jobs?
2. How would you rate these wants in their order of importance?

Later, managers and supervisors were asked to rate the same items in the order they thought employees rated them. Here is the outcome:

Areas of Job Satisfaction Wanted Most by Employees	*Employees' Rating by Importance*	*Management's Rating by Importance*
Credit for work they do	1	7
Interest in work	2	3
Fair pay with salary increases	3	1
Understanding and appreciation	4	5
Promotion on merits	5	4
Counsel on personal problems	6	8
Physical working conditions	7	6
Job security	8	2

In comparing the management and employee ratings, it is apparent that management expected employees to be primarily motivated by salary and job security, while the employees stressed satisfaction on the job itself. While management thought employees would show little or no concern for job recognition, employees pointed out that they wanted to be given credit for doing a good job. The results of this study (as well as others) seem to show that some managers and supervisors don't have a true awareness of the wants and needs of their workers; they also illustrate management's traditional emphasis on *primary* needs as motivators.

THE FRUSTRATION OF GOAL BLOCKAGE

The total satisfaction of human needs, of course, can seldom be met on the job, even when management is willing to try to do so. The realities and constraints of the job will result in certain goals being blocked from satisfaction.

Anytime an individual is unable to satisfy his needs and thereby reduce his state of tension, he will experience *frustration.*

Our previous diagram of the motivation process as goal-seeking behavior can be expanded to illustrate the blockage of need satisfaction (see Figure 2-3).

FIGURE 2-3. Blockage of Need Satisfaction

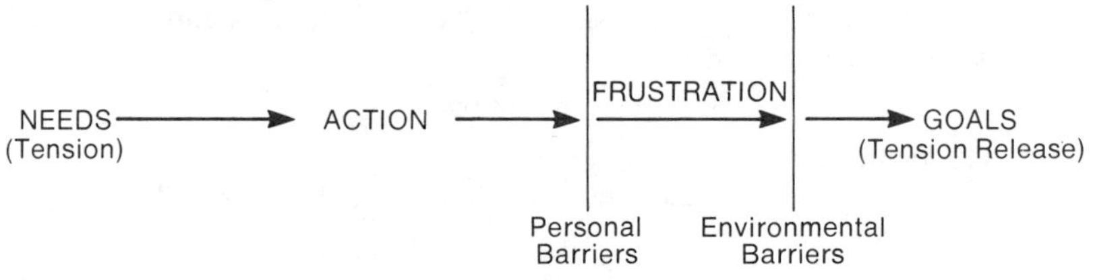

Personal and Environmental Barriers

The blocks that prevent a person's goals from being achieved can be either *personal barriers* (internal to the individual) or *environmental barriers* (external to the individual).[4]

Personal barriers result from the individual's overestimation or underestimation of his capabilities, either *physical* or *mental.* Examples are the person who does not have the physique to achieve fame as a pro football star and the man who lacks the intelligence necessary to graduate from college, even though these have been life-long goals; in both cases, the individuals *overestimated* their capabilities.

[4] S. G. Huneryager and I. L. Heckmann (editors), *Human Relations in Management* (Second edition; Cincinnati: South-Western Publishing Company, 1967), pp. 326-7.

Or, as an example of a personal barrier resulting from an *underestimation* of capabilities, consider an employee who desires to assume more responsibility or to learn to operate a new machine; lacking confidence in his ability to attain such goals, he may never attempt them or give up before reaching them.

Environmental barriers are those that exist in the situation in which the person finds himself. An example of this type of barrier could be the supervisor who stands in the way of a worker's promotion. The job itself or the organization may also be environmental barriers; for instance, a job that affords little or no opportunity for contact with other people represents an environment which precludes the worker from adequately fulfilling his social needs at work.

It is important to note that both types of barriers can be either *real* or *imaginary,* depending upon the individual's perception of the situation. As an example, the employee who is afraid to learn to operate a new machine might be imagining that he can't do so. However, since he *perceives* that he can't, the barrier exists. On the other hand, the 135-pound man aspiring to be a football star faces a very real barrier.

Reactions to Frustration

Employees caught in a state of frustration commonly react in ways that will protect their self-concepts and egos from the psychological pain of failure or defeat. These unconscious reactions to frustration are called *defense mechanisms.* Reactions will vary from person to person; some people will react in a constructive manner while others react in a defensive manner. Regardless, this reactive behavior to frustration can still be considered *goal-seeking behavior* in that it is **directed at the goal of defending the self-concept**. Unfortunately, it is often behavior not necessarily aimed at accomplishing the organization's goals.

The typical defense mechanisms can be conveniently grouped into three major classifications: (1) *aggressive reactions;* (2) *substitute reactions;* and (3) *avoidance reactions.*

Aggressive reactions

1. **Aggression**: *Direct* or *indirect* action is taken against the source of frustration. If the barrier happens to be a person, the action taken could be outright physical attack. However, in a work situation indirect action aimed at the barrier is more likely. For example, verbal aggression, antagonistic behavior, a scowl, subtle sabotage, petty thievery, absenteeism, tardiness, or "malicious obedience."

2. **Displacement**: Here, hostile feelings are *redirected* toward persons or objects *other than* the source of the frustration. In general, the substitute target is one that isn't capable of retaliation. For example, the supervisor who has just been reprimanded by his superior may in turn displace his aggression on a

subordinate worker who, in turn, may arrive home yelling at his wife or kicking his dog.

Lacking any nearby safe objects, the frustrated person may be limited to verbal abuse of such things as the state of the economy, minority groups, or women drivers. Because the world offers a multitude of such "irritations," the displacement of aggression to substitute objects is easy.

Substitute reactions

1. **Compensation:** This reaction is an attempt to overcome some real or imagined inadequacy. The individual redirects his behavior away from the unattainable goal toward a *substitute* goal from which he can gain satisfaction.

Thus, a worker who is unable to climb the management hierarchy may try to become a civic-club leader or a union official. Or, as another example, a person who has failed to achieve a desired level of social status in his community may expend a large proportion of his income on an expensive car, clothing, and other presumed material indicators of high status.

2. **Rationalization:** The individual concocts false reasons to justify failure of goal achievement in order to preserve his self-esteem; conclusions that the person *wants* to believe are arrived at through illogical thinking.

This popular type of reaction often involves blaming something or someone else for one's own failures; for example, an incompetent employee may blame obsolete equipment or those who are "against him" for his poor performance.

The person whose ego was severely injured by social contacts in the past may rationalize by saying, "I couldn't care less what other people think of me." This is his way of protecting himself from being hurt again.

Other examples include the employee who, failing to get a much-desired promotion, says, "I didn't want it anyway because it would require too much extra work," or the salesman who pads his expense account "because everybody else does it."

3. **Projection:** This reaction is an attempt to protect the individual from conscious awareness of his own undesirable feelings and attitudes by attributing (projecting) them to others; others are blamed for thoughts that are not compatible with the individual's self-concept.

For example, a subordinate who is having a bad relationship with his supervisor may feel that it is the supervisor who is being nasty and ill-tempered, when in fact this is the behavior of the subordinate.

Persons who cannot accept the fact that they are racially prejudiced (if this attitude is inconsistent with their self-concept) may ascribe this attitude to others and become "champions" for the cause of racial equality.

4. **Identification:** The achievements of a successful person become the conquests of the frustrated "little man." The individual gets pleasure from the success of another person when his own success is blocked. This process frequently leads to internalizing the beliefs and mannerisms of the person being

identified with; for example, the rank-and-file employee may start talking, dressing, and acting like his admired boss. Identification, of course, is what "hero worship" is all about.

Avoidance reactions

1. **Regression:** When confronted with frustration, some people attempt to return to immature, childlike behavior. This reaction evidently allows them to escape the realities of adult responsibilities. Desk-pounding, temper tantrums, horseplay, and a desire to return to "the good old days" are examples. Or, the supervisor who has been blocked in some pursuit may busy himself with clerical duties more appropriate for his subordinates.

2. **Repression:** The individual loses conscious awareness (or "forgets") incidents or feelings that would cause frustration and anxiety if permitted to remain at the conscious level. Thus, a subordinate may "forget" to tell his boss about a personally emabarrassing or painful incident.

3. **Withdrawal:** In this reaction, the individual retreats from reality by leaving the situation in which frustration is experienced. The withdrawal may be *physical* (actually leaving the scene) or *psychological.*

Increased absenteeism, extended lunch hours or coffee breaks, extra days off, and increased turnover represent examples of ways employees may seek to withdraw physically from jobs that provide little need satisfaction.

Fantasizing and daydreaming provide examples of psychological withdrawal from a frustrating work environment.

4. **Apathy:** The frustrated person resigns himself to the fact that a situation exists beyond his control. Typical behavior evidencing this reaction includes doing the bare minimum required to retain the job, doing nothing to correct a malfunction, or simply not caring if something is done right or not.

Implications for the Supervisor

You can no doubt think of examples of your own reactions to frustration that illustrate the basic defense mechanisms. All of us use these defense mechanisms at one time or another because they perform an important function in protecting our self-concepts and helping us adjust to reality. Thus, a supervisor should find a knowledge of them beneficial in understanding the behavior of his subordinates, as well as himself.

Unless carried to an extreme degree, such behavior is considered normal. However, when defense mechanisms dominate behavior (as is especially likely with the avoidance reactions), a serious personality problem may exist requiring professional help.

An understanding of defense mechanisms should give the supervisor greater empathy in his everyday interactions with subordinates. However, it is important to view such reactions on the part of subordinates as *symptoms* of underlying causes. Take the example of an employee who frequently takes longer than allowed for his lunch break. This might be a withdrawal reaction to an unchallenging, boring job. The supervisor's action in this case would best be aimed at eliminating the basic *cause* of the frustration (the boring and unchallenging job), not at severely reprimanding the employee for his tardiness (the symptom).

The employees' relative use of defense mechanisms can often serve as valuable clues to the degree to which their needs are being fulfilled. The supervisor can then help to reduce, when possible, the environmental and personal barriers to their goal achievement.

MOTIVATION IS INTERNAL

There are still some supervisors who believe that the only motivation needed to get a job done is a direct order: "Do it—or ELSE!" Such supervisors who think their authority is motivation enough will answer in any discussion about motivation, "I'm too busy to go around coddling my people. I give them an order and the job gets done; but if they goof off, they'll hear from me soon enough." This reaction is common, sometimes even understandable; but it also reflects a basic misconception about how people are best motivated.

If you are willing to accept our previous concepts of motivation, you can readily see that one cannot truly "motivate" anyone else. "Motivation" does not mean something that supervisors try to "do" to other people.

When you get right down to it, people must motivate themselves. Motivation should be viewed as coming from *within the individual* (internalized) rather than from his supervisor. As motivation expert Frederick Herzberg has said, "I can charge a man's battery, and then recharge it, and recharge it again. But it is only when he has his own generator that we can talk about motivation. He then needs no outside stimulation. He *wants* to do it."[5]

Actually, the only thing a supervisor can do to achieve genuine cooperation from his subordinates is to create an atmosphere in which each individual will want to move in the direction of achieving the organization's goals while at the same time achieving his own personal goals; in other words, the supervisor can provide a *motivating environment.* The supervisor cannot force the employee to accept the goals of the organization or to seek fulfillment of all his needs on the job. But the supervisor can create an environment, or an atmosphere, where the employee is encouraged and able to seek such satisfaction for himself.

[5]Frederick Herzberg, "One More Time: How Do You Motivate Employees?" *Harvard Business Review,* January-February, 1968, p. 55.

The supervisor must help his employees to satisfy *their* needs before he can logically expect the employees to achieve the goals of the organization.

McGregor's "Theories X & Y"

Much discussion has evolved out of Maslow's original concept of the need hierarchy, most of it indicating that the motivational methods that may have worked well enough a generation ago are increasingly ineffective today. Perhaps the most important effort along these lines is the work of the late Douglas McGregor.

McGregor saw the emergence of two basic sets of assumptions about human behavior that characterize management styles. He labeled these sets of assumptions "Theory X" and "Theory Y." These two theories reflect completely different approaches to the motivation of people and have spurred much of the research done since the early 1960s on leadership styles and motivation.

Theory X. Theory X represents the "traditional approach" to the management of people. According to McGregor, it assumes that people are inherently lazy, that they dislike work, and will avoid it if possible; that they prefer being told what to do, avoid responsibility, and have little ambition.

Managerial style under Theory X assumptions tends to depend on the methods of *coercion,* which uses the threat of termination as a means of compelling a person to work, and *compensation,* which uses the reward of money as a means of attracting the person to perform activities needed by the company. Both of these methods assume that people have to be subjected to some form of *external control* to insure productivity; in other words, the supervisor must maintain a close surveillance if the organization's objectives are to be obtained.

Whether we like it or not, many business organizations of today are modeled on Theory X beliefs; many management policies and practices seem to reflect these assumptions (for an extreme example, see Reading Selection 2). Is it small wonder that conflict and strain often develop between management and workers when management consciously or unconsciously communicates the way they feel about the people who work for them?

Theory Y. Theory Y, on the other hand, holds that, given the opportunity and incentive, most people want to work. People will not only accept but, in many cases, seek responsibility. McGregor contended that management, instead of depending solely on direction and control, should concentrate on creating an environment that releases man's potential, fully utilizes the employee's talents and training, creates opportunity, removes obstacles to individual initiative, and encourages individual growth.

A Theory Y environment integrates the organization's objectives with the individual's needs. If a worker is committed to the objectives of the organization, he will exercise *self-discipline* and *self-control.*

It is important to note that McGregor did not deny that human behavior in the average organization often reflects the traditional assumptions of Theory X. But he was sure that this behavior is *not* the consequence of man's inherent nature, but rather of man's experiences and conditioning under Theory X organizations. The traditional approach, according to McGregor, is based on the mistaken notion of what is *cause* and what is *effect.*

Certainly, the kinds of assumptions that a supervisor makes about people—whether Theory X or Theory Y—have a tremendous impact upon the things he says and does and lead to completely different approaches to motivation. In essence, Theory X implies that motivation is *external to the individual,* and Theory Y implies that motivation comes from *within the individual.* As has already been stated, we must support the latter implication.

MOTIVATION IN PERSPECTIVE

"How do I go about motivating my subordinates?" The answer to this frequently asked question is obviously of great importance to the supervisor who views his primary function as getting work done through people. Ultimately, getting the work accomplished is entirely dependent upon the *behavior* of the employees comprising the work group. Thus, the supervisor must have insight and knowledge about why people are motivated to behave as they do.

We have defined motivation as *goal-seeking behavior;* from a supervisory viewpoint, it is the stimulus for directing the behavior of subordinates toward the goals and objectives of the organization. It is every supervisor's responsibility to consider how he can more effectively provide a motivating environment for his employees; his task is to create work conditions that will get his employees to enthusiastically accomplish the organization's goals *because they want to.* The degree of effort exerted by an employee toward the accomplishment of his job and, to a large extent, the quantity and quality of his work are determined by the amount and type of his motivation.

The theories and concepts of the motivation process that we have discussed in this chapter may at times appear confusing and somewhat difficult to understand; their practical application on the job can admittedly often be even more difficult.

Nevertheless, the supervisor who has a basic understanding of human needs, who has the ability to estimate which need is predominant in an individual employee at a particular time, and who is able to supply a work environment that attempts to satisfy these employee needs will be far more effective in releasing the full potential of his employees than will a counterpart who lacks these abilities. In essence, to understand what motivates people to want to perform well on the job is, in large part, to understand how to be a good supervisor.

Certainly, we still have much to learn about human motivation and the practical application of motivation theories to the work place; but there are productivity gains waiting for the supervisor who, even in a small way, can put to work our present supply of knowledge.

Reading Selection 2

*HOW TO MOTIVATE?**

Jud Morris

It's a well-known fact that the great preponderance of aircraft *structural* failures are directly attributable to excessive air speeds. In short, insofar as structure is concerned, airplanes are conservatively designed and they're more than adequate as long as they're flown the way they're supposed to be flown!

Years ago, when I was employed as an Aeronautical Design Evaluation Engineer with the, then, Civil Aeronautics Administration, we were seriously concerned with ways and means of assuring that airplanes, particularly private airplanes, would, in fact, be flown the way they were designed to be flown. A major concern was: how to prevent pilots from exceeding V_{ne}, the "never exceed" velocity. Someone came up with the world-shaking suggestion that a red line should be placed at V_{ne} on the airspeed indicator! Naturally, structural failures plummeted—as did the airplanes!

Motivation is defined as "making an employee want to do what he is assigned or directed to do." It is unquestionably one of the most worrisome functions of the present-day manager—and, very probably, his most important one! I would like to suggest a few "red line" approaches which should eliminate this problem once and for all.

First, and most important of all, the manager must adopt formal rules for motivating "his" people. These rules should be issued in the form of official policies or procedures and should be clear-cut, well-defined, and unvarying in their application to all employees alike. Here are a few examples I have found to be most effective.

1. Whenever an employee makes a mistake, provide him with a written notice of deficiency, one copy to the employee and one to his permanent personnel file. This is invaluable in that it provides the employee with concrete evidence of his own inadequacy—and gives you something to sink your teeth into at the next performance interview. It will save endless arguments and discussions directed at finding out *why* the mistake was

*From *Manage* (October 1967), pp. 18-24. Reprinted with permission of The National Management Association.

made, and it will place the responsibility for determining how similar mistakes can be avoided in the future right where it belongs, on the shoulders of the offender!

2. Let it be known throughout your organization that merit increases are to be based primarily on the number of mistakes a particular candidate has made since his last increase (if any). There are numerous advantages to this rule. First of all, it's a well-known fact that everyone works for money. (We're not here just because we like to be here!) Dangling the threat of financial loss over an employee's head is just as effective as promising rewards for good performance; probably better because, in the latter case, he may make some mistakes in his effort to perform well, and everyone knows that it's better that he do nothing than that he do things incorrectly.

Secondly, a system such as this will insure excellent performance at review time and this takes a real load off the manager's back. Last but not least, the threat of financial loss promotes a real spirit of healthy competition. You will receive irreplaceable help in discovering mistakes you might not otherwise have even suspected. Everyone knows that the less money you hand out to other people the more there is for him. You will find that everyone pitches in with zest to help you find other people's mistakes. Actually, this sort of team spirit can make almost any job a real "fun" game! (It might be well if you were to post the "scores" on the department bulletin board so that everyone knows exactly where he stands—uncertainty is a definitely negative motivator!)

3. In all instances, the manager must make use of every available opportunity to demonstrate his own superior knowledge and ability in all matters. No one respects a man who doesn't know at least as much as he does. If, for example, you are expecting a report on interstitial conflabulation from one of your people, study up on interstitial conflabulation. Find some little-known facts on the subject and drop them casually during the report. If possible, try to discover some phase of the subject which may have been overlooked by your employee. There's nothing like catching him off guard to motivate him. If you are unable to acquire suitable knowledge to impress him, simply question his knowledge: "Well, *I'm* no authority on the subject but I don't have to take *your* word for it" will do nicely. If you don't even know what he's talking about, fake it! Chances are he won't "call you"; after all, you're the "Boss"!

4. The manager must never show outward enthusiasm for his employees' ideas. This will only lower you to their level and make you lose their respect. At all times play the "Devil's Advocate"—even if you agree with an employee, don't let him know it. Frown, look doubtful, purse your lips, and make some comment like, "Weeeel, I dòn't know . . . ." It's important that you make him "sell" you—otherwise, *you* may be blamed if the project is a flop or worse yet, he may get the credit if it's not! Let him know it too! Simply come right out and say, "Well, *I'm* the manager. *I'm* responsible for everything that goes on in this department. If things are O.K., you guys get the credit; if things go wrong I get the blame!" (Look him straight in the eye and he may believe this hogwash!)

5. Closely related to item 4, above, allow your employees to shoulder their responsibility. If, for example, the president is displeased with one of them, let him have his "day in court." Don't try to act as a "buffer" for your men. After all, *they* did it. If it's wrong, let *them* defend it. No one likes to have some third party present his case. Anyhow, if *you* try to speak in their behalf, the big boss is

liable to think that *you* were in some way responsible for the whole mess! Let your people know that you consider them to be mature adults—and that you're going to let them shoulder the blame for their own mistakes. This is the o-n-l-y way to make them acquire the responsibility so necessary to success in this dog-eat-dog world.

6. Probably one of the most subtle requirements for any manager worth his pay is the necessity for being supremely noncommittal. After all, *you* are the manager! *Don't* let subordinates "sluff off" their responsibility for decisions. Don't allow them to become dependent on your advice. You may know the answer—but let 'em figure it out for themselves. It'll do 'em good! Always qualify your statements. It is fatal to be found wrong, so leave yourself some sort of opening in case of emergency. "If you have a problem, don't hesitate to come to me—if it's really important." "Believe me, I'm behind you 100 per cent—as long as you're on safe ground." And here's the best one of all, "Don't do as I *say*, do what I *mean*!" That'll really separate the men from the boys!

It's also a good idea to pass a little of this "hedging" on to your people (after all, development is one of your functions too). Tell 'em to be completely honest in their opinions—but cautious. Suggest that what's really needed is more creativity, but add a statement like "Of course, we wouldn't want everyone going around being creative, would we?" Assure them that they are in complete charge of their projects—but always remind them that they're part of a team and that there has to be a captain for every team. (You might straighten your necktie at this point—or polish your fingernails on the lapel of your jacket.)

7. In order to assure real enthusiasm on the part of his employees, the manager should keep them in a state of general suspense. Give 'em something to keep 'em on their toes. It's a good policy to hint that there are going to be "certain important changes" in the not-too-far distant future. This will keep 'em guessing—and promote a healthy spirit of competition. Just as the Project Engineer on a certain project is leaving your office, you might say casually, "You know I'm thinking about making a separate group out of your project—supervisor and all!" Then, when he asks for details, just mumble, "We'll see, we'll see . . . ," or better yet, look him straight in the eye and say, "Of course, a lot depends on how things go for the next month or so . . . ." Never leave out the "or so." This is invaluable in building suspense—besides, it prevents you from ever being "tied down" on the matter.

8. The effective manager is, above all, detail minded. Nothing is too small, too insignificant, to merit his attention. People will admire your ability to pick the flyspecks out of the pepper. "Boy, can *he* spot the little things!" "Nobody can get anything past *him*!" "That guy could find a misplaced comma in a hundred-page report without even opening it."

That's YOU they're talking about! Sort of gives you a warm feeling right "here," doesn't it? Don't let them trap you into discussing principles or fundamentals. They may trap you into something where *you* are wrong! Stick to the unimportant details where you know you're safe. If a man is conducting an investigation of the entire production control system for you, be sure that he's using the right *forms*. If someone has prepared a highly technical report for you, look for split infinitives. If it's a new design of a complicated product, make sure that the arrowheads on the dimension lines are to your liking. Let 'em know that they're responsible for the survey, report, or design. *You* are going to be sure that those oft-overlooked details are in order. You'll get a tremendous reputation by doing this—and you'll always be on "solid ground."

9. We've already mentioned healthy competition a couple of times but it's worth a category all by itself. Competition is a wonderful thing. Under stress the average human can do almost unbelievable things. Keep 'em under stress! Be sure that there are always at least two candidates for each and every job—and that they are kept constantly aware of this fact. Let your people know that only the best of them are going to survive. Keep 'em fighting amongst themselves for the "plum" assignments. Let 'em know that there's liable to be a layoff and that you're just now trying to decide who goes.

Not only will this keep 'em working at their best, but it will also prevent their getting together except when absolutely necessary. Everyone knows that two people working *together* are a lot more effective than two people working separately. This effect gets worse and worse as the numbers increase and, before you know it, your job may be in jeopardy! No, sir! You wouldn't want *that*! A boss is a boss and you can't have people ganging up on you. Divide and conquer, *that's* the secret! Keep 'em fighting among themselves and you'll have nothing to worry about.

10. The manager who is a motivator is a prodder. He *never* loses sight of the fact that *he* is responsible for the ultimate success of every project under his cognizance—and he *never* lets anyone else forget it. Let the fellows know that you're interested. Even if they submit complete status reports, question them as a matter of routine. If a man tells you that he will be at a certain stage "by Friday," check up on him Monday, Tuesday, Wednesday, and Thursday. Let him know that you're staying "on top" of the program—that you're not depending on *him*! If things are on schedule, shake your head, frown, and walk away as though you were unable to believe it; if they're not, give him hell! (It might be a good idea to suggest that there are a couple of other people who could do it better. *That* usually sparks some action!)

11. There's an old saying, "What they don't know, won't hurt them." No truer words were ever spoken as far as motivation is concerned! Each and every man in the efficiently run organization has plenty to keep him busy without cluttering up his mind with irrelevant facts—like how business is going, whether the new man in the group is going to be put in charge, or why there haven't been any merit increases for over a year.

Things of this nature are strictly "management" information and there is no rhyme or reason in spreading such tidbits about the office willy-nilly! If they ask, be polite—but firm. Smile knowingly and say, "Sorry, I'm not allowed to say," or "That's for me to know and you to find out." It is important that each individual know exactly where he stands and, by letting him know that *he* is not "management," you've got this matter settled once and for all!

12. Just to make an even dozen suggested rules, let's talk about being open and above-board in all matters. It's the manager's duty and obligation to be completely open with his people at all times. If someone pulls a boo-boo, tell him so—right out in front of God and everybody! He'll respect you for your frankness and courage. Don't wait until you're in the shelter of your office to chew him out—he'll think you're a coward. Tell him off in front of the whole staff. That way *everybody* in the whole department will get the advantage of your wise words. Particularly, if there are people who report to him in the vicinity, let *them* know who's really "Boss." You can get the message across to an entire group in this manner (if you talk loudly enough).

As a matter of fact, it is often helpful to get such messages to the group by giving the supervisor what-for even if he doesn't deserve it. There's usually *someone* in the vicinity who will profit by a little "advice" so you might as well take advantage of the opportunity. The use of the "scapegoat" is an old and honorable means of asserting one's authority and importance. (It's also useful in clouding the issue and shifting the blame, a not inconsequential advantage under certain circumstances.)

Make no mistake about it, the above is not a comprehensive list of rules for accomplishing "motivation" in the true sense of the word. It is simply a set of guidelines for the uninitiated. It should serve to start one on the way toward outstanding and effective motivation. It is important, however, that these (or any other) rules be formally established and published for all to see. There are those who maintain that motivation cannot be set forth in arbitrary rules and regulations. This is a bunch of HOGWASH! People are people, the world over. We are all motivated by the same wishes and desires! Genghis Khan, Napoleon Bonaparte, and Adolph Hitler motivated whole nations by the application of simple rules such as those outlined above. Machiavelli, in his inestimable treatise, *The Prince,* outlined in 1532 a system for motivating people which has not changed in the past 435 years.

Oh, sure, there may be a few "oddballs" here and there who are not primarily interested in money, or security. We can always handle them by presenting them with loyalty buttons, efficiency pins, or an extra bookcase. However, they are the exceptions to the rule. They are the very special, intelligent few—like you and me—and we, of course, being members of management, are self-motivated! We motivate *them* simply by dangling promises of raises in front of their noses, holding threats of disciplinary actions over their heads, and dominating them by the sheer force of our superior personalities. They are, after all, inferior to us. We should handle them as we do teenagers—and with the same results! "Motivation" is a basic function of all management: use it to advantage.

EDITOR'S NOTE:

It is hoped that most readers recognized this article as a light-hearted parody on traditional "Theory X" motivation concepts. Admittedly, the ideas expressed are grossly exaggerated; however, we believe that the article presents some very realistic examples of the motivational attitudes *still* held by many supervisors (you may even know one or two who feel this way!). To be sure, this is a serious problem, but perhaps a little levity may provide a welcome relief to the conscientious reader.

Reading Selection 3

*THE HUMAN SIDE OF ENTERPRISE**

Douglas Murray McGregor

It has become trite to say that industry has the fundamental know-how to utilize physical science and technology for the material benefit of mankind, and that we must now learn how to utilize the social sciences to make our human organizations truly effective.

To a degree, the social sciences today are in a position like that of the physical sciences with respect to atomic energy in the thirties. We know that past conceptions of the nature of man are inadequate and, in many ways, incorrect. We are becoming quite certain that, under proper conditions, unimagined resources of creative human energy could become available within the organizational setting.

We cannot tell industrial management how to apply this new knowledge in simple, economic ways. We know it will require years of exploration, much costly development, research, and a substantial amount of creative imagination on the part of management to discover how to apply this growing knowledge to the organization of human effort in industry.

MANAGEMENT'S TASK: THE CONVENTIONAL VIEW

The conventional conception of management's task in harnessing human energy to organizational requirements can be stated broadly in terms of three propositions. In order to avoid the complications introduced by a label, let us call this set of propsitions "Theory X":

1. Management is responsible for organizing the elements of productive enterprise—money, materials, equipment, people—in the interest of economic ends.
2. With respect to people, this is a process of directing their efforts, motivating them, controlling their actions, modifying their behavior to fit the needs of the organization.
3. Without this active intervention by management, people would be passive—even resistant—to organizational needs. They must therefore be persuaded, rewarded, punished, controlled—their activities must be directed. This is management's task. We often sum it up by saying that management consists of getting things done through other people.
4. The average man is by nature indolent—he works as little as possible.
5. He lacks ambition, dislikes responsibility, prefers to be led.
6. He is inherently self-centered,

*Reprinted by permission of the publisher from *Management Review,* © November 1957 by the American Management Association, Inc.

indifferent to organizational needs.
7. He is by nature resistant to change.
8. He is gullible, not very bright, the ready dupe of the charlatan and the demagogue.

The human side of economic enterprise today is fashioned from propositions and beliefs such as these. Conventional organization structures and managerial policies, practices, and programs reflect these assumptions.

In accomplishing its task—with these assumptions as guides—management has conceived of a range of possibilities.

At one extreme, management can be "hard" or "strong." The methods for directing behavior involve coercion and threat (usually disguised), close supervision, tight controls over behavior. At the other extreme, management can be "soft" or "weak." The methods for directing behavior involve being permissive, satisfying people's demands, achieving harmony. Then they will be tractable, accept direction.

This range has been fairly completely explored during the past half century, and management has learned some things from the exploration. There are difficulties in the "hard" approach. Force breeds counter-forces: restriction of output, antagonism, militant unionism, subtle but effective sabotage of management objectives. This "hard" approach is especially difficult during times of full employment.

There are also difficulties in the "soft" approach. It leads frequently to the abdication of management—to harmony, perhaps, but to indifferent performance. People take advantage of the soft approach. They continually expect more, but they give less and less.

Currently, the popular theme is "firm but fair." This is an attempt to gain the advantages of both the hard and the soft approaches. It is reminiscent of Teddy Roosevelt's "speak softly and carry a big stick."

IS THE CONVENTIONAL VIEW CORRECT?

The findings which are beginning to emerge from the social sciences challenge this whole set of beliefs about man and human nature and about the task of management. The evidence is far from conclusive, certainly, but it is suggestive. It comes from the laboratory, the clinic, the schoolroom, the home, and even to a limited extent from industry itself.

The social scientist does not deny that human behavior in industrial organization today is approximately what management perceives it to be. He has, in fact, observed it and studied it fairly extensively. But he is pretty sure that this behavior is *not* a consequence of man's inherent nature. It is a consequence rather of the nature of industrial organizations, of management philosophy, policy, and practice. The conventional approach of Theory X is based on mistaken notions of what is cause and what is effect.

Perhaps the best way to indicate why the conventional approach of management is inadequate is to consider the subject of motivation.

PHYSIOLOGICAL NEEDS

Man is a wanting animal—as soon as one of his needs is satisfied, another appears in its place. This process is unending. It continues from birth to death.

Man's needs are organized in a series of levels—a hierarchy of importance. At the lowest level, but preeminent in importance when they are thwarted, are his *physiological needs.* Man lives for bread alone, when there is no bread. Unless the circumstances are unusual, his needs for love, for status, for recognition are inoperative when his stomach has been empty for a while. But when he eats regularly and adequately, hunger ceases to be an important motivation. The same is true of the other physiological needs of man—for rest, exercise, shelter, protection from the elements.

A satisfied need is not a motivator of behavior! This is a fact of profound significance that is regularly ignored in the conventional approach to the management of people. Consider your own need for air: Except as you are deprived of it, it has no appreciable motivating effect upon your behavior.

SAFETY NEEDS

When the physiological needs are reasonably satisfied, needs at the next higher level begin to dominate man's behavior—to motivate him. These are called *safety needs.* They are needs for protection against danger, threat, deprivation. Some people mistakenly refer to these as needs for security. However, unless man is in a dependent relationship where he fears arbitrary deprivation, he does not demand security. The need is for the "fairest possible break." When he is confident of this, he is more than willing to take risks. But when he feels threatened or dependent, his greatest need is for guarantees, for protection, for security.

The fact needs little emphasis that, since every industrial employee is in a dependent relationship, safety needs may assume considerable importance. Arbitrary management actions, behavior which arouses uncertainty with respect to continued employment or which reflects favoritism or discrimination, unpredictable administration of policy—these can be powerful motivators of the safety needs in the employment relationship *at every level,* from worker to vice president.

SOCIAL NEEDS

When man's physiological needs are satisfied and he is no longer fearful about his physical welfare, his *social needs* become important motivators of his behavior—needs for belonging, for associaton, for acceptance by his fellows, for giving and receiving friendship and love.

Management knows today of the existence of these needs, but it often assumes quite wrongly that they represent a threat to the organization. Many studies have demonstrated that the tightly knit, cohesive work group may, under proper conditions, be far more effective than an equal number of separate individuals in achieving organizational goals.

Yet management, fearing group hostility to its own objectives, often goes to considerable lengths to control and direct human efforts in ways that are inimical to the natural "groupiness" of human beings. When man's social needs—and perhaps his safety needs, too—are thus thwarted, he behaves in ways which tend to defeat organizational objectives. He becomes resistant, antagonistic, uncooperative. But this behavior is a consequence, not a cause.

EGO NEEDS

Above the social needs—in the sense that they do not become motivators until lower needs are reasonably satisfied—are the needs of greatest significance to management and to man himself. They are the *egoistic needs,* and they are two kinds:

1. Those needs that relate to one's self-esteem—needs for self-

confidence, for independence, for achievement, for competence, for knowledge.

2. Those needs that relate to one's reputation—needs for status, for recognition, for appreciation, for the deserved respect of one's fellows.

Unlike the lower needs, these are rarely satisfied; man seeks indefinitely for more satisfaction of these needs once they have become important to him. But they do not appear in any significant way until physiological, safety, and social needs are all reasonably satisfied.

The typical industrial organization offers few opportunities for the satisfaction of these egoistic needs to people at lower levels in the hierarchy. The conventional methods of organizing work, particularly in mass-production industries, give little heed to these aspects of human motivation. If the practices of scientific management were deliberately calculated to thwart these needs, they could hardly accomplish this purpose better than they do.

SELF-FULFILLMENT NEEDS

Finally—a capstone, as it were, on the hierarchy of man's needs—there are what we may call the *needs for self-fulfillment.* These are the needs for realizing one's own potentialities, for continued self-development, for being creative in the broadest sense of that term.

It is clear that the conditions of modern life give only limited opportunity for these relatively weak needs to obtain expression. The deprivation most people experience with respect to other lower-level needs diverts their energies into the struggle to satisfy *those* needs, and the needs for self-fulfillment remain dormant.

MANAGEMENT AND MOTIVATION

We recognize readily enough that a man suffering from a severe dietary deficiency is sick. The deprivation of physiological needs has behavioral consequences. The same is true—although less well recognized—of deprivation of higher-level needs. The man whose needs for safety, association, independence, or status are thwarted is sick just as surely as the man who has rickets. And his sickness will have behavioral consequences. We will be mistaken if we attribute his resultant passivity, his hostility, his refusal to accept responsibility to his inherent "human nature." These forms of behavior are *symptoms* of illness—of deprivation of his social and egoistic needs.

The man whose lower-level needs are satisfied is not motivated to satisfy those needs any longer. For practical purposes they exist no longer. Management often asks, "Why aren't people more productive? We pay good wages, provide good working conditions, have excellent fringe benefits and steady employment. Yet people do not seem to be willing to put forth more than minimum effort."

The fact that management has provided for these physiological and safety needs has shifted the motivational emphasis to the social and perhaps to the egoistic needs. Unless there are opportunities at *work* to satisfy these higher-level needs, people will be deprived; and their behavior will reflect this deprivation. Under such conditions, if management continues to focus its attention on physiological needs, its efforts are bound to be ineffective.

People *will* make insistent demands for more money under these conditions. It becomes more important than ever to buy the material goods and services which can provide limited satisfaction of the thwarted needs. Although money has only limited value in satisfying many higher-level needs, it can become the focus of interest if it is the *only* means available.

THE CARROT-AND-STICK APPROACH

The carrot-and-stick theory of motivation (like Newtonian physical theory) works reasonably well under certain circumstances. The *means* for satisfying man's physiological and (within limits) his safety needs can be provided or withheld by management. Employment itself is such a means, and so are wages, working conditions, and benefits. By these means the individual can be controlled so long as he is struggling for subsistence.

But the carrot-and-stick theory does not work at all once man has reached an adequate subsistence level and is motivated primarily by higher needs. Management cannot provide a man with self-respect, or with the respect of his fellows, or with the satisfaction of needs for self-fulfillment. It can create such conditions that he is encouraged and enabled to seek such satisfactions for *himself,* or it can thwart him by failing to create those conditions.

But this creation of conditions is not "control." It is not a good device for directing behavior. And so management finds itself in an odd position. The high standard of living created by our modern technological know-how provides quite adequately for the satisfaction of physiological and safety needs. The only significant exception is where management practices have not created confidence in a "fair break"—and thus where safety needs are thwarted. But by making possible the satisfaction of low-level needs, management has deprived itself of the ability to use as motivators the devices on which conventional theory has taught it to rely—rewards, promises, incentives, or threats and other coercive devices.

The philosophy of management by direction and control—*regardless of whether it is hard or soft*—is inadequate to motivate because the human needs on which this approach relies are today unimportant motivators of behavior. Direction and control are essentially useless in motivating people whose important needs are social and egoistic. Both the hard and the soft approach fail today because they are simply irrelevant to the situation.

People, deprived of opportunities to satisfy at work the needs which are now important to them, behave exactly as we might predict—with indolence, passivity, resistance to change, lack of responsibility, willingness to follow the demagogue, unreasonable demands for economic benefits. It would seem that we are caught in a web of our own weaving.

A NEW THEORY OF MANAGEMENT

For these and many other reasons, we require a different theory of the task of managing people based on more adequate assumptions about human nature and human motivation. I am going to be so bold as to suggest the broad dimensions of such a theory. Call it "Theory Y," if you will.

1. Management is responsible for organizing the elements of productive enterprise—money, materials, equipment, people—in the interest of economic ends.
2. People are *not* by nature passive or resistant to organizational needs. They have become so as a result of experience in organizations.

3. The motivation, the potential for development, the capacity for assuming responsibility, the readiness to direct behavior toward organizational goals are all present in people. Management does not put them there. It is a responsibility of management to make it possible for people to recognize and develop these human characteristics for themselves.
4. The essential task of management is to arrange organizational conditions and methods of operation so that people can achieve their own goals *best* by directing *their own* efforts toward organizational objectives.

This is a process primarily of creating opportunities, releasing potential, removing obstacles, encouraging growth, providing guidance. It is what Peter Drucker has called "management by objectives" in contrast to "management by control." It does *not* involve the abdication of management, the absence of leadership, the lowering of standards, or the other characteristics usually associated with the "soft" approach under Theory X.

SOME DIFFICULTIES

It is no more possible to create an organization today which will be a full, effective application of this theory than it was to build an atomic power plant in 1945. There are many formidable obstacles to overcome.

The conditions imposed by conventional organization theory and by the approach of scientific management for the past half century have tied men to limited jobs which do not utilize their capabilities, have discouraged the acceptance of responsibility, have encouraged passivity, have eliminated meaning from work. Man's habits, attitudes, expectations—his whole conception of membership in an industrial organization—have been conditioned by his experience under these circumstances.

People today are accustomed to being directed, manipulated, controlled in industrial organizations and to finding satisfaction for their social, egoistic, and self-fulfillment needs away from the job. This is true of much of management as well as of workers. Genuine "industrial citizenship"—to borrow again a term from Drucker—is a remote and unrealistic idea, the meaning of which has not even been considered by most members of industrial organizations.

Another way of saying this is that Theory X places exclusive reliance upon external control of human behavior, while Theory Y relies heavily on self-control and self-direction. It is worth noting that this difference is the difference between treating people as children and treating them as mature adults. After generations of the former, we cannot expect to shift to the latter overnight.

STEPS IN THE RIGHT DIRECTION

Before we are overwhelmed by the obstacles, let us remember that the application of theory is always slow. Progress is usually achieved in small steps. Some innovative ideas which are entirely consistent with Theory Y are today being applied with some success.

Decentralization and Delegation

These are ways of freeing people from the too-close control of conventional organization, giving them a degree of freedom to direct their own activities, to assume responsibility, and, importantly, to satisfy their egoistic needs. In this connection, the flat organization of Sears, Roebuck and

Company provides an interesting example. It forces "management by objectives," since it enlarges the number of people reporting to a manager until he cannot direct and control them in the conventional manner.

Job Enlargement

This concept, pioneered by I.B.M. and Detroit Edison, is quite consistent with Theory Y. It encourages the acceptance of responsibility at the bottom of the organization; it provides opportunities for satisfying social and egoistic needs. In fact, the reorganization of work at the factory level offers one of the more challenging opportunities for innovation consistent with Theory Y.

Participation and Consultative Management

Under proper conditions, participation and consultative management provide encouragement to people to direct their creative energies toward organizational objectives, give them some voice in decisions that affect them, provide significant opportunities for the satisfaction of social and egoistic needs. The Scanlon Plan is the outstanding embodiment of these ideas in practice.

Performance Appraisal

Even a cursory examination of conventional programs of performance appraisal within the ranks of management will reveal how completely consistent they are with Theory X. In fact, most such programs tend to treat the individual as though he were a product under inspection on the assembly line.

A few companies—among them General Mills, Ansul Chemical, and General Electric—have been experimenting with approaches which involve the individual in setting "targets" or objectives *for himself* and in a *self*-evaluation of performance semiannually or annually. Of course, the superior plays an important leadership role in this process—one, in fact, which demands substantially more competence than the conventional approach. The role is, however, considerably more congenial to many managers than the role of "judge" or "inspector" which is usually forced upon them. Above all, the individual is encouraged to take a greater responsibility for planning and appraising his own contribution to organizational objectives; and the accompanying effects on egoistic and self-fulfillment needs are substantial.

APPLYING THE IDEAS

The not infrequent failure of such ideas as these to work as well as expected is often attributable to the fact that a management has "bought the idea" but applied it within the framework of Theory X and its assumptions.

Delegation is not an effective way of exercising management by control. Participation becomes a farce when it is applied as a sales gimmick or a device for kidding people into thinking they are important. Only the management that has confidence in human capacities and is itself directed toward organizational objectives rather than toward the preservation of personal power can grasp the implications of this emerging theory. Such management will find and apply successfully other innovative ideas as we move slowly toward the full implementation of a theory like Y.

THE HUMAN SIDE OF ENTERPRISE

It is quite possible for us to realize substantial improvements in the effectiveness of industrial organizations during the next decade or two. The social sciences can contribute much to such developments; we are only beginning to grasp the implications of the growing body of knowledge in these fields. But if this conviction is to become a reality instead of a pious hope, we will need to view the process much as we view the process of releasing the energy of the atom for constructive human ends—as a slow, costly, sometimes discouraging approach toward a goal which would seem to many to be quite unrealistic.

The ingenuity and the perseverance of industrial management in the pursuit of economic ends have changed many scientific and technological dreams into commonplace realities. It is now becoming clear that the application of these same talents to the human side of enterprise will not only enhance substantially these materialistic achievements, but will bring us one step closer to "the good society."

QUESTIONS FOR REVIEW AND DISCUSSION

1. a. What is *motivation*?
   b. Can supervisors actually "motivate" anyone? Explain.
2. Employers are often heard to say, "Why do we have to worry about motivating people? We pay them a good salary, provide good working conditions, and have excellent fringe benefits—and yet, people don't seem to be willing to put forth more than a minimum of effort. They *ought* to be motivated to do a good job for us, shouldn't they?" How would you respond to such a comment?
3. a. Explain the basic needs stated by Maslow in the sequence in which they normally occur. Is it necessary for a supervisor to be familiar with the basic needs of man in order to motivate employees successfully? Explain.
   b. Explain what is meant by the "hierarchical" nature of these needs. How can a supervisor make use of the need hierarchy concept?
4. "Virtually any social group or clique which forms and functions during working hours is a potential threat to satisfaction of the company's goals." How would you respond to this comment?
5. a. It is often said that supervisors are frequently uninformed about their employees' needs for esteem and recognition. Do you agree? Why?
   b. Discuss various ways of helping employees satisfy these needs on the job.
6. a. "You can say what you want to about psychological needs. I still say money is the best motivator. In the final analysis, if you give a guy a raise or promise to give him one, you'll motivate him." How would you reply to this statement?
   b. What are some of the possible reasons other than salary or fringe benefits that might affect your decision to accept one employment

offer over another? Would these reasons outweigh a difference in salary of $100 per month? Relate your reasons to Maslow's need hierarchy.

7. If money is not a "true" motivator, how do monetary incentive plans achieve increased production in many companies?
8. a. Many changes are occurring in our society today that are seemingly responsible for a shift in motivational emphasis from the "primary" needs to the "secondary" needs. What factors do you believe account for this?
   b. Several recent polls of college students have shown a large percentage of them opposed to taking management or management trainee jobs. Top salaries and the chance to climb the "corporate ladder" are refused by many. At the same time, a growing number have chosen careers in social work and education—including those with degrees in business. What do you feel is motivating these people to reverse the trend of a few years ago?
9. A middle-level manager, whose future success seemed insured, quit his job four years ago at the age of thirty-one to become a writer. Since then he has sold very few stories and suffered a considerable financial loss. He maintains, however, that he is optimistic, happy, and satisfied with his work. How do you reconcile this situation with Maslow's hierarchy of needs?
10. a. What motivates *you* to do a good job?
    b. What is motivating you to take this course? Specifically, what needs are you attempting to satisfy?
11. Evaluate the merits of using *competition* among employees or groups in an effort to motivate them. What employee needs might this satisfy?
12. Is a proper program of employee training and development a necessary requirement for effective employee motivation? Explain.
13. a. Repeated efforts to unionize engineers have largely met with failure. Many engineers agree that as a group they would likely be helped by the unions, but they don't want to join. How would you explain this?
    b. What motivates an employee to join a labor union (irrespective of the "closed shop")? In other words, what basic needs are typically fulfilled by union membership?
14. a. Discuss how *level of aspiration* affects an employee's needs.
    b. What effect might level of education have on a person's aspirations?
15. How does a supervisor go about identifying the individual needs and aspiration levels of his subordinates? How may he use this knowledge profitably?
16. a. When does *frustration* occur?
    b. "Employees are not disagreeable and uncooperative simply because they want to be; more likely, such behavior is caused by the lack of fulfillment of certain basic needs on the job." Evaluate this statement.
    c. In what three basic ways can a person react in order to escape frustration? What is the primary purpose of these reactions?
    d. Recall a recent experience that proved to be quite frustrating to you. How did you react? What *defense mechanisms* did you employ?
17. "The needs of subordinates are not only different from, but often in direct conflict with, the needs of the organization that the supervisor must satisfy." Do you agree? Explain.

18. a. In McGregor's "Theory X," what are the assumptions a supervisor makes about his workers? Are these assumptions basically correct? Why?
    b. Do you believe that most organizations are based upon "Theory X" assumptions? Explain.
19. a. What are the fundamental differences between "Theory X" and "Theory Y"?
    b. Recall the approaches to motivating students used by different instructors under whom you have studied. Which approaches were the most effective in motivating you to exert extra effort? Relate these approaches to McGregor's "Theories X & Y."
20. In your opinion, why do some supervisors persistently resist changing their traditional concepts of motivation?

SUGGESTED ADDITIONAL READINGS

Because of the similarity of subject matter, suggested additional readings for this chapter are combined with those listed at the end of Chapter 3.

3

MOTIVATION THROUGH MEANINGFUL JOB DESIGN

Although it may not be fashionable to admit it, most people actually like to work. Have you ever noticed how much mental and physical work people will do without getting any pay for it at all? Take the worker who puts in his 40 hours doing a highly repetitive job. It's monotonous, and he hates it, maintaining that the only reason he works is to eat. Yet when his time is up each day, he rushes home to work in his garden, mow the lawn, paint the house, work on the car, go bowling, or take the family camping on the weekend. Why does he put effort into these tasks while lacking interest in his job? The probable answer is that he likes what he is doing—something he can't say for his job.

It is unfortunate but true that there is often a substantial *gap* between the needs employees bring to their jobs and the satisfactions derived from the jobs. Certainly in many jobs this gap is small or even nonexistent. However, there are many other jobs in business and industry where the gap is wide and seemingly unbridgeable; these jobs are typically characterized by highly repetitive, monotonous activities offering few opportunities for a motivating environment. One of the dangers of this type of job, in which a worker finds no challenge and little pride of accomplishment, is that even though he may show up every day, to all intents and purposes the company has lost him.

HERZBERG'S MOTIVATION-MAINTENANCE THEORY

A logical starting point for discovering ways to narrow this gap and making work more motivating and meaningful is an examination of the work of Frederick Herzberg and his now famous Motivation-Maintenance Theory.

In extensive studies, Herzberg concluded that motivation is essentially a *two-dimensional* problem. He found that some factors of a job, when not present, primarily *dissatisfy* employees. However, the presence of these factors does not build strong motivation. Herzberg called these factors *maintenance* or *hygiene* factors because they are necessary to prevent dissatisfaction.[1]

On the other hand, other factors were found which, if present, build high degrees of job *satisfaction* and thus motivation. If not present, however, they do not prove highly dissatisfying. These satisfying factors were labeled *motivators.*

Thus, Herzberg determined that the factors involved in producing job *satisfaction* are separate and distinct from those leading to job *dissatisfaction.* He came to use the term "motivation" in a restricted sense, applying it only to job factors or experiences that produce high levels of satisfaction, rather than in its more general sense.

As the Motivation-Maintenance Theory is admittedly difficult to understand at first glance, let us examine it in more detail.

The Motivators

When the subjects of Herzberg's studies said they were satisfied with their jobs, they most often described factors related directly to the job itself, i.e., *job content.* These job-centered *motivator* factors are:

1. **Achievement**: a feeling of personal accomplishment; meeting success in solving a problem; seeing good results from one's work; or completing a challenging job.
2. **Recognition for achievement**: being recognized for doing one's work well; receiving praise or acknowledgement from superiors, the company, fellow workers, or the public.
3. **The work itself**: performing creative or challenging work; liking the work one does.
4. **Responsibility**: having some responsibility for making decisions affecting one's own work; being permitted to work without close supervision.
5. **Growth**: The opportunity to learn new skills and knowledge; personal development.
6. **Advancement**: the opportunity for promotion.

Again, these motivator factors lead to strong satisfaction when they are present but do not cause much dissatisfaction when they are absent. In other words, the employee does not seem to miss them when they are not around. For example, if recognition led to a good feeling about the job, the lack of recognition was seldom indicated as a cause of bad feelings.

Not only do these factors tend to satisfy and, in turn, motivate employees, they also serve to develop employees rather than merely maintaining them at a constant level of competence.

[1]The term "hygiene" was originally used in a suggested analogy to the term used in preventive medicine.

The Maintainers

In contrast to the motivators derived from the content of the job itself, Herzberg's subjects reported that the job factors which were most often dissatisfying were related to conditions that *surround* the job itself, i.e., the *job environment.* These *maintainers* include:

1. **Salary**: anything involving compensation and fringe benefits.
2. **Working conditions**: things such as lighting, tools, air conditioning or heating, or parking facilities.
3. **Security**: feeling certain about the future; financial contentment.
4. **Company policy and administration**: the competence of management; the effectiveness of personnel policies.
5. **Behavior of supervision**: the supervisor's competence, ability to provide guidance, and fairness.
6. **Interpersonal relationships**: social interaction with fellow workers and the supervisor.

When any of these factors are deficient, employees are likely to become dissatisfied and to express this dissatisfaction in ways detrimental to the organization's goals. Thus, the supervisor must always be concerned with maintaining, in Herzberg's words, "a good hygienic environment." However, the improvement of the maintenance factors is not likely to provide satisfaction or "genuine" motivation.

Relationship of Motivators and Maintainers

It is important to reiterate that the factors involved in producing job *satisfaction* (and, thus, motivation) are separate and distinct from the factors leading to job *dissatisfaction.* Satisfaction and dissatisfaction, in this sense, should not be viewed as opposites. The opposite of job satisfaction is not job dissatisfaction but, rather, *no* job satisfaction. Similarly, the opposite of job dissatisfaction is not job satisfaction but *no* job dissatisfaction. This relationship can be seen in Figure 3-1.

FIGURE 3-1. Relationship Between Maintenance and Motivation Factors

	MOTIVATORS	MAINTAINERS
If Present	Job Satisfaction	No Job Dissatisfaction
If Not Present	No Job Satisfaction	Job Dissatisfaction

As an example, when wages are considered to be inadequate, the principal effect will be dissatisfaction. However, the principal effect of a wage increase will be to remove dissatisfaction, not to create satisfaction. At best, employees can be brought only to a *neutral point* by such maintainers.

Herzberg's studies have, however, indicated that when an individual is denied motivation opportunities, he may become preoccupied with the maintenance factors, i.e., a "maintenance seeker." Not being able to find any real satisfaction in the job, the individual continually strives to reach that neutral point of an absence of job dissatisfaction. In doing so, he is likely to find fault with the maintenance factors provided him.

When employees are motivated, however, they seem to have an increased tolerance for dissatisfaction arising from deficient maintenance factors.

Short-Term Nature of Maintainers

According to Herzberg, any job satisfaction associated with the maintenance factors is short-lived, and, with the passage of time, a feeling of deficiency recurs. Just as eating a meal doesn't prevent a man from becoming hungry later, a salary increase has only a temporary effect; it doesn't prevent an employee from becoming dissatisfied eventually with his new wage level.

Herzberg says that wages motivate only in the sense that employees are motivated "to seek the next wage increase." He contends that, "benefits are no longer rewards; they are rights."[2]

Motivators, on the other hand, tend to have a longer-term effect on employees' attitudes. They are more continuous in nature. For example, unlike the pleasure of a raise in pay or a larger office which soon lose their impact, the satisfaction derived from meaningful work is a daily occurrence as long as it lasts.

Relationship to Maslow's Need Hierarchy

Herzberg's Motivation-Maintenance Theory differs from Maslow's need hierarchy in that it is more specifically related to motivation on the job. However, there is also much similarity, enabling us to roughly interpret Herzberg's findings within Maslow's framework (see Figure 3-2).

Herzberg's maintenance factors roughly parallel the lower-order needs listed by Maslow, encompassing the *physiological, security,* and *social* needs. Herzberg views these lower-order needs as having little or no motivating force in today's work situation, only the ability to dissatisfy when absent.

The motivators roughly parallel Maslow's higher-order needs—*esteem* and *self-actualization.* Herzberg implies that most of our society's employees have

[2]Frederick Herzberg, "One More Time: How Do You Motivate Employees?" *Harvard Business Review,* January-February, 1968, p. 55.

FIGURE 3-2. Relationship of Need Hierarchy to the Motivation-Maintenance Theory[3]

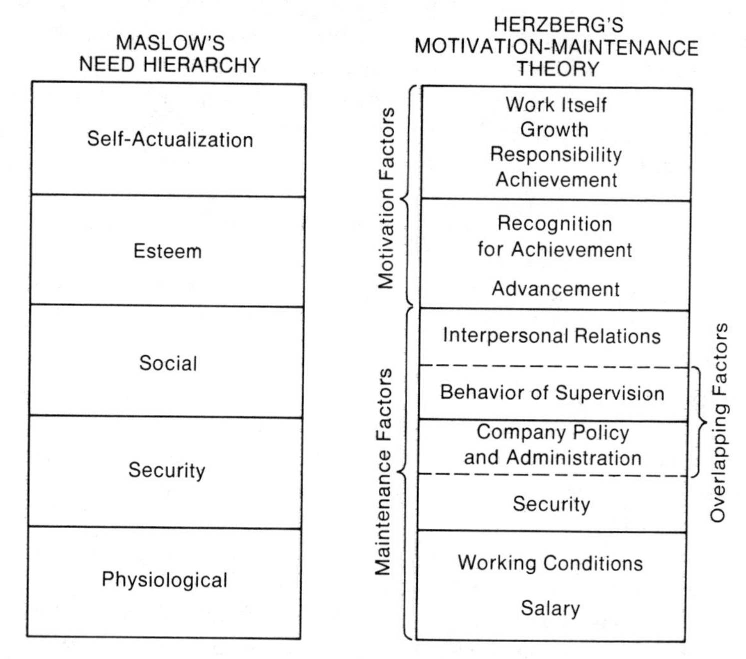

achieved a level of economic and social progress such that these higher-order needs are the only genuine motivators.

However, just as the lower-order needs in Maslow's hierarchy must be reasonably satisfied before the higher-order needs are activated, Herzberg concedes that the maintainers are a *prerequisite* for motivation even if they do not motivate in and of themselves.

Implications for Supervision

The fundamental implications of Herzberg's work for the supervisor are that "maintaining" the employee, while quite important, only avoids dissatisfactions; the absence of the maintenance factors can make employees unhappy, but their presence will seldom make them want to work harder or more efficiently. Making jobs truly motivating requires designing them to give the employee challenging work in which he can assume responsibility and fulfill his higher-level needs. The maintainers simply meet people's expectations, while the motivators move them to do things.

[3]Adapted from Keith Davis, *Human Relations at Work* (New York: McGraw-Hill Book Company, 1967), p. 37.

Thus, supervisors who traditionally approach motivation from a solely maintenance angle are seriously handicapping themselves. Instead, they might better concern themselves with the nature of the work itself and making it more challenging and meaningful; in other words, more attention should be given to making jobs *intrinsically satisfying.* Expenditures beyond that needed to provide a basic maintenance level might better be spent on programs to increase the responsibility and development of the individual employee; in the long run, this could well be less expensive than sole reliance on maintenance.

The basic question for the supervisor then becomes: What can be done to increase the presence of such motivator factors as achievement, recognition, satisfaction of the work itself, responsibility, advancement, and growth? For the answer, the *design* of the job itself must first be closely examined, for this defines the satisfactions that employees can derive from it and sets definite limits on the degree that Herzberg's motivators can be provided by the supervisor.

THE TRADITIONAL APPROACH TO JOB DESIGN

The *traditional* approach to job design is based upon five general rules:

1. Skills should be specialized.
2. Skill requirements should be minimized.
3. Training time should be minimized.
4. The number and variety of tasks in a job should be limited.
5. The job should be made as repetitive as possible.

Thus, the most common way to design jobs has been to simplify them. Work is divided into smaller parts with each employee producing one minute

"Same work for five years—never anything new"

portion of it over and over again. The object is to permit the hiring of minimally qualified employees at lower wage rates and to reduce the chance of errors.

We are not questioning the basic advantages of specialization; no organization could possibly function without it. In fact, our entire mass-production economy is based on the concept of specialization. It is *over-specialization* that is now being questioned by many management experts who feel that we have carried the original concept to extremes, at the expense of the employee's need satisfaction and his job performance.

Negative Effects of Over-Specialization

Specialization, when carried to extremes, has brought disadvantages in recent years along with its hoped-for advantages. In many cases, it has generated boredom, fatigue, apathy, higher turnover, absenteeism, more grievances, reduced productivity, and work stoppages, just to name a few. By slicing a worker's job into what is only a piece of a job, his imagination has been stifled and any interest and challenge eliminated; any satisfaction to be derived from performing a whole job has been smothered.

Many studies have shown that hourly-paid workers frequently report that their work has little meaning and just seems to go on endlessly and monotonously. Repetitiveness, when it leads to boredom, has also been shown to reduce quality rather than to increase it. In the long run, these negative effects of over-specialization seem to outweigh the cost savings that specialization is intended to bring about.

Current social trends in our country tend to indicate that over-specialization of jobs may cause even greater problems in the future. In the first place, today's employee is typically much better educated and more independent than the typical worker of only a generation ago. Companies that once employed elementary school dropouts now often hire men and women with two or more years of college, people whose entire education has encouraged them to think for themselves. This better-educated work force wants more meaningful and challenging jobs. Faced with the tedium of specialization, many workers expend their excess mental energy in creating problems for the supervisor.

A second alarming problem is that young people now tend to shun preparation for many skilled manual jobs, preferring instead to prepare for professional or managerial careers. Perhaps one of our greatest challenges is to upgrade the status of these jobs by giving them at least some intrinsic job satisfaction, for we must find enough qualified workers to replace those now performing them.

Although industrial jobs offer the best examples of jobs that are often not intrinsically satisfying, there are others equally guilty. Many retail and clerical workers, for instance, experience the same frustrations. Retailers, who have come to depend a great deal on minimally-trained, low-paid personnel, seldom offer meaningful or motivating jobs at the lower levels, which undoubtedly partially explains why most two-year or four-year college graduates tend to ignore retail careers; experiences derived through part-time retail employment have led many to believe that this is not "where it's at." In return for meaningless jobs, retailers are increasingly plagued by higher sales costs, higher turnover, employee theft, and persistent efforts to unionize retail sales personnel.

"Healthy Reactions to an Unhealthy Environment"

Chris Argyris, a noted authority on human relations in organizations, has long been critical of excessive specialization, commenting that:

> From an employee's point of view this means that he is asked to be more passive than active; more submissive than responsible; to use his shallow, surface abilities and ignore his more complex and deeper abilities. Such conditions are better suited to the world of infants than the world of adults. This is why, in several instances, where work has been highly simplified, the mentally retarded and insane have outproduced healthy human beings by wide margins.[4]

Employee apathy and lack of effort are not, according to Argyris, simply a matter of laziness. Rather they are often healthy reactions of normal people to an unhealthy environment. Argyris contends that the typical organization places most of its employees in roles that provide little opportunity for responsibility, self-reliance, or independence. On the contrary, too many jobs are designed to make only minimal demands on the individual's abilities.

To the extent that employees are relatively mature adults, they feel frustrated under such conditions; work becomes a necessary evil rather than a source of need satisfaction. As we have seen in Chapter 2, frustration arises when employees are unable to obtain need satisfaction. Argyris says that the common reaction of the employee's withdrawing his interest from the job–treating it with indifference or even a certain amount of contempt–is a necessary defense maneuver to protect his self-respect. Obviously, the costs of such reactions to the company are high.

The costly strikes that have recently been so prevalent in our economy may well be, in large measure, a spontaneous expression of the bitterness workers hold toward their jobs. Their frustrations may not reflect their low incomes so much as their inability to utilize their abilities in a significant way. In other words, they need a sense of pride and accomplishment; instead, they find their work neither stimulating nor dignifying.

In fact, Argyris feels that many workers view higher wages as a "penalty payment"–a sort of "fine" that they can periodically levy against employers to compensate them for the frustrating elements of the work situation. The

[4]Chris Argyris, "We Must Make Work Worthwhile," *Life*, May 5, 1967, p. 56.

employee says, "O.K., if you want me to work under these conditions, pay me!" He feels that the answer to any job dissatisfaction is more and more money.

JOB ENRICHMENT

Job enrichment is an approach which attempts to solve some of the motivational dilemmas created by over-specialization by making the employee's work more meaningful. Although a relatively new technique, job enrichment has achieved impressive results in building motivation. It seeks to get from the employee not the least he is capable of doing, but the best he is capable of doing.

Job enrichment can be simply defined as **the enlargement of a job's responsibility, scope, and challenge.** In the context of Herzberg's Motivation-Maintenance Theory, we can view an enriched job as including the factors of achievement, recognition, satisfaction from the work itself, responsibility, growth, and advancement.

Focusing primarily on job redesign, job enrichment has the objective of creating a job situation where the worker can obtain intrinsic motivation from his work. Under a job enrichment program, the design of jobs takes into account the human needs of employees as well as the technical production requirements and the economic needs of the company. Thus, attention is given not only to the prescribed tasks to be performed, but also to the aspects of these tasks that will heighten the motivation of the employee.

The job is made more challenging than before. The worker becomes aware of a completeness, or wholeness, to his task, which provides him with a greater sense of accomplishment. Of equal importance, the employee is developed to the extent that he is better prepared for future assignments.

Horizontal vs. Vertical Expansion

Enrichment of a job can be brought about through *horizontal* or *vertical* expansion or, preferably, both. *Horizontal expansion* of a job is characterized by the addition of a variety of similar functions or activities. *Vertical expansion,* on the other hand, is achieved by providing employees with increased opportunities for planning and controlling their own work.[5]

Horizontal expansion. One very satisfactory method of horizontally expanding jobs is the "total job concept." In this approach, each employee becomes responsible for an entire product or a complete component part of the

[5]M. Scott Myers, "Every Employee A Manager," *California Management Review,* Spring 1968, pp. 1-2.

finished item. An electronics assembly plant has been quite successful in implementing this concept. For example, in one department employees assembled a number of different models of electronic apparatus called "hot plates," using a normal assembly line operation. Without making any other changes in the department or its personnel, jobs were redesigned so that each employee assembled an entire hot plate, rather than its individual parts. Marking a positive reaction to the change, employees made such comments as, "Now it's *my* hot plate." To further demonstrate the positive aspects of the change, controllable rejects dropped from 23% to 1% in the next six months while absenteeism dropped from 8% to less than 1%, and productivity increased 84% in the second half of the year.[6]

Another common method of horizontal expansion is *job rotation,* in which employees are regularly switched from one job to another to provide variety in what they are doing and to prevent boredom from setting in; it also allows employees some physical movement and helps to reduce the psychological fatigue effects of repetitive work. An added advantage is that it helps to develop a broad base of highly skilled employees within the department.

Horizontal expansion, however, seldom offers the enrichment opportunities provided through vertical expansion. In many applications, it involves little more than adding meaningless additions to an already meaningless job. Job rotation, for example, accomplishes little in terms of added meaning if an employee is rotated from one inconsequential job to another of no greater consequence; as Herzberg has warned, this can be likened to "washing dishes for a while, then washing silverware."[7] For change to be really effective, meaningful activities and responsibilities must be added.

Vertical expansion. The key idea of vertical expansion is that employees (at least some employees) are capable of managing themselves to a much greater degree than they currently do; jobs are expanded to include some of the normal managerial functions of *planning* and *controlling* the work, as well as the actual *doing* of the work. Employees are increasingly encouraged to exercise their own judgment and discretion in making decisions about their work, to participate with the supervisor in problem-solving and goal-setting, and to offer ideas, suggestions, and opinions. (Employee participation in decision-making is fully discussed in Chapter 4.) They are therefore allowed to contribute with their minds as well as their skills.

Not only is the employee's work made more meaningful and intrinsically motivating, but the supervisor is also freed from many time-consuming routine management functions, allowing him to devote more time to higher-level planning and decision-making.

[6] Edgar F. Huse and Michael Beer, "Eclectic Approach to Organizational Development," *Harvard Business Review,* September-October, 1971, pp. 103-7.

[7] Herzberg, *op. cit.,* p. 59.

In contrast to horizontal expansion, vertical expansion provides opportunities for the employee's psychological growth rather than merely making a job structurally bigger.

Limitations of Job Enrichment

It is easy to paint pretty pictures of the potential advantages to be derived from enriching work. We must recognize, however, that in many cases the road to actual practical application of job enrichment is not an easy one. Not all jobs *can* be enriched, nor do all jobs *need* to be enriched.

Certainly there are many lower-level jobs that simply do not lend themselves to job enrichment. There are few jobs more lacking in potential motivators than the production worker on a typical assembly line, for example. To suggest that an assembly-line supervisor develop in his subordinates a sense of achievement, responsibility, and satisfaction in the work itself may be unrealistic at best.

It is also reasonable to assume that there are many employees (fewer than popularly supposed) who would not respond to additional responsibility, scope, and challenge. We cannot generalize that the worker with a routine, repetitive job is of necessity bored and frustrated; there are doubtless many people who actually prefer to work under conditions of routinized small jobs. We must remember that what may be monotonous for one individual can be interesting and absorbing to another; "the beauty of the job is in the eye of the beholder."

So, when we talk of trying to design enriching jobs that will fulfill man's higher-order needs, we hopefully are not speaking of an organizational utopia. We fully recognize that every firm has a certain amount of routine, dirty (but necessary) work to do. Most employees realistically expect to do some unattractive work as part of their jobs; life requires learning to mix the bitter with the sweet. Job enrichment merely seeks to devise a more satisfying mixture.

The Importance of Each Employee's Contribution

Regardless of whether a job can or cannot be enriched in the true sense, it can often be made more meaningful by simply letting each employee know the importance of his contribution to the success of the company as a whole and the results of inadequately done work.

Many employees seldom see the total operations of the company; they see only the small and often uninteresting part to which they are assigned. It is therefore not surprising to discover how many workers are actually unaware of the importance of their work to the finished product or of how their own work affects the work of others in the same company. If employees don't know where they fit, they cannot have a sense of importance or identification.

As an illustration, consider the old story about a lesson learned by the captain of a battleship after Pearl Harbor. Finding himself in a situation where victory depended on a burst of speed, he decided he wanted an extra five knots. His order was passed down the line, finally to the man who had his hand on the throttle. But the word came back up the line: "Can't be done." The captain exploded: "Why not?"

"We've got boiler scale," came the reply from the boiler room. (Boiler scale has to do with the rated maximum capacity of the boiler; beyond that, the men were not supposed to pile on extra speed.) The captain groused and griped to his exec and others of his top brass. His fury was noticed by the chaplain.

"Captain," said the chaplain, "those men don't feel they belong to the ship. All they do is turn valves and watch gauges and oil pressures; they have no idea what's going on topside. Yes, they get orders. But there's no feeling of urgency attached to your orders. None that means anything to them. They never know when they'll be blown to bits. Their work is important, Captain. Yet they get no recognition for their work."

The captain thought about what he was told. Finally, he said, "I see what you mean. What do you propose?"

"Put an officer behind a microphone on the bridge," said the chaplain, "and let him give a running account over the public address system of the entire strategic and tactical situation as it unfolds. Emphasize those items of immediate importance to the men in the boiler room. Have your officer give a blow-by-blow description of each engagement, the disposition of the enemy, and the ship's battle status at every instant."

"Good idea!" said the captain. He found his man and put him to work.

The officer did his job well during the next battle engagement. After it was over, the captain said, "Lieutenant, give me the mike. I'll announce the box score." When he finished, he added, "This is peanuts compared to what we could do if only we could overtake the enemy squadron to westward. But we need an extra five knots to do it."

He got the extra five. They overtook the squadron exactly on schedule and clobbered the enemy. The captain grabbed the mike from the officer. "You men down in the engine room," he shouted. "You did it! We all did it! Thank you for those five knots!"

JOB ENRICHMENT—A FEASIBLE SOLUTION TO MEANINGLESS WORK

There is little doubt that the majority of employees comprising today's work force is capable of exercising more initiative, creativity, and responsibility than is presently required or allowed by most lower-level jobs. In his recent best-seller, *Up the Organization,* Robert Townsend put it this way:

> All you have to do is look around you to see that modern organizations are only getting people to use about 20 percent—the lower fifth—of their capacities. And the painful part is that God didn't design the human animal to function at 20 percent. At that pace it develops enough malfunctions to cause a permanent shortage of psychoanalysts and nospital beds.[8]

To fulfill the supervisory duties of developing subordinates and meeting production demands, the potential of the employee must be tapped. Tried and true—but obsolete—management methods are not accomplishing this. Today's problems can't be solved with yesterday's solutions.

The solution may very well be found in *job enrichment,* where the supervisor's basic task is to create wherever possible an environment where workers can contribute the full scope of their talents in accomplishing the goals of the organization. Entirely consistent with our previous discussions of McGregor's "Theory Y" and the Herzberg theory, job enrichment attempts to expand the areas in which workers can exercise *self-direction* and *self-control* as they develop greater insight and ability.

Fortunately, many routine meaningless jobs have already been eliminated by automation, and certainly more will be—but these jobs are only a small part of the problem. The concept of job design must be changed if the challenges of a better-educated work force and a rapidly changing business world are to be met.

[8]Robert Townsend, *Up the Organization* (New York: Alfred A. Knopf, 1970), p. 140.

Reading Selection 4

*JOB ENRICHMENT—WHAT IT CAN DO FOR YOU**

A common complaint these days is that people have lost pride in their work. They have so little pride in what they do that they merely try to get by with a minimum amount of effort. The evidence is everywhere to be seen, but *why* is pride in good performance at such a low ebb?

In plain and simple language, many workers are bored to death by their jobs. "What can we do?" management asks. "We've made their work as easy as possible. We've given them good pay and a better fringe package. They're still not satisfied. What else is there to motivate them?" The problem with this line of thinking is that it searches for external solutions to a motivational problem which is essentially internal: the work an employee must do.

MANAGEMENT'S TRADITIONAL APPROACH

Our traditional theories of management have called for stripping away from a worker's job any aspects that might call on him to make a choice. Presumably, the reason was to avoid placing the worker in a situation where he might be forced to make a decision. Because management was afraid he'd make a mistake, it divided the worker's job into smaller parts, none of which would tax the intellect of the individual worker. It was made so simple that anybody could learn to do it.

Management got more or less what it had asked for. To the degree that it forced the worker into a tiny corner of a job and made his work less meaningful, it got an increasingly recalcitrant worker who cared less and less for his job and what it produced. Management was not looking for ideas from workers and it got none.

RECLAIMING THE LOST EMPLOYEE

Contrary to what our traditional managers appear to have believed, when the worker becomes merely another cog in the vast machinery of

*Edited and abridged from *Job Enrichment* (Waterford, Connecticut: Bureau of Business Practice, 1970).

industry, pushing a button or doing the same meaningless task over and over, you've lost him.

How do you bring him out into the open again? The answer is to make his job more meaningful. Enrich it. Broaden the range of the worker's responsibility. Instead of developing a man who is highly skilled and highly paid but does a basically small and simple job, call upon him to manage himself in a way that is more consistent with high pay and high skill.

A means of passing along to the worker the sense of pride and self-sufficiency that we're talking about is the concept of *job enrichment.*

* * * * *

Linda Henson was one of 14 women who prepared the payroll for a large factory. She was responsible, along with a couple of other women, for computing the payroll deductions for the entire plant. When the pay records came to her, they were complete as far as gross pay was concerned. She deducted federal and local taxes, withholdings for health insurance, payments to the company credit union, and the like.

Linda didn't make many mistakes. But the job of two of the 14 people was to check the transcriptions and computations of the other 12. Despite all efforts and intentions, however, errors did occasionally creep into paychecks—such as the time the boss's monthly check was $14.00 instead of $1,400. *That* caused a crisis.

This error caused Linda's supervisor to come head to head with a problem that she knew existed but didn't know how to solve. People were human, and they could make mistakes. How could mistakes be prevented?

Linda's supervisor decided that maybe her payroll people were tired of doing the same old thing day after day. "Perhaps if I vary the routine they'll be more interested," she thought. So she did. The workers switched jobs, and before long she had everyone trained in every aspect of the payroll. She had 14 people who could prepare and check any payroll computation from start to finish.

No one thought to give it a name like job enrichment. But it was only a small step to letting individuals be responsible for the complete payroll computation. The work was evenly divided with each girl handling so many accounts. Linda—and the others—developed a sense of responsibility that was lacking before. *She,* and no one else, did one-twelfth of the company's payroll. If she goofed, someone didn't get paid. When she realized this, her attitude toward her job changed. The realization that someone out there *depended* on what she did while she was at work made a big difference. The error rate dropped to almost nil. Linda's supervisor, over a period of time and with conscious effort and thought, had resolved a problem so fundamental that most people wouldn't even seriously consider how to come to grips with it.

* * * * *

Managers wonder how they can put some pizzazz back into the worker. The answer is job enrichment. As Linda Henson showed us, it can be a great success, even if disguised under a different name. It may be hard to do under certain conditions. But, if you can excite the worker about his job, even a little bit, the results are bound to be better.

WHAT IT IS

Job enrichment is a wide-open concept. No single term can describe it adequately, and it undoubtedly exists under different names at different companies. Certain elements characterize it, however.

Central to the process is the notion of giving the worker more say in the way the job should be done. Along with this goes the increased responsibility of seeing that the job is done correctly.

One of the effects of job enrichment is that each worker becomes his own manager to a greater degree than before. As he gets broader experience, he is called upon more and more to make decisions: how best to proceed with a series of operations; how to set his own goals; responsibility for the rate of production and the excellence of the product. In some types of assembly, the worker may become responsible for production of an entire unit, from bottom to top.

JOB ENRICHMENT AT WORK

Shop Supervisor Bob Newton shook his head. "I just can't see any reason for it. This fellow just walked into my office and announced that he was leaving—that he'd found a better job with another company and would be leaving in two weeks. If this were an isolated case, maybe it wouldn't bother me so much. But it isn't. I've had more than I like to admit."

"Like I say, I just can't see a logical reason for it. Working conditions are as good as you'll find anywhere in the area. Salaries, too. And everyone knows that the company's fringe benefits are excellent. And it isn't as if these workers who've left are malcontents or anything like that. Some of them were showing a lot of potential—this latest one especially."

"You've brought up a serious problem, Bob," commented Bill Marsh, the plant's manufacturing manager. "And it's not one that is confined to your department alone. We've done some listening," Marsh continued, "and we've come up with some interesting things on the way many of our employees feel about the work they are doing. The general reaction among them is that the work is 'boring, monotonous, deadening.' In short, to them, the work is meaningless."

"But what can a supervisor do about it?" asked Newton. "I mean we've been doing everything we could think of and nothing seems to work. Where do we go from here? When a guy signs on in the shop, he knows there's going to be a lot of drudgery. He's a fool if he doesn't."

"Actually, management has a program in the works that attacks just this point," Marsh replied. "It's called job enrichment, and it's designed to take the 'drudge' out of a job and make it more meaningful for the person who does it."

By the time the job enrichment program was ready to be put into effect, Bob Newton had received about 20 hours of orientation and was thoroughly convinced that the program could work. But he wasn't convinced that his department would go for the idea without a fight.

When he first discussed the program with them, he knew he'd been right. There was a clear undercurrent of discontent. "What are you trying to do, get more work out of us?" one worker asked.

Newton stepped right in. "First, let's get it straight that this isn't some crackpot idea that somebody thought up to make your lives miserable. It's been tried by other companies and we want to see if it will work for us. This is what's happened. We've decided that some changes are in order that will improve your jobs and make them more meaningful."

"How are you going to make *my* job 'meaningful'?" asked Harry King, a bit sarcastically.

"Well, we haven't actually decided yet, Harry," Newton answered. "You'll have something to say about it, though. But since you've brought it up—and I bet the rest of you are wondering the same thing—let's take your job and see what could be done with it to make it better."

Newton continued, "You operate a machine, right? You've been at it for about 10 years, and you do it pretty well. But I know for a fact that you don't want your kids to have to work here in the shop the way you've had to. Why don't you want your boy to run a machine the way his 'old man' does?"

"I guess it's because I've got a 'nothing' job. I put a piece of stock in a machine, push a button, and the machine does the rest."

"Would you say the job is boring? Or is it a challenge?"

"BORING!" Harry shot back with a laugh. "There are times when the biggest challenge it gives me is trying to stay awake."

"Who does the setups and the inspection of your work? You or somebody else?" Newton asked.

"You know as well as I do the setup men do all the prep work. I just push the buttons and feed the machine."

"Do you think you could handle your own setups?"

"I suppose I could," King answered tentatively. "I've seen them do it often enough."

"Well, under this program, it might be decided that if you were qualified to handle an extra part of your job, you should have the responsibility for it. You might carry it right through from setup to inspection—putting your own stamp of approval on each and every step."

The first step completed, Newton made a survey of the attitudes of his men toward their jobs. Then individual and group conferences were held with the workers to develop ideas on how their work could be made more meaningful. As it turned out, it was decided to make each worker responsible for the setup of his machine from blueprints. When this was accomplished, they would begin taking on greater responsibility for the inspection of their own work. Workers who proved themselves capable of handling their own inspections would also maintain their own quality records.

Of course, the end result of this program was that the jobs of many setup men and inspectors would be eliminated; but they weren't eliminated right away. Instead, setup men were put to training those individuals who didn't have the necessary skills to take on this added responsibility. They also checked the setup work done by the workers until it was obvious that the workers were capable of doing it accurately on their own. This training and checking process was also given to inspection personnel as the machine operators moved into this area of responsibility. As setup and inspecton jobs were eliminated toward the end of the program, these people were offered jobs as machine operators within the department. All but three accepted.

Reviews of changes in employee attitudes toward their work were made at six-month intervals over the next two years to see whether the desired improvement had been achieved.

At the end of a two-year period of the test, Bill Marsh prepared a final report summarizing the program's primary achievements. In abbreviated form it stated that while certain additional expenses had been made necessary by the program, these expenditures would be more than offset by reduced cost for setup, inspection and other benefits:

1. Product quality had been improved. Since the program had been implemented, a substantial reduction had taken place in losses due to units that failed to pass inspection and to scrap. It was felt that this reduction was due, in large part, to the increased responsibility employees were taking on in their work.

2. Both machines and operators were subject to less idle time. Previously an operator had to wait for a setup man, but the operator was now qualified to do this work himself.

3. Lateness, absenteeism, and turnover were significantly reduced. The variety and responsibility introduced into workers' jobs resulted in an increased sense of interest and involvement on the part of the worker. As he was made responsible for an entire work segment—and knew that it wouldn't get done unless he was there to do it—he no longer felt he was an unimportant cog in a big machine that could easily get along without him.

HORIZONTAL VS. VERTICAL LOADING

Jobs can be looked at in two ways: *horizontally,* which means the several operations that are required to produce the product or service, and *vertically,* which means the management or supervisory actions and decisions involved in producing the product or service.

Horizontal job enlargement expands the worker's involvement by assigning him additional related work segments—as Harry King did in our case. Although this method may prove adequate in some instances, often the worker is inclined to view horizontal enrichment merely as a speedup, *unless it is accompanied by vertical enrichment.*

Vertical enrichment can be carried out by allowing workers to participate in such normal management functions as planning, goal setting, problem solving, methods improvement, and personnel assignments. Because job enrichment must be a continuing process to be truly successful, progressively greater employee participation in these activities should be considered as the employee gains experience and becomes more qualified.

Naturally, if you give a worker responsibility for management functions, you are delegating authority that once was confined to your hands. There's nothing wrong with this. Obviously, you don't delegate a job and then completely forget about it. There must be follow-up and feedback. A job well done should be talked about to reinforce the employee's pride in the job he's doing. A job poorly handled will require patching up. Gradually, however, a feeling of independence will grow in the worker. He won't want his supervisor around checking up on him. Doing it himself and doing the work as well as anybody can do it—these objectives become a fertile source of excellence of work and pride in the job.

CHANGING ROLE OF THE SUPERVISOR

Job enrichment is not a concept that will apply only to the line employee or clerical worker. If it is possible to enrich the employee's job, it then becomes possible to enrich the supervisor's job.

Because job enrichment cannot be applied at successively higher levels until it has succeeded at the worker level, a very definite pattern emerges. When workers begin to take a greater interest in their jobs, some of the pressure of constantly checking up to make sure things are done correctly will be removed from the supervisor. He then has the time to pay more attention to the concepts of management. Thus, job enrichment for the supervisor is an *effect* of having enriched the job of the average employee.

As already mentioned, vertical job enrichment for the worker causes some changes in the supervisor's traditional role; however, the changes aren't so drastic as they might at first seem. The delegation of some supervisory duties to the workers doesn't mean that the supervisor has lost control over them or that he has given up the final responsibility for their proper completion. He has simply given someone else the opportunity to do the work and enriched their jobs and his in the process.

The supervisor is no longer the supreme authoritarian who plans, orders, and punishes when performance is below his standards. That supervisor is gone. Instead, the new supervisor is *goal*-oriented. He provides employees with information about the company's goals and then helps employees set individual goals to ensure that company objectives are met. He monitors performance and provides feedback and earned recognition.

In short, the supervisor's new role gives him time to *manage.* And that is what he is there for anyway.

INITIATING THE PROGRAM

Top management, of course, must give its approval to a plan for job enrichment and set the limits within which it wants the program to operate. It then becomes the function of line managers and department heads to educate their subordinate supervisors in the techniques of job enrichment.

Before attempting to enrich a worker's job, you must have the answer to one key question: Where are we now? Without a clear picture of the work as it is presently set up, improvement would be haphazard at best. A systematic analysis of each job in the department is necessary before attempting to improve it. To determine those areas where improvement is needed, questions such as the following should be asked:

Does the job in question
- –utilize the worker's skills effectively and provide a challenge worthy of his attention?
- –provide boredom-reducing variety for the worker?
- –enable the employee to see the relationship of his work to other operations in the overall production cycle?
- –lend itself to being combined with some other job to save time and effort and to make the two more meaningful?
- –have a satisfactory work cycle, neither too long nor too short?
- –give the employee adequate feedback on his performance so he can tell how well he is doing?
- –enable the employee to see how his work contributes to the value of the company's product or service?

Can the employee
- –do things that are currently being done for him?
- –make decisions that are now made for him?
- –set his own production?
- –take on additional training to help him prepare to operate at a higher level of competence?

Get the facts. Find out *how* the job is done and *why.* When the answers to these questions have been determined, you can start looking for ways to enrich the job's meaningfulness for the worker. Another way of making this analysis is to ask the worker who is doing it. After all, who should know more about the job than he?

Of course, not all jobs can be enriched, and enrichment may not always be a good idea. Many occupations already provide challenge and variety and would be difficult to enrich further. But there are many more jobs that can be enriched. Their very routineness and lack of challenge identify them.

Employee Resistance

Any company implementing a job enrichment program must be prepared to face at least some resistance from its employees. Why, if the program is actually designed to make their work more meaningful? Workers removed from the "safety" of their daily routine, even if they haven't enjoyed it, are fearful of the effect these changes might have on their jobs. "What happens if I don't make it?" they wonder; "Will I lose my job?" Others are very suspicious of anything which "smacks" of manipulation by management: "Is it a speedup?" they ask.

To the worker, these fears are real enough, and management must be prepared to answer their questions to the workers' full satisfaction if these fears are to be relieved.

Different industries may have varying degrees of difficulty in implementing job enrichment. Generally speaking, small companies should find it easier than large ones; nonunion shops will have less difficulty than union-organized plants.

In any case, the big changes will take time, and must have top management approval at the outset. Changes will be small and gradual at first.

Breaking the News

The success of job enrichment hinges on employee understanding of what management seeks to do through the program.

Thus, one of the first tasks facing the supervisor in job enrichment is that of letting his people know what changes are coming and why. Discuss it early, with all the facts at your disposal. By announcing a change and explaining it fully before the change is actually made, you give the workers a chance to get used to the idea. Time to adjust means that they won't have to make overnight changes in work habits that they've grown accustomed to over the years.

The first announcement is critical. For a good example of how this announcement should be made, take another look at the way Supervisor Bob Newton handled it in our case. Note that he had anticipated that his workers would be somewhat skeptical and fearful about the new changes, and he was ready. He could have announced the job enrichment program and let it go at that, using a take-it-or-leave-it attitude. Instead, he worked to show his workers just what this concept could mean to them as individuals.

ENRICHMENT IN PROBLEM AREAS

A formal job enrichment program as presented here isn't always the answer. In some instances, the requirements of complex production and assembly lines have made it impractical to implement changes in the actual work employees are doing. Some companies have encountered resistance from their unions and have backed off to avoid what they felt might be a potential labor crisis.

Does this mean that job enrichment cannot work for these companies? Certainly not! A formal program may be ruled out, but many of job enrichment's basic concepts may still be applied. And in most cases, all that's needed is a shift in emphasis from the enrichment of an employee's actual work to the enrichment of the climate in which he works.

There are two key things you can do to make your employees' jobs more meaningful and provide increased job satisfaction in the process:

1. Keep each employee informed about how his job contributes to the success of the entire operation.
2. Set attainable goals which challenge the employee to do his best at all times.

"That's the most critical part in the whole apparatus." **"It is?"**

Keeping Employees Informed

Here's how one supervisor solved the problem of letting his machine operators know the importance of their jobs. Gene O'Hare happened to be walking through the cafeteria one day when he overheard some of the gear-grinding-machine operators complaining about the tolerances they were being asked to hold. "Don't know about you guys," one commented, "but I can't see any reason for it. The old tolerances worked, didn't they? So why tighten them?" In this case, the gears were being used in a new calculator; its speed and accuracy depended on precise gearing. When he heard that remark, O'Hare realized that he'd better fill them in on why the new tolerances were so important.

The first thing O'Hare did after lunch was to visit the advertising manager. "Do you have any brochures or advertisements that explain how accuracy is obtained in the new Mark IV calculators?" he asked. "Some of my operators don't understand why they have to hold such tight tolerances, and I figured that the brochures would be a good way to get the point across to them."

"You bet I do," the ad manager replied. "That's one of our most important product advantages. If your men don't give us precision gears, we come up with inaccurate calculators. This could mean that we'd end up spending a lot of money for trouble-shooting, not to mention the possibility of finding ourselves with a lot of unhappy ex-customers."

After showing O'Hare the brochure that told the calculator's precision story, the ad manager said, "I'll have the warehouse send you a supply right away, and you can pass them around. And how about an ad reprint that lists some of our major customers? That'll show them that we're playing in the big leagues. A lot of the companies listed are household names all around the world."

O'Hare agreed, and when the materials arrived he made a point of seeing that everyone in the department got them. "I just thought you'd be interested in seeing why those new tolerances are so important," he told them. "A lot of companies use our equipment and depend on its accuracy. Take the aerospace industry alone. If you take a look at that ad reprint I gave you, you'll see a lot of key companies on there. And in a sense your work is helping them do their jobs. It may not seem like much, but when you really stop and think about it, the job we're doing is pretty important. Even I was surprised."

O'Hare's tactics worked. Not at first–that would have been too much for him to expect. But he kept them up. When new products were introduced, he explained to the department precisely where their work was fitting into the over-all scheme of things. He told them how their work made the product better than the competition's. He gave them something they could be proud of. And when they worked on a special project, he told them who the customer was and how the finished item was going to be used. After a while–and it didn't take too long–results began to show. Workers were taking more pride in their jobs. O'Hare had helped make them more meaningful.

Setting Challenging Goals

When tackling the second part of the task of giving employees a feeling of satisfaction on the job, the manager must be on guard for two major pitfalls: setting goals either too high or too low.

Any time a goal is set too low, it's robbed of its challenge for the worker. When it's met, the worker has no sense of achievement because he knew he could do it all the time. Although goals must be set high enough to represent a challenge to the worker, if they are too high they will discourage any effort. When employees are frustrated over their inability to reach the goals that have been set for them, they often lose the desire to work well at anything. They figure that if they're going to fail anyway (and they've convinced themselves they will), why bother? The result is an across-the-board lowering of quality and productivity.

Consequently, you must walk a thin line when setting goals for your employees–neither too high nor too low, but always a challenge. To make this easier, follow these guidelines:

–Any time you set a new target, be sure it's an improvement over what is being done now.
–Don't ask the impossible.
–Be specific whenever possible. Generalities accomplish little because the employee isn't sure of what you expect of him.
–Whenever possible, give your employees a say in setting their own goals, which gives them a sense of participation and helps them see the need for improvement. There's no need to be afraid that they will take advantage of the situation and set ridiculously low goals for themselves. Experiences have shown that more often than not, you'll have to curb their enthusiasm somewhat to keep the goals they set for themselves within the realm of reality.

IN PERSPECTIVE

Industrial psychologists recognize that modern production methods have taken away much of the opportunity for workers to feel that their labor is creative–that by working they build something that is meaningful to the society in which they live. It is said that man's inherent "laziness" caused him to invent all the work-saving devices that we have today. Perhaps this is true, but it oversimplifies. More fundamental even than the desire to avoid work is the awareness that man must work in order to live. Work is part of man's nature.

The prime motivator is the job itself. If a worker finds his job meaningful, he will bring to it an interest and an involvement which far surpasses any that could be forced out of him by a threat of "Do it—or *else*!" And that is how job enrichment works; it is intended to dissolve that elusive and hard-to-detect sympton known as worker apathy. It strives to make work meaningful for the employee, allowing the motivation for increased productivity and better quality to come from within, where it does the most good.

Job enrichment is a valid concept and more importantly, *it works.* To the degree that you can contribute to enriching someone else's job, you have made an important contribution to the life of the worker himself and to the welfare of the group in which he works. Additionally, what you spend in the way of effort to benefit the individual comes back as a benefit to your company in the long run.

QUESTIONS FOR REVIEW AND DISCUSSION

1. What role of importance does work play in a person's life? Analyze this question in relation to your own work experiences and what you have read in this chapter and Chapter 2.
2. Older employees are often heard to say, "People today just don't care about putting forth the effort on their jobs like they used to." Do you agree? Why?
3. a. Explain Herzberg's motivaton-maintenance theory and the extent that you feel it applies in actual work situations.
   b. Do you feel that the motivation-maintenance theory is equally applicable to blue-collar workers as to managerial and professional workers?
   c. What factors do you personally believe cause satisfaction or dissatisfaction in working at a job?
4. "Negative motivators can be dissatisfiers too, but not so frequently as the maintainers. For example, while *achievement* is a motivator, *failure to achieve* can be a dissatisfier." Evaluate this statement.
5. "We supervisors give a great deal of lip service to the importance of developing our subordinates and really helping them to grow. Yet, most of us tend to keep our people in a dependency relationship with respect to us. We prefer individuals who turn to us for the answers—individuals who can't make a move until we call the shots for them." Do you agree with this statement? Why?
6. a. How important is job design in employee motivation?
   b. Comment on the statement: "Job design in industry is strictly an engineering problem."
7. What is the usual effect of excessive job specialization on an employee's motivation and productivity? Explain fully.
8. Experiments have shown the feasibility of using employees with less than average intelligence in very routine jobs. Handicapped workers have also been successful in routine jobs. Does this constitute manipulation of these people? Is there any implication from these experiments for the very common policy of hiring nothing less than a high school graduate?
9. The number of people suffering from mental illness has increased at an alarming rate during the time that most job content has been reduced in significance. Is it unrealistic to attribute at least part of this increase to the traditional approach to job design?

10. The quality control manager of a company blames the high rate of waste and rejects on poor training. What factors other than training might be at fault?
11. Why might a particular job be satisfying to one individual but not to another?
12. Explain in detail what is meant by *job enrichment.*
13. Distinguish between *horizontal expansion* and *vertical expansion.*
14. How do you feel your own job could be enriched in the sense of making it more intrinsically satisfying? Consider both horizontal and vertical means of expansion.
15. a. Do you feel that retail jobs lend themselves to job enrichment concepts as readily as industrial jobs?
    b. In what ways could a typical department store salesperson's job be enriched? That of a checker in a supermarket?
16. Should individuals participate in determining how their jobs should be enriched?
17. a. How would you predict that union leaders would react to the concept of job enrichment?
    b. What problems might be encountered in implementing a job enrichment program in a union shop? What might be done to overcome these problems?
18. Is the concept of "work simplification" the natural enemy of the concept of job enrichment? Are the two in direct conflict or can they peacefully coexist?
19. How can a supervisor best go about letting each employee know the importance of his individual function to the success of the company as a whole?
20. This chapter presented a pretty strong case for job enrichment. Can you visualize any potential pitfalls in this approach to motivation?

SUGGESTED ADDITIONAL READINGS

Ackerman, Leonard. "Let's Put Motivation Where It Belongs—Within the Individual," *Personnel Journal,* July, 1970, pp. 559-62.

Anderson, John W. "The Impact of Technology on Job Enrichment," *Personnel,* September-October, 1970, pp. 29-37.

Argyris, Chris. "We Must Make Work Worthwhile," *Life,* May 5, 1967, pp. 56-68.

Guest, Robert H. "Better Utilization of Skills Through Job Design," *Human Relations in Management,* S. G. Huneryager and I. L. Heckmann, editors. Second edition. Cincinnati: South-Western Publishing Company, 1967. Pp. 793-810.

Hampton, David R., Charles E. Summer, and Ross Webber. "The Individual in the Organization: Psychological Factors in Organizational Behavior," *Readings in Management Strategy and Tactics,* John G. Hutchinson, editor. New York: Holt, Rinehart and Winston, Inc., 1971. Pp. 22-38.

Herzberg, Frederick. "One More Time: How Do You Motivate Employees?", *Harvard Business Review,* January-February, 1968, pp. 53-62.

Huse, Edgar F., and Michael Beer. "Eclectic Approach to Organizational Development," *Harvard Business Review,* September-October, 1971, pp. 103-12.

Maslow, A. H. "A Theory of Human Motivation," *Human Relations in Management,* S. G. Huneryager and I. L. Heckmann, editors. Second edition. Cincinnati: South-Western Publishing Company, 1967. Pp. 333-55.

Myers, M. Scott. "Every Employee A Manager," *California Management Review,* Spring 1968, pp. 9-20.

Myers, M. Scott. "Overcoming Union Opposition to Job Enrichment," *Harvard Business Review,* May-June, 1971, pp. 37-48.

Myers, M. Scott. "Who Are Your Motivated Workers?", *Harvard Business Review,* January-February, 1964, pp. 73-88.

Repp, William. "Motivating the NOW Generation," *Personnel Journal,* July, 1971, pp. 540-43.

Roche, William J., and Neil L. MacKinnon. "Motivating People with Meaningful Work," *Harvard Business Review,* May-June, 1970, pp. 97-110.

Sorcher, Melvin, and Herbert H. Meyer. "Motivation and Job Performance," *Personnel Administration,* July-August, 1968, pp. 9-21.

Townsend, Robert. "People," *Up The Organization.* New York: Alfred A. Knopf, 1970. Pp. 137-43.

Wolf, Martin G. "The Psychology of Executive Motivation," *Personnel Journal,* October, 1968, pp. 700-04.

4

PARTICIPATION BY SUBORDINATES IN DECISION-MAKING

By definition, a supervisor is one who accomplishes his goals and obtains results through his subordinates. Thus, as subordinates are directly affected by most of the supervisor's decisions, they often express considerable interest in them. Because of this possible interest, it is only logical that they may desire to *participate* in the making of certain decisions about matters that affect them. Such desires certainly cannot be considered unusual, when one takes into account our society's deeply-ingrained democratic traditions.

THE PARTICIPATIVE APPROACH TO SUPERVISION

The participative approach to supervision is based on the premise that **many employees want to participate in decision-making and, furthermore, that they very often have the ability to help shape better, more meaningful decisions.**

The concept of participation can be defined as **mental and emotional involvement of a person in a group situation, which encourages him to contribute to group goals and share responsibility in them.**[1]

Thus, the supervisor draws on the ideas of his subordinates who will be affected by the decision. He attempts to get them to think about issues of the problem and actively seeks their comments and suggestions before he makes a decision. The supervisor obviously cannot consult with employees on every problem, but he can set a *climate of consultation* by being genuinely receptive to the ideas of his people and providing them with a voice in the affairs that directly concern them. This, in many cases, may prove to be highly motivating and contribute to the meaningfulness and enrichment of the individual's job.

[1] Keith Davis, *Human Relations at Work* (New York: McGraw-Hill Book Company, 1967), p. 128.

Autocratic vs. Participative Styles of Supervision

Participative supervision can generally be considered the opposite of autocratic or authoritarian styles of supervision.

The autocratic supervisor *centralizes* all authority and decision-making within himself. In this style of supervision, all planning, goal setting, work standards, organization, and information dispersion are highly structured and are exclusively within the province of the supervisor; he assumes full authority and responsibility for the complete work situation. Employees are simply informed of the supervisor's decisions and expected to carry them out and do what they are told.

The participative supervisor is far from being an autocrat. In contrast, the use of participation *decentralizes* managerial authority. Whenever possible, decisions affecting the group are not made unilaterally by the supervisor, as by the autocrat, but individual members of the group are brought in and encouraged to offer ideas and suggestions on current problems facing the supervisor. However, it is important to understand that the participative supervisor still must retain the *ultimate responsibility* for his unit's operation; in using participation, he is merely sharing some of this responsibility with those people who actually perform the work.[2]

Dispelling a Common Misconception About Participation

Now that we have a working concept of what participative supervision is, let us at this point also mention what it is not, in order to avoid confusion later. Many supervisors, at the mere mention of the word "participation," immediately reject the concept because of oversimplified notions of what it really is.

It is not to be thought of as "pure democracy" in the political sense, with every employee having the right to vote on all major decisions, with the majority ruling; pure political democracy can rarely be equated with participative or democratic supervision within a business organization. Therefore, keep in mind that when we refer to participation by employees in planning and decision-making we are referring not to direct democracy but rather to individual or group participation in making *some* (but not all) decisions that affect the way things are to be done in the group. The supervisor still reserves the right to make the final decision and is accountable for it. But before doing so, he takes into consideration the needs and opinions of those working for him, actively soliciting rather than merely tolerating or attempting to squelch their contributions.

[2]*Ibid.*, pp. 105-7, 128.

THE PROCESS OF DECISION-MAKING

Before continuing our discussion of allowing subordinates to participate in decision-making, perhaps we should take a quick look at what the decision-making process really involves.

Solving problems and making decisions are, of course, the supervisor's "bread-and-butter"; they are what he gets paid for. A college professor was once overheard to say (hopefully in jest), "If we could only figure out some way to get rid of all these damned students, we could have a smooth running college." Of course, a college without students would mean no need for professors. This analogy can also be applied to supervisors; without problems to solve and decisions to be made, there would be no need for supervisors.

Needless to say, wise decisions are crucial to supervisory success; but we often fail to understand all the things involved in arriving at an intelligent, rational decision.

Decision-making of any kind on the part of the supervisor involves **a choice or selection of one alternative solution from among a group of two or more alternative solutions to a particular problem.** In its simplest form, the decision-making process involves these four steps:

1. **Identification and diagnosis of the basic problem:** Decision-making is never an isolated activity; it is always related to a problem, a difficulty, or a conflict. Decisions bring about an answer to the problem or a resolution of the conflict.
2. **Identification of all alternative courses of action available for resolving the problem:** True decision-making necessitates that a choice be made from two or more alternatives. Obviously, if there is only one choice, there is no decision to be made. Several possibilities are available for resolving a problem from which the ultimate selection must be made.
3. **Evaluation and comparison of the alternative courses of action:** This involves weighing the *advantages* and *disadvantages* of each possible alternative, and considering the *probability of success* and the *risks* of complications inherent in each alternative. Naturally, all pertinent data that can be tracked down should be assembled and related to the alternatives at this stage.
4. **Selection of the final solution from among the available alternatives:** Decide which course of action promises to be most successful, recognizing the strengths and weaknesses of your chosen solution.[3]

[3]The reader may argue that, in reality, a supervisor does not always *consciously* go through these four steps in making all decisions—especially in making simple routine decisions. The point may be argued; however, the authors would still contend that, regardless of the routineness or complexity of the decision to be made, any intelligent, rationally-made decision requires the supervisor to go through the four steps, on either a conscious or an unconscious level. Many poor decisions are the direct result of neglecting to devote adequate consideration to one or more of the steps.

POTENTIAL BENEFITS OF PARTICIPATION

Although there are several potential benefits to be obtained from participative supervision, **the primary purpose of practicing participation—and the primary benefit to be derived from it—should always be to improve the quality of supervisory decision-making and the total performance of the supervisor's work unit.**

Other benefits that we will discuss—*raising the level of employee motivation* and *increasing the acceptability of decisions*—are best viewed as by-products of the primary purpose of achieving improved decision-making.

Improving the Quality of Decision-Making

Frequently, subordinates are able to point out factors of problem situations that might be overlooked by the supervisor who makes certain decisions solely on his own. In soliciting the ideas of those employees directly involved in the problem and affected by the decision, decisions can many times be made more efficiently. For example, it is seldom if ever possible for a supervisor to have knowledge of all aspects of a problem, all alternative courses of action, or all consequences and risks related to all the decisions he must make.

Subordinates often can shed practical ideas on the problem from an *operative standpoint;* by discussing certain problems with subordinates and drawing upon their practical experiences, the supervisor may actually find that he has not completely explored the problem. The interchange of ideas and different views of the problem can often give the supervisor a much broader view of the situation.

Importance of attitude projected by the supervisor. To effectively utilize participation in this manner, the supervisor must project to his subordinates an attitude reflecting the fact that he recognizes that his employees have talents and abilities that can enhance the quality of decisions—that they have the ability to think and come up with new ideas. He must be *genuinely* receptive to employees' ideas, perceiving their ideas as useful. In fact, in order to work properly, participation requires that both the supervisor and his subordinates sincerely believe that the final decision will be a better one because the ideas of two or more people have been integrated into it.

Furthermore, the supervisor must admit that he doesn't always know everything about every problem, which of course requires a certain degree of humility—something that many supervisors seem to lack (!). However, if thi attitude is not displayed when using participation, employees will usuall quickly perceive the supervisor's participative efforts as being a superficial facade, interpreting it merely as a *manipulative tactic* rather than a genuine desire for their ideas.

Freeing the upward flow of communication. Because of the barriers often existing in the upward flow of communication from subordinates to management in most organizations (discussed fully in Chapter 6), much valuable information and ideas possessed by subordinates that can be vital to a decision are often withheld and never reach the supervisor; ideas go unrecognized and untapped in most organizations in enormous numbers.

A climate of participation within the supervisor's work unit is one tool that can help to break down some of these barriers to upward communication, making information available to the supervisor that may improve the quality of his decisions. Involving employees in problem-solving allows them to voice attitudes and feelings that may go unheard in any other way.

Raising the Level of Employee Motivation

Although participation should be used to achieve improved supervisory decision-making primarily, a welcome by-product is that it often improves the level of employee motivation and morale; not only can participation be a source of many practical suggestions that can improve the efficiency of the work group, it can also be highly motivating and intrinsically satisfying to the employee who comes to feel a sense of involvement in the group's goals.

Intrinsic job satisfaction. If employees are allowed to participate in various steps in the decision-making process, they can find an important source of satisfaction and meaning in their work.

The key to the potential success of participation as a motivator, of course, rests upon *ego involvement.* As our earlier definition of participation implied, a person who plays a meaningful role in decision-making can become ego-involved in his job instead of merely task-involved; this can motivate the person to contribute more fully to the organization's goals and to accept a greater degree of responsibility. In the use of participation by the supervisor, the employee's need to feel important and to contribute is recognized and utilized.

Additionally, most employees derive a sense of personal satisfaction from being able to solve problems; challenging the employee with a problem and then having him report back his ideas and possible courses of action can be a positive motivating factor in supplying the employee with a sense of achievement and recognition. For the employee to know that he can freely express his ideas and that he can help shape the final decision can be a definite source of intrinsic job satisfaction.

Teamwork and commitment to group goals. Participation can also motivate employees to develop *teamwork.* Teamwork results when individual employees form a closely-knit work group that has a unity of purpose to which each employee becomes dedicated. Employees come to feel that they are an integral and important part of the group; this feeling of belonging and being needed not only helps to satisfy their social needs but also encourages employees to accept responsibility in their work group's activities.

Employees who can become ego-involved in their jobs as a result of the participation process tend to have a much greater feeling of identification with the company and its goals. In a sense, **participation helps to bring about a coincidence of the individual employee's personal goals and the organization's goals.** The employee recognizes that helping the organization to accomplish its goals will, in turn, enhance the satisfaction of his own needs. When employees feel a personal stake in the organization's goals, they will usually be more willing to do what is needed to accomplish them; job problems then become "ours," not "theirs."

Furthering the individual development of employees. In motivating employees to contribute through participation, the supervisor is also providing the opportunity for subordinates to release their own resources of initiative, creativity, and ingenuity; he is creating a climate in his work group conducive to individual employee growth and development, where new skills and knowledge can be learned. When the employee is given the opportunity to suggest and question instead of the traditional pattern of following rigid sets of instructions, he usually can develop into a more mature and responsible individual.

In contrast, autocratic supervision may well pay off in terms of dollar profits, but it can seldom offer a climate for human growth and development.

Thus, in the choice of a supervisory style, "human costs" should be considered along with a desire for high productivity and profits; in the final analysis, the two usually complement each other.

Increasing the Acceptability of Decisions

In general, it has been found that decisions that subordinates have been allowed to participate in making are more acceptable to them than those decisions that are arbitrarily forced upon them by the supervisor. As the old saying goes, "The fellow in the boat with you never bores a hole in it."

Of course, it is often argued that it may actually be easier and more efficient for the supervisor to make departmental decisions without bothering to involve his employees; as we shall see later, in many instances this is true. However, we need to keep in mind that the supervisor's job as a problem-solver does not end with the making of the decision; he also is responsible for the *implementation* of the decision. Thus, in reality, he has two things that must be accomplished: (1) **the making of the decision itself** and (2) **the activities required to carry out the decision.** The latter frequently requires cooperation and acceptance on the part of subordinates.

As a result it is entirely plausible that, in many cases, the supervisor may well do better by taking the extra time to discuss problems with his employees and, on occasion, perhaps even to accept suggestions that he believes may be somewhat less efficient than his own in order to obtain employee acceptance and cooperation in carrying out the decision. In other words, **solutions of lesser quality accompanied by a high degree of employee acceptance might be more effective in some cases than solutions of higher quality without employee acceptance.**[4]

Such a choice should not be interpreted as "buying" cooperation or manipulating subordinates by letting them participate. Again, we emphasize that, in using participation, the supervisor's first concern is **improving the quality of the decision.** The supervisor by no means has to accept solutions that he considers to be poor or incompatible with the objectives of the organization; acceptance of a poor solution certainly accomplishes nothing in the way of improving the group's performance. If the supervisor believes he has a substantially better course of action than has been offered by subordinates, he should present his reasoning and evidence to support his viewpoint.

Even if employees' suggestions are not accepted, **the mere fact that they have been consulted can make the final decision more understandable to the employees, less likely to be misinterpreted, and generally more acceptable.** As decisions arrived at through participation are more likely to take into account the needs and interests of all parties, supervisory control is less likely to seem arbitrary and threatening.

[4]Raymond E. Miles, "Human Relations or Human Resources?" *Harvard Business Review,* July-August, 1965, p. 150.

Overcoming resistance to change. Participation has proven to be especially useful in reducing resistance to the introduction of change. (The topic of "change" is fully discussed in Chapter 5.) Employees tend to react adversely to decisions that impose changes upon them. The supervisor can often minimize this resistance by drawing the employees affected by the change into participating in the planning and implementation stages of the change; employees who are consulted and allowed to participate in the decisions about the change are normally able to more easily adjust to the change.

PREREQUISITES FOR SUCCESSFUL IMPLEMENTATION OF PARTICIPATION

It is necessary to emphasize that the benefits of participative supervision that we have discussed are merely potential benefits and can be successfully derived only in the proper situations and circumstances. Thus, we must guard against the tendency to overgeneralize about these benefits, because they by no means automatically follow from the use of participation; their success is entirely dependent upon the manner and conditions under which participation is applied. In fact, there is much evidence that participation in many situations may not be desirable at all.

Keith Davis, in the first reading selection in this chapter, lists seven *prerequisite conditions* that must be met by both the supervisor and his employees before participative supervision can be successfully applied. Viewed together, these prerequisite conditions simply mean that **participation works better in certain situations than in others**; in some situations, it is best not used.

Choice of a Style of Supervision to Fit the Situation

A supervisor cannot simply choose to use or not to use participation in making all his decisions. The essential question that he must ask himself is: "Under what conditions is participation likely to be beneficial or not beneficial?"

In this chapter's second reading selection, Tannenbaum and Schmidt view the use of participation as existing on a continuum ranging from little or no participation under a highly autocratic style of supervision to almost complete democratic participation with a minimum of imposed authority (see Figure 4-1). In other words, the use of participation on any specific problem may fall anywhere between two extremes. On the left side of the continuum, the supervisor maintains a high degree of control and complete centralization of decision-making authority, merely announcing his conclusion and attempting to get his subordinates to carry out his plan; at the other extreme, on the right side of the continuum, the supervisor completely delegates decision-making authority to the subordinates.

FIGURE 4-1. Continuum of Leadership Behavior[5]

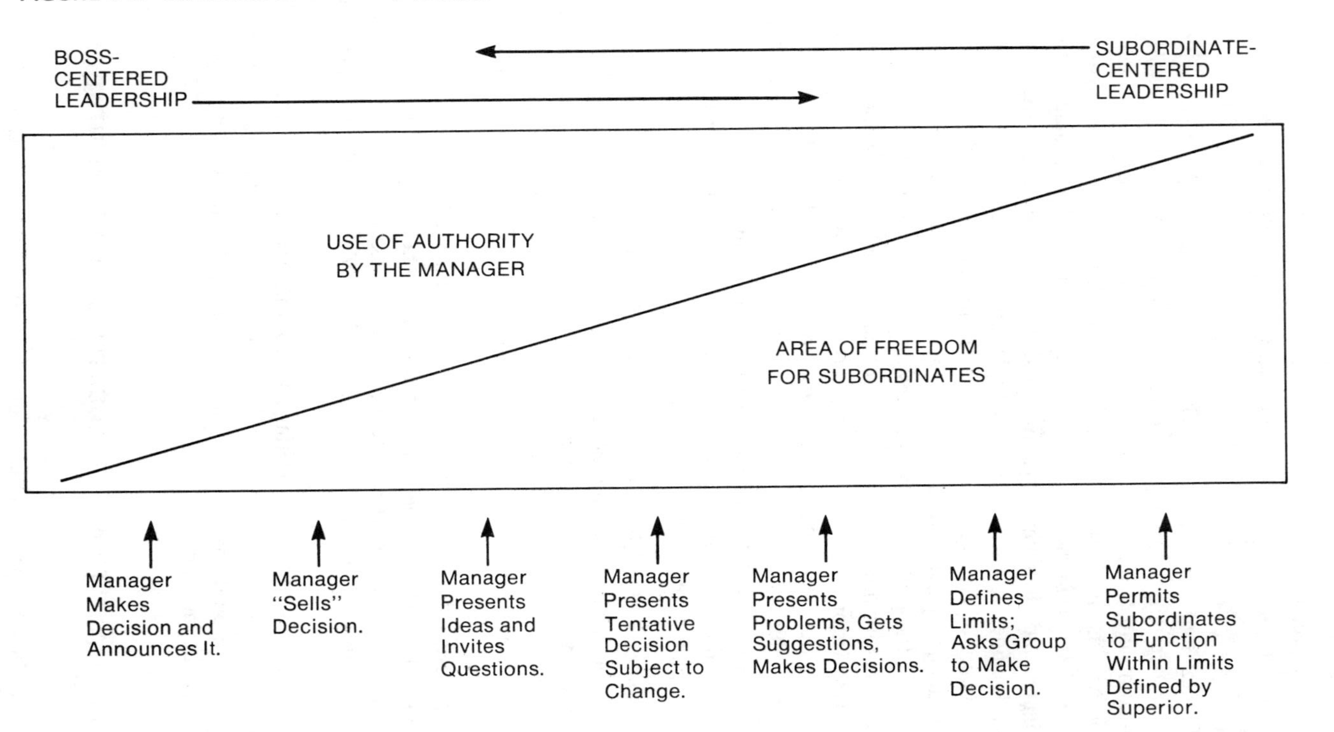

[5]Robert Tannenbaum and Warren H. Schmidt, "How To Choose a Leadership Pattern," *Harvard Business Review*, March-April, 1958, p. 97.

As the continuum illustrates, a number of supervisory styles can be employed between the two extremes; within a period of time, an effective supervisor may well practice varying degrees of participation along the continuum.

Variables to be considered. Thus, in reality, supervisors can seldom be totally autocratic or totally participative in all situations. According to Tannenbaum and Schmidt, the appropriate degree of participation used or the style of supervision chosen to fit a particular situation depends on the interaction of *three primary variables*—**the supervisor and his characteristics, the subordinates and their characteristics, and the circumstances of the immediate decision.** Included in these primary variables are such factors as the value system and personality of the supervisor, the supervisor's confidence in his subordinates, the subordinates' personalities and their capacities and willingness to contribute, the nature of the problem, economic restraints, and pressures of time. All these and other factors must be taken into account in determining the appropriate style of supervision in a particular circumstance, as any of them can restrict the courses of action available for solving a problem. As the restrictions become greater, the value and desirability of participation becomes less. Certainly, in a case where there are restrictions and participation cannot add to the quality of the decision, the supervisor should not try to fool his subordinates into believing they are helping to reach what is already a foregone conclusion.

Maintaining flexibility in supervisory style. Hence, the "ideal" style of supervision on the continuum is nonexistent; the uniqueness of each work group and situation prevents us from prescribing a "one best way" to supervise people that will be appropriate in all circumstances. A participative style is no more effective than an autocratic style if it is not adaptable to the demands of the situation.

The most effective supervisor is the one who is adaptable, maintaining a sense of flexibility so that he can cope with different situations. He may have a typical style that lies somewhere between the two extremes on the continuum, but his flexibility allows him to "tailor-make" a style for each particular situation.

As in all attempts at motivating and working with employees, this requires that the supervisor be *empathetic*—knowing his subordinates, their needs, attitudes, and aspirations—in order to effectively judge the degree of participation that will be most appropriate.

PROBLEMS TYPICALLY ENCOUNTERED IN IMPLEMENTATION

Even though the basic concept of participative supervision has been around since early in the human relations movement, great difficulty is often still encountered by supervisors in understanding and applying the concept.

Application Within a "Theory X" Framework

Undoubtedly, the not infrequent failures encountered by supervisors in implementing participation can be partially attributed to the fact that they have "bought the idea" but have applied it within the traditional "Theory X" framework and its assumptions; consciously or unconsciously, they consider participation mainly as a way of manipulating their employees rather than as a means of improving decision-making and developing their people.

Obviously, a change from an autocratic style of supervision to a more participative style necessitates a change in attitudes on the part of the individual supervisor; namely, from those attitudes about people associated with McGregor's "Theory X" to those supporting "Theory Y" (see Chapter 2). For many supervisors, such a change can be quite difficult to justify or accept, as attitudes that have been formed over years of experience are always difficult to change. Nevertheless, the change is a prerequisite for the success of any of the supervisor's participative attempts.

Moving Too Fast

There is also much evidence that participative supervision can get into trouble if it is implemented too fast. Participation simply can't be put into full-scale practice overnight; this is particularly true where employees have been conditioned throughout their entire work experience to expect traditional autocratic styles of supervision.

Yet, many supervisors decide one morning that they're going to be more participative with their work group, only to conclude by the afternoon that it doesn't work. The authors have had supervisors in human behavior seminars who have rushed out and tried to use participative techniques immediately and, a week later, woefully and dissapointedly complained to the class that it was a complete failure. Their subordinates typically had reactions ranging from feelings of manipulation and distrust to contentions that the supervisor was becoming mentally ill (!), or to feelings of "that's what supervisors are paid for–to make decisions–so don't bug me with your problems!" Such reactions are common when you move too fast; many employees aren't as ready for participation as one might think. Unfortunately, when the supervisor feels his participative efforts have failed, his frustrations usually erupt into an immediate revival of his former autocratic approach to any problem.

You simply can't abruptly order employees to start participating and taking on more responsibility; where participation is suddenly imposed on all group members, it may well create as much resentment as highly autocratic methods.

One explanation lies in the employees' *role expectations* and *perceptions* regarding their own role within the work group and the previous role behavior of their supervisor in relation to them. For example, many employees have an "authoritarian set" to their personalities, deriving a sense of security and dependency from working within a strong authority structure; in their work experiences, they have come to expect strong autocratic supervision. If their supervisor has never asked for their opinions and suggestions, they naturally do not expect him to do so. When they are suddenly confronted by a supervisor who asks them to participate in decision-making, they are often bewildered, reacting quite adversely to this new experience.[6]

If, on the other hand, their expectations about their supervisor's role can be gradually changed and their perceptions about the degree that they should participate can be raised, participation may in time become more acceptable to them.

Thus, the solution is simple: *Move slowly;* begin in a small way. The supervisor must gradually expose his subordinates to participative experiences, which requires a continuing effort to *condition* subordinates to participating in decisions that affect them in their work. As their abilities expand and they become accustomed to their new role, the supervisor can then expand their participation and responsibilities step-by-step.

In reality, it is not uncommon to find that a complete transformation to a participative climate may take several years. Thus, an evaluation of participation's success too early in the game will not necessarily give an accurate indication of its ability to produce the desired results.

Miscellaneous Pitfalls

There are other inevitable pitfalls and shortcomings that the supervisor must be prepared to encounter in his early participative efforts. For example, employees whose ideas and suggestions have been rejected may become alienated. In attempting to be more participative, the supervisor may well meet resistance from his more apathetic and dependent workers who prefer to let him do all the thinking and take all the responsibility. Some employees may never wish to participate, nor can it be assumed that all are capable of contributing to problem-solving. Other employees will be able to take on only *limited* responsibilities, regardless of how much the supervisor tries to give them. Participation may actually lead to greater group cohesiveness *against* management if the goals of the group are contrary to the goals of management. Subordinates may expect further increased participation that the supervisor is restricted from providing. Finally, union leaders are sometimes antagonistic toward participation, fearing that it will draw the loyalty of workers away from the union and closer to management.

[6]Davis, *op. cit.*, pp. 105-106.

IN PERSPECTIVE—A MODEL OF PARTICIPATIVE SUPERVISION

Although management experts have not yet agreed on any one consistent concept of participative leadership, the following model offered by R. E. Miles may be helpful as a summary of the subject:

Attitudes Toward People

1. In addition to sharing common needs for belonging and respect, most people in our culture desire to contribute effectively and creatively to the accomplishment of worthwhile objectives.

2. The majority of our work force are capable of exercising far more initiative, responsibility, and creativity than their present jobs require or allow.

3. These capabilities represent untapped resources that are presently being wasted.

Kind and Amount of Participation

1. The supervisor's basic task is to create an environment in which his subordinates can contribute their full range of talents to the accomplishment of organizational goals. He must attempt to uncover and tap the creative resources of his subordinates.

2. The supervisor should allow, and encourage, his subordinates to participate not only in routine decisions but in important matters as well. In fact, the more important a decision is to the supervisor's department, the greater should be his effort to tap the department's resources.

3. The supervisor should attempt to continually expand the areas over which his subordinates exercise self-direction and self-control as they develop and demonstrate greater insight and ability.

Expectations of Participation

1. The over-all quality of decision-making and performance will improve as the supervisor makes use of the full range of experience, insight, and creative ability in his department.

2. Subordinates will exercise responsible self-direction and self-control in the accomplishment of worthwhile objectives that they understand and have helped establish.

3. Subordinates' satisfaction will increase as a by-product of improved performance and the opportunity to contribute creatively to this improvement.[7]

As we have seen, participation has its dangers and limitations, as well as its often cited advantages; when applied in inappropriate situations, it can become a miserable failure. In spite of this, there is enough evidence to indicate that, when used under the proper circumstances and in the proper manner, participation has considerable potential as a management tool. Of course, like all other manage-

[7]Miles, *op. cit.*, p. 151.

ment tools, it must be completely understood, carefully considered, and cautiously applied by the supervisor.

Certainly, it is not the answer to all supervisory problems; however, if the supervisor is interested in (1) improving the quality of decision-making, (2) raising the level of employee motivation, and (3) increasing the acceptability of decisions, he might well seriously consider the use of participative supervision.

Reading Selection 5

THE CASE FOR PARTICIPATIVE MANAGEMENT*

Keith Davis

Participation is an overworked word in business and government, but an underworked activity. The idea sounds good to most managers, but they are frequently unsure of what to do with it. Some grossly misinterpret what it is, so that when they say, "Participation is great," they are really talking about something else; others are not sure when to apply it or how far to go with it.

One reason for the slow growth of participation is that it is a difficult philosophy to understand, and even more difficult to develop in a group. Genuine social science skill is required to make participation work. Many supervisors get in over their heads in a burst of enthusiasm and, after experiencing a rebuff, tend to withdraw from further efforts at participation. It appears that improperly applied participation may be worse for productivity and morale than simply doing nothing. Ineffective attempts to secure participation may make a group feel manipulated, resentful, confused, or lacking in objectives.

In spite of the difficulty of developing participation, it does have enormous potential for raising productivity, bettering morale, and improving creative thinking. The need of people to participate is not a passing fancy. It is rooted deep in the culture of free men around the world, and it is probably a basic drive in man.[1] Because of its significance and permanence, participation is a method to which leaders need to devote long-range efforts. Means of tapping this source of creativity and of using its cohesive power for teamwork need to be developed. Participation affords a means of building some of the human values needed in a group. It can create an asset in

*From *Business Horizons,* Vol. 6, No. 3 (Fall, 1963), pp. 55-60. Reprinted with permission.

[1]Comparative studies in England and the United States suggest that participation is a basic human drive rather than a cultural acquisition. *See* N. R. F. Maier and L. R. Hoffman, "Group Decision in England and the United States," *Personnel Psychology,* XV (Spring, 1962), p. 86.

morale so that when necessary orders are given, people will respond more cooperatively because they are participating in their group, although they did not participate in determining the instruction they have most recently received. The importance of participation has been described as follows:

"Two thousand years ago we put participation in the religion which has come to dominate the Western world. Two hundred years ago we put this essential element in our political and social structure. We are just beginning to realize that we ought to put participation in business as well."[2]

CLASSICAL EXPERIMENTS

Classical experiments by Roethlisberger, Bavelas, and Coch and French confirm our belief that participation is extremely valuable. Roethlisberger and his associates originally sought to show the relationship of physical change in environment and output. In the course of their experiments, new relationships, many of them involving participation, developed between workers and supervisors, and workers and experimenters. The results convincingly showed that these social changes improved both productivity and morale. Although participation was not the whole cause of these improvements, it seemed to be a significant cause.[3]

Bavelas worked with a group of women performing a sewing operation on a group incentive basis. For his experiment, he chose a superior group whose production averaged about 74 units hourly, with a range of 70 to 78. He asked them to set their own production goal. After considerable discussion they agreed unanimously on a goal of 84 units hourly, which they exceeded within five days. A goal of 95, set at a later meeting, could not be met. The goal was then reduced to the relatively permanent level of 90 units. During the next several months, the group's output averaged about 87 units with a range of 80 to 93. The net increase after participation was about 13 units hourly.[4] Coch and French achieved similar results in experiments with sewing machine operators.[5]

The benefits of participation are evident in the experience of a large aircraft manufacturer, who employed from 5,000 to 20,000 shopworkers during the decade following World War II. The company used a safety committee system in which each department was represented by one worker. During these ten years, not one person suffered a disabling injury while serving as safety committeeman. This record was made despite the facts that hundreds of workers served on the committee during the decade, and accident-prone workers sometimes

[2]Ralph M. Besse, "Business Statesmanship," *Personnel Administration,* XX (January-February, 1957), p. 12.

[3]F. J. Roethlisberger, *Management and Morale* (Cambridge: Harvard University Press, 1941), p. 14.

[4]Norman R. F. Maier, *Psychology in Industry* (Boston: Houghton Mifflin Company, 1946), pp. 264-66. Lawrence and Smith have since repeated Bavelas' experiments with similar results. *See* Lois C. Lawrence and Patricia Cain Smith, "Group Decision and Employee Participation," *The Journal of Applied Psychology,* XXXIX (October, 1955), pp. 334-37.

[5]Lester Coch and John R. P. French, Jr., "Overcoming Resistance to Change," *Human Relations,* I (No. 4, 1948), pp. 512-32 and John R. P. French, Jr. and Alvin Zander, "The Group Dynamics Approach," in Arthur Kornhauser, ed., *Psychology of Labor-Management Relations* (Champaign, Ill.: Industrial Relations Research Association, 1949), pp. 73-75.

were appointed to the post in order to make them safety conscious. Although some committeemen probably returned to work earlier than they should have after an accident in order to preserve their record, the facts still show a significant difference between committeemen and other workers. Part of the difference was surely due to the fact that the committeemen were participating in a safety program.

Participation is especially important in encouraging people to accept change, a persistent pressure on all of us in our dynamic society. Participation is helpful both in planning and installing change, because when employees understand the objectives and content of a change, they are confident that management is not trying to "pull a fast one" on them. Participation may actually improve carefully devised management plans, because it elicits the ideas of the persons who are most thoroughly acquainted with the working effects of those plans. It may cancel a poor plan and thus save management many headaches. In any case, it broadens the outlook of those involved and helps them feel that they have an active part in what is taking place.

When a change is within management's control, such as the determination of a new work method, best results are realized when the group participates in the recognition of the need for change. Participation is less effective if it begins only after management has decided that a change is necessary.

KEY IDEAS IN PARTICIPATION

Participation is defined as an individual's mental and emotional involvement in a group situation that encourages him to contribute to group goals and to share responsibility for them. This definition contains three important ideas.

First, participation means mental and emotional involvement rather than mere muscular activity. The involvement of a person's *self,* rather than just his skill, is the product of his mind and his emotions. The person who participates is ego-involved instead of merely task-involved.[6] Some managers mistake task-involvement for true participation. They go through the motions of participation, but it is clear to employees that their manager is an autocrat who does not really want their ideas. Employees cannot become involved in this kind of situation.

A *second* important characteristic of participation is that it motivates contribution. Individuals are given an opportunity to direct their initiative and creativity toward the objectives of the group. In this way, participation differs from consent,[7] which uses only the creativity and ideas of the leader who brings his idea to the group for their approval. Participation requires more than mere approval of something already decided. It is a two-way psychological and social relationship among people rather than a procedure imposing ideas from above.

A *third* characteristic of participation is that it encourages people to accept responsibility for an activity. Because they are self-involved in the group, they want to see it work successfully. Participation helps them become responsible citizens rather than non-responsible automatons. As individuals begin to accept responsibility for group activities, they become

[6]Gordon W. Allport, "The Psychology of Participation," *The Psychological Review,* LIII (May, 1945), p. 22.

[7]Mary P. Follett, "The Psychology of Consent and Participation," in *Dynamic Administration: The Collected Papers of Mary Parker Follett,* eds. Henry C. Metcalf and L. Urwick (New York: Harper and Brothers, 1941), pp. 210-12.

interested in and receptive to teamwork, because they see in it a means of accomplishing a job for which they feel responsible. A person who is actively involved in something is naturally more committed to carrying it out. Of his own free will, he creates responsibility rather than having it forced upon him by delegation. By making himself responsible, he gains a measure of independence and dignity as an individual making his own decisions, even though these decisions are heavily influenced by his group environment.

Managers often ask, "If I share decisions with my personnel, don't I lose authority? I can't afford to give up authority because I'm responsible." This is a perfectly normal worry of an executive who is considering the values of participation for the first time, but it is hardly a justifiable worry. The participative manager still retains his authority to decide. He shares his problems with the group by means of a process that may be called social delegation. Social delegation in the human relations domain is comparable to formal delegation in the organizational domain. Neither type of delegation weakens a manager's organizational authority. No manager of the future—say twenty years hence—will object to a certain amount of social delegation through participation under normal conditions. It will be as much his stock in trade as formal delegation is today.

PRACTICE LIMITATIONS

These experiments (and the conclusions drawn from them) have a number of limitations that managers cannot ignore. Their success is no guarantee that all similar practices will be successful. The experiments described were performed by professional men skilled in human relations; similar efforts by ordinary supervisors undoubtedly would not produce such consistent results. The step from experimentation to practice is a long one indeed. The experiments were mostly one-shot efforts in a narrow work situation, using small groups who were doing repetitive work and undergoing changes. Participation in large work groups may be more difficult. In any case, managers should not go overboard for participation as they once did for scientific management. The latter was a worthwhile development, but managers' failure to recognize its uses and limitations in particular situations nearly ruined it.

In developing participation, we must be able to strike a precarious balance between counterfeit participation, which would arouse distrust, and excessive participation, which would consume valuable work time and destroy unified direction. Many issues are involved. Counterfeit participation may be tinsel and ribbon to make people happy, or it may be a more insidious tool handled by skilled social scientists, the engineers of consent.

Another danger of participation—as was true of scientific management—is that practitioners will get lost in the procedures of participation and overlook its philosophy. The substance of participation does not automatically flow from its procedures; there is no such mechanistic connection. Rather, when procedures are used at the right time and in the right circumstances, they enable it to develop.

Another issue concerns a person's right not to participate. There is no evidence that advanced participation is required for everybody; there is evidence that many persons do not want to be bothered with participation. Shall we force them into a mold merely because we think it is good for them? Some persons want a minimum of interaction with their supervisor and associates. The role expectation of many employees is to work for an autocratic supervisor, and consequently they produce effectively with this type of leadership. Research shows that the more authoritarian personality derives less benefit from participative methods, while the more equalitarian personality is more favorably affected.[8] Sometimes a group can be kept participating only by pressure from above. When that pressure is released, the group reverts to patterns of less participation.[9]

PREREQUISITES FOR PARTICIPATION

Finally, it should be emphasized that the success of participation is directly related to how well certain prerequisites are satisfied. Some of these conditions occur in the participants; some exist in the environment. Taken together, they mean that participation works better in some situations than others—and that in certain situations, it works not at all.[10]

The first prerequisite is that ample time must be allowed to participate before action is required. Participation may not be appropriate in emergency situations. Second, the financial cost of participation should not exceed the values, economic and otherwise, that it produces. Third, the subject of participation must be relevant to the participant's organization, something in which he is interested, or he will regard it as mere busy work. Fourth, the participant should have the abilities, intelligence, and knowledge to participate effectively.

Fifth, the participants must be able to communicate in order to be able to exchange ideas. Sixth, no one (employee or manager) should feel that his position is threatened by participation. Seventh, participation for deciding a course of action in an organization can take place only within the group's area of job freedom. Some degree of restriction on subunits is necessary in any organization in order to maintain internal stability; subunits cannot make decisions that violate company policy, collective bargaining agreements, or similar restraints.

Since participation is a deep-seated need of man, it is worth trying: (1) if the manager understands what he is doing; (2) if he has developed some social science skill; (3) if he will meet the prerequisites; (4) if he will respect the role expectations of his people; and (5) if he will begin in a small way, rather than shooting for the moon in the first few months. Managers should proceed with caution, building each improvement upon past success – but by all means, they should proceed.

[8]Victor H. Vroom, "Some Personality Determinants of the Effects of Participation," *Journal of Abnormal and Social Psychology,* LIX (November, 1959), pp. 322-27.

[9]Robert N. McMurry, "The Case for Benevolent Autocracy," *Harvard Business Review,* XXXVI (January-February, 1958), pp. 82-90.

[10]For further explanation, *see* Robert Tannenbaum, Irving R. Weschler, and Fred Massarik, *Leadership and Organization: A Behavioral Science Approach* (New York: McGraw-Hill Book Company, Inc., 1961), pp. 88-100.

Reading Selection 6

HOW TO CHOOSE A LEADERSHIP PATTERN*

Robert Tannenbaum
Warren H. Schmidt

"I put most problems into my group's hands and leave it to them to carry the ball from there. I serve merely as a catalyst, mirroring back the people's thoughts and feelings so that they can better understand them."

"It's foolish to make decisions oneself on matters that affect people. I always talk things over with my subordinates, but I make it clear to them that I'm the one who has to have the final say."

"Once I have decided on a course of action, I do my best to sell my ideas to my employees."

"I'm being paid to lead. If I let a lot of other people make the decisions I should be making, then I'm not worth my salt."

"I believe in getting things done. I can't waste time calling meetings. Someone has to call the shots around here, and I think it should be me."

Each of these statements represents a point of view about "good leadership." Considerable experience, factual data, and theoretical principles could be cited to support each statement, even though they seem to be inconsistent when placed together. Such contradictions point up the dilemma in which the modern manager frequently finds himself.

NEW PROBLEM

The problem of how the modern manager can be "democratic" in his relations with subordinates and at the same time maintain the necessary authority and control in the organization for which he is responsible has come into focus increasingly in recent years.

Earlier in the century this problem was not so acutely felt. The successful executive was generally pictured as possessing intelligence, imagination, initiative, the capacity to make rapid (and generally wise) decisions, and the ability to inspire subordinates. People tended to think of the world as being divided into "leaders" and "followers."

New Focus

Gradually, however, from the social sciences emerged the concept of "group dynamics" with its focus on

*Reprinted with the permission of *Harvard Business Review,* Vol. 36, No. 2 (March-April, 1958), pp. 95-101.

members of the group rather than solely on the leader. Research efforts of social scientists underscored the importance of employee involvement and participation in decision making. Evidence began to challenge the efficiency of highly directive leadership, and increasing attention was paid to problems of motivation and human relations.

Through training laboratories in group development that sprang up across the country, many of the newer notions of leadership began to exert an impact. These training laboratories were carefully designed to give people a first-hand experience in full participation and decision making. The designated "leaders" deliberately attempted to reduce their own power and to make group members as responsible as possible for setting their own goals and methods within the laboratory experience.

It was perhaps inevitable that some of the people who attended the training laboratories regarded this kind of leadership as being truly "democratic" and went home with the determination to build fully participative decision making into their own organizations. Whenever their bosses made a decision without convening a staff meeting, they tended to perceive this as authoritarian behavior. The true symbol of democratic leadership to some was the meeting–and the less directed from the top, the more democratic it was.

Some of the more enthusiastic alumni of these training laboratories began to get the habit of categorizing leader behavior as "democratic" *or* "authoritarian." The boss who made too many decisions himself was thought of as an authoritarian, and his directive behavior was often attributed solely to his personality.

New Need

The net result of the research findings and of the human relations training based upon them has been to call into question the stereotype of an effective leader. Consequently, the modern manager often finds himself in an uncomfortable state of mind.

Often he is not quite sure how to behave; there are times when he is torn between exerting "strong" leadership and "permissive" leadership. Sometimes new knowledge pushes him in one direction ("I should really get the group to help make this decision"), but at the same time his experience pushes him in another direction ("I really understand the problem better than the group and therefore I should make the decision"). He is not sure when a group decision is really appropriate or when holding a staff meeting serves merely as a device for avoiding his own decision-making responsibility.

The purpose of our article is to suggest a framework which managers may find useful in grappling with this dilemma. First we shall look at the different patterns of leadership behavior that the manager can choose from in relating himself to his subordinates. Then we shall turn to some of the questions suggested by this range of patterns. For instance, how important is it for a manager's subordinates to know what type of leadership he is using in a situation? What factors should he consider in deciding on a leadership pattern? What difference do his long-run objectives make as compared to his immediate objectives?

RANGE OF BEHAVIOR

Exhibit I presents the continuum or range of possible leadership behavior available to a manager. Each type of action is related to the degree of authority used by the boss and to the amount of freedom available to his subordinates in reaching decisions. The actions seen on the extreme left characterize the manager who maintains a high degree of control while those seen

EXHIBIT 1. Continuum of Leadership Behavior

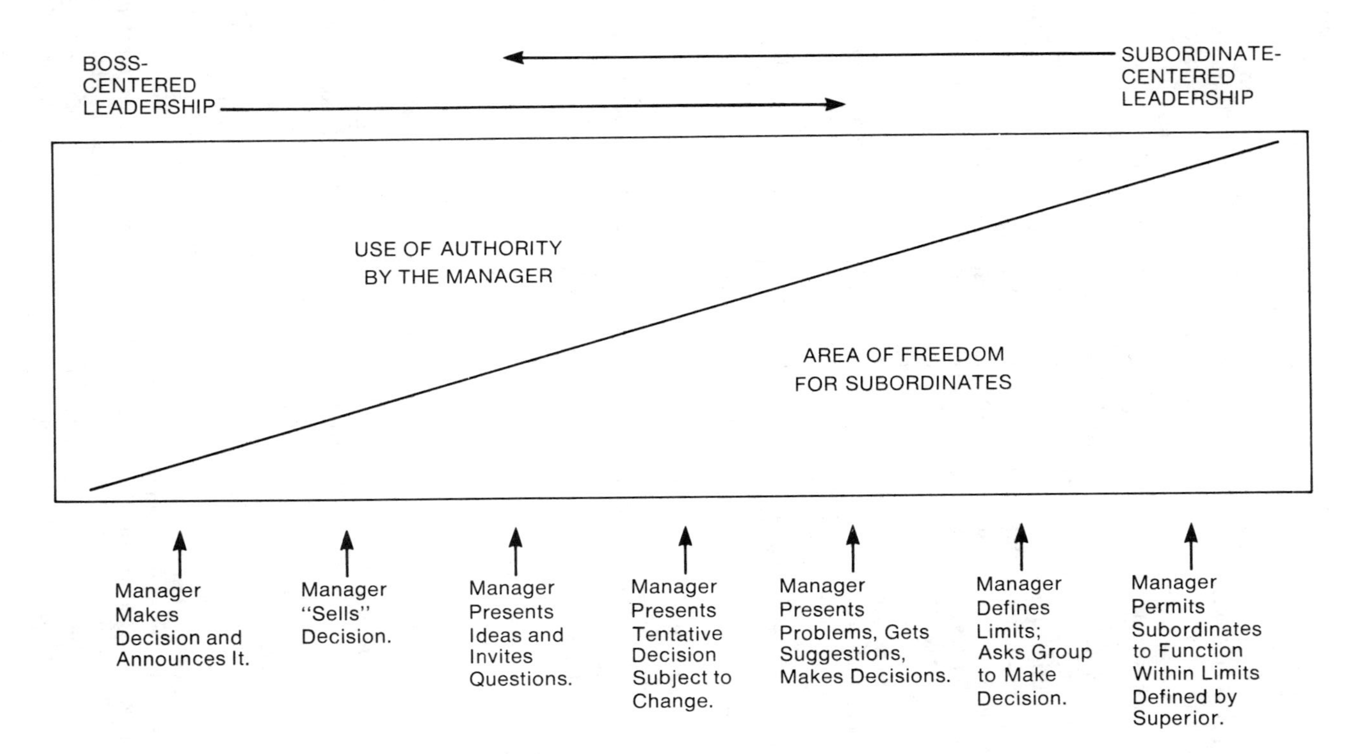

on the extreme right characterize the manager who releases a high degree of control. Neither extreme is absolute; authority and freedom are never without their limitations.

Now let us look more closely at each of the behavior points occurring along this continuum.

The manager makes the decision and announces it. In this case the boss identifies a problem, considers alternative solutions, chooses one of them, and then reports this decision to his subordinates for implementation. He may or may not give consideration to what he believes his subordinates will think or feel about his decision; in any case, he provides no opportunity for them to participate directly in the decision-making process. Coercion may or may not be used or implied.

The manager "sells" his decision. Here the manager, as before, takes responsibility for identifying the problem and arriving at a decision. However, rather than simply announcing it, he takes the additional step of persuading his subordinates to accept it. In doing so, he recognizes the possibility of some resistance among those who will be faced with the decision, and seeks to reduce this resistance by indicating, for example, what the employees have to gain from his decision.

The manager presents his ideas, invites questions. Here the boss who has arrived at a decision and who seeks acceptance of his ideas provides an opportunity for his subordinates to get a fuller explanation of his thinking and his intentions. After presenting the ideas, he invites questions so that his associates can better understand what he is trying to accomplish. This "give and take" also enables the manager and the subordinates to explore more fully the implications of the decision.

The manager presents a tentative decision subject to change. This kind of behavior permits the subordinates to exert some influence on the decision. The initiative for identifying and diagnosing the problem remains with the boss. Before meeting with his staff, he has thought the problem through and arrived at a decision—but only a tentative one. Before finalizing it, he presents his proposed solution for the reaction of those who will be affected by it. He says in effect, "I'd like to hear what you have to say about this plan that I have developed. I'll appreciate your frank reactions, but will reserve for myself the final decision."

The manager presents the problem, gets suggestions, and then makes his decision. Up to this point the boss has come before the group with a solution of his own. Not so in this case. The subordinates now get the first chance to suggest solutions. The manager's initial role involves identifying the problem. He might, for example, say something of this sort: "We are faced with a number of complaints from newspapers and the general public on our service policy. What is wrong here? What ideas do you have for coming to grips with this problem?"

The function of the group becomes one of increasing the manager's repertory of possible solutions to the problem. The purpose is to capitalize on the knowledge and experience of those who are on the "firing line." From the expanded list of alternatives developed by the manager and his subordinates, the manager then selects the solution that he regards as most promising.[1]

The manager defines the limits and requests the group to make a decision. At this point the manager passes to the group (possibly including

[1] For a fuller explanation of this approach, see Leo Moore, "Too Much Management, Too Little Change," *Harvard Business Review* (January-February, 1956), p. 41.

himself as a member) the right to make decisions. Before doing so, however, he defines the problem to be solved and the boundaries within which the decision must be made.

An example might be the handling of a parking problem at a plant. The boss decides that this is something that should be worked on by the people involved, so he calls them together and points up the existence of the problem. Then he tells them:

"There is the open field just north of the main plant which has been designated for additional employee parking. We can build underground or surface multilevel facilities as long as the cost does not exceed $100,000. Within these limits we are free to work out whatever solution makes sense to us. After we decide on a specific plan, the company will spend the available money in whatever way we indicate."

The manager permits the group to make decisions within prescribed limits. This represents an extreme degree of group freedom only occasionally encountered in formal organizations, as, for instance, in many research groups. Here the team of managers or engineers undertakes the identification and diagnosis of the problem, develops alternative procedures for solving it, and decides on one or more of these alternative solutions. The only limits directly imposed on the group by the organization are those specified by the superior of the team's boss. If the boss participates in the decision-making process, he attempts to do so with no more authority than any other member of the group. He commits himself in advance to assist in implementing whatever decision the group makes.

KEY QUESTIONS

As the continuum in Exhibit I demonstrates, there are a number of alternative ways in which a manager can relate himself to the group or individuals he is supervising. At the extreme left of the range, the emphasis is on the manager—on what *he* is interested in, how *he* sees things, how *he* feels about them. As we move toward the subordinate-centered end of the continuum, however, the focus is increasingly on the subordinates—on what *they* are interested in, how *they* look at things, how *they* feel about them.

When business leadership is regarded in this way, a number of questions arise. Let us take four of especial importance.

Can a boss ever relinquish his responsibility by delegating it to someone else? Our view is that the manager must expect to be held responsible by his superior for the quality of the decisions made, even though operationally these decisions may have been made on a group basis. He should, therefore, be ready to accept whatever risk is involved whenever he delegates decision-making power to his subordinates. Delegation is not a way of "passing the buck." Also, it should be emphasized that the amount of freedom the boss gives to his subordinates cannot be greater than the freedom which he himself has been given by his own superior.

Should the manager participate with his subordinates once he has delegated responsibility to them? The manager should carefully think over this question and decide on his role prior to involving the subordinate group. He should ask if his presence will inhibit or facilitate the problem-solving process. There may be some instances when he should leave the group to let it solve the problem for itself. Typically, however, the boss has useful ideas to contribute, and should function as an additional member of the group. In the latter instance, it is important that he indicate clearly to the group that he sees himself in a *member* role rather than in an authority role.

How important is it for the group to recognize what kind of leadership behavior the boss is using? It makes a great deal of difference. Many relationship problems between boss and subordinate occur because the boss fails to make clear how he plans to use his authority. If, for example, he actually intends to make a certain decision himself, but the subordinate group gets the impression that he has delegated this authority, considerable confusion and resentment are likely to follow. Problems may also occur when the boss uses a "democratic" facade to conceal the fact that he has already made a decision which he hopes the group will accept as its own. The attempt to "make them think it was their idea in the first place" is a risky one. We believe that it is highly important for the manager to be honest and clear in describing what authority he is keeping and what role he is asking his subordinates to assume in solving a particular problem.

Can you tell how "democratic" a manager is by the number of decisions his subordinates make? The sheer *number* of decisions is not an accurate index of the amount of freedom that a subordinate group enjoys. More important is the *significance* of the decisions which the boss entrusts to his subordinates. Obviously a decision on how to arrange desks is of an entirely different order from a decision involving the introduction of new electronic data-processing equipment. Even though the widest possible limits are given in dealing with the first issue, the group will sense no particular degree of responsibility. For a boss to permit the group to decide equipment policy, even within rather narrow limits, would reflect a greater degree of confidence in them on his part.

DECIDING HOW TO LEAD

Now let us turn from the types of leadership that are possible in a company situation to the question of what types are *practical* and *desirable*. What factors or forces should a manager consider in deciding how to manage? Three are of particular importance:

1. Forces in the manager.
2. Forces in the subordinates.
3. Forces in the situation.

We should like briefly to describe these elements and indicate how they might influence a manager's action in a decision-making situation.[2] The strength of each of them will, of course, vary from instance to instance, but the manager who is sensitive to them can better assess the problems which face him and determine which mode of leadership behavior is most appropriate for him.

Forces in the Manager

The manager's behavior in any given instance will be influenced greatly by the many forces operating within his own personality. He will, of course, perceive his leadership problems in a unique way on the basis of his background, knowledge, and experience. Among the important internal forces affecting him will be the following:

1. *His value system.* How strongly does he feel that individuals

[2]See also Robert Tannenbaum and Fred Massarik, "Participation by Subordinates in the Managerial Decision-Making Process," *Canadian Journal of Economics and Political Science* (August, 1950), pp. 413-418.

should have a share in making the decisions which affect them? Or, how convinced is he that the official who is paid to assume responsibility should personally carry the burden of decision making? The strength of his convictions on questions like these will tend to move the manager to one end or the other of the continuum shown in Exhibit I. His behavior will also be influenced by the relative importance that he attaches to organizational efficiency, personal growth of subordinates, and company profits.[3]

2. *His confidence in his subordinates.* Managers differ greatly in the amount of trust they have in other people generally, and this carries over to the particular employees they supervise at a given time. In viewing his particular group of subordinates, the manager is likely to consider their knowledge and competence with respect to the problem. A central question he might ask himself is: "Who is best qualified to deal with this problem?" Often he may, justifiably or not, have more confidence in his own capabilities than in those of his subordinates.
3. *His own leadership inclinations.* There are some managers who seem to function more comfortably and naturally as highly directive leaders. Resolving problems and issuing orders come easily to them. Other managers seem to operate more comfortably in a team role, where they are continually sharing many of their functions with their subordinates.
4. *His feelings of security in an uncertain situation.* The manager who releases control over the decision-making process thereby reduces the predictability of the outcome. Some managers have a greater need than others for predictability and stability in their environment. This "tolerance for ambiguity" is being viewed increasingly by psychologists as a key variable in a person's manner of dealing with problems.

The manager brings these and other highly personal variables to each situation he faces. If he can see them as forces which, consciously or unconsciously, influence his behavior, he can better understand what makes him prefer to act in a given way. And understanding this, he can often make himself more effective.

Forces in the Subordinate

Before deciding how to lead a certain group, the manager will also want to consider a number of forces affecting his subordinates' behavior. He will want to remember that each employee, like himself, is influenced by many personality variables. In addition, each subordinate has a set of expectations about how the boss should act in relation to him (the phrase "expected behavior" is one we hear more and more often these days at discussions of leadership and teaching). The better the manager understands these factors, the more accurately he can determine what kind of behavior on his part will enable his subordinates to act most effectively.

Generally speaking, the manager can permit his subordinates greater freedom if the following essential conditions exist:

1. If the subordinates have relatively high needs for independ-

[3]See Chris Argyris, "Top Management Dilemma: Company Needs vs. Individual Development," *Personnel* (September, 1955), pp. 123-134.

ence. (As we all know, people differ greatly in the amount of direction that they desire.)

2. If the subordinates have a readiness to assume responsibility for decision making. (Some see additional responsibility as a tribute to their ability; others see it as "passing the buck.")
3. If they have a relatively high tolerance for ambiguity. (Some employees prefer to have clear-cut directives given to them; others prefer a wider area of freedom.)
4. If they are interested in the problem and feel that it is important.
5. If they understand and identify with the goals of the organization.
6. If they have the necessary knowledge and experience to deal with the problem.
7. If they have learned to expect to share in decision making. (Persons who have come to expect strong leadership and are then suddenly confronted with the request to share more fully in decision making are often upset by this new experience. On the other hand, persons who have enjoyed a considerable amount of freedom resent the boss who begins to make all the decisions himself.)

The manager will probably tend to make fuller use of his own authority if the above conditions do *not* exist; at times there may be no realistic alternative to running a "one-man show."

The restrictive effect of many of the forces will, of course, be greatly modified by the general feeling of confidence which subordinates have in the boss. Where they have learned to respect and trust him, he is free to vary his behavior. He will feel certain that he will not be perceived as an authoritarian boss on those occasions when he makes decisions by himself. Similarly, he will not be seen as using staff meetings to avoid his decision-making responsibility. In a climate of mutual confidence and respect, people tend to feel less threatened by deviations from normal practice, which in turn makes possible a higher degree of flexibility in the whole relationship.

Forces in the Situation

In addition to the forces which exist in the manager himself and in his subordinates, certain characteristics of the general situation will also affect the manager's behavior. Among the more critical environmental pressures that surround him are those which stem from the organization, the work group, the nature of the problem, and the pressures of time. Let us look briefly at each of these.

Type of organization. Like individuals, organizations have values and traditions which inevitably influence the behavior of the people who work in them. The manager who is a newcomer to a company quickly discovers that certain kinds of behavior are approved while others are not. He also discovers that to deviate radically from what is generally accepted is likely to create problems for him.

These values and traditions are communicated in many ways—through job descriptions, policy pronouncements, and public statements by top executives. Some organizations, for example, hold to the notion that the desirable executive is one who is dynamic, imaginative, decisive, and persuasive. Other organizations put more emphasis upon the importance of the executive's ability to work effectively with people—his human relations skills. The fact that his superiors have a defined concept of what the good executive should be will very likely push the manager toward one end or the other of the behavioral range.

In addition to the above, the amount of employee participation is influenced by such variables as the size of the working units, their geographical distribution, and the degree of inter- and intra-organizational security required to attain company goals. For example, the wide geographical dispersion of an organization may preclude a practical system of participative decision making, even though this would otherwise be desirable. Similarly, the size of the working units or the need for keeping plans confidential may make it necessary for the boss to exercise more control than would otherwise be the case. Factors like these may limit considerably the manager's ability to function flexibly on the continuum.

Group effectiveness. Before turning decision-making responsibility over to a subordinate group, the boss should consider how effectively its members work together as a unit.

One of the relevant factors here is the experience the group has had in working together. It can generally be expected that a group which has functioned for some time will have developed habits of cooperation and thus be able to tackle a problem more effectively than a new group. It can also be expected that a group of people with similar backgrounds and interests will work more quickly and easily than people with dissimilar backgrounds, because the communication problems are likely to be less complex.

The degree of confidence that the members have in their ability to solve problems as a group is also a key consideration. Finally, such group variables as cohesiveness, permissiveness, mutual acceptance, and commonality of purpose will exert subtle but powerful influence on the group's functioning.

The problem itself. The nature of the problem may determine what degree of authority should be delegated by the manager to his subordinates. Obviously he will ask himself whether they have the kind of knowledge which is needed. It is possible to do them a real disservice by assigning a problem that their experience does not equip them to handle.

Since the problems faced in large or growing industries increasingly require knowledge of specialists from many different fields, it might be inferred that the more complex a problem, the more anxious a manager will be to get some assistance in solving it. However, this is not always the case. There will be times when the very complexity of the problem calls for one person to work it out. For example, if the manager has most of the background and factual data relevant to a given issue, it may be easier for him to think it through himself than to take the time to fill in his staff on all the pertinent background information.

The key question to ask, of course, is: "Have I heard the ideas of everyone who has the necessary knowledge to make a significant contribution to the solution of this problem?"

The pressure of time. This is perhaps the most clearly felt pressure on the manager (in spite of the fact that it may sometimes be imagined). The more that he feels the need for an immediate decision, the more difficult it is to involve other people. In organizations which are in a constant state of "crisis" and "crash programming" one is likely to find managers personally using a high degree of authority with relatively little delegation to subordinates. When the time pressure is less intense, however, it becomes much more possible to bring subordinates in on the decision-making process.

These, then, are the principal forces that impinge on the manager in any given instance and that tend to determine his tactical behavior in relation to his subordinates. In each case his behavior ideally will be that which makes possible the most effective attainment of his immediate goal within the limits facing him.

LONG-RUN STRATEGY

As the manager works with his organization on the problems that come up day by day, his choice of a leadership pattern is usually limited. He must take account of the forces just described and, within the restrictions they impose on him, do the best that he can. But as he looks ahead months or even years, he can shift his thinking from tactics to large-scale strategy. No longer need he be fettered by all of the forces mentioned, for he can view many of them as variables over which he has some control. He can, for example, gain new insights or skills for himself, supply training for individual subordinates, and provide participative experiences for his employee group.

In trying to bring about a change in these variables, however, he is faced with a challenging question: At which point along the continuum *should* he act?

Attaining Objectives

The answer depends largely on what he wants to accomplish. Let us suppose that he is interested in the same objectives that most modern managers seek to attain when they can shift their attention from the pressure of immediate assignments:

1. To raise the level of employee motivation.
2. To increase the readiness of subordinates to accept change.
3. To improve the quality of all managerial decisions.
4. To develop teamwork and morale.
5. To further the individual development of employees.

In recent years the manager has been deluged with a flow of advice on how best to achieve these longer-run objectives. It is little wonder that he is often both bewildered and annoyed. However, there are some guidelines which he can usefully follow in making a decision.

Most research and much of the experience of recent years give a strong factual basis to the theory that a fairly high degree of subordinate-centered behavior is associated with the accomplishment of the five purposes mentioned.[4] This does not mean that a manager should always leave all decisions to his assistants. To provide the individual or the group with greater freedom than they are ready for at any given time may very well tend to generate anxieties and therefore inhibit rather than facilitate the attainment of desired objectives. But this should not keep the manager from making a continuing effort to confront his subordinates with the challenge of freedom.

CONCLUSION

In summary, there are two implications in the basic thesis that we have been developing. The first is that the successful leader is one who is keenly aware of those forces which are most relevant to his behavior at any given time. He accurately understands him-

[4]For example, see Warren H. Schmidt and Paul C. Buchanan, *Techniques that Produce Teamwork* (New London: Arthur C. Croft Publications, 1954); and Morris S. Viteles, *Motivation and Morale in Industry* (New York: W. W. Norton & Company, Inc., 1953).

self, the individuals and group he is dealing with, and the company and broader social environment in which he operates. And certainly he is able to assess the present readiness for growth of his subordinates.

But this sensitivity or understanding is not enough, which brings us to the second implication. The successful leader is one who is able to behave appropriately in the light of these perceptions. If direction is in order, he is able to direct; if considerable participative freedom is called for, he is able to provide such freedom.

Thus, the successful manager of men can be primarily characterized neither as a strong leader nor as a permissive one. Rather, he is one who maintains a high batting average in accurately assessing the forces that determine what his most appropriate behavior at any given time should be and in actually being able to behave accordingly. Being both insightful and flexible, he is less likely to see the problems of leadership as a dilemma.

QUESTIONS FOR REVIEW AND DISCUSSION

1. What is meant by *participation?*
2. Explain the difference between "ego involvement" and "task involvement."
3. "It is fine to talk about the 'rational process of decision-making,' but how often does a supervisor have the time for such luxuries? Something happens and you have to act fast. This is where a supervisor earns his salary—making fast, intuitive decisions under pressure." How would you respond to this statement?
4. a. Recall a decision that you recently made. Did you go through the four steps in the decision-making process cited in this chapter? Trace your decision through the four steps, explaining each.
   b. Which of these four steps could a subordinate, friend, or associate have contributed to that might have improved the overall quality of your final solution?
5. Which style of supervision—autocratic or participative—is generally the easiest for the supervisor to practice? Why?
6. Discuss the major potential benefits of participative supervision.
7. As you see it, which is better—a decision reached by an individual or one reached by a group? Explain.
8. Many companies utilize *committees, departmental meetings,* and *suggestion systems* as devices for obtaining employee participation. How would you evaluate the desirability and benefits of these techniques? If you have had experiences with any of these techniques, relate to the class how they have been implemented and if they have been successful; if they have not been successful, how do you account for this?
9. a. What factors determine the degree of participation that should be used in a given situation?
   b. What are some of the "realities of life" in an organization that can restrict the use of participation?
10. What are the major implications for supervision of the "leadership continuum" presented by Tannenbaum and Schmidt?

11. Can the points on the leadership continuum be related to the degree that subordinates are allowed to participate in the four steps in the decision-making process? Explain.
12. Does the leadership continuum basically represent McGregor's "Theory X" at one end and "Theory Y" (discussed in Chapter 2) at the other end? Explain.
13. As you see yourself as a supervisor, what style of supervision do you (or would you) use most of the time? Why? Where does your style fall on the leadership continuum?
14. *Supervisor A:* "I always give my men directions in a few words, telling them clearly what is expected of them. When possible, I do this in writing to give them a permanent statement of what is required. If they have questions on what is expected they may raise them, but I don't encourage questions dealing with why a decision was made as it was. This way they are clear as to precisely what I want."
    Supervisor B: "I usually talk over my decisions with the men who carry them out to be sure they not only understand what is expected of them but why, and how what they do fits into the total picture. This way they see the reasons for my requests, and they can carry them out with higher motivation and greater perspective."
    a. Which points on the leadership continuum do you feel would typically represent each supervisor's style of leadership?
    b. Under what conditions might A be better? When would B be better?
    c. If you were receiving orders, which approach would you prefer?
15. In what ways can the use of participation by the supervisor aid in supplying the employee's job with Herzberg's *motivator* and *maintenance* factors, discussed in Chapter 3?
16. How does the concept of participation by subordinates in the decision-making process relate to (a) *horizontal expansion* and (b) *vertical expansion* of jobs, as presented in Chapter 3?
17. The basic concept of participation has been with us since early in the human relations movement. However, it has never attained great popularity with management and has apparently not been successful in all applications. How would you attempt to explain this failure to gain universal acceptance?
18. "Often I will consult with men who lack the interest or ability to make constructive suggestions. They don't really add anything to the quality of the decision, but it gives them a sense of importance. Besides, who knows? Someday, somebody might come up with a good idea." Do you believe that the supervisor making this statement will get the results he expects from the use of participation? Why?
19. Can you tell how "participative" a supervisor is by the number of decisions his subordinates make? Explain.
20. Does the supervisor lose a certain degree of authority, control, and influence when he allows his subordinates to influence decisions through participation?

SUGGESTED ADDITIONAL READINGS

Allbrook, Robert C. "Participative Management: Time for a Second Look," *Fortune,* May 1967, pp. 166-70, 197-200.

McMurry, Robert N. "The Case for Benevolent Autocracy," *Harvard Business Review*, January-February, 1958, pp. 82-90.

Miles, Raymond E. "Human Relations or Human Resources," *Harvard Business Review*, July-August, 1965, pp. 148-163.

Tannenbaum, Robert, and Fred Massarik. "Participation by Subordinates in the Managerial Decision-Making Process," *Human Relations in Management*, S. G. Huneryager and I. L. Heckmann, eds. Second edition Cincinnati: South-Western Publishing Company, 1967, pp. 592-605.

5

EFFECTIVE INTRODUCTION OF CHANGE

Today, sociological and technological change is taking place at a much faster pace than ever before. Change has of necessity become a way of life in most business and industrial organizations; those which have survived and will continue to be competitive are the organizations that have learned to effectively cope with this accelerated rate of change.

Change is inevitable for us all. Things can never be kept exactly as they are or as many of us might like them to be. There is no such thing today as standing still; we either move ahead or we slip back. Even though we know this is true, we also have a definite tendency to highly resent certain changes; at times we strongly *resist* them. The mere word "change" produces emotional reactions; it is certainly not a neutral word. To many people, it very often carries a threatening connotation.

Supervisors can be viewed as "change agents," responsible for the effective implementation of various changes within their work units. As such, successful supervisors must be equipped to understand the nature of change and to diagnose and resolve the natural human tendency of their employees to resist change.

In this chapter, we shall first look at what resistance is and then examine some means whereby resistance can be prevented or decreased by the supervisor. We should keep in mind, however, that our discussion of resistance to change is applicable equally to managerial and supervisory personnel and to rank-and-file employees. Resistance can be just as pronounced and stubborn in a white collar as in a blue collar.

THE NATURE OF RESISTANCE TO CHANGE

Human beings are creatures of habit and like to settle into a routine, especially on the job. Even if the way they are presently doing things is not the best, it's at least familiar and comfortable, and they're adjusted to it; there are no unknowns. Therefore, **people tend to resist any ideas that threaten to change their established way of doing things.** The fact that a change is even suggested seems to imply a criticism that the old way was not good enough; this often evokes the familiar question, "What's wrong with the way we've always done it?"

To give up well-established and therefore easy habits and to experience the possible threats of new work conditions are upsetting. Unless there is more to be gained than lost and unless the gain is made clearly apparent, people naturally resist having to change.

Of course, all changes are not resisted by employees; some are actually wanted. The tendency to resist change is somewhat offset by a desire for new experiences and for the rewards that may come from certain changes. In this sense, man is a curious creature. He seeks many changes and finds change resulting from his own efforts to be highly rewarding. But, almost paradoxically, he also seeks stability and predictability in his environment. It is when change is perceived as *imposed* upon him and is seen as a threat that he begins to resist.

"They're always changing something—never leave a guy alone."

Resistance Not Always Undesirable

All behavior representing resistance to change isn't necessarily undesirable. Some opposition to change on the part of employees may be perfectly logical and grounded on well-supported reasons.

Management tends to fall into the trap of assuming that change is always "good" and should be accepted without question, while those who oppose it are the "bad guys." However, we can all probably recall experiences where changes were introduced (for example, by politicians!) that proved to be unwise changes, and people were perfectly right in resisting them. Thus, there are actually two kinds of resistance to change—one based on *logical, rational analysis* and another based on *emotional reactions* to fear and real or imagined threats.[1] Although it is admittedly difficult to distinguish between them, it is to the latter that we shall direct our interest.

Perceived Threats to Need-Satisfaction

Huneryager and Heckmann, in this chapter's reading selection, suggest that any form of change creates a *state of disequilibrium* in the individual's environment that causes him to experience an *imbalance in need-satisfaction.*

This simply means that, before the change, the degree of satisfaction of the person's basic needs—physiological, security, social, esteem, and self-actualization (discussed in Chapter 2)—is relatively stable. The change is perceived as a threat to this stability; this threat, of course, can be real or imagined. In either case, the person becomes fearful that the change will decrease the level of satisfaction of his various basic needs.

Therefore, resistance to change can be viewed as **a reaction intended to protect the individual from a perceived threat to need-satisfaction**; anything which threatens such fundamental needs as job security, social relationships, self-esteem, or status may be desperately feared and resisted.

Fears Underlying Resistance to Change

The threat of change to the individual's need-satisfaction is evidenced through various job-related *fears;* typical of these deep-seated fears underlying resistance to change are:

1. Fear of unemployment, displacement, or demotion.
2. Fear of reduction in earnings.
3. Fear of a "speed-up" or of being forced to work harder in order to maintain existing rate of earnings.
4. Fear of having to break or alter established social relationships and/or having to establish new relationships.
5. Fear that the change implies criticism of the individual's or group's past performance.
6. Fear of losing power over an area that the individual formerly controlled.
7. Fear of impaired status and/or recognition within the group.
8. Fear of inability to learn new methods.
9. Fear of greater specialization, resulting in a boring, meaningless job and a decreased sense of achievement.
10. Fear of *any unknown* which the individual does not understand.

[1] Keith Davis, *Human Relations at Work* (New York: McGraw-Hill Book Company, 1967), pp. 393-95.

It is important to recognize that the same change may elicit different fears within individual members of the group, simply because **different people often perceive different meanings in the change.**

Furthermore, in those organizations where employee fears, insecurities, and frustrations are already present, even relatively minor changes in policies or procedures may evoke profound reactions of resentment and hostility; in other words, any added fears only reinforce and accentuate the existing ones.

Of course, as with almost any effort at effectively dealing with human behavior, empathy on the part of the supervisor—the ability to put himself in the employee's shoes—is essential in determining the probable fears existing in the group.

Forms of Resistance

People resist change for highly personal and unique reasons—sometimes reasons buried so deeply in the person that he himself does not know what they are. Thus, the behavior used by the resister can be expected to take many forms, depending on the individual, the nature of the change, and the particular situation.

The ingenuity of workers in devising various overt and subtle resistances is often astonishing and almost limitless. The form of resistance can range from direct or indirect aggression against the change itself or against the supervisor to such reactions as withdrawal or apathy; efforts may be made to block the introduction of new methods or to discredit them and force their removal after their implementation. In extreme cases, there may be outright sabotage of the new procedures.

PREVENTING AND DECREASING RESISTANCE TO CHANGE

The supervisor has the responsibility of implementing a change in such a way that there will be satisfactory acceptance and a minimum of resistance in his work group.

The supervisor's role in the change process basically involves three steps: (1) *unfreezing* (casting doubt on existing methods of operation); (2) *changing* (trying new methods of operation); and (3) *refreezing* (reinforcing the new, more desirable changes). This may appear simple enough; in actuality, moving through the process can be quite a challenge to any supervisor's ability.

Though the supervisor typically has the role of "change agent," we must keep in mind that it is really the employees who ultimately control the decision to *accept* the change, and they are the ones who determine the eventual success of the change. Therefore, employee support of the change is essential.

In order to obtain this support, employee resistance to change must be either prevented or decreased. Thus, we shall now turn our attention to some procedures and techniques by which this may be accomplished. Most of these are little more than common sense; all of them have been well tested and proven useful.

Prevent Excessive and Unnecessary Changes

Perhaps one of the most important ways to prevent resistance is to first determine if a proposed change is really necessary and advantageous. Any modification in policies or procedures that may be interpreted as a threat to employee need-satisfaction should be carefully considered, anticipating and identifying all probable consequences of the change.

Change merely for the sake of change serves little purpose and frequently produces adverse reactions that far outweigh any supposed advantages. In the long run, therefore, it is sometimes better not to make trivial, moderately needed changes because the disturbances they cause may be more costly than will a continuance of current methods.

Move Slowly

If it is finally decided that a change is necessary and must be made, it is wise, whenever possible, to move slowly.

A proposal to change things immediately arouses fear of the unknown and the unfamiliar. Many good ideas for change that ought to work fail simply because they are put into effect too abruptly and rapidly. The same plan introduced more gradually in a step-by-step manner, with time for employees to adjust their thinking and get rid of some of their fears and objections, will normally meet with greater success.

Disrupting surprises can be avoided if the supervisor *prepares* and *informs* his employees (and himself) well in advance of any changes that will affect them. This can do much to allay the fears that a sudden change typically arouses; there will probably still be some remaining anxiety about the change, but advance preparation can help to minimize it.

Of course, how much preparation a supervisor is able to provide depends to a great extent on where the plan for the change originates. For example, if it is the supervisor's idea and affects only his department, he can usually prepare everyone in plenty of time to ensure a smooth transition. However, if the proposed change comes from higher-level management, the supervisor's time for adequate preparation may be greatly restricted.

Adequate Preparation through Effective Communication

Once a change has been announced, the maximum possible information should be communicated to employees about it in order to allay as many of their potential fears and anxieties as possible.

Resistance can be expected when the change is not made understandable to those who will be influenced by the change; **what employees don't fully understand, they typically suspect, fear, and resist.**

On the other hand, resistance is almost always lower if the nature, goals, benefits, and drawbacks of the change are made completely clear; in general, **the greater the degree of effective communication, the greater the employees' willingness to accept and support the change.**

Complete explanation of the change. A full statement must be given explaining the need and reasons for the change and indicating how the company, the department, and, especially, the employees themselves will benefit from the contemplated change.

Employees are much more likely to accept change if they can see the immediate or the long-range benefits. If they can be made to see that the proposed change will make their jobs easier, faster, more challenging, safer, more productive, or better in some other way, there is that much more chance that they will accept it with only minimal resistance.

"What's wrong with the old way?"

In his explanation, the supervisor should make every attempt to relate the needs for the change as closely as possible to the employees' own personal needs and interests. In a very real sense, the supervisor must use the same approach in "selling" a change that successful salesmen use in selling goods and services: **Tell the user what's in it for him.** If employees perceive the change as primarily benefitting only the company, rather than themselves and their fellow workers, greater resistance is likely to be encountered.

Needless to say, the supervisor himself needs to fully understand the change before attempting to explain it to his group, and his presentation must be planned with care. For example, let's assume that top management decides on a new cost-reduction program. Before any supervisor can help fulfill his company's new goal, he must understand (1) why the new program was initiated and (2) exactly what is expected of him and his work group.

Also, in the case of a company-wide change or one instituted by higher-level management, the supervisor may at times find *himself* resisting the change; nevertheless, it is his responsibility to present the new policy or procedure to his workers in a favorable light, whether or not he completely agrees with the change.

Establishing a continuing dialogue. To this point in our discussion of effective communication as an aid in preventing and decreasing resistance, we may have inadvertently given the impression that the *direction* that such communication takes is only one-way—*downward* from supervisor to subordinates. Nothing could be less desirable.

Because of the emotional nature of resistance to change, a direct, logical, one-way presentation of the merits of the change is seldom enough. What is really needed is an explanation of the change followed by a *two-way* dialogue or discussion whereby members of the work group can become highly involved in expressing and discussing their ideas, attitudes, opinions, and suggestions about any aspect of the change with each other and the supervisor. In fact, this feedback from employees is the only means the supervisor has to determine if the information he has transmitted about the change has been properly understood and accepted; in addition, it can often allow employee fears and anxieties to be expressed and perhaps dealt with on the spot.

Yet, all too often, supervisors, along with staff personnel (especially technical specialists such as engineers, job analysts, and accountants), become so convinced that the change is logical, technically correct, and beneficial that they see no need to *discuss.* They simply *tell,* and they consider any opposition to "their" change as coming from obviously bullheaded and ignorant people. Anyone who feels this way should keep in mind that, regardless of the "facts," employees still may perceive them as a threat and respond accordingly; complete information about a change can be distorted just as readily as incomplete information.[2]

Through discussion, freedom to ask questions, and the sharing of ideas, the group's level of resistance to change tends to decrease, while their understanding and "trust" of the change increases. Obviously, face-to-face communication is much more desirable in accomplishing this than any form of written announcements.

Furthermore, effective communication in the change process cannot be viewed as a "one-shot" presentation or discussion. Rather, it should be looked upon as a continuing dialogue taking place as needed up to the time of the actual implementation of the change—and frequently continuing even after the implementation.

[2]Davis, p. 396.

Tensions and hostilities will almost invariably arise both before and after the change is put into effect. Thus, it is advisable to provide employees with ready outlets, for example, periodic informal meetings or "gripe sessions" (either on an individual or group basis) for "talking out" and relieving their accumulated anxieties, fears, and resentments from time to time. Complaints and grievances should actually be invited during the transitional period of the change.

There is definite value in being able to "blow off steam" without fearing reprisal from the supervisor. (Psychologists call this "catharsis.") A good gripe session often clears the air, and employees are then able to return to a reasonable discussion of how they can best adjust to the requirements of the change.

The desirability of establishing a continuing dialogue after the change is put into effect is also illustrated by the need to keep employees fully informed of the results and progress of the change and of how well they are doing in terms of the change; good performance by employees should be rewarded and recognized. Additionally, the supervisor needs to continue to express his confidence that all employees will be able to adjust to and benefit from the new methods.

Employee Participation in the Change Process

Employee participation is another effective means for building support for change. People who are consulted and allowed to participate in making decisions about a proposed change are normally more receptive and able to adjust better to the change. (The topic of "participation" is discussed fully in Chapter 4.)

Therefore, whenever possible, give those affected by change an opportunity to have some degree of influence on such decisions as the *nature, direction, rate,* and *method of introduction* of the change.[3]

As a general rule, **resistance to change increases when change is arbitrarily introduced from above and pressure is put on employees to accept it, and it decreases when employees are allowed to have some "say" in the planning and implementation of the change.** The use of force in dealing with human behavior, as in physics, breeds counter-force—often aimed at discrediting or sabotaging the new methods; but when employees are able to offer suggestions, ideas, and comments concerning the change, they at least feel that they are involved and have had an opportunity to be heard.

Even when employees' contributions are negligible or their suggestions are not practical, the chance to participate in the early stages of change can alleviate many fears and misunderstandings, while giving workers a sense of having some control over their own destinies; employees are more likely to support any change of which they are, even to a minor degree, the co-architects.

[3]The relative *degree* of employee participation used in effecting decisions about a change depends on the variables present in each individual situation, as discussed in Chapter 4.

Ideally, employees should be involved as early as practicable in the planning stages of the change; in so doing, they can often aid the supervisor in making a diagnosis of what needs to be changed and why. This process of diagnosing the existing situation and discovering problem areas for themselves can lead to a definite "unfreezing" of employees' present attitudes, thus increasing their recognition of the need for new methods of operation.

If employees are able to develop their own understanding of the need for change and the benefits that can be derived from it, they are in a much better position to develop their own internal motivation to achieve the change; voluntary steps are taken to change the existing situation instead of having the boss order that the change be made.

Through group participation, employees also tend to become more *committed* to seeing that the change is carried out successfully. If they are involved in the change right from the start, it is possible for the new methods to become "their" new methods, and suspicions and resistance can, to a great extent, be eliminated. Furthermore, commitment to take part in a program for change is much more meaningful when expressed by an individual in a group setting, rather than in private with his supervisor; commitment expressed in a group usually means that the employee intends to carry his commitment into action.

Although early employee involvement in the planning stages of the change is usually preferable, participation can be useful even if the supervisor says, "This much about the change has already been decided; I now would like your thoughts and suggestions on the rest; although I can't guarantee to accept all of your proposals, I will certainly consider them." In other words, the supervisor can establish broad guidelines for the objectives to be achieved in the change and then leave the details of implementing the proposed change to be worked out by the group.

Preventing and decreasing resistance to change should certainly not be considered the only reason for soliciting employee participation, however; adding the contributions of those who will be directly affected by the change can also improve the overall *quality* and *success* of the change. Employee participation can prove to be invaluable in spotting potential difficulties in the change that haven't been anticipated. Those who actually perform the work often see problems from a completely different perspective than their superiors do and frequently spot bugs and oversights that may otherwise go undetected. Even the most appealing and obviously beneficial idea for change can have something wrong with it that hasn't occurred to its initiator. So, why "bull" ahead when it is so easy to utilize employees as a "sounding board" for evaluating a proposed change and to tap the group's ideas and suggestions for improvement?

Of course, the success of any of the supervisor's participative efforts rests on the extent that employees view them as legitimate and honest; the group must be convinced that their ideas and suggestions are sincerely wanted and will be given serious consideration. "Pseudo-participation" is a waste of time for everyone; nothing communicates itself as rapidly as involving employees in decision-making when, in fact, nothing that they offer will be incorporated into the final decision.

Needless to say, participation should not be asked for if there is no flexibility in the plans for the change and a course of action has already been settled on; if all decisions about the change have, by necessity, been determined, then there is no need for participation. In this case, the supervisor must depend on other methods for gaining employee support for the change.

Don't Expect Miracles

Lastly, **be patient.** Getting people to accept change is difficult and frequently takes a great deal of time.

A mistake made by many supervisors—and one that can be fatal to the introduction of change—is the belief that, once the change has been put into practice and the employees have seemingly adapted themselves to it, the supervisor can then relax his efforts.

The supervisor who does this forgets how powerful a force habit is. A high level of contact must be made until you're certain, on the basis of frequent observation, that there is no danger of employees reverting to their former habits.

IN PERSPECTIVE—HOW TO INTRODUCE CHANGE

Every imposed change in methods, even a relatively minor one, is almost certain to face some degree of resistance. Change disturbs complacency—that comfortable feeling that all's right with the world; when this comfortable state is threatened, people naturally resist. Even changes which are obviously advantageous to employees are often objects of attack.

Even though some forms of employee resistance may appear to the supervisor as irrational and illogical behavior, there are definite causes of it; therefore, the supervisor would be wise to first concentrate on the reasons that resistance to change occurs. If the supervisor recognizes that the natural reactions to change are not the result of mere stubbornness or stupidity but are caused by basic fears, anxieties, and perceived threats to need satisfaction, a much more understanding and empathic view can be taken of the phenomenon. With this background, the supervisor can effectively concentrate his efforts on preventing or decreasing the resistance.

In reality, of course, there is no single technique for introducing a change that will insure employee adjustment with a minimum of resistance. We have suggested several techniques, however, which can aid the supervisor in accomplishing the three basic steps in the change process (*unfreezing, changing,* and *refreezing*). Some of these techniques may be combined and used consistently, while others are best used as the particular situation dictates.

Realistically, resistance is seldom totally conquered. However, the supervisor who realizes the reasons for resistance to change, understands his employees, and properly implements change can overcome much of the workers' resistance. Thorough groundwork by the supervisor can reduce the effects of negative attitudes that are typically associated with change.

Reading Selection 7

ORGANIZATIONAL CHANGE*

S. G. Huneryager
I. L. Heckmann

In order to remain stable and flexible and to insure long-run success, most organizations must operate within a dynamic environment. This means, in essence, that management must be alert to, must plan for, and must adapt itself, the company, and employees to myriad changes that are necessary for the efficient operation of a business enterprise. If this is not done—that is, if dynamism, flexibility, and adaptability do not exist—then there is great danger that complacency and stagnation will set in. The result, particularly in highly competitive industries, could well be serious damage to or even termination of the organization concerned.

WHY PEOPLE RESIST CHANGE

Because change of every conceivable type and form is highly important to the success of an organization, it is unfortunate that many people have the tendency overtly or covertly to resist it, frequently to the extent of seriously impeding or completely thwarting its effectuation. Perhaps a basic reason why this resistance occurs, whether it is manifested in the form of apathy and indifference or in the form of opposition and rebellion, is that most changes disturb the equilibrium of the situation and environment in which individuals and groups exist. To overcome this dis-

*From S. G. Huneryager and I. L. Heckmann, *Human Relations in Management* (Cincinnati: South-Western Publishing Company, 1967), pp. 656-62. Reprinted with permission.

equilibrium and to return to a state of balance requires people to go through a period of adaptation and adjustment to the change. If this inevitable process of adjustment is facilitated, especially prior to initiation of the change, so that a new state of equilibrium can be quickly achieved, then little or no resistance usually results. On the other hand, if management ignores this fundamental facet of human behavior and does nothing to help people adjust, then resistance will occur and a state of disequilibrium will continue to exist. How serious this situation will be is, of course, impossible to say, because it will depend upon the nature of the people and the change concerned.

Although disequilibrium is the result of change and the cause of resistance, it is important to recognize that the state of disequilibrium which exists is actually an imbalance in need satisfaction. The assumption here is that prior to a change the individual exists within an environment in which the satisfaction of his needs has reached a high degree of stability. When a change occurs, particularly in the absence of adjustment facilitation, there is immediately manifested a threat to motive satisfaction. In other words, there now occurs the possibility that the change may prevent or decrease need satisfaction. Whether or not the change actually has this result makes no difference at this stage. The important point is that, until proven otherwise, the person believes or assumes that this threat will materialize. As a consequence, he feels his needs are no longer satisfied to the degree that they were satisfied and a state of imbalance exists. Only when he recognizes that the change will not affect his need satisfaction, or when he adapts himself to a change that in fact does decrease or prevent the satisfaction of a need, will equilibrium return and resistance disappear. In either case, however, some degree of adjustment must occur.

TYPES OF CHANGES THAT CREATE DISEQUILIBRIUM

The types and kinds of changes that cause disequilibrium and resistance are legion. They range in nature from attitudinal changes, such as a supervisor changing a positive attitude toward a subordinate into a negative attitude, to fantastic technological advancements, such as a new machine that will displace twenty old machines. Because it would be impossible to consider here every conceivable form of change, we shall devote our attention only to those types of changes that are likely to occur in most organizations. No attempt will be made to rank them in order of importance, because changes affect people in different ways; çonsequently, a change that causes great resistance in one person may create little or no disequilibrium for another individual.

Changes in Tools, Machines, and Equipment

Almost every organization has experienced difficulty with employees who resist the installation of new tools, machines, and equipment. Whether such changes are the result of technological advancement or managerial efficiency makes little difference—a threat to security, status, and other basic needs has occurred. Consequently, even if the change is potentially beneficial to the employee, resistance usually results.

Like all changes, those concerning the mechanisms and devices with which people work establish an element of the unknown. In the case of a new machine, for example, especially one that has the potential to displace workers, people resist its introduction because they do not know how it will affect them. Accordingly, they begin to wonder about things such as whether or not the machine will displace them, if they will have the skill required to operate it, and so on. Until these unknowns are resolved, people will assume without realizing it that their fears and suspicions will be confirmed. This is particularly true of any change in machines that actually poses a threat to job security. In fact, it could be said that resistance to automation is one of the chief areas of resistance that management is faced with today, primarily because the results of technological advancement have actually resulted in the displacement of people and the loss of jobs.

Changes in Methods and Procedures

It is frequently said that we are creatures of habit. Although this statement connotes a detrimental characteristic of man, it should be recognized that habit, especially in the context of a business organization, does possess several distinct advantages. Perhaps one of the most important of these concerns the fact that the way we habitually do things, assuming that these habits are correct and efficient, can lead to the development of greater proficiency in doing work. In other words, by doing the same thing over and over, we can acquire a high degree of skill in performing various aspects of our jobs.

When a change occurs in a method or a procedure that we have been habitually accustomed to using, we have the tendency to resist it because it may decrease our proficiency and hence the pride we take in our work. In addition, we sometimes feel that the change was directed at us, that is, that we were not performing the job correctly and that we have lost face because we did not perceive and effectuate the change in the first place. Although such reactions sometimes border the ridiculous, they are nevertheless very real to those who experience them and hence are powerful motivators of behavior. How many times, for example, have we heard someone say "it won't work" when we know very well that the individual concerned definitely does know it will work? Changes in methods and procedures, therefore, like all other changes, establish many unknowns that must be clarified if adjustment is to take place.

Changes in Personnel

A change that frequently results in a great deal of covert resistance in many organizations occurs when a subordinate is placed under the supervision of a new superior. Usually the degree of resistance developed in such a situation is correlated with the length and the satisfaction of the previous superior-subordinate relationship. In other words, the longer and more satisfied we were with our "old boss," the more we visualize and fear the unknowns created by the appearance of a new boss, especially if he is a total stranger. Until proven otherwise, we suspect and fear the worst about his ability to perform his job and to perceive our proficiency. Most important of all, we wonder what sweeping changes he will make (as many new bosses do) and what effect they will have on us. Without being able to express what has happened to us, we have lost in one moment much of the feeling of stability we had in need satisfaction. Until we bring back into balance our desire for belonging, recognition, status, and other motivating forces, we shall continue to view the new man with suspicion. Unfortunately, the attitudes that result from these fears become the very barriers that hinder the new superior in proving his worth to his employees and in providing the means or opportunity to satiate their basic needs.

Changes in Formal Organization Structure

The creation of a formal structure, as the section on organization pointed out, establishes lines of authority and responsibility in an organization. Along with these lines there are also created channels of communication and interpersonal relationships. When changes in this formal structure occur, unknowns about future lines of authority and relationships develop. We wonder who will be responsible for what and why, who our new boss will be, what opportunities it will take away from us or create for us, and so on. The result of these worries is that we no longer maintain equilibrium in our need satisfaction. Consequently, faced with the possibility of loss of status, prestige, belonging, recognition, and so forth, we become involved in a state of imbalance and resist the change.

Another aspect of formal structure concerns the question of who has the authority to make a change. Quite frequently employees resist changes, not because of the change *per se,* but because of the person who initiated or requested it. An example of this would be the foreman of Department B telling a worker in Department C to use a new procedure in the performance of his work. Although the new procedure may be very efficient and acceptable to the employee, he resists it because the foreman has no authority over him. The same type of reaction also occurs when changes are made by people who have the authority to make changes but whose authority is not known or accepted by the worker. This frequently happens when staff people have been delegated the authority to initiate changes. An illustration would be the industrial engineer who has been given the task of developing and installing better job methods. Because the employee tends to view his own boss as the only person who has a right to tell him what to do, he also tends to resist and reject any change proposed by the engineer.

Changes in Informal Organization

The informal relationships established between people in an organization become a very important part of our existence, basically because many of our primary motivational forces find their satisfaction in these relationships. Our urge to belong, for example, finds satisfaction in the many informal groups and cliques with which we associate. Our desire for recognition is satisfied by the accord given to our skills, talent, and abilities by various friends and acquaintances in the organization. Likewise, our needs for prestige, status, achievement, and many other basic sociological and psychological motives depend to a great degree on various aspects of informal organization for their satisfaction. Consequently, when management makes any change that disturbs the informal relationships established between people, there is bound to be created a state of imbalance and, hence, resistance to the change.

Of all the classes of changes that can disturb informal relationships, perhaps one of the most important for management to recognize and understand is that type of change which results in the separation of groups and individuals. Whenever people find it difficult or impossible to continue or maintain informal relationships, they find it equally difficult or impossible to maintain stability in need satisfaction. The reason for this, of course, is that the means to need satisfaction, namely, the people with whom we associate informally, no longer is present or easily accessible after the change. The result is that stability in motive satisfaction disappears and resistance sets in. It is no wonder, therefore, that people resist changes such as transferring an employee from one department to another or the simple moving of a clerk from one end of an office to the other end.

HOW PEOPLE RESIST CHANGE

Resistance to change can take many forms. At one extreme, people suffer a temporary disequilibrium in need satisfaction, ask a few questions about the change, quickly adjust to it, and resume their previous behavior. At the other extreme, reaction can take the form of open opposition, rebellion, and even destruction. In between these extremes lie many other forms of behavior, such as apathy, indifference, and antagonism. What type of reaction occurs in a particular situation is a function of the nature of the change and the people concerned. It is especially a function of how well adjustment to the change was facilitated.

Whatever general form resistance to change may take, it is important for managers to recognize that human behavior will always be influenced by it. This means that immediately or ultimately the change will exert an impact on employee performance. Depending upon the nature of the resistance, therefore, behavior can be reflected in such things as quantity and quality of production, absenteeism, tardiness, turnover, grievances, accidents, strikes, and so on. Unfortunately, many of these concrete results of resistance are very difficult to relate to the change that caused them, not only because of physical and organizational elements, but also because they are frequently so subtly manifested by employees that it is difficult to observe and measure them in the first place. This is just another reason why management must make every effort possible to effectuate the change properly and to facilitate adjustment to it.

FACILITATING ADJUSTMENT TO CHANGE

Several important points deserve mention here. One of the most important of these concerns the fact that preventing and overcoming resistance demands that managers respect and understand employee reaction to change. Altogether too frequently, people in leadership positions assume that, because a change will definitely be beneficial to people, it will be acceptable to them. Actually, nothing could be farther from the truth. Consequently, whether threats to need satisfaction are real or imagined, they must always be recognized as powerful motivators of behavior. As such, some manner or form of adjustment facilitation must take place.

Another important point for managers to understand is that there is no one simple panacea for preventing or overcoming resistance to change. Although it may be possible in one situation to rely exclusively on one particular method, such as participation, for example, it is most unlikely that such a technique will be universally and solely applicable in all resistance problems. What is more likely is that the manager (the leader) must utilize many different methods, techniques, and procedures to prevent and to remedy resistance to change situations. This means that, in addition to participation, he may certainly have to counsel and train employees, particularly if a change actually results in the prevention or decrease of need satisfaction. It may also mean that if the situation warrants it, he will have to dispense with the change or completely adjust his thinking about it. Most fundamentally of all, however, it means that he must determine and communicate to his employees the things they consciously and subconsciously want and need to know to resolve the unknowns that pose the real or imagined threat to the satisfaction of their motivating forces. In other words, preventing and remedying resistance to change demands efficient leadership and the practice of human relations.

QUESTIONS FOR REVIEW AND DISCUSSION

1. a. Explain why people resist change.
   b. Under what circumstances do people *seek* change?
2. Using examples from your own experience, discuss some of the ways in which employees typically resist change.
3. How does resistance to change differ from *reactions to frustration* (discussed in Chapter 2)?
4. Explain the difference between *technological* and *social* change. Which has the greater influence on employees? Why?
5. Would a supervisor who has recently taken over a department be in a better position than his predecessor, who was supervisor for three years, to install a new operating procedure?
6. "The successful supervisor is one who knows how to play the role of a change agent." Evaluate this statement.
7. Name and explain the three basic steps involved in the process of change.
8. Discuss the various methods for preventing or decreasing resistance to change. Which do you feel are the most useful?
9. Is it sometimes better not to make a change? Explain.
10. "By reducing unnecessary or trivial changes, employees' receptivity to future needed changes may be increased." Do you agree with this statement? Why?
11. Discuss the role of communication in the change process.
12. Why is a direct, logical presentation of the merits of a change often futile in overcoming resistance?
13. Because the supervisor must "sell" a change to his work group, must *he* be "sold" on the change before presenting it? If so, what should the supervisor do if he must implement a change which he does not completely support? Explain.
14. Some employees may have had good things happen to them after a change; others may have experienced hardship or unhappiness following previous changes. How might these past experiences affect responses to future imposed changes?
15. Because today's youth have been brought up in an environment of rapid technological and social change, are members of this younger generation generally more receptive to change? Explain.
16. The implementation of a job enrichment program (discussed in Chapter 3) necessarily involves change. If such a program were installed in your company, what degree of employee resistance would you predict? How would you suggest reducing this resistance?

SUGGESTED ADDITIONAL READINGS

McMurry, Robert N. "The Problem of Resistance to Change in Industry," *Human Relations in Management,* S. G. Huneryager and I. L. Heckmann, editors. Second edition. Cincinnati: South-Western Publishing Company, 1967. Pp. 663-68.

Reddin, W. J. "How to Change Things," *Executive,* June, 1969, pp. 22-6.

Watson, Goodwin, and Edward M. Glaser. "What We Have Learned About Planning for Change," *Management Review,* November, 1965.

Wickes, Thomas A. "Techniques for Managing Change," *Automation,* May, 1967.

Zander, Alvin. "Resistance to Change–Its Analysis and Prevention," *Human Relations in Management,* S. G. Huneryager and I. L. Heckmann, editors. Second edition. Cincinnati: South-Western Publishing Company, 1967. pp. 669-75.

6

COMMUNICATION–THE AVENUE TO UNDERSTANDING

It is often charged that communication is an overworked subject. An ailment called "lack of communication" has become a general explanation for all an organization's problems in interpersonal relationships; "better communication" is offered as a universal panacea for any ill. We may be tired of hearing this, but its validity is difficult to deny. Certainly, one of the greatest problems of all segments of our society (as well as the rest of the world) is the lack of adequate understanding among people.

From the first time man found it necessary to join another in achieving common goals, he has faced the necessity of communicating. A company is made up of a scattering of people; these people become an organization when they work intelligently together as a team to reach common goals. This teamwork, however, is attained only when they understand each other and communicate clearly. Coordinated effort toward common goals is impossible without effective communication of information and ideas, attitudes, and feelings among individuals and groups throughout the organization. Communication can be looked upon as a *network* that binds all the members of an organization together, making it possible for members to influence and react to one another.

Initiation and maintenance of a successful company communication program are primarily dependent on top management. If higher-level management establishes a sound climate of information exchange with its associates and insists that they do likewise with others, this climate tends to permeate the whole organization. This, however, does not relieve any other level of management of its responsibility for effective communication. In fact, although important at all levels of an organization, communication between a supervisor and his subordinates represents perhaps the most critical area in the organization because of the supervisor's direct influence on employees' behavior and motivation.[1]

Communication is really the heart of all supervisory activities. Fundamental to supervision, it encompasses all activities by which a supervisor in-

[1] Keith Davis, *Human Relations at Work* (Third edition; New York: McGraw-Hill Book Company, 1967), pp. 322-23.

fluences and interacts with others. Communication is the process by which all orders, instructions, praise, criticism, discipline, requests, and reports are exchanged. The supervisor exerts his influence only by conveying ideas, feelings, and decisions to his subordinates. They, in turn, must communicate with the supervisor if he is to appreciate their responses to his actions and their own personal ideas, opinions, and problems.

Of course, all the topics that we have previously examined—motivation, participation, and change—directly involve communication. Every aspect of human behavior is related in some way to the process of sending and receiving information. Communication, therefore, should be viewed not as an independent activity but as an essential adjunct to everything a supervisor does.

Are most managers and supervisors effective communicators? Unfortunately, in the majority of cases they seemingly are not. It is estimated that as much as 75 to 90 per cent of the average manager's or supervisor's time is spent in some form of communication—writing, speaking, listening, and observing. Yet available research indicates that as much as 70 per cent of all business communications fail to achieve their intended purpose. In fact, of all the abilities required for successful supervision, the ability to communicate effectively is commonly the one in which most supervisors seem to be deficient. Hence, is it any wonder that so many employees are unclear as to exactly what is expected of them, why certain policies are in effect, how their work ties in with the company's goals, why changes are needed, and so on?

So perhaps, as charged, communication is an overworked subject; but then, it is an overworked problem.

ANALYSIS OF THE COMMUNICATION PROCESS

Although the term has different meanings for different people, for our purposes communication can be defined as **the passing of information and understanding from one person to another by an effective means.** The word "understanding" in this definition would ideally be printed in red because without understanding we have no effective communication. Communication seeks to *inform,* but transmission of facts must be followed by *understanding.*

Because we talk to each other constantly, write memos and letters by the dozens, and see the technical marvels of modern communication equipment all around us, we're inclined to take for granted the ability to communicate. This assumption of communication in large part explains why most of us experience so many instances of "lack of communication." As W. H. Whyte, Jr., aptly put it, "The great enemy of communication is the illusion of it." The *illusion of communication* is believing that understanding has taken place simply because one person has spoken to another or because what has been written by one has been read by another.

An example of this error concerns a true story you may recall reading in the newspaper several years ago. A man whose car had stalled on the New Jersey Turnpike finally managed to flag down a lady motorist. "My car is stalled," he said. "Can you give me a push?" "Why sure," she said. Then he informed her that, "I have an automatic transmission and you'll have to get up to about 35 miles an hour." She responded, "Whatever you say." The man got back in his car and waited. Nothing happened. He waited a little longer and still nothing happened. Finally he looked in his rear-view mirror and saw her bearing down on him at 35 miles an hour!

After the tempers and metal were untangled, the man no doubt asked, "Why didn't she do what I told her?" The answer, of course, is that **what is expressed is not necessarily what is understood.**

Many supervisors ignore this fact. They think the mere act of telling someone something is sufficient. These people are the ones who are constantly surprised that their subordinates have misinterpreted their communication; they typically react in a tone of astonishment, "It's written right there in black and white; how could you possibly misunderstand it?"

The most successful communicators, in contrast, are those who assume that communication is not automatic, that it takes work and must be approached with care. The process of communication is much less simple than we ordinarily realize, and the meaning that gets across is more than a matter of transmitting logical facts.

The goal of all communication should be complete understanding, which means that the receiver interprets or perceives the message exactly as the sender intended. Full communication occurs only when one person receives both the same *intellectual message* and the same *emotion* that the other person sent and felt. Understanding, of course, neither assures nor necessitates that the receiver agrees with the content of the message or has the same emotional response to it as the sender; but understanding is necessary in *seeking* agreement.

In reality, there are always a myriad of barriers standing in the way of this ideal state of complete understanding, basically because no two people ever perceive anything exactly the same way. However, as in all aspects of the study of human behavior, recognition of the *real* does not prevent us from continually striving for the *ideal.*

One-Way vs. Two-Way Communication

Are you a one-way communicator or a two-way communicator? The answer to this question is of utmost importance to any supervisor. Picture a man stranded on a desert island crying at the top of his lungs for help. Is he communicating? Of course not. But how often are our business communications no more effective than this? Many people are conditioned to a *one-way* flow of words, believing if they speak enough words or send enough memos, the message will reach the right person and be understood.

In *one-way* communication, the sender presents his ideas but there is no opportunity for the receiver to indicate his response to the sender, to express his ideas, or to question the meaning of the sender's message.

In *two-way* communication, there is some form of interaction between the sender and the receiver. By having a two-way flow, the sender is able to not only express his thoughts but to check the effectiveness of his expression—whether he has made himself clear. In response to *feedback* from the receiver, he is able to modify his message if necessary to assure understanding of his presentation. At the same time, the two-way interaction provides a rich opportunity for obtaining suggestions from the receiver on the subject of the discussion.

A one-way communicator tends to think of the communication process as something akin to pouring water into a jug; in other words, you can communicate ideas by pouring them into someone's head. He looks at the subject solely from his own viewpoint and sincerely believes that if he describes his ideas and tells the receiver why he should accept them, the job is finished. If the receiver is unconvinced or misinterprets the message, this communicator is mystified.

The two-way communicator understands that communication starts with the other fellow's needs; he concentrates more on the receiver than on himself. His presentation remains flexible, constantly guided by responses from the receiver; and he keeps trying until he is sure he has "gotten through" or resolved the receiver's difficulties in understanding.

In addition to one-way and two-way communication, there is another type worthy of mention. This is "phony two-way," usually labeled two-way by the sender and one-way by the receiver. The supervisor who says, "Let's have a meeting to let the men voice their opinions before we tell them what we've decided," is a phony two-way communicator and will eventually be recognized as such by the receivers.[2]

Until supervisors accept the necessity of genuine two-way communication and become skilled in both transmitting and receiving information, they face problems in leading and motivating people to work efficiently.

Steps in the Communication Process

To improve our communication, we must first have a basic understanding of what actually happens in the communication process. The entire process of one person communicating with another involves six steps, regardless of whether they talk, send written messages, use facial expressions or hand signals, or use any other form of communication. The accompanying figure illustrates this sequence of steps.

Familiarity with these steps is valuable in analyzing and comprehending the barriers to understanding that typically occur.

[2]T. K. Lawson and A. F. Tate, "Heads Are Not Jugs," *Traffic Safety,* June, 1970. Also see N. Richard Diller, "Improving Communications On the Job," *Manage,* August, 1966, pp. 48-55.

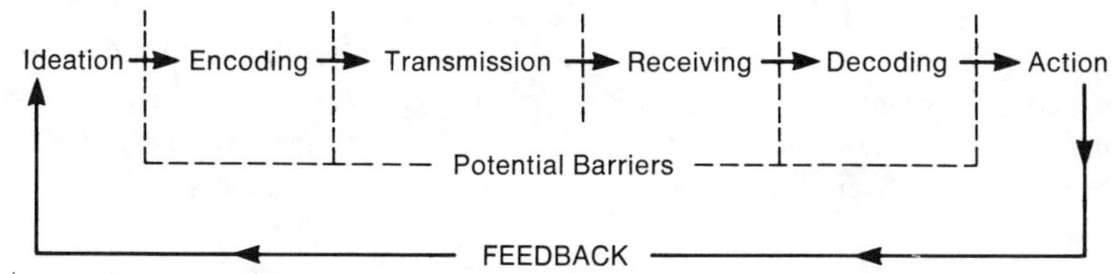

FIGURE 6-1. A Model of the Communication Process[3]

Ideation. The first step in the sequence is ideation—the creation of an idea—by the sender. This step forms the content or basis of the message. Obviously, you need to fully understand the idea that you want to communicate; for example, if you wish to effectively explain the operation of electronic computers, you must know the subject thoroughly. Yet, one of the most common causes of communication breakdown is that the sender is unclear in his own thinking about the subject. A message which is not clearly formulated or adequately planned in the mind of the sender is quite likely to be misunderstood by the receiver. Thus, the motto for this step might well be: "Don't start talking until you begin thinking."

Furthermore, as messages tend to become increasingly filtered, distorted, or diluted as they pass through each step in the process, this first step is crucial to the success of the entire process.

Encoding. In the encoding step, the ideas formulated in the first step are converted into a series of *symbols* that communicate the message to the receiver. Words, numbers, pictures, or gestures stand for something; they are symbolic. The key is to select a combination of symbols that have the same meaning for both the sender and the receiver and are appropriate for the situation.

At this stage, the sender often knows what he wants to express but is hampered in his ability to express it. How many times has the average teacher heard this excuse about an exam: "I knew the answer, but I just couldn't seem to put it into words"? This type of barrier is caused by various limitations—limited vocabulary, inability to write clearly, inability to precisely express oneself, and the like.

In addition to picking the proper symbols in this step, the sender must also choose the *medium* for transmitting the symbols, whether it be face-to-face oral communication, written communication, the telephone, or some other form. Like symbols, the medium also must be appropriate for the receiver and the situation.

Transmission. Transmission is the actual sending of the encoded message through the medium selected. For example, in using verbal communication, the words are spoken; in writing a letter, the letter is mailed.

[3]Adapted from Herbert J. Chruden and Arthur W. Sherman, Jr., *Personnel Management* (Cincinnati: South-Western Publishing Company, 1968), p. 327.

At this point in the process, the sender begins to lose control of the message. Such things as distractions, noise, interruptions, and breakdowns in mechanical means of communication can interfere with the message's transmission. This interference must be minimized if the message is to have a chance to reach the receiver.

Receiving. In the fourth step, the receiver finally enters the picture. Essential here is getting the receiver's *attention* so that he will "tune in" on the message. The best message is of little use unless the receiver listens or reads and attempts to understand it. No matter how brilliant and informative you and your message may be, if the receiver is uncooperative, defensive, disinterested, or not perceptive, your message is lost.

Yet, how often do we speak without listeners or speak when we should be listening? And, how often does the avalanche of memoranda, letters, and reports common to the business world fail to find readers? A partial solution may be to speak less and say more and to write shorter, fewer, and better messages.[4]

Decoding. In the decoding step, the receiver converts the symbols transmitted back into ideas, interpreting and evaluating the message. Encoding is message *creation,* while decoding is message *recreation.*

If understanding is to occur, the receiver must take from the message the meaning intended by the sender. However, as we shall discuss later, there are many subtle perceptual barriers that prevent this from happening; the receiver's perception of the message may never be exactly what the sender intended.

Action. Finally, the receiver acts or responds to the message in a certain way—ideally, in the manner intended by the sender. The receiver's action may take many forms; he may simply file the information in his brain for future reference, perform a specific function, ask for more information, or disagree (remember, there can be disagreement along with understanding). In any case, he must do something in response to the message.[5]

The Desirability of Feedback

No communication is ever completed with certainty unless some type of *feedback* is available to determine the degree to which the message has been received and understood (see Figure 6-1). This reinforces the desirability of *two-way* communication. **Without feedback, there is no guarantee that the message was correctly interpreted and acted upon by the receiver.**

The normal result of an attempt to communicate is partial misunderstanding. Through feedback, the sender can make the necessary corrections and

[4]Henry H. Albers, *Principles of Management* (New York: John Wiley and Sons, Inc., 1969), p. 461.

[5]Davis, *op. cit.,* pp. 317, 323-24.

adjust his message to fit the responses of his receiver. For example, in face-to-face oral communication, if the receiver looks puzzled, the speaker can repeat what he originally said or try saying it differently.

Feedback in communication can be likened to the thermostat that regulates your home air conditioner on the basis of feedback—namely, the temperature of the room. In human communication, you need some way of "taking the temperature" of the people with whom you are communicating so that you can adjust your message to their needs.

Every supervisor must accept the fact that at least some of his workers are going to misunderstand his communication efforts at least some of the time. The most effective attitude is to take nothing for granted. Some supervisors are content to rely on a simple question after involved instructions or directives are given: "Have you got that?" "Do you understand?" Such questions invariably obtain affirmative responses such as, "Yes, I have it," when what the employee often really means is, "No, I don't understand, but I'm too afraid or too proud to admit it." Rather than ask for clarification, the employee will muddle along trying to work things out by himself, sometimes with disastrous results. Why? Perhaps because he simply wants to convince the supervisor that he is a good worker and can do his job.

"Do you understand what the boss wants?" **"I think so but I'm not sure."**

The supervisor, in order to confirm that his communication has resulted in mutual understanding, needs to keep alert to any feedback available. Feedback can be solicited simply by asking subordinates questions designed to get them to repeat the gist of the message or by creating a climate in which everyone feels free to ask questions. In addition, you can observe whether the subordinate acts in accordance with the message. When direct observation is impractical, you can watch various reports or other results that may serve as feedback cues.

Only feedback can tell you what you're communicating or, in fact, whether you're communicating at all.

Transmission Media

Although there are an endless number of specific media for transmitting information (telephone, letters, conferences, reports, gestures, etc.), all fall into three general classifications: *oral, written,* and *nonverbal.*

Oral communication. Oral communication is the most frequently used business communication medium. Generally speaking, it is the most effective medium as well, especially when the communication is intended to be persuasive rather than factual.

With the exception of the telephone, a public-address system, or other such mechanical media, oral communication is face-to-face, allowing the advantage of *maximum feedback.* Because it encourages two-way communication, there is opportunity for immediate response from the receiver. Each party can question the other if the meaning is not clear, and different points of view can be voiced. The communicator can change or vary his approach according to the situation, thus making oral communication a very *flexible* medium. Added explanation and reassurance can be readily provided, and disagreements and misunderstandings can frequently be resolved on the spot.

In contrast with written communication, the spoken word is more natural, personal, and expressive. It is also usually more flattering to the receiver. By a smile, gestures, or the right tone of voice, you can communicate things orally—emotions, emphasis, and feelings—that could not be easily written.

Yet, day after day, people grind out letters, memos, and bulletins about subjects that could be better handled face-to-face. In some cases, people write memos to others whose desks or offices are located nearby! Before writing a memo or sending a message via a third party, stop and consider: Wouldn't it be smarter to do this in person? Or at least follow it up that way? If it is impractical to see someone, consider telephoning him. It is quicker and more personal than a memo and still gives him a chance to ask questions and express his opinions.

The major inherent disadvantage of oral communications is that it is usually filtered and distorted each time it is passed from one person to another. Whenever possible, tell your message to the man directly affected. As the number of intermediaries between the sender and the eventual receiver increases, the chances of distortion and dilution of the original message are also increased.

Written communication. Although less personal than oral communication, written communication is essential in any organization and is more effective in transmitting certain kinds of information than oral methods.

It can best be used when the message is lengthy, complex or technical, extremely important, has long-term significance and is needed for future reference (such as policies or procedures), or concerns many people and needs to be widely circulated. Written communication can be kept and referred to later as a guide for future action. It can be widely distributed so that everyone concerned gets the same story with a minimum of distortion. It can sometimes be more carefully thought through than spontaneous conversations or other oral communication and can be checked for accuracy before being issued.

Additionally, written messages are often used to supplement and reinforce orally transmitted information. On matters that are particularly important, easily forgotten, or subject to misinterpretation by subordinates, the supervisor can confirm his oral communication with a written message. In a similar way, oral communication can be used effectively to accompany or follow up written communication to provide added explanation and clarification, meet objections, and head off misunderstandings before they occur.

The primary disadvantage of written communication is its limited ability to provide prompt feedback and encourage a two-way exchange of information. Furthermore, skill is usually required in meaningfully conveying written ideas, and unless the writer is available for discussion his intentions may not be understood as he intended by the receiver. Because of its impersonal nature, it also tends to foster greater suspicion than oral communication.

Furthermore, written communication in business is typically expensive. *Needless* written communication is staggeringly expensive. One study done several years ago by a governmental agency discovered that a memo or letter of average length costs between $2 and $6, depending on the wage levels of the writer and the secretary, the time spent on each memo or letter, and the material costs. These figures take into account time spent in preparation, researching, dictation, proofing, signing, and the like by the writer and the secretary's time devoted to taking dictation, transcribing, proofing, mailing, filing, and so on. A more recent study by Bruce Payne and Associates, a management consulting firm, claims that the cost ranges from about $6.50 all the way to $15 on some letters. Regardless of whose figures you choose to accept, written communication is obviously time-consuming and costly when used unnecessarily.

Such costs, of course, do not include reading and "translating" costs at the receiving end; if the communication is not understandable, the cost skyrockets, depending on the number of receivers in the company. One writing-cost analyst figures that 15 per cent of all letters or memos are "fog-induced"—merely requests for clarification of a previous letter or memo. Obviously then, the extra time the writer gives to making his communication clear and readable the first time is economically spent, especially on a memo that takes thirty minutes to read and interpret when it should have taken only five![6]

Nonverbal communication. Of the three general media of transmission, oral, written, and nonverbal, the first two are always considered by communica-

[6]John O'Hayre, *Gobbledygook Has Gotta Go* (Washington, D.C.: U. S. Government Printing Office, 1966), pp. 91-95.

tors, while the latter is often dangerously overlooked. By our original definition of communication, "the passing of information and understanding from one person to another *by an effective means,*" it should be obvious that you are not restricted to the use of words alone, either spoken or written. You communicate through nonverbal means as well. Communication encompasses *all* human behavior that results in an exchange of meaning.

In fact, research has indicated that as much as 93 per cent of the impact of what you communicate to others is conveyed by nonverbal means. Even though it is such an important medium of transmission, many people seemingly don't realize that it even exists. An awareness of this type of communication is essential because, consciously or unconsciously, we all use it every day.

In its simplest form, nonverbal communication would assume the form of a child sticking out his tongue or an irate man making an appropriate gesture. Neither of these actions is verbal, but both do a great deal of communicating.

"From the way he looks, I think something's cooking. What do you suppose it is?"

In its more complex form and in relation to supervision, nonverbal communication includes such varied examples as the "look" in one's eyes, avoidance or maintenance of eye contact, a raised eyebrow, posture, a pointed finger, a shrug of the shoulders, the way a person walks, manner of dress, a man's buttoned or unbuttoned coat, a smile or a scowl, a firm or limp handshake, the manner in which a verbal message is conveyed, tone of voice, inflections, a slammed door, "noncommunication" (lack of explanation when it is needed or failure to give an employee recognition when it is expected or desired), signs, pictures, charts, or a demonstration. Any of these can communicate, either consciously or unconsciously, a message to others as surely as words can. Even silence can convey meaning and must be considered a part of communication.

Nonverbal communication can often be *planned* and *controlled* by the sender, as in the case of pictures, a demonstration, or a gesture. At other times, however, we *unknowingly* communicate either by some action or lack of action; if the resulting communication is unplanned, it is also uncontrolled and wide open to any number of interpretations.[7] This frequent lack of control over one's communication is, upon consideration, a bit frightening.

Nonverbal communication is often quite effective in transmitting ideas, attitudes, and feelings. For instance, a supervisor pounding on his desk may communicate very clearly the action he wants. Or, consider what usually happens when one person wants to terminate a conversation. He may shift his body, tap his fingers on his desk, divert his gaze from the speaker, or look at his wristwatch periodically. The more he fidgets, the more he communicates his boredom or disinterest in further conversation.

As another illustration, George has an appointment to meet Bill at 10 o'clock; due to unknown reasons, he arrives at 10:30. Their conversation is friendly, but Bill retains a lingering hostility. Why? Because George, through his tardiness, has unconsciously communicated that he doesn't think the appointment is very important or that he has little respect for Bill.[8] In each case, you can see the subtle power of nonverbal communication.

As the well-worn saying goes, "Actions speak louder than words." This is particularly true in supervision. In the long run, employees are influenced not so much by what a supervisor says but by what he does. When his actions, behavior, or attitudes contradict his words, employees will tend to discount what he says; their past experiences will lead them to know what is believable and what is not. Ralph Waldo Emerson put it this way: "What you are thunders so loud I cannot hear what you say."

The supervisor who tells his workers that he is interested in their problems but, in reality, ignores their requests for help or information is communicating that he is *not* interested in them. Similarly, it is useless for a supervisor to announce an "open door" policy if employees don't feel comfortable once they go through the door.[9]

The fact is that *every* action of a supervisor has some influence on the people who observe it. Meaning will be attached to his behavior, even if it is nothing more than a smile, patting an employee on the back, or closing his office door. Any supervisor should keep in mind that he is communicating almost all of the time–whether he intends to or not.

[7]Richard A. Hahn, "What Is Communication?" *Industrial Supervisor,* March, 1971, p.

[8]Edward and Mildred Hall, "The Sounds of Silence," *Playboy,* June, 1971, p. 139.

[9]Frank E. Fischer, "A New Look at Management Communication," *Personnel,* May, 1955, p. 495.

ORGANIZATIONAL NETWORKS FOR COMMUNICATION

You may have noticed by now that effective communication between members of this class is often difficult—at times seemingly impossible!—even though you are all students at the same level. It is easy to see then that when *hierarchical* relationships exist, as in a business organization, the process of communication requires even more attention and effort if it is to yield the degree of understanding necessary for efficient operations among the various levels of the organization.

Formal Communication Networks

Formal communication takes place between personnel on the basis of established lines of authority and according to established procedures and relationships.[10]

Formal communication is used in sending and receiving information between different organizational levels—to and from supervisors and subordinates—and between personnel at the same level—for example, between the production department and the marketing department. The type of communication flowing in this network is primarily *work-related;* it has a direct relationship to the operation of the work group or the company.

Generally, formal communication follows the lines or networks indicated on the company's organization chart. It may flow in any of three directions—*downward, upward,* and *horizontally.*

Downward communication. In downward communication, information flows from the top to the bottom of the organization, or from a higher level of authority to a lower level of authority, until it reaches the intended receivers. This is the most frequently used channel for transmitting orders, instructions, objectives, policies, feedback to employees about their performance, and so forth.

There are a great many barriers to effective downward communication as it passes through the various levels in the organization. A study conducted by Pidgeon-Savage-Lewis, Inc., of the communication efficiency of 100 representative business and industrial organizations reveals a tremendous loss of information as it passes from top management down to the rank-and-file worker. As shown in Figure 6-2, lower-level employees receive only about 20 per cent of the original content of a message. The validity of such findings is open to debate;

[10]Chruden and Sherman, *op. cit.,* pp. 330-31.

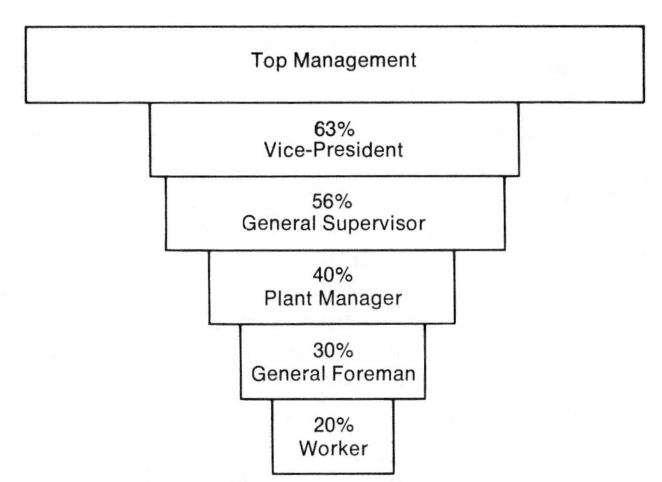

FIGURE 6-2. Loss of Information in Downward Communication

however, there is little doubt that sizeable dilution and distortion of downward communication are realities in most companies.

One difficulty is that personnel at certain levels are often not sure whether the communication is intended for their level alone or whether it should be passed on to a lower level. A second is that some people have a tendency to treat information as their personal property or to filter it according to what they think subordinates should or should not be told.

An effective system of downward communication is essential to any firm's success, but reliance on this channel alone allows little, if any, provision for feedback. It is strictly a one-way street.

Upward communication. In addition to downward communication, part of each supervisor's responsibilities includes having the needs, aspirations, ideas, attitudes, complaints, and problems of his subordinates conveyed to him through an *upward* channel of communication. If subordinates are unable to communicate freely with their supervisor, he will not receive much of the information he needs to supervise effectively.

Aside from giving the supervisor an excellent source of ideas, suggestions, and indicators of his work group's state of morale, upward communication is also his most important source of *feedback.* As feedback, it can provide a check on employees' reception, understanding, and acceptance of downward communication, as well as whether the intended action has been taken. In other words, did the message get through without distortion or misunderstanding?

The value of upward communication does not end with its feedback potential, however. As a by-product, employees' motivation will generally be greater if they feel free to discuss problems with their supervisor and to participate in decisions affecting them. Upward communication is thus one of the means that an individual can gain satisfaction from his work, feeling that he "belongs" and is important. If no means are available to assure that subordinates' ideas are heard, they always have recourse: They can simply close their minds to their superiors' ideas.[11]

Although "lip service" is frequently given to the desirability of upward communication, many organizations do not provide adequate outlets for such flow. We have already seen that communication efficiency *down* through the levels of an organization is often poor; but upward communication through the levels is apparently an even greater problem in many instances. In fact, one theory is that the major reason for the formation of unions and the willingness of workers to join them is the lack of effective upward communication channels within the company. This theory holds that unions become the only medium by which employees can convey to management their ideas, opinions, and needs.[12]

Why is upward communication often inadequate? Undoubtedly, part of the problem can simply be traced to poor listening habits on the part of the superior; far more attention is typically given to telling, informing, and commanding than to listening, asking, and interpreting.

The primary barrier, however, to the upward flow of communication is *fear of reprisal.* Fear of being criticized, disciplined, or denied promotion can often make even the strongest and most secure employee hesitate before presenting "all the facts" to his supervisor. Whether or not such fears have any basis in fact makes no difference; they are real in the eyes of the subordinate and cause upward communication to suffer. **Employees are reluctant to communicate anything that could have a negative effect on their relationship with the supervisor.** If they fear that a frank criticism, a voiced grievance, a suggestion, or a nonconformist opinion will be taken in the wrong way by the supervisor, they will ordinarily hold back, camouflage, or distort their upward communication to him.[13]

Many things can be done to keep upward communication channels open. The policy of the "open door" is suggested by many as a solution to the problem. Effective upward communication, however, normally requires more from a supervisor than just a statement that "my door is always open." If employees feel that the man behind the door won't really listen to them, allow them to talk out their problems, or take any action regarding their suggestions or complaints, the door is in effect still "closed." Furthermore, many supervisors who proudly point to their open door often mistakenly conclude that when no

[11] Saul W. Gellerman, *The Management of Human Relations* (New York: Holt, Rinehart and Winston, 1966), p. 65.

[12] S. G. Huneryager and I. L. Heckmann, *Human Relations in Management* (Second edition; Cincinnati: South-Western Publishing Company, 1967), p. 510.

[13] Harold Stieglitz, "Barriers to Communication," *Management Record,* January, 1958), pp. 3-4.

one ventures in to complain or talk about problems, there are in fact no complaints or problems. Such is seldom the case.

The idea of the "open door" is admirable in theory, and a *genuine* open door may be an aid to upward communication. Perhaps, however, as Keith Davis has stated, "the way the open door can be most effective is for a manager to walk through it and get out among his people. The open door is for managers to walk through, not employees!"[14]

Suggestion systems are another frequently offered solution. In many companies, employees' suggestions and ideas obtained through such systems have proven invaluable. When improperly used, they have also proven to be miserable flops in other companies.

The best place to start in freeing upward communication is to eliminate fear on the part of subordinates. This, of course, isn't as simple as it may sound. Basically, as Gary Gemmill advises in Reading Selection 8, it requires the building of a relationship between subordinate and supervisor which encourages and rewards complete disclosure; supervisors must continually encourage their subordinates to convey information upward, including information that is "bad news." The subordinate must have confidence that he can freely express his sentiments or "speak his mind" without the threat of direct or indirect reprisal by the supervisor. Upward communication will exist to the degree that it is allowed and encouraged by the supervisor.

In summary, management at all levels needs an awareness that communication *up* is a subject equal in importance with communication *down.* In fact, *downward* communication is likely to improve when a better understanding of the attitudes, opinions, and problems of subordinates is acquired through *upward* communication.[15]

Horizontal communication. The horizontal channel is used for the sending and receiving of information between people at the same organizational level; for example, a supervisor in one department communicates directly to a fellow supervisor in another department.

Horizontal communication is essential to assure *coordination* of the firm's various activities—production, marketing, finance, credit, personnel, and so on. It establishes an overall atmosphere of cooperation, building rapport and understanding between personnel involved in diverse functions. It encourages communication about common problems.

Personal rivalries and ambitions can create barriers in these channels; jealousy between functional areas or departments, infighting, and "empire-building" often arise, blocking the exchange of ideas and the sharing of information that could be beneficial to all.

[14]Davis, *op. cit.,* p. 346.

[15]Ernest G. Borman *et al., Interpersonal Communication in the Modern Organization* (Englewood Cliffs, New Jersey: Prentice-Hall, Inc., 1969), p. 190.

Informal Communication Networks

In contrast to formal communication networks, **informal communication ignores formal lines of authority and established relationships,** existing outside the official networks. Whereas the formal network is deliberately planned and designed by management, the informal network is unplanned, unrestricted, and spontaneous.

Informal communication is basically an attempt by employees to interpret their environment and make it more understandable. Although the formal network carries messages that the senders want the receivers to believe, the informal network usually carries messages that the senders themselves want to believe.[16]

The informal network is perhaps more commonly known as the "grapevine." As the name suggests, the grapevine is intertwined throughout the organization, branching out in all directions—up, down, and across the organization. It carries non-work-related information as well as work-related information. To a large degree, the grapevine is made up of *rumors, gossip, speculation,* and *partial or inaccurate information*—all spread with surprising speed. Even though it may lack access to official sources of information, its believability among employees is usually quite high.

Contrary to popular opinion, the grapevine is not always "sinister" and undesirable. Properly understood and controlled, the informal network can be an effective part of an organization's communication system, serving as a useful adjunct to the formal network.

The nature of rumors. Rumors sent through informal channels are based on uncertainty and insecurity. They flourish most often in companies where little reliable information is available to employees through the organization's formal communication network. If the company neglects to provide adequate information about its plans, operations, and anticipated changes, employees will supply their own answers through speculation and rumors. Even if their speculation turns up the "true story," the message passed from person to person along the grapevine is subject to progressive filtration and distortion. Each person who takes part in transmitting a rumor has his own ideas and perception of the subject, and will thus tend to omit certain facts and exaggerate others. Before you know it, an initially accurate statement such as "I hear they're going to transfer and retrain 50 people because of the new automated equipment" becomes "I hear those new machines are going to put us all out of work."

A manager at any level can contribute to the rumor mill whenever he chooses to withhold bad news for fear that it will be damaging to morale or when he decides not to comment on a problem in the naive hope that "maybe

[16]Gellerman, *op. cit.,* p. 60.

no one has noticed, so why call their attention to it?" Some perceptive employees most assuredly will notice, and not talking about the problem will start the grapevine buzzing, increasing subordinates' anxieties and stimulating speculation.

Information hunger. Rumors basically result from what Saul Gellerman has called "information hunger." According to Gellerman, "*information hunger* exists due to the tendency for people who already have information to assume that other people also have it."[17] We might also attribute it to the common assumption that others don't need the information.

Today's employees have an active desire to know more about their jobs and their company. Matters which directly affect employees and their jobs, such as promotion possibilities, company policies, working conditions, work methods, fringe benefits, and the importance and contribution of their individual jobs to the company as a whole, are naturally always of interest to them. However, they also like being informed about many higher level issues—more so than is normally expected. For example, information concerning the general welfare of the company, the company's profits for the year, progress in attaining general company objectives, sales forecasts, major expansion plans, and the company's contribution to social improvements in the community is often of interest to lower-level employees. Unfortunately, such information is sometimes made public through press releases before giving any consideration to the need for informing lower-level workers directly through internal company communication.

Employee newsletters or bulletins and company-wide meetings for all employees can be useful in keeping workers informed. But the immediate link between employees and top management is the supervisor; part of his job is to keep his work group up to date on what is happening within the department and the company. As an illustration of a simple "opening up" of communication, one company initiated a program whereby each supervisor held monthly meetings with his production employees. The initial format was simply for the supervisor to fill in his subordinates on what was going on in the plant and in their department. He discussed the monthly objectives of the plant, how it was doing with regard to its objectives, and how departmental objectives fit in with plant objectives. At the beginning, the meetings were rather formal and stiff with little two-way communication. This soon changed, however, with subordinates becoming truly involved. The content of their questions, complaints, and comments also changed. Discussions of specific worker-related topics such as vacation and sick-leave policies evolved into discussions of broader concern such as: What is our product being used for? Who is using it and what do they think of it? Are our quality standards high enough? The program became quite successful, and it was soon evident that employees wanted even more

[17] *Ibid.*, p. 64.

information about their jobs, how their jobs related to the company, and how the company was doing.[18]

The question usually arises, "How *much* should employees be told about the company's operations?" As much as might be of interest to them, so long as the information isn't of necessity confidential. Nevertheless, many supervisors firmly believe that company information is not really the employee's business; in other words, the rule is that the employee should do his job and management will run the company. Obviously, there will inevitably be an information gap under such circumstances.

Besides helping prevent needless fears and misunderstandings, sharing information with employees supports their sense of belonging. Employees come to believe that the company cares enough to keep them informed. And, when workers feel they are truly part of the organization—that management is honest and direct with them and that they know the facts they want to know—the rumor mill's level of activity is sharply reduced.

Guidelines for controlling the grapevine. The grapevine exists in every organization. As a result of the natural desire of people to communicate with one another and to make sense out of their situation, informal communication is sure to develop wherever a group of people interact.

The grapevine cannot be abolished or suppressed; the supervisor has to learn to live with it. But there are ways that the grapevine can be influenced and controlled. Here are eight guidelines and suggestions that can help reduce the number of rumors and keep employees supplied with reliable information:

1. Instead of ignoring the grapevine and hoping it will go away, *listen* to it and *study* it; learn what the grapevine is saying. Rumors not only reveal the hopes and fears of employees but also indicate the kind of information they need. However, you can analyze and prevent rumors from spreading only if you have *access* to the grapevine; you won't know what it is saying unless you have created an atmosphere encouraging upward communication, in which employees feel free to talk about anything that troubles them.

2. Encourage employees to ask about subjects they feel might be rumors. Then, play it straight. Answer questions honestly and thoroughly. When you don't know the answer, admit it, and tell the questioner you'll find out. Don't bluff an answer, and always follow through on getting the information.

3. Report any distortion of facts you hear circulating to your own superior. Rumors grow out of anxiety; the *cause* of the anxiety rather than the rumor itself must be discovered and corrected for effective rumor control.

4. Counter false rumors with a presentation of the correct facts. Rumors can be stopped or weakened only by getting out the full story as quickly as

[18]Edgar F. Huse and Michael Beer, "Eclectic Approach to Organizational Development," *Harvard Business Review*, September-October 1971, pp. 109-10.

possible. In accomplishing this, face-to-face communication is generally more effective and believable.

5. Keep workers informed about what is going on concerning their jobs and the rest of the company. Tell them everything that might be of interest, and be sure that what you tell them is correct. When explaining a directive or a change, make certain through feedback that employees understand it thoroughly.

6. Never consider a rumor "silly." Many times, people who know the true situation tend to dismiss an unfounded anxiety as only a "silly rumor." While false or exaggerated ideas may sound ridiculous to you, they are no laughing matter to the employee who is hungry for the facts.

7. Think twice before deciding that anything must be kept secret. Because of its ability to cut across organizational lines and deal directly with people "in the know," the grapevine often cracks even the most tightly-controlled "secrets" anyway.

8. Always remember: Rumors *start* when information *stops.*

Reading Selection 8

MANAGING UPWARD COMMUNICATION*

Gary Gemmill

The problem of upward communication appears to be endemic to superior-subordinate relationships. It is a common observation that subordinates in their relationship with superiors often conceal and distort their real feelings, problems, opinions, and beliefs because they fear disclosure may lead superiors to punish them in some way. Decisions by subordinates not to disclose such information results in a superior being unaware of how his actions affect them. This lack of feedback may prevent him from changing his managerial style or from correcting misperceptions on their part. Similarly, he is put in a position where he is unable to share knowledge with them that might lead to improvements in their performance. Perhaps most important, however, from a manager's perspective, is that this lack of communication may cut him off from some essential information.

Given that concealment and distortion by subordinates can be costly, is there anything a superior can do to lessen it? Is it possible for him to lower the probability that subordinates will

*From *Personnel Journal,* February, 1970, pp. 107-10. Reprinted with permission.

conceal or distort their communication with him? If it is possible, what must he do in his relationship with subordinates? How can he manage their upward communication?

WHY SUBORDINATES DISTORT THEIR UPWARD COMMUNICATION

An understanding of the factors that lead subordinates to distort upward communication is a prerequisite for managing it. One frequently cited reason for such concealment and distortion is that subordinates believe their superior may penalize them in some way for disclosing their real opinions, feelings and difficulties. Stated in a propositional form:

If a subordinate believes that disclosure of his feelings, opinions, or difficulties may lead a superior to block or hinder the attainment of a personal goal, he will conceal or distort them.

According to this proposition, a subordinate enters an organization with such personal goals as moving upward as fast as possible, achieving stable or increasingly higher earnings, or doing work that leads to growth in his abilities. In pursuit of these goals, he evaluates contemplated actions in terms of how he believes they will facilitate their attainment, attempting to avoid actions he believes may hinder. At various levels of personal awareness, he may conceal or distort his opinions, difficulties, or feelings when he believes disclosure may lead a superior to do something to block or hinder attainment of his goals.

For example, if he receives a salary increase he considers unfair, he tells his superior it is more than fair because he is afraid that by expressing disappointment he may injure his promotion prospects. He may believe the superior would consider him an ingrate or interpret his remark as an insult to his managerial proficiency and hold it against him when his name comes up for promotion. This belief, however, may not be grounded in reality since the superior may not actually attach a penalty to the expression of disappointment. But if the subordinate believes there may be one, it is sufficient for him to distort his feelings to avoid the possibility that the superior might react to disclosure by blocking or hindering the attainment of his personal goal of upward mobility. This may be done consciously. In some situations, however, the subordinate may not be fully aware that he is distorting the feedback to his boss.

THE ORIGINS OF DISCLOSURE BELIEFS

Subordinates acquire beliefs about the types of information to avoid disclosing to superiors from many sources. For example, subordinates who have worked for a superior for a number of years may instruct new subordinates that, careerwise, it is unwise to express ideas for improvements to him. They may even cite a case where a subordinate was purportedly penalized by him for rocking the boat. While this belief may lack an objective basis, if the new subordinates accept it, the probability that they will disclose ideas for improvement is reduced.

Some beliefs are undoubtedly founded in general social norms or corporate "folklore." For example, "subordinates should not display emotions in the presence of superiors" or "subordinates should never question the decisions of superiors." If subordinates have internalized such a norm, the probability is great that they will make decisions not to disclose their feelings or criticisms of decisions handed down to them. Indeed, they may even consider it legitimate for a superior to reprimand them if they make such disclosures.

Some beliefs originate in a subordinates' direct observation of types of disclosures that he perceives his superior dislikes. For example, when he disagrees with a superior who becomes emotionally upset and defensive he may say to himself: "I shouldn't have disagreed with him even though he told me he wanted me to feel free to do so. It's obvious he is upset by it. He may hold it against me when my name comes up for promotion or a new assignment. I'd better play it safe in the future and refrain from voicing my opinions." Rightly or wrongly, he considers the superior's reaction to disagreement to be a threat. He perceives the superior as being capable of blocking attainment of his personal goals and acts in a way to avoid it.

Where subordinates have not directly or indirectly acquired beliefs about the types of disclosures that may be penalized, they frequently operate on an uncertainty principle. When they are unable to predict if a superior will reward or penalize disclosure, to avoid the risk of a penalty they make a decision not to disclose. When in doubt, they say nothing.

EMPIRICAL STUDIES OF UPWARD COMMUNICATION

There are a number of empirical studies that offer support for the proposition that subordinates make decisions not to disclose their feelings, opinions, and difficulties because they are afraid that their superior may punish them in some way for doing so. Vogel, in a study of approximately 2,000 employees in 8 companies, found that almost a majority of them believed that if a subordinate told his immediate superior everything he felt about the company, he would probably get into a "lot of trouble," and that the best way to gain promotion was not to disagree very much with a superior.[1] This study, however, identifies only the prevalence of these beliefs and not how or where they were acquired.

Read, in a study of fifty-two superior-subordinate pairs in three companies, found that the accuracy with which subordinates disclosed their difficulties to superiors was negatively related to their desire for upward mobility.[2] The greater the desire of subordinates for upward mobility, the less likely they were to accurately disclose their difficulties to their superiors. The amount of inaccuracy in the upward communication, however, was affected by the perceived influence of the superior over their careers and how much they trusted him not to hold disclosures against them in considering promotion. The greater his perceived influence over their careers and the lower their trust in him, the more inaccurate their upward communication of difficulties. Read points out, however, that even when subordinates trust their superiors not to hold disclosures against them or block mobility, high mobility aspirations militate against disclosure.

Blau and Scott in a study of agents in a federal law enforcement agency found that the agents were reluctant to take their work-related problems to superiors even though

[1] A. Vogel, "Why Don't Employees Speak up?" *Personnel Administration*, May-June, 1967.

[2] W. Read, "Upward Communication in Industrial Hierarchies," *Human Relations*, Vol. 15, 1962, pp. 3-15.

they were officially expected to do so.[3] They believed that exposure of problems might be interpreted by superiors as a lack of independence, resulting in a low rating. Perceiving the possibility of a goal block by superiors, they decided not to disclose their difficulties in order to avoid it.

Argyris has also found that subordinates often conceal their feelings, opinions, and difficulties from superiors because they are fearful that they may be penalized in some way for such disclosure.[4] He suggests that one of the primary reasons for lack of disclosure is that many organizations place a high reward value on rational-technical aspects of behavior and discourage or penalize emotionally based behavior. When, for example, a subordinate expresses feelings in a discussion, the superior tells him to keep his feelings out of it. The subordinate thus learns not to disclose his feelings to avoid a career penalty of being labeled as too "emotional."

MANAGING UPWARD COMMUNICATION

The important question remains: What, if anything, can a superior do to lessen the probability that subordinates will conceal or distort their real feelings, opinions, and difficulties when communicating with him? Unfortunately, there has been little if any research directed to this question. Thus, the intent here is to conceptually examine factors that would appear to have a significant role in managing upward communication.

It seems clear that an awareness that subordinates tend to filter upward communication is a necessary condition for lessening it. Given awareness, diminishing the probability would seem to require a change in their perception of penalties for disclosure. The crux of the problem is establishing a relationship where they feel they will not be penalized by the superior for disclosure. Is it possible for a superior to create such a climate? If so, how can he do it?

Changing the Basis of Perceived Penalties

If the superior's control over the personal goals of subordinates were decreased, their fear of receiving a penalty for disclosure would undoubtedly decrease. It is perhaps unrealistic, however, to expect this to be a feasible alternative, given the type of organizational structure prevalent in our society. It is a fact of organizational life that a superior has a fairly high degree of control over the means of satisfying the personal goals of subordinates. He can often, for example, fire, lay off, block promotion, block salary increase, or hold back developmental assignments if he doesn't like what he hears from a subordinate. Even though he may claim there is no penalty for disclosure, and, in fact, can refrain from applying one, as long as the subordinate believes there may be one, or believes he can't hold back a penalty even though he wants to, he in all probability will refrain from disclosure.

Eliciting Disclosure Decisions Through Rewards

While it may not be feasible to create a situation in which a superior

[3]P. M. Blau and W. R. Scott, *Formal Organizations,* San Francisco: Chandler, 1962, pp. 128-134.

[4]C. Argyris, "Interpersonal Barriers to Decision-Making," *Harvard Business Review,* Vol. 44, March-April, 1966, pp. 84-97.

lacks control over the personal goals of subordinates, it may be possible for a superior to improve the chances of openness by rewarding incidences of disclosure. Stated in a propositional form:

The more a superior rewards disclosure of feelings, opinions and difficulties by subordinates, the more likely they will be to disclose them.

To create a relationship in which subordinates perceive disclosure as rewarding or not threatening, a superior can begin by telling them he expects them to have problems and disagreements and that he would like them to disclose them.

Obviously, simply telling them that they should feel free to discuss their feelings, opinions, and difficulties is not enough. They want to know if such actions on their part will, in fact, be rewarded or punished. Here, again, words by the superior to the effect that there will be no penalty are not sufficient to bring about a decision to disclose. Subordinates realize there is often a difference between what a superior says he wants to hear and what he actually wants to hear. The problem from their viewpoint is one of determining if he means what he says. How would he really react to disclosure? What types of disclosure can he tolerate? If he didn't like what I said, would he hold it against me?

These questions deal with the subordinate's perception of the consistency between the superior's words and actions. Are his actions consistent with his statement? It is a common belief in our culture that actions speak louder than words. Thus, it is perhaps not surprising that subordinates test out the consistency of a superior's words and actions by observing how he actually reacts to disagreements, expression of emotions, or reports of difficulties. If his response is a hostile or a demeaning one, they may conclude that there is a penalty for disclosure, even though he tells them there is not. In short, they may feel that his actions contradict his statements of the behavior he says he really wants, and they give priority to his actions. Because of the perceived penalty for disclosure, they learn to conceal their problems and disagreements from him.

At a minimum then, managing upward communication requires a superior to reinforce verbally stated expectations of leveling with actions that lead subordinates to view disclosure as a rewarded response or, at least, a response that does not result in a perceived penalty or threat. When subordinates make decisions to disclose, the superior must act in such a way that they will find the situation rewarding or at a minimum non-threatening. Sometimes this means that he must act contrary to his natural inclinations. Any expression of hostility or impatience will be perceived by subordinates as a threat or a perceived penalty which will seal off disclosure in the future. To increase the probability of future disclosure, he must reward instances of disclosure, since rewarded responses tend to be repeated while unrewarded ones tend to be eliminated.

To further increase the probability of disclosure by subordinates, a superior may use himself as a disclosure model in his relationship with them or his own superior. When talking with them, he makes a practice of disclosing his feelings, opinions, and difficulties, demonstrating that he practices what he preaches. Stated in a propositional form:

The more a superior discloses his own feelings, opinions, and difficulties to subordinates and his superior, the more likely subordinates will be to disclose theirs.

Such modeling would tend to reinforce his verbally stated desire for disclosure, thereby increasing the probability of disclosure.

To sum up, managing upward communication involves building a relationship with subordinates in which disclosure is encouraged and rewarded. It must be a supportive relationship—one in which subordinates feel that the superior will not take advantage of them if they fully speak their minds. For full disclosure to occur they must know that they can express their feelings, difficulties, and opinions without fear of reprisal. They must look upon the superior as a source of help rather than as an all powerful judge.

QUESTIONS FOR REVIEW AND DISCUSSION

1. Diagram a model of the communication process. Briefly explain each of the steps in the process.
2. a. What is the difference between *one-way* and *two-way* communication?
   b. How would you describe the supervisor who is more likely to prefer one-way over two-way communication? What are the likely results of his practices in terms of employee satisfaction and performance?
   c. Is two-way communication always more effective than one-way communication? Why?
3. a. What is a *symbol*?
   b. Name as many types of symbols as you can that are commonly used in communication.
   c. Can you think of any examples of communication breakdowns that have resulted from people's confusing the symbol with the thing or idea represented?
4. a. What is *feedback?*
   b. Can effective communication take place without feedback? Explain.
5. a. Name as many specific types of communication *media* as you can think of.
   b. Why is face-to-face communication usually more effective than other media? Under what circumstances would other media be more effective?
6. "*Failure* to act is an important way of communicating." Evaluate this statement.
7. Is the same nonverbal behavior perceived in the same manner by different societies, ethnic groups, and cultures? Discuss.
8. What nonverbal connotations can written communication convey?
9. a. What are the three directions in which formal communication may flow? Briefly explain each.
   b. Which of these directions is the most important to an organization's efficiency? Why?
10. a. What are the benefits of *upward* communication?
    b. Discuss some of the typical barriers to upward communication.
    c. What are some of the means whereby upward communication can be improved?
11. a. Do you feel that the company you now work for encourages upward communication? Why?

b. Could you freely communicate any message (good or bad news) to your supervisor without in anyway diluting or distorting it?

12. "Receiving only a few complaints or grievances is a good sign of high morale in the work group." Evaluate this statement.
13. We sometimes find ourselves telling strangers things about ourselves that we don't tell those close to us. How would you explain this?
14. a. Explain the difference between *formal* communication and *informal* communication.

    b. Why are informal communication networks usually formed?
15. Under what circumstances are rumors most likely to arise? How can they be prevented?
16. Discuss some of the ways that the grapevine can be influenced or controlled.
17. Would it ever be advisable for a supervisor to spread information informally via the grapevine? Explain.
18. To what extent is a supervisor the key man in an organization's communication network? Explain.
19. "As the complexities of an organization increase, so do the difficulties of efficient and accurate communication." Discuss this statement.
20. How can effective communication increase an employee's motivation?

SUGGESTED ADDITIONAL READINGS

Because of the similarity of subject matter, suggested additional readings for this chapter are combined with those for Chapter 7.

7

ROADBLOCKS IN THE AVENUE TO UNDERSTANDING

As discussed in the previous chapter, the ultimate goal of communication—complete understanding—is seldom achieved. Because of the countless barriers to communication that litter our avenue to understanding, we must often accept less than complete understanding. Perhaps, when we consider the magnitude of these barriers, we should not be dismayed that communication is frequently poor but wonder that it is as good as it is!

Fortunately, these barriers are usually not *absolute* blocks to communication. Rather, by screening and distorting the original meaning of the message, they reduce the *degree* of success in achieving understanding.

COMMON BARRIERS TO EFFECTIVE COMMUNICATION

Many of these barriers were necessarily examined in our prior discussion of the communication process and its relation to organizational structure. Several others are pointed out by Leonard Sayles in Reading Selection 9. However, we feel that special attention is due four specific barriers that commonly create communication breakdowns. The fifth barrier presented—poor listening—we believe to be of such importance that a separate section is devoted to it. Hopefully, a basic understanding and awareness of these barriers by the supervisor will mean that he can start to win the battle of overcoming them.

Differences in Individual Perception

As we have continually stressed, **no two people perceive or interpret the same event in exactly the same way**. This single fact constitutes the major obstacle to effective communication; in fact, all of the other psychological barriers to communication are directly related to this one principle.

Many problems and misunderstandings arise because of people's perceptual differences. An old World War II story provides a humorous example of this: On a train in Europe, an American grandmother, her young and attractive granddaughter, a Rumanian officer, and a Nazi officer occupied one of the train's compartments. As the train passed through a dark tunnel, a loud kiss, followed by a vigorous slap, was heard. After the train emerged from the tunnel, the grandmother thought to herself, "What a fine granddaughter I have. She can take care of herself. I am proud of her." At the same time, the granddaughter was saying to herself, "I am surprised what a hard wallop grandmother has; why should she get so upset over a little kiss?" The Nazi officer was meditating, "How clever these Rumanians are. They steal a kiss and have the other fellow slapped!" And the Rumanian officer sat chuckling to himself, "What a smart fellow I am. I kissed my own hand and slapped the Nazi."

Each individual brings to the communication process his own set of experiences, attitudes, values, interests, motives, assumptions, and expectations. Collectively, these components form the person's perceptual *frame of reference* –the key concept in communication because it determines how the individual perceives and interprets whatever he sees or hears.

Communication is, of course, best between people who have similar frames of reference. Unfortunately, such an ideal state seldom exists, since no two sets of experiences, attitudes, etc., are ever exactly the same. Whenever the frames of reference of the sender and receiver are not relatively homogeneous (as is more frequently the case), meaning will be difficult to convey between the two.

The obvious implication for supervision is to **accept and consider another's frame of reference and then communicate in terms of it.**[1] How often have you asked (or been tempted to ask) someone, "Why can't you see things *my* way?" Your concern might better be focused on how and why the other person perceives the situation as he does. What are his background, viewpoints, biases, current position on the subject, intelligence, educational level, age, race, occupation, and position in the organization? All of these things can affect his perception of your message and should be taken into account if you are striving to achieve understanding with him. Thus, communication is influenced not only by how the *receiver* perceives the sender and his message, but also by how the *sender* perceives the receiver and his frame of reference.

This, once again, points out the universal importance of *empathy* in everything a supervisor does in interacting with others. To be an effective communicator, the supervisor must attempt to put himself in the frame of reference of the other fellow; i.e., to empathize and to sense his feelings about the matter. After considering the characteristics of the receiver, the supervisor can then try to fit his communication to the other person's needs.

[1]Keith Davis, *Human Relations at Work* (third edition; New York: McGraw-Hill Book Company, 1967), p. 350.

Although the field of psychology has offered a variety of individual factors that influence the complicated process of human perception, our limited space dictates that we examine only a few of the more significant ones:

Expectations. People tend to perceive what they *expect* to perceive. If a communication is not in keeping with what the individual expects, he may unconsciously reject or distort the objectionable part of the communication. There is truth in the often-quoted statement, "He hears only what he wants to hear."

Two people rarely meet with what is called an "open mind." Instead, each has preconceived ideas or expectations about the other person and the topic of their communication; any information which doesn't fit these expectations is filtered or distorted.

For example, if an employee has had a bad relationship with a previous supervisor, he may perceive anything his present supervisor says or does with distrust and dislike. His earlier experiences are used as a basis for his current expectations. In a similar way, teachers have been known to unconsciously grade a good student's test paper disproportionately higher than a poorer student's paper simply because they expect the better student to make a higher grade.

Mental set. Probably one of the most prevalent and difficult of the perceptual barriers to successful communication is known as *mental set.* Quite similar to expectation, mental set is a psychological term used to describe the tendency or readiness to react in a particular way. We tend to perceive something in the way that we have become accustomed–or set–to perceiving it. From early childhood, people begin absorbing attitudes, values, and ideas to which they continue to cling. When developed over a period of years, a mental set may become so rigid that it is often practically impossible to change.

Perceptual selectivity. Perception is *selective.* In other words, we seldom pay attention to everything that is communicated to us. Rather, we are inclined to select or focus on those things that particularly interest us. In a meeting with ten people, each individual will leave with a somewhat different view of what occurred; each filtered the communication that took place, sifting out those ideas that he agreed with or found important.

Emotional state. An individual's current emotional state or mood can greatly influence his perceptions. Just as the heavy drinker may view the world more cheerfully today than he will with tomorrow's hangover, you will perceive things differently when you are angry, emotionally upset, or simply have a bad headache from when you're reasonably calm, happy, and healthy.

Semantics

If words are to effectively communicate ideas between the sender and the receiver, they must have the same meaning to both people. The problem is that **words have varied meanings.** Because of different perceptions, the meaning intended by the sender may vary greatly from the meaning understood by the receiver.

It is difficult to believe, but the *Oxford Dictionary* lists an average of 28 separate meanings or definitions for each of the 500 most frequently used words in the English language. Is it any wonder that we encounter semantic problems in communication? To compound our difficulties, dictionaries are overflowing with definitions that are outmoded and seldom used anymore, and people are overflowing with definitions dictionaries have not yet chosen to include.[2]

A frequently overlooked principle is that **words do not convey meaning; only people convey meaning through their use of words.** Or, put another way, the meanings of words are in the minds of the sender and receiver, not in the words themselves. Words are simply *symbols* that represent something; they have meaning only because people in a particular society or culture *give* them meaning. As we grow up, we learn to associate words with their specific meanings.

Since people come from varying goegraphic, ethnic, social, educational, and occupational backgrounds, the same word (or, for that matter, nonverbal action) often has entirely different meanings to different people because of each individual's perceptual frame of reference. Each person interprets words according to his past experiences; as no two sets of experiences are exactly the same, perceptions of words may be different.[3]

Do the same words mean the same to the college graduate and the person who left school after completing the sixth grade? Frequently not. As another example, the language of a company vice-president is obviously different from that of the janitor, and communication between the two may not always be presented in terms that are understandable and familiar. This is not to imply, however, that you should "talk down" (or "write down") to someone. The

"I thought I explained it clearly" "But you didn't check to make sure."

[2]John O'Hayre, *Gobbledygook Has Gotta Go* (Washington, D. C.: U. S. Government Printing Office, 1966), pp. 17-18.

[3]Harold Stieglitz, "Barriers to Communication," *Management Record*, January, 1958, pp. 2-3.

vice-president talking to the janitor would be well advised not to talk like a janitor, but he certainly shouldn't talk like a vice-president either.

The sender must communicate in terms of the receiver's background and frame of reference. In selecting your words, always consider your receiver and his likely interpretation of the words you choose. As N. R. Diller has colorfully put it, "Words should be developed to shape, mold, and express thought. They are capsules of mental effort and must be projected toward the target in order to be effective. If this is not done, they are like so many blank shells or 'duds' which make a feeble sputter and fizzle out."[4]

"Gobbledygook"

Closely related to semantic barriers, but deserving of separate attention, is the use of "gobbledygook"—wordy and generally unintelligible language—in oral and written communication.

Occasionally, many of us use words or phrases that are really meant to *impress* more than *express.* As a supervisor, your job is to *inform,* not to impress others with your extensive vocabulary. Officious four- or five-syllable tongue-twisters may sound very eloquent; but, if they are not understood by the other fellow, they are useless. Simpler words that are more easily grasped by the receiver can be used to convey the same meaning.

This is illustrated by the old story of a plumber who wrote to a governmental agency, the Bureau of Standards, inquiring if his longtime practice of cleaning drains with hydrochloric acid was harmless.

The Washington bureau replied: "The efficacy of hydrochloric acid is indisputable, but the chlorine residue is imcompatible with metallic permanence." In gratitude, the plumber wrote back saying that he was glad they agreed with him that it was harmless.

With a note of alarm, the Bureau rapidly replied: "We cannot assume responsibility for the production of toxic and noxious residues with hydrochloric acid and further suggest you use an alternate procedure." Flattered by Washington's interest, the plumber expressed in another letter that he was happy to find that the Bureau still agreed with him.

As the story goes, he received an immediate reply which very concisely read: "Don't use hydrochloric acid; it eats the hell out of the pipes!"

The point of the story is simply that *true* communication and understanding existed only at the end. It also illustrates the need to communicate in terms of the receiver and his frame of reference.

The use of gobbledygook is especially serious in *written* communication where the receiver is often unable to obtain additional clarification of the message. And let's face it—many of us don't know *how* to write simple, clear English. In fact, we are seldom even *exposed* to it. Many textbooks (perhaps even this one) are perfect examples of complicated, verbose, pompous, and often

[4]N. Richard Diller, "Improving Communications On the Job," *Manage,* August, 1966, p. 53.

meaningless language. As E. A. Stauffen has said, "If you think good writing comes easy, then you either don't write, or if you do, you don't know how yet."[5]

Technical jargon, common to almost all trades and professions, is another frequent nemesis to understanding. At times, various trades and professions seem to be *competing* with each other to see who can come up with the most status-seeking, complex terminology! We are not implying that technical jargon is "bad," for it certainly has its place. When used among people in the same technical area, it efficiently conveys meaning. But it is dangerous when used to communicate with people in other fields or with someone who hasn't been on the job long enough to learn the jargon. To make the point that technical jargon is understood only by those within a trade or profession, see if you can figure out this statement made by a printer: "I can't put her to bed; she pied when I picked her up." What is the printer trying to communicate? Simply that he couldn't put a job on the press because when he picked up the form, the type fell out. To a fellow printer, the statement would be quite clear. But to an outsider, it is sheer gobbledygook.[6]

In summary, the aim of communication is *not* to test the receiver's literacy; it is to reach mutual understanding.

Facts vs. Inferences

Inferences—conclusions drawn from observation of facts—are an essential part of our communication. However, it is wise to recognize that there is a distinct difference between inferences and facts. At times, inferences may prove to be correct; at other times they give a wrong signal that can result in misunderstanding.

As an illustration, consider the hypothetical case of Frank Cain, an accounting clerk for the XYZ Company. For years, Frank has dressed in a casual, unassuming manner, usually wearing a sport shirt or sweater. Today, Frank arrives at work attired in a dress shirt, a flashy tie, and a sports coat. In this situation, the only available *fact* is that Frank is indeed dressed differently from usual. However, a variety of *inferences* can be made from this single fact. His boss may *infer* that Frank's "new look" is an attempt to impress him. A fellow accounting clerk might infer that the change is a result of the boss berating Frank about his previous sloppy dressing habits. The guard at the plant entrance may infer that Frank has received a promotion. The attractive office secretary may decide that Frank is making a play for her attentions. Perhaps *one* of these inferences may be correct; then again, *none* of them may be correct. In each case, Frank's nonverbal behavior (which may or may not have been a conscious attempt to communicate anything) would be misinterpreted. Who knows? Further investigation of the facts might simply reveal that all of Frank's sport shirts and sweaters were dirty!

[5]O'Hayre, *op. cit.*, p. 27.

[6]*Ibid.*, pp. 25-26.

What are the implications for a supervisor? First, when inferences are mistaken for facts, you can get in a lot of trouble. For example, suppose one of your employees has come to work fifteen minutes late for the last four days. This is an observable fact. You, as his supervisor, might infer that the employee has become apathetic and irresponsible and has lost all interest in his work. Your inference may impulsively lead you to take immediate disciplinary action against him. Would your inference and action be correct? You can't be sure unless you make an attempt to discover additional facts about why the man has been tardy.

Secondly, you need to remember that people will make inferences from *your* words and actions which could possibly lead to misunderstanding of the facts you intend to communicate. By anticipating probable inferences that employees may make, you can furnish them with sufficient factual information to lessen the possibility of unwarranted inferences.

LISTENING—THE NEGLECTED AVENUE TO UNDERSTANDING

Listening is one of the most important—and most neglected—skills in communication. Few people really give much thought to the time they spend listening. Generally speaking, a breakdown of the total time a supervisor spends in communication during a normal day shows that 9 per cent of his time is spent writing, 14 per cent reading, 32 per cent speaking, and *45 per cent listening.* In other words, he does more listening than anything else. This is obvious when you stop to consider all of the instructions, information, advice, criticism, complaints, etc., that the average supervisor is confronted with each day. And, as he rises on the management hierarchy, the time devoted to listening is apt to increase even more.

How well do most of us listen? Is there any need to improve listening skills? We can answer both questions by citing the findings of research conducted by Dr. Ralph Nichols of the University of Minnesota. Nichols' studies of the listening aspect of communication indicate that most people retain only about *half* of what they hear immediately after listening to a short talk. After a few weeks, the same people will recall *only about 25 per cent* of what was said. Put another way, the majority of us operate at a 25 per cent efficiency level when listening; this finding is a bit unnerving when applied to business and industry, where management likes to talk in terms of 90 per cent or higher efficiency in the company's operations!

The poor listening ability of the average person was pointed out by one of our students in a salesmanship class. We were discussing the importance of promptly recognizing customers in a retail store. One student who was a salesperson in a large department store told the class that all of his store's personnel had been instructed to greet customers with a friendly "Hello, how are you today?" Another student, who frequently shopped in this same store, told us that he always smiled back at the salesperson and answered, "I have ten days to live, thank you." His weird sense of humor rarely received any reaction from the salesperson, who probably expected to hear the usual "Fine, thank you."

Although Mother Nature has wired us for sound, most of us evidently transmit better than we receive. And yet no communication is ever complete until there is understanding on the part of the receiver. Our problems in communication are not solved by seeking only to be *understood;* equally important, we must seek to *understand* others—i.e., to be a good listener.

Nichols has suggested that our country's educational system has overlooked an important subject—refining our ability to listen. Our schools teach writing and reading skills (even though the average high school graduate still reads at the eighth-grade level) and offer courses in speech, but relatively little attention is given to listening, the form of communication that occupies the greatest amount of our time.

Advantages of Effective Listening

The biggest plus for effective listening by the supervisor is that it encourages beneficial interpersonal relationships with subordinates. Of all the sources of information available to the supervisor for knowing and accurately "sizing up" the people in his work group, listening to the employee is the most important. Additionally, it indicates a willingness to understand and respect the other man; he, in turn, will be more willing to understand and respect you.

If you want to stimulate upward communication and a two-way flow of ideas, you must be a good listener; the only way you will get a person to be willing to talk is to be willing to listen.

Yet, too often in a discussion about listening, a supervisor will exclaim, "I don't have time to listen carefully." The obvious response is, "You don't have time *not* to listen carefully!" Effective listening *is* a difficult, time-consuming process, but the return justifies the investment by paying handsome dividends. Failing to listen to the people in your work group invites many problems that might otherwise never develop.

The Difference Between Listening and Hearing

Don't fall into the trap of confusing *listening* with *hearing.* Many of us who consider ourselves good listeners might be better described as good hearers. Hearing is merely a physical act and is almost impossible to avoid. Listening, however, requires more than just remaining passive and silent while the other fellow speaks; it involves more than just hearing words. Listening is an *active, conscious* act, requiring as much, if not more, mental effort and concentration than speaking.

Hearing is with our ears; listening is with our minds. If you only hear people, you're probably missing valuable information, suggestions, and ideas.

Common Bad Listening Habits

No one is born with the ability to listen effectively. Just like all other communication skills, good listening must be *learned.* To a great extent, this involves forming good listening habits and breaking bad habits. Here is a short test that, *if answered honestly,* will give you an idea of whether you have any bad listening habits:

1. You think about four times faster than a person usually talks. Do you use this excess time to think about other things while you're keeping track of the conversation? . . . . Yes No
2. Do you listen primarily for facts, rather than ideas, when someone is speaking? . . . . Yes No
3. Do you avoid listening to things you feel will be too difficult to understand? . . . . Yes No
4. Can you tell from a person's appearance and delivery that he won't have anything worthwhile to say? . . . . Yes No
5. When somebody is talking to you, do you try to make him think you're paying attention when you're not? . . . . Yes No
6. Do certain words or phrases prejudice you so that you cannot listen objectively? . . . . Yes No
7. Do you turn your thoughts to other subjects when you believe a speaker will have nothing particularly interesting to say? . . . . . . Yes No
8. When you're listening to someone, are you easily distracted by outside sights and sounds? . . . . Yes No
9. When you are puzzled or annoyed by what someone says, do you try to get the question straightened out immediately, either in your own mind or by interrupting the speaker? . . . . Yes No
10. Do you catch yourself concentrating in a conversation more on what you are going to say when it's your turn to speak than on what the speaker is saying? . . . . Yes No

If you truthfully answered "No" to all the questions, you are a rare individual–perhaps a perfect listener. (You may also be kidding yourself!) Every "Yes" means you are guilty of one of the ten bad listening habits that we shall now examine.[7]

Wasting thought power. We listen and absorb ideas at a much faster rate than most people talk. On the average, most of us *talk* at a rate of 125 words per minute. Yet, we can easily *think* in terms of 400 or 500 words per minute. Unfortunately, this difference between speech speed and thought speed is responsible for many *mental tangents;* in other words, instead of concentrating on the speaker's message, your mind frequently uses its excess capacity for thinking about some other subject. At the same time you are listening to a conversation or speech, you can periodically ponder your plans for the weekend, your hobby, that new secretary, last night's party, or Sunday's football game. Before you know it, your mind wanders too far away and "tunes out" the speaker altogether.

What is the solution? Obviously, if you have the ability to think four times faster than a person can talk to you, this can be turned into a listening asset. By disciplining your thoughts, your spare thinking time can be used to think about the speaker's subject and improve your listening comprehension. How? By

[7]The framework of this presentation is taken from Ralph G. Nichols, "Listening Is Good Business," *Management of Personnel Quarterly,* Winter 1962, pp. 2-10.

anticipating the speaker's next point, reviewing or summarizing the points he has made, and listening "between the lines" to get any hidden messages that may go unspoken.

Listening only for facts. One common mistake made by poor listeners is attempting to remember all the facts. Instead of memorizing a series of facts, try to get the gist or main ideas of the speaker's message. Facts are understood and retained only when they are tied together to support a concept, principle, or generalization.

"Throw-in-the-towel" listening. Many people quit listening if they think the speaker is going to talk about something that is technical or difficult to understand. And, little wonder; we are *conditioned* to evade difficult material. You only need to watch a night of TV–"the vast wasteland"–to recognize the widespread tendency in our society to listen only to light, recreational, unchallenging material. Many of us are simply inexperienced in listening to difficult material; others are just out of practice and in a rut.

Don't shy away from tough subjects or those outside your field. As you continue to listen, you may find that the subject isn't so hard to understand after all.

Criticizing the speaker's appearance or delivery. It is easy to criticize a speaker's appearance, delivery, dress, mannerisms, or eccentricities. However, when you react in this manner, you are not listening effectively and are shortchanging yourself by closing the door on what might be useful information.

If an employee stops to offer a suggestion, but he has long hair, do you think you might say to yourself: "Anybody who has long hair can't have much to say"? Be careful, the man may have a good idea that can solve one of your biggest problems. Dr. Nichols provides another illustration:

> Suppose that right now a janitor interrupted you, yelling in broken, profane English, "Get the hell out of here! The building is on fire!" You wouldn't lean backward and say, "Please, sir, will you not couch that admonition in better rhetoric?" You would rush pell-mell out of the room, as you know. That is my point. The message is ten times as important as the clothing in which it comes.[8]

Concentrate on the *content* of the message, not the speaker's dress or mannerisms. The speaker must have something worthwhile to say, so why not dig it out? Give him the benefit of the doubt; in the long run, you'll pick up some excellent ideas from "dull" or "eccentric" speakers.

Faking attention. Many people only go through the motions of listening; they figure that if they pretend to listen, no one will notice the difference. They are wrong in two ways. First, you seldom can fool the speaker. Even though you appear to be listening intently, the speaker can tell from your reactions that you haven't heard a thing; and, when subordinates brand their supervisor as a phony listener, they will cut off upward communication to him. Second, you are shutting yourself off from a potentially good source of ideas and information.

[8]*Ibid.,* p. 6.

Submitting to emotional words. Another bad listening habit is allowing emotional words—often called "red-flag" words—to block rational listening. Examples of words that are currently emotion-laden to some people are *automation, taxes, mother-in-law, union, women's lib, bussing, Vietnam, welfare, insurance, computer, hard-core,* and *big business.* The mere mention of such words can make some people "see red" and miss or distort the entire message. You can probably think of many words that personally turn *you* off. But remember, words are only *symbols* of something; so why let a simple word disrupt your listening efficiency?

Calling the subject uninteresting. A seventh bad listening habit is to immediately declare a speaker's subject uninteresting. Naturally, the most attention-getting subjects are those you are personally interested in; because of your personal interest, you *want* to listen. If, however, the subject doesn't appear to directly involve you or seems boring, you may go off on a mental tangent, feeling that there is no reason to listen.

Nichols suggests that, inasmuch as you're "trapped" and can't gracefully walk away in such a situation, you should concentrate on sifting, screening, and hunting for *something*—even if only a few words—the speaker says that is meaningful and useful to you. This can be a very profitable activity. Actually, there is no such thing as a talk completely lacking in useful information.

As G. K. Chesterton said many years ago, "In all the world there is no such thing as an uninteresting subject. There are only uninterested people."[9]

Tolerating or creating distractions. Poor listeners are easily distracted by other sounds or sights going on around them. A good example is the supervisor who is always willing to see an employee but who allows the conversation to be interrupted time and again. He talks to anyone who sticks his head in the office and answers a continuous stream of phone calls.

One of the authors once attempted a conversation with an administrator who prided himself on being able both to listen to someone and open and read his mail at the same time! Perhaps there are some people who are able to pull off such amazing feats successfully. However, such persons are likely to convince those talking to them that they really have no interest in listening attentively.

"I-can't-buy-that" listening. When you find yourself disagreeing with a person, do you start mentally planning a rebuttal before he is finished talking? Do you tend to prejudge or make assumptions about what is said before your comprehension is complete? To do so is to allow your emotions to affect your objectivity and reduce your listening effectiveness. And, if you jump to a conclusion about what a person is getting at before he actually makes his point, you may find yourself embarrassingly wrong.

We all have certain sensitive topics and prejudices that can cause us to get emotionally involved with the speaker's message. But this is no excuse for

[9]*Ibid.*

becoming over-emotional and argumentative. Wait for the speaker to finish talking before judging and evaluating his ideas. Hear him out; if you still disagree, then offer your opinion in a calm and rational manner.

Similarly, we sometimes find ourselves not listening to another person because we don't like him personally. In other words, we don't like the man, and therefore we don't like his ideas. Here again, when you react in this emotional manner, you are closing the door on what might be useful information.

"Open-mouth" listening. One of the most prevalent causes of poor listening is impatience to have our "say." Silence is difficult for many of us. We like to speak more than we like to listen. Thinking that we must say something each time the speaker catches his breath, we often concentrate more on what *we* are going to say next than on what the speaker is saying. Obviously, this is part-time listening, at best.

Choke off the temptation to "butt in" or dominate the conversation. Let your speaker know he has your full attention. An occasional nod or a comment like "that's interesting" or "I see" will work wonders.

Perhaps we should keep in mind the warning of an old proverb: "Nature gave us two ears and only one mouth so that we could listen twice as much as we speak."

General Suggestions for Improved Listening

Aside from overcoming the bad listening habits discussed above, here are some suggestions that will improve your listening and help you discover a world of useful information:

Listen empathetically. The key to effective listening is *empathy* (there's that word again!). You must attempt to get yourself into the speaker's frame of reference and sense his feelings about the topic of discussion; try earnestly to see his point of view in light of his background, attitudes, and needs.

When listening empathetically, you listen *nonevaluatively,* without passing judgment on what is being said at the time. This opens the way for a subordinate to talk freely about his ideas and feelings without worrying about justifying every statement he makes.

A supervisor's empathetic listening can actually be therapeutic for the subordinate. Very often the mere act of listening to an employee's problems and letting him "get it off his chest" helps him to work things out for himself.

The ability to listen with genuine empathy and understanding is rare, but it can be acquired through desire and practice.

Listen between the lines. A supervisor must not only listen to what is said, he must also try to hear what is not said. Consider this illustration. One of your subordinates, Al Gandy, has just approached you to report:

"Well, I finally finished up the order for the Ace Publishing Company. Man, what a mess! But you said it was an emergency job, so I saw to it that it went out today. You know, I've been here every night this week to finish that darned thing up. My wife may throw me out tonight! Ace's specifications were ridiculous, but the order is on its way. And let me tell you, if I never see another job as tough as that, I'll be happy. That one was blood, sweat, and tears!"

If you should answer, "Great, Al; now let's get back to work on the Wilson order," you haven't really been listening, have you? What was Al really trying to get across to you? We can't be sure, of course, but it's doubtful that he was simply saying the Ace order was difficult. More likely he was saying, "How about a little recognition for a job well done?"

The sensitive supervisor will look beyond words for the meaning and sentiments the speaker is attempting to convey; he will hear what the other fellow is often inhibited from saying directly.[10]

In order to better analyze the speaker and his message, you should also note any change in his tone of voice, his gestures, facial expressions, and body movements. Such things can be important clues to the real meaning of the message. Be careful to evaluate these visual signs only in connection with what is being said, however; otherwise, they may only become distractions to your listening.

Anticipate the speaker's next point. Good listeners try to think ahead of the speaker, anticipating his next point or line of reasoning. If you guess correctly, learning is reinforced. Even if you guess wrongly, you have forced yourself to concentrate on the subject.

Make mental summaries. Periodically make quick mental summaries of what has been said to that point. Not only does this reinforce learning, it helps utilize the differential between thought speed and speech speed.

COMMUNICATION IN PERSPECTIVE

Further pleading the cause for communication following our lengthy discussion of the topic in these last two chapters is surely superfluous. Little shrewdness is needed to realize that the job of supervision—getting work accomplished through others—requires effective communication. Communication is a basic skill of supervision and the foundation upon which all cooperative group activity rests.

However, every communication situation poses a challenge to those involved in it. Effective communication requires an understanding of the basic processes of communication and the organizational structure that furnishes its environment. These were our goals in Chapter 6. There, we examined the six

[10]Norman B. Sigband, "Listen to What You Can't Hear," *Nation's Business,* June, 1969, pp. 70-72.

steps in the communication process and continually stressed the desirability of two-way communication and feedback. Advantages and disadvantages of oral and written communication, as well as the often-overlooked nonverbal medium, were presented.

Next, we looked at the supervisor's role in formal and informal communication networks. We saw that a formal system for transmitting and receiving information up, down, and across is a basic requirement for any organization depending upon human cooperation. Interwoven with the formal structure, however, is an ever-changing and complicated network of informal communication channels that cannot be ignored by the supervisor.

In Chapter 7, we have tried to further illustrate the complexities of person-to-person communication and the various obstacles to understanding.

The future will doubtless bring increased recognition of the value of effective communication both to individuals and to organizations. As business and industrial organizations continue to grow more complex and larger, the need for people with communication skills at all levels of management will also increase. We are now at the point where lip-service to the need for effective communication is no longer adequate. We must begin practicing it. Regardless of our field of specialization, each of us is in the midst of an information and knowledge explosion, and our communication skills must keep pace.

You will undoubtedly, in time, forget many of the details presented in these two chapters. Make it a point, however, to remember this: There is nothing simple about communication; it cannot be taken for granted. There are so many psychological and physical barriers that the normal result of any communication effort is partial misunderstanding.

No one's communication skills will ever be perfect, but they can be improved; indeed, they must be. All of us must begin with an awareness of our own present level of competence as communicators, one which involves a clear and honest evaluation of one's current abilities and practices. Armed with this self-awareness, you can then begin striving for continual improvement.

One of the authors now has a sign on her office wall as a constant reminder of the difficulty encountered in achieving understanding:

I know you believe you understood what you think I said, but I am not sure you realize that what you heard is not what I meant.

Definitely wise words to live by!

Reading Selection 9

*ON-THE-JOB COMMUNICATION**

Leonard Sayles

PART I: WHY ISN'T IT EASIER?

Watch two old friends talking to each other. Do they have difficulty communicating? Probably not. They might not even have to use complete sentences—often a single word or a raised eyebrow conveys all the meaning necessary. Since the friends know each other thoroughly, key words or signs are all they need to exchange their ideas.

For the supervisor at work, communicating isn't that easy. In giving a simple order to a subordinate, asking why an assignment wasn't completed on time, or listening to a suggestion from an employee, the supervisor is faced with many communication barriers that almost never exist between close friends.

Let's look at these barriers, along with some specific examples of how they can impede communication between a supervisor and his subordinates.

The Speaker and Listener Differ in Experience and Background

A supervisor tells one of his key men that the company may have to cut back production because some important orders were lost. But the employee hears: "You can expect to be laid off soon."

Why? In other companies where he's worked, lost orders always meant he was out of a job.

Our understanding of what we hear depends largely on our own experience and background. Instead of hearing what people tell us, we may hear what our mind tells us has been said. There is often a vast difference.

Differences in experience often influence the way workers respond to incentive plans. A company offers to give merit increases and higher-paying jobs to superior employees. Some workers fail to respond with enthusiasm—even though they want to earn additional money. Why? It may be that they have never gained anything from being good workers. Perhaps they belong to an ethnic group that is often ignored when better jobs are filled. Perhaps they've worked in companies that "cut the rate" when employees made more money by working harder. Whatever the reason, they hear the company's announcement this way:

"Certain workers whom we choose will get benefits by working harder; others will get nothing."

We Fail to Convey the Information the Listener Needs and Can Understand

For example, a supervisor may fill a trainee's mind with information he is not ready to grasp. In one survey, cashier-trainees in department stores

*Reprinted by the permission of the publisher from *Supervisory Management,* © July 1962 by the American Management Association, Inc.

reported that much of their induction training was meaningless to them. The reason: Without any experience on the job, they didn't understand how they could apply the information. It was only after they were on the job handling sales slips that they could have absorbed the knowledge. For this reason, training is more effective when the supervisor can simulate actual on-the-job problems to which the new information can be applied.

It is the supervisor's job, too, to make sure that the information he *gets* from subordinates is what he needs. Often, a subordinate is in the dark about what information his boss wants from him. The boss then complains that the subordinate is failing to keep him informed in vital areas or that he is deluging him with information he doesn't need.

Our Stereotypes and Beliefs Influence What We Hear

A man with a strong prejudice is often confronted by information that contradicts it. But the prejudice may be so powerful that he will twist the information to support it.

For example, let's say a supervisor is convinced that because one worker in his department belongs to a certain ethnic group, he is, therefore, always looking for the easy way out. One day, the worker comes up with a carefully worked out, practical shortcut on his job. Instead of praising him for his initiative, the supervisor thinks to himself: "Just proves they're all alike—always trying to get away with less work."

Look at how a supervisor can come to three different conclusions about the same situation, depending on his preconceptions. The situation: He sees a group of employees laughing together.

1. If he believes that hard work has to be unpleasant, he decides the employees are wasting time and should be given tougher assignments.
2. If he believes that good work and cheerful attitudes go together, he will congratulate himself for being a good manager.
3. If he is personally insecure, he may assume that the laughing employees are making jokes about him.

Our Emotional State of Mind Colors What We Hear

The worried, fearful employee finds threats in everything he hears. Let's say new equipment is being introduced in a department. The employees fear the worst. As a result, everything seen and heard is interpreted as confirmation that they will suffer: "I saw the supervisor looking at the seniority list—it looks as though they're going to lay off half the department after that new machinery comes in."

We're Dead Set Against a Speaker's Message Because We Suspect His Motivation

The classic example of this particular barrier is to be found in labor-management relations. Many union members are convinced that management is out to weaken their union, and they refuse to believe anything management tells them. Similarly, management may regard all grievances as political maneuvers designed to win union votes. Both sides are sometimes right, of course. But too often this closed-mind attitude makes it impossible for the two sides to reach each other.

The same suspicion can impede communication between supervisors, too. Often one supervisor may reject worthwhile ideas from an associate simply because he's convinced that the man is trying to show him up.

In dealing with subordinates, the supervisor can be at the receiving end of such disbelief. If an employee is convinced that his boss is trying to manipulate him, all the human-relations techniques in the book—no matter how sincerely they are used—will be unsuccessful.

Let's say an employee makes a cost-cutting suggestion to his supervisor. The supervisor says, "Thanks, I'll think about it." If the subordinate believes that the supervisor isn't really interested in developing people, he'll hear this as, "Stick to your own job and let me take care of the thinking around here."

On the other hand, if he thinks the supervisor genuinely wants to encourage initiative, he'll hear: "I'm pleased that you came up with this suggestion—I'll see if there is some way we can use it."

We Fail to Evaluate the Meaning Behind What We Hear

Sometimes we go to the opposite extreme—instead of judging what we hear entirely by the speaker's imagined motivation, we completely ignore the possible latent meaning of his words. We forget that most statements are a combination of fact *and* feeling.

An employee comes over to his supervisor and says disgustedly, "This lousy machine is broken again." An alert supervisor will wonder if there isn't more in this complaint than just a maintenance problem. Could the employee be saying, "I don't like this job" or, "I think I'm getting a raw deal"? These possibilities deserve investigation.

We Fail to Realize That What We're Saying Has Symbolic Meaning for Our Listeners

What we say often has a far greater meaning than it appears to on the surface. That's why we sometimes get a surprisingly strong reaction to what we consider a rather mild statement.

Recently, for example, a production supervisor told his men, "We're going to start using plastic for these parts instead of chrome steel." He reassured them that no one would lose his job, and there would be no changes in earnings or working conditions. It was simply an economy move to reduce the cost of this particular component.

Yet the morale of the whole department was shaken. The supervisor didn't realize that the men were proud of the superior appearance and durability of the chrome-steel component. The phrase "chrome steel" was loaded with symbolic meaning: product prestige, a feeling of superiority, a determination to be the best even if it cost more.

We Forget That Words Mean Different Things to Different People

Words and phrases often lead to trouble because the speaker and listener interpret them differently.

For example:

A supervisor spots a dangerous pool of oil on the shop floor near a machinist. As he passes, he says, "Get that oil wiped up as soon as you can—it's a real safety hazard." The machinist nods.

Ten minutes later, the supervisor is called back—an inspector has just taken a bad spill on the oil. The supervisor bawls out the machinist for failing to follow his instructions. But the machinist says:

"You told me to get it wiped up as soon as I could. I thought you could see that I was working on a delicate cut and had to finish that first."

To the supervisor, "as soon as you can" meant immediately. To the machinist, it meant as soon as he had finished the piece on which he was working.

Our Reference Group Often Dictates the Way We Hear a Message

The group we identify ourselves with—psychologists call it the reference group—tends to shape our opinions on many matters. The result is often another block to true communication. Here's an example:

A night-shift operator finds a note left for him by the day man who runs the same machine: "Don't expect to get any good work from this—I didn't. It needs cleaning and some decent maintenance for a change."

The day man was just trying to be helpful, even though he didn't know the night man. But the night man read the note this way: "Your sloppy maintenance is to blame for my difficulty."

How come? Based mostly on imagined slights, the night man's reference group—the rest of the night shift—had developed a resentful attitude toward the day shift. Influenced by this attitude, the night man interpreted the note as a slap at him.

PART II: IT'S EASIER WHEN YOU KNOW HOW!

A large group of supervisory trainees listened intently as their instructor gave them elaborate directions on how to arrange five dominoes in a certain pattern. They were not allowed to ask any questions of the instructor.

In another room, the same directions were being given, but here the trainees were allowed to ask as many questions as they wanted of the instructor.

The results were startlingly different. In the first room, only three trainees were able to arrange the dominoes correctly. In the second room, only four trainees did *not* arrange them correctly.

This experiment in communication points up what is perhaps the single most important technique in better communicating: feedback. There are other weapons in the supervisor's communications arsenal—and we'll get to these later—but feedback is probably packed with more potential than any of them.

That's because feedback can tell the supervisor *if* he is communicating and *what* he is communicating to his listener. It turns communication from a shot-in-the-dark that may or may not be hitting the target to a two-way process that leaves both speaker and listener better informed.

Let's look at what feedback is. Actually most of us use this principle constantly without recognizing it. Put simply, it means modifying what we say and how we say it according to the response we get from our listener. This is the same way a thermostat regulates the amount of furnace heat on the basis of feedback, which in this case is the temperature of the room.

When a supervisor uses this method deliberately, he can develop better ways of learning what is being understood by the subordinate to whom he's talking. Various experiments have revealed that the accuracy of communication increases with the amount of feedback. Limiting the listener to "Yes" or "No" responses (asking him, for example, "Do you understand that?") is less effective than encouraging him to ask his own questions.

Face-to-face Communication

The first essential for maximum feedback is face-to-face communication. Only then can the communicator find out if the receiver understands, if he agrees, if he's sympathetic, indifferent, hostile, or just confused. The feedback comes not only through the listener's words, but through his nonverbal behavior, too.

We can watch for expressions of puzzlement, anger, or comprehension that may flicker across his face. Gestures and other physical actions can reveal impatience, animosity, or agreement.

With the set of his lips, the movement of an eyebrow, a listener can often tell us more than he does in hours of talk, because these expressions may indicate attitudes that he is reluctant or unable to express in words. For example, a subordinate is understandably unwilling to challenge the orders of his boss. Even when he has information that makes him skeptical of the success of a proposed plan, he may still want to keep his misgivings to himself. But in the course of an informal, face-to-face discussion, an alert supervisor can detect a lack of enthusiasm in his tone of voice and his facial expressions.

While a supervisor should not—and probably doesn't want to—think of himself as a psychiatrist, he should learn to "listen with a third ear" to what a subordinate is saying. What is the employee really trying to say? Is the problem deeper than he's letting on? What isn't he saying? What subjects is he avoiding, and why?

Interpreting feedback is not always easy. What we say may symbolize something to our listeners that is not apparent to us. One such case occurred recently in a large merchandising company. To help him in the preparation of market analysis, a new district sales manager asked his salesmen to compute certain correlation coefficients on the basis of their sales records. The task was not difficult—they simply had to use an easy formula. But they failed to do it. One excuse followed another: The computations were too complicated, it was clerk's work, it wasn't in their job description, the coefficients were really useless anyhow, and so on. Their distaste for this task seemed to be out of all proportion to the difficulty involved.

Solving the Mystery

Why was the modest request greeted with such stubborn resistance? The sales manager came up with the answer after much investigation and interviewing. Three years before, the salesmen had had an authoritarian supervisor whom they thoroughly disliked. He had tried to introduce this same statistical technique. When the new manager brought it up, they immediately rejected it, because to them it had become a symbol of oppressive supervision.

Once the mystery had been solved, the sales manager decided to withdraw his request temporarily. After giving his men time to develop confidence in him, he reintroduced the request and had no trouble getting their cooperation.

Other Communication Aids

Vital as it is, feedback is only one of a number of aids the supervisor can use to improve his communicating. Here are some others:

1. *Projection.* Before you communicate something, put yourself in your listener's shoes. How is he likely to react to your message, and what should you do to make sure he understands it the way you mean it? For example, you tell an employee he is wanted in the front office. His silent reaction may be, "I'm in for a dressing-down from the big boss." If this isn't the case, you should make it clear to him.

   Often there may be a wide gap between the supervisor's experience and that of his listener. The supervisor must try to bridge that gap.

2. *Timing.* Once an erroneous belief has been established in employees' minds through rumor and misunderstanding, it is very difficult to dislodge—even with the facts. The answer is to get the facts across *before* misconceptions have a chance to gain a foothold.
3. *Believability.* Your words won't mean anything to employees if they're skeptical of your sincerity. Anything you tell them must be supported by your actions. And when something happens that contradicts what you've told them, you should give them a full explanation.
4. *Simplicity.* This is an especially important ingredient of your written communications. Every manager should put his bulletin-board announcements, policy statements, and directives in simple, direct language.
5. *Repetition.* Saying something over again often helps to make it stick. This is particularly true when you're giving an employee complicated instructions. If he misunderstands what you said the first time, he'll have a chance to catch it the next time around.
6. *Freshness.* There are times when you should avoid repetition and find new ways of saying things. Timeworn, overfamiliar phrases will be ignored by your subordinates—they'll figure they've heard it all before. Discussing this problem recently, one worker said, "I know just what the boss is going to say the minute he starts with that line about all of us being one big happy team—so I don't listen."

   It's a good idea to review your favorite phrases once in a while and replace them with fresh variations. You'll have a much better chance of gaining the attention of your listeners.

Good communication does not, of course, depend only on these techniques. It must be based as well on a healthy, cooperative relationship between the supervisor and his subordinates. The supervisor who has the confidence of his subordinates will find it much easier to explain, for example, why air conditioning must be postponed till next year than will the supervisor who hasn't. And using the techniques outlined here will help him get the message across to them.

QUESTIONS FOR REVIEW AND DISCUSSION

1. Recall a breakdown in communication that you have observed or have been a part of. What caused the misunderstanding and how could it have been avoided?
2. How do individual differences affect communication?
3. "The concept of *frame of reference* is the key to the entire communication process." Evaluate this statement.
4. "Most communication serves to reinforce one's already-held beliefs and attitudes." Do you agree? Why?
5. a. Why is semantics a problem in communication?
   b. How can semantic barriers to communication be overcome?
6. Why is it important to distinguish between facts and inferences?
7. What are some of the communication barriers likely to exist between a supervisor and a subordinate that usually do not exist between friends?

8. How important is *trust* in supervisor-subordinate communication? Explain.
9. a. What is the function of listening in communication?
   b. What supervisory problems may result from failure to listen effectively?
10. Keep a log of the time you spend engaging in each form of verbal communication—reading, writing, speaking, and listening—during an entire typical day. Compare your results with the percentages reported in this chapter. Do your results confirm the importance of listening as a major component of communication?
11. Is there a relationship between listening and upward and downward communication? Explain.
12. Is good listening by the supervisor helpful in his efforts to motivate subordinates? Explain.
13. Name and briefly discuss the ten common bad listening habits presented in this chapter. Can you think of any others that could be added to this list?
14. a. Why do people tend to react emotionally to certain words and not to others?
    b. What are some words that typically make you "see red"?
15. Most of us have been unwilling to accept ideas or information communicated to us only to find later that the communication was, in fact, valid. From your own experiences, discuss your reasons for rejecting the communication. As a group, try to determine if your reasons are similar or if each group member tends to have individual reasons for rejecting communication.
16. What are some suggestions for improving one's listening effectiveness? Can you offer any suggestions that were not presented in the chapter?
17. Why is it important for a supervisor to listen "between the lines" or with a "third ear"?
18. At which of the six steps in the communication process discussed in Chapter 6 do you feel that the most barriers to effective communication occur? Defend your answer.
19. Both Chapters 6 and 7 have suggested that the communication process is more complex than we usually think. Can you recall personal experiences in which you were conscious of the difficulty in communicating? In what ways were these situations different from those which did not seem difficult?
20. What benefits will be derived in an organization in which all relevant communication is passed to the right people?

SUGGESTED ADDITIONAL READINGS

Anthony, Philip, and William P. "Now Hear This: Some Techniques of Listening," *Supervisory Management,* March, 1972, pp. 19-24.

Barker, Larry L. *Listening Behavior.* Englewood Cliffs, New Jersey: Prentice-Hall, Inc., 1971. 154 pp.

Diller, N. Richard. "Improving Communications on the Job," *Manage,* August, 1966, pp. 48-55.

Fischer, Frank E. "A New Look at Management Communication," *Personnel,* May, 1955, pp. 487-495.

Gelfund, Louis I. "Communicate Through Your Supervisors," *Harvard Business Review*, November-December, 1970, pp. 101-104.

Grossman, Jack H. "Are Your Messages Provoking Conflict?" *Supervisory Management*, November, 1970, pp. 2-6.

Hahn, Richard A. "What Is Communication?" *Industrial Supervisor*, March, 1971, pp. 3-7.

Hall, Edward and Mildred. "The Sounds of Silence," *Playboy*, June, 1971, pp. 138 ff.

Nichols, Ralph. "Listening Is Good Business," *Management of Personnel Quarterly*, Winter 1962, pp. 2-10. Also see *Human Relations in Management*, S. G. Huneryager and I. L. Heckmann, editors. Second edition. Cincinnati: South-Western Publishing Company, 1967. Pp. 543-562.

O'Hayre, John. *Gobbledygook Has Gotta Go*. Washington, D. C.: U. S. Government Printing Office, 1966. pp. 112 Available from Superintendent of Documents for 55 cents.

Rogers, Carl R., and F. J. Roethlisberger. "Barriers and Gateways to Communication," *Harvard Business Review*, July-August, 1952, pp. 46-52.

Sigband, Norman B. "Listen to What You Can't Hear," *Nation's Business*, June, 1969, pp. 70-72.

Smith, Alton E. "Communication," *Manage*, April, 1966, pp. 50-55.

Stieglitz, Harold. "Barriers to Communication," *Human Relations in Management*, S. G. Huneryager and I. L. Heckmann, editors. Second edition. Cincinnati: South-Western Publishing Company, 1967, pp. 669-675.

Weiss, W. H. "Breaking the Fear Barrier," *Nation's Business*, July, 1971, pp. 64-65.

"Why Best Managers Are Best Communicators," *Nation's Business*, March, 1969, pp. 82-83.

Zeyher, Lewis R. "Improving Your Three-Dimensional Communications," *Personnel Journal*, May, 1970, pp. 414-418.

8

THE GROUP—WHY IT EXISTS AND WHAT YOU CAN DO ABOUT IT

With few exceptions, people belong to bridge or social clubs, professional or occupational organizations, unions, political parties, churches, families, and work-centered groups. In fact, groups are ubiquitous and inevitable. But what do we mean when we discuss a group? We shall define a group as **two or more persons working together toward a common goal.**

Every business organization automatically becomes a group when more than one person works for that organization. As the organization grows, subgroups are created when the work is divided into divisions and departments.

However, an organization is more than a series of boxes on an organization chart. It is a social entity composed of individuals who form groups. Each group affects not only the behavior of its members but also that of other groups within the organization. Furthermore, the success of the organization rests on the interdependencies and relationships that exist among these groups as each performs its necessary functions. These groups are the *formal* ones which are created to work together to reach organizational goals.

Along with these formal relationships exists a complex network of *informal* groups and relationships which performs functions vital to both the organization and the people comprising these groups. As both systems—formal and informal—are necessary and have similar characteristics, we shall examine both; however, we shall concentrate mainly on the informal organization.

Why should you as a supervisor study the work group? Perhaps these four reasons will explain why:

1. The formation of groups—both formal and informal—is inevitable. Understanding the reasons for group formation and behavior is likely to make the supervisor more effective in dealing with them.
2. Work groups strongly influence the overall behavior and performance of members.
3. Group membership has both positive and negative consequences for the individual and the organization.
4. Successful supervisors are usually those who effectively achieve results not only through individuals but integrate the group into a productive team.

As you, the supervisor, are charged with the responsibility of getting the work of your department done through others—and those "others" comprise a group—these reasons are quite significant. Certainly, the topics already discussed in this book—motivation and communication, for instance—are directly related not only to the individual alone but also to the individual as he is influenced by his group.

The formal relationships imposed by the organizational structure and most definitely the social traditions and relationships of informal groups are often annoying to the supervisor. Who among us at one time or another has not wished that he could simply wave a magic wand and banish the woes and exasperations of dealing with the tangled knot of problems encountered in coping with his employees? Like so many potentially great forces, these groups when mismanaged can be destructive; likewise, understanding the force makes it possible to direct it toward constructive purposes.

BASES OF GROUP FORMATION

The first reason for studying groups, the fact that they are inevitable, leads to the question, "Why and how are groups formed?" In answering this question, emphasis will be given to the formation of informal groups rather than formal groups—the ones that result from dividing the work of the organization. It is worth noting, however, that if those responsible for the formal division of work were more aware of the reasons for informal-group formation, the supervisor's job of dealing with groups might be easier.

Need Satisfaction

As discussed in Chapter 2, individuals behave in a manner designed to satisfy their needs. Becoming part of a group helps fill three of the needs described by Maslow's hierarchy: security, social, and esteem. As Richard Muti points out in Reading Selection 11, "Informal groups are formed because they satisfy human needs." It simply isn't an accident that most of us are actively affiliated with one or more groups; rather, it is one of the ways we use to satisfy our needs.

Group membership serves to directly satisfy the social need, the desire to belong. As our society and environment become more impersonal, we search for ways to replace the closeness of the small-town gathering, the support of the entire family in frequent contact, the interaction of the community. Large organizations with endless numbers of employees, a rush atmosphere, and far-flung operations find it difficult to meld their employees into "one large family." Therefore, the sense of belonging that the employee seeks is usually lost in the vastness of the organization. The immediate work group, however, offers the individual employee more than "a number"; he receives identification as an individual, recognition for his contributions, and acceptance into an identifiable organization. Keith Davis, in Reading Selection 10, further describes the provision of social satisfaction by the informal group.

From early childhood through school days, most of us have sought to be accepted by a group; in fact, many small boys have fought battles to "earn the right" to belong to the gang. Those who failed to make it "in" were often scorned as the "outs." **Being accepted by the group gives recognition to the individual and increases his feeling of esteem and importance in the working world,** just as it does for the boy seeking to join the gang. At work, too, as in our total society, some groups are more prestigious than others. Special skills, personal attributes, or seniority may qualify one for membership in a high-status group. Seeking to further the feeling of importance leads to joining with others to make the group one of which its members can be proud. Additional esteem may be sought and gained by individuals filling leadership or special roles within the group. In fact, part of the establishment of the group includes the process of selecting members to fill certain roles; those chosen are usually accorded special importance and recognition. Surely it's no surprise that people seek the recognition and status offered by a group when so many employees fill unchallenging, routine, and unrewarding jobs.

The search for security and protection usually leads to association with others who face the same challenges. Rather than face the battle alone (and perhaps feel helpless in so doing), **the security, assistance, and protection offered by a group is sought.** Assistance may be simply lending "a helping hand" to those needing advice about the job, lending tools, or cooperating to complete a job. Need satisfaction and security against unreasonable demands from management are common group goals. In fact, a rather disunited collection of individuals may form an active, functioning group should the individuals feel that they are "mistreated" by management. Unions are often the result of a group's feeling that management may threaten its established expectations concerning fair pay, overtime, treatment of employees, and the like. When employees determine that their customs, culture, or traditions (even though loosely established) are challenged, the group forms to protect their values. Being a part of a group that will stand behind us gives us the courage to face the problem.

Interaction and Communication

Closely related to need satisfaction, but more a function of the formal division of work, is the natural interaction and communication that results when people are in contact with one another. Because of the proximity of people working together, the demands of their jobs, or their interest in company activities, employees must communicate. Doing the same or related work, for instance, forms a bond of common interest. Employees may have lunch together and discuss the problems of the morning's work, the sale missed, the breakdown of equipment, the cranky patient, or the stubborn boss. As employees continue working together and build interest and friendship bonds, communication increases.

As discussed in Chapter 6, if formal communication channels do not provide sufficient information, the informal networks are created to relieve the "information hunger" of employees. Actually, many groups are formed and continue to function because the members need to know about the organization, company plans, departmental happenings, what's expected of them, and employee attitudes. As employees interact and discuss information of mutual interest, the group is formed. Additionally, if the atmosphere of the formal organization fails to communicate to the employee that he is an important, contributing individual, he must seek that satisfaction elsewhere, namely, in the informal group.

Although Davis separates communication as a function of the informal group from social satisfaction, communication undoubtedly provides many of the social needs of the individual. Knowing what is going on and increasing our understanding of our co-workers results from interaction and socializing. As individuals find satisfaction from this association, the group becomes important to them.

Interaction, communication, common interests, and need satisfaction occur at all levels in the organization. Although there is a tendency to consider informal groups a phenomenon of operative-level employees, they exist in management as well. The functions of the group and the reasons for their existence are universal; an examination of your associations as a supervisor is likely to reveal that you, too, are a part of at least one informal group.

THE INFLUENCE OF THE GROUP

The second and third reasons for studying the group pointed out that behavior and performance are influenced by the group and emphasized that both positive and negative consequences for both the individual and the organization occur. The next logical questions to consider may be "How does the group exert its influence?" and "Just what are the consequences of group action?" This section provides some brief answers to these questions; some of the points are expanded in the reading selections in this chapter.

Enforcement of Group Standards

As we have already said, the most significant basis for group formation is fulfillment of the individual's needs for security, social acceptance, and esteem. There is, however, a "price to pay" for this need satisfaction. Groups put pressure on members to accept group standards, routine, and opinions about supervisors and the formal organization, and even select favorite eating places. In general terms, it can be said that **groups strongly influence the attitudes, beliefs, and behavior of their members.** For instance, the group may hold the attitudes that the corner office is most desirable, higher education worthwhile, Jim Jones is a good supervisor, the company cheats them, doing a good job is "right," or hour-long coffee breaks are justified. It's almost a certainty that the group will establish norms for the quality and quantity of work produced by members.

Conforming to group standards almost always leads to rewards—specifically, to acceptance by the group along with the security and esteem that accompany group membership. The person who steps outside or fails to support group standards is subject to group censure or "punishment." As this punishment may be quite severe and reduce the individual's need satisfaction, he is likely to accept the group's judgment. In fact, most research indicates that even when the individual's personal standards conflict with the desires of the group, the norms of the group prevail. Rather than face possible ostracism or "razzing," the individual accepts and conforms to the group's expectations.

The norms of the group can help *meet* the objectives of the formal organization as well as *hinder* the reaching of these goals. For instance, the salesman who produces below quota, the stenographer who delays a report, or the custodian who cleans sloppily may be regarded with disdain or even contempt by their co-workers. In many cases, companies have found that group relationships encourage low absenteeism. Employees may actually come to work, even though physically ill, just to associate with other people.

Potential Benefits to the Formal Organization

It becomes apparent, then, that the formal organization may either benefit from the group's standards or conflict with the group. Supervisors tend to look on the dark side of the issue, but it is important to recognize the benefits that the formal organization may enjoy as a result of group existence.

As indicated above, group membership may encourage such positive aspects as reduced absenteeism and favorable attitudes toward work. A stable work force may also result from group influence. When employees belong to a group, are accepted by co-workers, and enjoy satisfactory need fulfillment, they are reluctant to quit. Lower turnover reduces recruiting and training costs and usually results in a better-trained work force. Not only the individual benefits from this satisfaction of his needs, but the organization as well.

Davis notes that a closely knit work force makes communication easier. As discussed earlier, the employee may be induced to become part of a group through interaction and communication with others. However, the better communication that results from group existence may also be beneficial to the organization. Formal communication networks, plans, and policies are often tied to an inflexible organization structure. The informal group, though, may blend with formal procedures, communicate quickly, and take action immediately to get the job completed.

The supervisor who has been successful in building a cooperative group will have an easier job of managing. The group usually assumes some of the control function, making it less necessary for the supervisor to check constantly on work progress. Through cooperative efforts among members and group pressure to conform to expectations, the group insures that the job is completed. Often, in fact, supervisors find that the group is much more effective than they are in making sure that individuals perform as expected. The group may also fill in gaps in the abilities of individual members, or even of managers. With this kind of support and confidence, the goals of the organization can be more easily met.

The presence of a strong group also influences the supervisor to manage more carefully than he might otherwise. Although the pressure may seem slightly negative, the supervisor who realizes that the group will react to arbitrary or unwise action on his part usually "thinks twice" before he acts. As a result, his decisions may be more effective, as he is forced to weigh his alternatives and consider the consequences of his actions.

The influence of the group is quite significant, both to the individual and to the organization. Whether the negative or the positive aspects of group influence are felt by the organization depends upon whether the goals, attitudes, and expectations of the group are contrary to those of the organization and upon the degree to which the group can pressure members to conform.

GROUP COHESIVENESS

Continuing to examine the influence of the group and the possible positive and negative consequences of that influence leads us to examine questions suggested by the preceding section. "What determines the degree to which the group influences members?" "Should supervisors encourage strong group action?" "How can supervisors build unified groups?"

Whether or not individuals are influenced by a group may be judged by the extent to which there is a "we" feeling expressed, as opposed to an "I" feeling. The "we" feeling, or *group cohesiveness,* refers to the degree to which the members of a group desire to remain in the group. Thus, the members of a highly cohesive group, in contrast to one with a low level of cohesiveness, are more concerned with their membership and are, therefore, more strongly motivated to contribute to the group's welfare, to advance its objectives, and to participate in its activities.[1]

[1]Dorwin Cartwright and Alvin Zander, *Group Dynamics* (Third edition; New York: Harper and Row, 1968, p. 91.

Determinants of Cohesiveness

Why are some groups cohesive and others disunited? Several factors determine this:[2]

1. *Size of work group.* As the group increases in size, cohesiveness decreases—largely because of communication problems. Small groups can more easily and frequently interact.
2. *Dependence of members upon the work group.* As members receive increased and continued satisfaction from belonging to the group, cohesiveness increases.
3. *Achievement of goals.* This factor has a spiraling effect: as the group reaches its goals, it develops increased cohesiveness; more-cohesive groups tend to reach goals more easily.
4. *Status of group.* As more stature and recognition is given to the group, membership becomes more valuable to the employee. High-status group membership is often avidly sought.
5. *Management demands and pressure.* Should management make what group members deem excessive demands or threats to job security, the group jells to present a solid front. Any threat to satisfaction of group goals usually causes strong resistance.

Other important determinants of cohesiveness are:

6. *Similar work.* Those engaged in the same or similar work have a natural bond. This joint interest may be slightly less, however, if the higher earnings of one member result in lower earnings for another member.
7. *Common background.* Cultural and religious orientation, age, sex, or marital status likenesses create more natural interests and friendship bonds.
8. *Length of association.* The longer the group exists and satisfies its goals and its norms become deeply entrenched, the stronger is the attraction of the group.

When factors favoring cohesiveness are present, attractiveness of group membership increases. Cohesiveness seems quite natural when the elements of friendship, common interest, background, need satisfaction, and opportunity are present. This is not to imply that everyone will want to be a part of the group. Certainly, too, some members find more satisfaction than others from participating in group activities.

Desirability of Cohesiveness

Should the supervisor encourage cohesiveness in his work group? Much of this discussion has revolved around the benefits provided by the group, both to

[2]Adapted from James H. Donnelly, Jr., James L. Gibson, and John M. Ivancevich, *Fundamentals of Management* (Austin, Texas: Business Publications, Inc., 1971), p. 170-172.

the members and to the formal organization. The importance of building good teamwork has been emphasized. Does this mean that the supervisor should always encourage cohesiveness? There is no one answer to this question. Rather, it depends on the degree to which group goals are integrated with the goals of the formal organization.

Numerous research projects have shown that cohesive groups have certain characteristics: (1) They are either more or less productive than less cohesive groups—depending upon the norms of the group. (2) Members tend to work together smoothly with less bickering and bad feelings. (3) Morale is usually higher in the more cohesive group. However, high morale is sometimes the result of the group's achieving goals detrimental to the organization!

Therefore, **if the group's goals and activities are compatible with the efficient operation of the organization, the supervisor should encourage strong group ties.** There is also the possibility that the supervisor may be able to work toward integrating and harmonizing the goals of the formal and informal organization.

Building Cohesiveness

Should you conclude that a cohesive work group is desirable, what can be done to build such a team?

1. Identify the group. The supervisor should think and talk about the group; the use of the word "we" may help. Give the group a history and tradition. Unusual or outstanding events have undoubtedly happened in the past and will continue to occur; the group exists, and things happen to it. Recalling these events emphasizes their common bonds.

2. Set attainable group goals. Working with the group and establishing goals that can be met as a group increases its identity and purpose for existing.

"These are the fellows who really deserve the credit."

Reaching attainable goals builds a success cycle and increases the status feelings of members.

3. Give group rewards. Certainly individual contribution shouldn't be ignored, but the benefits of teamwork should be reaped by the entire group. Make sure that others in the organization recognize that the efforts of a team have been responsible for success.

4. Recognize those factors which determine group cohesiveness. While the supervisor probably couldn't (in fact, probably wouldn't want to) utilize all the factors that lead to cohesiveness, certainly he should consider their implications for his group. If he really wants to build a team, these factors are necessary.

THE QUESTION OF HARMONY

The last reason given for studying the group suggests that the most successful supervisors are those who are effective in dealing with groups. "Business organizations are founded upon the principles of teamwork, which in turn is based upon cooperation and the coordination of individual efforts."[3] Building this required teamwork and cooperation emphasizes the need to integrate group goals with organizational purposes. Unless this is accomplished, conflict—not harmony—will exist. Specifically you may ask, "How can this integration be brought about?"

The result of the integration of goals indicated in Figure 8-1 is harmony between the formal and informal organizations. Examination of each of the

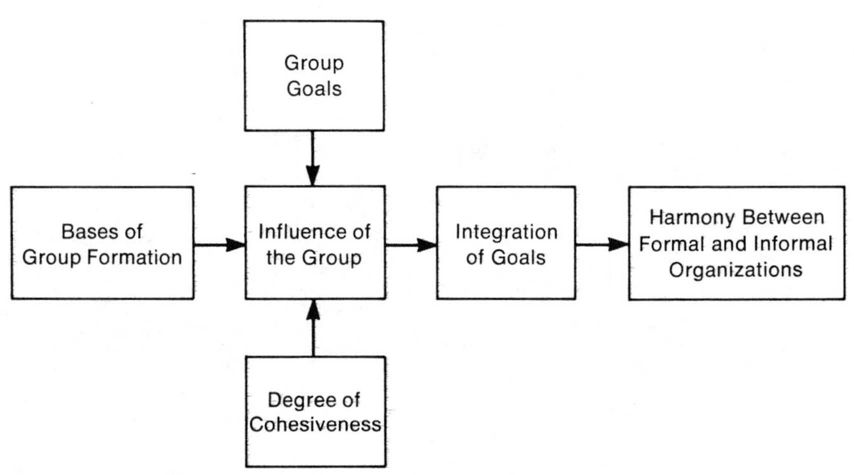

FIGURE 8-1.

[3] Leon C. Megginson, *Human Resources, Cases and Concepts* (New York: Harcourt, Brace & World, Inc., 1968), p. 38.

factors preceding such harmony—as presented in this chapter—makes it clear that this is no simple task and that no simple answer to the problem exists. In fact, harmony between the formal organization and the group isn't always possible. What is really desired is harmony when possible and integration of goals to the extent that it is feasible.

Prerequisite to the supervisor's attaining harmony in his group is the application of the behavioral principles and human skills presented throughout this book. Without careful consideration of how his people are motivated, utilization of subordinates' talents in decision making, careful initiation of change, and effective communication with his group, the supervisor may only succeed in encouraging group norms that conflict with organizational goals. As groups are formed to satisfy human needs, supervisory action that threatens this fulfillment is certain to invite defensive action by the group.

Some specific actions the supervisor may take to integrate goals should be helpful:

The supervisor must recognize that he is working with a team—a team with established standards of behavior. Rather than viewing these standards as enemies of the organization, consider them carefully for formal adoption. As mentioned earlier, group norms are often compatible with and helpful to the organization. Don't discount group standards just because of their origin; rather make the most of encouraging those which may be beneficial.

The efforts of individuals working together as a group is greater than the efforts of individuals working separately. Therefore, consider forming integrated task teams charged with the responsibility of completing an identifiable job. This proposal relates directly to the discussion of job enrichment in Chapter 3. Each member's contribution to the task becomes more important and visible to him while the group enjoys the rewards of accomplishing a goal together.

As Muti suggests, **the wise supervisor recognizes the presence of and builds a good relationship with the informal leader of the group.** All too often supervisors react (probably quite normally) to informal leaders with venom and regard them as "troublemakers." However, the opposite tack is actually the desired approach. When informal leaders exist, they usually represent the group's goals and possess influence on other members. Take time to communicate with the leader, ask his advice, and respect his position. Rather than treating him as an adversary, enlist his assistance in explaining and attaining your goals.

Take every opportunity to demonstrate to your group where they fit into the entire organization and their importance to its success. Capitalize on the need to belong, and don't leave the entire satisfaction of that desire to the group. Make the "we" feeling of the cohesive group extend to include the formal organization as well. No matter what aspect of life is considered, the fact remains that when an individual feels himself to be a needed, significant, and recognized contributor to the success of something, he becomes committed to the accomplishment of its goals. For too long the premise that success in achieving organizational goals means suppression of individual and group goals has been accepted as "just the way it is." Recognize your group for its contributions and give the members pride in their accomplishments.

Building an effective group is not an easy task; it requires dedicated, concentrated effort and understanding of your group. Whether you supervise a group in harmony with you and the organization or one specializing in destructive conflict may depend upon your skill in knowing why the group exists and what you can do about it.

Reading Selection 10

GROUP BEHAVIOR AND THE ORGANIZATION CHART*

KEITH DAVIS

Apart from the clean lines on a company's organization chart and the concise statements in the job descriptions, there is a highly interesting complex system of social relationships known as the informal organization. This organization arises from the social interactions of people. It is significant to management because of its powerful influence on productivity and job satisfaction.

Like the formal organization, the informal one has basic functions or activities. As it performs them, it develops certain abuses or problems as a natural consequence of its actions. The problems may be called the reciprocals of the function, since they arise from the function, often in proportion to the degree in which it is performed.

For example, one of the basic functions of informal groups is communication. A reciprocal that unfortunately arises therefrom is rumor. Another function is social control of members. The reciprocal is undesirable conformity.

This type of analytical framework offers a useful way to examine the role of informal structures in our complex industrial society. In the discussion that follows, however, only one principal reciprocal will be described. There are, of course, more than one.

The informal communication system is familiarly known as the grapevine,[1] and rumor, the reciprocal, is defined as the injudicious or untrue part of the grapevine.

Rumor is a devastating disease that sweeps through an organization as fast as a summer storm—and usually with as much damage. Consequently, management must not only be prepared to deal with it, but must know how and what to do. It is a serious mistake to strike at the whole grapevine merely because it happens to be the agent which

*From *Advanced Management—Office Executive,* (June, 1962), pp. 14-18. Reprinted with permission.

[1]For further details, see Keith Davis, "Making Constructive Use of the Office Grapevine," American Management Association, *Office Management Series,* No. 142(1956), pp. 25-35; and Keith Davis, "Management Communication and the Grapevine," *Harvard Business Review,* (Sept.-Oct., 1953), pp. 43-49.

carries rumor. That approach would be as injudicious as throwing away a typewriter because of a misspelled word.

The best approach when dealing with rumor is to get at its causes—the preventive approach. Trying to kill the rumor after it has already started is a tardy, curative approach. . . .

IT MAY MEAN SOMETHING ELSE

. . . A second function of informal organization is to provide social satisfaction. Informal organizations give a man recognition, status, and further opportunity to relate to others.

In a large office an employee may feel like only a payroll number, but his informal group gives him personal attachment and status. With his group, he is somebody, even though in the formal structure he is only one of a thousand clerks. He may not look forward to posting 750 accounts daily, but the informal group can give more meaning to his day. When he can think of meeting his friends, eating with them, and sharing their jokes, his day takes on a new dimension that erases any disagreeableness or routine in his work.

Of course, these conditions can work in reverse: A group may not accept a worker, thereby making his work more disagreeable and driving him to transfer, or to be absent, or to resign. These are reciprocals of the social satisfaction function. However, the main reciprocal which tends to develop is role conflict.

The quest for group satisfactions often leads members away from organizational objectives and, hence, into a role conflict in which formal and informal roles are pulling against each other. For example, a motivated employee may want to be productive in his role of employee, but he may also want to be the less-productive "good Joe" in his role as a fellow worker with others—hence, two roles in conflict.

PERFECT HARMONY NOT FEASIBLE

Much of this role conflict can be avoided by carefully cultivating mutual interests with informal groups. The more the interests, goals, methods, and evaluation systems of formal and informal organizations can be integrated, the more productivity and satisfaction can be expected. However, there must always be some formal and informal differences. This is not an area where perfect harmony is feasible.

An interesting example of role conflict is one in which two electricians used an unusual situation to gain informal status with their peers and with a staff engineer—an attempt in which glory soon faded!

A young electrical engineer was assigned the job of mapping the underground cable system of a shipyard which, after five years of abandonment, had been taken over by a new chemical firm. No blueprints of the cable system were included in the property transfer, and management was unable to discover any. The only visible evidence was locations where cables entered and left the ground.

Two plant electricians at the chemical firm had formerly worked at the shipyard, and the engineer went to them to see if they remembered any of the cable paths. Preliminary discussion and a tour of the grounds indicated that the electricians could be helpful, so the engineer started working with them regularly.

To establish rapport with the two electricians, the engineer frequently bought them morning and afternoon snacks, and engaged them in long bull sessions and in walks around the grounds. He felt, too, that this practice jogged their memories and helped them recall the cable paths.

DELIGHTED WITH NEW STATUS

The electricians were delighted with their new status and importance, so much so that their memories of the cable paths seemed slower and slower, though still surprisingly accurate. Meanwhile, spurred by a completion date, the engineer worked even harder to be nice to them.

One day the engineer was with the electricians when an emergency occurred requiring knowledge of a cable location not yet found. One of the electricians, without thinking, walked over to his locker and unrolled the complete original set of blueprints of the electrical cable system remarking as he found the cable in question, "Here it is, Joe, right by the north end of number 7 shop." At this point, he looked up and saw the engineer five feet away!

A third function of informal organization is social control by which the behavior of others is influenced and regulated to help the group achieve its satisfactions. Social control is both internal and external. Internal control is directed toward making members of the group conform to its culture. In an accounting office, for instance, an employee wore a bow tie to work. Comments and "razzing" from other workers soon convinced him a bow tie was not an accepted style in the group, so thereafter he did not wear it.

External control is directed toward those outside the group, such as management, union leadership, or other informal groups. Pressures of external control can be quite strong, as when a walkout strike occurs.

SUPPOSED EVILS OF CONFORMITY

Although social control is necessary, its undesirable reciprocal is conformity. Much has been written in fiction and nonfiction[2] about the supposed evils of conformity as it has developed within formal organizations. In both cases, writers have tended to assume that, since conformity existed in formal organizations, the formal organizations were the cause of it.

However, the informal organization appears to be an equal cause of employee conformity. Certainly the informal culture can be just as brutal in its demands for conformity as formal organizations can be. Evidence the fads and fashions of teen-age speech and conduct, and the work restrictions in the factory.

There are two types of conformity—action and attitude. Uniformity of action is called group standards. Standards are essential to coordinate large work groups, and where standards derive from the work requirements themselves, there seem to be no overtones of conformity. Only when standards are arbitrarily required does the charge of conformity arise. Although business and government certainly do have some arbitrary conformity, much of what appears to be conformity is simply a requirement of the work process itself, but is not understood as such by the employee. No human boss arbitrarily requires employees to conform.

MUCH EVIDENCE TO THE CONTRARY

In fact, business organizations are known for their encouragement of initiative and difference. They have been one of the strongest world-wide supporters of individuality. There is little evidence that conformity is a hallmark of business culture, as compared with government, church, or labor unions. But there is much evidence to the contrary in the business record of innovation, research, and employee advancement.

One study of managers, for example, showed that those who were

[2]See, for example, William H. Whyte, Jr., *The Organization Man* (New York, Simon and Schuster, 1956).

different (idiosyncratic) were regarded as superior administrators. Another study reported that managers who valued conformity least were rated most effective as managers.[3]

A more serious matter is conformity of action away from work. Here, again, formal organizations do not seem to be the main influence.

The most serious conformity is of attitude. If attitude conformity can be induced, then man loses his individuality, and he can be manipulated by unscrupulous leaders. Group requirements for attitude consistency are known as norms, and the group whose norms a person accepts is a reference group, whether he belongs to it or not. Informal norms and reference groups are a powerful force in work society. They consistently guide opinion and wield power contrary to the leadership of formal management or formal union.

The great danger of informal group conformity is not its dull loss of personal difference, which is bad enough, but rather that the members become subject to the willful control of the informal leader who can skillfully manipulate them for bad as well as for good.

The informal leader is a leader in just as strong a sense as a formal leader is, but without the controls and weight of responsibility which constrain the formal leader. In this fashion the informal group becomes a prime instrument of manipulators and inciters of conflict who move into the informal structures of society to influence people toward their selfish ends.

In short, people themselves may be the chief cause of their own conformity—rather than their bosses, as current writers would have us believe. Indeed, informal organizations can be just as autocratic, destructive, and conforming as formal ones. This possibility is to be expected: both groups are made up of people—often of the same people!

A fourth function of informal groups is to perpetuate their culture. This function helps preserve the group's integrity and values. As a reciprocal, there develops a resistance to change—a tendency to perpetuate the status quo and to stand like a rock in the face of change. What has been good *is good and shall be good!*

If, for example, job A has always had more status than job B, then job A must continue to have more status—and more pay—even though conditions have changed to make job A inferior to B by other standards. If restriction of productivity was necessary in the past with an autocratic management, then it is necessary now, even though the management is becoming participative.

BOUND BY CONVENTION

Although informal organizations are bound by no chart on the wall, they are bound by convention, custom, and culture. Whenever managers deal with change, they especially need to understand informal organization, because the resistance will be a key to the success or failure of the change. In fact, fear of change can be as significantly disrupting as change itself, because the former reproduces identical anxieties and reactions.

That an informal group is made up of persons with high I.Q.'s or advanced degrees does not necessarily mean the group will better understand and accept change. Often the opposite is true, because the group uses its extra intelligence to rationalize *more* reasons why a change should not be made.

The more intelligent the group is, the more reasons it can find for opposing a change. Intelligence can be used either for or against change, depending on how management

[3]Edwin E. Ghiselli, "Individuality as a Factor in the Success of Management Personnel," *Personnel Psychology* (Spring 1960), pp. 1-10; and Edwin A. Fleishman and David R. Peters, "Interpersonal Values, Leadership Attitudes, and Managerial 'Success' " (Yale Univ., unpublished manuscript, 1961).

motivates the group. Often, therefore, intelligent high-level groups cannot be sold new methods as easily as average groups can be.

To summarize, each of the key functions of informal organization brings with it certain abuses or problems as reciprocals. The work environment might be better without these reciprocals, but managers learned long ago that informal organization cannot be abolished, starved, or hidden under a basket. It is here to stay, and the reciprocals are part of the package.

All the manager can do is develop a mature understanding of informal organization and chart his course toward minimizing the abuses and maximizing the benefits. Informal groups can be blended with formal organizations to make an immensely workable system for getting the job completed.

Reading Selection 11

THE INFORMAL GROUP— WHAT IT IS AND HOW IT CAN BE CONTROLLED*

RICHARD S. MUTI

When Joe Simpson reported for his first day of work at the Wilson plant, Harry Eaton, the shop supervisor, introduced him to the ten men he'd be working with in the die shop. After a brief tour of the shop, Simpson settled down at his machine, anxious to begin the day's work. By mid-morning, he had turned out half his day's quota of dies, and it seemed a cinch that he'd beat the standard output by at least a hundred. Not bad for the first day on the job, he thought. But he wondered why the standards were set so low. It didn't seem right that a new man should be able to step in on the first day and exceed the output that the company had set for its more seasoned workers. He shrugged it off, and continued to turn out the dies at an even pace.

Just before noon, Ed Morgan, one of his coworkers in the shop, stopped at Simpson's machine.

"Hey, Speedy Gonzales, you got a light," said Morgan, taking a cigarette and offering the pack to Simpson.

Simpson laughed. "Sure," he said. He stopped work and accepted one of the cigarettes, happy for the pause and grateful for Morgan's friendly gesture. After both cigarettes were lit, Morgan spoke first.

"What do you think of Eaton, the supervisor?" Morgan asked.

"He seems like a real nice guy," replied Simpson.

Morgan grunted. "It's all an act, believe me. He'd sooner turn you in than look at you. You've got to watch what you say around him. He's a 'company man' all the way."

"Oh," said Simpson.

"You know, I've been watching you all morning, Joe," said Morgan. "You're going to kill yourself the way you've been working. You ought to slow down and take it easy like the

*From *Personnel Journal* (August, 1968), pp. 563-571. Reprinted with permission.

rest of us. Say, you don't own part of this company, do you?"

Simpson laughed. "No," he said, "but I could sure use some of that bonus money they pay for beating the standard."

"We all could use the money, Joe, but don't you see what'll happen? We all start turning in work over the standard and, sure, they'll pay us the bonus for a while, but then what happens. The first thing you know, they go and raise the standard on you. Then where are you—breaking your back, turning out more work for the same money you got in the first place. It doesn't make sense, does it?"

"You know," said Simpson, "I never thought of that before."

"Listen, kid," said Morgan, "You'll do all right around here. Stick with me and I'll teach you the ropes in no time. Say, why don't you come to lunch with me and the guys. We always go to this little place around the corner."

"Say, that'd be great," said Simpson.

"See you later," Morgan said as he walked off, "and remember—*slow down.*"

Simpson turned to his machine and began work again. That Morgan is quite a guy, he thought. He really knows what the score is. He unconsciously settled back into the same, efficient pace, punching out the dies with an easy economy of motion. But after a few minutes, he caught himself, and slowed his pace noticeably. He looked up from his machine at the faces of his coworkers. They were all smiling at him, nodding their heads in approval.

Joe Simpson has just been introduced to an informal group. He has met the group's leader, Ed Morgan, who set him straight on what the group thinks of Harry Eaton, the supervisor, what the group feels is a fair day's work, and where the group likes to eat lunch together. In time, Simpson will be taught all the group's norms and values. The pressures to conform will be great, probably too great for an average man like Simpson to resist.

The situation described above is fictional, of course. There is no "Wilson plant," as such. But the exchange between Simpson and Morgan, with only the names changed, probably takes place many times daily in the plants and factories across the country. A new man joining a small work force is taught the informal group's standards and norms, instructed in the proper attitude to have, and given time to conform, or else. It occurs at every level. Shop space or office space, blue collar or white collar, manager or operator—every echelon of American business is rife with informal groups.

Not every informal group is antagonistic toward management, as was the case in the die shop at the Wilson plant. Indeed, some groups can be extremely cooperative, policing their members with regard to tardiness or absenteeism, or even exceeding managerial demands for output. For example, a group of salesmen might have as its goal high sales, the higher the better. Management might do well to cultivate such a group, to encourage its growth and strength. An informal group can also be neutral, with goals purely social in nature. Caution is necessary in dealing with neutral informal groups. By restricting fulfillment of the group's social needs, management can easily turn a neutral group into an antagonistic group, at odds with the company at every ground.[1]

ORIGINS OF THE STUDY OF INFORMAL GROUPS

Not until the early 1900's did management really begin to recognize

[1] Robert Dubin, *Human Relations in Administration* (Englewood Cliffs, N.J., 1961), pp. 84-85.

the existence of informal groups. The problem of restricted output was perceived as early as 1911 by Frederick W. Taylor. He and other scientific managers felt that the problem could be solved by having management, rather than the workers, determine production rates.[2] Time-study men went to work to help management set production standards, but they probably only increased the workers' determination to regulate output, since retiming of a job almost always meant a cut in pay. Workers felt, especially during the depression, that by working slowly, they could make their job last longer. It was, for them, a defensive device to protect them from the whims of management. It indicated a basic distrust between management and the workers.

Henri Fayol, one of the leading proponents of the Universalist school of management, felt that the interests of the company should prevail over the informal group. In 1916, he stated that combating the ignorance, ambition, selfishness, laziness, and weaknesses that cause the interests of the company to be lost sight of is "one of the great difficulties of management." He suggested three ways to effect this subordination of the individual to the company: firmness and good example on the part of superiors, agreements as fair as is possible, and constant supervision.[3]

Although Taylor and Fayol were among the first to identify informal groups, their studies contributed little to the understanding of group structure and behavior. There were still many unanswered questions. Why did informal groups exist? How were they formed? What factors affected group behavior? The first really definitive study of the informal group was the bank wiring room phase of the Hawthorne Experiments, which began in November, 1931. This study stands today as one of the major accomplishments in this field. It exposed for the first time the inner workings and hidden mechanisms of the informal group, and for this reason, it is dealt with in some detail here.

In this phase of the Hawthorne Experiments, fourteen male operators in the bank wiring room of the Western Electric Company were observed during the period November, 1931, through May, 1932. An observer, stationed with the group, followed certain rules to gain the group's acceptance. He assumed no formal authority, he tried to be noncommittal in any argument, he respected all confidence, he tried not to be overimposing in gathering information, and he became, through speech and behavior, as much a part of the group as possible.[4]

The observer found that the fourteen workers had an intricate, informal social organization of their own. There were sub-groups, cliques, and isolated individuals. The personal relationships of each operator in this informal organization "determined to a large degree his status in the group, the expectations of the other members, and the kinds of satisfactions and expectations he had of himself."[5]

[2]Loren Baritz, *The Servants of Power* (Middleton, Conn., 1960), p. 96.

[3]Henri Fayol, "General Principles of Management—From Division of Work to Espirit de Corps," in *The World of Business,* ed. by Edward C. Bursk, Donald T. Clark, and Ralph W. Hidy (New York, 1962), p. 1691.

[4]F. J. Roethlisberger and William J. Dickson, *Management and the Worker* (Cambridge, Mass., 1956), pp. 388-389.

[5]Baritz, pp. 92-93.

The group set standards of behavior for its members, and enforced its standards by using ridicule, sarcasm, or "binging"[6] to keep its members in the fold. They also set standards of production. By adjusting production reports, the group effectively circumvented the "bogey"[7] set by management. The workers liked to have some completed work saved up and ready to turn in on days when output was low. Consequently, they reported a consistent output that often differed from the actual output.[8]

In an attempt to explain differences in output among individual operators, dexterity and intelligence tests were administered to the group. The lowest producer of the group ranked first in intelligence and third in dexterity. It was concluded that no direct relationship between performance and ability to perform as determined by dexterity or intelligence tests existed.[9]

The sentiments of the group were: (a) don't be a "rate buster," (b) do your share of the work; don't be a "chiseler," (c) don't be a "squealer," and (d) don't put on airs (i.e., if you are an inspector, don't act like one).[10] At first glance, it would seem that the group was antagonistic toward management. But the researchers point out that, in fact, there was no conscious effort on the part of the workers to oppose management.[11] The workers were not hostile toward management; the Western Electric Company had a reputation of being very fair with its employees. The restriction of output in the bank wiring room could not be blamed on poor management or inefficiency, either. Actually, the bank wiring group's output compared most favorably with similar work of other companies. What, then, caused the regulation of output? The researchers concluded that "noneconomic motives, interests, and processes, as well as economic, are fundamental in behavior in business."[12]

The findings of the bank wiring room phase of the Hawthorne Experiments created great interest in human relations in industry. It seemed that management had two alternatives—either change the informal group's thinking so that it paralleled management's or neutralize the group's power to control standards. Perhaps a better understanding between management and workers could more closely align the logic and sentiments of the informal organization to the formal organization. By asking for suggestions

[6]Roethlisberger, p. 421. "Binging" is a physical attempt to control workers who deviated. It was used to regulate the output of the faster workers. The observer in the wire bank room remarked, "one of them walked up to another man and hit him as hard as he could on the upper arm. The one hit made no protest, and it seems that it was his privilege to "bing" the one who hit him. He was free to retaliate with one blow. One of the objects of the game is to see who can hit the hardest. But it is also used as a penalty."

[7]Roethlisberger, p. 418. "Bogey" is the standard output as determined by management. Wire bank workers feared that if they consistently met the bogey or exceeded it, management would raise the bogey or cut the piece rate, causing an operator to work harder to make the same pay.

[8]Roethlisberger, p. 426.

[9]Roethlisberger, pp. 442-443.

[10]Roethlisberger, p. 522.

[11]Roethlisberger, p. 535.

[12]Roethlisberger, p. 557.

and criticisms, the workers could have had a more active role in the decisions concerning them. The Hawthorne experimenters, more closely attuned to management policies, failed to adequately explain the informal organization, merely terming the workers' behavior as irrational.

The work of many early human relations experimenters is suspect. Many of them believed that industrial cooperation meant that labor should do as management said. Elton Mayo, the head researcher at Hawthorne, failed to recognize that the informal organizations of workers may have been necessary antidotes to an overbearing management. In fact, the Mayo school barely touched on the idea that management, itself, was filled with informal organizations, that managers, just like workers, could act "emotionally and irrationally." This anti-labor, pro-management attitude of Mayo and his colleagues has caused much of their work to be severely criticized by some social scientists.

Management's reaction to the informal group at odds with formal policy was limited. Either the group had to be destroyed or its thinking changed. The bank wiring experiment showed that the group's power exceeded management's. It seemed that the second alternative—promoting friendly informal groups—would more likely meet with success. Amid cries of manipulation, management sought to encourage groups to think constructively along managerial lines.

Sociometry, the study of personal likes and dislikes, provided a technique for greater understanding of informal associations. In 1934, Jacob L. Moreno introduced this technique of learning about the group through study of its individuals. Using this approach, it became possible to "speak of the degree of cohesiveness of a specific group and to make comparisons between one group and another."[13] Sociometry asked questions of individuals such as: whom do you like best, least in your shop? whom do you like to work with best, least? A sociometric map or sociogram provided a means of displaying these social choices of the shop workers.

In a further attempt to understand group behavior, several men tried to classify the informal work group. Elton Mayo and George F. Lombard formed three classifications. The "natural" group, composed of six or seven members, functioned automatically, unguided by supervision. The "family" group, about thirty members, had a core of regulars that provided an example for the other members. The "organized" group was large and had a direct relationship with management (e.g., the "whole factory" concept).[14]

Leonard R. Sayles probably came closest to a realistic classification of informal work groups. He placed the groups into four basic categories. The "*apathetic*" groups are those least likely to make complaints or to join together to pressure management. They are characterized by a dispersed leadership, not clearly identified or accepted, internal frictions that cause low cohesion, and undercurrent of discontent, but little action to change things. Their jobs are usually in a noisy environment, with little interaction between members.

The "*erratic*" groups are easily incensed over minor, insignificant issues, or can remain inactive when confronted with more important grievances. When they do take action, they are poorly controlled and inconsistent. This type of work group is most susceptible to conversion to good relations with management. They have a strong, independent leadership, but high turnover lessens their cohesiveness. Their jobs consist mainly of crew

[13]Baritz, p. 177.

[14]Dubin, pp. 88-89.

operations or groups performing similar tasks.

The "*strategic*" groups are the shrewd instigators, searching for loopholes, comparing economic benefits, reacting to unfavorable management decisions. They are highly cohesive groups with a strong leadership that uses group pressure tactics to best advantage. Men in the strategic groups are the most active union participators. They maintain high work standards in their jobs, which usually consist of crew or assembly type operations.

The "*conservative*" groups are composed of highly skilled workers with high status, engaged in individual operations throughout the plant. They are the most stable, most likely to give warning before taking any action. They are least likely to be union participators. Members of the conservative groups are characterized by self-assurance, success, and patience.[15]

CHARACTERISTICS OF THE INFORMAL GROUP

A small group can be defined as two or more people who interact with one another in face-to-face relations over an extended period of time, who differentiate themselves in some way from others around them, who are conscious of belonging to the group, and whose relations with one another are taken as an end in itself.[16] It's impossible to set an upper limit on group membership. The only limiting factor is that all members must have direct personal contact with one another. This would probably necessitate a group no larger than fifteen or twenty members.

Informal groups are formed because they satisfy human needs. Every human being has a need for companionship, for identification. This need to belong is most easily satisfied at one's own level. One needs understanding from one's friends to combat life's frustrations and tensions. The informal group provides answers for its members; it serves as a "guide to correct behavior." It helps solve work problems. Teamwork can get the job done more easily and enjoyably, and can promote either efficiency or work restriction. Protection for its membership is another function of the informal group. There is strength in numbers—strength to resist changes, or to fight managerial demands for greater production. The methods the group uses to oppose management can vary from merely cutting down on the work pace to outright sabotage of the work.[17]

Satisfying these individual needs of belonging, prestige, recognition, etc., is the primary function of the informal group. The informal group is a natural unit in which work decisions and judgments are reached. It provides an atmosphere for testing new procedures, and creates standards of conduct for its members.

Group standards of behavior pervade the informal social organization. They can take many forms—eating lunch together, following certain customs to make the job easier, and regulating production, to name a few. Management may either benefit or suffer from the group's standards and group pressure to conform. It depends on how close the goals of the group are to the goals of management.

"There are also group standards of attitude—or norms."[18] "This job is great," or, "that foreman should be fired," are examples of what group norms might be. These attitudes could

[15]Dubin, pp. 90-95.

[16]Bernard Berelson and Gary A. Steiner, *Human Behavior* (New York, 1964), p. 325.

[17]Leonard R. Sayles and George Strauss, *Personnel* (Englewood Cliffs, N.J., 1960), pp. 56-60.

[18]Sayles, p. 65.

be completely unfounded, but to the group they are real, and management must recognize they exist.

The group member experiences certain pressures to conform to group standards and norms. The individual point of view becomes aligned with the group's point of view, and since the group satisfies the member's social needs, he accepts the group's goals. He wants to be "well regarded" by the other members. A member who exceeds the group's accepted level of output may find himself ostracized. Any deviation from group standards may cause the member to be isolated, given the "silent treatment." He may be left out of group activities. More direct methods of pressuring the individual to conform include letting management know of the deviant's "mistakes", flooding his desk with work, or even sabotaging his equipment.

The enforcement of group standards and norms is a four phased operation. First the new man is educated. He learns what the group expects of him. Then he is watched by all the group members to see if he conforms. He is bound to make mistakes, and for any deviation, a warning is given, and surveillance continued. Finally, disciplinary or rewarding actions ensue.[19]

The sum total of forces acting on group members, causing them to remain a part of the group, is called group cohesiveness. As cohesiveness increases, so does the power of the group over the individual increase. There is more pressure to conform.[20] Many factors affect group cohesion. Size is one factor. The smaller the group, usually, the more cohesive it will be. Lack of homogeneity will decrease cohesion. There will be a tendency for sub-groups and cliques to form, made up of members with like interests and backgrounds. Easy communications between the members and physical isolation of the group from other groups will both increase cohesion.

Supervisory practices can influence cohesion. For example, if management promotes competition between group members, there will be a lessening of cohesion. Likewise, rewarding team work builds cohesion. Outside pressure is a factor. Threats from outsiders result in increased cohesiveness that tends to remain, even after the danger or inequity is removed. Successful group ventures, which cause the group's status as a unit to increase, also build cohesiveness.[21] Other contributing factors are a high degree of dependency upon the group, stability of the group, the presence of ritual in the daily contacts of the members, and strong leadership.[22]

The group's leader tends to be the member who most closely conforms to the group's standards and norms, or the one who has the most information and skill related to the group's activities. The leader must enable the members to achieve their private goals as well as the group's goals. Consequently, leadership must simultaneously satisfy two conflicting needs of the group—that for initiative and guidance, and that for harmony and mutual acceptance. Often, a leader may begin by satisfying both these needs, but before long, he can effectively assume only one of these roles.[23] "As a result, there are often two leaders: a task or work leader and a

[19]Joseph A. Litterer, *The Analysis of Organization* (New York, 1965), pp. 110-111.

[20]Richard P. Calhoon, *Managing Personnel* (New York, 1963), p. 480.

[21]Sayles, pp. 74-76.

[22]Litterer, pp. 92-100.

[23]Berelson, pp. 343-345.

social-emotional specialist."[24] When given the choice, most leaders prefer the popular role. The controlling role loses its player popularity.

The informal leader can sometimes mold and change the group's goals and norms. When he speaks, the group listens, and is influenced. But if he tries to change things too fast, he can lose his leadership role.

Informal groups overlap. People belong to a number of informal groups, a fact which sometimes causes conflicts and stress. When an individual is a member of two conflicting groups, he will experience emotional strain, which he will attempt to reduce by resolving the conflict in favor of the group to which he is most closely tied.[25]

MANAGING THE INFORMAL GROUP

The first step in any scientific method is defining the problem. Managing the informal group begins just as basically. Management must first recognize that informal groups exist. Once this is acknowledged, management should gather as much information as possible about the existing groups. Who belongs to which informal groups? What are the goals of the different groups? Are they opposed to the company's goals? What are the operating techniques of the groups? How cohesive are they? On-the-spot managers are probably in the best position to find out this information. They should be trained in group behavior and human relations so they may deal more effectively with the informal groups they supervise.[26] The supervisor is the key to good management-informal group relations.

The supervisor can gain cooperation only by respecting the group's standards and norms. Supervisors have been characterized as the "men in the middle." They are formal leaders, but must rely on more than the authority of the formal organization to get successful results. They must build acceptance of themselves by the informal group, and, in effect, attain some portion of the role of informal leader. Formal authority alone will not be enough to give the formal leader sufficient influence.

A good supervisor knows what the group expects of him, and adjusts his behavior accordingly. He makes *fair* demands of the group. He must emphasize "getting the job done," rather than use authority for its own sake. Rules imposed on the group should be reasonable. Time honored customs should be respected whenever possible, although there are times when such customs are in direct conflict with managerial desires. At such times, action should be taken to thwart the custom, but perhaps not by frontal assault. Management must weigh the implications carefully before taking a position at odds with the accepted practices of the group.

More positive action would be to give the informal group an opportunity to participate in decision making. Group discussion of problems can gain acceptance for decisions. Management seems least willing to give the group decision making powers in production areas: output standards, production planning, use of equipment, changes in technology. It seems more willing to let the group handle areas like absenteeism, tardiness, health, and discipline. It is most willing to let the group decide in areas

[24]Litterer, p. 116.

[25]Berelson, p. 329.

[26]George S. Odiorne, "Put Cliques to Work For You," *Nations Business* (August, 1958), pp. 50-53.

where there is a common goal, like accident prevention.

"Letting the group decide on its own production goals is the most certain way of getting the group to accept them."[27] Of course, management cannot be certain the group will make the right decision. Whether the decision is left to the group depends on what management knows about the group. Are they hostile to the company? If this were the case, they certainly wouldn't be given decision making powers in an area as vital as production. But if the group is not openly antagonistic, management would be wise to let the group take an active role in decision making. "The mere fact that the group is given the power to enforce and implement rules makes the group more likely to accept the rules themselves, even rules to which they might otherwise object."[28] If management does give some decision making powers to the informal group, it is most important that the gesture be sincere. The group can readily detect insincerity. Nothing could be more detrimental to promoting good relations with the group than taking a patronizing attitude.

Encouraging group discussion and decision making will help to develop group responsibility. Unimportant and trivial jobs increase the group's feeling of irresponsibility. Management must build group responsibility by making the job more important, or at least, by making the people in the job feel more important. Allocating work assignments at the group level, decentralization, and decreasing specialization will result in added group responsibility, and ultimately increase the effectiveness of a cooperative group.

"Leaders of small groups tend to direct the group's activities along lines at which they themselves are proficient and away from those areas where they are less competent."[29] Management should give informal leaders a chance to gain recognition by working with rather than against management. Build good relations with the informal leader—pass information to him, ask his advice, have him train others. But beware of the dangers. It is sometimes hard to identify the group leader. The group spokesman is not necessarily the leader. There may be different leaders for different group functions. A close management-leader relationship may cause the leader to lose status (and eventually, his leadership role) in the group. He could get the reputation of being a "company man." This could happen if the leader were asked to deviate from the group's norms. It is important not to build cooperation so far that it becomes favoritism.

Should management try to build cohesiveness? There is no clear answer to this question. Cohesive groups display teamwork, higher morale, lower turnover and absenteeism, and are easier to supervise. But high cohesive groups may not readily accept new employees. They may not cooperate well with outsiders. Consequently, competition and hard feelings between rival groups can develop. Does high cohesiveness increase productivity? Studies show that a highly cohesive group produces either somewhat higher than the average or somewhat lower, depending on the attitudes of the group. Cohesiveness means that the group members will follow more closely the group's norms, be they beneficial or not to the company.

If the group is cooperative, or even neutral, management should obviously try to encourage cohesion. The use of sociometrics to avoid the formation of sub-groups and cliques is one tactic. Helping to bring isolated individuals into the group will increase each employee's identification with the group. Stability promotes cohe-

[27]Henry Clay Smith, *Psychology of Industrial Behavior* (New York, 1964), p. 155.

[28]Sayles, p. 167.

[29]Berelson, p. 343.

sion, so management might cut down on transfers in and out of the group. When new workers are assigned to the group, a "big brother" type system to help them gain acceptance more quickly would contribute to cohesion. Group piece rates rather than individual piece rates develop teamwork and cohesion.[30]

If management feels that compatibility between informal and formal goals is not possible, it should work toward weakening or destroying the group. This could be accomplished by moving personnel about, particularly the informal leaders. Stressing dealing with individuals rather than the group will lessen cohesiveness. Since group standards will be strengthened in areas where external standards are weak,[31] beefing up company policies and standards may be necessary in some areas.

Resistance to change by the informal group can be disastrous to a company in an industry where change is imperative. "But we've always done it this way," is the cry most often heard. This resistance is natural. We all fear the unknown, and that is basically what change is. Therefore, if it wants to get a change accepted, management must furnish accurate and meaningful information about company plans through either formal or informal channels. The group should be informed why management made a decision that concerns them. Any objections from the group should be cleared up as quickly as possible. A trivial matter unattended to could lead to more deep-seated problems.[32] It is usually more effective to try to influence people as group members rather than as individuals. Even so, it is still difficult to change the group, because of the support members receive from each other.

CONCLUSIONS

The existence of informal groups within formal organizations can no longer be ignored. They must be dealt with effectively—on friendly, cooperative terms, if possible, or on decisive, not-so-friendly terms, if necessary. Cooperation between formal and informal organization is desirable. Lower turnover and absenteeism, higher morale, higher production—these are the rewards when a strong, highly cohesive group's goals are closely attuned to managerial goals. If this is the case, management should do all it can to create a permissive atmosphere for the formation of informal groups. If an informal group is antagonistic to the company, management should try its best to change the group's attitude. But failing in that, it should attempt to weaken or destroy the power of the group.

Effective action is impossible without a thorough knowledge and understanding of informal groups at all managerial levels. Managers should be trained in group behavior and human relations. This is especially important at the supervisory level, where day to day encounters take place.

Above all, it is important that management, itself, maintain an open-minded realistic attitude about informal groups, and not be led into the trap of thinking that management is always right, the group always wrong. If there is a better way to do something, the group will probably be the first to find it. Informal groups perform necessary functions—they satisfy human needs. Management should help satisfy these human needs whenever possible, thereby encouraging group goals and company goals to coincide.

[30] Sayles, pp. 178-179.

[31] Berelson, p. 334.

[32] John T. Doutt, "Management Must Manage The Informal Group Too," *Advanced Management* (May, 1959), pp. 26-28.

Of course, there will always be a gap between manager and worker. Understanding is the only power that can fill that gap.

QUESTIONS FOR REVIEW AND DISCUSSION

1. How does a knowledge of why groups are formed and exist assist the supervisor?
2. "Informal groups form because the formal organization is viewed by the group as being illogical, inefficient, and immature." What is your reaction to this comment?
3. From your own experiences, recall why a group to which you have belonged came into existence. What benefits did you receive from this group membership?
4. Why might an individual choose not to join an informal group?
5. In what ways does the informal group differ from the formal work group?
6. a. As the supervisor cannot fully control the informal group, is he responsible for any problems which may arise from its action?
   b. Should the supervisor attempt to become a part of the informal group?
7. a. Have groups formed within your class?
   b. From your observations, what do you believe to be the bases for their formation?
8. Davis describes an undesirable reciprocal of each group function. Does the presence of these reciprocals negate the benefits that arise from the group functions?
9. Members of groups perform certain roles within the group. From your own experiences, relate how you came to fill a role within a group.
10. a. What functions may the informal leader of the group perform?
    b. How does one become the leader?
11. a. Should management encourage cohesiveness in the work group?
    b. If so, what factors should be introduced to encourage cohesiveness?
12. Do you belong to a group which is cohesive? If so, why do you believe it to be so?
13. "Success breeds success." How does this adage apply to group cohesiveness?
14. a. Recall a personal experience or observation of a group's rewarding an individual member who supported the group's standards of behavior.
    b. Recall an experience or observation of a group's "punishment" of a member who did not meet the group's norms.
15. How can the supervisor integrate the goals of the formal and informal organizations?
16. Muti suggests that supervisors should attempt to destroy groups that are "anti-organization."
    a. Do you agree or disagree with this proposal? Why?
    b. What may be the consequences of attempting to break up a group?

SUGGESTED ADDITIONAL READINGS

Brown, J.A.C. "The Informal Organization of Industry," *The Social Psychology of Industry*. Baltimore: Penguin Books, Inc., 1954. Also see Robert A.

Sutermeister. *People and Productivity.* Second Edition. New York: McGraw-Hill Book Company, 1969., p. 305.

Likert, Rensis. "Group Processes and Organizational Performance," *New Patterns in Management.* New York: McGraw-Hill Book Company, 1961, pp. 26-43. See also *Human Relations in Management,* S. G. Huneryager and I. L. Heckmann, editors. Second edition. Cincinnati: South-Western Publishing Company, 1967, p. 622.

Seashore, Stanley E. "Group Cohesiveness in the Industrial Work Group: Summary and Conclusions," *Group Cohesiveness in the Work Group.* Ann Arbor, Michigan: The University of Michigan Press, 1954, Ch. 7, pp. 97-102. See also Rober A. Sutermeister. *People and Productivity.* Second Edition. New York: McGraw-Hill Book Company, 1969, p. 330.

Stagner, Ross. "Motivational Aspects of Industrial Morale," *Personnel Psychology,* Vol. II, 1958, pp. 64-70. See also Robert A. Sutermeister, *People and Productivity.* Second Edition. New York: McGraw-Hill Book Company, 1969, p. 343.

Stieglitz, Harold. "What's Not on the Organization Chart," *The Conference Board Record.* November 1964, pp. 7-10. See also Keith Davis and William G. Scott. *Human Relations and Organizational Behavior: Readings and Comments.* New York: McGraw-Hill Book Company, 1969, p. 174.

CASES AND ROLE-PLAYING EXERCISES

INTRODUCTION TO THE STUDY OF CASES

The cases in this volume place the student in a simulated position of a decision-maker handling practical supervisory problems. What is a case? A *case* is a description of people and events in a realistic situation that represents a problem to be analyzed and a decision to be made. Although the names of people and companies have been disguised, the cases in this book are based on problems and events that actually took place.

The case method of learning forces the student, not the instructor, to do in-depth analysis of a particular situation. The major responsibility for analysis rests on the participants; learning is promoted by their search for solutions to the problem. Thus, the case method *requires full student participation;* its effectiveness is entirely dependent upon the student's willingness to become *involved.*

This approach is based on the principle that learning that draws upon the learner's personal initiative and involvement produces more lasting and effective results than learning that is acquired simply through passive absorption of knowledge. In other words, learning is enhanced if the learner takes an *active* part in the process.

The instructor's role in case analysis is keeping the group aware of its responsibilities, posing questions, suggesting additional lines of exploration, and summarizing progress. His role is *not* to spoon-feed the group, supply it with pat answers, or impose his own opinions upon the participants.

EMPHASIS ON DECISION-MAKING

One of the prime objectives of the case method is to sharpen your decision-making skills. This objective is of no small consequence because decision-making is one of the most important functions of any supervisor.

In pursuit of this objective, all cases in this book are descriptions of situations calling for a *decision on future action,* along with an appraisal of past action. It is not enough to criticize what has transpired in the case; instead, you must decide *in detail* what should be done to improve the current situation in the case.

Each case calls for a careful review of the situation in terms of defining and analyzing the problem, weighing alternative courses of action, and offering a feasible solution. The stress is on logical analysis, developing a framework for decision-making, and the necessity of thinking through problems in a straight-line manner.

SUGGESTED APPROACH TO SOLVING CASE PROBLEMS

There is no one best way to study and prepare a case problem, nor is there necessarily a standard outline or form in which to present a case analysis. But here are a few suggestions that should prove helpful, whether you are preparing a written or oral analysis.

First, *read* the case thoroughly and carefully—usually several times and as far as possible in advance of when you plan to do a *serious* analysis. Think about the situation and try to involve yourself in it. Then, put the case aside for a while and let it "incubate." Allow the facts to simmer in your mind and let your subconscious work them over. Then *reread* the case. You'll likely find that your second impressions are somewhat different from your first.

Throughout the process of analyzing the case, ask yourself questions. Questions for consideration might be: "Why are the people in this situation acting like this?" "Why has the present situation developed?" "What is the basic problem in this situation?" "What caused this conflict?" "What alternative solutions are available to solve this problem?" "What are the chances of success for the various solutions?", and so on.

Additionally, you are encouraged not to disagree with *facts,* but to "read between the lines" in a case and question the *opinions* and *judgments* of the people quoted in the case.

To start your thinking and help you to explore as many areas as possible, questions are appended to each case. These questions are by no means meant to limit you. In fact, some of the questions may never even be raised in a discussion of the case.

In keeping with the objective of improved decision-making skills, here is a suggested model for case analysis that has been well tested in actual practice and may be used as a general outline to guide your thinking:

1. **State what appear to be the major issues in the situation.** An *issue* can be defined as "the question to be resolved" or "the decision that must be made." Examples of issues are: "What should be done to meet the sales

quota in Department A?", "What steps should be taken to insure employee acceptance of the new cash registers?", or "How can we help Joe improve the quality of his work?".

2. **Diagnose the problem(s) underlying the major issue.** Decision-making is always related to a problem, a difficulty, or a conflict. Whenever things are not going as expected, there is a problem. Decisions bring about an answer to the problem or a resolution of the conflict.

   Thus, the first, perhaps the most difficult, and often the overlooked phase, is a thorough diagnosis of the problem to be dealt with. The question of problem definition is very important; unless the problem is wisely defined, a poor case solution is almost inevitable.

   A common error in diagnosing problem situations is confusing *symptoms* with the problem itself. Essentially, your task in problem diagnosis is finding the *root causes* for the current situation in the case. The same symptoms can result from numerous causes. Clearly, if the wrong causes are assumed, your solution will also be ineffective.

   In trying to find this root cause (problem), it may be helpful to view the process as a "gap" between *what we would like to happen* (i.e., our ideal state or objective) and *what is happening now in the current situation.* What *obstacles* are standing in the way of reaching the desired objective?

   For example, consider a department that is experiencing a high degree of turnover. A superficial diagnosis might indicate the problem to be "low morale." Of course, an even less sophisticated response would be "the problem in this situation is high turnover"! What is *causing* high turnover? What is *causing* low morale? Low morale is not the problem; it is only a *symptom* of the problem. Perhaps the real cause of the situation is lack of proper training. Again, however, would this be the *root cause? Why* is training inadequate?

   Hence, we should continue moving from *superficial causes* (symptoms) to *root causes* (problems). A good way of getting beyond symptoms to the problem itself is to keep asking "Why?". "*Why* does John have a poor attitude?" "*Why* is Larry a lousy communicator?" "*Why* is Mary continually late for work?"

   So, in analyzing the problem, the question should *not* be "What should be done in this situation?" but rather "*Why* did this situation develop? What *caused* it?" To put it simply, problems are the reasons for your having to resolve the question or make the decision that you have stated in Step 1.

3. **State all alternative courses of action available for resolving the problem.** Decision-making necessitates a choice between two or more alternatives. If there is only one solution available, then there is really no decision to be made. In a problem situation, there are always numerous possibilities available from which we must make a selection.

   Imagination and originality are needed at this stage. The goal in this step should be *quantity* of alternatives, not particularly *quality* of alternatives. Don't reject an alternative because at first glance it seems improbable or impractical. There may be elements in it that can contribute to the ideal solution. Only by considering all possible alternatives can you be confident you have not overlooked any opportunities to get the results you want.

4. **Select and state the two or three most reasonable alternatives available.** Evaluate briefly the several courses of action stated in Step 3. From them select the two or three most reasonable proposals.

   The first alternative that occurs to you probably represents your usual approach to this type of problem. But remember that the seemingly "one" right or obvious solution is not always the best answer, because the first idea to come to mind is frequently triggered by preconceived notions held before the problem was analyzed.

5. **Analyze and compare the alternatives.** Weigh the *advantages* and *disadvantages* of each alternative. Consider the *probability of success* and the *risk* of complications for each and forecast the consequences. Determine both the *strengths* and *weaknesses* inherent in each course of action. All pertinent data should be assembled and related to these alternatives.

6. **Make your decision and plan for its implementation.** After weighing the pros and cons of each alternative in Step 5, decide which course of action promises to be the most successful. Also, consider *how* you would carry out your plan of action, what steps should be taken, etc.; in other words, give thought to the *implementation* aspects of your course of action. Remember, a poorly implemented, good decision may be no better than an expertly implemented, bad decision. Whenever possible, translate the course of action into a complete statement indicating *who, what, when, where, how,* and *why,* as appropriate.

Notice that each step in the above model for solving case problems builds on the foundation of the previous steps. Success at each step is dependent upon the successful achievement of the preceding step.

COMMON ERRORS AND FRUSTRATIONS TO AVOID

1. Inadequate definition of the problem. By far the most common error made in case analysis is attempting to recommend a course of action without first adequately defining or understanding the problem. Whether presented orally or in a written report, a case analysis must begin with a focus on the central issue and problem represented in the case situation.

In a traditional classroom situation, we normally expect the instructor to state the problem. In using cases, on the other hand, the problem is usually buried under a large number of facts and opinions that confuse and complicate the process of problem definition. Realistically, this is as it should be; in the real world of the supervisor, as opposed to a pure classroom environment, problems are seldom easily identifiable.

As stated earlier, unless the problem is adequately diagnosed and defined, there is little chance of proposing a useful solution to the problem.

2. The search for "correct answers". Most of us are used to receiving set answers to questions and problems raised in a classroom. Yet, in using cases, there are no clear-cut solutions. Thus, this approach to learning often tends to be frustrating at first.

Keep in mind that an objective of case studies is learning through discussion and exploration (and, occasionally, even argument). There is no one "official" or "correct" answer to a case. Rather, there are usually several reasonable alternative solutions—some perhaps better than others. Depending on the problem situation and the individual skills of the problem-solver, many approaches or solutions could be successful in a particular situation.

Therefore, it is quite normal for group members not to agree upon a single black-and-white solution or not to reach a neat conclusion at the end of a case discussion. Indeed, you can never, even after the most conscientious analysis, *be sure* your solution (or anyone else's) is correct.

Even though this lack of a "correct answer" tends to be frustrating, it is ironic to note that when classroom cases *do* provide answers there are almost always strong objections from participants who claim that the answers given are wrong!

3. "I need more information". You may often complain that there isn't sufficient information in some of the cases to make a good decision. There is justification for not giving you "all" of the information. As in real life, a supervisor seldom has all the information he would like. Time and financial constraints dictate that the supervisor often makes decisions with only the information available to him at the time. The challenge is to find a feasible solution *in spite* of the limited information.

Certainly, it will be necessary to project yourself into the case situation and make *assumptions* based on the facts provided. But, in all the cases in this volume, sufficient information is provided to allow you to select alternative courses of action and to reasonably predict their chances of success.

4. Use of generalities. In analyzing cases, *specifics* are necessary, not *generalities.* For example, a suggestion to resolve a particular problem situation by "calling the employee in to counsel him" is unsatisfactory and quite naive. *Specifically,* how will you attempt to solve the problem by counseling? What will you do and say?

5. "If the situation were different. . . ." Considerable time and effort are sometimes exerted by students contending that "if the situation were different, I'd know what course of action to take." Or, "If the supervisor hadn't already fouled things up so badly, we wouldn't be in this mess." Such reasoning ignores the fact that we cannot change the events in the case that have already happened. Even though analysis or criticism of past events is necessary in diagnosing the problem, we must in the end address ourselves to the present situation and the decision to be made.

6. "Narrow vision" analysis. The cases presented in this book are not conveniently categorized into problems of "motivation," "communications," "participation," and so on; they do not merely illustrate the concepts covered in any one chapter. Rather, most of the cases involve application of *several* aspects of supervision and require you to consider all these aspects in your analysis and recommendations. This is by no means unrealistic, in that it corresponds with the whole-problem challenges facing the supervisor in real life. Thus, at times you may wonder why you aren't able to fit a particular case to a certain chapter or why you can't seem to find all the answers to a case in this book. Admittedly, the process can be very frustrating—again, just as real-life supervisory problem-solving can be frustrating.

THE VALUE OF GROUP DISCUSSION

Central to the case method of learning is *group discussion* of the cases. Discussions invite and draw out the experiences of group members so that, in effect, they teach one another.

Each person exchanges his opinions, attitudes, and interpretations of the case with others. In so doing, he can see a variety of possible points of view about facts he may have considered to be quite obvious. For example, in discussing a case, a group member may find that he hasn't completely explored the problem. Or, he may discover that the group has been able to identify many more alternative solutions than he could find. During an open discussion, he may also find that his ideas (as well as everyone else's) are influenced by individual attitudes and values that are not completely free of bias or prejudice; other group members may challenge these attitudes and values, causing the person either to defend them or modify them.

By allowing free expression, the discussion exposes everyone in the group to new ideas, new information, and various ways of looking at and solving supervisory problems. It can also help each individual gain insight into his personal thought patterns and ways of perceiving his world. Acquiring such self-awareness is one of the keys to becoming a better supervisor and increasing one's capacity to deal effectively with people.

As an additional benefit, skills developed during group discussions are easily transferrable to the job during staff meetings, committee work, and other group problem-solving situations.

GUIDELINES FOR ROLE-PLAYING

As you analyze the cases that follow, you will notice that many of them indicate that you should be prepared to *role-play* the situation. To role-play a situation means to simulate the situation through acting the roles of the people involved—attempting to show their attitudes and reactions to the events of the case. Unlike the possible connotations of the term, role-playing is a serious activity with worthwhile objectives. It is particularly useful when it evolves as a natural extension of case discussion and analysis. In trying to portray the people involved in a problem situation or in a proposed decision, the participants are forced to use empathy, broaden perspective powers, improve communication skills, and sharpen analytical abilities.

Role-playing can be quite helpful in evaluating the alternative solutions to a case. In simulating the implementation of a proposed decision, the participants assume the positions of the people involved in the decision. For instance, if the alternative were to "have a talk with Jim to determine why he has been late to work for the past two weeks," the participants would enact the discussion proposed by the decision. It's sometimes easy to say, "I would do 'such and such,'" and quite a different matter actually to carry out that decision. Through role-playing, you have an opportunity to see how others interpret and respond to the decision, to see "loopholes" in your strategy, and to understand how your communication efforts are received.

Reversing the roles (taking the position of the other person) helps one to understand the feelings and attitudes of another, thus building ability to empathize and to see how the situation looks from another's viewpoint.

Role-playing can also assist in developing ability to find the problems causing an undesirable situation. By acting out the background information presented in the case and putting yourself in the situations that have evolved, you may be able to understand why the people have reacted as they have, to recognize how you might have felt if you were in their situation, and to recognize the factors that influence actions and opinions.

This understanding should make it easier to see beyond the symptoms of the problem. Through analysis of the case information and then putting yourself into the circumstances of the situation, you may be able to spot the root causes of the problem.

In order to role-play a situation intelligently, participants must be adequately prepared. Preferably, most of the case analysis procedure outlined above should precede role-playing activity. That is, the case should have been read several times, the situation analyzed, and alternative courses of action formulated. Therefore, participants will already have a good idea of the attitudes displayed, the actions of the people involved, and the influences that have brought about the situation. Certainly you will be limited in your ability in "being" another person; however, repeated role-playing can help to develop your ability to empathize.

Group members other than those actually taking part in the role-play should watch for important happenings. These observers should keep several questions in mind: "What attitudes are being expressed?" "Do my perceptions of the people and events match those being portrayed?" "What was said that resulted in agreement—or conflict?" "What stimulated emotional responses in the participants?" These observations should be valuable in discussing the role-playing activity and making a final decision on problem diagnosis or implementation of alternatives.

Usually, two or three groups will role-play a situation. Almost always someone feels that he has an approach to the problem that will result in a better resolution of the question. Observing and analyzing the different approaches develops better understanding of the feasibility of various alternatives.

Role-playing increases the opportunity for learning through involvement of the student in a realistic situation. Through enacting a situation, lasting and effective learning can take place. In addition to the experience of analyzing the case and the individual's involvement in case discussion, role-playing allows the student to feel that he is actually a part of a situation while attempting to implement a decision.

TRY IT: SEE HOW YOU LIKE IT!

David Cisco supervises the first-shift maintenance crew at a large manufacturing plant. The company is in a city that has recently undertaken a campaign to encourage major employers to hire the hard-core unemployed. About 50 people from the ghetto area have joined the company.

One of these new employees has come into Cisco's department. He is Roy Grant, a black man with a wife and four children; according to his personnel forms, this is his first regular work in several years. Up until now, he's had odd repair jobs here and there, but nothing with any promise of permanence. His wife, however, has worked steadily.

David talked with Grant before he was hired and felt confident that he had the skills needed to work in his department. He seemed anxious and uneasy, but Cisco figured that was only to be expected under the circumstances. Beneath Grant's nervousness, Cisco could detect a strong desire to make good.

Because the crew is fairly large, Cisco handles most of the scheduling and paper work and lets his assistant, George Klenk, work directly with the men. Klenk didn't seem too keen on the idea of the company bringing in a group of hard-core unemployed, and few of the workers showed much enthusiasm either. Cisco explained the project to Klenk ahead of time, stressing that it would be up to everyone—himself, Klenk, and the whole crew—to make a success of it. This is a program that top management has undertaken voluntarily, and it'll be watched closely. Cisco didn't stress the fact that normal hiring standards would not apply to the project, but it was common knowledge anyway. It was fairly obvious that Klenk wasn't enthusiastic about the idea, but David hoped that he would come to accept Grant as just another worker.

After Grant came to the department, Cisco introduced him to Klenk and recommended that he be put on carpentry jobs, as Grant had said those were what he did best. From time to time after that, Cisco asked Klenk how he was coming along, and Klenk said, a bit grudgingly, that Grant seemed to be okay.

It's now three weeks since Grant started working, and Cisco was thinking a little while ago how satisfied he felt at the way his hiring Grant seemed to be working out. As if that were a bad omen, Klenk burst into the office just then, obviously steaming over something.

"This stuff about hiring the hard-core might sound great to people who don't have to work with them," he exploded, "but I just want to know if I have to take whatever they hand out!"

"Now, hold on, George. Just what are you talking about?"

"That new guy, Grant. He's been real touchy all week, and this morning when I corrected him for something, he blew up like I'd insulted his mother. If I have to use kid gloves on him, I don't want him! This is a shop, not a nursery!"

"Did you correct him any differently from the way you correct the others?"

"Heck, no! I just made a routine check of the work he was doing and pointed out something he'd overlooked. It was no big thing, but he blew his stack. Look, I treat him the same as anyone else. Maybe I didn't think so much of the idea of bringing all these inexperienced guys in, but that's beside the point now. I've got one of them, and I don't want problems with him any more than from the others."

"Okay, George. Why don't you cool down and ask Grant to come by here so I can talk with him."

A few minutes later, Grant was in Cisco's office. He looked apprehensive yet defiant. Cisco motioned for him to sit down, and began by asking how he liked his work so far. Still cautious, Grant said he liked it just fine.

"Klenk says you're doing a good job," Cisco added. "But I understand you and he have had a few words. Is something or somebody giving you a hard time?"

Grant hesitated, then said, "Not so much in the open. But I know how they feel about me being here. For a while I thought things were working out real fine. Then, last Friday, I went to my locker after coffee break to put my Thermos away and I heard two or three guys on the other side of the partition. They were talking about the hiring program, bringing in people like me. One guy said his nephew tried to get a job here and was turned down, that they told him nothing was open. He said he guessed you have to be black or a dumb dropout to get work these days. Somebody else said we were nothing but lazy bums, why didn't we go back where we came from and let people have the jobs who deserved them."

"Well," Grant continued, getting more heated, "I'm not as dumb as they think! I was working the best I could before now—a job here, a job there, whatever I could get. And my wife was working steady all the time. How do you think that feels—my wife keeping a job and I couldn't? I know they don't want me here, and I know they're watching me every minute, looking for mistakes to show up to get me tossed out. I've been thinking about it all week, and when

Klenk said something about the job I was doing, I thought he was in on it, too, and I blew up. This is the first real job I've ever had, and I'm not letting anybody take it away from me!"

"I think you're overreacting to this," Cisco said. "After all, it is Klenk's job to check the work and if something isn't right to point it out."

"I know that," said Grant, "but it was the way he did it. He seemed glad he found an oversight. Another thing, how come he calls everyone else by name—but always calls me 'boy'?"

It's obvious by now that the tension has reached an explosive point as far as Grant is concerned. David didn't doubt for a minute what Grant says he overheard; he knew the other men well enough to know that many of them would feel just that way about it.

Cisco wondered what he should do now. Grant promises to be a good worker; but with this atmosphere, it's likely that a fight will break out which could lead to Grant's discharge. That is, unless Cisco can think of a solution.

GUIDES FOR ANALYSIS

1. Why do the other men react to Grant as they do?
2. Can Cisco change the attitudes of the crew by talking with them?
3. Is Grant overreacting to the situation? How would you feel if you were in his place?
4. Recommend a course of action to Cisco.

THE MOONLIGHTING FARMERS

"Cass, I mean it. I think the company made a bad mistake moving out here. These people just don't want to work."

The speaker was Steve Marcyk, a foreman in the small plastic extrusion plant that had just moved into a rural area. Because of high taxes and labor costs, management had decided to pull up stakes and move from a city suburb to a farm area where labor costs were reasonable and taxes low. But in the first few months at the new location, operations had not gone smoothly. There was no trouble hiring all the workers needed, but high absenteeism during the day shift was beginning to threaten production schedules.

"Steve is right; they just don't want to work," echoed Wayne Hadlock, the other production foreman confronting the plant superintendent, Cass Campbell. "Every time one of these jokers is out it's soybean planting time or else he has to hoe corn or bale hay. We've let them have time off without pay, but there's got to be a limit."

"Now, wait a minute, Wayne. Both of you were told what to expect with people who had never worked in industry before. Like the Old Man says, they've got to be 're-educated.' "

Marcyk snorted. "Re-educated! Come off it, Cass. You don't believe that psychological bunk any more than Wayne and I do. The Old Man's been sticking his head in too many books and listening to too many 'experts.' These farmers are playing us for saps."

"I'm not saying you should coddle them," said Campbell patiently. "All I'm saying is that both of you have got to be a little more understanding. Those are good people out there and they learn fast. Sure, they have to adjust to us, but we have to adjust to them, too."

"Just how are we supposed to 'adjust,' Cass?" said Hadlock, obviously not convinced.

"Maybe by using your brains instead of threatening to use your authority."

"We *are* using our brains, Cass, and our brains tell us that if we don't crack down on absences the Old Man is going to crack down on you and you're going to crack down on us. We'll all get it in the neck," said Marcyk, ruefully. "A couple of years ago in the old plant we started having the same problem, remember? And when we got tough, people started showing up on time."

"But that was with men who had worked in factories for years," Campbell pointed out. "Besides, they were completely dependent on their jobs for income. These people aren't. Most of them still work farms part-time."

"That's the trouble," said Marcyk, an exasperated edge to his voice; "they're too independent. From now on, no time off for farming."

"Get-tough policies like that usually cause more trouble than they clear up," said the superintendent with a shake of the head. "But if you're so set on it, go ahead and try."

"Thanks, Cass, we think we know what we're doing," said Hadlock with a grim smile, and both foremen headed back to the shop floor, with Campbell watching them thoughtfully.

The next morning Wayne Hadlock had the chance to test his new get-tough policy. Norman Johnson, one of his extrusion machine operators, showed up at work after a two-day absence.

"What's the excuse this time, Norman?" the foreman asked without looking up from the absence report.

"Corn plantin'."

"A couple of weeks ago some of you guys were out because it was 'soybean plantin' time! What's it going to be in two more weeks—pumpkin harvest? Johnson, if you're absent again for any kind of farming reason you're fired. Understood?"

"Yup."

"O.K., get to work. We're already behind on half our orders."

Marcyk had a similar showdown that same morning with one of his men and handed out the same kind of ultimatum.

"Looks like they're getting the message, Wayne," said Marcyk to his fellow foreman as they were eating lunch together that afternoon.

"No doubt about it, Steve. I saw Norman Johnson talking to some of the other men at coffee break this morning. Whatever he said seemed to sink in. And they were pretty quiet the rest of the morning. I think we've got it licked—pass the mustard, will you?"

But at the beginning of the first shift the next day, Marcyk knew he had trouble. Nearly a quarter of his crew had called in sick. Then he saw Hadlock walking over, and he didn't need to guess why he wasn't smiling.

"Some of your men out?"

"Yeah, I'll have to juggle to keep the line going. Better go tell Campbell and face the music. He was against a get-tough policy from the beginning, and now it looks like he was right."

Five minutes later the two foremen were standing in front of the superintendent's desk.

"All right, your hard-nose policy obviously hasn't worked," said Campbell looking over the absence report. "We'll have to get this mess straightened out quick, or we'll start slipping on production schedules. I'm giving you fellows one more chance to solve your absence problems yourselves. I'll expect some concrete suggestions from both of you by tomorrow morning."

GUIDES FOR ANALYSIS

1. What kind of suggestions might Cass Campbell be looking for?
2. How did the farmers perceive their jobs at the plant?
3. In what ways is the work of a farmer likely to differ from that of an industrial worker?
4. How would you advise these two foremen to handle the absence problem? Be specific.

ONE ROTTEN APPLE

"The trouble is they're just kids," thought Bill Massingale, the second-shift foreman, as he headed toward the shouting and laughter coming from the Section 20 electrical cable test area. "And it's that wise guy Harvey Harrington who's taking them down the path."

The sounds grew louder as Massingale hurried up the aisle toward the test pens. Just as he rounded the corner of the safety fence, Randy Deckert and

Floyd Hanley, the two youngest guys on the shift, came whizzing past, one pushing the other in a dump cart. Heading toward the wall, the cart and its occupant sped right past the foreman, missing him by inches.

Massingale released his breath slowly; a bit closer and he would have had a broken leg. "Deckert, Hanley," he said with as much control in his voice as he could muster. "Put that cart back and get to work. You're wasting time and you could have hurt someone pretty badly with that thing. Who put you up to this foolishness?"

Massingale didn't need to ask that question; he could hear the sound of barely muffled laughter as he slowly turned to look down the aisle of the test area.

There at the end he could see Harvey Harrington busily sweeping up cable scrap. He knew, although he couldn't prove it, that Harrington had started the horseplay.

That was the real problem. The fellows were good workers, but Harrington just seemed to be turning them bad—fast.

The whole crew had been warned before about their fooling around, but Massingale didn't want to fire all of them, nor could he without causing a lot of headaches. Good workers were scarce. Nevertheless, he had to do something before Harrington, who seemed to be their natural leader, completely corrupted the rest of them. But what?

Then he had an idea. Give him some responsibility. It might just work.

The next night he called Harrington aside. "I'm going to make a deal with you," Massingale began. "Even though I know you've been at the root of all the goofing off around here lately, I'm . . . ."

"That's not true, and you can't prove it," Harrington interrupted as he played with his cigarette lighter.

"Never mind that," replied Massingale, trying to keep his cool. "Let's just say from now on bygones are bygones. Anyway, I think you have leadership potential, and that's why I'm appointing you temporary shift leader for this crew."

"You're kidding," Harrington said, smiling incredulously.

"No, I'm dead serious. But I warn you, Harvey, I don't want any more horseplay. You'll be responsible for the performance of the crew. I won't accept any alibis. What do you say?"

"Suits me." Harrington thought for a moment. "But wait a minute." Harrington rubbed his fingers and thumb together and looked at his foreman inquisitively. "There's a little extra bread, isn't there?"

"A five-cents-an-hour increase," said Massingale a little abruptly.

"Well, that sure ain't much, but I'll take anything I can get. When do I start?"

"As of right now the crew's your responsibility," said the foreman and turned on his heel and walked away.

For the next several nights Department 20 functioned like a carefully run machine, the crew buckling down to the job of packing and moving the drums of cable. Bill Massingale began to think his gamble was paying off.

But one evening, about a week after he had appointed Harrington shift leader, the foreman suddenly became aware that the test area was too quiet.

"Matter of fact, I haven't heard a sound from that crew for the past three hours," he muttered to himself.

Sure enough, there was no one in sight as he surveyed the row after row of unwrapped drums. A forklift stood in the center of the aisle, its motor turned off.

At that moment he caught a glimpse of cigarette smoke curling up from behind a large cable drum in test pen nine. Massingale walked quietly over to the pen, squeezed between two cable drums and peered along the gap between the row and the wall.

There, protected from prying eyes, sat Harvey Harrington and the rest of the crew deeply absorbed in a poker game.

Massingale stood looking at them for a moment, unnoticed until Harrington happened to glance up. Not taking his eyes off the foreman, he slowly laid down his cigarette and began casually to shuffle the deck of cards. The rest of the crew followed his gaze, but then looked down at the floor guiltily.

GUIDES FOR ANALYSIS

1. Was Massingale's idea of giving Harvey responsibility a good idea?
2. Did Harvey and the crew know what his new responsibilities were?
3. What do you think of Massingale's "let's make a deal" approach?
4. Is there any hope left for Harrington?
5. If you were Massingale, what action would you take?

THE SUBSTITUTE SUPPLY CLERK

It was one of those days in the supply department at the Crescent Chemical Company. Everyone in the plant and office seemed to have requisitions that should have been filled the day before. The four order clerks were busily trying to fill the requisitions that kept coming in one on top of the other.

Supervisor Tom French appreciated the way his people were working, but he realized that some more help would make it easier on them. His eyes caught young Lynda Donnell, who checked invoices and supplies as they came from the vendors. That Monday, Lynda had her usual work load and was working at her normal pace while the other people were really pushing it.

Noticing that the supply clerks were falling further behind, French went over to Lynda and said: "Lynda, I need you to give the supply clerks a hand. Go over there, and Marianne will show you what you have to do." Half to himself French mumbled as he started to turn away, "Why does everybody have to have everything today?"

"I have some more of my own work to finish," Lynda said.

"I said I needed you over there now," French retorted, rather frustrated at Lynda's stubbornness. "We've got to keep this place running and that work has to be done immediately."

"But what about these supplies I have to check in?"

"Just leave them there. Anyone can handle that job. You can do it later when you get a chance. Filling these requisitions is more important," French almost yelled at her.

Lynda, somewhat reluctantly walked over to Marianne Atkins, the supply clerk. "What do you want me to do?" she asked sullenly.

Marianne quickly pulled out a bunch of requisitions and showed Lynda how to fill them in. Lynda worked the rest of the day without saying another word—not to French, not to any of the girls. Even at lunch time, she ate by herself in the company cafeteria. And at the end of the day, she walked out of the office without her usual cheery "Good night." Everyone was so busy they hardly noticed.

The next day Lynda was back checking incoming supplies and invoices, the department was back to normal, but Lynda's mood hadn't changed. She grumped only the most perfunctory greeting to her co-workers and didn't even nod in French's direction. She was usually very accurate, but this day Marianne found three miscounts when she was filling requisitions.

As the week went on, everyone in the department knew that something was bugging Lynda. Wednesday, French stopped Lynda. "Lynda, you're way behind. Just look at this mess around here." Linda just shrugged her shoulders and walked off. French was really puzzled. What could be causing this, he wondered. Something was surely wrong, because Lynda wasn't her usual self. Lynda had been a friendly, outgoing person, and always seemed to pride herself on doing a good job. All this week, supplies and invoices were stacked around her. She'd done only about half her work, and you couldn't get a decent word out of her. One of the girls was convinced that Lynda was having a hard time at home. Another felt that she must be having trouble in the night-school classes she was attending. But no one was sure.

On Friday, Lynda went to the Office Manager, Pete Mason, and asked to be reassigned to another job, preferably as a supply clerk.

"I thought you were happy with the work you were doing, Lynda. We've been very proud of the job you've been doing, and we really don't need another permanent supply clerk, either. What made you decide to ask for a change?"

GUIDES FOR ANALYSIS

1. What was Lynda's attitude toward her job before becoming a substitute supply clerk?
2. What was Lynda's attitude toward her job after serving as a supply clerk?
3. What possible reasons could exist to make her attitude change?
4. Did Tom French contribute to the change? Did he do anything to hurt Lynda's morale?
5. Recommend a course of action to Pete Mason.
6. Be prepared to role-play Lynda's and Mason's following conversation.

BRIGHT YOUNG MAN GOES "PFFFT"

Lloyd Lawson had been very glad—and felt very lucky—to welcome young Jerry Robinson to his division. Lloyd, accounting division manager for Stephens', a local chain of department stores in the large southwestern city, had long needed another ambitious young man in his division.

Robinson, a 22-year-old veteran, had just completed two years of college. Recently married, he had decided that his new responsibilities required him to work full time and continue his education at night. An accounting major with some part-time work experience, Robinson represented "a real find," Lawson thought.

Lawson introduced Robinson to Jim Positan, head of the section to which Robinson had been assigned. "Jim, here's that young man we've been looking for. After you work with him a while, I know he's going to take a real load off your shoulders. By the way, take care of him, will you? His older brother is my buddy John, the buyer for the men's department in the downtown store."

Positan was glad to have some help, but John Robinson's brother! He knew that Lawson and the older Robinson had worked together for about five years and had become close friends. "Well, guess I have to tread lightly with this one," thought Positan.

A couple of months later, Jim Positan was ready to agree with Lawson's introductory remarks. Jerry had proven himself to be a hard-working, ambitious young man. Seemingly anxious to learn, he sometimes stayed after hours studying procedures in the department.

Lawson, during the early months of Robinson's employment, had left Jerry and Jim pretty much alone. About six months after Jerry came to work, though, Lawson kept noticing Jerry "coming and going" a great deal. It seemed like everytime he looked up, Jerry was walking down the hall, out the door, going somewhere. Lloyd decided to ask Jim about it.

The next week, though, because of a store-wide clearance sale, everything in the division was rather chaotic. He was so busy, he just forgot to speak to Positan about Jerry.

Immediately after that, Lawson went to the downtown store for a company management meeting and ran into John Robinson.

"Say, Lloyd, how's my little brother doing? Some kid, huh? He's a smart one—always making the dean's list at school, right in the middle of the student government at college."

Lloyd felt almost trapped; he hadn't talked to Positan so he hadn't been able to check on Jerry—and all that running around—"You're right, John, with all that 'smart' he really ought to go places."

"Well," replied John, "I really hated to see him have to quit going to school full time, but after he got married he just couldn't keep up all his activities and make a living, too."

Lloyd returned to the store and immediately contacted Jim Positan. "Jim, how's Jerry doing? I've been meaning to talk with you about him, but you know how it gets around here."

Remembering Lloyd's friendship with John Robinson, Jim decided that he should be a little tactful. "Jerry's ability is tops, he catches on fast, and his first few months he really jumped into it. Lately, though, I don't know. . . . Maybe he's just settling down into a routine or something, but a lot of his 'fire' seems to be fading."

"Exactly what have you had him doing?" interrupted Lawson.

"Mainly," responded Positan, "he works on the accounts receivable, but he actually does several clerical jobs that I've assigned him. Sometimes lately, he gets a little behind with some of his work."

"Did he have any trouble learning the new assignments?"

"Well, no, not really; he seems to be a little careless about some of it now, though. I didn't want to say anything, but I had to talk to him about a few mistakes he made—nothing serious, understand."

"Jim, why don't you send Jerry down here and let me talk to him. Maybe he'll open up and talk. I'll tell him I saw John downtown, that might make him feel a little easier."

"Great," replied Jim, "I don't know what to do with him. I'll go back and send him down." Positan was glad to let Lawson talk to him—after all, he was his friend, maybe he could straighten him out.

Within five minutes, Jerry strolled through Lawson's door. "Well, Lloyd, I hear you reported to John," he began.

Lawson, rather surprised at that as a beginning, replied slowly, "Yeah, I ran into him at a meeting downtown. He seems to be pretty proud of you. . . . Well, tell me, Jerry, how are you doing here with us?"

"Oh, I don't know. It seems easy enough, not really hard at all. Man, that Positan, though–just make one little mistake and you hear about it. But I guess he told you about that."

"Actually, Jerry, Jim told me a few months ago that you were getting right after it. Did something happen?"

"He thought I was doing okay?" questioned Jerry. "I never heard a 'peep' out of him; he just sorta threw some work at me and didn't say a thing till I messed up a few times. Considering all the help he gave me, I thought I did pretty well."

Lawson thought he might ease away from an obviously touchy situation, "How about the work–what you're doing–do you like it and the department?"

"Oh, sure, it's okay, I guess. Nothing exciting especially. I wouldn't mind getting a promotion though, something a little more challenging. And the extra money would help. I'd really like to move up before long. With John doing so good with the company and everything. . . ." he trailed off.

"Okay, Jerry, I'll talk with Positan. Maybe we can figure out something. We'll get back together."

After Jerry left the office, Lloyd decided that he and Positan would have another talk tomorrow. After all, Jerry did have the ability. Maybe together they could figure out what was going wrong.

GUIDES FOR ANALYSIS

1. What do you think Jerry Robinson wants from his job?.
2. What could Jim Positan have done to keep Jerry from "losing fire"?
3. Has Lloyd Lawson played a role in forming Jerry's attitude?
4. Recommend a course of action that might resolve the situation.

WHAT, ME WORRY? *

When he arrived home Friday evening, Max Gerson immediately took a tranquilizer tablet. It was an hour later before he was relaxed enough to tell his wife of the latest incident involving Terry Mellon, the young new supervisor of the Information Services and Data Processing Unit.

*Reprinted with permission from the August, 1971, issue of *Training in Business and Industry* ©MCMLXXI Gellert Publishing Corp., and the author, Robert D. Joyce.

Gerson is now Director of Administration after 23 years with Amercade Products. Starting as a production stockroom clerk right out of high school, he performed all tasks given him with efficiency and filled a dozen or so positions over the years. Gerson had known and worked for just about every type of supervisor: dictators, egomaniacs, perfectionists, slackers, politicians and softies—the good guys and the bad—and he had learned a little from all.

Above all, Max Gerson had learned that you eventually get to the top by hard work; that even a college diploma (which he earned after seven years of night school) couldn't guarantee success. Hard work also meant playing ball with the Boss—no matter what!

Gerson felt that he had fewer personnel problems than most managers, but Mellon was something else again. . . .

As his wife, Edith, listened attentively, Max recalled the six weeks since Mellon was hired.

"He certainly made a good impression during the employment interview. He was neatly dressed, aggressive but not overbearing, and relaxed as if he already had the job. He obviously knew his business, too—a B.S. and an M.S. in Information Theory, plus solid progressive positions in two prior companies. I felt he would be an outstanding choice as our Supervisor of Information Services although he had no prior supervisory experience.

"About two weeks after he was hired he began to wear sport shirts and came to work several times in sandals with no socks. Then there was the beard! We had a long talk at that point about the interests of the company, his role as a supervisor, and his personal rights. He kept the beard, but I got him to wear socks.

"Later, when Mellon became involved in a complex simulation project, he started working all hours of the night and came in at one or two o'clock the next afternoon. He also had some of his people doing the same thing and there were times when their work area was practically deserted. I was about to read the riot act to him when he announced that his group had completed the simulation programming except for documentation! Under Ben Otter, the manager prior to Mellon, the group had fooled with that same problem for months and appeared nowhere near a solution."

"I knew that," Edith responded. "What happened this week?"

"Well," sighed Gerson, "it started on Monday. I was reviewing some classified material with Terry when he went off on a tangent about the foolishness of security. He rambled on about how we keep documents on government projects classified secret—you know, key drawings, specifications, and so forth—only to find the same information later on page 10 of an aviation magazine or a perfect small-scale replica plastic model kit of the thing sold to kids.

"He had a point and I agreed that some of our security practices were poor. I thought the whole matter was over and done with, but Tuesday I heard him joking in the cafeteria about how he had gotten into the facility that morning by quickly flashing a pack of cigarettes to the guard instead of his badge! I told him that he was out of line and that this would have to stop immediately. He apologized but appeared surprised that I didn't see anything funny in the incident."

Gerson continued. "Thursday the whole area was giggling over another Mellon antic. He evidently clipped a picture of that comic-book character Alfred E. Neumann—you know, that "What, Me Worry?" boy with the moronic face—and pasted it over his own picture on his badge. Apparently he wore it that way all day before anyone noticed. I was ready to have it out with him once and for all, but by the time I saw him the picture was gone.

"This morning about 8:15 I received a call from the guard at the main entrance. He said that Mellon didn't have his badge when he arrived and refused to accept a 'temporary.' The guard told him that no one entered that plant without a badge and he had his choice of a temporary badge or going home. Then he said that Mellon turned abruptly and walked off. Terry Mellon never showed up today at all and wasn't home when we called.

"Edith, this guy borders on genius but he's a *kook*! I don't know what to do with him."

"You want my opinion?" asked Edith.

"Yes, I do."

"Fire him! You've got enough other problems. If you continue to be soft, he'll make you the laughing stock of the company."

GUIDES FOR ANALYSIS

1. How would you handle this situation?
2. Could the problem have been prevented? How?
3. Would you answer this differently if:
   a. Mellon were a programmer and not a supervisor? Explain.
   b. Government security were not involved? Explain.
   c. Mellon were not so talented? Explain.
4. What is the attitude of your company (department) relative to unusual dress or work habits?
5. Can restrictive organizational policies limit individual creativity? Explain.

HORTON'S DEPARTMENT STORE

Horton's, a local full-line department store, is one of a chain of ten stores located mostly in medium-sized cities throughout the Midwest. In the three years that Jim Owens had been the store manager, the store's business had just about doubled, as had the population in the area which the store served. The store had 100 regular employees and usually added another 30 temporary workers for holiday help.

Jim Owens was known among his managerial staff as an efficient person, although he left most of the day-to-day operations to his division managers. He wasn't one to fritter time away on anything that wouldn't contribute to the growth of the business and spent a great deal of effort in doing public-relations work in the community. He served, for instance, as president of the local Kiwanis Club. Although he presented a rather cold image to most of the employees, most of the "old-timers" felt a certain respect for him.

The staff of the store included an accounting department (three employees), three secretaries, a personnel manager, and the two division managers, Charles Stout in hard lines and Mike Laird in soft lines.

Jim periodically reviewed all phases of his operation. Right now, he was looking over a review of the labor turnover figures which the personnel manager, Miss Lyons, had given him. Part of the labor picture was fairly stable: Miss Lyons had been with the store for four years, Stout and Laird had been there three years. The accounting department and secretarial pool suffered from a high turnover rate; in fact, there had been 10 different girls in the three secretarial positions in three years. Accounting department employees seemed to last about six months.

What really bothered Owens though was the turnover in salespeople. To maintain an employment level of 70 regular salespeople, they had hired 165 people during the past year. Part-time employees seemed to last about three months. Of the 30 temporary helpers employed, only five had ever returned for another holiday season.

Extremely disturbed over these high turnover figures, Jim decided to call a meeting of the division managers, department managers, and the entire office staff to see if they could present any ideas for this costly situation. He set the meeting for early the next morning.

Jim greeted the group the next morning and proceeded to lay his cards on the table. He wanted to give them the facts and find out the true story behind the picture. Having presented the labor turnover situation, he continued.

"I just don't understand what's happening and perhaps you can tell me. Our salary scale is 5 cents an hour higher than the other retailers in town, and we've tried to take care of our employees. Last year we set up the new employees' lounge—even put in a television set and vending machines so they could relax on their break—and started the new vacation program after a year's service. So what is it?"

There was silence around the table in Owens' office. Finally, Stout spoke, at first hesitantly.

"Good, hard-working people just don't want to work for what we can pay them," he commented. "Why, I have to keep a constant watch on everyone of mine, or they'd just let customers wander off without even trying to sell anything." He seemed to warm to the subject and was about to continue. Therese Rich, Ladies Accessories department manager, interrupted.

"You're right, Charles. Just last week I had to terminate one of my girls. When she made her fourth error on the cash register in a week—well, that's just too many. They're so bad they can't even learn a simple thing like ringing up sales!"

Charles Stout broke back in, "Most of them don't care if they do what they're supposed to do or not, and when you try to tell them where they're wrong, they just quit."

Jim Owens, not believing that the employees were all incompetent people, pondered, "Well, what about the suggestion system we started last year. Did we get any ideas from that about what we could do to improve the situation?"

"No, not really," interjected Mike Laird, soft-lines manager. "I heard a lot of them laughing about it, though. I told them they would get a reward for a good suggestion, but very few were submitted."

Miss Lyons, personnel manager, had kept quiet. But now, she added, "You just don't get good applicants any more. It seems that we used to have about five applications for every job, but not now. And what you can get just want to show up, and that's all! Having to put up with part-timers is a real pain, too. Most of them don't want to work in retailing as a career. They're just here to make some spare money. Just try telling some of them what to do, and they're gone in a flash."

Karen Oxford, one of the secretaries, spoke up. "You all sound alike—and just like her," nodding at Miss Lyons. "She isn't even my boss, but no matter what the secretaries do, it isn't right. She's always telling us that she does something another way."

Miss Lyons, obviously disturbed, jumped up. "Somebody has to tell her how to get things done around here. If it weren't for me, none of these girls would ever do anything right."

Jim Owens, seeing the heated atmosphere between the two women, decided that he'd better break it up at once. Still, he was concerned; he wasn't sure that he had heard the real story. He interrupted,

"Let's close this meeting now. But I want you to be thinking about the situation; surely there must be some answers to this turnover problem. After all, ours, according to industry figures, is way out of line. I'm going to do some investigating and thinking of my own. Ask one member from each department to come to a meeting at ten in the morning, and I'll see what I can learn from them. You people (indicating the entire group present) come up with some ideas before we meet again next week."

At ten the next morning, the departmental representatives slowly gathered in Mr. Owens' office. There was a steady buzz of wondering what the meeting was all about.

Jim Owens greeted the group cordially, attempting to put them at ease. "I know you are all curious about why you're here. We have a real problem that simply must be solved. I've talked with the managers and asked them for their ideas. Now perhaps you can help too." Glancing around he noticed several wary looks and continued.

"Our labor turnover rate is extremely high; our employees seem to leave just about the time they're broken in. It's bound to be affecting sales and that means it affects you. Can you help me find out why so many people are leaving?"

Blank, hesitant faces stared at each other. They certainly hadn't expected this.

Finally, Harold Samuels from the TV department commented. "Well, we lost one man last week. He was a pretty fair salesman—he'd had some sales training before he came here. But he and Mr. Stout just didn't see eye-to-eye on some things. He just couldn't take any more and quit."

Lee Davis of the men's department looked up. "Mr. Owens—you really want to know why we quit? The money isn't much, but mainly, oh, I don't know, just the way some people act around here. . . ." he trailed off.

Suddenly, Marty Simmons of the girls' department started, "It's the managers!" she stopped, as though backing off. Slowly, she began again, "Sometimes they're a little rough on you, you know, jumping on you for little mistakes, giving orders. . . ."

Mr. Owens, feeling uncomfortable, slowly came to his feet.

"I wonder if this attacking of supervisors is really getting us anywhere. We're all in this together and we have our problems. You have a job to do, maybe everything your managers do isn't right; but perhaps if you did what you're supposed to do, they wouldn't jump on you. I'm about to think this meeting was a mistake. Even so, if any one of you have any good, constructive ideas about why people quit, I'd appreciate your coming by and telling me."

Jim Owens dismissed the meeting in a state of confusion. The managers complained that the salespeople wouldn't work; but something was definitely wrong. Just what did these employees mean about the managers? He determined that he would have to get some help in finding out the real problems that existed.

The next day, six salespeople gave notice of quitting. One of the six was Marty Simmons, who had said a few things at the meeting. This time, she accepted his invitation to let him know how she felt. She left the following note for Mr. Owens:

Mr. Owens, you wanted to know why we quit. Since I'm leaving anyway, I guess I can tell you without it hurting anything—it's already ruined anyway. Being dirt under anybody's feet is no fun, being yelled at is embarrassing. Everybody expects you to know how to do everything—automatically! And when you don't—watch out. Probably a lot of others have left for the same reasons.

Marty Simmons

Jim Owens scanned the note and pondered all the things it could mean. Sadly he shook his head and wondered, "What now?"

GUIDES FOR ANALYSIS

1. What attitudes are displayed by the two groups toward each other?
2. Can you draw any conclusions about the seeming lack of a training program?
3. Have the managers, including Owens, contributed to the problem?
4. What appears to be the philosophy of management displayed in the store?
5. Recommend a course of action to Jim Owens.

WHAT DOES IT TAKE?

Grady Hull carefully parked his new Corvette in the company lot and walked across the road. His work clothes were clean, his lunch pail full. In three years, he'd come a long way from the Kentucky hollow he'd lived in until he was twenty-four.

The stainless-steel mill here in northern Indiana was the greatest thing that had ever happened to Grady. He was making more than twice as much money as he'd ever made, the work was twice as easy, and everyone acknowledged that Grady ran the angle-straightener better than anyone else and put out far more production to boot.

The straightening machine had long been a headache to Claude Miller, supervisor of the processing department. For years he had mentally groaned whenever he saw a large order for angles on his schedule. The machine was old, its adjustments were wrong and there was no tried-and-true way to run it. Yet, angles were a minor part of over-all production—not important enough to justify the purchase of an up-to-date straightening machine, according to the plant manager.

But Claude's headache had eased considerably when Grady Hull arrived. This lean mountaineer knew instinctively, it seemed, exactly how to make that machine behave. The operators on the other two shifts continued to have their difficulties, though, and whenever possible Miller moved them to other machines in the department, giving Grady overtime. Of course, this brought some protests from the other men and the union—but not as many as if the other operators had been anywhere near as capable as Grady. There was no question, Grady was in a class by himself.

There hadn't been an assistant foreman's job open until recently. And that was when the trouble started. Grady had ambitions. He'd long since made sure Miller knew that he thought he deserved to be made assistant foreman and would like to be considered for it when an opening came. But Claude Miller, however much he respected Grady as a worker, simply didn't feel he was foreman material. If he'd had to put it into words, he'd merely have said, "He isn't the type." Of course, he'd have denied that it had anything to do with Grady's being a "hillbilly," although he would have admitted that the other men didn't have much use for hillbillies in general or Grady in particular. Not that Grady minded. Loners never do.

So last week Miller had picked Ronnie Ball. Ball was a crane follower. As such, he'd had to keep track of all the orders on the floor, take a finished bundle of steel from a machine, put it where it was supposed to go next, and replace it with whatever other bundle the schedule called for.

But he'd never been a ball of fire. Many's the time both operators and foremen had to go scouting for him when they wanted something moved. Still, he made few mistakes. And he did have a pretty good understanding of what went on in the entire department. Besides, he was captain of the bowling team and had once run a gas station, factors that carried a lot of weight with management.

To Grady, however, Ronnie Ball was just a goof-off—someone who would go far out of his way to avoid a good day's work. In fact, he'd argued with Ronnie over many an unmoved bundle. Ronnic's getting the job came as that much more of a blow.

Last week, when he'd heard the news, he'd told Claude, "I can see that the way a man gets to be a foreman around here is by goofing off."

Claude gave this little thought until he began noticing Grady's production figures. Formerly, Grady had always turned out at least twice as much as anyone else on the job. But for the past week, his production rate had dropped to what would be normal for the other operators—in other words, not nearly enough. If it kept up, Claude estimated, his schedule would be in serious trouble soon!

Sure, he'd confronted Grady with the figures. "What about this, Grady?" he'd asked. "Haven't you been feeling well or something?"

"Been feeling fine, Claude," Grady had replied. "What makes you think I haven't?"

"Look how you've dropped off."

"I don't know what you mean, Claude, I'm doing just as good as the other guys, aren't I?"

It was true. Grady was doing as well as the other operators. That was just the trouble.

The supervisor sat down at his desk and tried to figure out what had gone wrong and, more importantly, what he might do to right it.

Had he, a production-minded supervisor, really considered Grady for the job? Or would he have favored Ronnie no matter what Grady's qualifications? Had he, Claude Miller, done as much as he might have these last three years to help Grady make himself more promotable? Ah, no sense crying over spilt milk. But he still had to find some way to get Grady back on the beam again.

GUIDES FOR ANALYSIS

1. From Grady's viewpoint, what should be the basis for promotion?
2. Why did Miller select Ronnie Ball for the job?
3. What did Miller really think of Grady?
4. Does the supervisor have a responsibility for developing his subordinates?
5. If you were Miller, what would you do now?

UP THE LADDER

"Fallon? Good kid, real good kid. I spotted him the first day he started as a general helper over in Department 20. When I had an opening I asked the foreman to release him for a transfer. Haven't been sorry yet," said Art Eversole, trim and assembly department foreman, to Sid Hazleton, the casting department supervisor. "He's smart, you know?" Eversole winked and tapped his head. "And ambitious. Reminds me of myself fifteen years ago."

Hazleton smiled and relit his pipe. "Glad to hear it, Art. I noticed him working the other day, and he looks like he can handle that trim machine."

"He sure can. Took him about a day to reach production on it, and now he's my best man. I'm telling you, Sid, that kid's on the ball. You know what he buttonholed me for after lunch? He wants to move up to an assembly machine! Really gave me a sales talk. After only three months on the trimmer, he's the fastest man in the department, and now he figures he's ready for the assembler."

"He's hungry," said Hazleton, puffing on his pipe.

"I know it, just like I was when I was his age. His wife's got a baby on the way, and he wants that 10-cents-an-hour increase. Well, he's earned the job. Matthews is transferring to nights next week, and Fallon can have his spot." Eversole sat there musing for a moment. "You know, if I just had one or two more kids like him, my department might start setting some production records around this place."

"Art, you'd better enjoy it while you can. Up-and-comers happen along only once in a while, and when they do, they don't usually stay in one department too long. They're always ready to jump at the next spot up the ladder. And Fallon will do just that. He wants to learn, and he needs the money, too."

"Look, with his speed he'll make out on that assembly machine like a bandit," said Eversole, irritably. "He'll be making more money than most young guys around here, and he'll want to stay on the assembly machine for at least a couple of years, once he gets the hang of it. If I'd had the chance to make that kind of dough when I was just starting out, you can bet I wouldn't have jumped around so much."

"Yeah, and you probably wouldn't be a foreman right now, either–and hoping to make assistant supervisor in a couple of years," replied Hazleton with a chuckle.

Almost six months went by, and Hazleton began to wonder if he hadn't been wrong. Young Fallon had seemed to settle down to the trim and assembly department for an extended stay. After the first couple of months learning the ins and outs of the assembler, he had, according to Eversole's glowing accounts, increased his productivity until he was number two man in output. From what Hazleton could observe, Fallon appeared to be a team man in trim and assembly, getting along well with the other men and his boss and enjoying his work. But then a few weeks later Hazleton found Fallon waiting for him near his office on his return from lunch. "Do something for you, Eddie?" "Hope so, Mr. Hazleton. Hear you got a slot open on one of your casting machines, and I'd like to try out for it."

"Yes, I do, Eddie," said Hazleton, stuffing his pipe into his shirt pocket, "but I thought you were doing real well on that assembler."

"I am. I'm making the highest rates in the department now," he said proudly. "But now I think I'm ready for a casting machine, and I'd sure like to get a crack at that 30 cents more an hour."

"It's okay by me, Eddie, but you better let me talk to your foreman first about a transfer. He'll probably be a little unhappy to see you go." Hazleton realized what an understatement that was when he went into Eversole's office a few minutes later and saw an angry man hunched over his desk.

"You already know what I came over here for, don't you, Art?"

" 'Course I do. The kid was over in your department, wasn't he? What else was he there for except to ask for that casting-machine job?"

"Well, I said I'd try to get him the transfer," said Hazleton, a little warily.

"You did, huh? Listen, friend, I can't spare him. He's the best operator I got, and he stays in this department. Now, if you don't mind leaving, I got some work to finish."

GUIDES FOR ANALYSIS

1. Why does Eversole want Fallon to remain in his department?
2. Does Fallon's achievement record say anything about his goals?
3. Eversole has gladly encouraged Fallon's progress within his department; does he have a responsibility to let him on up in the company?
4. What would you do if you were Sid Hazleton? Remember, Eversole spent months training Fallon to be a productive member of his department.

ASSEMBLY TWO

Clay Hagen is the supervisor of the assembly department of a medium-sized electronics company, Space-Age Industries. The company has been a fast mover in a rapidly growing industry. Until four months ago, all of the assembly work was done in a single department with around 55 women employees. Then Space-Age developed a new product, something really different in the industry, which required a new assembly department.

To keep a balance of experienced employees in both of the departments, Hagen transferred 15 of his veteran, though average-producing, employees to the new department. All of them seemed happy to make the change—in fact, several others wanted to change, too. New employees were hired for both departments, 15 new employees for each.

The production standard for the old department—now called Assembly One—is 100 units an hour. The women receive a 1 per cent hourly bonus for each unit they produce over this standard. Each employee in Assembly Two must perform two additional operations, and the work is slightly more complex. Methods engineering therefore set their production standard at 80 units with the same incentive bonus.

Hagen and Doug Turner, a member of the Training Department, trained the 30 new employees. Turner spent ten days in the new department, while Clay divided his time between the new employees in Assembly One and helping train in Assembly Two. Both were really amazed at the progress in Assembly Two. Training time to reach standard in Assembly One had usually run about five days, but Hagen had expected Assembly Two to take a month to reach that, since they had to do not only more operations but more complex ones, too. Assembly Two employees really caught on to their jobs.

Within 10 days they were producing up to standard; at the end of the first month, they were averaging 100 units per hour for a 20 per cent bonus.

It looked like everything was rolling along smoothly. Until yesterday. That was when Hagen heard the "buzz group" in Assembly One. As they returned from their afternoon break, Clay heard Jill Hawthorne, one of the veteran assemblers, talking to Sandra Crawford, one of the new employees in Assembly One.

"I average 110 units for a 10 per cent bonus, and that's just about right for Assembly One, as we are now called. But you know, Sandra, those gals in Assembly Two get a 20 per cent bonus for less work," complained Jill.

"That doesn't seem fair for them to turn out less and get paid more," agreed Sandra. Some of the other workers chimed in their general agreement, too.

Clay started to talk with them, to try to understand what was going on. But the telephone distracted him.

Clay knew he should have been prepared. The next day, Jill, Sandra, and five others stopped him on his way through the department. Jill led the discussion and repeated just about what he heard the day before. She continued, however,

"We think the standard rate for us ought to be reduced to 80 units or their standard in Assembly Two raised to 100. It's not right for us to get less for more work."

Not really knowing how to answer the argument (and realizing that the other assembly women really had made standard quickly), he promised,

"I'll check with Methods Engineering to make sure that they couldn't have made a mistake in setting the standards." The women weren't too happy with that, but it seemed to pacify them.

Well, Clay wondered, what else. Oh yeah, those rumblings in the non-incentive workers—mainly in Quality Control. They aren't on incentive because their work requires analysis and problem solving, elements that can't be timed. Most of them were at the top of their salary range. Even though they earned more than the girls in Assembly Two, they felt the difference was too little.

Clay returned to his office and called Larry Schmidt in Methods Engineering.

"Larry, recheck your standards for my new Assembly Two, will you? Those gals hit the standard mighty fast, and I'm about to have all kinds of trouble with my girls in Assembly One."

Larry countered, "I have the figures here, Clay. Those standards are correct. I was especially careful with that. In terms of the additional operations and their complexity, those women in Two have a lot more to do than those in One. There must be something wrong in One, but it isn't the standards. They're right for both sections."

Hagen spent the next hours mentally reviewing Assembly One. He couldn't think of anything wrong there—till this gripe came up, anyway. There wasn't anything there to keep them from making just as much bonus as those in Assembly Two: the work is easy, there's nothing to delay them, he concluded.

Well, thought Clay, there has to be an answer. He had to find it. He'd told Jill and Sandra that he'd talk with them tomorrow. Maybe by then something would show up—or even they might give him some clues.

GUIDES FOR ANALYSIS

1. Why might employees have asked to change to the new department?

2. What factors may exist which encourage higher production in Assembly Two?
3. Recommend a course of action for Clay Hagen.
4. Be prepared to role-play Hagen's meeting with Jill and Sandra the following day.

SIMMONS SIMULATOR CORPORATION

The Simmons Simulator Corporation was founded in 1942 by Lionel Simmons, an aeronautical engineer, to provide simulator panels for training naval pilots. Since its inception as a single-product war baby, Simmons has grown into a multimillion-dollar company with sales and rentals on more than 17 basic simulation systems. These systems range from small, relatively inexpensive devices used for testing depth perception and reflexes, to elaborate systems used in the aircraft, missile, and space industries. The large systems, typically, are rented at fees that run in excess of several thousand dollars a month.

The Simmons company sought not only to build high-quality equipment but also to assure its productive use by developing an outstanding service organization. As the company expanded into more and larger systems, Simmons saw even greater importance in guaranteeing major customers immediate service and maintenance. Building a team of servicemen with an intimate knowledge of Simmons' equipment has proven to be a costly but invaluable step in the company's continuing growth and profit. Several of Simmons' customers have commented that while other companies offered comparable equipment at lower cost, they have stuck with Simmons because of assurance of quick and competent maintenance.

To assure this service, Simmons has developed a highly trained, well-paid group of 60 to 70 "Service Engineers" who operate out of 16 district offices. As the major customers are closely clustered around ten of these offices, Simmons normally is able to put a Service Engineer in a customer's facility in less than two hours after notice of difficulty. Given the extremely complicated nature of the system, however, it may take as many as six hours to diagnose and remove the cause of a system's failure. Although such a situation is unusual, when it does occur, typically it is in a large, rented system. Thus, every hour spent on diagnosis is costing the company dollars of lost profit and, typically, is delaying important tasks in the customer's facility.

In an effort to increase the speed and accuracy of diagnostic work by the Service Engineers, George Nichols, director of service engineering, has worked with a large computer company on a "diagnostic assistance" program.

The reason for, and mechanics of, this program are given in the following memorandum from Nichols to the ten district managers reporting to him.

To: District SE Managers
From: G. W. Nichols
Subject: Diagnostic Assistance Program

As a result of the increasing difficulty in the maintenance and repair of our large rental systems, we have virtually completed plans for the installation of a diagnostic assistance program. Please arrange your schedules to make it possible for you to be in Houston on October 20 in my office for a two-day briefing. More detailed plans will be forwarded to you prior to the 20th, but it may be helpful to give you an overview of the program as it is now envisioned.

With the introduction of the Series G simulator last year, our records indicate a 15 per cent increase in the average time required to isolate causes of systems failure. Moreover, with the Series F-A2 simulator now being used in the Neptune project in three locations, we have been experiencing increased problems in locating the causes of systems failure. Fortunately, with both systems, we have had a very low failure rate, but we cannot expect to hold our market without improving the speed and accuracy of diagnostic work. As you know, Sim-Test has been our strongest competitor in both of these markets and is bragging about its "larger and better-trained" field staff.

I recognize the pressures our Service Engineers are under and do not want to appear critical of their work on these series. Rather, the diagnostic assistance program is designed to make their job a little easier. We have virtually completed a program for our home office computer which will allow for extremely rapid and accurate diagnostic assistance. We plan to connect your offices directly to the computer on January 1 of next year for data-processing purposes and will use the same input-output devices to handle diagnostic problems.

In a nutshell, the system will allow your field people, when they encounter a system failure which is not readily diagnosable, to call your office and provide symptom data which you will send through to the control computer in Houston. Based on tests of this system in several computer companies who use it to repair their own equipment, you should get a request for additional data or a diagnostic estimate within 15 seconds after sending in coded symptoms.

There are many bugs in the system that we will have to work out, and I will look forward to getting the benefit of your ideas on October 20.

One final point: until we have completed our review of the project, I would prefer that you do not discuss it with your people. After the recent incident in San Diego, we do not wish further trouble due to misunderstandings.

The San Diego incident referred to by Mr. Nichols caused quite a stir in the company. Although hourly workers in Simmons' plants are unionized, the Service Engineers are not. Three months ago, 9 of the 16 service engineers working in the San Diego branch office requested the right to hold a representation election to determine whether the Service Engineers wished to join an international electronics workers' union. The company's director of labor relations, Alex Michak, advised the men of their rights, and after several days' discussions the matter was dropped by the men. Michak reported that it really had stemmed from a "misunderstanding about company policy on tuition refunds for technical courses." Michak explained:

Tom Snow, who has been with the company for 17 years, is one of the top Service Engineers in the San Diego branch. For more than six months he has been trying to get permission to take a new course in electronics under the company's tuition-refund program. His district manager, Bart Dunn, had sat on the request because he didn't want Tom tied up in a course when he might be needed for emergency overtime because of problems with the FA-2 simulators. Besides, Bart told me that the only reason Tom wanted to take the course was so that he could qualify to be put on the new Series G simulator. Bart told me that he didn't really need Tom for Series G work since he had two new men who had just joined the company and who had the academic background to specialize on Series G maintenance.

When Snow learned that Dunn had not acted on his request, he and several other of the older Service Engineers in the district became quite upset about the way they "got pushed around" and sought the union election. Snow said:

I've been with this company a long time, and I like the work because it's always a real challenge. You really have to know the equipment inside out to maintain and repair it. If something goes wrong, it's a real test to see whether you can figure it out and fix it. We know that the faster we do our work, the more our customers like us and the more revenue for our company. But for most of us the real challenge is knowing we figured it out. Well, by now I know the Series FA-2 simulator inside out and, while there's an occasional tough one to fix on the Neptune project, I can handle that equipment blindfolded. The challenge has gone, and I want to get over to the new Series G stuff and see whether I can handle it.

George Nichols calmed Snow and the others down by assuring them that there was no company policy against high-seniority employees taking courses under the tuition-refund program. He pointed out, however, that the company found it much harder to shift men like Snow to the new systems because they were so good in their present specialties. "Besides," he pointed out, "the pay's the same regardless of what system they work on."

Tom Snow is presently enrolled in the technical course, which meets after working hours, and two other senior Service Engineers in San Diego have applied for the same course next term.

Nichols was quite relieved when things settled down because, as he put it, "Experienced men like Snow are scarce as hen's teeth. Sometimes they act more like primadonnas than repairmen, but right now they're in the driver's seat."

GUIDES FOR ANALYSIS

1. To what extent will the new program conflict with the needs of the service engineers?
2. Discuss the possible informal group reaction of the service engineers to the "diagnostic assistance program."

3. How would you recommend that the new program be explained to the service engineers?
4. If you were asked to advise G. W. Nichols, what basic problems do you foresee in the implementation of the new program? Give your recommendations on how these problems should be avoided or resolved.

THE GREAT TICKET TRAGEDY

As usual, the regular Thursday afternoon meeting of the division and department managers of the Westgate branch of Mason's department stores was in progress. Clyde Lowery from the downtown accounting department was presenting some new procedures that would be implemented in three weeks.

Stan Marvin, manager of the furniture department, impatiently drummed his fingers on the table as Lowery discussed the changes. Stan, who had been "mentally griping" suddenly tuned in on Lowery.

". . . in addition to these new steps to get sales reports to you, your salespeople will begin making the tickets on sales items which are delivered from the warehouse differently. As you know, the warehouse has often charged your departments the regular rather than the sales price on delivery merchandise. To make sure that all the inventory and charge records are kept straight, have your salespeople include the regular price, the sales price, and the difference on the tickets."

Stan, greatly concerned since a large part of his furniture sales were warehouse items, interrupted.

"What? My people will have to do all that? Isn't the merchandise number and sales price enough? Can't you keep the warehouse straight on the other stuff? We shouldn't have to do all those calculations."

Lowery, slightly startled by the outburst, replied, "Yes, we could and do try to supply the warehouse with price information. This way, though, we can be sure that every charge against your department is correct. Now, some sales information and price changes are overlooked."

Stan, still not satisfied, slumped back and muttered, "Looks like that's that. Just something else for us to do that they can't handle."

Ron Blake, store manager, continued the meeting amidst the stony stares of Stan Marvin and the somewhat less than enthusiastic expressions of the Home Improvement manager, Joe Mattern, and the Major Appliance manager, Jeff Stubblefield. These three departments sold mostly warehouse items.

At the conclusion of the meeting, Stan Marvin left hastily, thinking to himself, "Well, Lowery said to tell the salespeople now about the tickets. You bet I will. They won't like it, but it's just like always. Those guys figure they can change things around, make us do more work, and be real bigshots."

Mattern and Stubblefield likewise went to their departments to explain the new procedures. Both, however, before talking with their salespeople did some thinking. They recognized that Lowery had been right—there were mixups and this would probably help the problem. Not that they were overly enthusiastic about it; surely it meant some extra work. Both decided that the advantages were worth the trouble. After explaining the procedures, the employees in their departments generally accepted the idea.

When Stan got to his department, though, it was a different story. Striding briskly into the department, he called loudly to the two salesmen present: "Norman, Doug, come over here."

Reacting to Stan's apparent upset mood, Doug inquired, "What's up, Stan?"

Sarcastically, Stan replied, "We just had our meeting; and Lowery, the chief accountant, just put the monkey on our backs. Starting in three weeks, you're going to have to make out the tickets for the warehouse differently. From then on, you have to put the regular price, the sales price, and the difference on the tickets. Just because the warehouse can't keep their prices straight, we have to figure all that. I don't see what they're up to—probably trying to see if we're pushing sales merchandise or something. Who knows what!"

Norman ventured, "Just like those guys—think we don't have enough to do. If they did their jobs they wouldn't have to spend so much time checking on us."

"I don't like it any better than you do," replied Stan, "but I just work here too. . . ."

The grumbling continued later in the day when Stan relayed the message to the other employees in the department. For the next few days, the new ticket procedure was the main topic of discussion in the department.

Three weeks passed, and almost everyone had just about forgotten about the situation. Stan received notice that the new procedures were to go into effect. "Okay, fellas, this is it," he told them that morning. "You remember the new warehouse tickets—start that mess today. Don't gripe to me. I can't help it."

Doug, Norman, and the other employees shrugged their shoulders and walked off.

Two weeks passed. Whenever Stan happened to write up a ticket, he grudgingly but silently followed the new procedure. He didn't mention it to the others.

Thursday afternoon came and the managers meeting convened. Ron Blake distributed the various reports to the managers, including the warehouse distribution sheet. Attached to Stan's was a stack of tickets.

"What's all this on here?" questioned Marvin, pointing to the tickets.

"Well," replied Blake, "rather than give you an incorrect accounting of your warehouse sales costs, they sent copies of the tickets back."

" 'Incorrect'. . . 'costs' . . . what are you talking about?" sputtered Stan.

"They weren't sure what may have been sales merchandise, because of all your department's tickets only yours have all the calculations on them. All the others are figured like regular price."

"What? That makes my profit ratio look bad! I told those guys to figure the tickets the new way," retorted Marvin.

"Maybe they didn't get the message, Stan," replied Blake. "If you want a complete, accurate picture, you'll have to figure out the best way to get the information."

Stan was stunned. He wondered, "Those dummies–why did they mess up all these tickets?"

Meeting over, Stan left determined to give his guys "a piece of his mind." "Make me look bad, will they?" he thought.

Bitter over the embarrassment he had faced at the meeting, the extra work he faced, and his employees' failure to follow instructions, he rushed toward his department.

GUIDES FOR ANALYSIS

1. Why do you suppose the employees in Stan's department failed to make out the tickets properly?
2. Did Stan in any way contribute to the situation?
3. Did the attitudes of the other department managers toward the change influence the way they presented the new procedure to their employees?
4. "Stop Stan before he gets to his department." Recommend a course of action for him to follow.
5. Be prepared to role-play Stan's meeting with his employees,
   a. without having heard your recommendations.
   b. with your recommendations.

THE GUILTY PARTY

"Five hundred and fifty today, Dad. How many did your boys push out?" The speaker was Len Bagley, the young assistant foreman–one of two in the fractional motor department.

"Enough," Dan Ross replied without looking at Bagley. He was the other assistant foreman in the department. "And don't call me 'Dad,' " he added.

"Why not?" asked Bagley, grinning. "After all, you're plenty old enough to be my father—not that I need another father!"

"Don't think for a minute I'd want a wise-guy like you for a—oh, forget it."

"What's the matter, Dan?" asked Bagley, walking with the older man. "You don't look like you feel well."

"I'm just a little tired, that's all," said Ross.

"Could be the competition is getting to you, Dad." Bagley's voice returned to its former mocking tone.

"Listen," muttered Dan Ross in a savage undertone. "I don't know where you get this idea you and I are competing, but my advice is to cut it. My men put out a decent day's work, and that's all a decent foreman can expect of 'em—and Phil Blocker is pretty decent. Now, if you want to stay on your men's tails all the time just so you can make a hero out of yourself, that's your business. I'm not built that way."

"Okay, okay—don't get yourself shook," said Bagley. "Tell me one thing, though. If Phil is so damned decent, how come he set it up like this in the first place?"

"What are you talking about?"

"You know what I'm talking about. He didn't have to split the line up into two parts, right down the middle, so that we'd have almost the same equipment and manpower to work with."

"The way he's got it set up is his business," said Ross. "He's the foreman, isn't he? Besides, common sense would tell you that two of us splitting it down the middle is the only fair way."

"You think there's always going to be two of us? We're the only department that has this set-up. When Phil moves up to assistant super, there's gonna be one foreman—the guy that's got the best record. *Me.*"

"Baloney. Phil doesn't think like that. He's always told me that how you get along with your men is just as important as production."

"You just go on thinking that, " said Bagley, taking off his shoes. "But some time," replied Bagley with a slow grin, "get Phil to show you the chart he keeps on both of us."

"I got other things to do besides stick my nose in where it doesn't belong," muttered Ross, uncomfortably.

Three days later, Len Bagley was in Phil Blocker's office. "Look, Phil, if anyone else besides Pete Case had spotted this I'd have never come to you. But you know what a bigmouth Pete is, and I thought you'd better hear it from me before he blabbed it all over the place."

"You're sure there couldn't be any mistake about this?" asked Blocker.

"I just wish there was, Phil. I saw Dan transferring those cases from the reject bin back to the on-line rack for two days running. Hell, you can probably spot him youself if you keep an eye out after the shift goes off tonight."

"I guess that's what I'll have to do," said Blocker, thoughtfully. "Dan's been with me for over fifteen years."

"I know how it must be, Phil," said Bagley. "But I think he's been doing it because he's worried about keeping up with my unit production. This way, he wouldn't have that rework time on his record. I thought there was something funny about the way he was turning out way more than he used to."

"You're the last guy I thought would ever pull a stunt like this, Dan," said Blocker the next day.

"So am I," muttered Ross, his misery plainly showing on his face. "I don't suppose it would do any good to say it'll never happen again?"

"Maybe, if just you and me knew about it; but it's already gone all over the plant. I wouldn't be surprised if the Old Man has gotten wind of it."

Dan Ross sighed. "I guess I'm just out of luck. I should never have let that Bagley kid get to me with his talk of who was going to make foreman around here."

"What did he say?"

"Something about how you set it up so that whoever got the most stuff out the door would make foreman."

"Well, I did have something like that in mind," Blocker replied after some hesitation.

"I wish you'd told me about it, Phil. Then I might not have had to play catch-up all of a sudden."

Ross looked directly at Blocker. "Okay, I'm guilty," he said. "What happens next?"

GUIDES FOR ANALYSIS

1. Is high production over a short time indicative of good leadership?
2. Would you blame yourself in any way for this situation if you were Phil Blocker? If so, how would that affect the way you handled it?
3. What does happen next? What would be your course of action if you were Phil Blocker?
4. Be prepared to role-play the ensuing conversation at the end of the case when Dan Ross says, "What happens next?"

THE PRIMA DONNA

It was just a month ago that Bill Jordan, head of Research and Development for Quality Chemicals, had given Mike Elkins the good news that he was to become the supervisor of Quality Control the next week.

"Mike, you've only been with the company five months," Bill had told him, "but we feel that with the unusual flair you've shown for engineering you shouldn't have any trouble with the department. That's a pretty sharp group over there."

Mike and Bill reported to Quality Control the next Monday. After Bill introduced Mike as the new supervisor, Mike went into his new office. He felt that he really had a lot to learn; the former supervisor was already gone, but Mike reasoned that surely he'd be able to find out how the department really worked if he studied the records.

The men in the department hadn't exactly welcomed him as he would have liked. He hadn't gotten to know them personally. Right now it seemed more important that he learn the operation of the department; he could get to the "personal bit" later. Anyway, the men seemed to accept the fact that he was the new supervisor.

The past month had gone pretty well. Mike reflected as he sat in the office that he really would have to consider himself off to a good start, and he couldn't see any real problems ahead. He felt pretty secure in the job; studying the records and procedures had really helped. Then, too, Bill had been right about the crew—they were a pretty good bunch who seemed to be able to carry the ball without too much from him. Even though he had stayed in his office most of the time since he'd been there, he had a pretty good feel for their capabilities from the test reports.

Suddenly, the phone rang. It was Bill Jordan.

"The testing section will be running a special series on load capabilities starting Monday," Bill told him. "They need someone from your group to help keep an eye on it. It'll be a temporary assignment, probably no more than two or three weeks. But they need someone with a lot on the ball. I hate to say it, but what we need is the best you've got."

Mike hesitated a moment. "Then I guess that would be Gene Hock. I hate to lose him right now, but he seems to do a good job and be on the ball."

"Good, that's whom I had in mind, too. It's a pretty important series, and they need someone who can think," replied Jordan. "Have him report to Testing on Monday."

Mike hung up the phone, glanced at the clock and noted that it was late—right at quitting time in fact. Well, he'd better go see Hock. Here it was Friday—that wasn't much warning.

"Hi, Gene," Mike said as he approached Hock's station. "Got a moment?"

Hock put down the part he was inspecting and said cautiously: "Sure, what is it?"

Mike began, "Jordan just called me. They need a man in Testing starting Monday. They're going to be doing some special series for about three weeks. They need someone from our department, so I told them I'd send you. Bill said they'd give you all the details when you report first thing Monday."

Gene turned slowly and began, "Just some more bother, huh? You told them you'd send me?"

Slightly puzzled by Gene's seeming reluctance, Mike replied, "Yeah, just go on over there Monday like I said."

Hock stared, glared actually, then very loudly said, "Why pick on me to go over there? Aren't I doing okay here?"

Mike started, really startled at the reaction, "Of course, you're doing okay here, but they needed. . . ."

Gene interrupted, "I probably know more about this job than you ever will, Elkins. But as soon as somebody says they need an extra man, who gets sent? Hock! Yeah, I know, as far as you're concerned, I'm dispensable. All you need is your little stack of reports. We just do the work."

By now there was quite an attentive audience. The other inspectors had stopped their work to listen.

Mike, struck silent by the outburst, thought, "He looks like he's got a lot more to say; what brought this on? I'd better do something fast!"

GUIDES FOR ANALYSIS

1. What does Gene Hock feel that Mike Elkins is saying to him?
2. Why has Hock misinterpreted Elkins' feelings about him?
3. What can Elkins do now to straighten out the situation?
4. Be prepared to role-play the rest of the conversation between Hock and Elkins.

SOUTHWESTERN FABRICATORS

Southwestern Fabricators, a division of a large national concern, employed about 200 people—most of them skilled workmen. The nonunion company had a history of fairly good employee relations. In fact, Bob Portwood, production supervisor, was proud of his company's low turnover. Of course, the company paid good wages and had a good fringe-benefit package for all employees.

However, Bob was slightly puzzled right now. Last week, production in the machine shop had been very erratic—up one day, down the next—and there just wasn't any logical explanation for it. This week, it was even worse. Something was going on, he knew, because at least three times during the week he'd noticed clusters of his men engaged in rather heated discussions. He hadn't been able to learn what they were talking about because the groups always broke up whenever he appeared. Once he had inquired if they needed him to work out something, but they had just sort of mumbled and gone back to work.

Portwood did notice that most of these groups had one thing in common, however, and that was Larry Walker, a veteran lathe operator. Walker had always been a satisfactory performer, above average in many respects, but whenever there was controversy in the department, it was a good bet that he'd be involved in some way. Walker had been with the company for about ten years and seemed to know everyone who worked there. Many of the younger workers in the department seemed to look up to him and regarded him as "someone in the know."

On Friday, Portwood once more encountered a group of men. This time, though, he heard a little of what was being said before they rapidly broke up: they were talking about a layoff! Portwood decided to take Walker aside and try to get to the bottom of these meetings and this "layoff talk."

"Larry," he asked, "what do you know about this talk about a layoff?"

Walker looked at him for a moment and then smiled. "Finally going to give us the news, eh? Well, I just know what I hear—a layoff's in the works and it could hit any time. Now's the time, huh?"

"Wait a minute. I didn't say there was going to be a layoff!"

"They already laid off five guys in the other shop. I heard about that last week," countered Walker.

Portwood bristled. "Well, you're wrong this time. Dead wrong." He wanted to add that he thought Walker was at the bottom of the talk but thought better of it and didn't.

"No layoff?" Walker asked in mock amazement. "Come on, Bob, you can level with me. I've been around here long enough to know a layoff's coming when I see it. All you've got to do is look around you—there're signs all over the place. It's as plain as the nose on your face."

Portwood knew that Walker was probably referring to two ominously empty work stations from which machines had been removed a couple of weeks ago. "If it's those machines we took out that're bothering you, why didn't you fellows ask me about them before you went off halfcocked and jumped to crazy conclusions? That equipment was so outmoded it was pathetic—you know that—so we got rid of it.

"Well, the last time you took out some machines was right before that layoff," interrupted Walker.

"But we've got some replacements ordered, and they should be here in a few weeks. As for those guys in the other department, they were trainees who just didn't have it."

"No kidding?" Walker asked, still not convinced that he wasn't right about the impending layoff. "Well, if that's the case, I guess the guys in the other shop were wrong. I heard that everybody would be cutting back just like they did. Maybe nothing's behind all this we've been hearing. Just been worrying for nothing." And with that he went back to work.

Portwood wasn't sure that he'd been able to convince Walker, however. After all, the department had been hit by a layoff a few months before, and it always took a while for confidence to rebuild after something like that. At any rate, he'd made up his mind that he'd have to keep an eye on the situation.

His nagging suspicion that there might be problems was confirmed in less time than he imagined possible. Tuesday morning, John Cook, a young worker who'd been stationed near Walker, handed in his notice.

"I thought you liked it here," Portwood told him. "Is something wrong?"

"Sure I like it here," Cook answered. "The work's great. But I've only been here a few months, and when the layoff hits I'll be one of the first to go. The other three guys who started when I did feel the same way. I might stick it out and take my chances; but I've got a family to think about, too. So I lined up this job over at. . . ."

"Layoff!" Portwood blurted out. "What layoff? There's not going to be any layoffs around here."

"But I've been hearing about it for weeks," Cook told him. "What with those guys in the other shop going and taking the machines out. . . ."

"Well, you can forget about what you've heard," Portwood said heatedly. "Look, have you actually agreed to take this other job? Because if you haven't, I want you to sit tight. And as far as that layoff goes, you can take it from me that there isn't going to be one."

"Well, I don't know," responded Cook. "I would rather stay here, I'll think about it a couple of days. I don't know about the other guys, though. Larry Walker told us about the layoff, and he seems to know what's going on around here."

Until Cook tried to hand in his notice, Walker's storytelling had always struck Portwood as being harmless—the sort of thing that goes on in every shop. But now he could see that it was affecting morale and that something would have to be done before it got any further out of hand.

Now, to find Walker and talk to him!

GUIDES FOR ANALYSIS

1. What position does Larry Walker hold in the work group?
2. How has Bob Portwood created this situation? Or has he?
3. What was the men's source of information?
4. What has management communicated to the men?
5. Advise Bob Portwood on the course of action that he should follow.
6. Be prepared to role-play the coming confrontation between Portwood and Walker.

SO, DO ME SOMETHING

Jack Orman, the sub-assembly foreman, read the petition on his desk for the third time in the half hour since he'd received it. He'd been a foreman now for six years, and this was the first written protest he'd ever received from his crew.

The petition was from the workers on the "E" line—one of the five five-man groups that did the sub-assembly wiring on the vending machines that the company made.

It read: "We, the undersigned, do not want to work with Louis Walsher any longer. He has been a disrupting influence ever since he was hired and assigned to break in with us a year ago. Furthermore, although he has learned the work, he deliberately works slower than the rest of his fellow employees and impedes their progress, thus preventing them from making their full rates on the pool. We, the undersigned, have tried every way we know how to get this fellow employee to cooperate, but he just does not want to do so. Therefore, either we would like to have him replaced with someone who can get along with other human beings or we want to be transferred to another department."

"This is pretty bitter stuff," said Jack Orman to Al Lauder, the lead man of the "E" group and one of the signers of the petition. "And it's also a hot potato that you've dropped in my lap. You know as well as I do how closely the Old Man has been working with the state handicapped-workers program. That's how come Lou is working here in the first place. And it's supposed to be a compliment to you guys that you'd be understanding enough to take in a guy like Lou. Don't think the front office hasn't been keeping an eye on how he's getting along—him and all the other handicapped we've hired."

"That's the reason we all signed this thing, Jack," said the lead man. "It isn't as if only one or two of us feel this way—we all do. And don't think we don't feel lousy about the way it's turning out. The thing of it is, it's not the fact that he's in a wheel chair that's causing the trouble—it's the guy's personality. He is just no damned good. He's a trouble-maker. He can do the work all right, but all he's interested in is lousing the rest of us up. Hell, we've even told him to get lost somewhere, but he just sticks around and gets in our way. Believe me, we've tried everything we can think of."

"Have you invited him in on all the different things you guys do?" asked the foreman. "Maybe you've been making him out to be a cripple, and he doesn't like it."

"Come on, Jack—you know better than that. We wouldn't do that to a guy. He won't play cards with us, he won't stop for a beer, he won't do anything. We've tried to get him to go bowling with us, but he just makes one of those sarcastic remarks of his—something about bowling being for creeps like us—and he won't eat lunch with us—just goes off and listens to that transistor radio of his. We've given it a good try, but it just hasn't worked."

"There must be something we can try that'll make this thing work out." The speaker was Tom Drucker, the personnel director. He, Orman, and Walt Frost, the superintendent of Orman's department were sitting in Drucker's office. "I don't mind saying that this isn't going to look good for anyone if we have to get rid of Walsher or transfer the rest of the crew."

"I don't care so much about looking good, Tom," said Jack Orman. "I just don't want to lose my best group of assemblers."

"You may," said Frost, "unless you can get them in line. The way I understand it, there's a lot at stake in this handicapped program. There are some mighty good customers of ours in back of it."

The personnel director nodded. "That's about the way I see it, too. We've got to make more of an effort than we have so far."

"You'll get it when I'm good and ready!" Lou Walsher's voice came loud and clear and irritably from the section in which he and the rest of the group were working.

"Damn it, I just have to tighten this one flange up," said one of the other assemblers. "You can spare that wrench for two seconds."

"The hell I can!"

Jack Orman walked up to the work area where the argument was taking place. His intention was to have a heart to heart talk with Lou Walsher. "Why can't you let him use that, Lou?"

"Because he's got one of his own that he lent to someone, that's why. Now he's just gonna have to wait 'till I get through. I got my own work to do."

"But you're all supposed to be working together as a team," said the foreman.

"So go ahead and do me something," said Lou Walsher, sitting in his wheel chair.

GUIDES FOR ANALYSIS

1. Why may Walsher have declined to take part in the group's activities?
2. Should a group be prepared by management for the addition of a "different" worker such as a handicapped person?
3. Is Lou Walsher's attitude understandable?
4. Is the group's attitude understandable?
5. What would you do now if you were in Jack Orman's shoes? You're not permitted to replace Walsher. On the other hand, if you don't do something about his attitude toward the rest of the crew you stand to lose them all.
6. Be prepared to role-play the confrontation between Walsher and Orman at the end of the case when Walsher says, "So go ahead and do me something."

THE FRIENDLY SUPERVISOR HEARS NO EVIL

While driving to work, Bill Dossey, day-shift supervisor in Maintenance, remembered that this morning he had an appointment with Dave Snell, one of his arc welders. Dossey recalled that Snell, who had been with the company about five years, had asked at least a half-dozen times for "conferences" with him. They usually ended up with Snell asking about some trivial matter, like the time he took 20 minutes to ask for a new pair of safety gloves. "Well, I guess I'll have to go through with it and see what he has to complain about," Dossey thought to himself.

He prided himself on being friendly and putting his men at ease when they wanted to talk to him, even though most of them didn't seem to have any really important problems to discuss. In fact, half the time most of them just wanted to talk about their families or fishing or something like that. He knew them pretty well and always made it a point to go to their informal departmental gatherings.

Later that morning, Snell walked into Dossey's office. "Sit down, Dave," Dossey said. "Say, did you watch that movie on television last night?" the supervisor asked. "I don't remember when I've laughed so much."

"No, boss, I didn't. What I came in here to talk with you about is. . . ." Snell began.

"The trouble with old movies is that they remind you of how quickly time flies. We were all 15 years younger when it first came out," Dossey said, leaning back in his chair. "What I wouldn't do to be 15 years younger. Know what I mean?" Dossey asked, chuckling to himself.

"Sure thing," Snell answered. "Mr. Dossey, for the past couple of weeks my wife hasn't. . . ."

"Say, how is Marilyn?" Dossey interrupted. "I haven't seen her since our Christmas party. We really had a good one–we'd better all be getting together again soon."

"Well, Marilyn's what I wanted to talk with you about." Snell said quickly. "You see, for the past couple of weeks she hasn't felt well, and Monday I finally talked her into seeing a doctor."

"Nothing serious, I hope," Dossey responded, learning forward on his desk.

"No, it's not serious, but the doctor suggested that she take it easy for a few weeks and. . . ."

"Oh, glad to hear it. You just never know these days. Seems like so many terrible things happening around you all the time. Give her a good rest and it'll be okay though, huh? That's good news."

Just then his telephone rang. "Dossey speaking," the supervisor said. "Oh yes, Mr. McDonald . . . . Sure I can come up right away. . . . No, I'm not busy. One of my men is in here, but it's not that important. I'll be right up."

"Uh, Mr. Dossey, what I wanted to ask you was. . . ."

"Save it for later, Dave. When the boss calls, I've got to move."

"But Mr. Dossey, I've got to. . . ." Snell almost pleaded.

"Come in and see me anytime, like tomorrow afternoon. We'll get to it then," Dossey said, slightly irritated, as he got up from his desk and started toward the door.

Heading for Bob McDonald's office, Dossey wondered what Snell had wanted. All he had done was give him a rundown on his wife's health; probably wanted to complain about the doctor bills.

That afternoon, Dossey received a second call from his boss. "Bill," McDonald said, "if there's no one in your office right now, I'd like you to come up here."

When Dossey walked into his office, McDonald got right to the point. "Listen, Bill, one of your men was just in here to see me, and he was pretty upset."

"I don't know what or who you're talking about," Dossey began, obviously puzzled.

"I'm talking about Dave Snell," McDonald said.

"Snell! I saw him this morning. He told me something about his wife being ill, but that the doctor had said that it wasn't serious. I gather that all she needs is a few weeks of rest. That's all he had to say. Oh, yeah–he wanted to complain about the doctor bills or something, but I needed to come up here."

"Well," McDonald said, rather irritated, "I don't know exactly what happened in your meeting, but Snell feels that he received short shrift. The whole point of his wanting the appointment was to ask for permission to take time off to drive his wife to her sister's house. He thought she could take care of her. He wasn't looking for sympathy or to give you doctor's reports. He was making a perfectly reasonable request, which you evidently turned down."

"But he never asked for time off; so I didn't turn him down. I would have let him off for something like that. Why didn't he get to the point?" Dossey asked, his face flushed from the dressing down.

"Well," McDonald continued, "I told him I would talk to you about the situation, so we'd better figure some way to straighten this out and see that it doesn't happen again."

GUIDES FOR ANALYSIS

1. Why did Dave feel that he had been treated "poorly"?
2. What did Bill communicate to Dave? How?
3. Why did Bill feel that his men "usually didn't have any important things to discuss"?
4. What do you recommend that Bob McDonald do to "straighten this out" and "see that it doesn't happen again"?

WHAT AM I DOING HERE?

James Monroe had suddenly begun to ask himself, "What am I doing here?" After his promotion and transfer to the southwest branch of Barrington's, a local

EXHIBIT 1.

barrington's

houston, texas

From: J. Monroe To: Area Staff

Greeting from the new idiot of your areas. Even though I've talked to most of you already, I'd like to say now pleased I am that I am now in the new areas. Of course, most of you realize that all of these areas are "Christmas Areas" and that I am totally unfamiliar with the merchandise, personnel, stock areas, figures, and even the department numbers. I urge all of you to help me learn as fast as my feeble mind will allow me to do. In the same turn, I am a total new "project" for you, and you do not know my way of managing, methods of operation, expectations, and goals. Thus, the age-old problem of mankind--that of co-existance is forced upon us. This means, we must each try to live with each other, understanding, helping, and most of all cooperating with each other for the bettermend of the area. (And our jobs)

First of all, I feel that I do not have 13 departments (or whatever the exact total might be) but that I am responsible for an area. I feel that each of you are qualified for movement into another area (not technical areas, such as cameras) but from one into another. Even though, previously, you were a china lady, or silver lady, etc, but now I expect each of you to remain in your most familiar area, but remember, you are not tied there. If I should ask you to move areas to cover a lunch, break, or while stock is being cleared, I do not want to hear "that's not my area," because it is, as long as I am responsible for area 4, 14, and 10.

I have also requested that all 5:30 totals be called in by Barbara White, and then put on my desk. On her day off, she has assigned that task to someone else.

Any paperwork, (transfers, <u>and</u> new orders coming in) that accompanies merchandise into my area will be put in the bottom drawer of my file cabnet, according to the department number. Also, any merchandise leaving the area, (except BITUC) the pink copy will be put into the file in the top drawer marked "Goods Transferred Out).

When I receive a "Price Revision Notice" I take it from my mailbox and make a Xerox copy at once. I then put that copy in my file in the top drawer, marked New Mark Downs, Ups,.....and then put the original in your mail boxes (on my desk top also)....when you have

houston, texas

completed the counts you will go to the New File, remove the copy, and fill it in according with the figures on the original copy and replace it to the file marked "Markdowns Completed"....and put the original in my mail box on the right hand side of the desk.

I have a pet-peave about having things left ix on my desk that have no messages, reasons, or instructions left with them....so please, if you leave anything on it...please let me know why, or what it is there for.

When I receive a proof from the ad department, I usually look over it, then place it in your mail box, and ask if "we're well stocked, or have enough, etc! If we are in trouble...LET ME KNOW IMMEDIATELY.... so that I mightxxxxxx take the necessary steps to help us out of it.

On my right hand drawer, I keep a file of Advertising by the month... it is up to each individual to see that you are aware of what is "happening" in your individual department...you might get a little notebook, and write down what ads are running when, so that we can be on the "lookout" for any trouble that might arise....such as no merchandiss. These are <u>usually</u> 2 weeks in advance, but occasionaly change, so check it periodiocally and we wont slip up. (like every 3 days)

If I receive phone calls on the floor, and you cannot find me, ask them if they can leave a message, or a phone xxxxxx number, (and a name) so that I might call back. DO NOT say that you dont know wheere I am and let it go at that.....that makes you look a little silly, and me a ghost. THE Take the message and leav it on my desk as soon as you get a free moment from all your custommers, or if you should xxk spot me coming, hand it to me personally.

Finally, xif I am with another person, Mr. Metcalf, Knapp, another Area Manager, buyer, and I have a phone call, ask them for a message also, and give it to me, but do not , (unless of course it is extremely urgent) walk up and say that I have a phone call....merely give me a message on paper, and I shall handle it.

I"m sure that these seem a little harsh as compared to some of your previous rules and regulations, but I am a very organized persnn (or try to be ha ha) and get very "uptight" when xxxxxx anything is "out of order" or in total confusion.

As far as our stock rooms go, I will be asking each of you for a little more manual labor this week and next, as you know Gourmet Shop is set up on Monday, and all of our Christmas Gifts, Candles, Records, Candy etc. is coming in each day in great quanity, and I'm being xx bombarded with questions on "where to put it"....I certainly wish I knew....so please, bear with me.

houston, texas

Again, I"m very pleased with my new areas, and I only hope that we can accomplish a good x rapport between us....and please, IF ANYONE HAS ANY QUESTIONS, GRIPES, PROBLEMS, ETC.......TELLXXME....AND IF I CAN IN ANY WAY HELP YOU I WILL, IF NOT I"LL SEND YOU TO SOMEONE WHO CAN....BUT DONT WAIT TILL LAST TO TELL ME...THAT WONT SOLVE ANYTHING......

In case we"re so swamped in the near future, or should I have a nervous breakdown by then end of December......Merry Christmas.....

J Monroe

department-store chain, James' life had been in a continuous state of turmoil, all seemingly coming to a climax this afternoon. "What have I done to deserve this mess?" he again pondered.

Only nine days ago, he had been quite contented as Housewares Department Manager at Barrington's downtown store. The Christmas season was only a couple of weeks away when the personnel manager, Mr. Sewell, unexpectedly informed him of his promotion to Area Manager at the branch store, making him responsible for a total of 13 departments.

Mr. Sewell mentioned something during their conference about the present Area Manager at the branch store being replaced suddenly because "he just couldn't handle the job." He also commented on the man's "loose operating style" that the company apparently was not pleased with. The personnel manager had continued, "I have full confidence, James, that you're ready for the move and can handle the new situation. There are some good department heads at that store, and I know they'll help you get started in any way they can. It'll take you a little while to get oriented, but that's to be expected. If you hit any snags, let the department heads help you out; they know their operation, so don't hesitate to ask their advice if you need it."

At first, it was too great to believe. At age 28, James had thought it would be at least another year before he could even be considered for promotion; he had had his own department for only slightly over a year.

The first week on the new job had been spent in trying to get a grasp of his new duties and responsibilities as quickly as possible; twelve- to fourteen-hour work days became common for James. He made an effort to meet as many of the personnel in his area as he could and tried to know everyone by name. Contrary to what Mr. Sewell had said, however, the department heads weren't all that cooperative. It almost seemed that they considered him to be in their way.

James was determined to gain control of the situation, however. In an effort to gain the support of everyone in the area and to communicate his methods of operation, James sat down at his typewriter and composed a memo that was distributed to all area department heads and sales personnel. (A copy of this memo is presented in Exhibit 1.)

The memo had been sent out two days ago, and yet everything seemed to be going wrong today. "What is wrong with these people? Surely, they've read the memo by now," thought James.

The day had started out all wrong when James had walked into his office only to find a stack of miscellaneous notes, invoices, and other papers strewn across his desk. It had taken him almost an hour to shovel through them and file them properly.

Several of the papers pertained to the Linen Department, so James walked over and asked the manager, Mrs. Craig, if she would please file the paperwork in the appropriate places as he had requested in his memo.

Although James thought he had asked her in a reasonable tone of voice, the woman exploded, "I don't have time to be your file clerk; I've got a department to run."

"I fail to understand your attitude," replied James, nearly in a state of shock. "It was a reasonable request, I believe."

He decided to let the matter drop for now, but knew that some action would have to be taken later.

On top of that, he received a phone call from Mr. Kravitz, the store manager, asking why James had failed to return his phone message informing him of a management meeting that took place earlier in the morning.

James uttered clumsily that he had not received the message and was quite sorry he had missed the meeting. Just then, he spotted a scrawled note taped to his door reading simply, "Call the Old Man."

As if all this weren't enough, two salespeople in the Lamp Department called in with what was supposedly the "flu." He had asked Mrs. Thompson of the China Department to fill in in the Lamp Department. She whined, "I can't do that Mr. Monroe; I know absolutely nothing about lamps. I'd do more harm than good in that department."

James threw his arms in the air, hung his head and shook it slowly, wondering half aloud, "What in the . . . ." as he heard the incessant ringing of his phone in the background. Stumbling to the office, he snatched the phone and answered with a very gruff "Hello."

"James," came the startled voice from the phone, "this is Mr. Sewell. You sound a little upset. Is something wrong?"

"No, Mr. Sewell, everything's fine–just great, in fact," James replied wearily. "All I have to do now is figure out what I am doing here!"

GUIDES FOR ANALYSIS

1. Has James created any problems for himself? If so, how has he done so?
2. What did James' memo communicate to his employees?
3. Have the employees reacted as you would have predicted?
4. Recommend a course of action to James.

LARKIN'S LAST LAUGH

Annie Larkin was furious. She'd been a lead woman assembler for almost five years; and now that there was an opening for foreman of her department, they were trying to tell her that she wasn't even going to be considered for the spot. "You say it's tradition! she said, angrily. "I say it's prejudice! That's right– PREJUDICE! Pure and simple. But go ahead and laugh all you want. We'll see who has the last laugh around here!"

"But I wasn't laughing at you, Annie," said Stan Shutz, her general foreman on the first shift. "All I was saying was. . . ." But she'd decided that she'd heard enough, so she didn't wait to hear Shutz finish. She stormed out of his office, slamming the door behind her.

"Boy!" exclaimed Stan, laughing to himself. "Women!"

Bert Strong, the day foreman that Annie wanted to replace, laughed with him when Shutz told him about the incident. "I've heard some screwy ideas in my time, but I never thought I'd be hearing them come from Annie. I always thought that she was pretty level-headed as a rule."

"Yeah, but they're all alike, basically," said Shutz. "Once they get it into their heads that you're trying to do 'em out of something, they try to get back at you any way they can. I'll bet you dollars to doughnuts that the next guy to hear about this is Al Sloan."

"Think he'll listen to her?" asked Strong.

"Al? Not a chance," answered Shutz. "He didn't get to be top man on this shift because he hasn't got good sense, you know. All Annie's got to do is hit him one time with that screwy idea of hers about being foreman, and he'll throw her right out of the office—politely, of course. Come to think of it, he might even take her lead-woman job away from her. I wouldn't put it past him, you know. He doesn't have time to fool around with crazy ideas like that."

"He'll break her heart if he does," commented Strong. "She waited a long time for that job, and I know it means a lot to her."

"Well, no one asked her to stick her neck out like she's doing," commented Shutz, emphatically. "Her trouble is that she's getting swell-headed. Just because she can handle a bunch of temperamental women, she thinks that she can step right in and order a bunch of guys around, too. Whew! When I think of what might happen if she ever got that job—I don't even like to think about it.

"I wish you hadn't told her that you're being transferred over to the other plant, Bert. It would've been better for everybody if she'd found out about the opening after we'd already found somebody else to fill it. Of course, who'd ever have thought that she'd think of putting in for it?"

The doors opened and Jake Dobbs, one of the inspectors, walked in. Spotting a chance to get some supporting evidence for his point, Shutz asked him, "How would *you* like it if you had to work under a woman foreman, Jake?"

"Are you kidding me?" asked Dobbs in return. "You'd better be, because it'll be a cold day in Hell before you'd catch me working for a woman. My brother did for a while; and from what he told me, I don't want any part of it. Besides, my old lady pushes me around enough at home. I figure good jobs aren't that hard to come by."

Shutz looked at Strong and smiled. "What'd I tell you?" He knew he'd made his point. Annie could try all she wanted to get a foreman's position, but the men would never accept her. And that meant that she'd never get it.

Shutz was right about Annie Larkin. When she left his office she was steaming with rage. She knew that she was the most qualified candidate for the vacancy, and she wasn't going to let them pass over her just because she happened to be a woman—at least, not if she could help it. So, she went straight to Al Sloan to have it out with him. When she finished telling him her story, he told her that he was sorry that she was so upset and that he'd look into the matter as soon as he could.

Later that afternoon, as Annie walked through the shop to the section where the women did the assembly work, she was greeted by some men who'd heard about her run-in with Shutz. "What do you say, boss lady?" called out one, and another brought himself to attention and gave her an exaggerated salute. "All right, all right," said Annie, trying to pass it off with a smile. But by the time she reached her section, she was beginning to wonder whether she hadn't made a mistake by saying anything about that foreman's job in the first place.

Early the next morning, she was called into the office of Sid Trask, the company's personnel man. "I'm only talking to you because Al Sloan has asked me to," he told her. "I don't really have much to add to what you've been told already. You see, we've always had a man in that spot, and I don't think that we're ready to change that policy at the present time. I understand that the boys on the floor have been giving you a rough time since they learned about it."

"That doesn't bother me, Sid," answered Annie.

"Well, I can tell you that it sure bothers me," Trask commented. "My job is rough enough without any new problems popping up, especially problems like this one. As I said, it would take a change in company policy to get you this job, and the policy isn't going to be changed. And if you're thinking about taking it to a higher court—like Mr. Ramsey—I can tell you right now that you'll be wasting your time. I had a hard enough time as it is convincing him that you were qualified to handle the job you've got."

Annie's jaw thrust forward. "Well, I can tell you that I definitely was thinking of going to him about it," she said defiantly. "Especially since all I've been getting so far is the runaround. This company has government contracts that state in black and white that you can't have any discrimination because of race, color, creed, or sex. I've been a lead woman for five years, and I know that you don't have anyone that's more qualified for the job. And what's more, I think a court of arbitration will agree with me—if it has to go that far!"

"Court of arbitration?" asked Trask. "Where'd you hear about that?"

"In the newspaper, that's where," she answered, as defiant as ever. "There was a case almost exactly like mine out in California last month. Would you like to guess who won?"

"All right, Annie," said Trask, grinning. "Why don't you let me talk to the Old Man about it. I can't promise you that anything will come of it—just don't be too surprised if he blows his top, though."

Two days later, Stan Shutz called Annie into his office. He didn't look very pleased. "I'm not sure what you told Trask or what he told the Old Man," he told her grimly, "but you're our new foreman—or perhaps I should say 'forewoman.' God only knows what's going to happen now. We'll probably have half the crew quitting by the end of the week—that or asking for transfers to other departments."

As Annie left the office, Stan wondered what he should do now.

GUIDES FOR ANALYSIS

1. Was Annie right to push her case?
2. What opinions do the men seem to have of Annie? Have they changed?
3. What role has Stan played in creating this situation?
4. Recommend a course of action to Stan.
5. Be prepared to role-play Stan's next conversation with the men in the department.

*ALBATROS ELECTRICAL COMPANY**

In the fall of 1959 the Albatros Electrical Company built a refrigerator assembly plant in Asheville, North Carolina. Among the original work force was John Franks, who was hired as a cleaner. A cleaner's job was to keep the floors swept and to remove all empty cartons and boxes from the work areas. The job paid a low wage and was considered undesirable by most job applicants. John was forty-nine years old at the time he was hired and was the oldest member of the cleaning section of the maintenance department. In the fall of 1960 the plant was organized by an international union, and John Franks was appointed shop steward for the cleaners.

The maintenance department consisted of four groups: the electricians, the mechanics, the layout engineers, and the cleaners. Each group was organized into a section whose supervisor reported to the plant engineer. In the cleaning section there were usually about twenty-four workers reporting to the supervisor. In 1966 the average age of the cleaners was forty years, and their average educational level was the seventh grade.

John Franks had a dominant, persuasive manner which enabled him to have considerable influence with the other cleaners. For this reason the plant engineer was not pleased with John Franks's appointment as shop steward. A few days after Franks became steward he presented his first grievance. The bargaining contract described the general procedure for complaints and grievances as follows:

Complaint Procedure: Any employee, or group of employees, having a complaint shall have the right, either himself or through his Union shop steward, to

*From *Human Relations at Work* by Keith Davis. Copyright 1967. Used with permission of McGraw-Hill Book Company.

present such complaint verbally to his immediate supervisor (assistant foreman or foreman) in an endeavor to reach an adjustment. An earnest effort should be made to settle and dispose of such complaints between the parties noted in this paragraph. If the complaint involves a matter subject to the grievance procedure and no satisfactory settlement has been made, the complaint may be presented as a grievance as hereinafter provided.

Grievance Procedure:[1]

Step 1: Any employee or group of employees having a grievance shall present the matter to his or their steward, who shall make investigations and, if the grievance is found valid, take the matter up with the general foreman of the section in which such grievance arose for adjustment. Failing adjustment in this manner within forty-eight (48) hours (Saturdays, Sundays, and holidays excluded), the matter shall be submitted to Step 2.

Step 2: The grievance shall be referred by the steward to the Business Manager of the Union or his designated representative, who shall take the matter up for adjustment with the Personnel Manager or his designated representative. Failing adjustment in this manner within seventy-two (72) hours (Saturdays, Sundays, and holidays excluded), the matter shall be submitted to Step 3.

Step 3: In the event the grievance is not satisfactorily adjusted by the procedure in the foregoing steps within the specified times, the grievance shall be considered by the Grievance Committee (who may be accompanied by the Business Manager of the Union or his duly designated representative, and/or a representative of the said brotherhood) and the Plant Manager of the Company and/or his duly designated representative. In the event it is not satisfactorily adjusted within five (5) days, it shall, at the request of either party, be submitted to a board of arbitration.

[A fourth step provided arbitration.]

In the cleaning section the plant engineer was equivalent to the "general foreman" specified in Step 1 of the grievance procedure. Franks's first grievance, which he presented to the plant engineer on the form provided, was that Pleasant Williams of the cleaning section was being denied promotion to an existing vacancy for which he was eligible. Williams was eligible for upgrading to a vacancy in the stock-handling section, but Williams had been told by his foreman that he could not be promoted until his replacement was hired. Williams had waited ten days, and no replacement was yet available.

The plant engineer was receptive to Franks's presentation of the grievance because he had not previously known of this problem. His investigation disclosed that the facts were substantially those presented; however, Franks did not first present the grievance orally to his cleaning supervisor as required by the complaint procedure. Since this was the first grievance in the department and the plant engineer wished to build good union relations, he arranged for Williams to be promoted the next day.

As a result of this event John Franks's prestige increased greatly among his co-workers in the cleaning section. John was aware of his new status. He made the following comment to several of the cleaners, "I am going to get that plant

[1]The Grievance Procedure could be invoked for any matter pertaining to the labor contract.

engineer straightened out and make him give the cleaners a fair shake." John Franks then began a campaign of seeking and presenting complaints and grievances. During the next six years he filed fifty-four formal grievances for cleaners, winning seventeen of them. During this period the number of cleaners in the department varied between eighteen and twenty-seven. Following are some of the typical grievances he filed:

1. Cleaners needed a special rest room and clothes locker room. (Not allowed; ended at Step 1.)
2. Make earlier distribution of checks on pay day so that cleaners can cash checks during the hour lunch period or give checks to their wives for cashing before the banks close. (Allowed for all shop employees; ended at Step 2.)
3. An additional cleaner is needed to allow other cleaners to rest periodically. (Not allowed; ended at Step 1.)
4. Women cleaners should have uniforms furnished by the company. (Allowed; ended at Step 1.)
5. Cleaners should not have to load cleaning waste into tote bins for trucker to deliver to junkyard. (Not allowed; ended at Step 1.)
6. The overtime list should be posted prior to Thursday noon. (Not allowed; ended at Step 1.)
7. Casey Porter's assigned cleaning area should be reduced in size because it requires too much work. (Not allowed; ended at Step 1.)

In one instance in 1964 Franks was censured by the plant engineer for taking up company time with an "absurd request." This grievance asked that production supervisors have their employees place all empty cartons and boxes in barrels which would be provided in the production area for that purpose. This, in some cases, would require a production employee to stop his job to place the cartons in the barrels. The request was denied by the plant engineer.

Early in 1965 the plant engineer felt that he had "reached the end of his rope" and called the union business manager for a conference about Franks. The business manager agreed that Franks was "hunting" grievances and was presenting many grievances without first discussing them with his supervisor. Then John Franks was called into the engineer's office for a discussion of his attitude. Both the plant engineer and the business manager reminded Franks that he should "use judgment" and present only those complaints and grievances that appeared to be contract violations. Franks said very little, except to assure the two men that he would cooperate at all times. Near the end of the meeting the engineer gave Franks a formal reprimand for presenting a grievance six days earlier without first discussing it with his supervisor. The reprimand and a summary of the meeting were placed in Franks's permanent personnel folder.

During the following months Franks filed several grievances without first discussing them with his supervisor, but the plant engineer took no further action. He later commented, "I hoped Franks would soon improve, and I did not want to create any incident which would undermine my good working relations with the union."

Near the end of 1965 it became evident that Franks was not changing his attitude, and the plant engineer again called the union business manager for a conference. After some discussion the business manager agreed to suspend Franks as shop steward and to try to get a replacement elected. In January 1966, the business manager suspended John from his steward's job and put out feelers for a successor. The problem became difficult when the business manager learned that the cleaners felt Franks was the only man for the job. Not one cleaner would consider taking the steward's job. This condition was allowed to continue for two months with the hope that a newly hired cleaner might be persuaded to become steward. Finally, due to pressure of the cleaners, the business agent reinstated Franks as the shop steward of the cleaning section.

John Franks's first act upon being reinstated as shop steward was to file a formal grievance to the effect that Mary Parker had been "forcefully persuaded" to transfer to the night shift. When the plant engineer checked this grievance, the foreman said that Mary had asked for night work but that Franks had talked her into wanting back on the day shift and had made her feel that she had been coerced into asking for night work. Mary admitted that she asked for the transfer, but she claimed that, from the way the foreman described the job, she had thought second-shift work would be easier, but it was not. When Franks was confronted with the evidence of the investigation, his reply to the plant engineer was a curt "so what?"

GUIDES FOR ANALYSIS

1. Why do you think Franks was originally chosen as shop steward? Why has he continued to keep the job? What has the company done to help him keep it? What has Franks done?
2. Why do you think the plant engineer reprimanded Franks in their conference early in 1965? What assumptions was the engineer making about Franks? Franks's supervisor? The function of the grievance procedure? The business agent? The engineer's own job?
3. What should the engineer do now? What should the business agent do?
4. Be prepared to role-play the meeting in 1965 of Franks, the plant engineer, and the union business manager, at which time Franks was given a formal reprimand.
5. Be prepared to role-play the meeting at the end of the case when Franks says, "So what?"

ABOUT DES KENNEDY'S FICTION

The Garden Club

"A beautifully written, funny, hopeful book."
— Jane Rule

"A truly delightful novel that uses gardening as the medium to enter and vicariously savour the lives of several west coast island dwellers."
— *Saskatoon StarPhoenix*

Flame of Separation

"A gem of a book . . . an open-hearted novel the likes of which are too rarely seen."
— *Vancouver Sun*

"Kennedy's writing style weaves the idea of a parallel universe so persuasively that the reader is prepared to accept the paranormal as an extension of the natural world."
— *The Globe and Mail*

Climbing Patrick's Mountain

"You will be well entertained, have no fear, not only by the unfolding itself, but by the bathos, the chat, the humour, the unexpected, the Irishness of it all, woven together by a master craftsman."
— *Celtic Connection*

"A notch above many best-sellers, ushering it into the realm of literature, a near-allegory simultaneously ancient and modern, a universal tale of Everyman's potential tragic ruin and possible redemption, a book well worth reading."
— *Scroll Press Literary Journal*

BEAUTIFUL COMMUNIONS

OTHER BOOKS BY DES KENNEDY

FICTION

The Garden Club
(Whitecap, 1996)

Flame of Separation
(Insomniac, 2004)

Climbing Patrick's Mountain
(Brindle & Glass, 2009)

NON-FICTION

Living Things We Love to Hate (Whitecap, 1992)

Crazy About Gardening (Whitecap, 1994)
Italian edition: *Tutti Pazzi per Il Giardinaggio*

An Ecology of Enchantment: A Year in a Country Garden
(HarperCollins, 1998)
U.S. edition: *This Rambling Affair: A Year in a Country Garden*

The Passionate Gardener: Adventures of an Ardent Green Thumb
(Greystone, 2006)

The Way of a Gardener: A Life's Journey
(Greystone, 2010)

Heart & Soil: The Revolutionary Good of Gardens
(Harbour, 2014)

beautiful communions

DES KENNEDY

RONSDALE PRESS

RONSDALE PRESS
3350 West 21st Avenue, Vancouver, B.C. Canada V6S 1G7
www.ronsdalepress.com

Typesetting: Julie Cochrane, in Granjon 11.5 pt on 15
Cover Design: Julie Cochrane
Cover Photo: "Garden Wall" with houseleeks & stonecrops © Iperl | Dreamstime
Paper: Ancient Forest Friendly 55 lb. Enviro Book Antique Natural (FSC), 100% post-consumer waste, totally chlorine-free and acid-free.

Ronsdale Press wishes to thank the following for their support of its publishing program: the Canada Council for the Arts, the Government of Canada, the British Columbia Arts Council, and the Province of British Columbia through the British Columbia Book Publishing Tax Credit program.

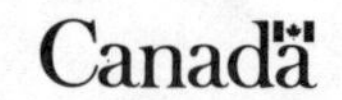

Library and Archives Canada Cataloguing in Publication

Kennedy, Des, author
Beautiful communions: a novel / Des Kennedy. — First edition.

Issued in print and electronic formats.
ISBN 978-1-55380-532-8 (softcover)
ISBN 978-1-55380-533-5 (ebook) / ISBN 978-1-55380-534-2 (pdf)

I. Title.

PS8571.E6274B43 2018 C813'.54 C2018-900526-2 C2018-900527-0

At Ronsdale Press we are committed to protecting the environment. To this end we are working with Canopy and printers to phase out our use of paper produced from ancient forests. This book is one step towards that goal.

Printed in Canada by Marquis Book Printing, Quebec

for Sandy

&

to the memory of

Melda Buchanan

Chris Pielou

Ruth Masters

ACKNOWLEDGEMENTS

I am much indebted to Jim Conlon, a philosopher and longtime friend, for his insightful assessment of early versions of this story as well as his ongoing support. Thanks also to H.M. for encouragingly reviewing the work with suggestions for specific and significant alterations. I deeply appreciate the favourable recommendations of two truly outstanding writers: Ronald Wright and Lorna Goodison. Their writings are internationally admired and I'm humbled by their gracious comments. Many thanks to publisher Ron Hatch and the good folks at Ronsdale Press. Besides admiring the many fine authors who find a home at Ronsdale, I was inspired by the fact that Ron, like myself, had managed to get himself convicted of criminal contempt of court for defending the ancient forests of Clayoquot Sound. The three women to whose memory the book is dedicated were old comrades who for years acted as fearless defenders of the environment on Vancouver Island. I hope something of their strength and grand humour is conveyed through these pages. Thanks lastly to my dear companion Sandy who inspires and enlivens all of it.

". . . let them see the beautiful blendings and communions of death and life, their joyous inseparable unity . . ."

— JOHN MUIR, *A Thousand-Mile Walk to the Gulf*

→I←

The Outrun

One

All Chrissie's thinking is Big. She's standing on a super-sized verandah at the heavy wooden door of an imposing stone house. Spacious grounds all around and huge old trees. Like a park. She raps on the door using the brass knocker that's big enough to take to a street fight. Even the old lady who opens the door is bigger than what old ladies are supposed to be. She's wearing blue jeans and a plaid shirt as if she's just come in from a logging camp or something, not how you expect old ladies to dress. And her hair! She's got this crazy mop of white frizzy hair, like an Afro that's been bleached to a blizzard.

"Hello, dear," the old babe says with a broad street smile. "I'm *so* pleased to meet you." Chrissie's on the small side to begin with, but she seems almost like a kid beside this towering old lady.

They sit down together on the verandah, her and the old gal, on big rattan furniture that makes you feel like a bird in a cage.

Chrissie's passed this place before on her bike. Lots of times. From the street you can hardly see what's in here because of all the trees and bushes, plus there's an iron paling fence around it, like some Gothic mansion or something. Gothic, yah. Like she's stepped through some crazy time warp into a Faulkner novel.

Chrissie's sort of done herself up for the interview — blouse and sweater in muted greens, leather mini over black tights. She fishes her notepad and smart phone out of her pack and does a quick check for messages. Nothing. She's half hoping for maybe an emergency somewhere so she can make this real quick and get out of the mausoleum back to the land of the living.

"All set to go?" the old lady asks with a Fruit Loops smile.

"Um. Yeah. Sure." Chrissie flips open her notepad and dives back into her ratty pack for a pen. Maybe she ought to be recording the interview, but she's learnt the hard way that some of these old monkey-mouths gotta tell you everything they can think of before the lights go out. Hours and hours of meandering that you have to listen to all over again for a couple of measly quotes. No way. Now she just waits for a juicy bit and writes it down. Simple.

"Good to go," Chrissie says, forcing herself to smile back at grandma. She hadn't wanted this assignment in the first place, but Harold Harding had insisted, the dumbard editor of the *Shetterly Standard*. TA DAH! Dorkiest newspaper ever printed. Chrissie wouldn't line her canary cage with it even if she had a canary. Harding could easily have sent Watts for this gig, it's the kind of syrup she loves. But oh, no, it's got to be Chrissie to *really* get the story, Harding says, and then that pukey smirk as if the two of them have a special thing going. Dumb cocknocker.

"I love the scents this time of year, don't you?" the old lady asks, maybe thinking she's got to break the ice or something. She's nodding out across the lawn to where masses of blue flowers are blooming under the big old trees. There is a weird smell in the air for sure, like smelly underwear maybe, but Chrissie wasn't going to mention it.

"Right," she says instead, "so, um, Mrs. Uh . . ."

"No, honey, puleez, I'm not Mrs. Anybody. Why don't you call me Ginger. Everybody else does."

"Ginger?"

"Yes."

Okeydoke, Chrissie's thinking, let's just pop another Valium and get on with it.

"And is Chrissie short for Christine, or what?"

"No, it's not short for anything." To herself: Why do people always ask that same bo question?

"It's your real name?"

"Uh-huh. My parents named me for Chrissie Hynde who was like a rock star when they were young." (Parents is a stretch, but easier.)

"Of course. Yes, I liked Chrissie Hynde myself, come to think of it. Like, I suppose I should say; she's still going strong you know?"

"No way, I thought she was dead from an overdose or something."

"Not at all," Ginger says, "big in the vegan scene apparently. And PETA."

"Cool," Chrissie says, "but she must be ancient by now, isn't she? Oops! I didn't mean . . ."

"Like me, you didn't mean?" Ginger slaps the arm of her wicker chair with delight. "Give praise for the ancient ones, honey," she says, chuckling, "because we know how the game's fixed."

"Huh?" Chrissie's flipping possibilities. Seems like this old babe's got some authentic piss in her.

"May I ask about your tattoo?" Ginger asks, like suddenly the two of them are getting to be soul mates or something.

"What about it?" Chrissie thought she'd got it covered. Besides, she's supposed to be asking the questions here.

"Oh," the old bird says, "it put me in mind of some I saw on a gorgeous young Maori once upon a time. A warrior, he told me he was, and I do believe he was. Body to drool over. The tattoos were beautiful against his dark skin, just as that one of yours is."

People don't usually say things like this to Chrissie, being as she's what's referred to as a Person of Colour, but this old Ginger's obviously a different piece of work. "Very interesting," Ginger says, even leaning over to run her fingertips across the skin of Chrissie's forearm. "Who did it for you?"

"Guy in Toronto, on West Bloor. Guy's a total genius, right, only hardly anyone knows about him. He's from Ethiopia or someplace. A Sufi, I think, so his designs are like really mystical. Doesn't do all that dragons and hearts and big tits kind of crap. I . . ."

Suddenly there's a commotion around the side of the house and a freaking black dog comes bounding up the front steps and charges straight at old Ginger in a frenzy of energy, all tapping claws and swishing tail and slobbery panting. It plunges its snuffling head into the old lady's lap and Ginger starts rubbing the mutt all over with her gnarly hands and laughing like crazy, the two of them, the dog and old dame, wriggling and snuffling like animals.

Chrissie's totally freaked. Very slowly she pulls her legs up and folds them under her in the chair. She's trapped here in this chair, cornered like a rat. Then without warning the dog comes lunging towards her and Chrissie screams in terror. She hadn't meant to, it just came out, but the fucking dog has a huge pink tongue hanging out of its mouth and long goobers of slobbery slime and vicious looking fangs. Chrissie can see them sinking into her flesh, crunching her bones. Tearing her to pieces.

A single sharp whistle sounds from somewhere around the corner and the dog instantly drops to the floor as though its battery just went dead. It's staring at Chrissie with huge brown evil eyes. She can see intention in those eyes. Cunning malice. There's something thick and clotty stuck halfway down Chrissie's throat, afterbirth of her scream, preventing words or . . .

"Oh, you frightened of dogs, honey?" Ginger asks her like a fidiot.

Oh, no, Chrissie almost says back to her, I'm just crapping my pants here to put a little colour in them.

At that moment a man appears at the foot of the steps. He's wearing high rubber boots and brown khaki pants, a battered sports jacket over a denim shirt and a lazy slouch cap. Lord Toppenpot playing at being a farm hand. He glances curiously from Ginger to Chrissie and back again but doesn't say a word. Chrissie's not sure he even saw her. The dog's breath pants up at her in furious rank gusts.

"Oh, Peter," Ginger says to him, and you can tell she's trying really hard not to laugh, the old bastitch, "I'm afraid Shep's given our poor visitor a bit of a start."

The guy gives another quick whistle and the dog instantly bolts down the steps and heels alongside him. "Sorry," he says to Chrissie in a barely audible voice, but not looking at her, not speaking to her really. Like he's sorry for everything in general. He reaches down and caresses the dog's head absently. Absent is what he seems like. Already Chrissie feels the terror draining out of her, gurgling away scummy as bathtub water. Something like shame comes seeping in to replace it, which she hates. She'd prefer it be anger, but it isn't. This dog and weird whistling man.

"Oh, Shep here wouldn't hurt a flea, would you, darling?" Old Ginger speaks directly to the dog and in answer the mutt gives two quick yips and swishes its tail across the ground like a broom. "See, dear?" Ginger says, looking at Chrissie, as though the frickin' dog is smarter than she is.

"Chrissie," Ginger then announces with mock formality, "this is my beloved son Peter and his faithful sidekick Shep."

The guy half bows towards Chrissie, touching the peak of his slouch cap. She can't tell if he's being smartass or not, but the gesture confirms her first impression that there's something off his box about him, something out of whack.

"Certain people like to imagine that Peter's the faithful sidekick and Shep's the one in charge," Ginger adds, smiling fondly at her son and his dog. "An understandable perception, I suppose, when you consider that border collies aren't really dogs in the conventional sense of the term, are they?"

"Huh?"

"More like highly evolved beings in the guise of sheepdogs whose purpose is to show us fool humans how to conduct our affairs with greater dignity."

Is this a put-on or not? Chrissie's got to restrain herself from rolling her eyes, being as she's got no time for this kind of Chakra Cookie BS.

"Chrissie's a reporter with the *Standard*," Ginger explains to son Peter, "and is interviewing me for salacious details about various townspeople, so best watch your words."

Chrissie smiles lamely at the tired joke.

Peter glances towards Chrissie again, still avoiding eye contact, probably thinking she doesn't look much like a reporter, which is what everybody thinks, but his attitude is inscrutable, at least to Chrissie. Not hostile, but not warm either. Indifferent. Like one of those loony county bachelors in British detective shows who emerge from seclusion and are gossiped about as being pervs. Or worse. Dark secrets. Gay, maybe, Chrissie speculates, though he's not the least bit swishy. Slow perhaps. Shut down for sure. Chrissie nonchalantly puts her feet slowly back on the floor, though the mutt's still watching her and looks like it could lunge at her again any second. Weird how the guy won't look at her at all and the dog won't look at anything else. Could be he's blind and it's a seeing-eye dog. She'd anticipated being bored to death on this drain bramage assignment, not scared shitless and then mystified as a kicker.

"Are you still going to tackle the roses this afternoon?" Ginger asks the loony as though everything was just as it should be.

"Hmm," he half replies, gazing out distractedly across the lawn. Still could be blind. Then half turns again towards Chrissie, nods once more by way of repeated apology and, with dog at heel, retreats behind the house.

"Sorry about the scare, Chrissie," Ginger says. "Are you all right?"

"Yea, it's just . . ."

"Have you always had a fear of dogs?"

Chrissie knows precisely where her fear of dogs began. When that Dicksmoke Chuck moved in with her mum and her. Him and his two fucking Rottweilers. But she's not going to get into that whole episode with someone she's only known for five minutes.

"They don't usually bother me," she says instead.

"What about when you're on your bike?" Ginger nods down to where Chrissie's bike is stashed at the bottom of the steps. "I can always remember being chased by dogs when I was cycling."

"Uh-huh," Chrissie says, "I carry a can of bear spray. Coupla shots of that and they learn pretty quick to leave you alone."

"I suppose so," Ginger chuckles.

"Um, I'm feeling like we better get on with the interview," Chrissie says.

"Of course," Ginger agrees, smiling. She's got a smile about a mile wide, all wrinkles and laughing eyes, but you can't really tell if she's being straight or not, or if something else is going on you don't know about.

Chrissie clears her throat professionally. "Now, the thing is, the town is a hundred years old this year and so is this house, correct?"

"Quite right," Ginger says, and plunges into her story. "Ah, it was boom town back then by all accounts. Fast money moving in and out. That's when the city hall got built and the cathedral. Big Dream times. And this place. Shortly before the First World War." She pauses for a moment, pondering, so Chrissie's unsure if the old duck's finished what she has to say. But she hasn't. "Fascinating, isn't it, how you have these times of incredible frenzy, a sort of collective mania that then morphs into an orgy of slaughter. Homo sapiens only not so sapiens." She smiles peculiarly at Chrissie. "I saw it myself as a child with the second war," Ginger carries on. "Anyway, yes, back then they were dreaming big, the town fathers, as they fancied themselves. New frontier. Unbounded optimism. All the usual delusions."

"Huh?" Chrissie's drifted for a minute into remembering those damn Rottweilers.

"Of course, this house was far grander than the average," Ginger continues, as though she hadn't noticed that Chrissie had been off in the ozone. "Built by a wealthy German family. I don't know where their money came from, banking perhaps, maybe armaments, I'm not sure, but they spared none of it putting this place up. Designed by a *wunderkind* architect from Chicago. But what a hodgepodge: Victorian Gothic Revival layered over Baronial Gothic and a splash of Beaux-Arts for good measure. All imports, of course, hankering after bygone splendours. Ornate mansions and pastoral fantasies. So often boom times and ostentation seem to go hand-in-hand, don't they?"

"I guess so," Chrissie says, wishing she'd taped all this stuff because most of it's zooming over her head like dirty birds.

"But it's usually a bad idea," Ginger says with a dismissive wave of her hand, "attempting to create an overnight sense of history by hurling money at something. Believing you can ensure permanence through piling up huge-enough stones. Ozymandias. The decay of that colossal wreck. A house for the ages this was supposed to be. Trying to make an impression, at best they succeeded in creating a folly."

"You don't like the place?" Chrissie asks. She's thinking of the little clapboard dump she and Chazz share with a colony of roof rats and several hundred cockroaches.

"Like it? Oh my, that's a tough question, Chrissie. The grounds are gorgeous, as you can see, the trees and lawns and gardens, but the house? On one level it's rather hideous, a monster home before people even knew about monster homes. Far too big to keep clean or keep warm. I feel like Miss Haversham or somebody rattling around in it on my own. Of course, Peter's here now, and Shep, which helps enormously, but still, can you imagine having a place this big when you know there's people out there sleeping in refrigerator cartons?"

"Yea, I get what you mean," Chrissie says.

"On the other hand," the old bird continues with a hand cocked sideways like it was holding up something, "it's where my brother and I grew up and where my own kids grew up for the most part, Peter here and his sister. So there's memories in pretty much every room. Not all good, nor all bad. I'll take you around if you like. You'll see how it's massive sandstone block construction; two huge fireplaces; every window's leaded glass. At its worst it half feels like one of those dreadful faux German hunting lodges with the heads of dead animals hanging on the walls. My parents worked for years trying to humanize the place, even though they were rather dour characters themselves, and Peter and I have done our bit too. The blue trim on the doors and windows helps a bit, don't you think?"

"Hmm, yeah, I guess so," Chrissie says, still trying to get her brain around someone living in a mansion and dissing it. "Did your parents buy it or your grandparents or what?" She tilts her head sideways, like she's seen inquisitive reporters do on TV.

Just then a Frisbee comes gliding across the big lawn, out towards the trees, and that frickin' dog's roaring across the grass in pursuit. Just as the Frisbee starts to drop, the mutt leaps into the air and plucks it perfectly in his teeth, lands a bit awkwardly, then stands for a moment with the Frisbee dripping slobber from his mouth.

"Well done, Shep!" Ginger shouts out, clapping appreciatively, and even Chrissie has to admire the dog's athletic grace, how it seemed to hang suspended in the air before snatching the Frisbee. Like a dancer almost. The nutter whistles again from somewhere around the house, and Shep speeds off with his prize.

"Now, where were we?" Ginger wonders, "Ah, yes, my parents bought the place during the Great Depression. Real estate had gone belly up like most everything else around here and I think they got it for a fraction of its worth. Monetary worth, I'm talking about. The original owners were long gone by then. I guess there'd been a lot of anti-German feeling coming out of the war, and that may have been what chased them off, I don't know. Stupid war to begin with, on all sides, stupid and venal. Anyway, the house was taken over by a fellow who was connected with mining somehow, but he ended up losing everything in the great crash and committed suicide."

"Here?" Chrissie gestures towards the house.

"Oh, yes, in the master bedroom, no less. Put a pistol in his mouth and blew his brains out. I heard all about it from old Phillips who was the gardener here when I was a girl. Loved talking about the follies of his employers, Phillips did. Dead long ago, of course. You can still make out a tiny dent in the ceiling plaster where the bullet lodged." Ginger shakes her head in wonderment. "As if anything is more precious than life. Nothing is, you know? Life is the thing. Terrible. Terrible the extremes that people are driven to."

Chrissie's feeling totally creeped out about somebody offing himself right in the house. But intrigued too. "Do you, um, still use that room for anything?" she asks.

"Of course!" Ginger says, grinning. "It's the master bedroom and it's got a lovely balcony with a marvellous view. It's one of the redeeming features of this pile. Are you imagining his ghost might still haunt it?"

"Well, ah . . ."

"No, I sleep in there every night. Well, sleep may be a bit of an exaggeration. Let's say I lie there every night trying to remember people's names or what the book I just finished reading was about, and doze intermittently. Sometimes I look at where the bullet left its mark,"

Ginger points upwards as if she can see it above her now, "and I think about living and dying, all sorts of grand notions. One of the perquisites of age, you see. It's a gift, actually, that sad little dent in the ceiling."

"Really. But there's no ghosts?"

"Oh, there's ghosts in the house all right," Ginger replies with a perhaps wink. "But not in that bedroom especially, no."

"But ghosts?"

"Most certainly. No, you can't have a place this old, that's housed so much tragedy and so much beauty without there being spirits lingering in it, voices to be heard in it, can you?"

After touring the girl around the house — at least the downstairs floor with entrance hall, library, dining room, kitchen and drawing room — piling on the anecdotes as they went, and startling Chrissie with a farewell hug, Ginger's back on the verandah, musing, the springtime light full of golden mischief.

Well it happens sometimes doesn't it? As if I didn't know any better. You start jabbering away about ghosts and how could I resist, the child was so obviously intrigued and then you've got ghosts on the brain for the rest of the day. Old songs the same: Will I see you in September. Not bloody likely. What was his name that mining man, I should remember it, Kinnear or Connor or something like that. No. No damnit it's gone. For now anyway. Peculiar how something can be absolutely gone one day as though it will never return and then it reappears in its own sweet time later on. Antechambers of the brain getting locked and unlocked by something other than yourself. Memories draped by the beneficent spider. T.S. Eliot, if I remember. This constant sliding away of things. Slip sliding away. Thank you, Paul S, prescient as ever. Slipping and sliding all along . . . Van the Man, another one. Named for Chrissie Hynde she said. Most interesting. Did I tell her I was named for Ginger Rogers? Probably not. I'm not even sure that I was but it seems like Mother said something of the sort. Poor Mother though, poor Mother and poor Dad. Speaking of ghosts. Trusting souls ruined by religion. Or maybe saved by it, who knows? You'd think being so Christian right down to their toenails they'd have named me for some saint or other. Philomena, perhaps. I'd have made a passable Philomena in the early years at least. Later on, maybe not. Too bizarre that such a pair of bible thumpers would name their daughter for a Hollywood starlet. Did they secretly love Ginger Rogers? I don't know. I don't even know if she was famous yet when I was born. Oh of course she must have been she did all those films with Fred Astaire in the thirties. Lord how those two could dance. Funny though since they didn't believe in dancing, dear Mother and Dad. Perhaps a more biblical name you'd have thought, Judith or Elizabeth, say. Chrissie Hynde and the Pretenders. Intriguing child though wasn't she? Tats and 'tudes as they'd say. And so terrified of Shep you'd have thought he was a grizzly bear to see her. But I shouldn't have laughed, fear's fear. Irrational or not it's still real. Yes, it's true Nigel could dance, not as smoothly as Astaire but close. People said that too at big occasions, that Nigel and I danced just like Fred and Ginger. Some of the hambones even nicknamed him Fred. Hmm. But Peter surprised me, being so stiff and withdrawn towards the girl. How long has it been now? Must be three years at least. Maybe not unreasonable after only three years, I must have moped at least that long after Nigel. Fool that I was. Bigger fool that he was. Don't get started on that. Why do fools fall in love? Wonderful song. Joni Mitchell's version is the one that plays in my head. With the, er, oh who was it backing her? The Persuasions? Maybe that was later. Afterwards. Still I can hear the original, back in the fifties it must have been. But who was singing it? Couldn't have been the Persuasions too. Maybe the Persuasions had nothing to do with any of it. I'll look it up. Make a note. Oh, yes, I remember dancing to it with Nigel. Must have been one of those dreadful faculty affairs. All those tweedy old professors trying to peek down your dress but pretending not to. Fools of another sort. But I like this little Chrissie. Rough and tender I'd say. Sweet beneath the scarring. Child survivors. Floaters is what that lovely young doctor called those spots in my eyes. Little amoebas floating across your vision. Oooh but that laser she shot into my eye was painful. Like hot needles jabbing. Why do they tell you something isn't hardly going to hurt at all when in fact it's so excruciating. You always hurt the one you love. Could have been Nigel's song. Except he couldn't sing any more than I could. And I'm not at all sure he could love either. But dance, Oh good Lord yes he could dance.

When Peter and Shep return from their chores they find Ginger snoozing peacefully, her face fallen in repose and mapped with the lines of age that seem to smooth away when she's awake and animated. Even so, she's beautiful. Shep approaches and softly licks the back of her hand so that Ginger slowly returns from wherever dreams have been carrying her.

"Well, there you are," she says awakening fully and straightening up in her chair, "culprits returned to the scene of the crime."

"Sorry about that, Mum," Peter says coming up the steps. "I think that must be the first time ever that Shep has scared anyone."

Shep glances from one to the other, as he always does when being talked about.

"But you weren't exactly the epitome of cordiality yourself, dear Petrus, were you?"

"Oh God, it was really bizarre," Peter says shaking his head. Leaning against the fluted verandah post, he reimagines the moment. What had he been doing? Fiddling with a pair of loppers, something like that. Then out of nowhere a piercing scream flinging him instantly back to a scream he'd never heard but hears echoes of still, even after three years. "There was something in her scream," he tells his mother.

"Ah. I guessed as much. A Munch moment for you?"

"She must have thought I was a total case. I mean, I couldn't even look at her for fear of seeing Cecilia."

"She's so *not* Cecilia a glance might have helped."

"Perhaps. I hope you covered for me," Peter says, the contrite choirboy.

"Not a bit of it. If she gives you a good roughing up in her story you've nobody to blame but yourself."

"Or Shep," he says.

"True," Ginger laughs, "Shep's the real villain of the piece!" By this point Shep's sprawled on the floor eyeing both of them with the detached bemusement humans so frequently require.

"Anyway, moving right along," Peter says, sitting down beside his mother, "what I really came to tell you is breaking news about our beloved Congregation of the Great Convergence. You haven't heard, have you?"

"Not a whisper," Ginger says in her love-a-bit-of-juicy-gossip voice, "do tell."

"Feature piece on CBC this morning. Child abuse scandal right at the top echelons."

"Good lord, no."

"Yep, dozens of kids involved apparently. Forcible confinement. Sexual assault. Child porn, you name it."

"I can hardly believe it," Ginger says, "I mean, they're such a puritanical self-righteous crowd, I wouldn't of thought they'd have the imagination for it."

"You'd wonder, wouldn't you."

"But, still, those poor kids. It beggars the imagination how people can behave that way. To innocent children? Pah!" She stares off across the lawns, lost for a moment. Then throws off her disgust like a dirty coat. "Do you think it will have consequences for this place?"

"Dunno," Peter says, "usually these things end up with massive compensation claims. If that were to happen, who knows what might become of Stone House."

"Whatever it is would be better than having it used for their filthy perversions."

"Agreed," Peter says. "But we shouldn't be getting ahead of ourselves. These are only allegations at this point. I don't think there's even been any charges laid."

"So no need to talk to the lawyers just yet?"

"I should think not."

"And I shouldn't be packing my bags?"

"You'd make a really unconvincing bag lady, Mother."

"But you'll keep an eye on it?"

"Like a hawk," Peter says, patting her hand reassuringly.

⋙⋘

Chrissie's freewheeling on her bike, flying down the near-deserted streets of town, legs pumping like frenzied pistons, heart flaring, lungs whooshing like pneumatic doors. A cool breeze streams across her face and arms and slithers in under her clothes to dry off the sweat from that bizarre interview. Booya, that was something else. Old Ginger showing her around that ginormous place, kinda mocking it the whole time, what did she call it — *nouveau riche* ersatz grandeur. Most people would kill to have a place half that size, and she throws shade on it like it was nothing. And the Barney son, I mean what was he about? Appears and disappears like some fracking ghost. But mostly that dog of his. Scared the living shit out of her. And, worst of all, took her right back to the crapbox in Scarborough. What she escaped. She peddles harder, legs and lungs pushed to the max, as though bitter memories were chasing her down the sunwashed streets.

"Oh, Chrissie, we're home!" she remembers her mum calling out. "Come meet your new step-dad!" One look at him was all it took. Scrawny little fucktard trying to be the tough guy.

"Pleased to meet ya, Chrissie," he says, sticking out his hand while her mum smiles stupidly like she's just made the greatest catch ever. Yuggh. She had to wash her hands three times afterwards just to get the stinking touch of him off her. He wasn't the first, there'd been three previous "step-dads," each one stupider than the one before, but Chuck took first prize for lifetime loser.

"C'mon out to the truck and meet my pups," he says to her that first day.

"Yea, honey," her mum chirps in, "it'll be great for you to get to know Chuck's dogs.

He just about drags her outside. A blazing hot sun beating down on the dusty weed patch outside their trailer. Chuck's rusted-out Datsun pickup with a wooden cage made from 2x4s in the back. She didn't want to go anywhere near it, but Chuck kind of pushes her forward until, when they were only a few feet away, two huge black dogs rose up snarling and lunged against the side of the cage, so the old truck swayed and threatened to topple over. Chrissie jumped back in terror, but Chuck was right behind her and held her in place, his fierce yellow fingers gripping her shoulders like scrawny claws.

"That's Satan," Chuck said pointing to the dog on the left, "and this one's Black Bitch. Ain't they something?" Chrissie, all of twelve years old, gawped at the caged beasts in terror. She felt a warm trickle down her legs and wanted more than anything to die.

Round and round the town she cycles now, fleeing everything, sucking in great draughts of leafy green air, conscious of bird chirps everywhere. Soon enough the memory starts blowing away in fragments until it's gone, and that bizarre interview too, gone, stripped away with all the other shit, down to the instinctive, the animal, cycling on until she hits it, that pure state of motion, intense exertion, like a dancer, hey, or a long distance runner. Up over the top, finally, and Geez, she feels great, flying out of time, imagines herself riding through deserts and mountains and across great plains, through towns without names, swarming with people who wave as she passes, spinning through places she's never even seen, with no plans of return, just going and going, afwhooo, pure freaking gliding forward without purpose or endpoint.

Already late and by now not giving a shit, swooping past a lumbering garbage truck, freewheeling down Maple Avenue hitting every green light as she goes, she decides in a flash she'll stop in and see Chazz before she heads back to the office because he was asleep when she left for work this morning and she really wants to see his kooky face, scraggly beard and all. Chazz is like antitherapy, right, he makes her forget all the things she needs to not remember. Just like her bike. Where everything else is like mud and slush, he's the solid fixed point from which her journey has finally started. She hangs a right at Second Street and goes whistling along for three blocks through a shower of small green-golden confetti petals shaken loose from the boulevard trees. She brakes hard at the house, a little clapboard box hunkered low and needing paint, or maybe demolition. Four yellow tulips are blooming in an old paint can at the front stoop. Beautiful.

"Hey, babe," Chazz greets her from the couch as she bursts through the door, kinda panting and wanting to laugh, "what's happening?"

"Oh, Chazzateer, I was just so hot for you I couldn't go back to that stupid office without I tear your clothes off first." She bounds across the tiny living room and pounces onto the sagging couch beside him.

"Whoa, chiclet, maximum caution with regards the axe!" Chazz says, holding his guitar away by the neck so's it doesn't get smashed between them.

"You composing?" Chrissie asks him, running her hand through his tousled hair and down across his cheek. Her fingertips linger on his cheekbones that are chiselled to the finest. There's the yeasty scent of beer on his breath, which she's just plain fuckin' crazy about. She sees several beer cans on the coffee table. It's amazing how Chazz always does his best work when he's had a drink or two.

"Yea, I got a little tune coming along," Chazz says, placing the guitar on the floor, "but nothing that can't wait, right." Looking super droll, he pulls Chrissie up against his chest then slides his hand under her short skirt and gently up her thigh. Ooooh. Chazz being a musician is like the greatest turn-on ever for Chrissie. His torn blue jeans and dirty *Grateful Dead* tee, that long, lanky body, even his crazy big feet, it's like instant start-me-up for her. Every time. Oh, and his fingers, of course, so long and slender and artistic. She couldn't help herself even if she wanted to. She unzips his jeans and slips her hand inside. As usual, Chazz isn't wearing underwear, which drives her insane thinking of his boss genitals rubbing up against his jeans and just a quick zip away. Yow.

"Oh, baby," Chazz says as she pulls him out and takes him in her mouth, his hands cradling the crown of her head. She works him gently, pleased with herself that she's got her tongue pin and lip ring in just the right places. Chazz swells and swells. Over and over again she's astonished at the size he can achieve. Truly unbelievable. She works her tongue and lips around him until his whole body is bent upwards off the couch, only his elbows and feet holding him, as though his cock was tied to a sky hook winching the rest of him up towards the ceiling. "Oh, baby," he's repeating like a mantra, "Oh, baby." Just as she senses he's about to come, she pulls off and finishes him with her hand so that he instantly erupts, moaning, his stretched body convulsing as though from a high voltage jolt. Holds the high arch for a moment, then, like a deflating balloon the bow of his body collapses and he's sprawled back on the couch, legs splayed, eyes closed, mouth slack, as if he was blootered. "Oh, baby," he murmurs again, his head lolling towards her, his blue eyes half open in that dreamy kind of way that drives her wild like when he's playing his guitar for her. "You are so fucking fantastic," he tells her, "I would die for you, I'd die without you, maybe I'm going to die right now, a happy man." He closes his eyes and smiles like some goofy plaster saint in a church.

Her man. They've got something real special, she knows that. They're good for each other, each better than when they're not together. She doesn't like to think about the times before she was with Chazz, except maybe for Sol. He was cool too, but he wasn't her anchor, he wasn't her bedrock the way Chazz is. Back in the trailer park with her crazy mum, a scrawny little black kid without any real friends, she never would have dreamed of being with a prince like this guy. Her heart can hardly hold it, it's so big.

Chrissie gives him a quick kiss on the mouth and jumps up. She straightens her dress and checks herself in the bathroom mirror. No incriminating evidence. She runs her fingers through her close cropped hair, kind of a butch marine look, and gives herself a knowing wink in the foxed mirror. Hot. As she leaves through the front door, Chazz is still sprawled on the couch, maybe asleep.

⁂

Peter catches himself thinking about the girl as he steers his pickup truck off the side road and onto the long driveway running into his farm. How her scream sliced into his brain, recalling. Everything. Couldn't bring himself to look at her. She must have thought he was extremely strange. Which he is, but not really, just now. Just since. "And you didn't help matters much either, did you, tiger?" he says aloud to Shep who's sitting upright in the passenger seat, tense with excitement, his attention riveted to a cluster of sheep grazing in the pasture off to the right. The fields are roaring green with springtime growth. As the truck rumbles up the dirt driveway both man and dog begin to feel the familiar power of the place, a frazzled turmoil of happiness, longing and grief. Peter's accustomed to it now, this insistent tugging at his heart that the place exerts. "Home again anyway, eh?" he says, reaching across to scratch the dog's neck. Shep shivers with delight but can't break his fixation on the sheep.

The truck pulls up in front of a massive wooden barn, its shingles and barn boards silver with age and endurance. Peter hops out of the truck and signals Shep to follow.

"Yo, Peter," a young guy in overalls greets them from just inside the barn's open door. Shep bounds forward joyfully and the man, stepping out into sunlight, bends to caress the dog's head.

"Hiya, Ron," Peter says, glancing up at the pattern of long veins that weather has exposed in the vertical barn boards. Wearing away a microscopic skin of wood every year, gouging out the softer parts and leaving the dark hard lines in relief.

"Okay," Ron says, straightening up, "what can I tell you? So far so good." He raises his right hand with fingers crossed.

"Yea?"

"Oh, yea. She saw the doc just yesterday. Said everything's looking real good."

Peter smiles and nods. Shep trots over to the fenceline where he sits upright, fixated on the distant sheep.

"Boy you should see her," Ron carries on, "like she's got a prize-winning pumpkin under her skirt."

Both men chuckle, exchanging a momentary closeness born of their shared remove from the wet, fleshy depths of womanhood. Peter's strangely cheered seeing in the young man that mixture of pride and near terror that accompanies the imminent birth of a first child. Not that Ron's any stranger to birthing. He and Lois have been through two lambing seasons since taking over the farm and have had their share of dicey situations. Breach births a couple of times, tangled umbilical cords, all the things that can go sideways trying to assist new life into the world. But they've done well, Peter knows. He's helped them a bit here and there, but mostly they're making a go of it on their own.

Plus, they've done a bunch of really smart things, like selling fresh organic produce to the better restaurants in town, something that wouldn't have occurred to him. Then they helped start up the farmer's market every Saturday morning through the summer, and that's been a real success story. No, these young folks have done well so far, and Peter's never regretted having chosen them to look after the place. Letting go of it for himself, oh shit, yes, he's regretted that every day for the past two years; but not that Ron and Lois were the ones who took it over. They plainly love it as he did. Does.

The official version of why Peter abandoned the farm, the version that Ron and Lois know, is that Peter needed to move back to town for his mum's sake. That she could no longer cope with the demands of Stone House on her own. And there was an element of truth in that. But the vastly larger and more complicated truth was that Peter made the move for his own survival. The memories embedded in the farm had grown so toxic he had to get out.

Ignoring the men, Shep stares fixedly at the distant sheep, as though they're calling to him, requiring him in some way. From having lived the first few years of his life on this farm, its fields and woods are embedded in his spirit. The scents of its grasses and herbs. The pungent smells of chickens, rabbits and geese. The rustling of hens as they settle to roost in the evening. The taste of milk still warm from the udder at milking time. And above all, the thrilling scents and sounds and movements of sheep. All of these connect the dog to this place and all come alive again in him each time he returns to it. His essence is here in a way that it will never be at Stone House, although he must be there because Peter's there. And he adores old Ginger, who wouldn't? But this is where Cecilia is, where he belongs and where he longs to be.

"You want a hand with the firewood?" Ron asks. "Or do you want to give Shep his workout and do the wood after?"

"I'll tackle the wood myself," Peter says quietly, "work Shep afterwards." He doesn't explain, or need to explain, that he knows Ron's got a lot on his plate just now, with Lois so close, and the last thing the young guy needs is to be spending time humouring his landlord. Not that it would be just that. But still.

"You sure?" Ron asks him.

"Uh-huh."

"Appreciate it," Ron says. "You want to work this little group over here?" He cocks his thumb to indicate the sheep Shep's staring towards. "Should be pretty good. None of them sour at all. Kinda miss doing it with you, but you're right, I got a lot on the go all of a sudden."

Peter smiles, slapping the anxious dad-to-be on his shoulder. "Love to Lois, okay?"

"Sure. Thanks." And Ron repeats his boyish finger-crossing.

Peter and Shep get back into the truck and continue slowly down a narrow dirt track that leads to the woodlot at the back end of the farm. They're hemmed in by hedgerows of hawthorn bushes just breaking into leaf and intertwined with rampant berry vines. A jungle in the making, waiting. Past the last field, they enter the other world of the woods. Big deciduous trees mostly, lots of maple and oak, widely spaced with a low understory of grasses and ferns. Dappled sunlight and thrown veils of shade. At the heart of the woodlot the truck wheezes to a stop alongside a pile of blocks. As soon as the engine noise dies, the woods come alive with all the chirps and rustlings and whispers of spring. The forest floor's seething with new baneberry, toothwort, mayflower and false Solomon's seal. High above, branches and limbs sigh with the sweetness of rising sap.

"All right," Peter tells Shep, "we both know you're not worth a damn when it comes to splitting firewood, so why don't I take care of it and you can go explore." At the wave of his hand, the dog bounds off and takes to rummaging around in the litter of last year's leaves, plowing his muzzle crazily through the duff into excellences of smell. Disturbed by the commotion, a fat brown toad emerges from a pile of leaves and takes a few uncertain hops. Shep crouches close by and stares at it, flinching each time the toad hops. Instinct urges him to herd the toad back towards Peter, but intuition tells him there'd be a loss of dignity involved, so he simply watches as the toad eventually wriggles its way under a rotting log, its ridiculous back legs and webbed feet disappearing last.

Peter takes a heavy splitting maul and two steel wedges from the back of the pickup and sets up one of the larger rounds to serve as chopping block. He places a smaller round on the block, lifts the maul above his head and swings it down with a vigorous blow. The block flies apart in two separate pieces. He repeats the action. Then again. And again. This is what he craves, purposeful activity, the more vigorous the better. He could tow in a mechanized splitter to do the work far more quickly and less strenuously, but he's not interested in quick and easy. He wonders if perhaps it's penance he's doing. He continues working steadily, not hurrying but with a measured rhythm. This is good tight maple, primo firewood. The heft of it, even when seasoned. The satisfying thunk as each piece splits apart. Tougher blocks with twisted grain or stubborn knots he has to hammer apart with the steel wedges. The heap of blocks dwindles as the pile of split pieces grows. When the splitting's done, maybe two or three hours, he stacks the pieces in a long row with a crib end of alternating pairs of pieces at each end. The wood will finish curing over summer.

Gratified, he pulls off his work gloves and fetches a thermos and chocolate bar from the glove compartment. He sits on a large fallen maple trunk sipping coffee and nibbling the dark chocolate. No question it's an optimal kind of day for bully-boy labour, not too hot, though he's worked up a bit of a sweat. The muscles of his arms and legs tingle pleasantly from exertion. Shep ambles over to see what's on offer and Peter throws him a Milk Bone. Shep catches it in his teeth with a primness that indicates a Milk Bone, while not to be entirely discounted, is among the lesser of the farm's excitements.

Peter scans the awakening woodlands, feeling a type of contentment here that he finds nowhere else, and some measure of relief, for the moment at least, from the residual disease in his spirit. He knows he could sit here for a whole lot longer and be as close to at peace as he is likely to get. Because, of course, she's here. Cecilia. Somewhere in a golden grove nearby. She might be dancing with the baby, her gypsy skirts and veils twirling; or musing over a poem by Blake while the baby sleeps beside her. She would be beautiful. Shep senses her proximity too. He sniffs the air for trace of her, ears twitching for a telltale sound from the deep woods where her spirit lingers.

"All right, I've done my work," Peter eventually announces to Shep, "time for you to do yours." They hop into the truck and turn back towards the fields. Within minutes the truck emerges from the dappled shade of woods into sunny meadowland. Sitting upright on the passenger seat, Shep's keenly aware that the earthy-mold smells of the woodlot have given way to the musky scent of sheep. He's rigid with excitement, eyes flashing from one direction to the next. His blood knows what awaits, his muscles and sinews vibrate with ancestral cues, every molecule acutely aligned towards the animal magnetism of sheep. Sheep of every description. Asiatic mouflons from which the rest descended. Damara sheep, bred by the Hamites of Gross Damaraland, later herded by the Himba and Tjimba people. Wiltshire Horns from the Chalk Downs of England. The Cholistani from Punjab Province. The Faeroes, mountain sheep of Old Norwegian and Icelandic ancestry. Reddish-brown Hazaragie from Central Afghanistan and Mehraban from Hamadan province in old Persia. The Adals, the Ghezels and dozens of other breeds swarm through the dog's ancestral herding grounds.

Peter smiles to himself at Shep's barely contained excitement. Even after years of doing it, working with sheep hasn't lost a smidgeon of gratification for either dog or man. Each has an instinctive desire to work alongside the other. In the fields, at least, and perhaps even beyond the fields, they form two halves of a whole.

Peter steers the truck to a stop in front of the barn again. Peter and Shep walk together to the pasture gate. The dozen or so sheep are scattered at the extreme end of the pasture, lazily cropping grass. With the gate latched behind them, man and dog stand together for a minute surveying the meadow. Inflated cumulous clouds fluff up against the eastern horizon foaming into a meandering white dreamscape between blue sky and green fields.

"Almost too pretty a scene to be spoiled with work, don't you think?" Peter asks Shep. As required, Shep swishes his tail and gives the imploring eyes look. This is part of their routine, this tantalizing extension of the moment before engagement begins.

Standing at his post, Peter gives the tiniest of signals and Shep's away running low to the ground, tail extended, paws barely touching the turf as he streaks through the outrun. As he approaches the sheep, he curves to the left in a perfectly pear-shaped line that takes him in behind the sheep. Of course he's just far enough away so as not to alarm them. "Stand!" He hears Peter call, although Shep's perfectly aware of the need to stop at the back side of the flock. What would be the point of just running past them? But Peter likes his little games and you're never quite sure what new wrinkle he might come up with.

Shep's standing rigid behind the flock ready to begin the lift, having the sheep move under his influence according to Peter's instructions.

All three players in position. The sheep — robust looking Suffolks with black faces and legs and barrel bodies covered in short white wool — are now on their guard, but surely not dogged. If there's one thing Shep really dislikes it's sheep that have been worked too much already. Wise to the game, as soon as they spot you, they go tearing off across the pasture and gather around the handler like a pack of dolts. Either that or they bunch up and refuse to be moved no matter what you do to them. Dogged sheep are beneath a good dog's dignity.

"Come-Bye!" Peter calls, and Shep turns squarely to his left and runs at a constant distance from the sheep, flanking them. The flock begins to tighten on that side. "There!" Peter calls, indicating that the required flanking's done on that end. Already Shep can tell that these are not light sheep, the kind that can be easily moved and perhaps even flighty enough they'll dash off in all directions. Better light than dogged, but not Shep's preferred type either.

"Away to me!" Peter calls and Shep bolts back in the opposite direction, flanking around the right side. "There!" Peter's call again checks his run. The flock bunches slightly more, but now Shep gets a hint of their character. Several large ewes turn to face him, offering a challenge. So, there will be a contest of wills after all. Perfect.

"Walk on!" Peter calls, and Shep moves directly towards the sheep in a calm and purposeful fashion. Two of the ewes refuse to move or turn away. Shep knows all about heavy sheep, stubborn creatures that insist on making it tough for even an expert dog and handler to move them. Usually larger breeds, they can be really aggressive, up to the point of attacking you, trying to shatter your confidence. Early in his training with Cecilia, Shep came to understand that sheep have an amazing ability to sense weakness in a dog and to exploit it. Crouching lower to the ground, Shep continues his steady advance, determined to impose his will upon the sheep. Drawing closer and closer to the renegades, he keeps his "eye" on them — an intense, almost mesmerizing glare that will compel sheep to go as they're directed. Here's the crucial moment at which they will or will not submit. Shep's advance is relentless. The rebels shift nervously, calculating their chances. Shep will accept no less than their complete obedience. He sees their courage deserting them. Then they falter and turn, all thoughts of resistance abandoned, and cluster with the others, all of them shuffling skittishly.

"There!" Peter calls again and once more Shep pauses in place, allowing the flock to settle. "Walk on!" Peter calls and Shep moves steadily towards the flock, nudging them slowly forward.

From this point on it's just fun, fetching the group down to Peter, darting this way and that to prevent any fools from bolting, continuously nudging them into a clump, bringing them along sweet and easy, eventually driving them around Peter and then back up the meadow again. Then maybe a bit of shedding, dividing the flock into two and moving each group independently. Or singling a lone sheep out of the group. Peter throws in a few new wrinkles here and there just for novelty, to keep Shep on his game. The whole time Shep moves with and through and around the flock as though they were one white woolly organism floating in a sea of green grass. Sheep, man and dog united in ancient triangulation.

Two

Six decades earlier, an expectant hush settled over the crowded lecture hall as Assistant Professor Nigel Childes strode to the podium at centre stage. He smiled drolly across the assembled throng, as though he'd wandered into the wrong room by accident and was now required to give an accounting of himself. "Good morning, my good historians," he announced with a tony British accent straight off BBC Radio. "Our topic this morning, you'll be delighted to hear, is the Tolpuddle Martyrs."

The student body burbled with green and eager earnestness. Childes was perhaps only a decade older than most members of his audience, tall and slender, impeccably attired in a tailored dark suit with conservative blue tie. His facial features were delicate, but a slightly receding chin and rather large forehead subverted what otherwise might have been thought a classically handsome face. His eyes were outstanding — not so much their colour, a muted hazel, but because they flashed bright and quick as though with mischief. A commanding presence at the podium, certainly, with a touch of the mercurial about him. In only his first year on the faculty at Carlyle College, he had, without apparent effort, already achieved star billing. Wit and flamboyance to burn. Oscar Wilde, some said. Noel Coward. He taught Late Georgian and Victorian Britain, a specialty dull enough to induce narcolepsy, but his lectures were invariably packed with fervent and attentive students. Insightful, passionate, humorous, he was hailed as a verbal magician whose lectures unscrolled with such panache and fluidity an hour would fly by in what seemed like minutes.

But not today, not for Ginger Flynn at least. For her the hour ticked slowly past, one tripping moment after the next. Perched in a third row aisle seat she was watching Childes with particular interest, her attention not entirely absorbed by the grievances of agricultural workers in nineteenth century Dorset.

"And so you see," Childes was saying, "this was, unhappily, one of the final bleats to be heard from the oppressed rural labourers before they subsided into another generation of stifled dissent and simmering but unexpressed outrage." The student body dutifully murmured its distaste for social injustice and other uglinesses.

But Ginger Flynn was far more intrigued at the moment as to why Professor Childes had surprised her on her way into the lecture hall with a discreet hand at her elbow. "Miss Flynn," he'd said to her with a delicacy perhaps aimed at excluding prying outsiders, "are you free for a moment this afternoon? Say around two?" Yes, she was, she said, in a flutter of surprise and speculation. "Lovely. In my office, then; you know where it is?" Yes, she did. "Excellent! I'll see you at two." And on he'd swept with his little entourage of acolytes in tow.

What was he possibly up to, she wondered. He'd never spoken directly to her before; there was no recent assignment or exam result to discuss. Yes, of course she was intrigued by Childes, as most of the few women on campus seemed to be. After all, he was single and sparkling, and she knew for a fact that at least two of her dorm mates were cultivating sizeable crushes on him. She herself was not. For one thing there was Jonathan to consider, back home in Shetterly, waiting faithfully for her, as he'd promised. As each had promised. But more to the point, for reasons she didn't fully apprehend, but felt intuitively, she wasn't entirely convinced that Nigel Childes was everything he was cracked up to be. Oh, yes, he was chic and cheeky enough to get the average sophomore girl wet between the legs, but how much sincerity, how much integrity lay beneath that glossy surface, she wasn't at all sure. Something about the man excited wariness in her. And so she spent the hour of this particular lecture largely ignoring the plight of the Tolpuddle Martyrs in favour of speculating as to what the enigmatic Assistant Professor Childes might have in mind for her.

That afternoon she tapped softly with two knuckles on the pebbled glass of his closed office door.

"Come!" The voice was peremptory, almost a summons.

She entered charily. She could barely make him out, rearranging a file of papers on his desk in a brilliance of backlighting from sunshine slashing against the windows behind him. The room had a close smell of old books and erudition, conjuring ghosts of wizened professors dead for decades.

"Yes?" he said, looking up. "Ah, Miss Flynn."

"Yes." She was uncertain if she should call him Sir, or just what.

"Please," he said, gesturing across the desktop to a wooden office chair, "won't you sit down." He'd removed his suit jacket, replacing it with an expensive looking cardigan in olive green that went well with his eyes. It had leather patches at the elbows, perhaps a bit too conventionally professorial. The blue tie was still knotted in place. She thought, idiotically, of her mother's sartorial axiom: blue and green should not be seen.

"Now," he said, setting the papers aside and placing both hands on the desktop, palms down, as though to steady things, and looking straight into her eyes, "I've asked you to stop in on a personal matter, nothing to do with the course at all."

"Personal?" she said, puzzled.

"Indeed. Is that all right with you?"

"Yes, yes, I suppose so," she said, looking down, having no idea, feeling disconcerted both by his topic and by the forcefulness of his gaze. Such glaringly intense eyes. As though he were challenging her in some way she didn't understand, almost as if trying to subdue her. Made aware of how her fingers were playing together skittishly in her lap, she sought to steady her nerves. She was not a young woman easily frightened and would not now admit to herself that she was unnerved.

"This might be somewhat painful for you," he said, his head tilted in a pose of solicitude, "but I hope not. I certainly don't want to upset you."

Geez, she thought, glancing up at him again, what on earth is he going on about? Is this some foolish flirtation he's attempting? He was smiling at her with the gentlest and kindest of smiles, though his eyes didn't seem to smile at all. It was disorienting how the smile said one thing and the eyes another. She smiled weakly back but could think of nothing to say. Instead she stared at a tiny stain on the front of his cardigan. Tomato soup it looked like.

"Did you by chance have a brother named Frank?" he asked gently, leaning forward across the desk.

Caught entirely off guard, and disconcerted already, she was swirled into something like vertigo and began to tremble. Frank. Her lovely, sweet, dead brother. Frankie. How . . . ?

"Oh, listen, I'm dreadfully sorry." She heard Childe's voice as though from a distance and paid it no attention. With rising panic she was searching in her mind for her brother's familiar image. But he would not come to her so suddenly and unexpectedly. He remained a shape, a shadow, something disappearing just beyond the edges of recognition. Surely her memory of him hadn't faded so completely. The memory of a dream. Frankie! Jesus, Frankie. No, it wasn't so. Just at this moment. The unexpectedness. This professor she scarcely knew.

There was a hand upon her shoulder, a discreet mere brush of a hand. Glancing up she saw that Childes had come around the desk to stand above her. "Look," he said, all concern and solicitude, "I'm terribly sorry. If I'd known . . ."

"No. No. It's all right," she said. "Really. It's just . . . oh." She didn't know what it was just. A brief heart seizure of some sort, perhaps, or a streak of lunacy only touched for a moment. Terrifying, though, that bottomless hollow. The not knowing, not remembering. Already the sensation was receding. She glanced towards the windows where sunlight still flashed in fractures. The shelves of old books stood gravely by. As suddenly as it had struck, her spasm of panic had passed. She'd be all right. Yes, she'd be all right. "I'm fine," she said, "really, I'm fine." Then, mumbling a brief apology, she stood and left his office.

⁂

Weeks went by and still Childes had not approached the Flynn girl again since that first unfortunate interview. Naturally he'd been startled and embarrassed by how upset she'd become over his mentioning her brother's name. Perhaps a bit of an overreaction, he'd concluded afterwards. After all, it was five years since Frank Flynn had been killed in the war and although Childes himself could not think of it without a certain emotional stir, the girl's response had been so extreme, you'd have thought the tragedy had occurred only recently.

Nevertheless, the resemblance between brother and sister was absolutely startling. Nigel had noticed it almost immediately, before he discovered who she was. Early in the term he was lecturing one afternoon and scanning his audience as he liked to do for dramatic effect when suddenly he saw her, sitting quite near the front, apparently very attentive. She was difficult to overlook, even amongst hundreds, taller than most of the men, with that head of unruly and extravagantly copper-coloured hair. He realized then that he'd noticed the hair previously without paying attention to her face. But on this occasion he'd paused in mid-sentence, knocked entirely off his train of thought, and instantly thinking: Frank. Frank Flynn. Picturing him in his army uniform, that silly grin of his, wartime London, the thrill and terror of it all. He'd forced his mind back into the lecture, not sure how long he'd been away, and tried to put the incident out of mind.

Truth to tell, he hadn't really thought of Frank Flynn all that much in recent years, but some things aren't designed to stay out of mind and, once reintroduced, Frank became one of those. Especially with the girl reappearing at his lectures, always seated close enough to the front to be easily seen. He'd checked her name in the enrollment and, sure enough, there she was: Ginger Flynn. Those high cheekbones and firm chin, the fine line of her nose, full lips — they were young Frank's features exactly. He would have sworn the two were twins had it not been for the age discrepancy. And the hair: Frank's had been straight and flaxen, forever flopping down across his forehead, nothing like the coppery conflagration of the girl's.

The more he saw of her, the more frequently random fragments of memory bloomed in Nigel's mind. How he and Frank had first met, the instantaneous mutual attraction. That marvellous hike that they had taken together across Dartmoor — the exhilarating sense of freedom they'd both felt roaming those wild hills, the illusion of being in another, far better time. Then a sudden storm hurtling up out of nowhere and pelting them with drenching rain. How they'd huddled together hopelessly against the crumpled stone remnants of an old tin mine, rain streaming down across Frank's face, a silly giddiness as they laughed together at their predicament.

As remembrances of Frank had stirred within him, Nigel had convinced himself that he should talk with the sister. Straighten out the leftover business from the war as best he could. He'd been fascinated to realize that the prospect had given him a small shiver of excitement, as though it involved something forbidden, something a prudent person would consider most carefully before undertaking. And in hindsight, he obviously should have thought it through more thoroughly. The girl had simply been unwilling, or incapable of discussing her brother with him and he felt rather a fool for having blundered into the situation so artlessly.

Afterwards he remembered the letter and was surprised with himself that he had not considered it until now. He must have it still, he was quite sure. After rummaging around a bit, finally in a tin biscuit box commemorating the coronation of Queen Elizabeth II, amid a clutch of old mementos, cards and letters, he found what he was looking for. A soiled and crinkled envelope addressed to himself at King's College, Cambridge. Inside, a single piece of writing paper crowded with Frank's neat handwriting in pencil.

October 25, 1943

My dear Nigel,

I can't tell you how much it meant to me to receive your letter yesterday. I was feeling a bit in the dumps, I don't mind telling you. We'd lost two good fellows a couple of nights previous, picked off by snipers we hadn't known were there. Chucker was from Saskatchewan, Hrechuk I think his name was but everyone called him Chucker. A big farm boy, and all he wanted to do was get back to his beloved grain fields. I think he had a girl waiting back there for him too, but he was too shy to talk about her. Then suddenly there he was, sprawled in the dirt with half his brain blown away. The other one was Hooles from someplace in small town Ontario. He wanted to become a doctor once this madness was over, and he'd have made a darn good one too, I'm sure of it. I sat and cried that night, cried and cried and cried and couldn't stop. They weren't the first we'd lost, God knows, but it was like the straw breaking the camel's back. Too much, just too damn much to bear.

I'm sorry to sound so gloomy. Especially since it seems at last the tide has turned in our favour. Everyone's talking about the end of the war and mostly about getting home again. For the longest time we didn't allow ourselves to think too much about it, because it made what we were doing that much more intolerable. But now there's a light at the end of the tunnel, thank God.

I am writing to you just now, rather than my family, because I don't want to have them worrying about my gloomy mood. We are not a family that easily expresses emotion among ourselves. Speaking of them, I do want to ask one huge favour of you. If by chance I'm killed before this thing is over, would you please get in touch with my family at the address on the reverse. Tell them how much I loved them. Tell my sister Ginger that she was the sweetest, dearest thing to me of all, and that my greatest regret is not being able to live a full, long life with her as a part of it.

Thank you, my dear friend. I miss you dreadfully and long for the day when I shall see your smiling face again.

Yrs,
Frank

Ps. I'm sorry I haven't talked more about your letter and how much comfort it gave me.

Nigel read the letter through a second time, then again. He glanced at the reverse side, to see what he knew wasn't there. Frank had forgotten to include his family's address. Nigel smiled to himself, rueful over the reminder of his own negligence. After all, he might have made enquiries once the war was over, might have tracked the family down and given them perhaps some small solace from Frank's words. Because he'd learned that his friend had been blown to pieces under a heavy artillery barrage only a day or two after writing this letter. But he hadn't made good on Frank's last request, for a dozen or more perfectly legitimate reasons, none of which he could now remember, and one less admissible reason which he could.

So Nigel determined to speak with Ginger Flynn again, if for no other purpose than to fulfill the obligation entailed in Frank's letter in the event of his death. But there was another reason too, even if Nigel didn't fully grasp it yet. Certainly he remained intrigued although somewhat uneasy about the reawakened sense of Frank and of their relationship, brief as it had been, brought about by the repeated appearance of Ginger Flynn at his lectures. In recent weeks he'd several times found himself dwelling a bit obsessively on certain memories of Frank. That cockeyed smile of his — he'd yet to see the sister smile in the same way, but imagined she must. Frank's way of sauntering down a street, his cap at a jaunty angle, as though he hadn't a care in the world, much less the Führer's tanks and cannons facing him. Now, inextricable from the memories somehow, here was this sister whom he knew Frank had loved above everyone else.

As part of her course work she had submitted a lengthy essay on the depopulation of the English countryside during the early Victorian years. Very thoughtfully composed, Nigel judged, and really rather elegant in its expression, at least in places. He noted the entirely apt emphasis she had placed upon the role played by teenage girls moving from rural life into domestic service. Reading through it had only reinforced how intriguing the girl's presence had become for him; but just how much of her appeal derived from her being Frank's sister, and how much from something else, he was reluctant to consider.

He composed and addressed a note to Ginger Flynn at her residence:

Dear Miss Flynn,

Since we spoke several weeks ago about a subject I had abysmally failed to anticipate would be so upsetting to you, I have felt considerable remorse for my unpardonable clumsiness. I hope that you have found it in your heart to forgive the inappropriateness of my conduct.

However, I need you to know that I have in my possession a letter written to me by your brother which I have good reason to believe may have been his last communication with any of us before his tragic death. The letter entails an obligation upon myself to speak with you specifically, and I regret that half a dozen years have elapsed without my discharging this duty. If it is at all tolerable to you, I would very much appreciate the opportunity to speak with you further on this delicate matter.

Yours sincerely,
Nigel Childes

Ginger was sitting at her desk in dorms when she opened the note. She was not at all surprised to receive it; in fact she'd been half anticipating some approach by Professor Childes ever since that unfortunate incident in his office. She'd never done anything quite like that before, completely breaking down in the presence of a stranger. Oh, yes, she'd sobbed her heart out over Frank's death often enough. She was only fourteen at the time and up until then had never suffered any loss more severe than being snubbed at school by some pimply boy she fancied. Then, suddenly, this. Her brother, her handsome, smart, funny, loving brother lying dead in some filthy European field. Stupid. Stupid and meaningless. Everything had stopped for her, the world she knew disappeared into a horrible murky twilight. She lost interest in everything. Her schoolwork suffered as she slid from top of the class to barely passing grades. She wandered around Stone House and its grounds hating it. Hating everything. Perhaps fearing that their own grief would worsen hers, her parents didn't speak with her about Frank's death other than in hopeless clichés and platitudes. A hero for his country. At least he didn't suffer. Didn't come back a vegetable like so many of those other poor boys. All the usual rubbish. As she remained mired in depression, they fretted and wondered and consulted as to what should be done for her.

But nothing was done and eventually time, as time does, set about restoring Ginger to herself. She started picking up the pieces of her life and gradually began to get on with things. A new high school sweetheart, dear Jonathan, helped, as did the dream of going to college, an ambition that not a single other girl in her graduating class shared. It began to feel as though the shattering reality of Frank's death was finally being laid to rest.

It was all the more startling, then, that she'd suffered that embarrassing emotional firestorm in Childes's office at the mere mention of Frank's name. She'd ended up by rather rudely excusing herself and leaving his office without any explanation. Afterwards she'd tortured herself over it for weeks, imagining that Childes must have thought her a completely unbalanced twit to have carried on that way. She thought numerous times about approaching him, in part to apologize for her behaviour and in part because she was intrigued by his connection with her brother. She presumed that he'd met Frank, but where, she wondered, and how. Had they been friends? She'd continued to muse over the unlikely connection of Childes the Cambridge scholar with Frank, a soldier from the colonies. She'd studied Childes closely during his lectures, knowing in her heart that sooner or later she would need to speak with him about the unfinished business between them.

During the course of all this, she recognized that she had come to revise her opinion of Childes somewhat. Certain of his mannerisms that had at first struck her as rather affected, now seemed less so. Yes, he was still a bit too clever for his own good, no doubt about that, and rather more pleased with himself than was appropriate, but perhaps he wasn't quite the phony she'd previously suspected. She began to consider the possibility that he was in reality as charming and insightful as he appeared in public. That he was something more than a highly polished performer. Plus, she had to confess, she'd derived great pleasure from the praise he'd accorded her essay on Victorian country girls going into service. He'd even quoted a brief passage from it in one of his lectures.

Ginger knew better than to share Childes's note with any of her dorm mates. She liked the three of them well enough, Dorothy, Patsy and

Diane, but none was a confidante, and all three would have instant antennae twitching at even the slightest suggestion that Professor Childes was showing a particular interest in Ginger, no matter what its root cause. Patsy, for one, seemed to imagine that Childes quite fancied her and was only restrained by his position from making an advance. All three of them had razzed Ginger about Childes quoting from her paper at which she'd been flustered enough to blush, which of course only egged them on.

Ginger addressed a short note to Professor Childes thanking him for contacting her and indicating that she would be pleased to meet with him at his convenience. After what seemed an interminable delay of three days she received another note from him suggesting a meeting at his office on the following Tuesday.

Once again she rapped on the pebbled glass and was summoned to enter, far less peremptorily than before.

"Ah, good afternoon, Miss Flynn," Childes said, rising from behind his desk and coming around to shake her hand. "Thank you for coming. Here, please take a seat." He guided her almost deferentially to the wooden office chair.

"Thank you," she said, seating herself and smoothing her skirt so that her legs were almost fully covered. She'd dressed a little more carefully than usual for this interview and had spent more time than normal on her makeup. She noticed that Childes hadn't changed into his cardigan but had kept his suit jacket and tie on. Today the tie was in a bold fuchsia pattern.

"Now," Childes began, taking his seat again behind his desk, "I wonder if we can start off by laying the ghost of our last meeting to rest? My clumsiness and . . ."

"Oh, no, not at all!" Ginger interrupted him. "You weren't the least bit clumsy, it was just this weird oh I don't know . . ."

"You're very gracious," Childes told her, smiling. "Anyway, let's start afresh, shall we?"

"Yes, I think so." Ginger folded her hands demurely in her lap. She was aware that the fierce, almost feral sharpness that had frightened her before was now gone from Childes's eyes and his whole manner was softer, less overpowering than it had been. She felt no fear of him this time. "You mentioned that you had a letter from Frank," she said.

"Yes, I do," he replied, pulling open a desk drawer. His desk top was almost completely bare except for a large blotter and writing pad, an expensive looking fountain pen and a telephone. Not like some of the profs' desks she'd seen that looked as though a tornado had passed over them hurling books and papers in its path. His desk, indeed his whole office, spoke to her of serenity and good order, an abhorrence of confusion or disarray. "Here it is," he said, extracting the soiled envelope from the drawer. "I wasn't at all sure that I still had it, but after seeing you, I thought I should rummage about and, sure enough, I found it amidst a collection of old letters." He paused for a moment before handing it over. "Now, you're quite sure you want to see it, are you?"

"Oh, yes," she said, "rather desperately in fact. We never did receive anything like a final letter from him. Foolishly, I suppose, I'd had no real sense that I'd never see him again. There was no final goodbye, none of what you'd say to someone you loved and were about to lose forever. He just vanished and it left a dreadful hole in all our lives. I don't believe my parents ever really got over it." She was talking too fast and feared that she might begin to babble. "So I do want to read it, absolutely."

"Would you prefer to take it with you? Read it in privacy and return it later?"

She hesitated for a moment. "That's very thoughtful of you," she said. It was a sensitive thing for him to have offered and she was touched by the delicacy of his gesture. "If you don't mind," she said.

"Not in the least," he said, holding the envelope out to her across the desk.

She leaned forward and took the envelope from him.

"Let me just say," he added, "that I deeply regret not having contacted you and your parents far sooner. It was something Frank asked me to do and I failed him badly by not doing so. I have no valid excuse other than the general turmoil of the times, which is no excuse at all. Please don't think too badly of me that I proved so negligent in what was, after all, a sacred duty of sorts."

"Of course not," she said, carefully placing the letter in her satchel and bidding Childes good afternoon.

Ginger was mildly surprised when, a few days later, Professor Childes took her aside after one of his lectures and suggested that they meet off campus for tea rather than at his office. This was not exactly against the rules, but there did exist an unspoken yet implicit understanding that extracurricular fraternization among faculty and students was frowned upon at Carlyle College. The faculty was by and large aged to the point of near decrepitude and thus the likelihood of impropriety existed, if at all, on the most distant of horizons. Childes, of course, was younger and unmarried, and thus perhaps in greater need of circumspection than his colleagues, but due to his popularity and his aura of sophisticated charm, Assistant Professor Childes gave the impression of someone not necessarily constrained by entrenched mores. Even though slightly taken aback, Ginger agreed to meet him later that afternoon at a certain tea shop in town.

She had Frankie's letter with her still and had read it over so often she probably had it unintentionally memorized. She'd made a copy for herself and would now return the original to Childes. The letter had roiled up a great confusion of emotion in her and for the past several days she'd felt beset by episodes of grief, loss, frustration, anger. She teared up repeatedly over that sentence of Frankie's: *Tell my sister Ginger that she was the sweetest, dearest thing to me of all, and that my greatest regret is not being able to live a full, long life with her as a part of it.*

That's how she felt as well, that a part of whom she was meant to become had been torn away from her and lost forever. That Frankie was her soul mate, someone she loved in a way that she could and would never love anyone else. Ever. *My greatest regret*. Oh, yes, yes it is. She'd felt the same way back when they first learned of Frankie's death, but not with the depth of understanding with which she'd now re-experienced it. Back then it had all been wild sorrow and lamentation, whereas now it was a far deeper and more abiding desolation of spirit.

Then, after having run that bitter course to its unsatisfactory end once again, she repeated the exercise of setting Frankie's memory free.

What remained was the mystery of Frankie's relationship with Nigel Childes. *Thank you, my dear friend. I miss you dreadfully and long for the day when I shall see your smiling face again.* That was not how she imagined young men communicated with one another, although admittedly she knew almost nothing about how young men communicated amongst themselves. *My dear Nigel. My dear friend.* How intriguing. She wondered if it would be appropriate to probe or best to simply leave the thing be, let Childes say whatever he wished to say without any inquisitiveness from her.

When she got to the tea shop, a pokey little place on a crooked back street, one that she'd never visited before, she found Childes waiting for her at a small table in a corner nook. Two older couples were sitting by the front window where they were being waited upon by a youngish woman dressed in a ridiculous maid's outfit; otherwise the place was deserted. Childes beckoned to Ginger from the table and rose as she approached.

"Well," he said as he held her chair for her, "is this suitably *outré* for your tastes?"

It was an odd little place indeed, with walls of white wainscoting and pink roses wallpaper, chintz curtains and bouquets of dried flowers. With a faint scent of lavender, it seemed fusty and old fashioned and not the least bit hip. She wondered if he'd chosen it as the least likely place in town to attract any students.

"Best tea in town by a long shot," he told her, as though needing to justify why he'd chosen such an antique venue. Having held her chair like a true gentleman, he seated himself across the tiny table from her. "Only real tea in town, so far as I can make out. These dreadful tea bags they insist upon using in this country. Absolutely revolting, wouldn't you agree?"

She couldn't tell how much of his feigned dismay was real. If any. It was a peculiar thing about the man — in his lectures he was invariably pitch perfect so that there was never a moment's doubt as to whether he was being ironic or sarcastic or absolutely sincere. And yet in personal discourse, as she had already discovered, his meaning was often blurred, not quite one thing or the other. What she couldn't decipher was whether the blurring was intentional or simply an inadequacy on his part. He was not someone with whom you associated verbal inadequacy of any kind.

Before she had time to respond to his question with anything more than a polite smile, the waitress approached their table. "May I help you?" she asked, all her attention on Childes, her hip slung forward just enough to be slightly provocative, her glossy lips pursed a touch coquettishly. It occurred to Ginger that this might not be the first time the waitress had flirted with Childes and that the girl's coquetry might be every bit as much an attraction to him as the establishment's marvellous tea. She told herself that she didn't care one way or the other, that the only aspect of Childes that was of any interest to her was his shared history with Frankie.

They ordered tea and scones.

"I've brought Frankie's letter," Ginger said, handing it over to him.

"I do hope it didn't reopen old wounds," he said, taking it from her and placing it gently on the table between them.

"A bit," she confessed, looking at the envelope. "But I'm glad to have read it and I really want to thank you for giving me the chance to see it."

"However tardy I may have been," he said with a self-consciously rueful grin. He was, she could see, fishing for absolution.

"I was wondering," Ginger said, hesitating, "um, how was it that you and Frankie came to know each other?"

"Ah, a remarkable crossing of paths, I can assure you," Childes said, obviously pleased to have been asked. "It was in the City, London I mean, in the evening, almost dusk as I recall. I was down from Cambridge for some do or other, I don't remember just what, but we were in evening dress, some classmates and myself, you know, white tie, top hat, tails, all the trimmings. Ridiculous in hindsight, but I'm sure we thought ourselves rather grand at the time." Childes smiled at her in a self-deprecating way she found rather charming.

"Do go on," she urged him, smiling herself.

"Anyway," he continued, "we were walking along, Tottenham Court Road it may have been, when a tremendous gust of wind lifted the topper right off my head and sent it scudding towards the gutter. I thought for sure it would be crushed completely under some dirty bus or taxi or something when, lo and behold, this young soldier stepped calmly off the sidewalk, almost into the traffic, then reached out and caught the topper with the most graceful grasp of his hand. Well, I tell you," Childes was beaming with pleasure at the memory, "we were thunderstruck at the audacity of the gesture, the pure panache. Several passersby stopped to clap and cheer as well. It was partly the war thing, of course, that here was one of these brave young fellows from abroad preparing to perhaps go risk his life . . . ah." Here Childes paused, and it didn't seem to Ginger as though he checked himself only to spare her sensibilities. There was sadness and loss lurking here for him too.

"Please go on," she said. Just then the waitress returned with their tea and scones, allowing them the distraction of making a fuss over pouring and stirring while the difficult bit passed over and away.

"Well," Childes resumed, placing his spoon carefully on the saucer, "I started towards him and he towards me, and as he handed the hat over I had the most extraordinary sensation that this was somebody I had known for a considerable time, someone with whom I had shared a great many experiences."

"But of course you hadn't."

"No, no, of course not," Childes said, his hands flittering in disavowal. Not for the first time Ginger noticed his hands, the fine thin fingers with immaculately manicured nails. "I knew from his uniform that he was Canadian and as soon as he opened his mouth, I realized that this was not a voice I'd ever heard before. But still, there was something about him that was entirely compelling. 'Good catch!' I said to him, just for something to say, as one does, and he told me we could credit it to his having been something he called a flanker. I had no idea what he meant, and must have shown it, because we both burst out laughing, right there in the middle of the street."

Childes took a sip of his tea and nibbled at a scone. "Well, we had to get on," he continued, "my friends and I, because of whatever it was we were attending, otherwise I should certainly have taken this flanker for a drink. I was ever so grateful for his having saved my hat, of course, as I told him, but . . ." Childes paused, lost for a moment in reverie.

"But what?" she prodded him.

"Well, it's difficult to put a finger on it really, but it was certainly more than that, more than simple gratitude for his heroics with the topper. I suppose I recognized that there was something about him, something numinous that I didn't want to withdraw from straight away. So we made a hasty arrangement to meet the following afternoon for a drink."

"And did you?" Ginger was entirely absorbed by the story and knew already from the letter still lying between them on the white tablecloth that there was far more to be revealed. Or not.

Three

The *Shetterly Standard* is housed in a square cinder block box painted a pukey salmon colour and squatting along the margin of a dispirited industrial zone. Only a few small windows squint from high in the walls, preventing any view of the outer world. A bunker, almost. As Chrissie wheels her bike into the parking lot, she sees Harold Harding's old Volvo wagon is sitting in its "Reserved for the Editor" parking slot alongside Larry Illinger's gleaming BMW in its "Reserved for the Publisher" slot. Shit, she thinks, what's Illinger doing here? Whenever he shows up something's fucked.

Being as there's no bike rack outside, like any civilized place would have, Chrissie has to wheel her bike in through the big glass front door and stow it inside.

"Hey, babe," she calls to Connie the receptionist as she breezes past. Connie waves distractedly in reply and keeps making um noises into the phone, probably because it's her mother talking at her.

Just as Chrissie's passing Harold Harding's office as quickly and quietly as she can, his door opens and Mr. Illinger appears in the doorway. He's dressed in a dark business suit like usual. "Well," he says, hand on the doorknob, "speak of the devil! How are you, Chrissie?"

"Fine," Chrissie tells him, "how are you?"

Illinger's an unusually small and slender man, scarcely taller than Chrissie herself, but he commands big space. His smile is all fake. Over his shoulder she can see Harding lurking like a dorkwad. Chrissie's seriously on her guard.

"Lovely," Illinger says, trying to look encouraging. Chrissie views Illinger as a shrewd little prick, as insincere as he is unprincipled. She knows he's the only reason she has this job as cub reporter for his paper. Most employers would take one look at her and show her the door, if she'd even managed to get through the door to see them. But the thing is, Illinger owns the paper and he also happens to have a son name of Chazz who happens to be Chrissie's guy. Connect the dots. Illinger's got Chrissie on staff, not out of any great generosity towards her, nor from any desire to do a favour for his son; no, she's here because Illinger wants to use her to keep a leash on his son.

Chazz and his dad don't really talk except by coded messages usually sent via Chrissie. No secret that Chazz dislikes his old man and is into heavy avoidance. But Illinger's a more slippery fish. Disappointed in his son and determined to change him, but unsure how. Latching onto Chrissie as the key. It took her a while at first to figure out what was happening and why. Several times she got caught in weird shit by Illinger exploiting her as a go-between. But even now that she's on to the game, she sometimes can't figure out what he's up to until it's too late. One thing for sure, she's got Chazz's back. Always. Like total OTP. Okay, so maybe he's not exactly what you'd think of as your classic breadwinner, but whether his father approves or not, Chazz's 110 percent on his career as a musician. He figures he'll catch a big break sooner or later and, once he does, they'll be on that street called Easy. Meanwhile Chrissie's doing this bumblefuck job as a reporter, and putting up with Illinger's vomit, to pay the bills. Everybody gets something here.

"Might I have a word?" Illinger asks her. His voice is dry and kinda whispery.

"Sure," Chrissie says with a shrug. What now? she thinks to herself.

"Harold," Illinger asks, turning back to Harding, "I wonder if Chrissie and I could commandeer your office for a few minutes?" Even though he's the publisher, Illinger doesn't have his own office here and is hardly ever around. He has a bunch of other what he calls "business interests" around town. Ultimate Bourgie.

"Sure, sure," says Harold, all grovelly and jovial. He waddles out past Illinger and winks lewdly at Chrissie as he passes.

Illinger closes the door, then he and Chrissie sit down at opposite ends of Harding's big leather couch. Chrissie places her pack on the couch between herself and him. Not that Illinger's got loose hands like Harding does, but still.

"Well, how are things?" Illinger asks her, folding his arms in a fake relaxed way.

"Fine," Chrissie says, "I'm working on a story about that big stone house and old Mrs. Um . . ." She's forgotten Ginger's name.

"Excellent," Illinger says, smiling approvingly, though you can tell he doesn't give a shit. "And how are things at home?"

"Fine," Chrissie says, like always.

"Good. Good. Chazz working away on his music, is he?"

This is twisted even by Illinger's standards, as Chrissie knows for a fact that Illinger despises the whole idea of his son as a musician. Chazz is supposed to become a lawyer or investment banker or something. Dad's setting bait.

"Now," Illinger says, turning fully to face Chrissie, "I wonder if I could ask you a little something about Chazz?"

"What's that?" Chrissie pulls her skirt down a bit because it's riding kind of high. She hears the warning horn like the highways guys use before they blow off a section of rock face.

"Well, this is rather a delicate matter," Illinger says, "and I'd rather it be kept just between the two of us, all right?"

"Sure." Illinger always says stuff like this when he's trying to work some angle with Chrissie. And the only time he ever talks to her is when he's working some angle.

He clears his throat and places his hands primly on his knees. He looks directly at Chrissie, pale eyes like blue ice, and asks, "Has Chazz mentioned to you any recent involvement in making a movie?"

"A movie?" Chrissie says. "Chazz? Are you kidding?" She wants to say Chazz couldn't make pancakes, much less a movie, but she never says more than she has to when she's talking to Illinger.

"So he hasn't mentioned anything of the sort to you?"

"Nope."

"Hmm. That's troubling," Illinger says, looking at Chrissie sympathetically, implying that he and she share a bond of being equally deceived by Chazz. A line he's worked before, but not so brazenly. It had taken Chrissie a little while to figure out this part of his game, but once she got it, she got it. She keeps her face absolute deadpan. As though Illinger actually gave a crap about her. Chrissie knows that he hated Chazz getting involved with her and tried everything he could to prevent it, even tried to send Chazz off to some stupid university on the other side of the country. He thought she was a bad influence. What a fucking joke. *Him* thinking anybody else could be as bad an influence on Chazz as he is. Anyway, after he figured out Chazz and she were so tight he couldn't pry them apart with the Jaws of Life, Illinger decided to use her instead. One minute she's not good enough to be invited to the family Thanksgiving dinner — Chazz wouldn't go without her either and she loved him like sewage for that — next thing you know, she's offered a job at the paper.

Chrissie sits and waits for Illinger to say whatever.

"Well, no sense holding back," he says, as though he's got some great reputation for openness and honesty that he has to maintain at all costs. "I've been informed by a quite reliable source that Chazz has got himself involved in making a movie."

"You're kidding," she says. Chrissie can't picture it. Chazz is into music not movies. Plus, for sure he would have told her. They don't do secrets.

"I wish I was," Illinger says, solemn as Solomon. Now he's looking straight ahead, not at Chrissie, like this is all so fucking Significant and Serious.

Then Chrissie twigs. "What kind of movie?" she asks. Her bum is starting to get sticky on this cheap leather couch, like it always does when Harding's hitting on her while pretending to be discussing her work.

Illinger clears his throat again. "Not the kind of movie any son of mine should even be watching, much less participating in."

"Huh. You mean a pornie flick?"

Illinger's nostrils tremble with disgust. "I believe so, yes. Pornography."

Shit. Chrissie can't believe Chazz would be doing that without ever even mentioning it to her. Still, he has been away a bunch of times lately, though he said he was working on tunes up at a friend's cabin. Shit, Chazz. She could care less what the ratchet film is, but she's grieved that he wouldn't tell her. Just do it behind her back. Her and Chazz have always been unbuttoned. No hidden shit. It's like he's broke the code between them. If it's true. Or maybe it's just Illinger fucking with her head again. Another con to try to break them up, which has always been his endgame.

"I'm surprised he's said nothing to you about it," Illinger says, still working the scheme of him and her both being duped by Chazz. He pauses for a moment then turns towards her again, all friends and family like, and asks, "I wonder, Chrissie, if you'd be amenable to talking to Chazz about it? Find out if it's true. Who else is involved. Anything you can pick up."

"Have *you* talked to him about it?" Chrissie sounds more defensive than she'd meant to.

"No, I haven't," Illinger says, now all touchy-feely, as though he's the poor victim of everybody else's screw-ups. "I was hoping you might help me with this," he says, "since we both love Chazz and . . ."

Chrissie's about ready to puke.

"Well, I'll leave it with you then, shall I?" Illinger concludes, rising abruptly. "Thank you so much, Chrissie. I'm very grateful for whatever you can do. Really."

Chrissie hasn't agreed to do anything, but Illinger just assumes he'll get whatever he wants.

"Maybe give me a call in a day or two," he says, like they were arranging a party or something. "And, it goes without saying, this is strictly between the two of us, all right? I certainly don't want Chazz imagining I'm doing anything behind his back."

You analmuncher, Chrissie's thinking.

"I'll look forward to your call then," Illinger says. He bows his head ever so slightly towards her and walks stiffly out the office leaving Chrissie foxed on the couch.

Having gotten out of his office just before Harding can corner her there, Chrissie's retrieving her bike from the office corridor when Connie at Reception calls over to her: "Honey, there's a message for you, from a, uh, let's see, oh, yea, Ginger Flynn, I think. Yes, Ginger Flynn. Says you left your notebook at her place and do you want to pick it up or what."

"Shit," Chrissie says. Right now her head's totally about what Illinger's just told her. I mean, what sort of a fuck-up would pull a stunt like what Illinger says Chazz has. A pornie flick? And without even letting her know? She's still half shivered about whether to even believe any of it. All she really wants to do is go home and get clear with Chazz, have it out with him if she has to, but now she'll have to ride all the way across town to that mausoleum and get her stupid notebook. Jebus Crisp. Keeping in mind that there's stuff in the notebook that she doesn't necessarily want other people reading. Plus, there's that effing dog to deal with. She rummages in her pack and fetches out a can of spray to have on hand just in case, then grumbles her way out through the door.

Once she's on her bike, pushing hard, things get a bit clearer, like they almost always do. Maybe just as well not to run up against Chazz straight away, let the storm warning pass. She's sometimes had the experience of how, after an hour or two on the road, worries start peeling away like flaking skin. It's her therapy, and for sure a bike was the only thing got her through those bitchy years in Scarberia before she took off from home. Without her bike, she'd have been in the Ding Wing for life. About the notebook, she realizes she doesn't need to get stressed, because she's fairly certain that she didn't scribble anything too bad during the interview, as she's done sometimes when she's been interviewing a certifiable asshole. Or some of the doodles she's done. Jesus. No, actually she kinda got off on the old bitty. Plus, Ginger's the type who probably has some horse-and-buggy code of honour so she wouldn't even look in the book anyway. No worries.

She glides around a corner where the local high school kids have flocked for a smoke. And even if Illinger's right about Chazz, it's probably that he's doing like a soundtrack for the flick, not having his dick sucked by some slut with fake tits like she first imagined. Like he did with her yesterday, only that was love, wasn't it? Chazz loves her, she knows that, he's said it to her over and over. That's the difference. But still he should have told her, should have said something about it, right. Or maybe he was planning a big surprise when he got a fat cheque for his work on the film. That would be Chazz all over. One day he'd just saunter into the room all casual like, and then he'd say something like, "How does that look to you, bae?" as he dangles the cheque in front of her eyes. "Let's turn up," he'd say, and they would, they'd party hard for all that cheque was worth. That's how life is when you're living with a musician. Geez, whatever, she loves the guy like skunkstink.

Chrissie glides up the circular driveway to Stone House, hops off her bike in front of the wide stone steps that rise to the verandah and front door. And there it is: that friggin' dog lying on the verandah. Stretched out on its side, it's kind of twitching and making funny sounds, like it's trying to bark but can't. Its legs move in small jerky motions. Chrissie thinks maybe it's having some sort of epileptic fit or something, like her mother used to have. She stands, holding her bike as protection, fingering the bear spray, not knowing what.

As she remains immobilized, she's remembering dumb Chuck's Rottweilers, those huge black fuckers packed with muscle and menace. She hated Chuck more than any of the other dumb shits her mother had had as boyfriends, more than she'd ever hated anyone. He stunk, for one thing, and had rotten yellow teeth with bits of food always stuck in them. And he swaggered around in his cowboy boots and blue jeans and no shirt like he was some sort of high roller, though all he did was work part-time pumping gas at his cousin's garage. Asshole. And when he was screwing Chrissie's mum he'd make the stupidest grunting noises for the whole fucking neighbourhood to hear. Totally repulsive. Chuck the Fuck she used to call him, only to herself.

Then he started coming on to her whenever her mother wasn't around. Suckhole stuff, like did she want to sit on his lap. Would she like to have a little drink with him. Thirteen years old! Jesus. He knew she didn't like him, too. That's why he started tormenting her. Whenever he got a chance, he'd get those fucking dogs of his, which he kept in a pen in the back yard, he'd leash them and bring them over to her and he'd get them to force her backwards until she was pressed right up against a wall of the garage or the trailer, and he'd let those fucking dogs get right in her face, their big, slobbery jaws right up against her face, and they'd be growling and making like they were going to tear her face off any second. "Now you see why you should be nice to me, Chrissie, don't you?" he'd say with a sick laugh. Then he'd pull the dogs off and put them back in their cage.

And you could hardly believe it, but her mother comes home early one time and catches him at it, tormenting her with those dogs. "Oh, don't do that, Chuck," she calls out to the asshat as she's carrying the groceries in, "you know Chrissie's afraid of the mutts." Her own mother! Afraid of the mutts! Like it's her fault that this psychopath and his killer dogs are threatening her this way. That was maybe the moment she knew she was getting the hell out of there soon as she could.

Chrissie comes back from the past and stares at Shep. She has no way of knowing that Shep's miles away, herding sheep as big as cumulous clouds, their rumps ridiculously soft and slow. He's flanking them this way and that, but struggling because the sheep are so enormous and the fields go on forever and ever. Plus, Peter is not there; he can't find his handler anywhere, so he doesn't know where he should be fetching the giant sheep. He sprints back and forth, back and forth across endless green fields herding the floating, directionless sheep.

Suddenly Shep's awake, his ears up and twitching, and there below him on the driveway stands the funny little human with dark skin and the most alluring odours. Smells of fear for sure, but other scents too, especially a hint of Cecilia that Shep would like to investigate. She's standing absolutely still and staring at him. So he lies completely still himself and stares back at her. Her eyes are dark but large and strangely bright, and frightened in some way. Shep knows she is afraid of him and that he will do nothing now to make her more afraid, but her fear is more than that, deeper and older than that. It's the fear he sees when he first approaches a sheep that's never been worked before. A kind of unstable panic that requires special care.

They remain like that, the two of them, motionless, for what seems a very long time.

⋟⋞

Once a year Peter travels to the city to consult with his money managers. Used to be you could make the trip by train until the geniuses in charge of things decided trains were better deployed hauling dirty coal around than taking people where they needed to go. So he drives, borrowing his mother's Prius rather than use his pick-up. The hybrid hums along the highway smoothly, but he'd still rather be on a train.

There's an expert being interviewed, rather clumsily, on the radio about the psychological impact of disasters. The expert and interviewer jabber away about last week's earthquake in China that killed two thousand people and injured another ten thousand. "Not as bad as the Haiti quake in January, but still horrific," the expert says. Volcanic ash from eruptions under an ice cap in Iceland is still disrupting air traffic across western Europe. This week an oil-drilling platform exploded in the Gulf of Mexico, killing eleven workers and is spewing oil all over the gulf. "Still, it's no time for apocalyptic fear-mongering," the expert advises.

Peter's actually glad to be listening to this plummy-toned fool for entirely personal reasons. Because his own life disaster occurred along this very stretch of highway. An inescapable place of pain: passing the spot where Cecilia and Katherine Ginger were killed. For a while afterwards he couldn't drive this route at all, preferring a tedious detour on back roads around it. But on his last two trips he's stuck to the highway and each time felt his heart being battered as he neared and passed the killing abutment. It had never entered his mind to put up a roadside shrine as people do to honour loved ones lost to accident. He needs no reminder. He sees their blood still splattered on that awful abutment. Bitter as acid reflux, the taste of his guilt over what happened. After months of denial and bewilderment, he eventually learned how to prevent the truth of his guilt from lodging prominently in full consciousness. The memory suppression is ongoing work, though less than it was. Today the gruesome tales of thousands of Chinese killed in the Qinghai quake perversely help damp down his own sense of loss.

He enters the city as a stranger. Even in the few years he's been gone, so much has been torn down, torn up, reconfigured. Brick and wood swept away, replaced by glass and steel. Canyons of gleaming towers where he remembers trees and dignified old homes. Traffic ramped up to screaming intensity. Heterogeneous herds of workers on the move. He almost can't believe he once lived here, thrived here, mastered the arcana of this bewildering place.

Growing up at Stone House with his mother and Irene, a strong-minded sister twelve years older than himself, he'd naturally assumed the outside world was as solid and immutable as that sturdy building. The time-honoured predictabilities of small town Shetterly reinforced the illusion. When he eventually left home for university he was ill prepared for entropy.

Not quite knowing what he wanted to do with himself, he took courses towards a liberal arts degree, but then somehow wandered into the recently opened terrain of computer programming. He soon realized to his surprise that he enjoyed it and was good at it. He discovered the enormous thrills to be had out on that technological frontier, juking and jiving with other bright kids, geniuses some of them, everyone sparking off everyone else. The permanence of Old House gave way to constant fluidity, components being revamped, reordered, transmuted as though by magic. Completely enthralled, and much to his mother's amusement, he went on to get a masters, then a doctorate at MIT.

Not many years after leaving school he and a pal were the unwitting owners of an innovative small software company that quickly became so potentially profitable they had a number of industry heavy hitters banging on their virtual door wanting to buy them out. He laughed them off at first, but his partner Michael, who handled the business end of the business, wanted to sell before the next generation of hotshots vaulted right over them. Peter held firm for a while, but gradually what had begun as a terrific fun ride slumped into what more and more felt like administrative drudgery. The power breakfasts and endless meetings and Byzantine industry politics. A solitary soul by nature, he was increasingly being compelled to do all sorts of things he didn't enjoy with people he didn't especially like, while finding less and less time to do the things he wanted.

Trapped in being outlandishly successful at something he no longer much cared about, he was perfectly primed to bail on the whole thing when one bright spring morning he received a call from a honcho at one of the industry main players who offered them twenty-seven million dollars for their little company. After a quick and giddy meeting with Michael, they agreed to accept the offer and within weeks the deed was done. He was an instant multimillionaire and, more importantly, he'd gotten out of the inferno well before flaming out.

Or so he thought.

But suddenly he had this huge bag of loot that needed to be dealt with. There was no shortage of assistance in this regard because the buy-out had been widely reported and he soon found himself besieged by a bizarre cavalcade of hucksters and dreamers and do-gooders each of whom had the perfect plan for where he should place his winnings. He wrote several generous cheques to international aid organizations whose work he admired, bought the big farm outside of Shetterly, where he planned to spend the bulk of his time, and plunked the remainder into an ethical investment scheme to be managed by a highly regarded chartered accountant imposingly named Zigfried Palz, the very fellow he's now about to consult with.

The Prius glides silently into a parking spot Zigfried keeps reserved in his building's parkade for top echelon clients. The elevator's a glass capsule that slides up the outer wall of the office tower, with the churning city streets receding below. None of the other riders speak, other than into their cell phones. The last person remaining, twenty-six stories up, Peter steps into the leafy foyer of the accounting firm where Zigfried Palz plies his trade.

"Hello, there, Mr. Flynn," Zigfried greets him by the reception desk. The accountant's made a point of being ready to receive his client at the appointed time, just as Peter's made a point of being punctual. The two of them shake hands, cordial, mutually respectful. Zigfried's fortyish like Peter, and fastidious in every aspect of his grooming and attire. Peter likes to imagine the man's been polished to the sheen of shoreline pebbles by the ebb and flow of money. His one distinguishing characteristic is a bold but meticulously trimmed mustache.

Zigfried leads the way to a small office with a glass wall that looks out across the city.

"Big news," Zigfried says about as excitedly as he says anything, "we've got peregrine falcons nesting somewhere just up above us." He indicates out and up from the glass.

"Wow," Peter says, "I'm impressed."

"We're very pleased," Zigfried says.

"I bet. But the pigeons must be nervous."

"Wouldn't want to be a pigeon in this neighbourhood," Zigfried agrees without apparent irony. He motions Peter into a plush armchair. "Coffee?"

"Please," Peter says.

"Two coffees please, Irenya," Zigfried says into his lapel.

"Now, as we discussed," Zigfried begins, taking a seat, "I've arranged to have Sarah join us in thirty minutes which will give us sufficient time to review your portfolio before she arrives and then perhaps the three of us can do a bit of brainstorming."

"Excellent," Peter says. As always during this annual review of his financial situation Peter has to compel himself to pay attention. Truth to tell, it bores the bejeezus out of him.

A few minutes in, Irenya the assistant enters carrying a tray with coffees and designer pastries. Zigfried scarcely misses a beat. Eventually, right on schedule, Sarah Patterson arrives. She's younger than the men but brimming with striking energy and confidence. An investment consultant with a very impressive client list, Sarah is perhaps slightly less permissive towards Peter's quirks than Zigfried. Both are invariably helpful, as advisers are apt to be with clients who have as much money as Peter does, but he's fully aware that they consider him eccentric at best. For all their skill with numerical calculation, neither of them has much success in disguising their bafflement at how Peter could have amassed his wealth while retaining such indifference towards it. His only concern appears to them to be an excessive obsession that the money not contribute to plundering the planet or oppressing the poor. As if ethical investing wasn't *de rigeur* these days.

With the necessary options explored and decisions made, the meeting concludes with Peter thanking both for their wise counsel and escaping back to the elevator. Glancing up as it begins its smooth descent, he sees what must be one of the falcons returning to its nest. He remembers there's been peregrines nesting in the towers of Manhattan for years, which is maybe why Zigfried is so pleased.

With the burden of money-talk lifted, Peter re-enters the swirl of the city streets with a less critical eye. He's got one more chore to do before returning home, which is to pick up an iPad that he's ordered as a gift for his mother. Just released this month, with magisterial fanfare, the new device is in high demand and short supply, but through an old friend he's managed to have one set aside for him at the Apple store. He drives across town, miraculously finds a parking spot not too far from the store and makes the purchase from a young salesman whose enthusiasm for the tablet is almost religious in its fervor. Handel could be playing as the sacred tablet is handed over. Peter smiles back at the memory of himself at that age, similarly smitten, equally oblivious.

Then the most pressing item of the trip: Peter makes note of the precise time at which he has now decided to leave the city.

⁂

Ginger's wandering around in the library at Stone House while waiting for her visitors to arrive. The high inner walls of the spacious room are lined floor to ceiling with books, many of them leather bound and gilt edged, venerable old tomes that have sat largely undisturbed for decades. She especially loves to spend winter afternoons in this room, its dignified chill driven off by a brisk fire in the fireplace. She'll take down a solemn volume of Smollet or Gibbon and lose herself in the wonderment of old-world words. On quiet days she sometimes overhears various authors talking in subdued tones. Dickens and Dostoyevsky whispering conspiratorially in the bay window alcove. Jane Austen and Emily Dickinson enjoying a giggle together.

Ah, the quiet's lovely though isn't it? Now all my teachers are dead except silence — W.S. Merwin, if I remember. Especially after all that fuss yesterday. I'm surprised the girl hasn't shown up. Wonder if she got my message. You never know anymore what messages get through and what don't. Suppose I should be on Facebook or Twitter or one of those things. Maybe they're more reliable. Or not. Of course she might be afraid to come back because of Shep the Ferocious. Ha! Fear makes the wolf bigger than he is. One of Father's old proverbs, not that Father was one to talk about fear. Odd, though, the things we choose to cluster our fears around. It was Frankie's gift to me, I know that now, his dying. Because it was so awful, a worst fear realized. Get it over with early on. What's left to fear after something like that? Except. Yes, it's true, to have lost one of my babies or both of them, that would have been worse. Only I'd have been stronger too. Because of Frankie. Not like poor Peter. So odd that dear old Mum and Dad couldn't talk with me about Frankie and I haven't been a whole lot better trying to talk with Peter about Cecilia and the baby. Oh, that darling baby! Cagey I took to calling her, for Katherine Ginger. Silly. The thought of it though, that dreadful crash. And what can be said about it really? Just like with Frankie. The sounds of silence. Poor Peter. Robbing Peter to pay Paul. Peter Paul and Mary. Hail Mary full of grace. Yes she was, Cecilia, full of grace. Nobody deserves to die like that, especially a young mother. And little Cagey too. The way she would laugh and laugh and laugh at the silliest things. All dead except silence. Farewell. Such a dreadful time . . .

The antique chiming of the front doorbell echoing through the house lifts Ginger from her reverie. She crosses the foyer to open the big oaken front door. Her friends Garth Wilson and Sarina Chand greet her warmly with a hug from each of them. Ginger's delighted to see them both. Garth's a retired civil engineer with silver hair and perfectly trimmed goatee, wearing his typical blue jeans and rough cotton shirt. A widower, he's always been one of Ginger's favourites, steady, strong and highly principled. She remembers him as a fiery young guy in his prime and he still retains the robust energy of someone far younger. And Sarina *is* far younger — early thirties, wielding a degree in political science, teaches at the community college, very bright, very quick. Thoroughly modern in dress and manner, she has in Ginger's mind a suggestion of the exotic and timeless about her. The black hair and impenetrably dark eyes, a calmness at the centre. Or is this only . . . what do they keep calling it on the radio nowadays, racial stereotyping? Ginger's not sure.

One thing's certain: Sarina, who's only lived in Shetterly for a couple of years, has already proven herself a player. Perceptive and articulate, she has almost single-handedly revitalized the town's activist community, much of which had been tottering into its dotage. Ginger remains its nominal matriarch, but Sarina's the firebrand now that Ginger once was. Oh, yes, she was a hell-raiser in her day. After Nigel deserted her and the kids. It was almost as though he took away with him the careful and correct young woman she had been and left behind a rebel more like himself, fully prepared to kick whatever official plump butt needed kicking.

That was back in '65 when all hell was breaking loose: Blacks marching in Selma, the first SDS marches against the Vietnam War, "sexism" coined as a term. Dylan going electric at Newport, the Beatles at Shea Stadium. A single mum, stripped of girlish illusions, thoroughly pissed off at her fleeing ex-husband, Ginger had decided insubordination was the order of the day.

Forty-five years ago. Impossible.

"I thought we could meet in the drawing room just for fun," Ginger says as she leads them into the cavernous room, "so we can lounge on the overstuffed furniture and pretend to be gentry."

"No need for me to pretend," says Garth, seating himself with mock self-importance in a wing-back chair covered in green velvet. He's been in here previously and enjoys making fun of the place. Though a frequent visitor of late, Sarina, hasn't been in this room before and now stares at the enormous oil paintings that dominate the space. Hanging on three of the high walls, each has a faux Baroque frame of moulded and gilded plaster over wood and depicts a different grim biblical scene — Lucifer plummeting from heaven, Abraham preparing to kill his son Isaac as sacrifice, and Salome bringing Herod the severed head of John the Baptist on a platter.

Ginger, unsure what the younger woman might be thinking, says, "Not exactly uplifting, are they?"

"Well, they're pretty twisted for sure," Sarina says, "but my God they're powerful."

"Yes. They go back at least a hundred years. I believe the people who built the house brought them from Germany. Some lesser-known genius of the period. Even my parents, who were dreadfully religious but not in this bloodthirsty way, couldn't bring themselves to remove the monstrosities."

"And you can't either?" Sarina asks, sitting down alongside Ginger.

"Well," Ginger says with a smile, "I'm, let's say, constrained against making significant alterations to the house and furnishings."

"Heritage home regulations?" Sarina asks.

"More like inheritance constraints," Ginger says with a laugh. "It's a long story."

"Speaking of which," Garth puts in, "lots of chatter on the web these days about your evangelical overlords."

"Yes," Ginger says, "Peter had heard some of it. Sounds like a nasty bit of business."

"I'll say. Child abuse on a massive scale, it looks like," Garth says. "Could be real interesting, what it means for this place."

"We'll see," Ginger says, following Sarina's gaze up to the Baptist's bloody head. "But can you imagine being a little kid growing up with these fiendish images leering down at you? Mercifully we didn't spend all that much time in here."

The pious young puritan she'd been, before Nigel set her free, she had become in this house under the baleful influence of these morbid paintings. Even her brother Frankie's irreverent childhood pantomimes mocking the figures in the paintings hadn't succeeded in disempowering them; in fact, after Frankie's death their true ghoulishness returned with a vengeance.

"So," she says, "what mischief's afoot to bring you two calling?"

Garth and Sarina exchange a quick glance and Garth takes the lead. "Rumours mostly at this point," he says.

"Oh goody," Ginger enthuses. "Dish."

"Two things really." Sarina jumps in the way she does. "First, municipal elections this fall as you know. It appears more and more that McKrindle will be stepping down as mayor."

"Yes," Ginger says, "there have been signs and omens that His Worship won't be seeking re-election."

"Good riddance at last," Garth says.

"Oh, Garth, where's the gratitude for all those years of public service?" Ginger's attempts at sarcasm frequently fall flat, as this one does. Not enough bitterness, insufficient bite.

"The only people that guy serviced were himself and his developer cronies," Garth says. "So good riddance and good luck to him." There's a bit of the street fighter in Garth, always has been, which is part of why Ginger likes him so much.

"More to the point," Sarina interjects perhaps a bit sharply, "have you heard who may be taking a run at becoming mayor?"

"Not a whisper," Ginger says, "but I'm so out of the loop nowadays I wouldn't have heard a shout either."

"Larry Illinger!" Garth snorts, slapping the padded armrest in disgust.

"Oh, good Lord," Ginger says. "Well, it's not all that surprising really, is it? We've half expected it for years now."

"If he hadn't had McKrindle for his proxy I'm sure he would have tried it long ago," Garth says. "McKrindle at least had the advantage of being a likeable personality, which is something friend Illinger has never been accused of."

"True enough," Ginger agrees. "I can remember him way back as a schoolboy; he was in the same high school class as my daughter Irene.

From what she says, he was a manipulative schemer even then. Bullied by the jocks, of course, and avoided by the girls, but he weaseled his way through and look where it got him."

Garth's heard all this before, several times, but Sarina hasn't, so Ginger can be forgiven her weakness for juicy bits of backstory.

"Item two," Garth says. "I got a call from an old colleague the other day. He didn't have anything firm, but he says he's hearing lots of chatter about a mega garbage incinerator. Serve the whole region, maybe even trucking in garbage from farther off."

"Don't say the words," Ginger says to him.

"Afraid so," Garth says, shaking his head. "At least according to my friend, Shetterly's on the short list."

"You have to wonder if these people are completely mad," Sarina says.

"Or just not very bright," Garth adds, "and stuck back in time by several decades at least. Anyway, if the rumours are accurate, and if the talk about Illinger wanting to be mayor is also accurate, we've got a nasty convergence on our hands."

"I would think so," Ginger agrees. "Unless my old ears are deceiving me, I can already hear Larry Illinger banging his Jobs and Progress drum." She knows there's a campaign in the making here and that her friends have come visiting to seek not so much her help but her endorsement, her blessing.

A decade ago she would still have been in the thick of things, but nowadays she's equivocal about her own role in the great ebb and flow of local issues. Her memory for names and facts and figures is not what it once was, and so she's a bit more hesitant than she used to be about getting up in front of a crowd to speechify. But in addition, there's a kind of sweet dreaminess has begun to settle more and more upon her days. She'll sometimes sit for several hours just musing and remembering and savouring. The line between her waking states and the dreams that come to her at night or during her afternoon nap seems to be eroding, leaving her unsure at times what is real and what is not. Did somebody actually say a particular thing the other day, or was it something she read in a book somewhere, or did it come to her in a dream? It matters less now than it might once have. Her busybody conscience still tries to urge her to action or her worrywart element may start fretting about the onset of dementia, but their voices are dimming, hushed by a gentle . . . what? Not contentedness, certainly, with daily evidence of an imperfect world torn with violence and suffering. Resignation perhaps, not quite defeatism but a sense that what will be will be. In a mad moment she'll laugh to herself that enlightenment is attempting to move in on her.

Now, before she can say anything else, a sudden feeling comes to Ginger. Something is going on, she realizes, not in the room here. No. Outside. Something is calling to her from outside.

"Would you excuse me for just a moment," she says to her visitors, rising from her chair.

"Anything we can do?" Garth asks, instantly concerned.

"No, no, thanks," she says, "there's just something I must check on."

She slips out of the drawing room and across the marbled foyer with the grandly pretentious oak stairway rising off to her right. She's drawn to the front door, though she couldn't say why. Peter's away in the city and won't be back for hours, but something is stirring, some perturbation going on. As she draws open the heavy front door she spots Shep sprawled on the verandah at the top of the steps. Shep turns his head to glance at her, while down on the pathway below stands little Chrissie with her bike. The expression of absolute dread on the girl's face instantly evaporates.

"Hello, Chrissie," Ginger says. "I hope Shep here hasn't been terrorizing you for too long."

"Uh, no, I just got here," Chrissie lies, trying her best to appear ultra cool.

"I do hope you were properly welcoming," Ginger says to Shep, stepping forward and bending to caress the dog's head. Shep's tail bangs the verandah boards with the sound of a rug being beaten.

"Peter's away today," Ginger tells Chrissie, "and poor Shep's never entirely himself without his handler. We don't like to say Master, do we Shep?" Shep wriggles in a way that indicates Handler is far preferable. "Because, of course," Ginger says, smiling at Chrissie, "the mastery is a mutual thing, a shared experience between the two of them."

"Uh-uh," Chrissie says. "I guess I forgot my notebook."

"Oh, of course!" Ginger says, "I left it just here on the hall table." She turns to fetch it but then stops herself and looks back at Chrissie. "Say, would you like Shep to fetch it for you? As a token, you know."

"I, uh . . ." Shit! Chrissie's thinking.

"Only if you'd like," Ginger says. "It might help cement your relationship."

I don't have a fucking relationship with that dog, Chrissie says to herself, but can't say.

"Or if you'd rather . . ." Ginger begins.

"No, that'd be fine," Chrissie says, with a small catch in her throat. She's gripping her handlebars tighter than when she's riding down a mountainside.

"You're sure?"

"Yea."

"Very good," Ginger says, smiling. "Now Shep, would you be kind enough to fetch the notebook, please."

Instantly the dog bolts through the open doorway and returns with Chrissie's notebook held in its jaws. Shep sits upright alongside Ginger.

Cripes, Chrissie's thinking, how did that effing dog know to get the notebook and not something else? She wonders if the old lady has been training the mutt for just this trick, setting her up like.

"Would you prefer Shep brings it to you or should I?"

"Um," Chrissie licks her lips and swallows. She knows what's expected and she hates it. "I guess, er, Shep. Please."

"You're sure?" Ginger's admiring the girl's courage, comprehending her terror.

"Yea."

"Very good. Now, Shep," Ginger says to the dog, while signalling with her hand, "take the notebook to Chrissie, please."

Shep treads gently down the steps, carrying the notebook, as though partaking in a formal ceremony. At the bottom, he stops for a moment, then sits upright, staring intently at Chrissie.

Normally Chrissie doesn't like looking into eyes, they're too spooky. She could hardly ever tell you what colour a person's eyes were. But especially a dog's eyes. Not after those Rottweilers slobbering all over her face, wanting to maul her. But today, for some stupid reason, she's been looking into this mutt's eyes and she could swear to God the dog is seeing exactly what's going on in her brain. Totally freaky.

Ginger is watching the scene casually, letting it be what it is, not making any fussy old lady type moves, even though she's itching to tell Chrissie to speak to Shep and have him pass her the book.

The three of them are momentarily posed in perfect tableaux: girl with bike, dog with book, old lady with a soaring heart.

Chrissie clears her throat and says, "Good boy, good dog," then ever so slowly forces her right hand to pry its grip off the handlebar and then to slowly extend itself, fingers trembling, towards the sitting dog. Shep does not release her from his gaze, but smoothly rises and approaches her, holding the notebook only inches from her quivering fingers.

Chrissie waits what seems like a very long time, looking deep into the dog's eyes, feeling an unfamiliar calm settle over her, noticing that her fear is ebbing away. She swallows hard. "May I have my notebook, please, er, Shep," she says, inching her hand closer to the jaw of fangs.

Shep daintily releases the notebook into her hand and steps backwards like someone who'd just laid a wreath.

Chrissie takes the notebook and clasps it to her chest. Then suddenly, from out of nowhere, a tremendous gust blows through her body, an overwhelming rush of emotions and memories and Christ knows what, in which she's lost; uncontrollably, she's crying like a baby, great bawling big tearstreams sliding down her cheeks.

Four

The plan was that Ginger and her dorm mate Dorothy would meet outside the Galaxy Theatre on Friday evening at seven o'clock so that they could get good seats for the seven-thirty showing of *The Third Man*. Simply everyone was crazy to see the film, so the place would be packed. But Ginger had been standing outside in the chill evening air for twenty-five minutes and still no sign of Dorothy. It seemed unlikely Dot would have forgotten, because they'd both been as keen as everyone else to see the film, and Ginger was now worrying that something dreadful may have happened. Not before, but since the war, since Frankie, she lived with an acute awareness that disaster might strike at any minute. She wondered if she should return to the dorm and investigate. She was quite sure she couldn't go into the theatre on her own and certainly not enjoy the film while worrying the whole time about Dorothy.

She'd just made up her mind to catch a bus back to the campus when she heard a familiar voice call her name and turned to see Professor Childes approaching along the crowded sidewalk.

"Good evening, Miss Flynn," he said, with the slightest bow of his head. "I come as the bearer of significant news."

"What is it?" Ginger asked, not able to read him, fearing the worst.

"Oh, nothing to be worried about," he said, smiling, "quite the reverse, in fact. Namely that Dorothy Phelp's parents showed up unexpectedly this afternoon and she was unable to get word to you that she couldn't join you this evening. I happened to be passing in the corridor when I overheard her telling a friend of her dilemma and so I stepped in, rude though it may have been to do so, to say that I had planned to see the film myself this evening, as indeed I had, and would happily convey her message to you. So here I am!"

He bowed before her with a mock heroic gesture, then straightened himself and looked at her as though he were a Boy Scout who'd done his good deed for the day and might now expect a reward of some sort.

"Well," Ginger said, "thank you, I was beginning to worry about Dorothy."

"Yes, you are a bit of a worrier, aren't you?" he said, smiling. "If you'll excuse my saying so."

She wanted to say that she'd never been a worrier before, that she'd been as free and happy as any girl could be for years until . . .

Perhaps spotting his blunder, Childes reached out and placed a hand gently on the sleeve of her coat. "I'm terribly sorry," he said, "how hopelessly insensitive of me."

"No, no," she said, even though it was true. He seemed to have a habit of being insensitive and then apologizing profusely.

"Tell you what," he said, as though the thought had just occurred to him, "I came to watch the film alone, but how would you feel if we were to watch it together?"

"Well . . ." She didn't know what to say. Crowds swirled around her and noisy traffic jolted past.

"I mean if you'd care to," he quickly interjected. "Or, of course, if you'd rather not, I understand completely. I'd be happy to escort you home straight away if you'd prefer."

Ginger couldn't think clearly, there on the jostling sidewalk, in the cool evening air, with this charming man, her brother's dear friend, inviting her into the theatre with him. She certainly couldn't expect him to miss the film on her account. And she'd already bought two tickets for herself and Dot. Still, it didn't seem quite right, really, to be in a darkened theatre with your professor. Yes, she'd met him at the tea shop, but that was in broad daylight and perfectly above board. Well, almost. But this was different, this felt a little bit like a date to her, even though it wasn't of course. But she must decide straight away, the film was about to start and the theatre would be packed.

"Do you think we can still get seats?" she asked him, stalling for time.

"Oh, I'm sure of it," he said confidently, "especially as I notice you have a pair of tickets in your hand. It sounds to me as though you'd really like to see the film."

"Well, yes I would, actually," she admitted, "I'm dying to see it. It's just . . ."

"Good, it's settled then, is it?" He held out his arm to her as a formal escort would and after only a moment's hesitation, despite her misgivings, despite the disapproving frown she could imagine on her mother's face, she put her hand on his arm and together they entered the theatre.

She passed the tickets to Childes who in turn showed them to an usherette. Ginger noticed that he also discreetly slipped the usherette a dollar bill that she swiftly pocketed and then led them by flashlight down the aisle to what Ginger imagined must have been the best seats in the house.

The house lights dimmed almost instantly, and before she had time to consider or worry any more about what she was doing, Ginger became entirely absorbed by the film. The eerie backdrop of bomb-shattered streets in post-war Vienna, the haunting sounds of zither music, the complicated tale of betrayals. All of it entranced her. Only when Anna Schmidt walked coolly down the deserted street and indifferently past poor Holly Martins, leaving him to smoke his cigarette alone, and the film came to an end, did Ginger return to herself, realizing how completely she'd been swept away by the story. Professor Childes seemed to have been similarly transported as he remained staring at the screen without saying anything.

"Well," he finally said, turning to her and smiling as the house lights came up, "that was a masterpiece, wasn't it?"

"Brilliant," she said, "I absolutely loved it."

"Did you? I'm so glad."

By then she could admit to herself how relieved she felt that he had behaved throughout like a perfect gentleman. Some of her initial resistance to seeing the film with him, apart from appearances, was her apprehension that he might be inappropriate in some way, try to take her hand or put his arm around her in the darkened theatre, as her high school dates sometimes did. She would have squirmed with embarrassment at anything like that, but he'd done nothing of the sort, in fact had seemed to be as engrossed in the film as she had, and she now felt foolish for having mistrusted him.

When they emerged from the theatre the night air seemed less chill than it had, and the sudden lights of the cars and shops excited an almost carnival atmosphere. She felt a kind of giddy elation. He asked if he should flag a cab to take her home or would she prefer to walk. Still under the mesmeric influence of the film, she felt as though she did not want the evening to conclude so abruptly. "Well, I'd love to walk," she said, "but it's rather out of the way for you, isn't it?" Having made enquiries, for reasons she had not fully examined, she knew he lived somewhere in town, not on campus.

"Not at all," he said jauntily. "I'd be delighted to walk you home and then it's only a quick hop and a jump back to my place."

"Well, if you're sure," she said, conscious that she was inconveniencing him but not wishing to lose his company just yet. Their conversation at the tea shop, with his dramatic tale of meeting her brother by chance on a wartime London sidewalk, had unfortunately been cut short by the arrival of two other faculty members and, after a few awkward pleasantries, she and Childes had left the café with the story incomplete.

"I've never been more sure of anything," he said gallantly, swooping his arm out in the direction of the campus, and so they set off. Of similar height, they walked with long strides that matched each other's perfectly.

"Now tell me how you felt about the film," he said.

"Oh, my goodness," she replied, laughing, "where to begin?" She realized she wanted rather badly to impress him with her analysis. "Well, I thought Joseph Cotten was very good in his part, didn't you?"

"Yes, I did. Quite a subtle portrayal, really, of a naïf discovering how bitterly disappointing life can eventually prove to be."

"Yes." She could think of nothing to add.

"I understand the director wanted Jimmy Stewart for the role," Childes continued in a way that made her feel that he was speaking to a colleague.

"Really? Oh, I don't know if he would have fit so well."

"Nor do I. Anyway, the producer wanted Cotten and Cotten's who they got. What about Orson Welles?"

"Oh, he was terrific, wasn't he?" In her excitement she put her hand impulsively upon his forearm. "So corrupt on the one hand and yet so, so . . ."

"Luminous?"

"Yes! Luminous and charismatic. You hated him and yet in another way you didn't."

"Exactly. It's a wonder he didn't overrun the film completely, he's so powerful. You saw him in *Citizen Kane* didn't you?"

"Yes, but I think I was too young to appreciate it fully. I'd love to watch it again, after seeing him in this."

"Yes, it's a film that bears multiple viewings. As is this one, I think."

They walked on in silence for a bit, now passing through a residential neighbourhood of modest homes from which flowed the warm glow and muted sounds of families settling for the evening. After the treacherous streets of shattered Vienna, and really, for one of the few times since her brother's death, the world seemed to Ginger a benign and beautiful place.

"Did you like the Anna Schmidt character?" she asked him, not wanting to leave off talking about the marvellous film.

"I did, yes, though I don't know the actress at all. Italian apparently.

But again, I thought she brought a lot to the role, that rather fascinating blend of hardness and vulnerability."

"She was difficult to like, though, didn't you find?" Ginger asked.

"Well, I wouldn't say that exactly, no. Intriguing, I would say, and intriguing characters often have some darkness about them."

"Like Harry Lime too," she said.

"Yes indeed, like Harry Lime." He seemed to genuinely appreciate the insights she was offering.

They continued chattering away about the film as they walked the long boulevard leading to the campus, passing through multiple pools of light from the overhead lamps and stretches of darkness between them, so that they were repeatedly revealed and hidden to themselves. Then, unexpectedly, they'd reached Ginger's dorms. She was sorry to arrive so soon; she would have liked to walk and talk for another hour at least. She felt it was the most intelligent and stimulating conversation she'd had for ages.

"Well, here we are then," he said, stopping under one of the large elm trees whose sinuous limbs disappeared into the darkness above. "You know, Miss Flynn, forgive me for saying so, but in hindsight I must confess I'm gratified that the parental Phelps made their unannounced appearance and precipitated your fall into my villainous clutches." He smiled at her like a soft-hearted rogue. "But seriously, thank you for a lovely evening."

Now that they'd stopped walking, Ginger's legs were trembling and she had to clear her throat before saying, "Thank you too, Professor. I enjoyed it immensely."

"So!" he exclaimed, bowing slightly, "I shall bid you good night and like poor Holly Martins begin the long and dismal trek home alone."

She grinned at him, turned and walked swiftly to her dormitory entrance, resisting the temptation to glance back.

Still somewhat giddy from the evening's pleasures, Ginger was surprised to find all three of her room mates already home when she slipped quietly into the dorm. Not so much Dorothy who, like herself, was apt to be back in residence long before curfew; but Patsy and Diane were party girls and rarely home early on a Friday evening. Ginger knew instantly something was up just from the looks she was getting.

"Hi," she said breezily, taking off her coat and scarf and hanging them nonchalantly in her wardrobe. "Did you have a nice dinner with your parents, Dorothy?" she asked.

"Oh, yes, thank you," Dorothy replied rather formally. "I'm sorry I couldn't make it to the film. I hope Professor Childes caught up with you in time." Tiny and sweet, with short dark hair and abnormally pale skin, Dorothy didn't have a malicious bone in her body, which was more than could be said of Patsy or Diane. Behind her, the two of them were engaged in what looked like a childish pantomime of suppressed hilarity.

Ginger could feel herself starting to blush. "Yes, he did," she replied, "and I was so relieved because I was really starting to worry about you, standing there on the sidewalk for so long. You're always so punctual, I couldn't imagine what might have happened to you."

"Oh, I'm sorry if . . ." Dorothy started to say, but Patsy cut her off.

"So what did he say?" Patsy asked leaning around Dorothy.

"He was kind enough to let me know that Dorothy couldn't come to the theatre because of her parents arriving unexpectedly."

"And?" Patsy was trying to look knowingly suggestive. Her straight blonde hair was tied back in a ponytail, intensifying the fleshiness of her face so that it appeared to leer unpleasantly. "We heard he was going to watch the film as well."

"Yes, he told me so," Dorothy put in to clarify. "That's why he offered . . ."

"And did he?" Patsy pressed on, tilting her head inquisitively. Patsy could be a ton of fun when she was up and a nasty piece of business when she wasn't.

Ginger recognized that something more than gentle teasing was at play here. Dorothy, who was incapable of guile, looked uncomfortably as though she might now be participating in it, while the other two circled like jackals. "Yes, we watched the film together," Ginger said matter-of-factly, "as I'd already bought tickets for Dot and myself."

"Ah!!!" Patsy and Diane chimed simultaneously while exchanging knowing glances.

"And how was it?" Diane asked.

"Oh, the film was excellent," Ginger said, knowing that wasn't the question. She took off her shoes and slid her feet into her cozy lamb's wool slippers. "You really must go see it. It's . . ."

"And afterwards?" Patsy asked.

"Then I came home, of course."

"Ah!!!" Again the silly chorus between Patsy and Diane.

"We wouldn't have known who you came home with either, would we?" Diane said coyly.

"Except!" Patsy interjected.

"Except," Diane repeated then paused for effect, "except a certain little spy named Dot . . ."

"Oh, no!" Dot exclaimed, "I didn't . . ."

"Oh, yes," Patsy insisted, turning to point an accusatory index finger at Dorothy, "a little spy named Dot happened to be looking out the dorm window just now."

"Dreaming of men, I think, can you believe it?" Diane pretended to be scandalized.

Now it was Dot's turn to blush. Her porcelain pale skin had a remarkable capacity to blush like a ripening tomato.

Realizing that she'd been spotted walking home with Childes, even though they'd parted prudently on the far side of the great lawn, Ginger allowed herself to preen just the tiniest bit. "Yes, Professor Childes did walk me home," she admitted primly, "as any gentleman would."

"Ladies and gentlemen!" Diane intoned in a mock master of ceremonies voice.

"What did you call him?" Patsy asked. The poor girl was rather giving herself away, exposing her shabby envy with her aggressive questioning. "Did you call him Nigel?"

"Of course not!" Ginger laughed dismissively. "I called him Professor Childes, just as you would have done in similar circumstances, I'm sure."

Stuck for a smart response, Patsy held her sneer but said nothing.

"And what did he call you?" Diane asked, trying to help Patsy out.

Ginger paused for a moment while the three of them gazed at her expectedly. She wondered if each of them concocted private fairy tales in which Nigel Childes addressed them with endearments. Or were they just intent upon whatever minor scandal might be wiggled out of the evening's events? "He didn't call me anything, come to think of it," she said, which was nearly true. "Now, if you'll excuse me, girls, I'm going to get a good night's sleep." And with that, Ginger went off for her toiletries and when she returned in her nightie, climbed into bed, switched off her bedside light and said, "Sweet dreams," to her dorm mates, whose tepid replies gave clear indication that they were less than satisfied by how little had been made of the tasty morsel of Ginger and Nigel Childes being out on the town alone.

Lying in her bed, feigning sleep, Ginger was feeling none of the sang-froid she'd attempted to convey to her inquisitors. The evening she'd just spent in Nigel's company — she was aware that she now thought of him by his first name, as poor Patsy had intuited — had been absolutely marvellous. It was the intellectual stimulation that thrilled her most, or so she told herself. The talking as adult to adult, the sense of maturity and sophistication she'd experienced. This was new to her and entirely ravishing. Throughout the evening she had not thought of Nigel in erotic terms, but now, in hindsight, she felt a kind of terrible thrill at the thought of him sitting beside her in the darkened theatre. She'd been glad at the time that he hadn't done anything silly like taking her hand in his, but now she half desired it. Desired even more than that, if she'd allowed herself to think it. And, yes, there had been something undeniably romantic about that dazzling walk home through the reappearing obelisks of vaporous light and intervening darkness. It was only then, reliving the experience in memory perhaps even more fully than she had in the moment, that she realized with a start that they had not mentioned Frankie's name once all evening.

Arguably reckless as it may have been, given the narrow-mindedness of Carlyle College, his unexpected evening out with Ginger Flynn had pleased Nigel immensely. He'd taken genuine delight in the girl's company, finding her quick and charming and altogether a most agreeable companion. Yes, he admitted to himself afterwards, he would not at all mind seeing more of her. Ah, but this was playing with fire, was it not? The risks inherent in causing a petty scandal and provoking the high priests of Carlyle were unsettling enough — in his brief academic experience he'd already seen several cases of promising careers decapitated over what seemed to him in essence trivial misdemeanours — but beyond that, on a deeper level he recognized a more formidable peril.

The blunt truth of the matter was that being with Ginger Flynn had excited in Nigel a quality of arousal that he had not really experienced since those heady few months he'd shared with her brother Frank. In one instance during that charming walk back from the theatre he'd caught himself about to call her by her brother's name, which would have been a truly grotesque lapse. No question about it, she was bringing Frank back to him whether he wanted it or not, somehow embodying the spirit of that alluring boy in a way that memory had gradually ceased doing over the past half-dozen years. It was a most peculiar sensation, as though of something precious that had been lost, now found again in different form. Precious indeed. Dangerous absolutely.

Frank Flynn.

They'd met for a second time, as arranged, the day after that chance encounter on the Tottenham Court Road.

"No top hat today?" Frank had asked jauntily as they shook hands at the entrance to an old pub in the City.

"Thought I'd not make a public spectacle of myself two days running," Nigel replied laughing.

And that was the start of it. Their mutual attraction sparked from the very beginning, untainted by any trace of apprehension or reticence or suspicion. It wasn't the least bit logical — they came from different worlds really, with differing codes, manners and expectations — and yet they were drawn together as though two severed halves of a whole. Nigel had never experienced anything quite like it before. His instinctive caution let down its guard almost immediately, as if some greater power held sway between himself and his new friend. Like a true apostle of Wordsworth, he imagined them simply flowing into one another as though two streams conjoining.

He and Frank had lingered in the pub, then in a nearby café, that first afternoon far longer than either had intended, talking and laughing as though they'd known each other for years. He delighted in Frank's marvellous facility for telling tales about local characters back home, or sometimes of his army chums, tales laced with irony and an innocently wicked wit. Invariably the story would conclude with Frank bursting into laughter at the complete absurdity of it all. A diarist of the ridiculous. There was an innocence and fresh vitality about the Canadian, a sense of unaffected candour that Nigel seldom encountered among his privileged peers.

And Frank was beautiful. Not pretty or effeminate, but beautiful in the way of Donatello's *David*. And unconsciously beautiful, that was the great thing of it. No posturing or affectation. No preening, just artless beauty. Being with Frank reminded him of lazy summer afternoons spent immersed in Keats or Shelley, sojourning in dreams and glimpses of other worlds. By the time they left the pub that evening, with plans in place to meet again in two days' time, Nigel had already felt the stirrings of what he would eventually come to recognize as love.

Their opportunities to meet were infrequent. Frank's unit was stationed in Wiltshire where they were in training for what was rumoured to be an imminent invasion of the continent. A few precious days' leave every so often afforded them the only opportunities they had to be together. After each meeting, however brief, Nigel felt himself longing to be with his friend again. The chatter of his Cambridge chums seemed increasingly glib and superficial to him, and the waiting until he would next see Frank became less and less tolerable. He recognized his state of mind as an obsession of sorts, embarrassingly adolescent in the cold light of day, but an obsession he had no interest in attempting to dislodge.

Their jaunt together down to Dartmoor proved decisive. For two days they tramped the rough moorlands without a care in the world, sharing an exhilarating sense of freedom, imagining themselves as wild in spirit as the Dartmoor ponies they occasionally encountered. They slept out under the stars on those mild May evenings talking for hours about far-flung galaxies and favourite books and all the big ideas young men discuss when inflamed by affection.

Then a drenching rainstorm and their pelting dash for shelter.

Eventually, late in the evening, they came across a stony farmhouse in a little dell near Widecombe in the Moor. "We've only the one extra bed," the ancient farmer's wife told them apologetically, "I hope you lads are good that way. Now take off them wet clothes and I'll hang them by the fire overnight. They'll be outside the door here in the morning." Then leaving them, alone together in the bedroom, naked and shivering and giddy.

The sudden intimacy of the tiny farmhouse bedroom. How at first they lay stiffly side by side in the bed, feigning sleep, listening to a swollen brook gurgling beneath their bedroom window. Nigel agonized for what seemed like hours, chafing with desire to reach across and caress his friend's nakedness. There'd been nothing of the sort lying together out on the moor, but the storm had stripped them down somehow, rendered them naked and vulnerable in a way they had not been. It was Nigel who'd broken the spell, slowly reaching his hand across until it touched Frank's shoulder. Rippled with muscle but soft and cool and smooth. He ran his trembling fingertips slowly down the arm thrilling to its fluid beauty. Unsure if Frank was asleep or awake, he paused when his fingers detected the pulse throbbing at Frank's wrist. He lingered there, feeling the strong beat of his friend's blood, feeling his heartbeat, so it seemed. Then slowly, without a word, Frank rolled towards him and placed a hand gently against Nigel's face. They eased themselves together then, delighting in shared warmth neither had felt alone. Awkward and shy under the force of affection, finally they kissed, tenderly, and drifted into sleep in each other's arms.

They'd awoken the next morning in a tangle, roused by the sound of someone outside the bedroom door. They'd instantly separated, in part from shy guilt and in part from fear that the old farm wife might enter the room and catch them in *flagrante delicto*.

Nigel had never been with another boy like that before, nor with a girl. Yes, he'd been anxious about what the old wife would have made of her soiled sheets had he and Frank gone further than they did. But that was the least of his anxieties. What they had done in all innocence seemed to him both beautiful and shameful, and he knew it was the finest of lines that separated the physical closeness they'd shared from whatever else he imagined men do together in such circumstances.

Now, seven years later, all of that tentative first touching, as well as what was to follow, was again becoming vivid in his mind. More than vivid, because back then a floodgate had opened and in their few remaining times together the two young men gave themselves over to what soon became fierce and brilliant passion. Nigel had had sufficient funds that they could sequester themselves in discreet hotels where they'd spend whole days and nights twined together ardently devouring one another, feeding a keen fervency new to both of them.

Three months in all, a half dozen or so at most of these impassioned trysts, and then Frank came to tell him that his company was packing up in preparation for departure to the south coast.

"I shouldn't be long," he told Nigel breezily, trying to put a lighthearted spin on what each knew to be a far more ominous proposition than either would acknowledge.

"I'd give anything to be coming along with you," Nigel said, speaking truthfully too, because, as much as he'd initially given thanks for the heart murmur that had kept him out of uniform, he now wished more than anything to be sharing in the peril Frank would soon be facing.

A few brief letters between them over the ensuing months, the last of them ending with that yearning line, *I miss you dreadfully and long for the day when I shall see your smiling face again.* Then silence, as when artillery falls quiet after a bombardment. Nigel knew that Frank was dead long before the official confirmation. Not any precise moment of dying, just a general heavy gloom that settled over him within which there lingered the unshakable conviction that he would never see his friend again. He had not spoken with anyone about his friendship with Frank Flynn and he was reasonably confident that Frank had not disclosed the secret either. No comrade in arms had ever looked Childes up after the war in order to talk about Frank. There was a very real sense in which their relationship had existed nowhere other than between the two of them and that it, like Frank, had died a tragic death in the killing fields of France, a sense in which it ceased to exist, even in memory, as suddenly and unexpectedly as it had begun, there in the Tottenham Court Road.

⊁⊀

In the weeks subsequent to the evening of *The Third Man*, Nigel and Ginger had no further direct contact. She continued to attend his lectures — now dealing with the great transformations in the structures of power in Britain brought about by the emergence of the new merchant and industrialist class. His brilliance was undeniable, provoking radical insights and astonishing connectivity with contemporary issues. This was history that had real meat on its bones. Observing him in action, Ginger mused that neither he nor she could know what, if anything, the other might be feeling about what had occurred between them on their way home from the theatre. She certainly couldn't pretend that nothing had occurred and she wondered if it was the same for him. Or whether, having discharged his duty concerning Frank's letter, he had relegated her to one additional knot in a long string of adoring female undergraduates, no more memorable than Patsy or Diane. She itched to know if this was the case, wanting it not to be so, just as she longed to discover more about the relationship between the professor and her brother.

During this time, when Ginger received the latest letter from her boyfriend Jonathan back in Shetterly, she surprised herself by how indifferent she was to its panting tone. How he thought of her every day and couldn't wait to see her again. What were her plans for the Christmas break? Would she enjoy a few days cross-country skiing up at his parents' cottage? Shamefully, she was quick to judgment about the clumsiness of his handwriting and the several smudges from his fountain pen. The black-and-white snapshot of himself he'd enclosed showed a boyishly handsome young man, crew-cut and smiling eagerly, one penny-loafer foot perched on the running board of a shining new sedan at his dad's car dealership. A sweet boy, perfectly devoted to her, as she had been to him until . . . well. Re-reading the awkward letter and looking again at the photo, she knew instinctively that she no longer wanted to be spending time with him or to be thought of as "his" girl. It came to her as a sudden and shocking revelation that — notwithstanding their embraces and promises and tearful farewells when she'd left to begin her college year — she did not in fact love the poor boy at all.

And why was that? she asked herself, sliding the photograph and letter back into their envelope. What had changed? Not Jonathan surely, revealed as he was in the photograph, handsomely unimaginative and utterly devoted. Rather her perception of him, and more than that, her expectations. She tried, although not as mightily as required, to forbid the image of Nigel Childes from presenting itself by way of unfair comparison. She was not unkind by nature, nor disloyal, but neither was she able to deny that the professor's smooth sophistication threw a pitiless light on Jonathan's homespun limitations and by reflection on her own naivete as well. Although not proud of herself for doing so, and despite the fact that Jonathan had been instrumental in lifting her from the gloom that beset her after Frankie's death, she now recognized quite clearly that she must cut herself loose from her high school sweetheart if she were to have any hope of entering that other world she'd glimpsed while walking in the night with Nigel Childes.

Several days later, browsing in a bookshop in town, she glanced up from the opening page of *1984* to see Professor Childes, also with book in hand, smiling at her from down the aisle.

"Ah, Orwell," he said approaching her genially, "are you thinking to buy it?"

"I'm not sure," she replied, "I hear it's rather bleak. Have you read it?" She was sounding far more composed than she felt.

"Not yet," he told her, "although I do intend to. I have a certain weakness for cautionary tales."

Was he implying something? No matter. The briefest glimpse of his amused smile was all it took for her to recognize how thoroughly everything had changed since their last encounter. He was no longer just her professor, nor merely her late brother's friend. He was a man who excited arousal in her. She could feel it now, standing in the shop with a book in her hand, a sensuous warmth suffusing her body, her brain doing a foggy swirling thing, her throat constricting so that words were trapped. She glanced back down at the book to avoid revealing herself, prevent his seeing how entirely she was exposed.

Perhaps recognizing her discomfort, he showed her the book he'd selected, *The Hero with a Thousand Faces* by Joseph Campbell.

"I don't know the book or the author," she managed to say.

"Just published this year," he told her, "but people are extremely excited about it. He's an American working in comparative mythology. Very up-and-coming. Listen to this." He opened the volume, searching through the first few pages. "Here we are: *A hero ventures forth from the world of common day into a region of supernatural wonder: fabulous forces are there encountered and a decisive victory is won: the hero comes back from this mysterious adventure with the power to bestow boons on his fellow man*. According to Campbell, all the great stories, the myths, follow this pattern or a portion of it. Calls it the monomyth."

"It sounds fascinating," she said as an over-large gentleman smelling powerfully of pipe tobacco edged clumsily between the two of them. She wished they weren't in this crowded shop. More than anything she wanted to have another long and ravishing conversation with Nigel Childes. About monomyths, if necessary, but preferably about his friendship with her brother. Every bit as much as she wanted simply to be in Nigel's company, she still itched to know what it was had bound him and Frankie together with sufficient intimacy that Childes was the last person with whom her brother would communicate before his death.

"So," Childes said, "apparently Mr. Campbell's hero begins his quest by heeding a call to adventure, a journey into unfamiliar regions where he will encounter extraordinary and mysterious occurrences. But I wonder if, in contrast, I might suggest a cup of coffee instead?"

"Oh, yes, I'd enjoy that," she said before her scruples could get themselves assembled.

"Excellent," he said, "now let me buy old Orwell for you while I'm paying for the Campbell."

"Oh, no, I couldn't . . ."

"Of course you couldn't," he said, raising a mock-imperious hand, "but I could, you see, and what's more I will, as professor to student no less."

"Well," she said, reluctant and thrilled both. Surely this was a singling-out, something special, a gesture not extended to every Patsy or Diane encountered by chance in a shop.

"There, it's done," he said. "I love watching qualms and misgivings put to rout, don't you?" Before she could answer, he carried on: "Speaking of which, we have two choices. There's a decent little café just around the corner here."

"Yes, I know the place," she said.

"Yes, you and the entirety of our fine student body, I should think. Or, for a touch more privacy, we might repair to my little *pied-à-terre* which by chance is only a few blocks away."

"Oh, I'm not sure about . . ."

"Of course you're not sure!" he exclaimed. "I'd be scandalized if you were. Imagine an attractive young co-ed like yourself wanting to accompany her musty old professor back to his dim lodgings. Shocking!"

"No, I didn't mean about your being old," she said, feebly. In truth, the thought of being alone with him in his apartments gave her a forbidden thrill. Again she conjured their walk together back from the movie theatre. She wanted more than anything to experience again what she'd felt that lovely evening.

"Ah, well, I'm mollified ever so slightly," he said. He was being cheeky with her, but not in a condescending way at all. She didn't mind in the least.

"But do you think it's proper?" she asked him.

"Of *course* it's not proper," he said airily, "what would be the fun in it if it was proper? No, I'm a great believer in pursuing impropriety whenever the opportunity presents itself. What say you, Miss Flynn?"

She knew she shouldn't. She knew even more that *he* shouldn't. And yet she realized she would. She'd step into his world and have a closer look.

Five

When Chrissie gets back to her house there's no tracks of Chazz, no note or anything, but so what? He's probably out jamming with some friends. They're always forming a new band, him and his cuddies. New drummer one week, red hot sax player just blown into town the next. Somebody ODs, somebody gets busted, somebody else splits in a hurry. The band's about as stable as uranium. They spend half their time thinking up rad names for the band whenever new players join. Frenzied Finger Lickers. Strung Out Slobs. One thing doesn't change: Chazz is the main man because he writes the tunes. Plus, he's a serious musician, really professional, the rest of them are just goofers who can't be bothered workin' hard at it. Chazz is the one who pays his dues. That's why she's crazy about him, even though the whole house is a shitbox of full ashtrays and dirty plates and tangled blankets all over the place. She picks a couple of empty beer cans off the floor and puts them on the cluttered kitchen counter.

Chrissie needs to talk to Chazz about the shit Illinger's dropped, about the porn flick, but she's just as happy he's not here because her head's still doing a funny thing about what happened with that dog. It's not the kind of stuff Chazz is interested in. For example, she's tried to talk to him before about Chuck and his Rottweilers, but all Chazz could do was get excited about maybe calling the band Chuck and the Fucks.

She flops onto the sagging couch and stares at a poster of Kurt Cobain pushpinned at a tilted angle onto the opposite wall.

What *was* it with that dog? She feels like she's had a religious experience or something. That moment when the dog handed her the book — well dogs don't have hands, right, but you can't say mouthed her the book — that was like a very intense moment. Outside of yourself. Acid space material. Next thing you know she's fountaining uncontrollably. What? Too bizarre. I mean, who was she crying for? Was she seeing herself as a little kid, trapped with a screwy mum and her sociopathic boyfriend of the moment? Jeezis, that was a torture chamber, those years. Undiluted living hell. And her terrified of dogs ever since. Until today, when she has this goddamn sacred moment with that what-do-they-call-it-Shep.

It was like someone pulled a trigger and suddenly all this shit came boiling up inside her, like how you see volcanoes erupting on TV and — what is it — lava comes spewing out so hot and angry. So intense like nothing can contain it. That's how she felt. And you couldn't put words to it. You couldn't say, oh, I'm feeling so *this* or so *that* and it's because of this thing that happened or it's because of that. No. It was something way outside of words. Outside of ideas even. Just ultra hot lava boiling up inside of her and pouring out in scalding tears and sobs. *Sklugh sklugh sklugh*. It's not like she cries a lot. Hardly ever. Sometimes in a really schmaltzy movie when somebody is dying of cancer or something like that. But not in real life. From early days she grew a maximum thick skin because she knew the world was crawling with stupid and dangerous cockmockers.

Maybe it was because of her colour. Her dad was black, her mother told her, not that Chrissie'd ever seen him. There weren't any photos of him around, there wasn't anything of him around, except her. Something had happened to him, but her mother would never say what. Maybe she didn't know either. Maybe he was only around long enough for a quick fuck. And her mother was part Hungarian or something and part Chinese, so Chrissie was this crazy mixture. And maybe people, specifically lecherous Alfredos, thought that made her fair game in some way, even as a kid. She knew all about predators way before she knew the word. There was that science teacher in grade nine, he was another one, always with the hands, like she was some kind of dollar-store toy he could fondle whenever he wanted. She learned to turn it to her advantage, like getting way better marks in science than she ever deserved, but she never cried about any of it. Or hardly ever.

So how long did she bawl like that today? Could have been an hour or more, but probably not. God, she must have looked like a total loser blubbering and dripping away. Especially when Ginger's visitors, an old guy and Asian babe, came out to see what was happening, then excused themselves and left. Then Ginger taking her inside, sitting her in that big, comfy chair, bringing her a huge cup of chai, God it tasted good. And not asking her anything, not poking or prying or anything. And not trying to tell her everything's going to be all right, dearie, there, there. No, just smiling at her and touching her every once in a while, such gentle touches with those soft, old hands. Touching her face where the tears kept running down, and her arms and her neck. Smoothing gentle hands over her head. Like velvet. Or satin maybe. She couldn't remember ever feeling touched that way before, so tender and loving, not maybe since she was tiny and her mother wasn't full on crazy yet. A kind of tenderness that she feels inside herself but hardly ever, never, encounters from anyone else.

She's still feeling powerful energies pulsing through her body from the whole weird experience. She can't even remember the bike ride home, it was like she flew back or something. And that dog's eyes seemed to watch her all the way. Even now she can kinda feel that dog still watching her and, what's really weird, knowing everything about her. She doesn't believe in souls really, but if she did she would say that dog, that Shep, had looked into her soul. Yah.

All of what's going down right now seems totally radical. That dog. Illinger. Chazz. Old Ginger. You get the feeling stuff is shifting, like those tectonic plates or something. Pressures building. Something gonna give sooner or later. Still in a sort of daze she sets about running dishwater into the sink and cleaning up the shitbox.

⇢⇠

Ginger decides on a whim that she'll give her daughter a call. Irene — Ginger still resists calling her by that name, rather than Sophia as she was christened as a child — lives hundreds of miles away and the phone is their main lifeline. For the longest time they scarcely talked at all, barely more than required social niceties, but in recent years things have gotten easier between them. They even tried skyping a couple of times a while back, but by mutual consent soon retreated to the phone.

When Irene's rather brusque answering machine tells her to leave a message, Ginger says "It's me, dear," and waits a moment until her daughter picks up.

"Hello, Mum," Irene says. "What a nice surprise."

"Hello, dear," Ginger says. "Have I caught you in the middle of things, or do you have a minute?"

"Of course. Nothing wrong, I hope?"

Irene has a certain instinct for things going wrong, even when they aren't. "Well, two things actually," Ginger says, "but, first, how are you?"

"Oh, fine," Irene says, as she always does. "We're working like crazy on that new townhouse project, and Phil's running around in circles, the way he gets when he's overstressed, but it'll all work out."

"I'm sure it will. How's Crystal? And little Isha?"

"Don't get me started," Irene says with a cynical laugh. Irene's daughter Crystal and granddaughter Isha are a source of enduring concern. Crystal has been chronically depressed for several years, ever since her husband left her for another woman. Irene, who likes things in their proper places, can't find a place in which to put her daughter's distress, so she retreats to the comforts of vexation. A precocious child,

Isha is not doing well either, embittered by her parents' break-up and her mother's crumpling. Ginger sees very little of them, however much she wishes that she could help in some way.

"So what two things, Mum?" Irene asks instead.

"Hmm? Oh, yes. Well, I wondered have you been following the news about our favourite Congregation of the Great Convergence?"

"The Congregation of the Great Conmen, you mean?" Irene says. "Not really. Phil mentioned something about them the other day, some sex scandal down in the States."

"Yes, most interesting developments," Ginger says. "Well, horrible as much as interesting. Dozens of the higher-ups in the church apparently accused of child abuse."

"You're kidding!" Irene exclaims. "That bunch of holy rollers?"

"Not so holy after all," Ginger says. "Molesting kids, trafficking, child pornography, just dreadful things."

"Well, I guess it shouldn't come as any surprise. After what they did to your parents. Stinking hypocrites. And them getting Stone House on top of it. I try never to think about it because it just makes me want to scream."

"Peter's been following the story," Ginger says, before Irene gets too wound up. "Whether or not Stone House will be affected."

"Wouldn't that be great, though, if that pack of thieves were to be locked up for life and we could get the house back from them."

"Well, it's early days yet, dear, but interesting developments for sure."

"I'd say. So Peter's on it, is he?" Irene asks in a tone that manages to question whether Peter's quite the right man for the job. A tone that hints perhaps Irene herself might be better suited for whatever hard-nosed work will be required to reclaim their family home from the disgraced church.

"Yes," her mother says, "he's taken a very active interest. Quite the knight errant in his own funny way."

Irene's "Hmm," is equivocal. She chooses to drop the topic. For now. "And is number two just as juicy?"

"In its own way, yes, I think so."

"Well?"

"It concerns a certain Larry Illinger." Ginger lets the name drop with what she imagines is a hint of sly enticement.

"Oh, God!" Irene exclaims. "What's that little slime bag up to now?"

"Would you believe running for mayor?"

"Oh, yes. Yes, I'd believe that easily. Lying Larry we called him at school. Always up to some mischief, but you were never sure just what. I remember the time the yearbook committee wanted to describe him as Most Likely to Succeed and Then Be Murdered. But of course they weren't allowed to. Everyone disliked him, but he seemed impervious to it, almost as though he enjoyed it. He actually had the nerve to run for president of student council in our senior year, so it doesn't surprise me at all he'd run for mayor."

"If I remember correctly," Ginger says, "you had a hand in his defeat, did you not?"

"Both hands, Mum, and both feet too. God, he was a despicable little manipulator. Even though everyone loathed him, in a weird way people were frightened of him too. Even the jocks who mocked him knew not to push too hard. It was always like he had some inside information he could use against you if you crossed him."

"Which *you* did."

"Oh, yeah, big time. Funny, isn't it? How it all seemed so important back in the day. High school confidential."

"Maybe we'll have to bring you in on this current campaign," Ginger says jokingly.

"I don't think so, Mum. All of that was so long ago I can hardly remember it."

Like something else that happened long ago, Ginger's thinking, that you can't forget. It's an abiding sorrow for Ginger that the collapse of her marriage scarred her daughter so lastingly. What lies between them as a consequence feels like a puzzle still waiting to be solved. A puzzle made all the more vexing with the same story now playing out between Crystal and Isha.

The two of them chat, mother and daughter, at a distance for a little while longer.

⊁⊀

The reason Peter checks the time so precisely before leaving the city for home is because he and his mum are conducting a little experiment about Shep's possibly psychic powers. Okay. Ginger had noticed it first, how whenever Peter was away somewhere Shep would suddenly break from whatever he'd been doing, whether sleeping or playing or fastidiously licking his genitals, and move to a particular spot on the driveway to await Peter's return to Stone House. At first they thought it was just that Shep could recognize the sound of Peter's truck from a long way off. But, no, on several occasions Peter returned from the airport in a taxi and Shep was there to greet him just the same. At other times Shep would take up his position when Peter was nowhere close to home, so they began thinking that maybe it was just a random response on the dog's part, something that coincided with his master's return on certain occasions and not on others.

But the more times Ginger saw how purposively Shep prepared for Peter's return, the more convinced she became that the dog was responding not to the sound of an approaching vehicle but to something less tangible, extra-sensory. "You know," she said to Peter one afternoon, "I'm beginning to suspect that Shep's aware of when you're on your way home, no matter how far away you are."

"Mother, you're not going Rainbow Gathering on us, are you?" Peter teased her.

"Not in the least," she parried, "we both know I've always been by far the most sensible person in this house."

"More sensible than Irene?" Peter asked, arching an eyebrow of disbelief.

"Well," Ginger said, conceding somewhat, "perhaps not in a practical sense, but in a metaphysical sense most certainly."

"Sensible in a metaphysical sense?"

"Yes."

"Mother."

"And Irene's no longer here, so let's keep her out of it."

"Agreed."

So the two of them set it up that Ginger would try to record the precise moment at which Shep took up his position by the driveway and Peter would make a note of when he started his journey home. Their data-base was ridiculously small because Peter didn't go all that many places without Shep, and sometimes when he did, Ginger wasn't able to observe precisely when Shep made his move, but every once in a while conditions were right. And Ginger's wacko theory was proven true. On seven separate occasions now, they have found an indisputable correlation between Peter's starting for home and Shep's positioning on the driveway.

Today they're adding a new wrinkle: Peter has noted the precise moment when he *decided* to start for home, as opposed to actually starting the journey. If Ginger's around to witness it and Shep makes his move at exactly the moment of Peter's decision, they'll have incontrovertible evidence of inter-species telepathy. Peter also realizes that a part of it is having a little adventure to share with his mum, something other than the lingering sorrow that he does his best to hide from her. Impossible, of course, because Ginger somehow relates to his sorrow even though she's about the least sorrowful person he knows. She's had her share of tragedy, God knows — death of a brother early on, her parents essentially disowning her, her husband abandoning her, her baby grandchild killed — but none of it has permanently broken her spirit. It's totally amazing to him how she just carries on, strong and helpful as always, and — most amazing of all — with this joyful zest for life that she has. It's humbling really, almost humiliating, to consider oneself in comparison.

Although it lingers around him like a toxic mist, the death of his wife and child is simply not something Peter wishes to discuss with his mother or sister or anyone else. Not just from the pain of it; no, there's also a shameful component to that tragedy that he cannot bring himself to disclose to anyone. He envies the ritual of confession and absolution. Only when he's in the woods or fields, working sheep with Shep, is he able to entirely escape the bleakness that beset him after the accident. Three years on, the pain has subsided but not been replaced by any real pleasure in life or any enlivening sense of what he should be devoting himself to. He's still devoted to the memory. And the guilt.

Streaking down the highway home, he smiles to himself ironically over the bizarre full circle he's run. After selling his dotcom business, he briefly enjoyed a breeziness of spirit he hadn't felt for ages. He was thirty-two years old, ridiculously wealthy, and free to do whatever he wanted. But what did he want? In the fresh, clean space that opened up for him — he was perfectly aware of how few were ever given such a gift — he had time to ruminate about his repositioning. One morning, gazing into the bathroom mirror part way through shaving, he was startled to see looking back at him a lathered person almost totally devoid of substantive human contact. Yes, he was devoted to his mother, no question, but his older sister Irene and he were not at all close, and he scarcely knew her daughter, his niece Crystal, or her child. They all lived a long way off, but more than that, there was a distancing of another sort, a tacit understanding that closeness would entail encountering things best left undisturbed.

He'd enjoyed the affection of certain colleagues and had experienced several fleeting affairs of the heart, none of them satisfactory, due he recognized in hindsight to the almost obsessive single-mindedness with which he'd engaged in his career. The thing was, he hadn't even thought of it as a career; it was just something that had happened to him, like a fungal infection or religious fixation, which was suddenly, mercifully over.

Shortly afterwards Cecilia walked into his life and everything was again knocked sideways. Mooching around the city one evening, he'd wandered into a downtown bookstore where a poetry reading was about to begin. The poet, whom he'd never heard of, was an aging shaggy bear of a man with, he was to later learn, a considerable reputation and an ego to match. Peter might have slipped discreetly away if his attention hadn't been drawn to the young publicist accompanying the poet. As she hovered attentively around the Great Man, something about her ignited Peter's interest. She was delightful to look at, every gesture and movement — the precision with which she arranged a small table and placed on it a tall glass of water, her delicacy in realigning the books that were for sale — seeming to him a bit of poetry in its own way. Peter normally didn't notice such things, but in this instance he was quite captivated. The smartly coiffed hair, the slender body in a stylishly close-fitting black dress, and a certain elusive quality that somehow conveyed her love of fine poetry if not necessarily of this particular poet.

Peter barely heard a word of what the poet declaimed but, where normally he would exit unnoticed during an event of this sort, he lingered afterwards and decided he would buy a book of the verse he hadn't heard. *Blood on the Crags* was the volume he selected and took for the poet's signature. She was standing just behind the table at which the author sat for signing. Close up she was even more tantalizing. Peter looked for a wedding ring and saw none. In fact she wore no jewelry at all, nor did her charm require any. But how would he approach her? Accomplished in so many ways, he had no skill at all in this, nor any confidence. He felt himself a clumsy fool, but a fool ensnared. As he handed the poet his book for signing and provided his name, he glanced up, caught her eye and saw lightning flash between them.

"Thanks, friend," the poet rumbled, handing the book back and dismissing him. Peter shuffled sideways but could not turn to leave. Instead he stood lumpishly alongside her, clasping his book, agonizing over what he could possibly say without sounding absurd.

"A fan?" she whispered to him before he could think of anything.

"Well, not exactly," he admitted, whispering too.

"Me neither," she mouthed the words to him and winked.

He wasn't sure he'd seen the wink or just imagined it. "I do love poetry," he managed to murmur in an almost normal voice.

"Of course," she said, as though she'd known it all along, "and so do I." Her voice had a soft rustling quality that reminded him of the whisperings heard among late summer leaves.

The bookstore had provided coffee and biscuits for after the reading, thereby saving him the riskiness of asking if she'd like to go somewhere for coffee. They sat together at a bistro table and soon were laughing giddily over her stories about the perils of the publicist. Discreetly she wouldn't name names, but took mischievous delight in recounting the drunken antics of a "very highly regarded" novelist or the tendency of a particular cultural historian to disrobe in public places. It was only much later that she confessed she'd sat with Peter that evening not from any great attraction to him but in order to avoid the lecherous advances of her poet who'd been hitting on her throughout their publicity rounds that day.

Peter was smitten. It was her joy that was so infectious, the delight she seemed to take in almost anything. Panhandlers and postal workers, fire hydrants and french fries, even her previous lover, whom she'd sent packing a couple of months ago — everything seemed to dance and sing for her as though in some far-fetched romcom. Was she high on something? Peter wondered at first. She sure was, but not drugs. Not religion either. One part of Peter kept waiting for a shoe to drop, but it never did. She just stayed up there like she was breathing helium.

For really the first time in his life romantic passion swooped in upon him. For seven giddy months they courted and caressed each other, Cecilia and he, so that everything around them seemed to him transformed. Outlandishly, he imagined her a priestess, capable of repeated transubstantiations. And of scorching sex like he'd never known.

His mother and Cecilia hit it off straight away, as he'd suspected they would. The difference in their ages meant nothing. It was the mischievous humour they both shared, a quick flashing perception of the absurd where others might only see the everyday. When the two women were in full throttle, his mother and his lover, Peter would just sit back and watch their highwire antics. The witches of Beastwick, he called them. The two women he loved.

Within no time at all Cecilia and Peter were a bona fide couple. She happily abandoned the perilous existence of literary publicist to devote more time to her own poetry. "Vastly superior to that pretentious *Blood on the Crags*," Peter told her. She reminded him that they owed everything to *Blood on the Crags* and not to dismiss the handiwork of Fate so cynically. "It was the handiwork of that lecherous poet we should credit," he said, as they collapsed laughing and kissing on the couch.

The following spring they moved together to the farm at Shetterly, although the old farmhouse was a considerable come-down on the luxury scale from Peter's penthouse. But it was where they both wanted to be, and they settled into a honeymoon life together on the farm, laughing and tripping their way up a steep learning curve of horticulture and animal husbandry. "Damned if I know!" was their laughing mantra about every new twist the farm threw at them.

Shortly after arrival, Peter returned from town one afternoon with a small black-and-white pup that he presented to Cecilia with mock liturgical solemnity. "Oh, she's adorable!" Cecilia shrieked with delight, cuddling the pup and smothering it with kisses.

"Yes, she is," Peter said, kissing her on her forehead. "And so is this little chap who, as you can see upon closer inspection," — here he parted the little nipper's hind legs — "is a spirited male like myself." She named him Shep, a choice that Peter declared would surely win a blue ribbon for originality.

Not long afterwards the greatest gift: Cecilia was carrying their child.

But then in the blink of an eye, both mother and daughter were dead. When the accident happened, young Shep was as disconsolate as Peter himself. Both of them moped hopelessly for months. Almost inseparable now, the two of them carry Cecilia's memory between them, and Peter knows that a part of the dog's attachment to him is its lingering devotion to the woman they both lost.

He couldn't remain on the farm afterwards, not like that, encountering her in every room, expecting her around every corner, repeatedly thinking he'd spotted her coming up the lane. Her and the baby. Shep always watching for her too, always waiting. Teetering towards madness he moved back into town, ostensibly to be with his mother and help with the running of Stone House, but really to save himself. And he has been saved, he knows that now, even on this cursed highway that claimed their lives. Saved but not yet shriven.

Peter comes gliding silently up the driveway in the Prius and stops beside where Shep is excitedly waiting. Less excitedly, Ginger's sitting on the verandah, absorbing the last slanting caresses of late afternoon sun glow. "Well," his mum says to him as he climbs the front steps, dog at heel, "how did it go?"

"Great," Peter replies, "we're penniless but proud."

"Ah, good, Pride goeth before the fall," Ginger pronounces.

Peter sits down beside her. "I brought you a little something," he says, handing across the Apple bag.

"Thank you, dear," Ginger says. "This helps account for the pennilessness, does it?"

"It does. But there's no cost too steep when it comes to you."

Ginger gives him her you're-full-of-bullshit look and opens the package. "Aha!" she exclaims. "I was just reading about these gadgets the other day. All the rage, it seems."

"Transformative technology," Peter agrees. "If I'd come up with something like that, we'd be in clover now."

"We're in clover already, you fool. How much clover does anybody need?"

"I'm all over clover," Peter says, just to be clever. "That thing will need a bit of fiddling; I'll set it up for you later."

"Thank you, dear, you're very kind. They say these tablets are idiot-proof, so I won't have to spend all my declining years trying to figure it out."

"We'll see," Peter says. "Now, on to the real business of the day."

"Ah, yes. I marked" — she takes a scrap of paper from her apron pocket to be sure — "let's see: eleven minutes to four o'clock. How's by you?"

"To the minute precisely," Peter says. "Wow!"

They both look down at Shep who's pretending nothing of significance has occurred.

"Well, I dunno," Peter says, "I feel we should be calling the National Research Council or something."

"Oh, don't!" Ginger laughs. "They'll dispatch a whole team of crackerjack researchers to conduct idiotic experiments aimed at proving that nothing can be proven."

"I think they've fired all the crackerjack researchers already. Undermining national security with all their inconvenient truths about climate change, etcetera."

"I expect you're right. Still, you'd have to think our little secret would be an unspeakable threat to the established order of things, wouldn't it, smartypants?" she says to Shep, tickling the bliss spot under his jaw. Shep's immediately away in the meadows of euphoria conjured by a perfectly located tickle.

Peter's suspicion, one he doesn't share with his mum, is that Shep awaits his return so dutifully with an unending expectation that Cecilia will be returning with him, that it's really her the dog is waiting for with an optimism never dimmed by her repeated failure to arrive. Sometimes, he believes, she may appear to Shep in a form he himself can't see.

"We must be sure to repeat the experiment to confirm our findings," Ginger says. "Meanwhile, how was it with Sarah and, what's his name?"

"Zigfried," Peter says. "Perfect name for an accountant, eh? All's fine. No suggestion of the fortunes to be made from gold mines in Siberia or hedging against the collapse of the euro."

"Well I guess our splendid casino economy is just going to have to continue staggering along without you for a while yet," Ginger says. "Poor thing."

"Yea," Peter chuckles, stretching luxuriously to squeeze the evening's final few drops of sunwarmth before going indoors. Relieved to be home, he's wondering once again how he ever adapted so well to living in the city for what now seems like the madness of his dotcom meteor ride.

"Did you bring up the business of the church scandal with them?" Ginger asks.

"No, that's not their bailiwick really, but I am thinking I should maybe talk to Vaughn Krippen about it, give him a heads-up. There was another item about it on the news while I was driving home. Sounds like charges are imminent."

"So, there's more to it than rumours."

"Seems like. And this is around the stage in these sagas when assets start getting shuffled sideways. Remember that bishop in Wisconsin? Moved millions into the cemetery fund well out of reach of any litigants. And then a sudden bankruptcy, and not a penny left for restitution."

"But is Stone House actually one of their assets?" Ginger asks, just as the sun slides behind the treeline to the west.

"That's what I want to discuss with Vaughn," Peter says. "Whether the place can be sold and your lifetime tenancy transferred to a new owner."

"If memory serves," Ginger says, "which I grant you it does less and less, the will was quite specific about the place being held by the church and used exclusively for church-related activities."

"Yep. So our unholy rollers can hardly flip it to WalMart then take the money and run."

"Which doesn't mean they might not try," Ginger says. "God moving in mysterious ways and all that. You haven't spoken with Sophia about any of this have you?"

"Irene, as we call her nowadays," Peter corrects her gently. He had only ever known his sister as Irene, though his mother had never quite accommodated her name change. "No, I haven't but we should give her a heads-up, I suppose."

"She and I talked briefly about it, but only in the most general terms. It would be helpful if you'd give her a call."

"I will. How's she doing, anyway?"

"Oh, the usual. Soldiering on. Worried about Crystal and Isha."

"Well, fixed points in a changing world at least."

The evident lack of affection between her two children has long been a sore spot for Ginger, and she awaits the day of its disappearance as faithfully as Shep awaits Peter's return.

"Shall we go in?" Ginger asks. "It's beginning to get a bit chilly."

The two of them head indoors, followed by Shep who's imagining it's almost time for dinner.

"We had the most extraordinary goings-on here today," Ginger says as they make their way towards the kitchen.

"What goings-on?"

"Remember Chrissie, the girl who was here doing the interview?"

"Yea. Funny little specimen. Not a Kennel Club member, I think." Peter peers into the fridge, considering whether a beer's in order or not, distracted by the memory of the girl's scream.

"Never saw anyone as terrified of dogs," Ginger says, perching on one of the counter stools, "even as obvious a pacifist as old Shep here."

Shep's trying to appear mellow but without giving any misleading impression that food is entirely unimportant at this point.

"Well, she forgot her notebook," Ginger says, "and came back for it today just while Garth and Sarina and I were going at it hammer and tongs."

"Cripes, I'd be more terrified of you bunch than the dog," Peter says. He's decided on a glass of apple juice. Ginger holds up a hand to indicate she doesn't care for any.

"Well, during the meeting — Garth had picked up some scuttlebutt about a giant garbage incinerator, but that's a whole other story — anyway, in the middle of it all, I sensed something was afoot," Ginger says in her best Miss Marple voice, "so I came out on the verandah and sure enough there's Shep and little Chrissie staring at one another and frozen like a pair of figures in the wax museum. So I had the brightest idea — I *do* have one every once in a while, you know."

"Yes, a very long while admittedly, but good for you nevertheless," Peter says sipping his juice with exaggerated satisfaction. He does love bantering with his mother like this and always has. Really she's the only person with whom he's completely comfortable, entirely himself. Now.

"So I asked her if she'd like Shep to fetch the book down to her."

"Oh, you old provocateur!" Peter exclaims. "Have you no shame at all?"

"You could see she was terrified by the prospect, but she's a spunky customer, you have to hand her that," Ginger says while pouring herself a small portion of vodka, an occasional allowance that she prefers to sip straight like a civilized Russian. "So she said okay. Well, wouldn't you know it, Shep fetches the notebook down to her, good as gold and the kid finally takes it after this agonizingly slow reaching out. It was fascinating, really, seeing her strength and her terror grappling together. Shep, of course, behaved perfectly, watching her closely and giving her strength. Didn't you, darling?" Ginger questions Shep who's imagining that the story might be more succinctly told in order to get on with dinner.

"Most interesting," Peter says.

"But wait!" Ginger says and sips her drink. "Because here's the most remarkable part. When the girl finally took the notebook from Shep she clutched it to herself and began the most uncontrollable weeping and sobbing I've ever seen. Torrents of tears, running nose, the whole waterworks business."

"What was that about?"

"I have absolutely no idea."

"And you didn't ask?"

"No, no, I let her weep to her heart's content, just like I used to do with you and your sister."

"Ah, yes. Momma Tough Love herself."

"Of course poor Sarina and Garth had no idea what was going on and were forced to slink away like thieves in the night. Then once Chrissie had wept herself dry, she took herself off on that bike of hers and that was the end of it."

"Well, that's a damn sight more exciting than counting coppers with Sarah and Zigfried," Peter says, downing the dregs of his apple juice. "Okay with you if I go have a quick shower? Wash the grime of the day away."

"Of course, dear," Ginger says, "I'll feed Shep and maybe have another thimble of vodka. No rush at all."

After giving Shep his bowl, slipping in a few special treats because of how brilliantly he performed today, Ginger takes another discreet glass of vodka and sits at the breakfast nook table, musing on the remarkable events of the day.

⇝⇜

You could almost hear Roy Orbison wailing behind that poor girl's sobs. Weeping's what it was, not simply crying. Tears drawn from the deepness of the soul. Oh, my. What's that line from Shakespeare? — he's always got a line on everything — To weep is to make less the depth of grief. That's what it seemed like with Chrissie. Depths of grief. Saddest in the young. I must have cried like that over Frankie's dying. Oh, yes, I do recall sitting under the trees out there and plenty of tears, but they were silent tears somehow, the stealthy tears of death. Standing by the wailing wall. Voltaire's silent language of grief. Maybe the deepest of all. Different from a broken heart. The Tears I Cry for You. Or the tears of desertion. I never sobbed the same way over Nigel's going. Yes, I snuffled and blubbered with the best of them at the time, but my spirit wasn't drawn and quartered the way it was with Frankie's death. Or even the way this girl wept. All those sad songs back around the time of Nigel's leaving too; or are there always sad songs only we hear them more in sadness. Cry Baby. Who was it? Garnet somebody and the Enchanters, long before Janis. Crying in the Chapel — oh, the Elvis version was everywhere that year, but I loved how Ella F sang it back in the fifties. Nigel scoffed at it, of course, the tears of joy, the happy in the chapel. A malfunction of the lacrimal apparatus he called it. Sure, it was corny, but that's still better than hard-hearted. I'm with Dorothy Parker on lips that taste of tears being the best for kissing. Lacrimation. The globus sensation. Crying over you. Belt it out there, Roy.

Chrissie's at her office desk working on her feature story about Stone House. Open on her desk there's a tattered book titled *Shetterly and District: An Illustrated History* that's got a whole segment about the house, with archival photographs, including one of the suicidal mining man. Plus, old Ginger gave her some really interesting stuff during the interview, then took her on a tour of the place which blew her mind. So putting the pieces together is a total no-brainer. *Click click* goes her keyboard as she taps the innocuous half-truths into the standard marketable schlock the *Standard* specializes in. Ha ha, Chrissie giggles to herself, the standard *Standard*. Blah. She's got a real knack for writing this sort of copy even though it's bland Pablum, and she's taken it on as her particular challenge to out-bland the very blandest that the paper has to offer. It's like the total opposite of the silent language in her head, where she uses every wonky, wild word she can think of. Or makes them up. She just loves it, verbally kicking the world in the ass whenever there's an opportunity. She's far too shy and cautious to talk that way out loud, except maybe with Chazz a bit, but inside her head she's brash enough to take on anyone.

Back to the copy, she makes no mention of suicides or ghosts or of the psychic dog and its loonie owner. The real stuff. She gives old Ginger a patina of respectability in the piece — well, hell, almost everybody gets a gloss of respectability once they approach eighty, and Ginger deserves it far more than some of the washed-up old fossils she's had to reinvent for public consumption. Drunks and wife beaters and Christ-knows-who parading around as eminent citizens.

Chrissie can write rings around hacks mostly because of Sol. He was like her guru after she ran away from home at age sixteen and landed in Toronto with nothing to her name except a fat wad of bills she'd lifted from Chuck who'd been passed out on the kitchen floor. He had one of those wallets with a chain attaching it to his belt like truckers have. Captain Crackerfuck. So just ever so gently she slid the wallet out of his hip pocket while he was snoring and grunting away, a little dribble of slobber trickling from his mouth to the linoleum floor, and took all the bills. She figured it was owed her for all the crap she'd had to endure from that sadistic little creep. Then she was out the door and onto the Greyhound and goodbye, good luck to all that shit. She decided on the bus that she'd change her last name so Chuck wouldn't be able to track her down. Ever. Happens the guy across from her on the bus is reading the sports pages and she saw the name Crosby in a headline. Chrissie Crosby, she thought. Not bad. Later on she sent a card to her mother saying thanks for nothing.

Sol saved her from Frankenstein only knows what might have happened to her after that. She met him in a coffee shop right after she'd gotten off the Greyhound, totally clueless about what she was going to do. He was sitting alone in a corner booth writing something in a notebook. It was late at night and the whole place was almost deserted. She was feeling lonely and scared and he could have been some psycho creep for all she knew, especially with his scraggly dark hair and beard, but turns out he was a spoken-word artist instead. They get to talking and he offers her a place to crash until she gets settled, which she went along with even though it was supremely dumb. She trusted him somehow, and it turned out just sharp because there were about five or six other people living in an old house downtown, and all of them were like painters or actors or something, so there was nothing to be freaked about.

She fell for Sol like she'd been hit by a wrecking ball even though he was older than her and kind of sad and solemn about everything. It was only after a while that they started sleeping together, and it was fine except for the times when Sol would start to softly cry right in the middle of fucking. She'd feel his tears landing on her chest like raindrops and realize he was sobbing. She was clueless what it was about, and afterwards he wouldn't talk about it.

Still, they were good together for almost a year and a half, and that's how she learned about writing, from being with him, reading his pieces, going to readings in coffee shops and places. Partly to fit the scene, but also to prevent Chuck from ever spotting her on the street, she did herself over in Goth. She started writing poems herself and she knows now they were totally craptacular but Sol was so cool talking with her about them. What worked and what didn't and why.

She wonders sometimes what would have happened if she'd stayed with Sol, stayed in Toronto, because it was good for her there. But Chazz showed up out of nowhere one afternoon and crashed at the house for a couple of weeks. One day she arrives home and there's nobody there but Chazz. He's playing his guitar and kinda humming a tune. He tells her it's called "Dusky Lover" and he's written it with her in mind. Instantly she's moist all over, and before you know it, they're in her bed fucking like gonzo. And, shit, he was good; he knocked her over the moon like Sol had never done. After that they couldn't keep their hands off each other. Yah. She hated what it did to Sol after all he'd done for her. Kind of a betrayal. But she couldn't help herself, she was that gone. So she and Chazz headed out together, bound for Shetterly where Chazz was from.

Yeah, Chazz. She still hasn't called him out on the film thing. By the time he got home last night he was totally wasted and it's pointless talking to him when he's pissed. She's not really focused on Chazz right now anyway, it's like somebody's hit the pause button with him and her.

Instead she's caught herself any number of times riffing on old Ginger. Something about that woman gives her a buzz, something she can't figure out. Chrissie has zero experience of old people, no grandparents she ever knew, no great aunties or anything like that. Well, there was that ancient couple lived next door when she was a kid, two wizened gnomes you hardly ever saw except when one of them would sometimes peek at her in the bathroom from behind their kitchen curtains. On quiet evenings you could hear them singing hymns together inside their collapsing trailer. Not exactly wisdom of the elders types. But that's what it is about Ginger, isn't it, something about wisdom, life lessons learned, that kind of shit. Calmness beneath. Which Chrissie hardly ever detects in everyday monkeymouths and entirely not in herself. Yar.

Chrissie's just about got the piece finished, 750 words of unapologetic fluff, when she becomes aware of Harding approaching her from behind. She can tell it's him from the muffled grunting noises he makes as he moves, the kind of noise a giant slug would make if slugs made noise.

"Working late, Chrissie?" he asks her in that oily way he has of talking. "How's it going?"

Chrissie's made a mistake, she realizes, staying here late, with everyone gone, except Harding. She hadn't thought he was still around, but she's well aware that he has the predator's knack for lying quietly in wait until it's time.

"Fine," she tells him, "just finishing the Stone House story." From the side of her eye she can see the bulge of his belly just beyond her right elbow. Harding almost always wears polyester dress shirts in pale blue that stretch snugly across his plump stomach. Like it was a trophy or something.

She briskly saves her copy and logs out of her desktop. "There," she tells him, "I'll have it to you first thing in the morning." She gathers her phone and notebook and stuffs them into her pack, then rises to leave.

"Ah, say, Chrissie," Harding mumbles, "you know, I was chatting with Mr. Illinger this afternoon."

"Uh-huh." Chrissie slings her pack across one shoulder and turns to go. Whatever twisted pathway Harding's going to head down, Chrissie isn't going to follow.

"Well — strictly between you and me, Chrissie, okay? — he seemed a bit upset about something."

"Hmm." Chrissie's exuding total no-interest vibes while trying to leave but Harding won't let her go. He's kind of blocking her path, hands on his hips, as though he was somebody worth paying attention to.

"He mentioned your name a couple of times, you know, in a, well, an agitated sort of way." Harding's a major suckhole when he's trying to project heartfelt concern.

Chrissie's not biting. She doesn't know if Illinger and Harding have cooked something up together, or if this is pure Harding on one of his lurid fishing expeditions. And doesn't give a shit. She busies herself checking for nothing in her pack. But Harding's pressing in against her; she can smell his horking cologne and putrid breath.

"Well, I know you might think it's none of my goldarn business," Harding continues, trying his fake Mr. Nice Guy schtick, "but *I* think maybe it would be best for all concerned if I knew what exactly is going on around here."

"Did you ask Mr. Illinger?" Chrissie shoots back at him, casually defiant.

"Of course I didn't, Chrissie. Don't be a fool. Mr. Illinger tells me what he chooses to tell me, as is his right."

"Right," Chrissie says, "so it's fairly certifiable he wouldn't want me telling you something he wouldn't tell you himself."

"Ah!" Harding replies, raising a pudgy index finger and tilting his head so he's looking at her slantwise as if that's supposed to impress her. "But what *he* chooses to tell me and what *you* choose to tell me are two very different things, are they not?"

"I don't see how." Chrissie is inching backwards away from Harding but he keeps pressing forward so that he's always too close. So ratchet. His shirt has a dark sweat stain under each armpit. For a second or two Chrissie feels a tremendous urge to drive her fist as hard as she can into his protruding stomach. She can visualize it bursting open like a cantaloupe with Harding's pink intestines spilling out.

"Let me explain then," Harding says with patronizing ooze. "I work for Mr. Illinger and do exactly what he tells me, right?"

"Uh-huh."

"And you, Miss Chrissie, work for me and do precisely what *I* tell *you*, right?" The folds of loose skin on Harding's neck have turned a bruised shade of purple.

Why is he running this wolf tickets shit on her? Here she's all set to defend herself against one of his dead spermy attempts at seduction and instead he's coming at her like Mr. Ultimate Fighting. Well, fuck him. "Yea," she answers boldly, "except when I'm doing something for Mr. Illinger that doesn't concern you."

"Ah, but it does concern me, Chrissie," Harding says, bringing his jowly face so close to Chrissie's she can smell the oily sweat on him. She winces sideways to avoid his janky fleshiness but he carries on, oblivious, pressing closer against her. "It concerns me very much when members of my staff, especially valued members" — and here he permits himself a salacious leer — "are doing things for my boss that I know nothing about."

"But . . ." Chrissie's now cornered against an office divider, her torso twisted uncomfortably away from him, one of his fat thighs pressing against her leg.

"Except," Harding says, "that my boss is phoning me obviously upset about something or other. Something or other involving you. I'd hate to think there was anything improper going on, right under my nose, and that later I might be called to account for not exercising due diligence. You can appreciate my position, can't you, Chrissie? Can't you?" Harding's just about panting with excitement and Chrissie recognizes his deviance for precisely what it is: the hypocritical wayward husband's twisted mix of fear and daring and illicit sexual arousal. And bullying. Just another Chuck the Fuck but missing the Rottweilers.

"Mr. Harding," she says to him as calm as she can, "I'm sorry. I gotta go. There's nothing I can tell you. None of this has anything to do with you."

Chrissie wiggles herself free and turns to leave, but Harding startles her by reaching out and catching her by the wrist. His fat white fingers look like uncooked pork sausages curled around her wrist. She tries to shake free but he won't release her. "Mr. Harding," she says in as stern a voice as she can muster, "you're hurting me." But he still doesn't let go. "Mr. Harding!" she shouts at him.

Suddenly it's as if a switch had been flipped and something blinks on for him. His eyes kind of wobble crazily for a moment. "Ah," he says, looking down at his hand as though it's not part of him, as if he hadn't realized what he was doing. Instantly he lets go, leaving a harsh circle on Chrissie's wrist. "I'm so sorry," he says, suddenly contrite. "I didn't hurt you, did I? Here, let me see." He reaches out for her, but Chrissie's had enough.

"Stop touching me!" she screams at Harding. "And get the fuck outta my face, okay?"

"Oh, Chrissie, please, I only . . ."

Chrissie shoves past him and quickly retrieves her bike from the corridor. She wheels it to the front door. Locked. She pushes at the release bar but the door stays firmly locked. Harding comes slithering up alongside her.

"Listen, Chrissie," he says to her, "this is awful. I never meant . . ."

"Would you please unlock this door," Chrissie demands, staring down at the floor, radiating rage.

"Of course, of course," Harding says, fumbling in his pants pocket for his ring of keys. "Only, Chrissie, I can't have you leaving angry at me this way. You know I'm your friend, don't you? Surely you realize how much I care for you."

"You ever lay a finger on me again," she's almost snarling at him, "and I'll have you up for sexual assault, you hear me?"

"Chrissie, I never meant . . ."

"Now open the fucking door!"

Six

As Professor Childes and Ginger walked from the bookstore to his "digs" as he referred to them, she was beset by a rising anxiety that she was doing something both stupid and shameful. She did not think of herself as a prude; rather as someone who attempted to behave in a decent and honourable fashion, someone for whom deceit was inherently repulsive. And there was no denying that what she was doing at this moment, walking with one of her professors for an assignation in his private apartments, smacked of indecency. She'd be mortified, for example, were they to encounter someone she knew, one of her fellow students. Someone like Dot for whom innocence was second nature. Although she continued smiling at Nigel's clever banter, tossing her wild copper hair now and then for the romantic effect she knew it created, Ginger felt her own claim to innocence was being roughly compromised.

They turned together onto one of the side streets of the old town. A double colonnade of enormous elms lined the road. Stately old homes in red brick stood well back from the canopied sidewalk and seemed comfortably settled within their manicured lawns and subdued foundation plantings.

"Here we are then," Childes said, indicating one of the houses.

Although nowhere near as imposing as her childhood home at Stone House, the building and gardens spoke of wealthy accomplishment. She wondered how he could possibly afford such a place.

"Rather pleasant, don't you think?" Childes asked her, as he led the way around the side of the house and down a pathway enclosed by a high hedge of lilacs.

"Oh, yes," Ginger said, her voice surprisingly calm considering the tumult of anticipation she was experiencing. All her mother's measured advice concerning what respectable girls did or didn't do was being battered to pieces.

"Of course, I only have this modest apartment here in the rear," Childes said as he retrieved a key from his pocket and opened the locked back door. "The place belongs to the dean of the Fine Arts faculty," he carried on, "off on sabbatical, mercifully, leaving the estate in my capable hands. Here, do come in," he invited her through a small entranceway into a brightly lit living room that looked out through large sash windows onto the back garden. It was an unmistakably private, perfectly romantic place.

"Please, let me take your coat," Childes said, reaching to set her book bag on a hall table and helping her remove her coat.

"Thank you," she said. "It's lovely here."

"Make yourself at home," he said indicating a chesterfield of tawny corduroy positioned somewhat oddly so that it faced the windows rather than the room.

"Thank you," she said again, seating herself at one end of the chesterfield. She was feeling a peculiar removal from everything, as though she'd been dropped into an heirloom landscape painting.

"Now I wonder if we can be just the tiniest bit less formal, shall we?" he said as he hung her coat in a small closet near the door. He seemed always a step or two ahead of her.

"Yes, I'd like that," she said, although she wasn't sure just how much informality he had in mind. Indeed, at this point she wondered whether it much mattered. Whether she hadn't already crossed a line at which any proper young lady would have balked. She could not remember ever having been so wayward.

"Excellent," he pronounced, coming back to her, "so let us bid a fond farewell to Miss Flynn the student and to Professor Childes, grand companions though they've been, and welcome in their stead Ginger and your humble servant Nigel." He bowed formally towards her with his arm crooked out like a maître d' and she laughed rather excitedly, some of her simmering tension momentarily released.

On a first name basis. She remembered Patsy and Diane quizzing her sharply on what she and Professor Childes had called each other when they were together at the movie house. Although that evening really wasn't any such thing, she found herself thinking of it as her first date with Nigel.

"Now, if you'll excuse me for a moment, I shall fix us two cups of the promised coffee," he said, "to dismiss any trace of misapprehension you may have entertained that I'd lured you into my lair under false pretenses."

She smiled weakly, confounded by how frequently his observations seemed to anticipate just what she was thinking, or was about to think.

"Not that all pretense isn't false," he continued after a moment's reflection. "Falsity is at the heart of pretense, isn't it, so one scarcely needs the adjective." He smiled at her brightly and retreated into a small kitchenette at the back of the apartment where he began rattling around with cups and spoons.

She was disconcerted by this mention of falsity. Was she indeed being false, not to him but to herself? And could she really call him Nigel, she wondered, gazing out at a gnarly apple tree amid the branches of which small nervous birds were pecking for insects in the bark crevices. For a moment she thought of the trees at home, the safety and established order of things she'd known there. Her parents, however stunted by religious scruple, trying their best. She couldn't remember ever having been quite so torn between wanting and not wanting to be doing something. The dangers of being here, being alone with this intriguing man. She felt she had no power over the circumstances, that all impetus belonged with him, that what might or might not occur would be entirely of his doing. Incapable of any initiative, she felt both humiliated and absolved by her powerlessness.

Needing to occupy herself with something, anything, she reached across and picked up a book from the end table. It had a soft brown cloth cover with a small gold phoenix embossed on the upper left corner, but no title or author's name. She realized perhaps it might be his diary and so quickly put it back where she'd found it. But he was approaching as she did so and she could feel herself a child again, caught out doing something wrong.

"Dear Constance," he said, holding a silver tray before her on which sat two small coffee cups, white with black etchings in art nouveau design. A matching small plate held bread-like biscuits of a type she hadn't seen before. "Cream or sugar?" he asked her, and she thanked him, adding a bit of each and stirring with a small silver spoon.

"I thought you might care for a *cantuccini* as well," he said, placing the tray beside her on the little table. In doing so he removed the brown book, taking it along with his coffee and seating himself at the far end of the chesterfield.

"Mmm," she murmured appreciatively after taking a sip of his coffee that really was superb.

"One of the very few practical things I brought with me from England," he said, "was my Atomic coffee maker and I shall be forever grateful that I did so."

"What's that?" she asked him.

"Wonderful device," he said, savouring a sip himself. "Designed by an ingenious Italian, Giordano Robbiati if you can believe it. I managed to snare one in Paris shortly before leaving. The levers and knobs alone would cause you to gasp, but I simply couldn't face life in the new world if it entailed imbibing that bitter, muddy brew emerging from the dreaded percolator."

"I thought you preferred tea," she said, remembering him in the café being as florid about tea as he was now being about his Atomic coffee.

"No, no, the pleasure of one does not preclude enjoyment of the other," he said and took another sip. Although they'd declared themselves now on a freshly informal footing they seemed to be behaving, or at least discoursing, more formally than ever. "Do have a nibble at the *cantuccini*," he said again, "I have them specially sent in from Montreal where there's a marvellous Tuscan bakery and I hoard them in a most miserly fashion, saving them for only the most esteemed visitors."

She couldn't tell if he was pulling her leg or not. She picked up one of the biscuits and bit into it. "Mmm," she murmured again, "that's lovely."

"Made the traditional way: "eggs, sugar, flour, almonds and pine nuts. No yeasts or fats of any sort. Barely moist dough, cooked twice, once as a slab and then again in slices."

"I really like it," she said, taking another nibble.

"If you're feeling positively continental," he added, "you could consider dunking it in your coffee. Personally I prefer not to, but I do like how they serve these biscuits with the wine they call *vin santo* in Tuscany."

He appeared to be trying awfully hard to impress her and it occurred to her for the first time that beneath the silken social graces he might very well be as nervous in her presence as she was in his. Clearly there was a tentativeness between them that had not existed on the walk home from the movie house, almost certainly having to do with being in his apartment and the more dangerous possibilities that suggested.

"Now, as to fair Lady Chatterley," he said, holding up the brown volume she'd glanced at.

"Oh, is that what it is?" she asked.

"You've heard about the book, of course?" he quizzed her.

"Oh, yes." She had only the vaguest notions about the scandalous novel, gleaned from uninformed gossip among her fellow scholars, but enough for her to know it was a dirty book and had been banned, other than in heavily censored form.

"This is a privately printed limited edition," he said, laying a hand tenderly across the front cover. "Only five hundred copies and entirely unexpurgated, of course. You can't buy a copy of it in this country without risking the firing squad, and the Americans only permit a heavily censored and abridged version. Shocking, isn't it?" he said warmly.

"But you have it anyway?" she asked him.

"Oh, I don't mean the book!" he said, laughing. "The book's not the least bit shocking — well, a bit risqué perhaps and a few naughty words here and there. But really."

This is what she had heard. That the book contained unspeakable words, words like *fuck* and *cunt*. She couldn't believe that her professor would have such filth in his house and not even hide it away somewhere.

"No, it's the confounded censorship that's shocking," he carried on. "Bunch of addle-headed old clowns stuck in the worst aspects of Victorian prudery."

She couldn't quite believe what she was hearing. Oh, yes, his lectures were generously laced with irreverence, that was a large part of their appeal, but never anything so disturbing as this, nothing to set her moral compass spinning wildly the way it was spinning at this moment.

"I think it's Lawrence's attack on the class system they really find objectionable," he went on. "That one of their precious daughters, married into the aristocracy, would throw everything over for a lusty commoner. That's the shocker. The outrage over graphic language is all a diversionary tactic."

Back safely in her own bed in dorms, Ginger lay awake for much of the night puzzling over what was happening to her. True, they had both been a bit stiff under the irregular circumstance of being alone together in his apartments, and the atmosphere of forbidden pursuits had been enhanced by the unexpected appearance of Constance Chatterley. But nothing untoward had come of it; Nigel had behaved like a perfect gentleman throughout, and they had not been observed coming or going, so no one beyond themselves would learn of what might, if discovered, have soured into a minor scandal. But still she fretted over it. He was a vortex of sorts, no getting around it, and she sensed that some loss of herself, perhaps of her principles too, would be the price for her getting drawn into him. But how could she resist? Finding a good man to marry — how often had she heard the mantra from her mother — was definitely not what had brought her to Carlyle College, as it had Diane and Patsy and perhaps most of the women students. Nevertheless, here, for the first time in her life really, was this outstanding man of unlimited promise who was obviously quite interested in her. Her.

A giddy prospect of course, but was he the type of man her parents would be pleased to see her marry? It was plain that, for all his meticulousness concerning dress and diction and manners, he was at heart a nonconformist. He took pleasure in snubbing social norms. He wouldn't be reading filthy books and entertaining female students in his home otherwise. But yet. Still faithful to the moral rectitude of her God-fearing parents, she herself had no instinct towards rebellion. So his indifference towards, or perhaps contempt for social mores both intrigued and frightened her. What she was doing, being with him, was dangerous behaviour, not something to which she was accustomed.

Awakening the next morning to bathroom clatter, she was no surer of herself than she'd been when finally drifting to sleep last night. But, certitude be damned, she knew the path she'd take. With the first visit to his home safely behind her, she felt less hesitation about visiting him there again. And so she was drawn, both were drawn, to a second visit.

She came on her own this time and found him waiting. Wearing khaki pants and a perfectly pressed blue dress shirt, though no tie, he took her hand at the door, in a way he had not done before, and said how delighted he was to see her. She confessed she was pleased to be there as well, doing her best to pretend to herself that the touch of his hand hadn't provoked a tingling thrill in her. She'd dressed smartly for him in cadmium orange slacks and a rust-coloured sweater that showed her form to advantage. An enlivenment of power shivered through her. She was, she knew, at a point of embarkation.

As before, he prepared two cups of excellent coffee served with his prized *cantuccini*. Again they settled at either end of the chesterfield looking out at the rather mournful late autumn garden brightened somewhat by a show of brilliant red fruits on a crabapple tree.

"So, have you started on your Orwell yet?" he asked her.

She marked his preference for immediately steering their conversation well away from anything to do with the college, as though to efface their positions of student and professor as anything other than a source of mild amusement. She didn't mind in the least; it was part of his appeal, this engagement on equal footing, as though she were a woman, not a girl.

She had arrived determined to ask him more about Frank, but there was plenty of time for that and she was pleased to share with him her thoughts on *1984*. She said how she'd read about half the book already, struggling with it at first, disliking its gloom, but gradually finding herself drawn into its bizarre world of Newspeak, Thoughtcrime and Doublethink. "It's fascinating, really," she told Nigel, "how Winston's job — he's the protagonist — is to rewrite history; he changes old newspaper articles so they reflect what the ruling Party wants history to say."

"Ah, yes," Nigel said, puffing himself up in a plainly self-deprecating parody, "the glorious art of historical revisionism. Quite up my line, obviously."

"Oh, I didn't mean that you'd ever do such a thing," she said, although she was amused by his setting it up this way.

"But we all do it, don't we, bend the story to our own purposes."

"Do you think so?" Behind the banter she was unsettled by the notion. "Even scholars like yourself?"

"Especially scholars like myself," he said, grinning broadly. "And, worst of all, we do it freely, wantonly, without any coercion from Big Brother."

"But why?"

"That, my dear, is the question decency has us beg."

She was sufficiently startled by the term of endearment she could think of nothing to say.

"I believe we do it, each of us, with our own life story too," he continued in a less flippant tone.

"How's that?" she asked. She had a sense of descending into places of difficulty.

"Editing out the bits we're too ashamed of, shading events in memory so they're no longer quite what they were, even outright self-deception where required."

"Oh," she said, unsure if he was talking about himself, or if perhaps he was about to make some startling confession. Something she didn't want to hear. Crazily, she imagined him having a wife back in England whom he hadn't bothered to mention. Their conversation seemed to be drifting into murk not unlike the mood of Orwell's story.

"But listen," he said more cheerily, "we're getting — no, forgive me, *I'm* getting far too morbidly introspective. Let's send Mr. Orwell back down the road to Wigan Pier for the present, shall we?"

"Yes, I'd like that," she said, brightening, though not knowing the reference.

"Good," he softly clapped his slender hands together like a magician, "what shall we speak of instead?"

"I wondered about Frankie," she said a bit timidly, "we never did get back to the story of your friendship."

The change in his demeanor was immediate, as if from a smart slap, though she couldn't have said just how. "Did we not? Where did we leave off? Do you remember?"

"He'd rescued your top hat, then you'd met for a drink the next day."

"Ah, yes," Nigel said distractedly, almost, she thought after a pause, as though he were alone. "Poor Frank. I knew him only for a few months, you know."

"Really?" This was disconcerting, that Frankie had written with such emotion what proved to be his final letter not to her or their parents but to someone he'd known only briefly. The war did such things to people, she knew, but still. She said as calmly as she could, "It seemed from his letter that you were very fast friends."

"Oh, we were," Nigel replied, again with that air of abstraction, as though he had withdrawn from her, "in every possible connotation of the word."

She waited for him to say more. After an awkwardly long pause he turned and looked directly at her. "Shall I tell you the unvarnished truth?" he asked her.

"Please," she said, though something in his expression provoked such uneasiness she half wished she hadn't. She remembered that first encounter in his office, when his intensity had so frightened her.

"Frank and I were lovers," he said.

She caught the gasp halfway up her throat and quickly looked down so as to avoid his gaze.

Having said the words seemed to give him a sudden strength of purpose and he spoke sincerely now, without affectation. "I loved him, Ginger, more than I'd loved anyone before and more than anyone since."

"I see," was all she was able to say. He seemed to her completely vulnerable just then, trusting her in this way.

Lovers. Male lovers. It was entirely outside her imagining. Or had been. *Thank you, my dear friend. I miss you dreadfully and long for the day when I shall see your smiling face again*. Of course.

"Would you rather I hadn't told you?" he asked after a bit.

"Oh, no. No. Not at all." Her tongue and lips were dreadfully dry. "May I have a glass of water, please?"

"Certainly," he said, perhaps relieved to retreat from the intensity. He went to the kitchenette and returned with a tumbler.

"Thank you," she said, taking a sip and looking away, out the window. Anywhere.

"I debated, you know — whether to say anything. I never have before, not to anyone. But with you it seemed dishonest not to."

"Yes. Yes, I can see that."

"Has it upset you terribly?" She could tell this mattered to him.

"Not really," she said. "It's a shock; I won't pretend it isn't. But if you loved . . ."

"Of that you can be quite certain," he said, "believe me. Our souls caressed each other every bit as much as our bodies. He was the loveliest man."

"Yes, he was," she said. "And if you were happy together . . ."

"Ecstatic. We were ecstatic together."

"As lovers are."

"Yes," he said, "as lovers are."

⁂

In hindsight, after she'd gone, Nigel questioned whyever he'd disclosed so much to the girl. He could have said far less, described instead the friendships of young men, the robustness of masculine affection, rather than confess — yes, it had been a confession of sorts — that he and Frank were lovers. Meaning unmistakably that they'd been sexually intimate. But failing to convey the something larger. Laughter, absolute trust, shared dreams — there'd been so much else, even in so short a time, a caravanserai of jostling attractions gathered. And, yes, the sex. Brilliant fucking sex, truth to tell. Savage and tender and mad.

She knew it too, it was etched all over her reaction to the word. Lovers. Startling almost certainly, but she seemed not to be repulsed or offended. Still he'd been a fool to run the risk. One of his students after all, a sheltered child. She might easily have misinterpreted, seeing him as the seducer, the corrupter, the one who'd enticed her brother onto a path at the end of which lurked Death. Fanciful? Perhaps.

While not intending to make this sudden disclosure, he had certainly considered what, if anything, he should tell her. Having been effectively obscured for several years, his memory of Frank had clarified significantly since his involvement with Ginger. And there could be no denying that it was now an involvement. He liked spending time with the girl and felt an increasing tenderness towards her, believing she felt similarly, though neither had intimated anything of the sort. While he was perfectly aware that the more he saw of her the more he thought of Frank, it was only after his confession that he realized how conflicted he'd been in his dealings with her precisely because he had not revealed what needed to be said about himself and her brother. So while prudence might have argued against full disclosure, forthrightness compelled him to make it. He had been honest with her at last and would take the consequences.

Among the various scenarios he imagined — Ginger quitting his class or leaving the school or, in infrequent and particularly paranoid moments, denouncing him to the high priests of the college for both sodomy and an illicit affair with a student — he had not reckoned on the one that actually came about, which was that Ginger, for all her propriety, seemed if anything more drawn to him than ever.

Only a few days later she was back at his suite, comfortably ensconced on the chesterfield, giving every indication she was prepared to have their relationship unfold however it would.

"Do you miss him?" she asked, not needing to say who.

"I did for the longest bit, most awfully," he said. "But, truthfully, over time the pain subsided along with the sense of loss. Like that dreadful war itself, he became a memory of things best sealed and put to rest."

"I see," she said. Even to himself his words limped with disloyalty. He was aware of how closely she was watching him whenever he spoke, as though she were probing for whatever crouched between the words. On this deeper ground he was not the master of situations he was at the podium.

"You know," he said, turning slightly towards her as a person might turn in complete darkness, sensing something close at hand, "as I said at the time, I've never mentioned any of this to a soul before. And now, having done so, having told you . . ."

"I'm glad you told me," she said, smiling at him. Was it his imagination, or was there a heat emanating from her, a scent charged with danger. Lust had not been something overtly between them previously. Nor romantic fantasy. He'd not concerned himself with the possible textures of her flesh, or the taste of her. Now, however, for reasons he couldn't identify, he felt aroused by her in a way he had not until then experienced.

"Good. Yes," he said clumsily. "But what I mean to say is that I feel strangely unburdened by having done so."

"Unburdened how?" Her eyebrows arched with the question and he noticed subtle tints of gold in them.

"Well, that's the thing, you see, I'm not quite sure. I hadn't realized there'd been a burden until it was lifted." He paused and shook his head slightly. "Most peculiar."

"May I ask you something very, very personal?"

"Of course," he said. No further disclosure could be as consequential.

"Have there been others? Since."

"Men, you mean?"

She nodded.

"Not really. A few clumsy attempts. Brief encounters. Nothing close to what Frank and I had." He could scarcely remember their faces, their ardent bodies, even his own yearning for what would not be found.

"And women?"

"Same thing, more or less. Titillations at best. Nothing very satisfactory. Nothing enduring." Their ghosts were even paler than the memories of men.

"And do you think it might have been enduring with my brother?"

Did he really? Was there a future to even consider back in those days when everything was being blown to pieces. Didn't they just seize whatever they could, survivors in a storm surge, clinging to the moment. What would endure and what wouldn't not even worth considering. But the girl would not understand.

"I would have sworn so at the time, oh yes," he said. "Only . . ."

"Only what?"

What indeed? That he'd lost whatever faith in permanence he'd once had. That Frank's dying had in turn been a killing of something else. Something that might have lived if his lover had not died. He didn't know. He didn't know a goddamn thing after Frank's death. He'd eventually blotted the whole business out, leaving the country and all its despairing landmarks of loss, starting over in a new world that had lost nothing but its innocence.

"I would hope so," he said, almost whispering.

"Yes, I would hope so too," she said. Then she closed the gap between them on the chesterfield, enfolding him in her arms.

Seven

Why didn't he frighten me away, I wonder. Confessing such a thing. Run, run, runaway. So obviously at odds with the world, as his champion Lawrence said. Hey, little girl, where you gonna run to? Nowhere. I didn't run at all. Because of Frankie. Frankie and Nigel: old Aristotle's single soul dwelling in two bodies. That's how they seemed to me, what they had. From what Nigel said. More even than I'd had with Frankie. Each a sheltering tree to the other. Of course I should have been forewarned, forearmed, aware of the peril. But why wouldn't I love him, my brother's lover. A love's lifeline. No doubt I desired Nigel for himself, his ascending cleverness, but also because Frankie was lost to me. Lost and can't be found. Except through Nigel. But if a while I think on thee, dear friend. Should I have been afraid. Did I ignore alarm bells foolishly. Back to fools again. Rushing in. Fool on a hill. Or in Campbell's cave, the one you fear to enter, the place that holds the treasure you seek. But I didn't fear. You better watch out. I fear you're mistaken. Fear's good, I remember Aeschylus whispering in my ear back then, keeping its watchful place at the heart's controls. That's what I missed, a watchman of the heart.

Tucked into a south-east corner of the kitchen so as to catch the morning sun through its large windows, the breakfast nook is one of Ginger's favourite spots in Stone House. Spacious and almost institutional feeling, the kitchen's dominated by an Aga, a hulking cast iron cookstove that her parents had installed shortly after the war. Its cream-coloured vitreous enamel coating still gleams all these years later. She can remember her mother producing huge amounts of baked goods in its ovens, perhaps her way of trying to fill the emptiness all three of them experienced following Frankie's death. And she can still picture her father dutifully shoveling coal into the stove's burner, a futile attempt to take the chill out of Stone House. Ginger herself hasn't used the Aga for years, except as a heat-proof countertop, but has felt no need to dispose of it, partly because its bulk helps fill the space in the oversized room but also because she thinks of the Aga as still the warm heart of the place.

Expecting Garth and Sarina any minute, she arranges cookies on a plate while the coffee brews. They arrive in short order and Ginger has them sit at the small round table in the breakfast nook. As usual, Sarina's got her gunslinger satchel stuffed with documents and correspondence but she flops the satchel on the tile floor now, as though their present plight is beyond the redemptive power of papers. Yesterday Garth had sent around a link to a new video about accelerating methane gas emissions in the Arctic, attributable to ice thinning. Perhaps already unavoidable, the consequences for runaway global warming seemed terrifying. A sense that the current they're swimming against is getting darker and stronger. In recent years Ginger's role in this worsening saga has become one of gentle reassurance. Not a "Don't Worry Be Happy" cheerleader, but a weathered voice for the merits of strength and perseverance. A reminder that bitterness and despair never helped anything. Although conscious she's one of the lucky ones by virtue of birth and place, she's glimpsed more than enough horror and destruction in her eight decades. Despair has always been a near neighbour, but so have hope and joy, and she feels both gratitude that they have not deserted her and a sustaining purpose to embody them as best she can.

But today her visitors have more tangible and immediate concerns to discuss — the municipal elections, an enduring, sometimes laughable and frequently disheartening ritual.

"So it's official," Sarina starts right in, "Illinger's declared."

"As expected," Garth says.

"And nobody else at this point?" Ginger asks, fetching down three mugs from a cabinet.

"Nope," Garth says. "And I'm not sure if anyone will with Illinger already in. He can be such a nasty opponent."

"Nomination deadline's Friday," Sarina says, "so we've got three days to figure out what's what." Sarina's wearing a stylish blouse of apricot silk that perfectly complements her dusky skin and lustrous black hair, the diametric opposite of Ginger's electric white shock.

"Are you still considering the sacrificial lamb approach?" Ginger asks Garth as she places the plate of cookies slightly closer to Sarina than to him and winks. Garth especially favours her low-fat cranberry cookies, which she made a batch of this morning.

"Yep," Garth says, eying the cookies but resisting the temptation to reach. He's made no secret of his resolve that if nobody else comes forward he'll throw his hat into the ring, not with any expectation of winning, but as an opportunity to debate the issues, especially the rumoured incinerator.

"We've got the nomination papers filled out but we won't file until Friday," Sarina says. "Deadline's at noon, so we'll wait and see if anyone else comes forward. No sense in splitting the anti-Illinger vote."

"But you're okay with making a run if it comes to that?" Ginger asks Garth.

"I think it has to be done," he says. "That garbage incinerator's looking more and more like a possibility. Two of the other communities on the short list have already got active campaigns against it. If Illinger wins, our chances of getting stuck with that dioxin spewer go up exponentially. Word is they're looking at the city-owned lands up above Peter's place."

"Oh, Lordy," Ginger sighs, as she brings the mugs of coffee to the table and sits down herself.

"How come the city even owns that land in the first place?" Sarina asks them. "I mean it's miles outside the city limits."

"Quirky bit of business," Ginger says, "and ironically dear old Stone House here is right in the middle of it."

"How's that?" Sarina asks, staring into her coffee as though looking for omens.

"Mr. What's His Name — oh, I can never remember this fellow's name when I need to — you know, the mining man who used to own this place . . ."

"McCracken, wasn't it?" Garth offers.

"That's right!" Ginger says. "John McCracken." Garth's razor-sharp memory for names and dates, though admittedly impressive, can be disconcerting at times.

Garth does a boardinghouse reach for a cookie by way of reward.

"What about him?" Sarina asks, with a whiff of the impatience for backstory minutiae she's shown before.

"Well," Ginger explains, "he was involved with several mining operations back up in the hills."

"Penny ante stuff," Garth snorts dismissively, "probably more speculation than real."

"Whether he was the owner or manager of them, or just what, I'm not sure," Ginger continues, "but he owned that one block at least, well over a thousand acres. They didn't last long, those mines, and maybe their failure was part of what did him in."

"He's the guy who shot himself in Ginger's bedroom," Garth explains to Sarina.

She looks shocked.

"It was his bedroom then, not mine," Ginger clarifies for Sarina's benefit, as though her ancient reputation requires shielding from scandal.

Sarina's *pro forma* smile as much as says You can't help but love old Ginger, but my God she can meander.

"But the point is this," Ginger says, as though she's scented Sarina's thinking, "poor Mr. McCracken, shortly before shooting himself, was taken to court by the city for being delinquent in paying his taxes on this very house. The city won the case and was awarded that big chunk of land as recompense. You'd have thought they'd get the house, but maybe McCracken had friends in high places, or just what, who knows? Anyway the deal was the city got that land."

"Probably not worth more than twenty-five bucks an acre back in those days," Garth says, "so the town fathers never sold it off. Seems to me there was a grand vision that the town might one day expand all the way out there and reap millions from developing it. Ha!"

"And now this," Sarina says.

"Yep," Garth agrees, "our contemporary version of the dream: Pave paradise and put up an incinerator. But there'll be money in it for sure, lots of money. I can hear the blather already: a new municipal swimming pool, a senior's home, a park along the river."

"And no doubt enhanced honoraria for the city fathers," Sarina adds.

"And you know who'll suffer the brunt of it, don't you?" Garth says, putting into words what Ginger's already thinking. "The farmers in that valley, that's who, Peter's farm included. The 'facility' as they always call these kind of shitboxes will be uphill and upwind within a couple of miles of those farms."

"Not to mention the tasty poisons that'll be seeping into their groundwater in no time at all," Sarina says.

"But you can count on them having a boxcar full of technical experts ready to trumpet their *world class* abatement technologies," Garth adds. "Shit smoothers I call them." He rewards himself for this bon mot with another cookie.

"But surely," Ginger says, "beyond the whole issue of pollution, there's the larger issue of waste, of constantly throwing things away, destroying what we've made. I thought we'd started down a better path than that with the recycling and composting programs. This whole burner business feels like two steps forward ten steps back."

The three of them sit silent for a moment, sipping their coffees and considering implications.

"Still, she's not a done deal yet," Garth says, slapping the table lightly.

"Step one is to stop Illinger in his tracks. If we can. Then we go from there."

⊹

Up on the farm at that very moment, Peter finds what he's looking for in a back corner of a lean-to shed appended to the barn generations ago, presumably when expansion was the order of the day. He must have stacked the stuff in here himself but has no memory of doing so, part of the great blur of three years back. He's come up to the farm to tend things while Ron and Lois are in town for the birth. He arrived with no intention of unearthing the old trials hardware but something in Shep's expression had nudged him into it.

He locates a pair of drive gates first, coated in dust and webbed with the silk of spiders. He cleans each off with a rag and carries them out into the sunshine. Shep sniffs at them approvingly. Is it sheep smell on them or perhaps the scent of Cecilia? She'd made the gates herself, Peter remembers, his city slicker wife who didn't know a T-square from a plumb bob but had taken carpentry courses down at the community college and emerged from them a more skilled carpenter than he would ever be. Same way she'd gone off and found old Carlsen, a curmudgeon if ever there was one but damned good with dogs, and charmed him into taking her on as a sheepdog training apprentice. It wasn't single-mindedness on her part either; she tackled the systems of growing, harvesting and processing fruits and vegetables with the same zeal. Beforehand Peter had felt considerable apprehension as to whether his city sophisticate new wife could adapt to farm life, but in no time at all found himself dashing just to keep up with her. The amazing energy, the crackling lust for life that woman had.

She just about split herself in half with delight that spring day when he'd first brought Shep home from the breeder's. "Oh, my God," she'd gushed, "look at those gorgeous eyes!" After Shep's gender was clarified, she'd lifted him with both hands and pressed him to her chest, kissing him wildly. The pup, which had been trembling with fear of the unknown ever since being taken from the kennel, squirmed with excitement in her embrace and licked her neck so that she squealed with ticklish pleasure.

"Talk about bonding," Peter said to her, laughing.

Shep had barely been with them any time at all when Cecilia determined that he was a dog of exceptional brilliance and that she would like to train him to compete at trials. Eventually she sought out old Carlsen and began learning all she could about the training and handling of sheep dogs. Carlsen, who'd never been known to enthuse about much of anything, agreed with her that young Shep sure enough had possibilities.

"You can see it in the eye," the old guy told her, "even at this age, they've either got the eye or they ain't."

Peter wasn't entirely convinced that old Carlsen, a confirmed bachelor and misanthrope, didn't have an eye himself for Cecilia, and who could blame the geezer.

After her carpentry course, Cecilia set about constructing the gates and pens necessary for training a trials dog. Peter and Shep observed from the sidelines with interest. Shep really wasn't old enough yet to get into serious training, but that didn't deter Cecilia. She set up the gates and pens anyway and began what she called her "walk-throughs" with Shep, more fun and games than anything, using a soccer ball for Shep to steer around with his muzzle. All of it accompanied by hysterical shrieks and laughter and much rolling around on the grass. Even old Carlsen, previously unknown to smile for several decades, had a crooked grin on his face watching Cecilia and Shep with their antics.

By the following year, Shep was ready for more serious training, learning his commands and directions, deciphering the differences within her tone of voice or whistles, discovering the convoluted ways of sheep. As Cecilia had intuited, Shep was a natural, mastering increasingly complicated tasks with apparent ease. He had absolute confidence around the sheep and even as a young dog commanded their respect. His "eye" was formidable but never too much. True to his breed, he had an overpowering urge to please Cecilia. He and Peter both.

By the third year Shep had thoroughly mastered the routines of the sheep dog trial and was in everyone's considered opinion ready to enter the regional trials. But only weeks before the trials date, the fatal accident. Everything obliterated at a stroke. Stumbling about in grief, Peter stored the gates and pens in the shed, and that was that.

Brushing more curtains of spider webs away, Peter next pulls out four sections of a pen. She'd designed the pen so that the sides snapped together for quick assembly and disassembly and were light enough for easy carrying. "Spruce wood," she'd said, "light and strong." After she'd erected it in the field she teased him as to whether he thought it was an exhaust pen, a letting out pen or just a regular pen. He'd played along, considering the thing from every angle and finally announcing his certainty that it was a let's-go-make-love pen. "Yes!" she exclaimed, clapping her hands with glee. "That's just what it is!" And just what they did.

As he brings out a second pair of gates, he recalls they played the same silly game a few weeks later when she'd asked him whether he knew which of the pair of gates she'd just constructed were the drive gates and which the fetch gates. He'd told her then he'd like to fetch her and drive her both. "Away to me!" she'd cried out and he'd circled anti-clockwise in front of her. "Come-Bye!" she called and he quickly turned to a clockwise circling, then they collapsed together on the grass kissing and grasping while the pup cavorted madly around them.

He's remembering all this, but today somehow, for a change, more in sweetness than in sorrow.

Shep's having a dreadful dream about goats. There must be half a dozen or more of them, nasty big white things, with bony legs and barrel bodies. Mean creatures. Shep's darting this way and that, trying to get them to move towards Peter. But the goats won't budge. They stare at him with their strange oblong eyes, daring him to get closer. He crouches and advances, giving them the eye, but it has no effect on them. The goats have some ancient, desert-bred stubbornness about them, like thorny plants in harsh places. They lower their heads butting their menacing horns at him. Then take vicious short runs at him, forcing him to retreat. Peter's calling to him but Shep can't make out what directions he's giving. Shep circles this way and that, making quick darts towards the goats, but still they hold their ground, stubborn and willful, daring him to trespass. There's a dreadful smell coming off them, not at all like the lovely lanolin aroma of sheep.

Then suddenly the girl is in the field with them. She is smiling and she holds her notebook out towards Shep. He takes it from her in his jaws and she touches him on the head tenderly. Then she moves towards the goats and they at once begin to file obediently down the field towards Peter. When she turns back to Shep, the girl has become Cecilia. Laughing gaily she kneels on the grass and opens her arms to him. Shep bounds over to her and presses himself into her soft embrace.

Peter's sister Irene has been carefully considering what both her mum and then Peter have told her about the Congregation of the Great Convergence. The church's current legal problems have certainly rekindled her bitterness towards the sect as well as renewed her interest in the future disposition of Stone House. Mistrusting both her brother's and her mother's adeptness, she's been wondering if she shouldn't perhaps become more actively involved in the case.

Meanwhile, she has her own family business to attend to. Sitting in her office, sorting through a dreary list of accounts receivable, she's interrupted by the ringing of her desk phone. Typically, she's feeling a diffuse irritation brought on by the accounts, a sense that people ought to be, well, more accountable. Electricians, plumbers, drywallers — they all seem to her vastly more efficient at prompt billing than at speedily plying their trade. And as to that pack of shysters with their thundering heat pumps . . .

"Mrs. Welch?" a female voice enquires. Tentative. Almost timid.

"Speaking," Irene says firmly.

"I hope I'm not disturbing," the woman offers.

"What can I do for you?" Irene asks, suspecting already it's another worthy cause calling for a handout. Irene and her husband Phil have been more than generous over the years donating to various charities and naturally taking whatever taxation advantages their donations entitled them to. The problem now is, Irene suspects, there's information sharing going on in the back alleys of philanthropy so that any donation anywhere sets you up as a mark for all the other needy groups. Irene doesn't mind donating but she despises being gulled.

"This is a personal matter," the woman says, "and I hope I'm not being indiscreet in calling you at work like this."

"What kind of personal matter?" Irene asks, immediately imagining it's something concerning Crystal or Isha. There's no end of disquieting possibilities on that front, causing Irene frequent premonitions of disaster.

"It concerns your father," the woman says.

Something like a rubber bullet strikes Irene in her chest and she can feel herself wheeze for breath. "My father?" she manages to say.

"Yes," the woman replies.

"I haven't heard a word from or about my father in forty years," Irene says, almost accusingly, as though the caller is running some cruel hoax on her.

"I know," the woman says.

Irene's not quite keeping a grip on herself. This vexatious woman calling about her father. Her *father*! Dear old Nigel whom she's imagined dead, wished dead, for decades. Now this.

"What do you know about my father?" she asks the woman. Perhaps this is his grieving companion calling to inform her that he has just died.

"Only that he's living in a retirement facility over near Clarkston. A quite exclusive sort of place."

Ah. Bloody hell, Irene says to herself. She stares at her list of accounts, the precise and perfect meaninglessness of them.

"You're sure of that?" she asks the caller. "Sure that this person is my father?"

"Absolutely," she says. "Professor Nigel Childes."

"How . . . ?" Irene has a sense of falling from a great height, as she sometimes does in dreams, falling and falling.

The woman hesitates for a beat, as though considering something, then explains. "A cousin of mine works at the facility and came to learn a bit of Professor Childes' story. He obviously mentioned Stone House at some point, and when my cousin told me that, just in passing, you know, as people do, I got to remembering your mother because she had once done a great kindness to my own mother and I admired her so much. Your mother, I mean."

"Yes."

"From what my cousin said, it seemed as though your mother had no idea that the professor was at the lodge, but I had this, you know, funny feeling."

"What sort of funny feeling?" Irene's having a surge of feelings of her own just now, though funny would not be an adequate descriptor.

"Well, it's hard to put into words, really." Again the woman pauses for a moment. "It's just that I had a strange sense that the professor, your father I mean, had said what he said to my cousin because he wanted your mother to know where he was."

"Well, there's far more reliable ways of communicating a message than that," Irene says a bit too tartly.

"Of course," the woman agrees, "and I don't pretend to know the ins and outs of it all, but there was this sense — and my cousin felt the same way — that the professor wanted your mother, or perhaps yourself, to be informed, but in such a way that it was not him doing the informing."

Irene has little patience for this brand of shilly-shallying, but it fits her picture of her father perfectly. A picture coming into sharper and sharper relief by the moment.

"I wasn't sure if your mother was still . . ." the woman pauses, searching for a word, "*active*, if you know what I mean."

"Yes, I know; as it turns out, she's more active than most thirty-year-olds."

"Oh, I'm glad to hear it. But I didn't know, you see. The shock, and so forth, I mean. For an elderly person. I thought it best if I were to approach you with this information first. Perhaps I've overstepped . . ."

"Not at all," Irene says, "it was thoughtful of you to contact me rather than her."

"I do hope you don't imagine I'm meddling in your family's private business."

"No, no, I'm glad you've called, really. It's a bit of a shock is all." The shock Irene's feeling is really a surge of alternating current — a powerful contradiction of misery and elation at the prospect of Nigel returned.

"Yes, I'm sure it is." The woman says nothing further, as though her message has been delivered in full. That she'll intrude no further unless requested.

Irene says nothing either, even though a tempest's raging. Nigel. Fucking *Nigel*!

Neither woman says anything for a bit.

Finally Irene, really not wanting to know, but realizing that she must, asks, "Can you tell me the name of this facility he's in?"

"Of course. It's called Strathmere Lodge."

"Strathmere Lodge," Irene repeats, jotting the name on a scratch pad. "And what's your name, please?"

"Oh, I'd prefer not to say, if that's all right with you."

"Well . . ."

"I'd also prefer that you not tell anyone about this call. Except your mother, of course. I don't want my cousin getting into any kind of difficulty. Patient confidentiality and all of that, you know."

"I understand."

"Thank you. Well, my duty's done," the woman says with a light exhalation of relief.

"You've done me, us, a good service," Irene says, "and I appreciate it, truly. Thank you so much."

"Goodbye," the woman says and the connection goes dead.

Irene sits at her desk and stares at her accounts receivable as though they were Egyptian hieroglyphics. Nigel. Back from the grave. Now what the hell's she going to do?

Chrissie's at home still roaring in her head about Harding's assaulting her when she inadvertently discovers a DVD hidden in a bureau drawer. What the fuck is this? *Here, Pussy, Pussy*. Cover photo of some white babe kneeling naked on a shag carpet, thighs spread wide, hands cupping enormous silicone breasts. What is *this* doing here? Chazz. Goddammit. Chazz. Gullible as Gertie Greenhorn, she scans the cover to see if he's credited for musical score. Ha! No one's credited for anything, at least not by their real names. The lead so-called actors are Tamara Twot and Johnny Cocker. Jebus. The back cover photo shows a group grope in the middle of which — you can hardly make him out because he's got his face between some bitch's thighs — is Chazz. Naked and stupid Chazz.

Chrissie's just about to throw the piece of shit on the floor and stamp it into fractures. Moron! Liar and moron! To sneak behind her back like that. Workin' on some tunes, my ass. She'd kill him now if he dared walk into the room, she'd take a fuckin' carving knife and cut him in a thousand places. Betrayal, that's what it is. Disgusting, lying betrayal. That smarmy smile with his tongue hanging out like some kind of stupid sex toy. And who knows what fuckin' diseases he's picked up. She wants to hurt him, she wants to hurt him more than anything. Illinger was on to it. Yah. She should have listened to him instead of being Miss Spinny Idiot taking Chazz's side. She looks at the photo again. Jesus, what's she going to say to Illinger? First Harding hulking out on her, now this. And behind it all, Illinger waiting to pounce.

But even in her rage and hurt, she doesn't smash the disc as she'd started to do. Some angel seizes her by the arm and prevents her hurling it to the floor. Calming down. Breathing deep. She gets a Kleenex and blows her runny nose. Her mind is kinda blank in a big aloneness. Like that time she arrived in TO with no co-ordinates. But she survived that and she'll survive this. Slowly, strategies begin to shape themselves. Yeah, speaking of Illinger, that disc might just be real useful in the dirty dealing coming up. For starters she'll give Chazz the chance, but only one, to prove that he isn't lying through his teeth to her.

But right here, right now she can't stay in this dump another minute, with Chazz's stench all over it. Creep me out the door. She's gotta get out, get some air. Changed into sweats and trainers, she wheels her bike out into the yard, straddles it and pedals away into the sleeping town. Streets and buildings all a blur, nothing to be seen, nothing remembered, she's completely inside her head, seething.

After an hour's savage cycling she's sorta cooled out and ready to calmly kick some ass. She sees by the house lights that Chazz is back home when she comes wheeling in like an avenging angel.

"Hey, babe," he greets her from the couch. He's got a beer can in his hand and some laughtrack garbage on the TV. "How ya doin'?"

"Fine," she tells him, "just fine."

"Cool," he says, running slim fingers through his long hair, "had an ace night with the boyz."

"Yeah?"

"Coupla new tunes comin' along so fine."

"Uh-huh."

"You okay, babe?" he asks. She's supposed to be all over him by now, kissing and cuddling. He's used to it, come to expect it. King Chazz accepting loving loyalty.

"Fine," she says, in a voice that could split atoms.

"Whazzup, babe?" he asks in a fake-concern voice, but doesn't mute the laugh track.

"You oughta know," she says.

"What's that supposed to mean?" he says, taking a swill of beer as though the meaning didn't matter all that much anyway.

"Chazz," she says, walking towards him, "would you please kill that shit for a minute."

"Sure, babe, no probs." He hits the mute. "What's up?"

"I'm going to ask you just once, Chazz, and I want you to give me a straight answer, okay?"

"Sure." He gives her his best straight shooter look. All she can see is his dorkwad face leering from the cover photo.

"Chazz, tell me: are you in any way involved in the porn industry?"

"Wha? The porn industry? Are you kidding me?" He's got the perfect touch of righteous indignation over the suggestion.

"No, I'm not kidding you, Chazz, I'm askin' you straight up. Yes or no?"

"How could you even ask such a thing?" Now a trace of wounded dignity. He slaps the padded arm of the old couch so that a puff of dust erupts.

"Because your father told me he suspected you might be." Oops. There she's gone and done it, broken her word to Illinger. Opened the doors to the madhouse.

"My father?" Now she's gotten his attention. "Let me get this straight: My father asked *you* if I was into making porn?"

"That's right, Chazz man. He asked me, now I'm asking you." Chrissie's amazing herself at how steely she's being through this. "I said I'd ask just once; now, for the third time: yes or no."

She can see Chad's mind tripping all over itself trying to find a lie that will work for both her and his father.

"Why didn't he ask me directly?" Chazz says, stalling for time.

"That's between you and him. This is between you and me."

"Cool. So just *between you and me*," Chazz punches the words with a sarcastic emphasis, "the answer is *No*. And you can tell my father that too, since you seem to have taken on the role of his spy."

Chrissie recognizes the pattern, the rich boy's instinct for deflecting criticism by righteous counterattack.

"So you deny it?"

"Yes, I deny it. Categorically. Now kindly get off my case, why don't you?" When he's angry Chazz tends to talk more like the lawyer his father intended him to be.

Chrissie isn't going to fight about it because it doesn't matter any more. He doesn't matter any more. He doesn't care enough about her to even tell her the truth. Fuck him.

She goes into the bedroom and pulls her backpack out of the stuffed closet. She's halfway through packing her gear into it when Chazz comes into the room.

"What're ya doin, babe?" Now it's the innocent little boy routine.

"I'm packing, Chazz."

"You leavin'?" Over the top incredulity.

"That's right."

"How come?"

"Because you're lying to me, because you're nothing better than a third-rate Johnny Cocker."

"Oh, shit. So you found the disk."

"Yeah, I found it. And I gave you the chance to come clean on it, Chazz. But you blew it. You just fuckin' lied. Straight to my face you lied and treated me like I was some spying bitch. Which I'm not. I'd never spy on you and then rat you out to your father or anyone else. Because I think like love means you don't do that shit. But you have. And you're not even fuckin' sorry." She's promised herself not to fight with him about it, and here she is doing just that. She stuffs a couple of shirts into the bag. She can feel tears misting the back of her eyes like steam on glass.

"Babe, listen to me," Chazz says, dripping sincerity as he draws near, reaching out for her, "I can explain."

"You're going to explain Tamara Twot to me Chazz?"

"Oh, come on, gimme a break! Look: I would have told you, I would have talked it over with you, course I would, except for my fucking father."

"Uh-huh."

"Look, I knew you wouldn't care about it, you're so cool, but that he'd go ape shit if he found out. And you're in a vulnerable position, right? He could easily pressure you into telling, if you knew. So I thought it was better for you not to know, not to be put in that position. I was only trying to protect you, babe, because you matter so much to me. Really. Babe, look at me. Look at a dude who's crazy in love."

Chazz is so good at this, she like almost fuckin' falls for it. But then, out of nowhere, she's remembering how she cried and cried up at Stone House. After the dog. Realizing how scared and alone she really was. Needing kindness and gentleness. The old lady's loving hands. Something poured out of her and left her changed that day. She knew it too. Before that, right, she would have gone for Chazz's BS, thrown herself at him like always. Forgiven and forgotten. They'd have fucked crazy on the floor to seal the deal. Not any more. Zero chance. Whether it's Chazz or Harding or whoever, she's like done with the humiliation game. She's done being bullied and lied to. She finishes up her packing, probably forgetting all sorts of stuff, sniffling back the tears she's determined not to cry, at least not now, while Chazz grovels and wheedles to try to make her change her mind. One thing she doesn't forget to take is the DVD.

She doesn't even say goodbye at the door. She just slings on her backpack, mounts her bike and pedals off into the night.

Eight

Shortly after Ginger left Stone House for college her parents had shocked her with a sudden disclosure. For as long as she could remember, her parents, Mr. & Mrs. Dustin Flynn to the outer world, had been staunch adherents of a particularly dour sect of evangelical Protestantism. They had required that Ginger honour its stern precepts too, until her sixteenth birthday, at which point she was free to do as she chose. As a child, unaware of alternatives, Ginger hadn't resented the stifling piety, with its instinctive distrust of a world best avoided during the grim trudge towards redemption beyond the grave, but she had gradually come to see it as oppressive and, once given her freedom, had jettisoned its trappings as best as she could. Years would pass before she fully understood that a thoroughgoing religious upbringing, however absurd it may eventually appear, is seldom entirely extirpated either by cogent argument or conflicting passion. Do what you will, bits and pieces of the old coda cling in unexpected crannies like intertidal creatures hidden when the tide retreats.

Having gone her own way in matters of faith, if not morality, Ginger took it as a given that her parents would continue to plod along the narrow and stony path from which she'd never known them to diverge. But then a letter arrived from her mother. It was the first such letter she'd ever received and she was unsure what to expect, but she imagined it would hold the familiar platitudes and nostrums in which her mother dealt. Ginger casually slit the envelope open while sitting at her dorm desk.

Stone House
28 September 1949

Dear Ginger,

Your father and I do hope that you are well settled in at the College. Poor old Stone House certainly feels that much emptier without you here.

Nevertheless, we are doing well, and we have some unexpected but quite wonderful news to report. After a very great deal of prayer and reflection, your father and I have made the very difficult decision to leave the Church of Christ Triumphant in favour of a new denomination.

Ginger could scarcely believe what she'd just read. She went over the previous two sentences again to be sure. But, yes, there it was.

I know this may come as a bit of a shock to you, dear, as we have been devoted followers of the Church for many years, as were your father's parents before us. And, as you can appreciate, we would not remove ourselves from the Church on just any flimsy pretext. However, we have been called to what we fully believe is a higher spiritual station in life.

We have joined a relatively new ecclesial community known as The Congregation of the Great Convergence. It has as its fundamental tenet that all the great religions of the world, the Hindus and Muslims and Buddhists and all the rest, even the Jews, are destined to unite in one great fellowship under the ascendancy of Our Lord Jesus Christ. Your father and I are inspired by this message, for surely it is the one and only path to ending the dreadful divisions and conflicts like the one that claimed poor Frankie and leading us together to the Paradise our Saviour has promised.

Ginger laid the letter on her desk for a moment and considered what her mother was telling her. Remarkable. The old church thrown over and this new one taken up with its outlandish ambitions. For the first time Ginger saw her parents — her steady, successful and respectable parents — doing something entirely erratic. She read on.

The Congregation is represented locally by a most extraordinary person, the Reverend Jaimie Hinkus. He has been sent to us from the southern United Sates, Alabama, I believe, to assist in establishing the Congregation here. His preaching is a wonder, so is his laying on of hands. We are without a proper chapel in this initial phase, so your father and I have made the library at Stone House available for our Sunday gatherings. It's a glory to feel so much vibrant faith echoing through the old place for one day of the week at least.

So, Ginger concluded, they've fallen under the influence of a fabulist, a term she'd only recently heard from one of her professors. Laying on of hands, indeed. Are they talking in tongues too?

Well, dear, I must close for now. I do hope that you appreciate our enthusiasm for this dramatic turn of events. I shall keep you posted on our progress.

In the meanwhile, your father and I wish you all the best with your studies.

Your loving mother,
Mrs. Dustin Flynn

Ginger was unsure what, if anything, she should say in response to this news. Over the next several months, she received three more letters from her mother each one echoing the message of this first. Had she not been so preoccupied with her studies and above all with the gravitational pull of Professor Childes, Ginger might have taken their significance more seriously, perhaps become alarmed. But her parents' concerns seemed now to belong to a segregated time and place, some vague and hazy otherness in which she no longer had, or wanted to have, any significant position.

But then came the difficulty of Christmas. She was expected to be home for the holidays. As well, dear Jonathan, faithful to her despite the increasing aloofness she'd shown him by inadequately replying to his ardent letters, continued to press her on activities they might enjoy together over the holidays. But all of her desire surged towards Nigel. They had not yet become lovers in the fullest sense, and certainly not in any public way, but they had tumbled into a secret and passionate intimacy. In her heart they were all but inseparable. He would be on his own for the holidays and part of her — to be honest, all of her — wanted to be with him and no one else. But she was expected at Stone House. For a mad moment she thought of taking him home with her, but of course that was impossible. Eventually she struck upon a compromise of sorts: she could invite him, not as a house guest, but just for dinner on Christmas day. Her mother raised no objection. A Cambridge gentleman professor overseas far from his own family, and someone who'd known Frank briefly during the war. Of course, darling. Ginger, naturally, had not shown to her parents Frankie's final letter. Not with that explosive closing note of affection. So it was arranged that Nigel would travel to Shetterly independently, stay at a local hotel and appear brimming with innocence at Stone House on the afternoon of Christmas Day.

On Christmas Eve, as Ginger was helping her mother set the table in the dining room, she noticed there were six place settings rather than four.

"Who else are we expecting?" she asked her mother.

"Oh, didn't I mention it, darling?" her mother said with a guileless smile. "How thoughtless of me. Yes, we've invited Reverend Hinkus and his wife to join us for dinner. Like your professor friend, they too are far from home and family."

"Oh." Ginger immediately sniffed trouble. Ever since her arrival home she'd been worrying about Nigel's presence here. What her parents would think of him. Worse, what he would think of them. She realized how badly she'd underestimated the gulf between Nigel's values and theirs. She had forewarned Nigel prior to the visit, even while knowing that he was not a person apt to heed forewarnings. Indeed, a perverse part of him enjoyed flaunting forewarnings. She intensely hoped that he would conceal from her parents the disdain that he would almost certainly feel, that the charm he could turn on like a faucet when it suited him would overcome all, as it usually did. But now the presence of the preacher and his wife complicated things. Nigel, she knew full well, considered all forms of sectarianism abhorrent. She recognized too late what a mistake it was to have invited him.

"Plus," her mother continued, while meticulously aligning seven silver candlesticks in the centre of the table, "Reverend Hinkus will conduct a short service in the library at ten-thirty in the morning. You're free to join us, of course, dear, and I think you might actually find it rather edifying. He's a most remarkable preacher."

Ginger did attend the morning service, less from piety than from a pressing need to get some measure of this character who'd so thoroughly captivated her parents. When she slipped into the library there were fewer than twenty congregants in attendance, a nondescript collection of mostly elderly folks, few of whom Ginger recognized. Chairs brought in from the drawing room and dining room were arranged in a semicircle. The atmosphere was more solemn than celebratory. She sat beside her father while everyone quietly awaited the preacher's entrance. He came in like a winter wind, a largish man with beefy face and close-cropped hair, wearing an off-the-rack suit. Without preliminaries, he took as his text a verse from the prophet Isaiah "*The look on their faces testifies against them; they parade their sin like Sodom; they do not hide it. Woe to them! They have brought disaster upon themselves.*"

With a sudden stab, Ginger realized it was herself he was describing, shamelessly parading her sin like Sodom. Bringing her illicit lover into this house on a holy day for which he had only amused contempt. While she roiled with a shame she knew to be ridiculous, the preacher continued his tirade. There was precious little of Christmas in it, no angelic hosts or Wise Men or any of the standard piffle. He was all fire and brimstone, this fellow, working himself up into a near-hypnotic trance. He battered the poor congregants into repentance, demanded they renounce their evil ways and come forward for a laying on of hands through which the Evil One would be exorcised. One by one the congregants crept forward, all looking incapable of much vice beyond miserableness. The Revered Jaimie seized each of them in turn by the head with both hands and bellowed at the Evil One to depart. Ginger was amazed and horrified at the spectacle. But then her parents rose to join the file of supplicants and she knew she could not, would not submit herself to this degrading sham. She rose too and quickly left the room.

How had her parents ever succumbed to such transparent nonsense? Their former church had been a grim bit of business, God knows, but at least it retained a dignified coherence within its narrow confines. But this! This brash cracker tub-thumping. This simple-minded biblical biliousness. She couldn't get her brain around what she'd just witnessed. Comprehension simply collapsed around it. She excused herself from lunch and went for a long walk through the deserted town. Along every chilly street, things seemed to be snickering at her — pigeons on the sidewalk, crows on the wires overhead, even the shop window mannequins — all were having a good snigger at her expense. Small-town fool! Daughter of simpletons! She wished like anything that she knew where Nigel would be staying as she realized it was imperative that she talk to him before his arrival for dinner. Otherwise a sword-fight might break out before the first course was finished. At least he hadn't been there for that sordid exhibition this morning; she could hardly imagine the level of his contempt for it.

After walking for several miles around familiar old neighbourhoods, she lingered along the banks of the shrunken river that meandered forlornly through town. Several abandoned shopping carts lay sideways in its muddy swirl. She dreaded the dinner ahead and realized with perfect clarity that she must dissociate herself completely from this imbecilic cult, that perhaps she must cut her parents loose too, in order to retain Nigel's respect. Not to mention her self-respect. She would betray her parents in her heart. Eventually forced by the damp winter chill to move, she returned to Stone House only shortly before Nigel was due to arrive.

But dinner proved not near the debacle she'd feared. Nigel, impeccably attired in a bespoke Brooks Brothers suit, arrived with a bottle of brandy and a round of aged cheddar, both produced, he announced, by Benedictine monks who had the good sense to devote as much of their time to fermentation and distillation as meditation. Undeterred by the brittle silence that greeted this jest, he showed the greatest deference to Ginger's parents and spoke enthusiastically about various architectural and artistic features of the house. Even the hideous paintings in the drawing room were acknowledged for their spiritual strength of purpose. Ginger's father, who still taught at a small Christian college in town, tried but failed to establish any pedagogical common ground with her professor. Ginger had never seen him quite so threadbare as he now seemed alongside Nigel.

As though by unspoken agreement, Frank's name was never mentioned.

When the Reverend Jaimie Hinkus and his wife arrived, it was soon obvious that there would be no great clash of values between Nigel and the preacher. For all his theological thunder from the pulpit, the Reverend Jaimie was quite passive in social interactions and proved a surprisingly sedate dinner companion, deferring constantly to his wife, a sharp-eyed lady whose first name was not disclosed. Somewhat younger than her husband, she spoke in clipped Southern absolutes and appeared not to hear anything said by anyone other than her husband. Alongside Nigel, who was not showboating by any means but certainly carrying the conversation with wit and elan, the two older couples seemed to Ginger to compose a quartet of irrelevant church mice.

Afterwards she walked Nigel to the door and thanked him for coming. She wanted to say how grateful she was to him, how proud of him, and . . .

"Wouldn't have missed it for the world," he said, winking archly. He'd had several glasses of the blessed brandy, as, surprisingly, had the Reverend Jaimie Hinkus under the watchful eye of his wife.

"God, I need to talk to you in the worst kind of way," Ginger whispered.

"See you soon," Nigel said giving her a demure peck on the cheek and taking his leave.

⊁⊀

Five months later, with the school year drawing to a close, Ginger and Nigel decided they would marry. For Ginger, the alternative — the prospect of returning to Stone House for the summer, of being apart from Nigel for three months — was insufferable. Her conscience would not allow her to copulate with a man to whom she was not married, but neither would her passion endure restraint much longer. She wanted him, all of him, in every way. And so they decided to marry once the term was over.

Nigel undertook the necessary discussions with the authorities. Not entirely pleasant deliberations, they concluded with an agreement that Ginger would withdraw from the college and Nigel could continue teaching. A few of the trustees would as soon have given him the heave-ho, but his popularity within the student body, and the certainty that another school would snap him up the moment he became available, convinced the majority that they could live with this unseemly interlude, which would blow over in due course anyway.

Ginger was slightly delirious, jouncing between the disappointment of abandoning her studies and the elation of becoming Nigel's wife. She returned to Shetterly on a bright May afternoon, not to spend the summer as had previously been planned, but to announce to her parents that she would marry within a few weeks. She knew the news would not be welcome. After the Christmas visit, which Ginger had thought went reasonably well, there'd been a bit of a scene with her mother, mostly concerning the bringing of brandy into the house. Letters from her mother during the subsequent months invariably contained subtle, and sometimes not so subtle, aspersions against Nigel. Gradually it became apparent that the Reverend Jaimie Hinkus, too, did not approve of what was called Nigel's "worldliness." Now the unexpected wedding announcement blew the lid off everything. Her father stood up without a word and retired to his study to mark papers. Was he offended that Nigel hadn't asked his permission? Or had the revelation that the professor had actually seduced one of his students confirmed Mr. Flynn's worst suspicions? Or was he just an embittered oldster envious of the younger man's rising star?

Retreating to the kitchen, Ginger and her mother had a whispered but heated exchange such as they'd seldom had before. "Listen to me, darling," Mrs. Flynn had warned, "you're doing yourself no favours throwing in your lot with that fine fellow. He loves himself far more than he'll ever love you. His cynicism your father and I find particularly distasteful. That oh-so-sophisticated contempt for mere commoners like us."

Even though there was a distant ring of truth in what her mother was saying, Ginger thought the accusations categorically unfair. "That's not cynicism, Mother," she said, "he has a wonderfully refined wit is all, everyone on campus says so."

"Well, everyone on campus can say whatever they please. I'm telling you that if you hitch your wagon to that particular star you'll find yourself being dragged into some very unpleasant places. Believe me, for all his cleverness, that's not a fellow any decent Christian girl would want to have for a husband."

Ginger continued defending her decision, her love for Nigel, his integrity. She was not accustomed to being in conflict with her parents and resisted the temptation to describe how laughable a fraud she found the Reverend Jaimie Hinkus. She was aware, as her mother seemed not to be, that the two of them each had her champion and that of the two Nigel was incontestably the superior. That was the unspoken truth of the Christmas dinner, that Nigel had so outshone the preacher as to make him seem trivial. That Nigel's clever atheism appeared somehow more admirable than the Reverend Jaimie's plodding faith. This is what could not be brooked.

"Well it's your life, darling, and you're free to do with it whatever you choose," her mother said, rising from her chair to indicate that everything needing to be said had been said. "But you certainly can't expect to have our blessing for this disastrous decision."

Ginger had badly wanted their blessing beforehand, but by this point she perceived the gulf between them and knew that blessings were impossible. And now she no longer wanted it. She wanted nothing from them but separation.

Her visit was cut short. Her father would scarcely say goodbye. Her mother seethed like a pot of prunes. Ginger was relieved to get away from Stone House and its atmosphere of sanctimonious claustrophobia, but her parents' sourness was not so easily escaped.

The following week a letter arrived at school in her mother's elegant hand. Ginger opened it with apprehension.

Stone House
29 May, 1950

Dearest Ginger,

Your father and I have made some quite significant decisions that we thought it best to convey to you straight away. Your announcement last week that you intend to marry your professor friend, unwelcome as it was, has proved a blessed spur for us to do what we have long dreamed of doing but postponed for your sake. God moves in mysterious ways indeed.

Now that you have struck out upon an entirely independent course (one with which, as you know, we strenuously disagree) your father and I feel free to pursue a lifelong ambition to undertake missionary work in Africa, in the region of the Congo specifically, where the Congregation of the Great Convergence maintains several missionary stations.

Ginger could scarcely believe what she was reading. Her parents? Going off to Africa to convert poor heathens? They might as well sail to Antarctica and preach to the penguins. She read on:

Arrangements are already underway, though there's a frightful amount of preparation required, vaccines and visas and all that sort of thing. Nevertheless, we've booked passage on a ship departing in several months. Needless to say, we are wonderfully inspired by the prospect of doing God's work in that forsaken place.

In a similar vein, your father and I have made a decision on the disposition of Stone House. As you surely remember, we frequently discussed how perfect a place it would be for a religious centre of some sort, whether as a retirement home for returning missionaries and former ministers, or perhaps an evangelical training centre of some type, bringing in eminent speakers and so forth. Indeed these ambitions played a considerable, if not entirely conscious, part in our acquiring Stone House in the first place, and they have been greatly fortified by our joining the Congregation. Since we do not anticipate returning to Stone House ourselves within the foreseeable future, if ever, we are making arrangements through our attorney, Mr. Gilpin, for you to retain a life tenancy at Stone House, should you so wish, and upon your demise, or your prior termination of the life tenancy, for Stone House to become the exclusive property of our Congregation to be used for purposes such as those just mentioned.

Your father and I trust that neither of these decisions will come as a shock to you, as we have all had more then enough shocks this week already.

Do write when you have a minute, darling.

Your loving mother,
Maureen Flynn

Ginger carefully refolded the letter and slipped it back into its envelope. Such a sudden tearing down of everything! Having lost her brother, which had been more ghastly than anything, she was now to lose her parents and the family home. So much for permanence. The established order of things to which she'd been born and raised. An implicit expectation that certain values were timeless, that traditions and conventions would continue to endure as they had endured. A place where the footing was firm and roots ran deep. All gone. Old moorings and hold-fasts swept away. Partly of her own doing, no question about it. Her infatuation with a man who didn't at all fit into the old paradigm. She had chosen quite deliberately to break away, but now the breakage was far more severe than she'd imagined. And the pain of losing Stone House! To have it eventually pass over to that grasping Congregation rather than remain in the family. The rightful inheritance of the children she and Nigel might have. It was unjust, entirely unjust and mean-spirited. She almost hated her mother at that moment. To lose both your home and your family as punishment for stepping so slightly out of line. Africa would teach them a thing or two, she was sure of it. And almost gleeful at the prospect, she felt a spasm of sorrow seize her, whether for her credulous parents or for her own abandonment or for the detestable ways of the world she didn't know. Aloneness, that's what she sensed. That she was now truly alone in the world. Except for Nigel.

But once beyond initial shock, beyond the anger and sorrow, she felt not so much abandoned as released. Notwithstanding her mother's warnings, Ginger felt herself set free. Nigel would suffice, she knew he would.

Nine

Peter's busy at work setting up the trials gates and pens in a meadow down near the road. The meadow grasses shimmer with a blinding green brightness; the hedgerows are alive with nesting birds. He's still at the farm because Lois and Ron have had to go to a larger hospital in the city. Their newborn son is not doing well, something involving antibodies in his blood. Ron had been near to sobbing and not very coherent explaining it over the phone. After fishing for words of sympathy he felt but couldn't adequately express, Peter had told Ron that of course he'd be happy to look after the farm for however long it took, his own aged sorrow less pressing than the younger man's anxiety. So here he is, in the middle of a meadow on a brilliant spring morning, setting up his lost wife's pens and gates, for reasons he doesn't himself understand, but delighting in the feel of her deft fingers in every hinge and latch, her strength of purpose in each driven brass screw.

Shep is a more than willing participant, paying no attention at all to several plump sheep lazing around on the far side of a fence. For both man and dog this reassembly of the mothballed trials equipment has taken on the solemnity of ritual, a conjuring of sorts that might entice the spirit of Cecilia from wherever she lingers nearby. She would come with the child in her arms.

Ron's news of their newborn's troubles has naturally started Peter remembering his own daughter's birth here in the farmhouse. Cecilia had been quite adamant about a home birth. A hospital was out of the question and even Stone House, which was far closer to help in case of an emergency, had not appealed. She wanted to be on the farm attended to by her beloved midwife Sarah. "Nothing will go wrong," she insisted, "my whole body is telling me that this is the way to do it and that nothing whatsoever will go wrong. I understand your concern, Peter, but really I have to trust what my body's telling me."

Although Ginger would have loved to have the proceedings at Stone House, she backed Cecilia completely in her choice. They were a pair those two, his mum and Cecilia, almost like sisters in a peculiar way, ripe with subtle woman's mischief. He didn't have a snowball's chance against the two of them, and so a home birth it would be and at the farm it would be; he'd just have to swallow his anxieties about the safety of the newborn and the health of its mother. Even old Carlsen the dog trainer, who'd become something of a regular around the place, such was his devotion to Cecilia, had put his two cents' worth in.

"Them wimmin knows what's needed," he'd told Peter. "It's in their blood, all this birthing stuff. No point you or me tryin' to tell 'em anything. What the hell do we know about any of it anyway?"

Peter felt he did know quite a bit about it actually. He'd dutifully attended pre-natal classes with Cecilia, learned and practised the breathing techniques, massages and other laying on of hands, prepared himself for the timely fetching of hot water and towels and all the rest of it. Despite all of which he was scared half out of his mind as her due date approached. What if? What if? Niggling doubts and anxieties trailed around behind him all day as insistent as imprinted ducklings.

Shep, on the other hand, no longer a pup but not yet quite an adult, was far less anxious even while being painstakingly watchful. He was inseparable from Cecilia, but without becoming a nuisance under foot, accompanying her everywhere and contributing moral support whenever required. He'd readily learned to fetch her slippers or a magazine, never giving a smidgeon of indication that he'd prefer to be fetching sheep.

Sarah the midwife arrived by bicycle during a brief summer squall. "Rainbows!" she called, bursting through the back door. "Did you ever see more beautiful rainbows!"

Cecilia was sprawled on the bed in the downstairs bedroom, her contractions becoming more frequent, but even so, Peter and Sarah abandoned her for a moment to look outside. They stared in wonder at the enormous double rainbow, both arcs radiant with vivid colours, the lower of the two touching the ground at either end. Peter immediately drew back the sheer curtains in the bedroom so that Cecilia could catch a glimpse of them. Between contractions she smiled beatifically.

"Now, if ever there was a good omen for a birth," Sarah declared as she bustled into the bedroom, "that has to be it!" A large and robust woman, Sarah lived with her husband and three kids at a nearby farm. She and Cecilia had become pals even before the pregnancy, Sarah being one of the knowledgeable locals from whom Cecilia was eager to learn the skills and secrets of the farming life.

The midwife now went about her preparations with brisk efficiency and a business-as-usual attitude. Peter sat at the edge of the bed, holding one of Cecilia's hands between his own and doing his best to ignore the demons of fear that were assailing him. So as not to be in the way, Shep retired to a corner of the room and sat attentively, his dark eyes seldom straying from Cecilia. Peter winced each time a contraction wracked his wife with pain, and as the pangs intensified he began wanting it all to stop, wildly he wanted to reverse everything, to not have her moaning and agonizing this way. His sympathetic breathing seemed idiotic, his attempts at reassurance no better than saccharine platitudes. With all that money at his disposal, what was he doing having his wife enduring labour in a run-down farmhouse miles from anywhere, completely dependent upon a good-hearted but uneducated farmer's wife. He was near to panic, knowing they should be at a hospital with surgeons on call just in case . . . in case . . . oh, Christ, he couldn't stop imagining all of what could go wrong. Then after what seemed like hours of mounting crisis, finally, mercifully, that explosive, swelling moment of release as the newborn slid smoothly into Sarah's waiting hands while Cecilia gave a great moaning sigh as though the Earth itself had given birth. Exhalations of relief, all pain and fear swept from the room by gusts of joy. Giddy and unbelieving, Peter kissed Cecilia tenderly on her sweat-soaked forehead, then they laughed, sobbing, staring with wonder at their tiny newborn daughter.

Ginger arrived early the next morning, laden with foodstuffs, of course, relieved that the birth had suffered no complications (she had kept to herself her doubts about the wisdom of a home birth so far from emergency services) and near bursting with love for her new grandchild as well as her son and his lovely partner. It was without question one of the most perfect days that she had ever known.

That Cecilia was a treasure though wasn't she. How Peter ever found her. Then lost her. Found and lost and still lost. Why the best and the brightest must die. Who can truly believe in a loving God when everything goes so wrong. Poor little KG, Katherine Ginger they called her. Honouring the mothers Cecilia said, her own mother and myself. I called her Cagey for fun. So beautiful. I could stare at her for hours, same as Sophia when she was just a babe. How her tiny fingers moved and her little lips puckering and blowing. You could get silly; I did get silly. First with my own and then again with Cagey. A child is born. How blissful Cecilia seemed nursing the little one, and Peter beaming. Husband and father with the whole world at his fingertips. He's got the whole world in his. World of Wonder. I wonder as I wander. Finally coming into himself, who he was meant to be. He was beautiful too as a babe, the only thing that kept me going with Nigel gone. Thou art Peter and upon this . . . But no it couldn't hold. Even a joy so deep and true couldn't stand against . . . That dreadful accident. Far worse than Nigel absconding, even worse than Frankie getting killed. That gorgeous child and her lovely mother. Snuffed out in the blink of . . . Of all the sorrows

maybe the worst. Deep in earth my love is lying and the world's more full of weeping. We wore ourselves away with weeping.

⊁⊀

After leaving Chazz the chump pornographer, Chrissie's got nowhere to crash. She doesn't have any real friends of her own, just a few Janes attached to the guys in the band. Which says something too. Like pathetic. Don't matter to her, though, she'd just as soon sleep in a dumpster as in a bed with the all-star broken condom, but still. She's gotta be at work first thing tomorrow morning and can't show up with maggots in her hair, so decides to take a cheap motel room. She's got enough cash to cover it. Just. Plus, some money in the bank. She'll be okay. Like that time she landed in TO and fell right in with Sol. Good old Sol. And dumped him for this asshole. Yag.

She picks up a Subway sandwich and checks into a slimy motel just off the main drag. She's so scrambled in her head she hardly knows what she's doing. Like sleepwalking or something. Before you know it, there's a man shouting at her about mattresses, but it's only the radio alarm's gone off prodding her to get up and go to work. She showers in tepid water, knowing it'll never get any hotter, but happy anyway to be washing stuff off her, getting clean.

Back on her bike, cycling across town, Chrissie likes the look of the new day dawning. Thin ghosts of mist are lifting off the river and the bold springtime sun, still low in the sky, is painting golden false fronts on old red-brick buildings downtown. Could be the Rocky Mountains at dawn, could be Newfoundland or someplace. Even with the heavy pack on her back, she's feeling light and smooth. Gliding. Like when she ran away from her mum's. Only not scared now. But released in a way. Yah. Released.

She's high as a kite by the time she gets to the office parking lot. And then Thump! There's Illinger's car. And Harding's. Shit.

As Chrissie wheels her bike in the front door, Brenda at reception cocks her head towards Harding's office and makes an ugly face. Chrissie nods her thanks and unslings the pack off her back, stashing it alongside her bike. Normally Brenda would make some crack about "was Chrissie running away from home or something," but not this morning. Chrissie had thought about maybe asking Brenda if she could crash at her place for a few days, but she knows Brenda's got a young daughter with Down's syndrome, which is plenty to deal with all by itself.

Muffled male voices sound through Harding's closed door as Chrissie makes her way to her cubicle. She powers up her desktop and sets to work on a piece she's doing about the local food bank but her mind keeps missing links like a worn sprocket. She knows she's just marking time until something gives. Like those whaddaya-call-em tectonic plates that grind and grind together until something suddenly gives way. Then there's a quake and everyone's screaming.

She senses rather than hears Harding's office door open.

"Good morning, Chrissie," Harding says to her as though nothing happened. Except it did and she can see it written all over him, that oily passive aggressive cowardice. "Mr. Illinger would like a word," he says.

Chrissie gets up without saying anything and strides briskly into the office, finding Illinger once again perched primly on the couch in suit and tie.

"Ah, Chrissie," he says dryly, "do please close the door, will you."

Chrissie clicks the door shut and takes a few steps forward.

"Please," Illinger says with a pale smile, "sit here." His open hand pats the couch seat alongside him.

Chrissie would prefer to stand, but sits down anyway. She has nothing to fear from Illinger.

"Well," he says to her in his quiet, grey voice, "it appears you've been rather active in the last little while."

"Yeah, I rode my bike to work," Chrissie says, though she knows it's not what he means. She's learned to ignore the insinuations that slither around most of what Illinger has to say.

"Most commendable," Illinger says, "all this bike riding. Helping save the planet and so forth."

That's the kind of slops Chrissie knows to ignore. The sneer beneath. Again she's amazed at how calm Illinger remains; his voice, his posture, his entire manner is like mega-controlled. The whole time he's looking straight ahead, not at her, as though there was a movie playing on the opposite wall. Chrissie keeps her own focus on Illinger's small white hands, lying like fungi on the dark cloth of his suit pants. She doesn't look at his eyes but can see them anyway, the palest blue, like ancient ice. She waits for him to play his next card.

"I understand you've left Charles, is that correct?"

So he knows already. Chazz must have called him. And told him what?

"I realize your private affairs are really none of my business, except insofar as my son is concerned, of course, but do you mind my asking why."

Chrissie does mind, but it's like minding that a snake has venom. "Certain things happened," she tells Illinger, "and we decided we'd both be better off not being together."

"*We* decided?" Illinger echoes her words caustically. "My understanding is that *you* walked out on him; that he begged you to stay and you refused."

From day one Illinger has wanted her and Chazz broken up; now it's happened and he's all Mr. Weeping Violins. Gimme a fuckin' break.

"Depends which way you look at it," Chrissie says.

"Meaning?"

"Meaning you could say Chazz walked out on me."

"Could you?"

"Yep," Chrissie says. And you could say a whole lot more, she's thinking, but won't. Not right now anyway.

Illinger pauses for a minute, his thin lips doing a weird puckering thing. "You remember our last little conversation?" he asks her.

"Of course."

"Since I heard nothing from you, I assumed nothing came of it. Was I correct in that assumption?"

This is the hard spot from Chrissie's angle. How much to tell Illinger. What use he'll make of whatever she says. Whether against her, or Chazz. Or both. Would it be smarter to keep the info to herself, maybe use it later somehow. She's really not any good at this kind of shit. Before she can decide what to say, Illinger carries on.

"You do know that I have entered my name as candidate for mayor in the upcoming election?" he asks.

"Uh-huh," she says.

"And, needless to say, I would prefer not to have any embarrassing facts come to light during the course of my campaign."

"Yeah, I can understand that."

"Things, for example, like the issue I raised with you previously. About Charles."

"Yep."

"I would have imagined that it was perhaps that very issue that might have triggered your severing the relationship."

Chrissie doesn't bite.

Illinger pauses for a moment, considering. Chrissie focuses on the blue veins running down the backs of his hands, imagines intersecting highways on a map. Getting away.

"Let me be perfectly blunt with you, Chrissie," Illinger says, clearing his throat. "Charles tells me that you left him after he confronted you about your engaging in certain debased activities."

"What?" Chrissie jerks forward on the couch. This has caught her completely off-guard. "*Me?*"

"Needless to say," Illinger continues calmly, and you can tell he thinks he's scored a hit, "I would have discounted the allegations as no more than the vindictiveness of a jilted lover, except . . ."

"Except what?"

"Except that Mr. Harding has just now to some degree corroborated what Charles had told me."

"Harding? What does he know about anything?" Chrissie's got a jumpy sensation like of bad guys popping up from behind tumbled walls all around her. Sniper's alley.

"Mr. Harding knows you far more intimately than I do, Chrissie, and has had more extensive opportunity to observe your various behaviours. There's no easy way to say this, but honesty compels me to reveal that he has, however reluctantly, reported your making what can only be called lewd and suggestive advances to him."

"What the fuck?" Chrissie says, not meaning to. Harding. The lying pervert. After mauling her like that. Chrissie wishes she had video of that little episode too. Or his slobbering all over her.

"To a happily married man, Chrissie, a devoted husband," Illinger says, primly sanctimonious.

Chrissie's ready to barf. So that's the game. Chazz using her as a firewall. Harding covering his fat ass. And Illinger manipulating everyone. They're going to hang her out to dry, so they think, the innocent gang of three. She shoulda seen it comin, dammit. She's not fast enough for this game, maybe not mean enough either. Shit.

"Nevertheless," Illinger continues in the same grey monotone, "I still find it hard to imagine your engaging in the degraded activities Charles alluded to, but I must hear from you clearly and honestly whether or not this was the cause of the rupture. Otherwise, as I'm sure you appreciate, I cannot risk the scandal of having you in my employ."

That fuckin' Chazz, Chrissie's thinking. What a dirty, stinkin' trick. She can't believe he'd use her like that, like a piece of janky garbage.

"Well," Illinger says calmly, "what do you have to say for yourself?"

⁂

Ginger's sitting alone in the breakfast nook reading Chrissie's article about Stone House in the *Standard*. It's the only old-style paper she subscribes to, preferring to browse the web for news of the world at large. She used to use her desktop, which always felt rather like work, but now she's got the tablet Peter bought her, which allows her to roam across the universe from the comfort of her window seat. Riots in Cairo, the ravages of drought in Sudan, North Korea's nuclear ambitions: all appear miraculously at the touch of her fingertip. Instant, and awful, but ephemeral somehow, constantly changing, flickering away at a touch, almost without substance. Although the daily mayhem intrudes at every opportunity, she prefers longer range perspectives, measured reflections on the themes and revelations to be found beneath the noise. Mostly she craves considerations of forgiveness and compassion. So she keeps an eye on the Dalai Lama, Desmond Tutu and similar brave saints who continually emerge like small islands of hope amid the mayhem.

Forgiving yourself first off. Why is that so confoundedly difficult? Hardest of all. Easier to forgive an enemy than a friend. Blake, I think. Those who betrayed you. Stole what you had offered. Expanding the circle of compassion, loving your enemies. The beginning of wisdom. Path to true happiness. Climbing the stairway to heaven. Simple sounding yet so hard. A hard rain's gonna fall. Yes, it is. Falling already. I fall to pieces. Objects of compassion are they, the monsters and killers and destroyers. Not deserving of love at all. Still it must be given. Given what we know. That violence begets. As does compassion. Or does it? Forgive them for they know not what they do. No, they couldn't know. Not when what they do is so savage. Who could know and still do so? Or is there innate pleasure in inflicting pain? Despots and tyrants, sickos with assault rifles slaughtering schoolkids. Does the sight of blood excite, give pleasure as they say is the case with gangs of apes murdering other gangs of apes? Quantifiable pleasure chemicals seeping through the brains of killer apes. Forgive them. Please forgive me let me go. Nowhere to go. Except into the heart of compassion.

There she's drifted off again, dreaming and scheming, halfway through the article. She shakes the newspaper straight in a businesslike way. But it's true, you know, when it comes to real stuff, the grit of life in community, a local paper is invaluable. Not that most of it isn't dreadful — splashy promotions by car dealerships and shameless puff pieces from the Chamber of Commerce — but the obituary page, for one, is invaluable and nowadays Ginger pores over it like the Dead Sea scrolls looking for the latest old acquaintance now lost. You know you've turned a corner, she muses to herself, when the obits are more exciting than the What's On column. But getting back to Chrissie's article, she chuckles over a sentence in the piece that describes her, amongst other things, as *a venerable presence in the town*. Ha! Venerable indeed. How times change.

Just then the phone rings, startling her.

"Hello?" she says into the receiver on her old-fashioned desk phone, which she's steadfastly retained as a preferred medium for enlightened and leisurely gossip.

"Good morning, Gorgeous," Garth greets her.

"Hello Garth," Ginger answers, "yes it is a gorgeous morning, isn't it? The sunlight's slanting through the trees just now, throwing lovely patches of light on the lawn. And I can tell from your tone you've had your breakfast oats already."

"Wild oats," Garth parries, "but that was long ago."

"And far away."

"Yep. But not so far you couldn't see it."

"On a clear day you can see forever," Ginger says on cue, "but are you calling me just to be silly this morning?" She actually loves it when Garth lets down his hair a bit — usually over the phone rather than in person — giving her an occasional glimpse of the lovable goofy-guy he keeps well camouflaged beneath his serious exterior. Other than Peter, Garth's as much of a man in her life as she has. Or wants.

"See the piece in the *Standard* this morning?" he asks her.

"I was reading it just now when this wretched phone had to ring."

"Ouch!"

"That girl's a skilled writer and surprisingly observant," Ginger says. "I was just having a laugh over the *venerable* bit."

"Yes. Actually I was meaning more the opinion piece Illinger's got in there."

"Oh, no, I haven't read that far yet. What with all the interruptions."

"Well, first things first," Garth says. "I suppose one would want to linger a while over being hailed as venerable."

"Ouch, yourself!"

"Sorry, darling, but yes, I agree, that piece on Stone House was cleverly written."

Ginger can see something peeking out from the shrubbery at the far side of the sun-dappled lawn. A cat? No, a raccoon it looks like. Peter and Shep have gone up to the farm, not that it would have made much difference anyway because Shep, for all his many attributes, is entirely lacking in the ferocity required for scaring off unwanted marauders. "What's Illinger have to say for himself?" she asks Garth.

"Usual drivel," Garth says, "a declaration of his noble purposes for running, including a solemn pledge not to use his ownership of the paper to unfair advantage over his electoral opponents."

"Such high-mindedness. Funny, I was just talking with Irene about what a cunning little weasel Larry was even back in high school."

"Now here's the thing," Garth says in his getting-down-to-business tone, "I've been thinking a lot about this election."

"Me too," Ginger says, which is not entirely accurate, but needs to be said.

"I believe we're all in agreement that it's imperative we have a strong candidate to challenge Illinger every step of the way," Garth says. Ginger smiles at how a visceral dislike and distrust of Larry Illinger flows between Garth and herself like alternating current, generated long ago and carried forward with the tenacity of a village feud. She wishes it were otherwise, that there were no Illingers gnawing like rats at the fabric of what she holds dear, but time has taught her that there always are. Bush and Cheney, Pol Pot and Pinochet and the rest of them, inflicting their personal disorders upon the planet. All the way down to twisted little Larry Illinger, a truly pathetic embodiment of evil in the world. Objects of compassion indeed.

"Absolutely," she tells Garth, "it would be disastrous if he were acclaimed. Well, disastrous if he wins and humiliating if he wins by acclamation."

"Or just handily clobbers any idiot-fringe candidates."

"Well, that lets me off the hook, but not you," Ginger says. Actually, Ginger quite appreciates the wobbly outsiders who regularly run for public office espousing outlandish ideas and being heaped with general scorn for their efforts. She considers a vote for the outrageous preferable to abstaining. When there's been no better choice available, she's cast her ballot for the Rhinoceros Party candidate on a number of occasions, once for a Flat Earth advocate and another time for a most agreeable young man advocating holding city council meetings under the influence of LSD.

"Are you still willing to take a run at it?" she asks Garth

"Well, I've said all along I'd do it if nobody else would."

"But has anybody else come forward?" Just at that moment a large raccoon breaks from the shrubbery and scuttles furtively across the lawn towards Peter's vegetable patch around the south side of the house. Ginger feels she should get out there and swing a hoe or something at the intruder. Compassion has its limits when it comes to raccoons.

"Here's how it's shaping up," Garth continues, "and this may come as a bit of a surprise."

"Nothing surprises me any more," Ginger interrupts him. "As I've probably told you before, I'm a firm believer that at birth everyone receives an allocation of surprise and if you live long enough it all gets spent, so that eventually the most outrageous developments are taken as quite ordinary. Personally I consider myself a surprise survivor. But tell me anyway."

Garth clears his throat in a brusque hint that the serious business at hand will admit of no further levity. "Well," he says, "Sarina has indicated to me that she'd really like to take a run at being mayor."

"Really?" Ginger says. "That *is* a surprise."

Garth ignores the opportunity for a sally and says instead: "She's thought it through and her reasoning's really sound."

"Yes, it invariably is, isn't it?" Ginger says with the faintest hint of snip in her tone. Something has come bubbling up, but she's not quite sure why she's reacting the way she is to this unexpected news about Sarina. Surely at her age she's not silly enough to be miffed about not being consulted beforehand. Or could she be envious of the younger woman, her age and energy, so many active years still ahead of her? Out of nowhere Ginger has a sudden flash of her father's attitude towards Nigel.

"First off," Garth carries on in his businesslike fashion, "whether it's her or me, our chances against Illinger are not especially good."

"True enough," Ginger says, happy to scramble back onto the firmer ground of tactical thinking. "There *are* certain advantages to owning half the town and having the old boys' network at your bidding."

"But if Sarina could manage to place a respectable second against him this round," Garth says, "she'd have a good running start in the next election."

"As would you," Ginger replies, still scratchily resistant to the notion of Sarina as their candidate.

"Ah, yes, but would I want to run three years from now and then serve another three years beyond that? Maybe not. Point two," he continues, "there's a lot of work to be done researching this incinerator project, just in case it does come our way. I'm the best qualified among us to do that work."

"Absolutely. So you're thinking . . ."

"That running for mayor is one job and researching the project is another. Both more than half-time and both fairly urgent."

"And better done by two people than one."

"Yep."

"What about switching the roles around?" Ginger's confounding herself with her resistance. She really admires Sarina, she approves of her politics entirely. So what's the problem here?

"Thought about it," Garth says, "but for all her smarts Sarina doesn't have the technical background required to analyze the incinerator stuff. It's immensely complicated and you know the proponents will be spinning it like crazy. I can meet them on that turf in a way that Sarina can't."

"But has she really been here long enough, do you think? You know as well as I do that many of our good townfolk have an abiding distrust of anyone whose grandparents weren't born and raised in Shetterly."

"No question, she hasn't been here long enough for lots of peoples' liking. Maybe too long for some."

"Yes," Ginger says, "she certainly raised some hackles on the school board by siding with the teachers during that strike." Remembering Sarina's unpopular but principled stand during an especially nasty brawl involving the teachers' union and the provincial government, Ginger releases whatever it was had been snagging her.

"I believe a lot of people saw her position as highly principled, even if they didn't necessarily agree with it," Garth says. "She came out of that scrap better than she might have."

"Yes, she did. And she's got time to take this on, along with everything else on her plate?"

"She says so. Even if she won, I guess it wouldn't be all that much more of a commitment time-wise than being on the school board."

"Or researching the effects of burning garbage."

"That too."

"So," Ginger says, "I'm all for it. She has to file by tomorrow, right?"

Ginger sees the raccoon skulk like a retreating thief back across the lawn.

"Tomorrow, noon," Garth says. "You want to sign her papers with me? She said she'd be honoured if you did."

"Oh, I'd be the one honoured to do so," Ginger says, as the raccoon's ringed tail disappears into the shrubbery.

Phone in hand, Irene feels as though she's stepping out onto a high-wire strung between tall office towers. Not terrified, for she's not given to terror, but apprehensive.

"Good afternoon. Strathmere Lodge. How may I help you?" asks a female receptionist.

"Hello," Irene says, "my name is Irene Welch. I am the daughter of Professor Nigel Childes, who I understand is now residing at your facility."

"One moment, please," the voice says pleasantly and Irene is put on hold.

Whenever she's on hold Irene likes to speculate as to what is being said to whom on the other end. Underhanded things almost certainly.

"Thank you for holding," the voice says after several minutes, "I'll put you through to Mr. Levitt."

"Hello?" A man's voice. "Ms. Welch?"

"Mrs.," Irene says. "Yes."

"Ah, yes. Good. Now, I understand that our Professor Childes is your father. Is that correct?"

"Either that or he's an imposter," Irene says. She doesn't much care for the *our*.

Levitt makes the kind of *heh-heh* noise people make when they aren't sure if something's been said in jest or not.

"I haven't seen my father for a very long time," Irene says, "and had imagined I might never see him again. But now I find he's at your facility and I would like to speak to him. Is he able to come to the phone?"

"Well, ah," Levitt says, then pauses for a bit. "Let's see. In cases such as this, we do have certain protocols in place."

"What protocols?" Irene asks. She doesn't say what she's thinking which is that most protocols are elaborate exercises in butt-covering.

"Well, for example, in situations like your own, where family members have been estranged for a very long time . . ."

Annoyingly the fellow stops in mid-sentence, and it's not at all clear to Irene if he's going to complete his thought. She imagines he's scanning a screenful of protocols looking for something that fits. "Yes?" She prompts him.

"Well, you see, there are a number of difficulties."

"What difficulties?"

"Well, for example: Professor Childes, in his file you see, has indicated *no next of kin*."

Irene snorts. "The file's obviously deficient," she says, "I'm his daughter whether *the file* knows it or not."

"Yes, of course," Levitt agrees. "Still, as I'm sure you recognize, we have an obligation to proceed with due diligence, and, given the circumstances, I don't believe it would be appropriate for me to have you talk with the professor without our having verified — how shall I put this? — well, frankly, that you are who you say you are."

"You're telling me that you won't allow me to speak to my own father?"

"Not before we verify with the professor that he does in fact have a daughter and that he wishes to speak with you."

"This is preposterous," Irene says. "Go ask him then."

"Ah, well, no, I'm afraid it's not so simple as that," Levitt says. "We can't just spring something like that on an elderly person while you're waiting on the line. I'm sure you appreciate that this is a very delicate matter and that the well-being of our guests is our primary concern."

Guests, Irene says to herself sarcastically. More like inmates by the sound of things. "I would like to speak to your superior," Irene says. She's had enough of this treacly-voiced apologist.

"Unfortunately," Levitt says, "Ms. Menzies is away on vacation for the rest of the month."

"Great. Is there anybody else I can speak with?"

"I'm afraid not. You could call back next month if you'd prefer to speak with Ms. Menzies."

"No, I don't prefer to wait until next month. So, let me get this straight: your problem here is that you can't be sure that I'm actually his daughter, is that right?"

"Well, there is that, certainly, among other . . ."

Irene cuts him off. "What if I was to show up at the lodge, birth certificate in hand?"

"Well, obviously that would surmount the initial difficulty."

"What else?"

"Well we would have to speak with the professor, verify that he is in fact your father, and get his agreement to meet with you."

"And he's clear enough in his mind to know what's going on, is he?" For all Irene knows, he could be demented or whacked out on drugs or whatever.

"Oh, my goodness, yes," Levitt says with a small chuckle, "Professor Childes is still as sharp as a tack."

"Fine," Irene says, relieved somewhat that Nigel is still himself at least. And, truth to tell, relieved also that she doesn't have to speak with him just yet. Because she has no idea what she'd say to him. "So how about you do what you need to do," she tells Mr. Levitt, "and then let me know."

"Absolutely I will."

"Terrific." Irene provides her phone number and email, then ends the call permitting herself another snort of contempt.

→II←

The Fetch

Ten

The beauty of Sophia's birth. A blessed child, everybody said so, even the old faculty crustaceans, still sniffing at the temerity of young Childes to have wed and bedded — bedded then wed some said — one of his students. It wasn't done. It offended common decency. There'd been an outcry. Well, more like a grumpy muttering, covertly blended with envy. Should proceedings be initiated, some wondered. Expulsion or reprimand or just what. Nigel had taken advantage of an innocent, betrayed a sacred trust. The girl had flaunted herself shamelessly. Tut-tut.

But eventually the child broke the spell, or rather cast a stronger one. They'd thrown a party, she and Nigel, a smallish affair for colleagues and friends, a christening celebration of sorts. Of course Nigel's people did not come over from England. Although he'd said he had, Ginger doubted that Nigel had invited them or even informed them of this new member of their family. Perhaps they were still smarting from having received no wedding invitation. Perhaps they were indifferent.

Nigel never spoke badly of them, but he never spoke well of them either. They were a nothingness to him. A Christmas card every year signed "Love, Mother and Father" in his mother's hand. Other than that, seldom a word. As lost as her own parents, still deep in the Congo doing missionary work, poor souls.

The past had passed and did not matter. Everything now lay ahead. This gorgeous child, a limitless horizon.

Nigel continued teaching at Carlyle, his star slightly dimmed by his being a husband and father rather than princely bachelor, but his irreverent wit still glittered and his lectures were as popular as ever. At home with their baby daughter, Ginger missed the mental stimulation of her classes, the exhilaration of discovery, and, yes, to be honest, missed being able to attend Nigel's lectures and preen just a bit because he was her husband. To see again something of the look she saw on the faces of Patsy, Diane and Dot when she'd first told them that she and Nigel were to marry. The feelings she'd enjoyed at the time, of satisfaction near to smugness. Not particularly admirable, but delicious nonetheless.

Instead she worked at home in an informal way as Nigel's assistant, marking papers for him and doing research as required. But those tasks weren't sufficient to blunt the realization that the academic world she'd dreamed of entering was receding further from her every day. Even so, housebound at first and childbound as she then became, she didn't regret the choice she'd made, at least not at the outset.

Her baby made all the difference. Tiny Sophia released in Ginger a wellspring of tenderness and affection far different from her infatuation with her husband or the dutiful loyalty she'd felt towards her parents. So often this new form of love reminded her of her brother, of the joyful devotion she'd felt towards Frankie when she herself was a child. Even as a newborn there was something in Sophia's face, especially her eyes, that was uncannily evocative of Frankie. She was simply mesmerized by her baby and could sit for hours playing and cooing and just being silly with her.

It was enough, more than enough to sustain her. Even through the gradually emerging realization that her marriage to Nigel had been, as her mother had warned, a serious mistake.

She'd first glimpsed the scope of her error on their honeymoon in England. Ginger had naturally assumed that they'd visit Nigel's parents and see other members of his family, but it soon became apparent that he had no intention of doing so. He ignored his relatives entirely and became sharp with her if she persisted about seeing them. Instead they visited Cambridge, where Nigel excitedly toured her through his old haunts, then up to Shropshire where they stayed in a charming country inn and walked through lovely pastoral landscapes. In Wiltshire he showed her what were now farm fields but had been a great encampment where Frankie had been stationed before leaving for the continent. By the time they got to Dartmoor, Ginger was seeing glimmers that Nigel was in some bizarre way not so much celebrating his marriage to her as reliving his affair with her brother. Or was she imagining things? He remained as caring and thoughtful and charming towards her as ever, but something seemed missing, some elemental component.

Their lovemaking, chastely postponed until after the wedding, proved something of an anticlimax. Beginning with that awful episode on their honeymoon, in the Dartmoor farmhouse, when she sensed that Nigel's erotic imaginings were for her brother rather than herself. Untutored as she was in the arts of love, she had anticipated her husband would pilot them both smoothly through its mysteries, but her elegant beaux remained surprisingly ineffectual between the sheets, his efforts bent more towards keeping his eyes closed and moaning mournfully than to steering her into bliss.

Matters didn't improve much over time. The prudery of her own upbringing and Nigel's confused predilections continued to make their lovemaking awkward. They didn't speak of it, although she tried several times to broach the topic. She was reminded of her parents who seldom spoke, at least to her, about anything of emotional consequence. She dreaded the prospect of so soon becoming a conventional couple, predictable and inert as puddings. What a grand irony — that Nigel, who'd awakened her imagination to wildish dreams, should so rapidly become the agent of their extinguishment.

Instead it was her daughter who set her dreaming.

And Sophia was a quite extraordinary child, a gentle spirit, quick to laughter and lovingly tender. Ginger was repeatedly amazed at how instinctively thoughtful and kind the little girl was and how devoted to herself and Nigel. They talked about her constantly, every new development, the latest word she'd picked up, all the odd and endearing things she did. The child became, Ginger only later realized, a surrogate of sorts for the linchpin lacking in their marriage. The child was their talisman.

What they didn't talk about, although entirely obvious, was the growing resemblance between Sophia and Frankie.

Nigel's leaving came as anything but a complete surprise to Ginger. The timing of it, just as she was ripe with their second child, yes, that was totally bizarre. But not the abandonment itself. Truth to tell, she'd almost been expecting it. No longer the bright-eyed naif she'd been at their marriage, through the intervening dozen years and the learnings of motherhood she'd come to see how thin a stratum underlay her husband's polished performance. It had dismayed her at first, she'd stoutly resisted it, the gradual realization that his quick and clever charm, the erudition, all of it existed on the surface the way lichen lives on stone. Even more disturbingly, she came to understand that Nigel was less capable than lichen of sincere and enduring attachment. He was designed to flit, not to adhere. The possibility, even the likelihood of his leaving her — not from selfishness or spite so much as from a deficiency of spirit — eventually became apparent. For several years she felt herself like a person walking over a frozen lake just before break-up, where the ice is bending and crackling but never quite breaking.

While not entirely the narcissist her mother had judged him, Nigel did require discipleship in order to flourish and as Ginger advanced beyond the limitations of the acolyte his attentions increasingly veered away from his wife and towards his daughter.

By the time Sophia was nine or ten, she and her dad were inseparable, constantly dreaming up outings and adventures which all too often did not include Ginger. A decade earlier she might have chafed at being excluded this way, but now it felt like emancipation, not having to be responsible for keeping votive candles lit around the sanctum of her husband. And she did appreciate that he was taking such an interest in their daughter. As a male parent he was truly exceptional. She could see Sophia blossoming under her father's devoted attention, well on her way to becoming a self-assured and accomplished young woman, and this too helped blunt the lack of real intimacy between herself and her husband.

Dissatisfied with the role of wife and mother to two people more engaged with each other than with her, and consequently with time on her hands, Ginger began taking courses towards becoming a librarian. The year was 1963. Nigel had given her a copy of a new album by somebody called Bob Dylan. *Blowin' in the Wind*. Exactly. She'd listened to Martin Luther King Jr.'s "I Have a Dream" speech in August that year. A growing commotion, some instinct towards independence, was at work in her as much as in the culture around her. So she enrolled at Carlyle once again, the scandal of a decade ago long since forgotten, her husband now a tenured fixture of considerable influence. But how odd it was to be back on campus, a "mature student" of all things. And how different she now was from the impressionable girl she'd been.

But maybe not so different after all. How else could you explain Gary. A bit younger than herself, he attended several of the same classes she did, but she scarcely noticed him at first. Quiet and shy, not especially attractive, he was the kind of person one didn't notice. But then by chance he and she were paired up for a particular assignment and got on well enough that afterwards they sought each other's company, first for lunch in the clattering cafeteria, eventually for a quiet glass of wine after classes. The more she saw of him the more she came to appreciate his quiet manner. He was like a gentle respite after the incessant flash and glamour of Nigel. And he listened thoughtfully to what she had to say in a way that her husband no longer did. With Nigel, her ideas served mostly as cues for a nimble rejoinder. Being with Gary discussing course material was rather like sitting in a tranquil place while the busy world roared in the far distance. When John Kennedy was killed that autumn, it was in Gary's company that she found solace from the crushing sorrow of those days.

Although it became in some way an affair of the heart, you couldn't call it an affair really. There were no secret weekends of forbidden sex, nothing of that sort, just a fond hug now and then, eventually a bit of tender kissing before Ginger's better self put her foot down and made a stop to things before she could tumble into adultery.

Probably the last time she and Nigel made love, ironically, was when she became pregnant with Peter. The shock of it. Did she really want another child? A baby to love and lose herself again in the loving. She wasn't sure.

When she told Nigel the news she could see he wasn't sure either. "How wonderful, darling," he'd exclaimed and kissed her on the forehead, but whether he was being genuine, even to himself, she couldn't tell. During her pregnancy he was again as attentive and affectionate as he'd been in their first years and she wondered whether this second child might be another talisman, as Sophia had been, to hold them against the breakage.

It was a warming summer morning, she remembered that. Sophia was alone in the back yard of their rented house not far from campus. Ginger sat in the kitchen, huge as a hippopotamus, not relishing the prospect of another hot day. When Nigel emerged from his study carrying a suitcase, she felt such a lurch she feared the baby had dropped.

"What is it?" she asked him, although some part of her knew. "What are you up to?"

"Darling, I'm going away for a little bit," he said. "I realize the timing's dreadful, and I've wanted to put it off until after the birth, but I find I can't. It's absolutely essential that I leave now."

"Leave? Where are you going?"

"Just away for a bit," he repeated. He was unable to look at her. He was behaving like a thief caught in the act.

"I've made arrangements with Mrs. Walters," he said. "She'll help with shopping and cleaning and whatever else you need and she'll drive you wherever you need to go."

Mrs. Walters was a neighbour, a widow, good-hearted but inclined to snoop.

"I don't understand," Ginger said. She was in a kind of shock.

"You will," he said. "In time you will, and you'll thank me in the end, I'm sure. I do hope you'll be all right for the next little bit."

What end did he mean? "And what about Sophia — you're not taking her with you, surely?" She was thinking wildly, suspecting the worst of him.

"No, no, of course not. She belongs with you."

"But how can you leave her, knowing how she adores you?"

"Darling, I love her dearly just as I love you. Believe me, it tears me apart to leave you both."

"Then why?"

"I simply must. Explain that to Sophia for me, will you?"

"How can I explain what I don't understand?"

Whatever she said glanced off him like sunlight on open water. Had he planned this desertion in advance or was it an act of impulse? She knew him not to be an impulsive man.

"Is it another woman?" she asked him, on the edge of tears.

"Of course not, darling," he said, touching her gently on the shoulder. She knew it wasn't. Although, even as a married man, he still had his way of subtle flirting with the prettiest of his students. A man? She didn't ask.

"Goodbye, darling, I'll be in touch." He bent and kissed her on the forehead.

"Aren't you going to say anything to Sophia?"

"No, I think it's best not. It will only upset her. And, frankly, I'm not sure I could stand it myself."

"But . . ."

"I'll write to her in a day or two, I promise. But for today it's best if I just slip away. You must know I'll always love you. I'll love you 'til the day I die."

Then he was out the door and gone.

Ginger couldn't fathom what was happening. Or why. Frantically she scrambled for a foothold of any sort. Something to make sense. Could it be that his daughter had become a temptation to him? That he was fleeing the possibility of doing something truly grotesque. Or had he already done such a thing? That seemed unlikely too. Everything seemed unlikely. Causes and effects were all unhinged, disconnected.

Then it occurred to her: Gary. So obvious. Nigel must have heard something from someone, the campus being such a breeding ground of gossip, and likely a far more lurid version than what the facts allowed. Nigel must have concluded she'd been unfaithful. Of course. Worse still — why hadn't she thought of it at once? — that the baby she was carrying wasn't Nigel's at all. She lurched up out of her chair to go after him but before she got to the front door she heard the car pull away. She watched it disappearing down the block. She sat back down for a bit, bewildered. Slip away. Yes, he'd slipped away. Eventually she heaved herself up and went outside to her daughter.

Sophia took the brunt of it, no question. Nigel's leaving. What was she, twelve or so? Off goes Nigel without a word. And the word was made . . . Me big as a house with Peter. Same as what happened to Sophia's girl Crystal. Same old story. What pulls the pieces apart? I fall to pieces. Sweet Patsy Cline. Yes, I did, I fell into fragments. How could he do it? I still don't know. All those nights blubbering to myself. A blubber kind of lover. Trying to make sense of it for Sophia's sake. Saying over and over it's not your fault. Nor mine. Nor the baby in my belly's. But you can't give way to hate. Too much hate in the world already. Can't have kids hating their father. Our Father who art . . . Can't allow hatred even for yourself. And you get over it, don't you? Eventually. Get over yourself. Like with Frankie. But not Sophia; her scar's still there. Scares and scars. Peter never knew his dad. Maybe just as well. Wellwellwell, so I can die easy. Sophia loved him fiercely; maybe more than I did. At that age you do. Like when Frankie died and I wanted to die as well. Because. But Sophia was different. Never again, you could see her thinking even at twelve, I won't let anyone do this to me ever again. And she hasn't. Even me she stopped loving, her own mother. Just in case. But the price you pay. And her own daughter in turn. Crystal and her confused little Isha. I wouldn't worry so much except for the drugs nowadays. Crystal loves her daughter I know she does. But a love in chains. Unchain my heart. Love you like a ball and chain. Baby, set me free. Yea the baby set Nigel free and Crystal's sad Brad too. Freedom from what, for what. Wonder what became of him, dear old Nigel. Would have thought he'd have popped up in some

newspaper or TV show doing something clever. No end of cleverness, a born performer that fellow. All performance. Crystal's miserable Brad is a cheap knock-off in comparison. Absurd to think of myself occupying Crystal's role, but there it is. Certainly for the child. Just like mine, abandoned by Dad. At least Nigel had the good taste to disappear and remain disappeared. Plus, the decency to keep sending support payments even if they came through a lawyer. But never to see his kids, never even send a card. How could anyone just drop it all like that? Same way he dropped his parents. Where have all the young men gone? Wonder if he returned to England, joined the — who was it? — his beloved Tolpuddle Martyrs. I could have helped him with the martyrdom bit. Oh, Nigel, really how could you? I can recognize him in Peter more and more these days. That tainted genius. The same melancholy; perhaps remorse over something in the past that can't be changed. Or forgotten. I'm glad Peter's gone up to the farm. Do him good. Shep too. Chasing their silly sheep around. Same as the rest of us are doing anyway. Counting sheep. Mary had a little lamb. Plus Peter and Paul. If I had a hammer. Yes, the quiet's lovely. The peace.

Eleven

For weeks Irene has agonized over this day. The day she will go see her long-lost father. The potent fusion of contradictions she'd felt when the anonymous caller had first tipped her off about Nigel's whereabouts has scarcely abated. She's suffered long hours of purple rage against her father, perforated with moments of undeniable tenderness towards him, the memories of him as ideal dad, her schoolgirl idol. Curiosity overlaying it all, partly the urge to see what he's like in his final days, but mostly the need to know *Why?* Why did he abandon them so heartlessly. Never once make any kind of contact over the years. His behaviour was inexplicable at the time and has remained so ever since.

She must go see for herself.

Irene has discussed very little of this with her husband. Phil. Worthwhile in so many practical ways, like Irene herself, Phil is not a confidante, any more than she is. Irene does not discuss what softheaded people call *matters of the heart* with Phil or anyone else. Certainly not

Crystal with her moping self-absorption. Not even with her mother, who would be a likely choice, being who she is. What was it that strange caller said about Ginger: *because she had once done a great kindness to my own mother and I admired her so much*. Oh, yes, Ginger and her great kindnesses. Except to her own daughter. Not that there's blaming there, not at all. Irene was never in the market for her mother's kindness. Still isn't. Not to anything that would open the door to the howling hurts from long ago. Such as what she's planning now.

So she's said nothing yet to her mother about this visit. She's not entirely comfortable with that decision, but Irene is highly adept at setting aside uncomfortable realities until they can be dealt with in their proper time and place.

When Peter called out of the blue yesterday, which he hardly ever does, she almost told him what she was up to, but again something held her back. Peter wouldn't understand anyway. He never knew Nigel, and never expressed any interest in him. Lucky him. Of course Peter and Ginger are thick as thieves, and with them living together at Stone House, and Irene so far away, it's only natural that they'd be totally tight and she'd be on the outside. Lord knows what they say about her, them with their lofty ideas and peculiar friends.

Peter's called a couple of times to update her on the whole thing with the church and what it might mean for Stone House. She still resents that Peter's taking the lead on this. He's smart enough in his own offbeat way, and of course he's made a great wallop of money, but that was more luck than anything, a case of being in the right place at the right time. When it comes to real business, to hard-nosed financial transactions, Irene considers herself far better equipped than her brother.

Plus, she does have a real interest in the future of Stone House. It's a prestige property, no matter how you look at it. She and Phil sometimes speculate about what could be done with it — a tasteful development, maybe condos, maybe a boutique hotel, all kinds of possibilities — but never very seriously, as that wretched gang of religious hypocrites seemed to have it firmly in their grasp. Now, maybe not so much. Yes, indeed, there might be interesting days ahead. Anyway, she won't do anything just yet, but she'll definitely keep a close eye on things and, who knows, maybe going to see old Nigel, repugnant as it is on almost every level, will open a door or two for her that might otherwise not be opened.

"I still think this is crazy," Phil says, stuffing a suitcase into the back of the Subaru, "driving all that way to see a guy who never took the time to see you and never gave a crap about you or anyone else."

"Phil, we've been over this enough," Irene replies. "It's important for me to go; we've decided I'm going; why are we still talking about it?" Irene has a way of saying things that leaves not the finest hairline crack between her opinion and objective reality. Phil understands that, bless him. She knows it was one of her characteristics that first attracted him to her.

He seemed so wobbly back then, a gangly young guy with no sense of himself at all, while she'd long since honed her persona of a young woman who knew her own mind entirely. Over the intervening years of what might not be called marital bliss but could legitimately be considered reasonably smooth sailing, Phil has learned the utter uselessness of argument. You might as well argue with the water spilling over Niagara Falls. He has, by way of adaptation, and much to Irene's amusement, evolved into an accomplished master of compromise as well as a consummate grumbler. Never with outright defiance, nothing unnecessarily provocative, he could grumble and natter with sufficient skill to preserve his dignity, as he is doing now while helping Irene get ready for a trip that she had insisted upon taking but that he considers foolish.

For her part Irene puts up with his grouching for what it is, the feeble protestation of a man chronically in need of a firm hand. She knows full well that if she'd partnered with someone like herself the marriage would have become a Wagnerian opera only much shorter. Some women might want a stronger man, a more forceful character, but she had enough strength and force for both of them, thank you very much. She far preferred Phil's tractability and his loyalty. And there was no question of his loyalty — to her, to the family, to the proper way of doing things if you're going to make a success of yourself in this world. Unlike, for example, a certain party she's setting out to visit today. No, Phil has none of her father's slippery charm and none of his fecklessness either, and that's exactly why he and Irene have remained solid all these years.

"I hope Crystal and Isha don't have too much gear," Phil says, closing the Outback's rear gate. "You ready to go then?"

"I guess so," Irene says, looking in her handbag distractedly.

"So long, then," Phil says, giving her a hug and a passionless peck on the cheek. "Oh, and I programmed the GPS thingy for you, so you don't take a wrong turn."

That's the kind of little thing Phil does that Irene appreciates. Nothing showy. Just a slightly plump guy in casual slacks and a golfing-dude cardigan she'd picked out for him from a sales rack at Sears. Balding. Bifocals. But accommodating, that's what's so great. There's no way he wants her to go on this trip, but he's accepting it. For her.

"Okay," she says, "I should be back by tomorrow evening. Goodbye, darling."

"G'bye. Drive safely."

Wheeling across town to where Crystal lives, Irene's beginning to regret that she invited her daughter and granddaughter to join her on the trip. She did so partly from guilt, because she sees so little of them, and partly out of rescuing Crystal who is still in the funk she's been in ever since her marriage blew apart. Left alone with a precocious kid, the husband off with another woman already. Modern marriage, what a joke. No, you can't blame Crystal for moping about all day like a dirty dishrag, but who wants to be around her dripping self-pity for more than a few minutes. Irene despises self-absorbed brooding over one's troubles, something Crystal has developed into her own art form. Now there'll be two days of it in the confines of the car. Lordy.

It was never, or hardly ever, like this when she and Phil were raising Crystal. Most always the child did what she was told when she was told with a minimum of hassle. Why Crystal can't raise her own child the same way is a mystery. But not really. The variance is that she and Phil stayed together through thick and thin, whereas Brad and Crystal didn't, and that makes all the difference.

Although she has her own limitations, God knows, and she'd be the first to admit it, Irene is not a person accustomed to failure. She and Phil have together worked their little construction outfit up into quite a going concern. They've emerged as people of substance in the community, active with the Elks and Kiwanis and everything else. There's a level of respect there, a level of deference that Irene now accepts as just reward for their years of struggle. But Crystal's reckless marriage and the spoiled, undisciplined, disrespectful kid it produced are a horrible smudge on what would otherwise be a rather gratifying midlife outlook.

Anyway, she's stuck with the pair of them for the next two days and, even worse, she's got to confront her feckless father. Every mile is taking her further away from her comfort zone and she knows it.

When Chrissie's pissed, she's pissed. I mean, who did that fartbox Illinger think he was talking to, after everything she'd done supporting that deadbeat kid of his. The great musician, Yah! Unimaginative piece of shit, his music is like so over it's not even funny. And, you know what: If Illinger had a clue about the slimeball video she's got stashed in her pack, you can bet he'd have been a bit more tactful. Even stupid Chazz may not have realized she'd boosted it. Assholes. Harding too. Perverted screwball. Yah, that disc's a secret weapon, but how she'll use it or when, she's not sure. It was great, though, how she blew off Illinger and Harding. Up and walked out on them cool as cubes. Like she was supposed to suckhole for that crappy job and the opportunity to get molested by Harding whenever he fuckin' felt the urge. *Me!* Those scumbags accusing *me* of sleazy dealings. What a joke. She'll fix them, she'll fix all fuckin' three of them once she figures out how.

She's been riding around town aimlessly for at least three hours and her backpack is getting to weigh like a ton, but where's she gonna go? Not back to that scuzzy motel for sure. I mean how many bedbugs does any one person need? There's no hostel in town or anything. Kack.

Just then, while she's sitting on a park bench in front of city hall, who does she see but old Ginger walking towards her with that tall Asian-looking babe from the college, and an old guy. She's seen them before, those two. Oh, yeah, they were there, at Stone House the day she and Shep were doing their transmuting souls bit.

"Hello, Chrissie," Ginger says coming up to her, "fancy meeting you here."

"Hiya, er, Ginger," Chrissie says, "yea I'm just hangin' out."

"Off on a trip somewhere?" Ginger asks, nodding towards her backpack on the bench.

"Not exactly," Chrissie says.

"Oh, I'm forgetting my manners," Ginger says. "Chrissie, let me introduce you to Sarina Chand who's going to be the next mayor of Shetterly, and a considerable improvement at that. Sarina, this is Chrissie Crosby. She writes for the *Standard*."

"Hello Chrissie," Sarina says with a killer smile. Raven black hair, Indo-chic clothes, fingernails and lipstick in synch, totally fierce, Sarina looks more Bay Street than Shetterly.

Ginger's smiling broadly at her but Chrissie's aware she must look like some freaky street kid to them.

"Oh, and this is Garth Wilson," Ginger says to Chrissie, placing a hand on the old guy's forearm, "one of our more distinguished citizens."

"Pleased to meet you, Chrissie," Garth says to her. "Let me tell you, I've admired your writing in the paper and I especially liked that piece you just did on Stone House and its rather peculiar inhabitants."

"Thanks," Chrissie says, smiling at Garth but not really getting him. Ginger's boyfriend, maybe?

"We're on our way in to get Sarina's papers filed for the election," Ginger tells her, "but I'd really like to have a bit of a chat. Are you off somewhere now?"

"Nah, I got all day," Chrissie says. She's really got all life but she doesn't say that.

"You're not on assignment, then?"

"Nope. I quit."

"You quit your job at the paper?"

"Yep."

"Oh, dear. You've been the only good thing about it of late."

"Thanks." Chrissie's touched by the old babe saying that. Really.

"All the good ones quit," Garth says, "you could almost take bets on how long each new one will last."

"I guess." Chrissie doesn't know what to say.

"Well, listen, Chrissie, may I treat you to lunch after we've done our official business here?" Ginger waves her hand towards city hall. "This shouldn't take long, I would think."

"Er, sure," Chrissie says, realizing she's nangers from not having eaten anything all day.

"Be careful, Ms. Crosby," Garth warns her, "you're dealing with a pretty slippery customer here, and you do know there's no such thing as a free lunch."

"Yea, I heard that somewhere," Chrissie says, smiling at the old guy, who may be a bit of a cheese muffin, but at least he's no Illinger or Harding. He wouldn't be if he's with Ginger.

"Good, it's settled then," Ginger says. "Now, do you want to come in with us, Chrissie, or wait for us here?"

"Um, I'll wait," Chrissie says.

She watches the three of them slowly mount the stone steps leading up to city hall. They look like three gnomes or something going up a mountain because the building's pretty impressive for a town this size. It kinda reminds Chrissie of the old city hall in Toronto which was near where she lived with Sol and them. Sol loved architecture, she remembers. Romanesque Revival he'd called the place that was a court house or something now. Good old Sol, wonder whatever happened to him. Maybe going back to TO's the thing to do. Burn bridges and shit. Start over. But, you know, would Sol really want her back. Like hardly. Truth is she's got zero friends, no place to go and nobody she can rely on. Shit. She sits on the bench blankly watching a flock of starlings pecking at a discarded bag of corn chips.

Not so long later Ginger and the other two emerge from the building kinda laughing and carrying on as they descend the steps.

"On your mark!" Ginger calls out, coming up to Chrissie. "Sarina's filed, the race is on."

"Great," Chrissie says, standing up, "congratulations."

"Thanks, Chrissie," Sarina says with a dazzling smile, teeth so white they don't look real, "I do hope I can count on your vote."

"Er, sure," Chrissie says. She's never voted for anyone and vaguely doesn't believe in it. Whatever changes, right? Sol was deep into the anarchist scene and that seemed to make a lot of sense to her. Smash the fuckin' system; voting's just propping it up.

They've obviously cooked it up inside that the other two will take off while Ginger and Chrissie go for lunch, which is fine by her, food being top of her list. Chrissie wheels her bike, walking along with Ginger, which is not a whole lot slower than she'd usually walk. She's amazed that old Ginger has so much energy at her age. They go into a little sushi joint recently opened and empty of customers. They sit at a small table by the front window where Chrissie can keep an eye on her bike. Nobody in this frickin' town seems to believe in bike racks. If she was still at the paper she'd maybe write a piece about it. Yea, maybe.

"I'm surprised to hear you quit your job," Ginger says after they've ordered. "Rather sudden, wasn't it?"

How much should she tell her, Chrissie wonders. "Yea, it's a long story," she says.

"I love long stories, don't you?" Ginger says, smiling like she's Grandma Moses or somebody. "I've just started reading Tolstoy's *War and Peace*. Good lord, the names alone are enough to make your head spin. But there are certain books you want to read while you still can."

"I haven't read it ever," Chrissie says, "though I was really into Yevtushenko for a while. 'Til Sol found out he was like really a stooge of the Soviets."

"Yes, I believe he was. And who's Sol?"

"Oh, a guy I knew in Toronto. Really a good guy."

"Chrissie, do you mind if I ask what happened with your job at the paper? You were so good at it, I had hopes you'd settle in and keep us on our toes for a few years at least."

"Thanks." Chrissie's sort of embarrassed by the compliment.

"We've had several good ones like you in the past," Ginger says, "but they invariably move on to bigger things."

Chrissie knows most of what she wrote for the *Standard* was schlock, so the praise sounds phony somehow. Let's face it, she hasn't had a whole lot of practice responding to nice. She can see old Ginger's making moves, but she can't figure out what they are. For sure she's got nothing the old babe could need. All her instincts are to leave, but she has to say something.

"It was a whole weird thing," she says. "I was living with a guy who's the son of the owner."

"Mr. Illinger?"

"Right. You know him?"

"Oh, yes, Larry Illinger and I go a long way back," Ginger says with a weird smile.

"Uh-huh. Anyway, I left the guy — Chazz, his name was, well, Charles really — and his dad didn't like it for whatever reason. So he made these like crazy accusations."

"Accusations?"

"Oh, stupid stuff. And the editor, Mr. Harding, backed him up on it."

"What a surprise," Ginger says, just as their order's brought over by an almost invisible waitress.

"Yea, really. Anyway, I told them to go screw themselves and walked out."

"Good for you," Ginger says, "not so good for us maybe, but good for you." She takes a piece of sushi with a tiny dab of wasabi.

Chrissie swallows a sushi whole. "Mmm, that's good."

"So what'll you do for money now?" Ginger asks.

"Yea, well, I dunno," Chrissie says, smearing rather too much wasabi on a second sushi.

"And do you have a place to stay?"

"Not really," Chrissie says. She's looking out the window where a guy's checking over her bike.

"Those are your life possessions, are they?" Ginger asks, pointing to her backpack.

You can see old Ginger's brain ticking like an antique clock.

"Yep, travellin' light," Chrissie says with a laugh, relieved that the guy outside is moving on. Then suddenly she gets a searing flash of heat down her throat as the wasabi ignites then explodes up into her brain. Wow.

"I wonder," Ginger says, "would you care to come to Stone House for a few days, until you get things sorted?"

Chrissie hesitates, sensing a trap of some sort, meanwhile guzzling water to douse the fire in her throat. The back of her eyeballs feel scorched. "Well, er . . ."

"If it's the dog you're worried about," Ginger interrupts her, "there's no need. Shep and Peter are up at the farm for the next little while."

"Oh." Chrissie's clicking through possibilities. Her options are actually somewhere right around zero, but her associations with that house are pretty extreme. The dog, the weirdo son, that crying jag she got into the last time she was there. She's got tears in her eyes now too, but they're from the frickin' wasabi. Probably. "Well, uh . . ." again she hesitates, but old Ginger reaches out across the little table and takes Chrissie's hand in hers. Chrissie's hand looks like a little kid's in the big, soft leathery hands of the old lady.

"Listen, honey," Ginger says, "there's enough room in that house for a travelling circus and right now there's nobody home but me. As I told you the other day, I feel terribly guilty having all that space and comfort to myself while people out there are sleeping under bridges and in dumpsters. So you'd be doing me a favour, really. I don't want to twist your arm, but if you could use some space for yourself, it's there for you, no questions asked, no money exchanged, no expectations at all. You can come and go as you please and then move on whenever you choose."

Chrissie's got something else in her throat now, not burning but kinda swelling, like when she started blubbering that last time. She can't do that again, not sitting in a stupid sushi house. Ginger releases her hand and devotes herself to another bite. She's said what she has to say. Chrissie doesn't know how she knows, but she surely knows that if she accepts the offer, stuff's gonna happen. It isn't gonna be just a place to crash for a few days. Like the old guy — who's it? Garth — said, there's no such thing as a free lunch.

⊱⊰

On pleasant days, Nigel takes particular delight in being wheeled out onto the great lawn at Strathmere and left in peace to savour the beauty of nature. The lawn slopes gently to the southwest with a scattering of very fine old oaks and on days when the sun's uncomfortably warm, as it is today, he'll ask the orderly to park his wheelchair in the dappled shade of a tree. The landscape's reminiscent of his favourite haunts in England, Tennyson's retreats of ancient peace, now menaced by coach-loads of tourists consuming landscapes like potato chips. Beyond the lawn there's a working dairy farm where herds of big Holstein cows mooch about. Nigel appreciates the black-and-whiteness of them, how they plod methodically with bulging udders, their apparent contentedness. Once the orderly's gone, a reliable but stodgy fellow named Bruce, Nigel sets about extricating himself from the wheelchair so that he can sprawl on the cool, green grass. He remembers himself as a child, a baby at family picnics, lying in the grass, the smell of it and the miraculous movements of insects. He can't, however, quite remember what his parents looked like.

All things considered, Nigel's as content as the cows, or at least as content as one's dwindling days allow. In hindsight not the most sparkling of careers, anyone would admit, sabotaged as it was by what he came to call the Flynn Effect. First Frankie, then his sister Ginger, and the child Sophia. Once free of them — treacherously, that's how he'd felt at the time, free of them — he'd made do the best he could. But he was badly disarranged in the process, permanently as it turned out. He would continue his days in a state of disarrangement. All those years in Panama City teaching at that forlorn American college. Agreeable as they may be at home, Americans abroad invariably manage to be appalling. Unnecessarily assertive and generally a few decibels too loud. And, of course, not the least bit interested in Edwardian England, so he'd had to reinvent himself as a professor of English literature, specializing in the Romantic poets. Keats and Shelley were his long-time acquaintances anyway, so he was not dissatisfied to spend his days with them and their swooning set. He'd made a few friends among the expats, but none of consequence. They seemed to him a restless and unrooted group, just as he himself was restless and unrooted. Perhaps it's why he appreciates the gnarly roots of oaks, the cool, moist roots of grass.

How the years had skittered past, though. One into another until, suddenly, he's an ancient. A frail old fool sprawled on the grass, awaiting the day when they'll place him down among the roots and cover him up forever. He doesn't resent it entirely, this too-sudden implosion of the adventure. Because adventuresomeness had leaked out of it long ago. Certainly as a young man he had imagined himself making a mark, being someone who created a difference, a worthy who would be remembered. Instead, one whose name was writ in water, as Keats put it. Entirely insignificant. Nor was the world even a smidgeon better for his having been in it for ninety years; not a single life had been enriched because of him. Love had not been a companion. And, try as he might, he has been unable to convince himself that anything but oblivion awaits him after death.

Strangely, these final years have been among the better. Not too many aches and pains. The restlessness left far behind. The conjectures and striving and deciding. The endless tyranny of Should I? Nowadays just one's books and fine music and, marvellously, books on disc. Of late he's been listening to the stories of Alice Munro read expertly by a woman with a very fine voice. Far preferable to the flighty chatter of nearby strangers with whom you share nothing in common but advanced age. It's one of the reasons that he chose Strathmere as a place in which to spend his concluding days; because here he can do as he pleases, without being subject to wheedling suggestions that he join in groups playing pinochle or learning macramé. He will decline in dignity at least.

Suddenly he's startled out of his reverie by the figure of Ms. Menzies looming above him like the shadow of Death. A woman of consequence, she's the prime mover at Strathmere, respected if not necessarily admired. Nigel likes her enormously.

"You haven't fallen, have you, Professor?" she asks rather drily.

"Only in your high opinion, I'm afraid," he says, sitting up and brushing bits of grass from his clothes, matching sweatshirt and sweat pants in a rather hideous teal.

Menzies doesn't often prowl this far afield because the stiletto heels she favours tend to get impaled in soft ground. Today she's wearing sandals instead. Tan slacks and a complementary blouse.

"Now you do remember that your daughter is coming to see you tomorrow?" she asks him.

"Ah, yes, my daughter," he says vaguely. He gets slowly to his feet by rolling to a kneeling position then hoisting himself up using the chair for leverage. Menzies knows not to lend a hand unless requested to do so. He lowers himself into the chair and, wheezing somewhat, gazes down at the Holsteins.

"Beautiful creatures, aren't they?" he says to Menzies, pointing with a crooked index finger.

"Lovely," she agrees, "though perhaps a bit bovine." She pauses briefly then asks him: "And how are you feeling now about your daughter's visit?"

He senses himself being reeled back into the world of clash and bang.

"Oh, it's all right, I suppose," he says, "though truth to tell, I'd just as soon not bother. After all these years . . ."

"Are you feeling anxious over seeing her?"

"Anxious?" he asks. "Perhaps, but I don't really think so."

His voice is reedy, whispery, a long-ago echo of the sparkling lecturer who could mesmerize packed lecture halls at Carlyle. He never sparkled quite that way again, certainly not in Panama where sparkle would have been superfluous, too much like the noisy splash of everything else.

His daughter. Sophia. A child is all he can remember. A lovely child, but dangerous. She was a danger to him. He can vividly remember the sense of peril she embodied, born at least in part from her uncanny resemblance to Frank. He expects for a moment that a child is coming to visit him until he remembers that she would be an older woman herself by now.

"Well, I'm afraid it's too late to put it off at this point," Menzies says. "She's coming a great distance to see you."

"Yes, I suppose."

"I regret that I was away when this situation arose," she says. "And after you telling us that you had no living relatives. Really, Professor." Her tone is chiding but affectionate. "Then this daughter having changed her name from what you knew her as."

"Yes, that was all a bit confusing," Nigel admits.

"Most irregular," Menzies says, as though he were a favourite pupil caught out at some schoolboy lark. "Mr. Levitt was perhaps not the person best equipped to handle the complexities of the case."

"Poor old Levitt; what's become of him?" Nigel asks.

"Leave of absence," Menzies says, "paid, of course."

"Naturally. I believe you told me that already."

"Yes, I imagine so. Now, is there anything we might do to make matters easier for you tomorrow, do you think?"

"Easier?" Nigel repeats. He's noticing that the Holsteins are all on the move, methodically plodding back across their pasture. "No, I can't foresee there'll be anything easy about it."

"You have now arrived at your destination," the female voice in the GPS unit tells Irene as she swings the Subaru into the parking lot of the Lay Z Bones Motel.

"Thanks for nothing," Irene comments sarcastically as she kills the ignition.

Crystal's slouched in the back seat staring out the window as though mesmerized by the headlights of passing vehicles flashing and glittering on the nearby highway. Alongside Crystal, Isha is sprawled asleep, her mouth drooping open and all her I Want To Be a Big Girl sass evaporated back into childhood. It's been a long day, almost six hours on the road with only a brief and fairly revolting stop for lunch at a sandwich joint attached to a gas station in the middle of everywhere.

Irene and her daughter had spent much of the journey once again sifting through the wreckage of Crystal's failed marriage. But tactfully of course with Isha in the car, even though she was listening to kiddy rock on her MP3 the whole time and regularly checking her text messages. She's a smart little whip, that Isha, and you don't want to go saying too much with her around. Right away Irene had noticed that the kid was wearing lipstick and eye shadow, which was new. Her tight sweater revealed the swelling of pubescent breasts, or something to suggest them, and her jeans might have been spray-painted on.

Eventually exhausted by feelings of personal failure about her bastard ex-husband, Crystal took to staring out the car window at several hundred miles of nothing. Irene kept the car on cruise control, driving in silence and trying her best not to think about anything.

Big surprise, the Lay Z Bones Motel isn't quite as splish as what it had seemed to Irene by its website, but the evening's getting on and it's only for one night anyway, so in they go. The manager's a slender young man with an Eastern European accent they can barely understand. He tells them there's a steakhouse just around the corner where they can get dinner and gives them adjoining rooms on the ground floor on what he calls the quiet side, away from the highway noise.

Collapsing into bed after a morose meal, Irene still can't really grasp that tomorrow morning she'll be visiting her long lost father. She hasn't the slightest idea of what to expect, but as she drifts in and out of sleep she's aware of feeling an unfamiliar variety of dread.

The *quiet side* of the motel proves to be anything but. The people in the room above arrive after midnight and clomp around in jackboots for several hours. Successive interminable freight trains rumble past in the middle of the night, shaking the whole place and sounding close enough to be in the parking lot. Hardly an hour goes by without the shriek of sirens, from police cruisers or ambulances or fire trucks or Christ-knows-what. Awake half the night, Irene spends the restless hours mostly brooding about her father. She can't for the life of her pin down what it was had made her so urgently want to see him once she'd discovered where he was. Forty years with not a word from him or about him in all that time. She was fairly certain that her mum hadn't heard from him either. Not that they talked about him, but Ginger would have mentioned it. Probably. Though you never could count on anything when it came to Ginger and Nigel.

What's she expecting? she wonders repeatedly. He must be into his nineties by now, undoubtedly enfeebled, quite possibly demented, although that fool Levitt had told her that Nigel's mind was still sharp. Tossing around on the lumpy motel bed, she finds it impossible to imagine him as anything but young and dashing, the adorable dad she'd loved so well. Back then she'd revelled in what she thought of as a perfect childhood with the best imaginable parents. Right up until the day of his treachery. Nothing in life, not even poor Crystal's troubles, has wounded her more grievously than her perfectly polished father deserting her pregnant mother and herself. Nothing ever would.

The dread awakens with her in the morning, creeping into the room with the anemic light of dawn. Today's the day; she has to go meet him face-to-face. And do what? Shamefully she accepts the fact that a large part of her would far prefer that he be long since dead and buried.

Shaking off grogginess she puts herself in order and phones next door. Isha answers on the first ring but says her mom is dead. "Try get her moving," Irene tells her, "we'll meet for breakfast at eight sharp, okay?"

They assemble for breakfast at the Happy Family Restaurant next door. All three of them are out of sorts, and under the lurid fluorescent lighting their faces have the colour of pale greenish mushrooms. Irene orders a bowl of oatmeal and a plate of fruit. Crystal orders pancakes with maple syrup and whipped cream. Isha says she'll have waffles and bacon.

"I've been thinking," Irene says while they wait for their food to arrive, "that maybe it isn't the brightest idea that we all show up together first off to see granddad."

"Isn't he my great-granddad?" Isha asks, just to be a nuisance.

"Yes, he is, Isha," Irene says, smiling, "and he's my dad and your mum's granddad, which is halfway between dad and great-granddad, so we'll call him granddad as a matter of convenience, all right?"

"Sure," Isha says, with her pouty lower lip stuck out. She hasn't put any lipstick on today, thank God; maybe Crystal's had a word with her. Irene is hopelessly conflicted around being grandmother to Isha. She realizes she should be playing a positive role in the kid's development, filling in at least a bit for Crystal's inadequacies. Trouble is, the girl is part of a reality beyond Irene's control and thus of diminished interest to her. Even Crystal, her only child, is functionally a stranger to her.

"What I mean," Irene continues, "is that we have no real idea what sort of shape Dad's in . . ."

"You mean Granddad," Isha interrupts her.

"For fuck's sake, Isha," Crystal hisses at her, "shut the fuck up!"

"Okay, okay," Isha says, all wounded dignity.

Oh, Lord, Irene sighs to herself.

"You're probably right," Crystal says, wanting to smooth things out. "It may be a bit of overkill if we all go trooping in there together."

"So what I suggest," Irene continues calmly, "is that I go for a visit first. I'll drop you two off at that big mall we saw on the way and you can go shopping for a bit. I'll call you on Isha's phone after I've seen my father and then we'll decide what to do next. How's that sound?"

"Fine by me," Crystal says, trying her best not to appear pissed off that she's been dragged out of bed early for nothing. Good old Irene with her ass-backwards organizing.

"Isha?" Irene says.

"Sure!" Isha mutters, still smarting from her mom's outburst.

"All good," Irene says, just as their plates start arriving.

Twelve

Shep's as happy as mushrooms, still at the farm with Peter, the two of them preoccupied with the fine business of trials. Peter has set up Cecilia's pens and gates down in the big meadow near the road, just where she had first installed them for training Shep. Every so often a lone car or pickup will pass and sometimes slow down, the driver or passengers waving. A man and his dog working sheep, reaffirmation of old ways, of what endures despite what's lost.

It's taken no time at all for Shep to get back into trials trim. The smooth, straight outrun to the distant sheep. Never a cross-over, needless to say, the blunder of crossing between the sheep and handler, something only a fool dog would do, or an amateur. Curling behind the half-dozen sheep to left or right, as directed, then the steady and calm approach to the lift. Full control here, no giddiness or posturing. Perfectly cornered flanking, not crowding the sheep or causing needless agitation. Smooth, smooth. Just what Cecilia used to say to him back in their training days. "Oh, Shep, you're such a smooth beauty," she'd coo with delight when they'd finished, kissing and stroking him tenderly. It was a mutual smooth to Shep, himself and his virtuous handler. Oh, and the scent of her! The rapturous smell of that woman as they nuzzled together.

After the outrun, the fetch, bringing the sheep down to Peter on a line so straight you'd swear a surveyor had laid it out. The keen aromas of grasses and herbs trampled by the sheep. Everyone squeezing cleanly through the fetch gates, making sure no troublemakers miss a gate or try to double back through it. Then straight ahead, a tight little knot of sheep, their foolish bums bouncing in rhythm, going just where they're directed. Back and forth Shep darts, low to the ground, pivoting abruptly, utterly absorbed.

At the conclusion of the fetch, with the flock approaching Peter, the field's reversed for the drive. Will it be left hand or right? — pushing the sheep either clockwise or counterclockwise around the handler at his post. Peter waits 'til the last second to indicate he wants them to the right and Shep responds by marshalling the flock in a clockwise direction around Peter and then driving them on a diagonal line straight towards the drive gate on the right. Through the first gate, smooth as syrup, then horizontally across the field and through the second gate. The pure symmetry of the thing. The perfection of harmonized motion.

Once through the second gate, Shep nudges the little flock to the shedding ring, not knowing just what Peter might have in mind next. Some singling perhaps; Cecilia loved her singling, selecting a single sheep and moving it away from the rest, but then Cecilia loved all of it, and Shep best of all.

Then suddenly Shep stops. Something has changed, some shift in the atmosphere. He glances about, although Peter hasn't called a Look Back to indicate there's another group of sheep to be gathered. No, but out of nowhere, like the sudden apparition Shep perpetually awaits, there she is: on the verge of the road, just across the fence, the small dark girl standing with her bike.

"That'll do," Peter says, following Shep's stare and seeing her. Shep releases the sheep and returns to Peter's side.

"Hello, Chrissie!" Peter calls across to her, saying her name before realizing he still remembers it.

"Hiya," she calls back. "Wow, that's amazing what you're doing. What *he's* doing." She nods towards Shep who thumps his tail twice on the ground, gratified by the recognition.

"Ah, yes," Peter says, "when he's not roaring around terrorizing maidens, Shep's not a bad hand at herding."

"No kidding," Chrissie says, smiling at his joke. "I was just cycling by," she adds, "and saw you. I had to stop and look."

"I'm glad you did," Peter says. Shep glances from one to the other as each speaks. They're both having to rather shout because they're quite a stretch apart.

"Would you like to come in, have a look around?" Peter asks.

"Well . . ." Chrissie hesitates. She's remembering how weird he was that first time she met him at Stone House, though he sounds sorta normal now. "Uh."

"Only if you'd like," Peter says. "It just seems a bit silly to be shouting across the ditch this way."

"Yah, it does," Chrissie says. She thinks maybe she should get back on her bike and go. Except she doesn't have anywhere to go. Maybe if she talks to him she'll know about moving into Stone House. Because he's like going to be there too at least sometimes and she doesn't feature being inside a Gothic mansion with some loony roaming the corridors at night. Weirdly, she's reassured because Shep's here, that there's nothing to be afraid of. "Okay," she says, "where do I have to go?"

"Back down to the driveway entrance there," Peter says pointing, "then straight up. We'll meet you at the barn, okay?"

"Great," she says, still not sure it is.

But it is. He's like a totally different guy from before. Like he's happy to see her and interested in her. Maybe more at home out here or something she figures. But there's nothing in his vibe makes her think he's trending below the belt like most guys she meets. She wouldn't be out here in bumblefuck nowhere with most guys. And Shep is like *so* cool. He sits on the grass by the field-gate and waits for her to come to him, if she wants to. And she does. It's like there's an energy or something coming off the dog, radiating straight at her. Hesitating only for a second, she reaches out and lets him sniff her hand, then strokes the silky crown of his head. He makes the faintest noise, almost a whimper, but you know it's like joyful. She's remembering her terror when she reached for her notebook, what a skook she was, now that she's not scared of him at all. Of either of them. It comes to her in a flash she's dreamt of Shep a bunch of times without remembering the dreams.

"There's not many people Shep will abandon his sheep for," Peter says to her, "you should feel honoured."

"No kidding," she says. "I couldn't believe how he was moving those sheep all over the field. I mean, I've seen those dogs on TV, but I had no idea; it was like this kind of incredible ballet or something he was doing."

"Yeah, it's pretty neat working sheep with a dog as good as he is. Now what about a hearty glass of cold apple juice?"

"Sure," she says. "Thanks."

As they walk over to the farmhouse Peter offers her an apology for his discourtesy when she first visited Stone House.

"Oh, that's cool," she says, although she's pleased he's thought of it.

"I don't know quite what came over me," he tries to explain, "something about your scream took me to another place. A hard place. I do hope you'll forgive me."

Chrissie's not used to guys talking to her like this, even older guys. Illinger, for example, even though he tries to sound like this, doesn't.

"I feel like I'm the one should apologize for screaming like that," she tells him. "It's so stupid how terrified I was."

"Not at all," he says. "I'm guessing you've had some bad dog experience in the past, so an outburst of civilized screaming is entirely in order."

He's got a really funny way of saying things, like how people used to talk, like in the movies and stuff, but don't anymore. Mostly she's amazed over how different he is from the first time, when he wouldn't talk to her or even look at her. Like he was scared of her and she was scared of Shep and suddenly nobody's scared of anybody. She doesn't get it and it doesn't matter.

Once Peter's fetched two glasses of juice they sit on weathered Adirondack chairs on the front porch. The house is all wooden and kinda run-down, not Stone House at all. Shep settles on the worn plank floor beside them.

Between sips of juice Chrissie surreptitiously studies Peter's face. Very fine, she thinks, like an artist's maybe. Sensitive like. She's laughing to herself over her initial take on the guy, how he was maybe blind or retarded or a perv. So stupid.

"What a great place," Chrissie says, leaning back in her chair, pleased that she's wearing frayed jeans and her baggy yellow sweatshirt, like she could belong here. She doesn't know the first thing about farms or even the countryside but this place kicks. Meadows sloping gradually away, splashed sunlight and illuminated insects. Birdsong everywhere. Pure sweet.

"Yea, I love it here," Peter says, "and it's Shep's favourite place in the world."

"So is this your farm or what?" she asks him.

"Yep, I've had it a few years now. But the last couple of years I've rented it out to a young couple."

"I couldn't bear to leave it if I lived here," Chrissie says. "How come you stay in town, because of your mum?"

"Partly," Peter says. "Partly because this place has, uh, difficult memories for me."

"Huh?"

"I lived here with my wife and baby daughter until they were killed in a car crash," he says in a matter-of-fact manner, surprising himself.

"Oh." It's a shocker to Chrissie, what he's told her. She doesn't know if she should say she's sorry or what. And, she realizes, that's maybe why her scream fucked him around so badly.

The two of them sit silent for a bit, and even Shep seems abstracted in memory. But surely something's shifting here, Peter senses, because his remembering what he can't forget now seems tinted with an unfamiliar lightness around the margins of his sorrow.

"Can I ask you something?" Chrissie breaks the silence.

"Of course." Peter sets the sweet sadness aside. "What is it?"

"Um, do you know your mum has asked me if I want to move into Stone House with her?"

"Has she?" Peter's surprised by the news, since Ginger hadn't sounded him out on it, but not the least surprised that his mother would make the offer. Over the years there's been a steady stream of what Ginger calls her "pilgrims" staying at the place for various lengths of time. Several of them were profoundly disturbed characters for sure, and Peter worried for her safety at times, but the amazing thing is, in all those years, she's never once been ripped off or taken advantage of. Every so often a letter or card will arrive at Stone House from some far-flung place expressing the writer's gratitude to Ginger for her generosity. You saved my life. You rescued me. You kept me from drowning. Because it wasn't just free room and board they'd received; at *chez* Ginger you got your own little customized course of miracles. Now this girl. Not as desperate as some, maybe, but who knows?

"How do you feel about it?" Chrissie asks him. "I mean . . ."

"I think it's brilliant," Peter says. "Mum's quite an exceptional character, you know."

"Yah, I kinda got that. I don't think I ever met anyone like her."

"Probably not," Peter says with a smile. "She's definitely a limited edition. I know she'd love having you around, your energy. She misses having kids and grandkids around the place."

"So she has grandchildren?"

"Only one. Her granddaughter Crystal, who's my sister's girl. She's got a teenager of her own, but they're all the way over in Smithton, same as my sister and her husband, so we don't see them very often, hardly at all. We're not what you'd call a close family, but I know Mum wishes that we were."

"So Ginger's a great-grandma?"

"Yep."

"Yow, I always think of great-grandparents being really ancient and worn out. Not like her."

"No, it's the rest of us are worn out trying to keep up with her."

"Cool. So will you be living there too or have you moved back here?"

"No, I'm only house-sitting here until the couple who run the place get back."

"Then you'll be at Stone House? You and Shep?"

Lying between them, Shep opens one eye at the mention of his name. Truth to tell, he'd dozed off during all of this chat.

"Yep," Peter says, "though I pledge myself to a more civil hospitality than what you received last time. Shep, of course, has a bit of a crush on you already, so you'll get no trouble from him. But you do realize, I hope, that if you take her up on the offer Mum will be dragging you into all sorts of crazy schemes."

"What schemes? You mean like the election?"

"That for sure since her sidekick Sarina's taking a run at the mayor's chair."

"Yea, she's pretty amazing too, isn't she?"

"Sarina? Off the charts, as we used to say. She and Mum make quite a pair."

"Yea, I met them at city hall, her and your mum and an old guy."

"Garth, no doubt."

"Right. That's when Ginger, I mean your mum, asked me if I wanted a place to stay."

"Uh-huh," Peter says, watching a banty hen and her brood of chicks pecking in the driveway gravel. "Then there's a proposed garbage incinerator to be tackled — they want to build the damn fool thing up in the hills back here — not to mention routine drubbings of Larry Illinger, if he gets elected. No, there's no shortage of issues to get entangled in with dear old Mum on the prowl. She's not quite the whirling dervish she used to be, but still far more than is decent for someone of her advanced years."

"I bet you don't say that when she's around."

"Oh, I tease her all the time, as I hope you will too. She'd far rather have impertinence than phony politeness."

"Cool."

"But it's just occurred to me," Peter says, "that things could get a bit sticky for you with your boss once he discovers you're aligned with Mum. The magnificent Mr. Illinger's a highly reactive sort, as you no doubt know."

"No worries," Chrissie says, "I quit the paper."

"You did? Well, that's a good start."

"Yea, except I got no money and no place to live."

"So," Peter says, slapping the arm of his chair forcefully enough to startle Shep out of a particularly desirable doze, "Stone House it should be and the devil take the hindmost!"

After the girl's gone, Peter remains sitting on the porch. It's where he'd stood with the midwife staring at the double rainbow the day his daughter was born.

⁂

Ginger's peeling potatoes at the kitchen sink thinking, for no particular reason, about her parents. Remembering the day she received a letter of condolence from some functionary at their beloved Congregation advising her, with deepest regret, that Mr. and Mrs. Dustin Flynn had both passed away, within weeks of each other, unfortunate victims of a cholera outbreak. Their corpses had been cremated to prevent infection. Ginger had only recently moved back to Stone House with her new baby Peter and sullen Sophia. The year was 1967, the centennial year. Expo 67. What historian Pierre Berton would later call "Canada's last good year." Not so good for Ginger. On top of Nigel's leaving, now her parents were gone forever.

She'd had no real reconciliation with them, just a distant and formal exchange of occasional politenesses, and with news of their death, this again bruised her terribly. It was only later that she realized her relationship with them in the end had not been all that different from Nigel's connection with his own parents.

⁂

Mrs. Nigel Childes. That's what I was known as in the early days. So silly. All those corny old country songs about wooing women with a promised change of name. Oh, goody. What's in a name? That which we call. We laughed about it, Nigel and I, the Mrs. Nigel Childes honorific. He'd call himself Mr. Ginger Flynn and flounce about the house in patriarchal mockery. Proper names are poetry in the raw, he'd quote Auden. Like all poetry they are untranslatable. Always a clever reference in his back pocket, that Nigel. Name is a fence and within it you are nameless. Who was that? Paronen perhaps. Sophia was the first of us, changing to Irene soon after Nigel left. A disagreeable change to my mind, but necessary for her. A more brittle name, less subtle, less resonant. Don't know why I stayed as Mrs. Nigel Childes as long as I did. I wasn't that when he was there, much less when he wasn't. Stop! In the Name of Love. I Call Your Name. Did She Mention My Name? I remember I had that Mary Daly infatuation back in the '70s. Beyond God the Father. Women have had the power of naming stolen from us. Yes. Out went Mrs. Nigel Childes like last week's newspapers. It felt so fine to be Ginger Flynn again. Sophia, I mean Irene, changed back to Flynn as well; she couldn't stand anything associated with Nigel. In the name of the Father. Ha! Name of the game more like. Peter had been Peter Flynn right from the get-go, born as he was in the backwash of Nigel's desertion. I don't remember why, but we had an old quotation from Confucius written on a file card and taped to the refrigerator door. What was it: If names are not correct, language will not be in accordance with the truth of things. Exactly.

Irene drives slowly up the long straight gravel driveway leading to Strathmere Lodge. A colonnade of enormous pine trees lines the driveway and beyond them perfectly sheared lawns stretch away on either side. The lodge itself looms at the far end of the colonnade, a large brick building with a mansard roof of copper gone to green.

Having organized this visit, insisted upon it, in fact, despite the resistances of everyone else, Irene's again asking herself what the hell she thinks she's doing. What purpose can possibly be served. And why has she said nothing to her mother or her brother about this visit; why hasn't she even told them that she's discovered where the old reprobate is. The fact that she can't say, really, is not like her at all. Usually she knows exactly what she's about and makes no secret of it either. She doesn't like secrets or secretive people. She likes things out in the open, plain and straightforward. That's why Crystal can piss her off so much sometimes. At heart her daughter's a sneak, and a not very good one at that. It's how come her kid is so out of control, because Crystal isn't honest with her; she's always trying to sneak around the back of things to get her own way, and a kid can see it easy as pie. And of course Isha's becoming the same. Talk about sneaks. Ha! That kid's got duplicity written all over her smirky little face. Ah, well, what can you do? Phil, of course, tries his best to be sneaky but he's not smart enough for it. She can spot a lie coming from Phil even before he's said it. She calls it her dishonesty barometer and she has completely baffled her husband any number of times by cutting him short before he can get one of his pathetic little attempts at deceit airborne.

Still, it's a peculiar feeling for Irene to be doing something that seems underhanded in some way, even though it isn't. And even more peculiar to be doing something for reasons she doesn't quite understand. For years she's blacked her father out; she even took a course in positive thinking long ago to help her escape her memory of him. She learned and methodically practised the trick of seeing each negative thought about her dad as a branch on a tree that she could quickly snap off and discard. In a landscape littered with branches, his memory eventually grew a bit dimmer. But since she learned of his being here at the lodge, he's been creeping into her head like a bloody cat burglar, especially in recent weeks as this visit drew near. Random fragments mostly. She remembered quite clearly walking with him in a park on a summer day while graceful white swans floated across the glassy water of a lake and he recited wonderful words to her, poetry it must have been. Maybe it was the same time he took her to a theatre to see a play. Perhaps it was *A Midsummer Night's Dream*, but she can't remember. His voice was always more vivid in her memory than his face. She'd thought as a child that he had a magic voice, that his speech could summon visions of beautiful creatures inhabiting enchanted landscapes. Pah!

She snaps to, realizing she's slowed the Subaru almost to a crawl. Flustered at her own foolishness, she speeds up along the last little bit of driveway and wheels into the visitors' parking lot.

Well, she says to herself, trying to get her hazy memories as well as her residual bitterness towards her father into their proper pigeonholes, Here we are!

Irene explains who she is to the receptionist, a harried woman demonstrably trying to be pleasant even while beset by enormous responsibilities, and is asked to wait in a reception area until someone named Ms. Menzies can have a few words with her. There's not another person to be seen and a sombre hush pervades the place. Antique furniture, freshly cut flowers in crystal vases, ornate woodwork and marble flooring. Not exactly the last refuge of indigents, Irene's thinking.

"Good morning," says a brisk woman approaching her from an office doorway, her heels clicking smartly on the marble. "Mrs. Welch? How do you do? I'm Mary Menzies." They shake hands and the woman ushers her into an office and closes the door. Irene has an impression of plate glass, pastels and exotic house plants, an unexpected contrast to the traditionalist foyer. "Please be seated," the woman says, indicating a chrome and leather office chair.

Mary Menzies is perhaps a few years younger than Irene, very polished and professional and immaculately turned out. The kind of person who makes Irene feel just a touch shabby and consequently prone to irritation. The woman seats herself opposite Irene. "Well, quite the day for you," Ms. Menzies says to her with a knowing smile, "seeing a parent after all these years."

It's not clear to Irene whether or not the comment contains an intimation that she's been neglectful of her aged father. "Yes," she says, "he vanished without a trace many years ago and it's only recently we came to learn of his whereabouts."

"How old were you when you last saw him?"

"I was twelve, I think, maybe thirteen," Irene says.

"Still a child, then," Ms. Menzies says, nodding gravely. "You must have been terribly upset to have lost him." The woman has a way of posing her questions that subtly suggests she's heard it all a hundred times before, understands all, forgives all.

"*We* didn't lose *him*," Irene says steadily, "*he* abandoned *us*." She wants to say he fucked off, but restrains herself.

"Of course," Ms. Menzies says with delicately honed compassion. "And what was it that motivated you to track him down at this late date?"

Irene is beginning to resent this line of questioning, as though this nosy stranger has been authorized to screen her from her own father. "I feel that it's important I make contact with him," she says firmly. And it *is* important to her although she has no real explanation as to why. This is the sore point that Phil had been scratching at for weeks back home, Why? Why? Why? Irritated by his dogged persistence, she became even more annoyed with herself for pursuing a course of action for reasons she couldn't understand. Was it just curiosity, or something deeper, more sinister, some final retribution she wanted to exact on her miscreant father by letting him know how much pain he had inflicted on her mother and her? Or was there some part of her that he had taken away with him and that she could reclaim only from him? All of this butts up against Irene's intense dislike of everything touchy-feely.

As though sensing her perplexity, Ms. Menzies places her next question with especial delicacy: "Important for you or for him?"

"Perhaps for both of us," Irene responds straight away. "We won't know that until after we meet, will we?"

"Please excuse my prying," Ms. Menzies says diplomatically, "but I'm sure you appreciate that your father is over ninety years old and your sudden reappearance in his life might be very disturbing to him."

"I understand that," Irene says. "We discussed all this quite thoroughly by telephone already."

"That was with Mr. Levitt, was it?" Ms. Menzies asks, although it's obvious she knows it was.

"That's right. And after several very thorough discussions it was jointly decided that I should come for this visit, so here I am. As I understand it, my father has been informed of my visit, and quite frankly I'd prefer to get on with it." Irene likes her particulars cleanly cut and properly established after which there should be no further need for long-winded discussion, a commodity this Menzies woman obviously excels in.

"Of course," Ms. Menzies replies accommodatingly. She pauses for a moment, gently tapping the armrest of her chair with a forefinger, as though considering whether what she has to say next should be said at all. "Unhappily," she continues, "Mr. Levitt is on leave of absence at present. And, well, to be perfectly frank, I'm not at all convinced that the decision-making process he went through with you was one that I would myself endorse."

"What are you saying?" Irene's getting heated. "I've driven hundreds and hundreds of miles to get here, for the purpose of seeing my father and see him is what I intend to do." Irene had realized, dealing with him over the phone, that this Levitt was a fool, but she'd gotten what she wanted out of him, and that was that.

Ms. Menzies pauses before replying, a gentle oh-it's-one-of-these-kind-of-cases smile playing on her face. "But of course," she says at last, "I shall let the visit proceed, even though it's against my better judgment. But do please be aware that we cannot have anything go on that will unduly upset your father. Recriminations or accusations or anything of the sort serve no useful purpose with someone of his advanced years. Are we perfectly clear on this point?"

Irene nods curtly, swallowing the several tart remarks she'd like to deliver to this officious meddler. The schools and hospitals are full of this type nowadays, all living handsomely off the public purse, benefits up the yin-yang, gold-plated pensions, the whole bit. And the arrogance of it! She'll *let the visit proceed*, will she? As though she's been given the right to decide who can visit their own father and who can't. Just as well she jettisoned Crystal and Isha beforehand, Irene's thinking, or they never would have gotten past this pompous gatekeeper.

She's directed down a corridor to the solarium where Professor Childes is to be found.

➛➚

Crystal and Isha meanwhile are checking out sweaters on a rack outside Sassy Suzy's in the Paradise Corners Mall. A few desultory shoppers drift past like flotsam but mostly the mall's deserted. Bored salespeople in the clothing stores refold already folded items and dream of other places. Vapid mall music goes slapback in the void.

"Yuk!" Isha says holding up a sugary pink angora sweater with a triple band of sequins at the neckline.

"Yep," Crystal says, looking at her appraisingly, "even you wouldn't look good in something that hideous."

"Betcha," Isha says, holding the offending item against her chest, tilting her head and rearranging her lips to a precocious pout.

"Ah, honey," Crystal sighs, smiling for maybe the first time on the whole trip. Truth is she loves shopping with her daughter more than almost anything. Even in a loser mall like this one. As hissy as the two of them can be towards each other when they're around other people, when it's just the two of them in the shops, mother and daughter, checking out fashions or cosmetics or whatever, just eye shopping really, they become different people, or at least people in a radically altered relationship. The weariness that presses on Crystal most of the time lifts off and lets her breathe for a bit. And Isha has nothing to kick against for the moment. It's as though they give themselves over to the pleasures of merchandise and become better people because of it.

The real story is Crystal would kill to be sixteen again. Like the day she and Brad first clicked. Looking fondly at her daughter, she remembers it like yesterday. She was standing at her locker in Central High, rummaging for a textbook or something, and suddenly there he is, Mr. Hot. Not just passing. Stopping to check her out. He looked her up and down that day and she looked him right back. No fear. At least none showing. The best thing she'd learned from her mum: you hold your ground. Of course her mum wasn't talking about when the hottest guy in the entire school is hitting on her. Two years older, he shouldn't even be interested in a sophomore like her, but he is. She feels her clothes dissolving under his lazy gaze. "Go for a ride sometime?" he asks her, as though she won't get the double meaning. "Why not," she says to him, ultra cool, like it was no special offer. Like she didn't know he drove an old Mustang convertible with a revolving cast of pretty girls cuddled beside him. Like she was nobody's fool.

Except she was. Head over heels doesn't begin to describe it. She was off the charts crazy fucking panting. To be with Him. To be seen to be with Him. To have those snotty senior girls whispering about *her*, dead with envy. Yeah.

Why would she be surprised that her mum went spastic on her. Good old Nose-to-the-Grindstone Irene. Expecting her to end up with someone like Phil. Some nothing. And here she is instead with Prince Fucking Harry on her arm. Her mother didn't rage, that's not her way;

she just carped and grumbled non-stop about how Brad was a fake and a fool, how he lacked substance, how he'd fall flat on his face once his pretty-boy features faded. Jesus, she was tiresome, like some fucking foghorn moaning out in the darkness someplace.

Crystal didn't fight back, she didn't need to, because she'd won already. Defying everyone's expectations, she and Brad stuck. After graduation he took courses in real estate and caught on with a company downtown where he was soon their *wunderkind*, selling homes like he was born to it. Pretty soon he was their standard issue Salesman of the Year. He'd figured out right away it was the women who'd be deciding which house they wanted to buy, so he worked up his act especially for them. Same as he'd done for her. He was one smooth fucker, that Brad.

He tried all his tricks on Irene too, but she never bit. Never changed her opinion of him one tick, not even when Brad and Crystal got married. Through all the speeches and kisses and toasting, Irene sat there like a stone monument, seeing the smooth groom as just another Nigel in the making. She waited for Brad to fuck up, as she'd predicted he would. It took him a few years, but he managed it eventually. Her mum never said *I told you so*; she didn't need to.

Focusing back on Sassy Suzy's, Crystal recognizes for the billionth time that her daughter is one of the few things in life she actually gives a shit about. Her irritation with the girl comes from knowing that her daughter is growing up and will soon abandon her. Just like Brad did. "Honey, I've met someone," he says one fine day, like that's a reasonable explanation for walking out on the person you've taken a vow to love and cherish forever. Fathered a child with. In good times and bad. Jesus. Crystal tries to snap this string of negativity and get back to being a friend of her daughter footloose in the mall.

"Wanna go eat?" Isha asks.

"Hmm? Oh, yes, I suppose so. We should get something before your grandma picks us up. You got your phone on, don't you?"

"Uh-huh."

The two of them follow the signs to the food court, kind of bumping into each other as they meander along. They could be refugees stumbling down the tunnel of love.

"You think it's going to be all right?" Isha asks as they slide into the fixed plastic chairs and table in the food court eating area. The smells of chicken teriyaki, pulled pork and pizza drift hungrily among the plastic dieffenbachia plants scattered throughout the echoing court.

"What, this?" Crystal says looking at the cheeseburger and fries on her tray.

"No, silly," Isha giggles, "I mean with Grandma visiting her dad."

"Oh," Crystal says, dipping a french fry into a blotch of dinosaur blood ketchup, "yeah, I dunno. But, honey, that ketchup bottle's really icky. Maybe use a napkin to pick it up."

"Okay. It just seems like a really big deal for her, doesn't it?"

Crystal poises her bulging cheeseburger in front of her mouth just as the PA system blares a garbled message about a one-time special offer that will never be repeated.

"Yeah, I guess it is for Mum for sure," Crystal says then sinks her teeth into the oozing burger. A dribble of greasy juice runs down from the corner of her mouth. Isha picks up the ketchup bottle using a paper napkin and squirts a blob of ketchup onto her paper plate.

"Is it for you?" Isha asks her through a mouthful of burger.

"Not really. A grandfather I've never seen. What's to be interested?"

"So why are we even here?"

"I dunno. It was like something to do I guess. Plus, your grandmother was pretty insistent."

"Big surprise there," Isha says, twiddling a bloodstained french fry. "Why is she such a keener?"

"Well, he is her father after all."

"Hardly. Like the guy's been gone forever. I wouldn't go looking up Dad if he did that."

"He's already done that, honey."

"But it's not the same!" Isha insists hotly. "It's not like he's disappeared or anything."

"Well I sure can't see him," Crystal says, looking around. "Oh, maybe that's him over there" — she nods towards a mangy old guy with stooped shoulders who's forlornly sweeping up bits of litter.

"*Mo-om*," Isha complains, wanting to laugh but not wanting to laugh at her dad.

⊱⊰

It's pissing rain on the afternoon Chrissie moves into Stone House. She's sorta clueless about what she's doing but she can't hit on anything else. It's like a temporary fix, right? She'll get her shit together, figure out what comes next and make a move. Sure. Stopping at the farm that day, when Shep and Peter were herding sheep, kinda made it seem like this was the thing for her to do. Maybe loneliness or something. Maybe desperation. Yag!

Old Ginger's waiting for her at the front door, like a doorman at a fancy hotel except she's wearing jeans and a sweatshirt.

"Hello, Chrissie," Ginger says, "c'mon in and get yourself dried off." Like what a mother would say if you had a proper mother. Chrissie unslings her backpack and takes off her slick. Inside the house it's so quiet you can't even tell it's raining outside. Solid. Not Chrissie's kind of scene at all. A flash of panic. What the bump's she doing in this boogeesie place. Like picture where you most don't belong and tell me how different it is from this. She looks down at her muddy sneakers and wants to cry.

"You must be soaked to the bone," Ginger says, "how about a nice hot bath?"

"Well, er . . ." Chrissie can't smell it herself, but probably she's stinking the place out because she hasn't really washed for quite a while. She's basically been living in a laundromat downtown because it stays open all night and was warm and the guy who ran it, kind of a loony but harmless, was cool about her staying there. Not a long-term arrangement, let's say. And no showers. So her clothes are clean, right, but she's like pretty ripe. Probably old Ginger's being discreet. Which is cool.

"Sure," Chrissie says, "that'd be great. Thanks."

Ginger leads her upstairs — surprising how nimble the old babe seems going up that huge stairway, not even using the curving wooden bannister — and down a corridor with watercolour landscapes along the walls. "Some of my paintings," Ginger says with a self-deprecating laugh. "Don't look too closely."

"You did these?" Chrissie asks. "Wow. They're really good."

Ginger makes a scrinched up face and shows her into a bedroom that's like the biggest one Chrissie's ever been in. You could play a game of football on the bed it's so big. Huge windows with silk drapes right down to the floor. Even a crystal chandelier, a smaller version of the one downstairs. Cake-eater terrain for sure.

"You can put your gear in here," Ginger tells her, pointing to a big wooden wardrobe. "You think it'll fit?"

"What?" Chrissie doesn't know if she's being mocked.

"Ah, honey," Ginger says coming over to her and putting a hand gently on her shoulder, "just relax, okay? I want you to feel at home here. You don't have to be anybody but you, all right? You is just fine."

"Yea, sure," Chrissie says, "thanks." It's true, she's feeling really wired, probably from not sleeping so great for like a week. Plus, she's fighting against starting to cry because old Ginger's being so fucking nice to her.

"Now, here's your bathroom," Ginger says, marching over to a door off the bedroom. "There's towels hanging for you and more in the closet if you need them. There's a shower and a tub. Do you have a preference?"

"Not really," Chrissie says, sorta stunned that she's got a bathroom that big all to herself.

"I usually like a quick shower myself," Ginger says, "but, you know, every once in a while there's nothing I love better than to draw a nice hot bath, sprinkle in some Epsom salts and soak my old bones for a good long while. Especially on a foul day like today."

"Yea," Chrissie agrees. She can feel big globs of tiredness engulfing her.

"Oh, and I picked up a little something for you," Ginger says, going to the wardrobe and bringing out a lilac-coloured robe of deep pile. "I have one like it myself," Ginger says, "and I find it's just the thing for lolling around on a wet lazy day like today."

"Thank you," Chrissie says, sorta lamely. She takes the robe from Ginger and runs her hand across the incredibly soft material. "I mean, wow, you shouldn't have," she says extra lamely.

"Perhaps," Ginger says, beaming at her, "but, y'know, so often the things you shouldn't do turn out to be the most fun. Anyway, I'll let you get yourself settled in. If you need anything, I'll be down puttering in the kitchen. Later on we could have a cup of coffee if you like, but suit yourself."

"Thank you," Chrissie says, "I mean, really, thank you." She's afraid she's going to cry again.

"Ta," the old bird says and disappears, closing the bedroom door behind her.

Chrissie stands in the middle of the enormous bedroom, holding the soft lilac robe. She feels like she's in some stupid movie where some hooker gets fixed up with a handsome gazillionaire who falls in love with her and they live happily ever after. Chrissie doesn't believe in happily ever after. She doesn't believe in happily at all except for little bits, like when you run away from home or fall for a dude who's really cool for the first few months. Guys like Chazz. Who she'd be missing like stink if he wasn't such an asshole.

And she almost is anyway.

The bathroom attached to her bedroom is all like marble and gleaming tiles. There's a big cast-iron tub with claw feet and Chrissie says to herself, Why the fuck not? She runs a hot bath, pours in some bubble bath from a bottle that's on the ledge, strips off her sweatshirt, jeans and panties, then lowers herself into the gorgeously warm water. She feels like an ice cube melting, all those sharp little crystals dissolving.

Yea, Chazz. He's left her a bunch of text messages. Stupid shit like what was he thinking, how sorry he is, how he can make it up to her. Loser yap. She blows a froth of bubbles off the bathwater like she's blowing off all the losers she's ever known. Then she holds her nose and slides down triumphantly under the foaming warm water.

Thirteen

Irene is standing in the Strathmere Lodge parking lot feeling as though she's just awakened from an anaesthetic. She remembers pausing at the solarium doorway and how momentarily relieved she felt to see only one person in the sunlit room, an extremely old man, perhaps asleep or gazing out to the gardens. His face in profile looked pinched and thin, his posture upright. To Irene's eyes he appeared refined, what she would think of as aristocratic, and her misgivings suddenly ratcheted up to near panic. Her father. That dignified old gentleman sitting over there was her father, a perfect stranger. She was entirely immobilized. She knew at that moment that she absolutely did not want to enter the room, in fact wanted nothing at all to do with him. It had been a foolish idea from the outset and now was worse, immeasurably worse. The indignation she'd held against him for all those years had abandoned her. All her firm resolve to hold him to account melted to a puddle at her feet. She remembers struggling to compose herself, to find that core of strength that has carried her through far worse than this over the years. Really? Had there been worse than this over the years, this clumsy attempt at unearthing old secrets and betrayals that might better have been left undisturbed.

And why on earth hadn't she consulted her mum beforehand? Ginger may well have told her something that would have prevented this foolhardy venture that was now maybe about to blow up in her face. Yes, there undoubtedly were reasons, things to know which might have dissuaded her. Because her whole life has been steadfastly structured around avoidance of matters like these, she's hopelessly unprepared for this encounter with a father who abandoned his wife and kids for no apparent reason. This old fellow just up and bloody vanished. What can you say to such a person, how can you control your rage and bitterness and sadness. That preposterous woman in the office — what was her name? Ms. something-or-other, Ms. Menzies — perhaps she'd been right after all. That this was not a wise thing to be doing; that there was no upside to it, no prospect of improved outcomes. Only the likelihood of distress all round.

She remembers willing herself to step into the solarium and approach her father. They'd introduced themselves with an awkwardly formal handshake. He'd asked about her journey and then straightaway enquired about Ginger, her health, how she was getting on. But what happened after that is now a muddle in Irene's mind. They'd chatted amiably but stiffly for a while. Trivial things. Inconsequential morsels about her husband and daughter and grandchild. Not a word about the gulf that has yawned between them for four decades. Nothing by way of explanation or apology. While Irene felt enormously self-conscious during this stilted exchange, the old fellow gave no hint of discomfort. She sensed he was watching her from a distance, a height, at an emotional remove she had no idea how to breach. There was a coolness about him which she interpreted as indifference. Somebody brought a tray with tea and dainty sandwiches at one point, allowing them the distraction of sipping and nibbling, she in her disarray, he in his dignified remove.

And before you knew it, the visit was over. "Goodbye." "Lovely to see you." "Do give my regards to your mother." Then that confounded Menzies escorting her to the foyer and thanking her for visiting. "I'm sure it meant a very great deal to your father." "Goodbye." "Yes, yes, goodbye."

On the long drive home, nobody pays any attention to anyone. In the driver's seat Irene is gripping the steering wheel tight enough to choke it. Alongside, Crystal stares blankly out the window at the wastelands of exurban slosh. Isha's in the back seat, eyes closed, listening to bubblegum pop on her MP3.

Irene's far away and long ago, back to that day when her dad walked out on them, when she was still Sophia. The memory has a hazy, dreamlike texture: her sitting on the grass in dappled sunshine under a big sycamore tree in the back yard, watching a line of ants moving purposively along a narrow pathway they'd worn through the grass. She heard a car door slam and the squeal of rubber as a vehicle accelerated away down the street. She knew it was her dad. Perhaps a part of her had been waiting for this day, this loss. Pathos lunged at her but she beat it back savagely. She could have killed at that moment.

After a bit her mum came waddling across the lawn to her, smiling bravely, her tummy enormous with the baby that was due any day. "Come into the house for a minute would you, darling," her mum said. Sophia didn't want to go, she didn't need to hear, she was thirteen years old and knew already.

"What is it?" she asked.

"Please, dear, come into the house; I can't sit down here or I'll never get up."

"He's gone, hasn't he?" Sophia asked, still not moving from where she was sitting.

"Yes, I'm afraid so."

"Is he coming back?" She knew he wasn't.

"Perhaps. But, no, I hardly think so."

Sophia wanted to swear. She wanted to call her dad a dirty, lying, cheating, fucking asshole, but she knew if she did it would upset her mum. And she wanted to call her mum a pathetic suck, but she didn't say that either. Instead she stood up and took her mum's hand and together they walked slowly back across the cool grass towards the house.

"Why has he left us?" she demanded to know.

Her mum said nothing while she laboriously climbed the back porch steps and then flopped heavily into the swing rocker on the porch. "It's complicated, honey," Ginger told her.

But Sophia was in no mood for platitudes. "What's so complicated? You're going to have a baby. It's his baby too. And he leaves us right before it's born. I don't understand it."

"You will. Some day you will. Maybe I will too. In the meantime, we'll have to get along the best we can. And, Sophia, I do need to tell you this one thing."

"Yea, what?"

"I know it's very hurting for you that your father didn't come to say goodbye to you."

"I don't care." Sophia was determined not to cry.

"Of course you care. And so does he. But he was so broken up he just couldn't face you; he was so sorry he couldn't."

"I don't believe it." Truculently.

"Sophia, it's important that you do believe it, and it's equally important that you not hate your father."

"But I do hate him!"

"No you don't. You love him; you've always loved him. And it will be way better for you, and for me, if we don't let that love curdle into something ugly. Love's all we've got, honey. Throw that away and we've really got nothing."

But Sophia couldn't hear it, didn't want to hear it. Nobody had ever loved their dad more than Sophia did. How smart he was and clever and funny. How he sounded like a posh English actor the way he talked. He could make her laugh so hard. Phi he called her. Said it was something about a golden ratio in art and architecture. She loved the crazy things he said, even if she didn't have a clue. And all the neat places he took her to, like going all the way to Toronto by train one Christmastime just to see *The Nutcracker*. Or the times they went sailing together on the lake, skimming across the glassy water in a sleek sailboat. Yea, she'd loved him, more than she loved her mum really, because he was just that little bit further away from her. Like a magician, he had the added allure of inaccessibility, whereas her mum was always there for her, common as porridge.

But now he was gone. And she had no idea why.

Of course her friends at school had noticed eventually and asked her about it. She didn't know what to say; she told them he was away teaching at a different university, making tons of money and that pretty soon she and her mum and the baby would be joining him there. It was in California she said, to make them envious. Sometimes she half believed it herself.

But the "pretty soon" never happened and Sophia in the meantime set about sealing off the part of herself she'd shared with her father, the way a tree seals up the wound from a severed limb. Her eagerness for love and approval, her delight in the extraordinary, her expectation of awaiting wonders — all of it gradually retreated behind a fortification of brisk competence and diminished expectancy. She came to prefer reliability over excitement. She stopped using her name and insisted she be called by her middle name, Irene. Before she was out of junior high she was a chronic keeper of lists and schedules. She won spelling bees with daunting regularity but abandoned her piano lessons. She disciplined herself to never look back to that charmed childhood of poetry and laughter, to discount it as whimsy, ephemeral as childhood itself. Once graduated from high school, with no desire for the so-called higher learning of university that she associated with her feckless father, she took correspondence courses in accounting and business management, laying the groundwork for a productive and unsurprising career.

Only after the birth of her daughter had some of the banished gentleness returned to her, so that she became misty and tender with tiny Crystal pressed to her breast. She felt a faint echo of the same at the birth of her first grandchild, Isha, but her feelings were muted by her dislike of Crystal's husband, precluding any chance of unsullied tenderness.

Over the years her mother had tried to talk with Irene about her father, his leaving, but each time Irene had cut the conversation short.

"Water under the bridge," she'd said. "No sense looking back at things that can't be changed." So the gulf between mother and daughter widened. Plus, as the years went on, Ginger became increasingly eccentric in Irene's eyes. Getting involved in radical issues, marches and sit-ins and even civil disobedience, making a spectacle of herself for causes she didn't even fully understand. Irene didn't blame her mum for going off the rails; she blamed her dad for pushing her off.

All the more preposterous then for Irene to have insisted upon visiting her father once his whereabouts became known. It had become a kind of obsession, this insistent nagging that she go see her dad and smash, she imagined, the tension she couldn't deny still feeling after so many years. The stupidity of it, the recklessness, now leered at her between the passing signage for oil changes and furniture sales, casinos and real estate. It was the kind of stunt idiots pulled, losers watching Hollywood romcoms to discover the meaning of life. After years of careful planning and meticulous work to structure her universe in such a way that she'd never be blindsided again, here she is, back where she started, fighting with every ounce of strength not to burst into tears because of her goddamned father.

Ginger's sitting in the breakfast nook on a sunny morning, shaking off the muddle of semi-dreams from last's night's semi-sleep. She's trying to soothe herself by lingering over coffee while she checks the morning's news on her tablet, but the news is hardly soothing.

Fighting in Gaza again, rockets raining down. Still. Women and children screaming in the streets. Boys throwing stones. Raging. The rage of young men. All over the planet young men raging. Not Frankie though. Frankie went to fight with no fight in him. Duty and honour, not hatred. Still. Did he ever kill some young man, some lad like himself full of grace and promise. A farm boy from the Rhineland perhaps whose sweetheart or sister or mother gazed across the fields of home and wept as I did. Oh Frankie, how would you feel killing such a boy. Seeing him sprawled in a ditch his pale blue eyes staring blankly at the sky. Of course Hitler had to be stopped but did this boy's dreams? Helicopter gunships over Jerusalem. Slouching towards Bethlehem was it? Dear old Yeats. To be born and die young over and over. The good they do. Do not go gentle into. No wonder the young men rage against. Carrying coffins through the thrown-stone streets swearing revenge. He who seeks vengeance must dig two graves. Rupert Graves was it or was it Robert? No, Rupert Brooke. Yes. Some corner of a foreign field. To hold them with me through the gate of Death. Inside the Gates of Eden. Poor boys with no war for their rage. Not even stones to throw. But wanting to throw. To hurt. Like Crystal's Brad. Brad the Impaler. Yes, he impaled poor Crystal, didn't he. Such a beautiful child she was, like her own little Isha. Or Sophia. And like little Cagey as well. Wounded. Children of light. Down the dark of life. Learning how to die before time cries, to cry before time dies. Yes, Nigel mourned as I did Frankie's dying. We met in the shadow of death not knowing. No rage in Nigel at all. Sadness and fear rather. Like Peter. Hushed up secrets. Once I had a secret love that lived within the heart of. Glimpsed now and then in that old mirror I got from Yeats, the tarnished mirror of the world.

She puts the tablet down with a sigh. She glances from the miniaturized wizardry of that device to the Aga stove, as much a technological wonder near the beginning of her life as the tablet is near the end. Whenever she sees the neighbourhood kids on the street with their thumbs flickering over their smart phones like chickens after scratch, she feels really old. Old and irrelevant. Which she is. Obsolete. More Aga than tablet. Plus, she's finding the tablet a damn nuisance in many ways, constantly hopping around without being told to, crazy stuff popping up from God knows where and then refusing to leave. She knows it's her insufficiency, not the device's and Peter's been a dear with his wise guidance.

Oh, stop your foolishness, she chides herself, getting back to the business at hand; she's determined to find out whatever she can about the current scandal at the Congregation of the Great Convergence. With Peter up at the farm, where he dislikes spending any time at all in cyberspace, and who can blame him, she's now reimagining herself as the *de facto* internet whizz-kid who'll find virtual needles in haystacks. Sure enough, Google instantly throws at her dozens of sites she can visit to get the lowdown on the Congregation.

And, yes indeed, there are new developments. *The Huffington Post* has the latest:

> The child abuse sex scandal that has dogged a controversial religious sect in recent weeks has now resulted in criminal charges being laid against seventeen high-ranking members of the church.
>
> Justice officials in Atlanta today confirmed that the suspects, fifteen males and two females, were taken into custody late yesterday evening following coordinated FBI raids on facilities owned by the Congregation of the Great Convergence in several states. Documents, computers and other materials were seized in the raids.
>
> The suspects are slated to appear in federal court this morning to be arraigned on multiple charges believed to include kidnapping, aggravated sexual abuse, sexual exploitation of children, transportation of obscene matters for sale or distribution and sex trafficking of children by force, fraud or coercion.

Ginger puts the tablet on her table and allows it to blink off.

She's assailed by a swarm of emotions. Anger at these filthy hypocrites. A weeping sadness at young lives brutalized. Weariness over what seems humankind's limitless capacity for evildoing. Just now she can summon no compassion for these people. Yes, yes, she knows they're victims themselves, that many of them may have been brutalized as children in just the same way. Etcetera, etcetera. But right now, just in this moment, she'd accept seeing all of them gunned down and their corpses kicked into ditches.

Shocked by her own rage, she gets up and strides outdoors. She'll take it to the trees. Yes, she will. The cool air's freshly green and sweet with birdsong. Sunshine's splashing a Pollock patchwork through the trees. Halfway across the lawn, she stops to watch a mass of flying insects backlit by sunlight, their wings gleaming. Each tiny flyer darts up a couple of feet, hovers, then drops down again. Dozens of them in the nuptial dance, they look like a line of animated musical notes in a plainsong inscribed by mad monks. A broad smile breaks across Ginger's face. "Oh, dance away!" she calls out to them, "Yes, dance, you lovestruck beauties!"

Ever since she was a child barely able to walk, Ginger has been drawn to the trees surrounding Stone House. Big deciduous trees mostly, beeches, maples, oaks and horse chestnuts. They'd seemed enormous to her as a child, though they must have been smaller then than now. Walking beneath them, touching their rough or smooth bark, curling up among their roots on a hot summer's day, cavorting with Frankie in the fallen autumn leaves, burying themselves under huge mounds of leaves where nobody would ever find them except maybe old Phillips the gardener when he came muttering along with his rake.

Not surprisingly, the trees cast a similar spell over her darling son Peter as a child. She'd often discover him among them, perhaps sitting with his back against a trunk, poring over a book, lost in childhood reverie.

Even Nigel instantly loved the trees, that time they came for a visit with baby Sophia. Arrangements had been made with the people renting the house; they were away for a few weeks and had invited Ginger to make use of the place in their absence.

How very strange it had been, returning to her childhood home with her parents now gone from it. Still off in the Congo, their infrequent letters less and less coherent. Ginger's attempts to get information about them from the Congregation had been entirely futile. "Joyfully doing God's work," she'd been told. "Happy workers in the vineyards of the Lord."

Visiting Stone House without them in it had only ratcheted up Ginger's anxiety about them. Estranged or not — and that was how she thought of them, estranged — they were still her flesh and blood, and she feared they were being cynically exploited.

But while the house had seemed vacuous and cold without her mother puttering in the kitchen and her father shuffling in and out of rooms philosophically, the great trees, as always, had been a comfort. The horse chestnuts were in bloom just then and Nigel was in raptures over having them alongside stout English oaks. They reminded him, he said, of Croft Castle in Herefordshire where the ancient tree walk featured an avenue of Spanish chestnuts planted 350 years ago in the formation of the Spanish Armada, allegedly with chestnuts that had washed ashore on English beaches after the Spanish fleet was wrecked. Huge English oaks, Nigel reported with glee, now triumphantly surrounded the declining chestnut trees at the castle.

Touching the sinuous skin of an enormous copper beech, Ginger smiles to herself. What a silky bullshitter that Nigel had been. And while he took away from her far more than he was entitled to, he also left her a considerable bestowal. Beforehand, even as a giddy schoolgirl cavorting in these leaves, she'd been as careful and correct as a proper little Christian could be. She was her parents' daughter, dutiful and timid. But after a dozen years living with Nigel and then being abandoned by him, she was far less constrained by caution and conventionality. By the time she'd moved back to Stone House with the kids in 1965 she was, if not yet a firebrand, at least a passably radicalized modern woman. Nigel's contempt for all things orthodox, buttoned-down, stuck in the mud, had become her own.

Typically, he'd given her a copy of Simone de Beauvoir's *The Second Sex* after the first English translation appeared in 1953. He'd already read it himself in French and had rhapsodized to her about its revolutionary woman's perspective. How the great machineries of society grind women down to become passive, dependent and inward. "Just listen to this," he'd suddenly exclaim, translating from his book, "*at the moment when man asserts himself as subject and free being, the idea of the Other arises*. That's it! Woman becomes the Other! And therein lies her oppression. Do you see, darling?"

Of course she didn't see much of anything from these random asides, but after she'd devoured the book herself in its much-maligned English translation, oh, yes, then she saw. Saw in a way that Nigel couldn't possibly have done. Not and then walk out on them as perfidiously as he did. That was the thing about Nigel, how he could bring provocative ideas into play and then act in a way that completely confounded them. It was not the essence of the concept that attracted him, she finally came to understand, but rather its boldness, its daring to challenge old orthodoxies, to smash down derelict convention. It was among his many paradoxes that, although he belonged imaginatively back in Edwardian England, he took his greatest delight in seeing traditions smashed.

Perversely that radical streak attached itself to Ginger after he'd gone. Except for her it wasn't just a coda of incendiary ideas, as it was for Nigel. No, for her it became the stuff of everyday. The peace movement, women's liberation, environmentalism, the rights of blacks, gays, First Nations — she threw herself into radical activism and found in it a balm for the hurt of Nigel's desertion. Gradually Stone House became the incongruous hub for Shetterly's lefties, whose numbers could have been accommodated in a place far smaller and less grand. Meetings were convened. Plots concocted. Inflammatory pamphlets printed on an ancient Gestetner. Stoned House some took to calling it.

Which brings her full circle to the dirty business of the Congregation. The will her parents left with their solicitor before departing for Africa and ultimately dying there specifies that Stone House will be held in trust for as long as Ginger continues to live in it and then become the sole and exclusive property of the Congregation. "Over my dead body," she says with a grin, pressing herself fully against the smooth beauty of the reassuring beech trunk. "I don't know quite how, but we'll find a way to get you free of those devils."

Peter puts down the phone and gazes out the kitchen window at sodden fields and a beaten pewter sky. The news is not good. Little Isaac, Ron and Lois's new baby, is back in intensive care. The doctors are unsure, the prognosis far from encouraging. The leading people in the field are at the Hospital for Sick Children in Toronto and Isaac's best chances of survival might lie there. Plus, Lois's folks are nearby in Hamilton. Nothing's decided yet. Except. Ron was sobbing on the phone, obviously stretched to breaking with fear and anxiety and exhaustion. "I'm sorry," he kept apologizing to Peter, "I'm sorry we've let you down."

Peter had done his best to reassure the poor guy, telling him over and over that the baby's health is foremost, that the farm will be fine, not to worry, not to beat himself up, not to add to his troubles unnecessarily. Knowing all along that Ron wasn't hearing any of it, couldn't hear anything really except the roar of helpless panic.

Peter knows it intimately, in all its cruel twists, that particular genre of angst associated with the survival of one's child. There is no other terror quite like it. What would be the greater torment, he wonders, going through what Ron and Lois are now, with its slowly coiling uncertainty, or the swift and sudden loss he himself endured? To have a child poised on the cusp of life and death, with alternating hope and despair battering in your heart day after day; or to have a perfect child snatched away in an instant, replaced by a permanent backwash of grief and guilt.

When Cecilia's car slammed into that abutment, instantly killing her and little Katherine Ginger, Peter knew absolutely who was to blame. Not in the way that Ron's now castigating himself for his helplessness, because there's not a thing Ron and Lois can do except put their faith in what the doctors are saying, try to make the right decision, then hope and pray for their baby's survival. Peter was denied even that. Life one moment, death the next.

How many times has he gone over that conversation with the mechanic. Dieter his name was, stitched on a patch on his grease-smeared coveralls. Something in the steering column that needed replacing, Peter can't now remember what. "Could go any minute," the fellow had said, "I wouldn't recommend driving her very far or very fast in that condition." Maybe not driving it at all except back to the garage when the replacement part got delivered in three or four days. And how had this not registered with Peter. How had he made a mental note to bring the car back in the following week, but neglected to tell Cecilia that the car was unsafe to drive. Yes, yes, she'd told him a week earlier that she planned on driving to the city for something, but he hadn't connected the two.

There'd been a crisis on the farm that morning, his prized ram down and the vet late in arriving and before he knew it Cecilia had gone and he didn't know where. Then remembered she'd mentioned the city. Frantic, he'd called her cell, then again, and again, but couldn't get her to answer. Eventually he called the police, pleading with the dispatcher to see if they couldn't intercept Cecilia somehow. "I'm sorry, sir," the toneless dispatcher had said, "we've had a rash of incidents this morning and our resources are stretched very thin already. We'll do what we can and get back to you."

There it was: the moment of numbing powerlessness. He could do nothing, just as Lois and Ron can do nothing now. Yes, maybe he could've gotten in his truck and raced around aimlessly looking for her, but where to look? And she might return any moment. Please return. Please. Please. All afternoon he waited in torment, still trying to call Cecilia, still getting no answer. Shep took to nervous pacing up and down the laneway, as though he knew more than Peter did.

When the phone finally rang late in the afternoon, Peter's heart sagged. He almost dared not answer. The police. A license plate number. We're sorry. An accident. Best to come at once.

Almost three years now he's lived with it and the memory has had him by the throat for much of that time. Awake at night, he would torment himself with it, refusing to forgive himself for the unforgivable. He's never confessed his negligence to anyone. Never returned to that garage either, convinced the mechanic would know of his criminal stupidity. He imagines old Carlsen, Cecilia's dog-training guru, suspects him of negligence — perhaps criminal negligence — in Cecilia's death. His culpability's the reason he can't speak to Ginger, or anyone else, about the accident. How could he talk about his feelings without acknowledging that his carelessness was directly responsible for their deaths. Although he'd said it to himself a thousand times, these were words he could not speak to anyone.

All the more surprising then that he'd found himself talking so easily to the girl about the accident, only a brief mention, but nevertheless without the barbed hooks that can normally snag his heart. Perhaps he'd recognized in her a fellow-sufferer. She's an odd little sock, but strangely appealing. Some kind of kindred spirit. That first time he'd heard her scream, before even having seen her, it was like the echo of a scream he'd been trying not to hear for three years. Certainly there's something between Shep and her, something reminiscent of how Cecilia was with Shep.

Ron's call just now was distressing for its news of the baby's peril, but not because Lois and Ron would be leaving the farm. What's been brought into focus for Peter is that being back here at the farm has not entailed nearly the sorrow it previously did. Something fundamental has shifted, allowing the place to begin emerging from the gloom of his wrongdoing. He knows Cecilia and little Katherine Ginger are here as they are nowhere else. Shep knows it too. It's where they belong. For the first time since, Peter feels some measure of happiness about returning home.

Fourteen

Whenever Ginger and Irene talk on the telephone a lot of the words go missing. Swoosh, they're gone like strangers on a crowded street. Not so much unheard as unrecognized. Some get swallowed up in the past, like now, as Irene's talking once more about her father. For years not a word about him permitted, but lately a topic that can't be left alone. Yet not faced squarely either, rather poked at from the safer distances of irony. Ginger's aware in the flight of words that there's something her daughter wants to disclose but can't. It's conceivable that the disjointed chatter about Nigel is a façade intended to conceal, but Ginger thinks not. Irene, dear, analytical, methodical Irene, is not given to concealment. No, there's an inexplicability rummaging around inside her, looking for a way out, and it's got to do with Nigel. As beguiled by curiosity as the next person, Ginger knows not to press; Irene's got her own way of going about things.

As happens during these half-conversations, or later perhaps in the ensuing silence, Ginger takes to musing on what has become of her winsome baby girl. Ginger would like nothing better than to stop Irene in mid-sentence and describe to her daughter the feelings that had welled up inside her when she walked into that gathering of Nigel's colleagues with her miraculous new baby in her arms. How everybody clustered about, exclaiming and marvelling at perfection born again. The bee's knees. The cat's meow. Welcome into the world, Sophia Childes. You're one in a million, kid.

Same thing when she went walking with the baby in her pram. Complete strangers on the street going ga-ga. Girls not much younger than herself melting at the knees, treacly with sentiment. Poker-faced old duffers breaking into silly grins. Baby Sophia was a love charm, a touchstone of tenderheartedness. And later as a schoolgirl too, the golden years for her daughter, when Nigel took such an interest in her.

"There's something I have to tell you, Mother," Irene says. At last.

"Yes?" Ginger's attention meanders around the kitchen, resting for a moment on the hanging copper pots and pans, the Aga stove, the big oak sideboard holding her parents' too-good-to-use dinnerware. Herself as a solemn child tiptoeing around in the pious quiet of this huge home. Then later, after Nigel, moving back here with the kids because it was hers, sort of, and safe.

"It's about Dad," Irene says tentatively. Meaning something beyond the standard recitation of grievances against, which is what Irene has been engaged in recently. Now the cracking point. Something out of character for Irene, something heartfelt. Ginger waits, reupholstering her love for her daughter.

"The truth is, Mother, that I — well, *we*, Crystal and Isha and myself, but just really me — went to visit Dad a while ago."

Ginger can't absorb it for a moment, as though her daughter has suddenly started talking in Swahili. "Did I hear you correctly," Ginger asks, "that you've visited your father — *your* father, not Phil's?"

"That's right, Mother."

Deep silence on the line. Two brains whirling, not a word between. So.

"I'm missing something here," Ginger says eventually. "How on earth did you ever find him? Where is he?" For Ginger it's as though a ghost has walked into the room, as though poor Mr. What's His Name with the pistol in the bedroom had come downstairs looking for a cup of tea.

"Oh, a friend of a friend sort of thing," Irene tells her. "The how's not important." Irene's getting back to being Irene.

"Yes, that's so," Ginger agrees. "But the why?"

"I know, I know," Irene says. "It was like, once I found out where he was living, I had to see him. It became a kind of obsession. I wanted not to but I couldn't not. Oh, Mum, I've been in such a state about it!"

Here's a rarely seen side, near vulnerability, admission of helplessness. Irene — Sophia — was sometimes like that as a girl, as children are, up until that dreadful day when Nigel walked out on them. After that, scarcely at all. Bewildered on occasion perhaps, but seldom vulnerable. Ginger wishes they were not on the phone just now, that Irene was with her here instead. A comforting touch, who knows, perhaps even an embrace. The unaccustomed tenderness Ginger's feeling towards her daughter. Not quite herself from the shock of Irene's confession, Ginger can't find the right words to say.

But Nigel. Out of nowhere. After all these years. The whole notion seems preposterous. Not that she hasn't thought of him. Of course. Peter's not quite the spitting image of his father, but the resemblance is strong enough and some of Peter's mannerisms — an occasional turning of the head or sudden smile — are uncannily alike. So, yes, every once in a while she'd taken to wondering what had become of her wayward husband. If he was still alive. Where he might be. Whether chance might bring them together for a final passing moment. The faithful child support payments, halved when Irene turned twenty-one, ceased abruptly with Peter's twenty-first birthday. After that, nothing.

The odd thing is, she realizes, she has actually been thinking of Nigel quite a bit of late, certainly more than what she used to. Could it be that she'd somehow picked up on Irene's discovery, that she'd become subconsciously aware of Nigel's being found. Like Shep sensing Peter's returning home. When she first got the Internet, Ginger fought against but eventually succumbed to the temptation to search for him. She found a number of references to speeches given, papers presented at conferences, but all long in the past, nothing recent, nothing that gave any hint as to where he was or whether he was still alive. Neither Google nor Wikipedia had been any more successful at pinning Nigel down than she'd ever been. She sort of liked that about him, that he'd proven himself too elusive for the all-prying eye of technology. She could imagine him quoting Orwell back to her. At times she'd supposed he was already dead.

Now this. Allowing her surprise, Ginger's all curiosity. "Where exactly is he?" she asks.

"In a kind of retirement lodge over in Clarkston," Irene tells her.

"And his health?" Ginger asks.

"He seemed fine," Irene says. "He sat in a chair the whole time I was there, so I don't know how active he is, but he certainly wasn't lying in a bed with tubes stuck up his nose and throat."

"Good. I'm glad. And his mind?"

"Seemed fine too. Lucid, I would say. He asked about you right away. We chatted for maybe half an hour. Quite normal conversation really."

"Yes."

"Well," Irene adds, hesitating, "normal is perhaps not quite the right word."

"How so?"

"It's just that he seemed, oh, I don't know . . . he seemed *absent* the whole time we were talking. Not spaced out or anything, he was very alert, but as though he really wasn't there, like there was a glass wall or something between us. Afterwards, it was almost as though the conversation hadn't happened at all."

"Fascinating," Ginger says. "And what about your feelings towards him?"

"Oh, God," Irene says, "I'm all over the map. You should have seen me on the drive home. I think I scared poor Crystal and Isha half to death."

"Did they visit with Nigel too?"

"No, no. They went shopping in the mall. A good thing too. Mum,

I'm sorry I didn't tell you about him right away," Irene says, sounding more like her child than she has in years. "Once I found out where he was, I mean. I didn't know if you'd want to know, or if he'd want you to know, or what. So I thought the best thing to do would be to go see him for myself, find out what's what, and fill you in later. Put things in order, you know me, but a fat lot of good it did me."

"I understand," Ginger says, not conveying how much more fully she understands than Irene might imagine. "And I'm glad you've told me now. But I must say it's quite a shock. Quite a shock indeed."

"Tell me about it," Irene says.

Ginger waits.

"Mum, I think we need to talk about this, don't you?"

⇝⇜

Does she? Raking those old embers. Coals still smoldering. Maybe striking sparks. Oh, Nigel Nigel Nigel. Missing in action. Inaction all this time. Gone before the birth of your son. Gone with the Wind. Dust in the Wind. All We Are. Now there you are. At last. Still. Unwanted. Unbidden. Unforgiven. Couldn't just die and be done with it. Be done and be damned. Have you something to say for yourself after all the silence? Always something to say. Mellifluity himself. Until. That honeymoon in England, remember? Not even a courtesy call on your family. As though they didn't exist at all. Chasing Hardy's ghost around the Dorset hills. Dogbury Hill in Blackmore Vale. Bookham Knoll in the Dorset Downs. Ups and Downs. Shropshire should have been a hint: Dear A.E. Spent in star-defeated sighs. But Dartmoor threw a dart into the heart of it all didn't it? The parts you'd roamed together you and Frankie. Roamin' in the gloamin'. The tin mine ruins where you sought shelter drenched and besotted. Widecombe in the Moor. The old farmhouse by the brook. You pointing to the window of the room where you'd slept. Our taking the same room that night. Hearing the same brook running as you'd heard. How you couldn't look in my eyes for fear. Nor I in yours. I knew it then. He was there between us in the bed. Between us even as we coupled. I could feel you holding him inside my skin. Feel you entering him through me. I cried all night. For him. And for us. What had become of us? And now what has become of you re-entering the world you left? That dreadful poem I wrote that night while you slept blissfully. About a convict escaped from the prison of love now loose on the moors. And here you are loose again after all these years. Turn me loose. Turn Turn Turn. To everything there is. Oh, Nigel.

⋟⋞

Chrissie enters the crowded foyer of Shallowford High's auditorium where the all-candidates meeting is about to begin, then hears a familiar voice and freezes.

"Hey, babe."

Motherfucker if it isn't Chazz smiling down at her with that dumb grin she always loved. Schlurg. The low rumble of conversations all around her collapses into a hard knot in her stomach. Her hands clench into instinctive fists. What's truly freaky is that Chazz is like totally made over — hair cut short, styled even, stubble shaved clean, a choice suit. A tie and polished leather shoes. Blower. No big surprise that Chazz would be here tonight, except that maybe his old man would want to keep him out of sight. Hence Chazz the changed man. Chameleon man. Hmm. His dad's brought him to heel somehow. And there's only one "somehow" Chazz faithfully responds to. Like how do you spell money.

Chrissie's brain begins jumping over very high hurdles and hardly hitting any ground at all. She hasn't seen Chazz since. Hasn't wanted to see him except sometimes. She's a new person now, this is what she feels almost every morning when she wakes up in that mega soft bed at Stone House, knows it to her blood when she goes cycling the back roads and trails in wind and rain, hurtling away from the no-hoper she was. He was. They were. Drenched and exhilarated, she can almost believe that she's done with the need to bob and weave, to slip past Illinger and Harding. And, yea, by Chazz too, when you think of it. She refuses to accept the suspicion that all she's really done is run away from home another time. This is something else, more like busting a bad habit, getting clear of always thinking herself an add-on, some ratchet appendage to bigger things.

Now here they are, Chazz and herself, standing face to face in the crowded foyer of the high school auditorium where Chazz was king back in the day. His version anyway.

Her prince too, no question. Until the curtain got pulled away. The noise of the room surges back in, a hundred conversations bouncing off the cinder-block walls, large men laughing too loudly, compliant wives squeaking. Yes, she can hear them, everyone in agreement that the Illinger boy — such great promise, what a future ahead of him — is already Mr. Past Tense. Chrissie can hear voices now she never heard before. Chazz may have changed his look, but she feels she's changed a fuck of a lot more than that.

"Hey, Chazz," she says, staying big, "what's so?"

"Kinda been missing you, Chrissie," Chazz says, coming closer, all sincerity and cologne, cow eyes innocent of meaning.

"Yeh?" Chrissie's heart does the same caught fish flop it did the first time she ever saw him back in TO. Like high wire beautiful. She could keel over right now and lie flat on her back in the grass staring up at the songs moving in Chazz's eyes. Float out of time on the dark ripples of his lyrics. He'd sing for her, stroke her soul with sweet purple song. Yea, she loved him like a load of gelignite. Even now, even knowing, she can feel herself softening, beginning to liquefy under the influence.

Except. Yea, the lies, right? The smug indifference, trust destroyed. And except out of nowhere she suddenly has this flash of captain charisma here schnorting around in that cunt in the vid wearing nothing but the stupidest look on his face and, she can't help it, really, she starts giggling. She tries to pinch her arm hard enough to stop, but can't. I mean, that cow-eyed, slobbering tongue look on his face! Like some bammer gawping in a pool of enormous boobs and bums. She can't help herself it's so cunchy. She's trying, but she can't eject it and pretty soon she's laughing like a maniac. Right there in the foyer, with all the straights looking on, she's rolling like a loonie on uppers. Betty Boobs and John the Rod!! She just about shrieks with hysterical laughter. Decades of graduating classes, immortalized on the foyer walls in tuxedoes and gowns and "the world awaits you" inspiration, gaze down on her in dismay. She can't help herself. Starring Veronica Vulva and Buster Big Balls!! She stamps her feet up and down, going crazy with bizarre.

Uncomprehending, Chazz is losing more cool than a retreating glacier. "Um," he says, drawing closer, working the power that he knows works, "Chrissie, I've been doing a lot of thinking."

"Awesome," Chrissie says, finally subduing her laughter, "trying new things is way savage."

"Okay, Okay, maybe I was a bit of jerk," Chazz says, looking more a jerk than a bit. "Yea, so maybe I owe you an apology," he says with an aw-shucks staring-at-his-shoes little boy schtick honed to perfection in childhood for getting around his mother.

"Like for having me fired, you mean?"

"No, no," Chazz says, laying a hand on her arm. "I never got you fired. Believe me, I begged my old man not to do that. You gotta trust me on this, babe."

"That would be one of my debased activities, would it?" Chrissie says with a lewd wink that's totally lost on Chazz. "Trusting you?"

"No, what I been thinking," Chazz says, uncomprehending, stripped of charisma, "is we had such a fine thing, Chrissie, you and me. Solid, you know. Sweet and solid. So I been thinking maybe we should try again, you know."

Chrissie flutters her eyelids mockingly. She knows exactly what his game is. He wants the evidence back before it blows up in his face. Explodes the myth of Mayor Illinger the Good. The Holy Family. Trouble is, in trying to manufacture sincerity, Chazz has produced exactly the same dumb look on his face that he had on the video jacket, which launches Chrissie into laughter all over again. The more she looks at him the more screamingly absurd he seems. She's starting to cry she's laughing so hard. She's gonna piss herself. People are kinda gathered around, some of them starting to chuckle as well, like that's what it's about. Maybe some cray-cray theatre piece right there in the middle of the lobby. You never know anymore.

"Or maybe not, Chazzo," Chrissie finally says, wiping her eyes with her knuckles. "Maybe not." She fishes in her pocket, finds a questionable Kleenex to dab at her eyes and wipe her nose. "Sorry about that," she says, giggles still rippling, "I got friends waiting, I gotta go. See you round, Chazz, right?"

"Yea, devious," Chazz says, "au revs," picking up and dusting off his dignity and then giving his best imitation of a stud sauntering off like there's plenty more on the floor.

She stares after him. The songs, blood-red sex, that whole choreography of lust. Yah.

Too late, though, Chazzman, too late to date, honey, because I got the video. And you got a problem. So hang tight.

She turns a saucy pirouette and strides away.

⁂

"And how are you feeling about your daughter's visit?" Mary Menzies asks Nigel. They're sitting at a bistro table on the flagstone patio at Strathmere. There's a dozen or so other residents at scattered tables, everyone loosened up in the lazy afternoon sunshine. Hanging baskets of nasturtiums splash colours around the patio. Summer moving on.

"A most interesting experience," Nigel says, taking a sip of coffee.

"Surely you're not prepared to be cryptic on a glorious afternoon like this," Menzies says.

"Far from it," Nigel replies. "It's just that the experience was so entirely singular."

"Singular how?" Menzies asks.

"Well, here was this person," Nigel says, opening both palms towards her, "to all appearances a perfectly normal specimen. Not particularly interesting, but not disagreeable either."

"I found her a bit prickly at first," Menzies says, peering at him over the rim of her coffee cup, "but I suspect that may have been nerves."

"Yours?" Nigel asks, just to be impertinent.

"Of course not," she counters, "she wasn't *my* long-lost daughter come calling."

"But that's the thing, you see," he says, "I could not for the life of me relate to her as a *daughter*. As my own flesh and blood, to use a tiresome phrase. I can scarcely recall anything of her as a child and there's nothing about this woman that strikes any chord of familiarity or affection or anything else. She was to all intents and purposes a complete stranger, one with whom I was required to make polite conversation for half an hour and nothing else. It was one of those encounters that theoretically should be freighted with significance but was in fact rather tedious."

"I'm surprised," Menzies says. "She was so intent upon visiting you, and plainly a hard-nosed sort, I feared the worst. I pictured all sorts of old grudges and hurts emerging."

"No, there was none of that," Nigel says with a dismissive wave of his hand. "She was not the least bit forthcoming and, truth to tell, it got to be rather a strain trying to keep any conversation going. I was ever so thankful when the tea and sandwiches appeared."

"Had you expected something different?"

"From tea and sandwiches you mean?"

"*Nigel!*" Ms. Menzies gives him a look of mock exasperation.

"Ah, I see what you're getting at. Well, yes, really. To be honest, I'd rather dreaded her visit beforehand. Digging up old skeletons, all that sort of thing."

"And there would be skeletons, if one were to start digging?" Ms. Menzies has a gloriously offhand manner of posing tough questions as though they were discussing the weather.

Nigel looks at her appraisingly for a moment. "There are always skeletons," he replies. "And in a case like my own, where a marriage fell apart and children were left without a father, the skeletons are apt to be that much more malformed."

"And yet you and your daughter didn't speak of them at all?"

"Well, I certainly wasn't going to initiate any rooting around in the muck. Far better just to get on, it seems to me. I fully expected her to lay into me for being a — what do they call them nowadays? — a *dead-beat dad*; but there was none of that. Surprisingly. I got off rather lightly in the final analysis."

"Do you think perhaps she was intimidated by you?"

"Possibly. Although she didn't give the impression of someone easily intimidated."

"I agree. But something obviously held her back."

"Indeed."

"And you've no idea what it might have been?"

"Oh, I've all sorts of ideas beginning to rattle around. But I'd rather they didn't, you see. Pandora's Box and all that."

"Yes."

Nigel sits mulling for a few moments. Then asks her, "Do you remember that, after Pandora had inadvertently let all the evils of the world escape the box, what was the one thing that remained inside?"

"Hmm," Menzies says, thinking hard. "Oh, I believe it was Hope, was it not?"

"Very good! Yes. Hesiod has it as *Elpis*. Meaning Hope or perhaps Expectation."

"You've lost me, Professor."

"Simply that at this late date, I don't especially care to be entertaining either hope or expectation."

"Whyever not?"

"Far too much bustle and commotion."

"I suppose. But did your daughter's visit not leave you with the feeling there was unfinished family business?"

"Certainly there's unfinished family business; families are specifically designed for the production of unfinished business. But whether attempts ought to be made to finish it is another matter altogether."

"Do you think she'll be back? To try again?"

"Not alone anyway, I shouldn't think."

"Would you prefer I attempt to dissuade her from visiting again?"

Nigel pauses for a moment, staring off into the late blue summer sky. "Perhaps I should," he says at last, "but, no, all things considered, I don't think I would."

⊱⊰

Ginger and Garth are waiting for Chrissie at the foyer door. Though you'd never know it from her smiling manner, Ginger's still in a spin over Irene's bombshell. It's overturned her apple cart for sure, as she puts it to herself, and part of her would far rather be at home by herself this evening mulling over the churn of feelings that Nigel's re-emergence has provoked. But she knows she's better off here, in the present, with her friends, and Chrissie's clever grin makes her chuckle in spite of herself. Surprising really, how in no time at all she and the girl have become so close. Her instincts had told her straight away that Chrissie might be something special, and she really is. Spunky, tough, irreverent — so entirely different from the timid creature Ginger herself had been at that age. But a really fine tenderness beneath the tough plating. Ginger's glimpsed enough of it to know.

"You'll never guess what," Chrissie whispers to her conspiratorially.

"Neither will you," Ginger replies with a wicked wink, suddenly relishing the sidebar benefits that might be found in the new melodrama that's arisen from her past. How perfect if the Resurrection of Nigel Childes might in the end make for a more satisfying diversion than his miserable disappearance ever did.

Garth leads the way manfully as Ginger and Chrissie, hand-in-hand, wiggle together down the aisle of the crowded auditorium. Ginger's greeted this way and that by friends and admirers. She's thrilled to see so many of her old activist cronies in the crowd, but notices too that a lot of the seats are already taken by prim greyhairs and suits who are definitely not fellow travellers.

"Okay," says Garth as they continue down the aisle like the three musketeers, "they got their people out, we got our people out. Should be fun."

There's three seats up near the front by the aisle that have been reserved for them. Chrissie's never had a reserved seat for anything, except for one time when Sol did a reading in a coffee house downtown where the reservation was kinda unnecessary because there was hardly anyone else there. Sol was cool with that. "Poets and prophets," he'd said. "Not without honour, save." Probably would have freaked if the place was full of people.

Chrissie sits down beside Ginger who's got the biggest-ever grin going. She's nodding and winking to people all around like it's the most fun since you can't remember when. That's the thing about this old Ginger, Chrissie's quickly come to learn, she's totally high on life.

Even though it's almost over for her. Which doesn't seem to freak her out at all. "Oh, yes," she'd said to Chrissie just the other day, "I spend a lot of time — too much time, perhaps — thinking about death. What, if anything of me will survive when they lay me down at last. I have no clarity about it all. There's times I wish I did: that I was a rock-solid Christian, or a Buddhist for that matter, any one of them I suppose, so long as I had an unshakeable conviction about what lies ahead, on the other side."

"And why don't you?" Chrissie had asked her. "Did you ever?"

"Oh, of course," Ginger said. "I was raised with very strict Christian beliefs. I knew without question that God had made me and why. Those dreadful paintings in the drawing room were absolutely real to me as a child, that well-ordered universe of damnation and redemption."

"Including where you'd go when you died?" Chrissie asked. They'd been sitting in the Stone House library, reading on a wet and windy afternoon, but had somehow got talking religion. Chrissie had spent a long time that morning staring at the three lurid paintings.

"Yes, indeed," Ginger replied with a smile, "I knew absolutely that my choice was to live a virtuous life and be rewarded with eternal bliss in heaven, or to take the path of a sinner and be tormented forever in the fires of hell."

"I never got any of that," Chrissie said. "My mother thought it was all bullshit."

"Well," Ginger said, "that's another brand of unshakeable conviction, I suppose. What the best lack, according to Mr. Yeats."

Chrissie rolled her eyes and the two of them giggled like schoolgirls.

"No, I wouldn't myself go quite so far as your skeptical mother," Ginger said.

"She was more a junkie than a skeptic," Chrissie clarified. "Almost everything was bullshit for her." Chrissie loved that she could say whatever she wanted to Ginger without there being any blowback ever.

"I see," Ginger said, unnecessarily poking the burning logs in the fireplace. "I'm sorry that's how you got your start."

"Nah, I got my start when I got outa there." Chrissie almost wanted to say she thinks maybe she's really just gotten her start here at Stone House. With Ginger. But didn't.

"No, I still believe the Christian story's an intriguing narrative," Ginger continued, "as are the foundation stories of the other great religions, even though they all have a man at the top. And as I say, I envy the conviction true believers hold that a better life awaits them after death. But the dark sides of the great faiths — and they all have their dark sides, don't they? Sanctimonious cant, vicious sectarianism, morbid scrupulosity — have pretty much rendered them inoperable for someone of my advanced years. Still, on gloomy days I sometimes get to thinking it's petulance on my part, this refusal to latch onto a comforting lifeline, even if it is illusory."

"So why don't you?"

"Oh, all sorts of reasons, I suppose, perhaps none of them all that valid. Mostly I've come to really dislike Ismism."

"Ismism?" Chrissie made a what-the-fuck face.

"Yes, I've come to the conclusion that it's not the belief systems themselves that are the problem," Ginger said, "although some of them are so outlandish you'd have to be pretty far gone to put much stock in them; no it's that certain true believers of all stripes tend to get so fixated on the details of their particular ism — whether it's Judaism or Marxism or Hinduism or whatever — that what's real and important and wonderful in life gets leached away and replaced with a snarling *my ism is better than your ism*. To the point where people kill one another. It's one of humankind's more grotesque follies."

Chrissie didn't know if Ginger was just venting or what. "So you don't believe there's like anything after death?" she asked.

"Well, I do believe the cosmologists when they tell us every single atom of my body and yours was once a part of a distant star, maybe many different stars. And that every bit of me and you will eventually be recycled through the universe again. And again. I certainly believe that the configurations of atoms at any given moment are astonishing and at times spectacularly beautiful, as they are on this Earth at this point on its journey. I love this place, Chrissie," Ginger said, smiling, "and to have spent eighty years in such a benign and lovely place — not that everyone has been as lucky as I have — I think that's good enough for me. More than good enough. Whatever celestial discharge awaits me on the other side, I'll go a happy camper." Ginger grinned and poked the glowing logs in the fireplace again so that an erruption of sparks fled up the chimney.

⋗⋖

Chrissie had come along to this evening's all-candidates debate mostly to see how Sarina would handle that slippery lizard Illinger. Chrissie might have been here anyway if she were still working for the paper. Speaking of which she can see dumbard Harding and his wife on the far side of the crowd. He's got his hair plastered over his bald spot, fooling exactly nobody. Harding is nobody. Nobody's fooling anybody and nobody cares. Your time will come too, asshole.

Suddenly the door at stage left opens and out strides Sarina looking like the Queen of Choice. She's fitted perfectly in a dark business suit with a brilliantly aquamarine linen blouse underneath. Stiletto heels. Lip gloss that could stop traffic. There's a murmuring in the crowd at her appearance. Hell, dandelions in a vacant lot would murmur at her appearance. She comes right over and bends down to give Ginger a big hug. The two of them clasp, like lovers almost, Sarina's impossibly black hair and Ginger's silver frizz intermingling. Releasing Ginger, Sarina plants a sisterly kiss on Garth's cheek and the old guy beams like a lighthouse. Then she takes Chrissie's hand in hers and gives it a squeeze.

"Thanks for coming, Chrissie," Sarina says. "Wish me luck."

"Yea," Chrissie says, "you'll be great." Chrissie's dazzled by her, and Chrissie's hardly ever dazzled by anyone.

Sarina retreats to the green room and a few minutes later she and Larry Illinger and another guy and Rebecca Kleep from the local TV station file out onto the stage and sit in armchairs arranged in a semicircle. All of them have clip-on mikes. Subdued applause amid a rustling anticipation.

"Who's the other guy?" Chrissie whispers to Ginger. Turns out he's a local eccentric who runs at every election, never winning enough votes to even get his deposit returned. "No worse than most of them," Ginger whispers, "I even voted for him once." Vosher his name is, Paul Vosher. He's wearing a safari suit and has an overstuffed old satchel that he puts on the floor beside his chair. To his right, Larry Illinger seats himself primly. He's wearing a dark suit, white shirt and blue-grey tie. He has no notes. Neither does Sarina who sits between Illinger and Rebecca Kleep. Fortyish and well turned out in that TV kind of way, Rebecca is known for deploying her interviewing skills in a relentless pursuit of what she imagines is the truth. She's the moderator for tonight.

Once the crowd has quieted, Rebecca introduces the three candidates for mayor. "In the long history of this community," Rebecca says, "there has perhaps never been an election as truly significant as this one."

Grant and Ginger exchange a smile flit. "She says the same thing every time," Ginger whispers to Chrissie.

Each candidate is given seven minutes for an opening statement, the order determined beforehand. Paul Vosher goes first, delivering at breakneck speed and with considerable spittle a bitter denunciation of the community at large for its many shortcomings.

"All reasonably accurate," Ginger whispers to Chrissie during the lacklustre applause, "but not quite the way to ingratiate yourself with the electorate."

Chrissie's getting more and more nervous. She knows what a viper Illinger is and that he'll do whatever he can to tear Sarina to pieces. Sarina goes second and of course she's brilliant. Compared to Vosher she's like a high priestess of the positive, extolling Shetterly for its progressive and egalitarian attitudes, outlining policies to tackle homelessness within the community, improve transit and energy efficiency. Then raising the dark spectre of the proposed garbage incinerator. "That's what we'll be voting on in this election," she tells the audience in conclusion, "whether or not we want that anachronistic abomination blighting the town for years."

Rebecca Kleep has to wait for the applause to die down before she can begin introducing the final candidate, Mr. Larry Illinger. He leads off with a self-deprecating joke about his not having quite the sex appeal of the preceding speaker, the subtext being that sex appeal, if not outright dirty, is at best superficially titillating. Certainly no substitute for prudent civic management. Sarina sits attentive and calm. Despite his whispery voice, Illinger's a remarkably effective public speaker. There's a hush in the room as he painstakingly makes his way through a labyrinth of detail about the town's financial situation, the great difficulties that lie ahead, and the salvific benefits that will accrue from having a world-class trash-to-energy facility. He's like a finely tuned machine, unemotive and efficient.

Illinger sits down to applause at least as robust as what Sarina received.

It's only later, during the debate section, that Illinger's venom spurts. But cleverly, with a subtlety that would go unnoticed by many audience members: the great value of having business experience, because running the town is, in essence, running a business. The incalculable benefit of having lived here all one's life, leaving unsaid Sarina's newbie status. The repeated emphasis on "our" people's great beliefs and traditions, again as implicitly distinguished from Sarina's Asian muddlings. And, as Illinger's *coup de grace*, repeated reassurances that he is "a family man" with his dear wife and beloved son here with us today in the audience, at which low point Mrs. Illinger and Chazz rise from their seats and salute the crowd. The royal family redux. It was enough to bring on the barf bags. But a brilliant bit of theatrics, you have to admit.

"I have nothing against other people's lifestyle choices," Illinger announces, with a crocodilian smile in Sarina's direction hinting at a promiscuity that might extend to all manner of lesbian or bisexual or, God only knows, transgendered licentiousness, "but I do maintain that good old fashioned Christian values are still what most people in this community believe in."

Thunderous applause erupts from a sizeable segment of the audience.

Chrissie wants to scream, but doesn't. Garth looks really pissed too, but Ginger's still smiling away like soap suds. Then a token drops into the slot and suddenly Chrissie knows exactly what she'll do with the prodigal son's steamy video.

Fifteen

John Carlsen smells better than any other human. Not as complicated as Peter's scent, say, which is incredibly elaborated with mingled hints of city and sheep and sorrow. Or Ginger who smells soft and wise and tender as pastries. Carlsen smells bluntly of sheep and horse and dog. Especially bitches in heat. That fertile reek, pink and careless around the edges, swollen fiercely red at its centre. A scent to drive a good dog wild.

Shep can smell Carlsen from several miles off, as now when he came riding up the drive on his chestnut gelding, his smell of dams in heat overpowering even the horse's rich odours. Carlsen with his grizzled stubble and battered Stetson, wooden matchstick between his teeth and a hand-rolled cigarette behind his ear. He's in the habit of watching old western movies from his satellite dish, imagining John Wayne as the sort of man a man should be.

Carlsen hasn't visited the farm since Cecilia's death, but he's leaning against the barn wall now, as though against the wild west wind or the weight of sagebrush history. His horse picks carelessly at wisps of hay on the barn floor. Shep's in a mighty struggle against the desire to bury his muzzle into the legs of Carlsen's coveralls and the rapture to be found there. Instead he sits, fidgety and attentive to the talk of Carlsen and Peter. Big doings.

"Here's what I been thinkin'," Carlsen says after a long pause. With Carlsen one can never be quite sure if he pauses so much between everything he says because he's thinking deeply or he's so slow it takes him that long to figure out what he wants to say next. "Got a lovely little bitch name of Belle in season just now."

"Yes, I believe I saw her with you that one time," Peter says, strangely slowing his own speech to complement Carlsen's lazy drawl. Even though scarce with his words, the older man controls the conversation.

"Been thinkin' I'd love to pair her with your Shep here." Carlsen squints down at Shep appraisingly. "Two real good dogs. Could be a hell of a litter."

Peter knows the drill about background testing prior to breeding, considerations of genetics, temperament and health. He also realizes that Carlsen does things his own way.

"You know Shep's not registered," Peter says.

"I don't give a shit about registered," Carlsen says, "I'm lookin' for top-flight dogs, which your Shep surely is and, unless I miss my guess, so's that little Belle. She's smart and she's quick. Out of my Floss and a prime stud over Helton way. Her and Shep, might be somethin' real choice there."

Somewhere in the fields a sheep bleats plaintively, but even Shep's not interested today, not with all this Shep-talk going. He's watching the two men closely, knowing he's the subject of discussion, but not really catching the context. The whiff of bitch coming off Carlsen is just about driving Shep crazy trembling with sweet delirium.

"Well, fine by me, then," Peter says, "and I'm sure Shep won't object."

The two men look down at Shep and chuckle, which usually isn't a good thing, but this time maybe it is.

"He sired before?" Carlsen asks.

"Not that I know of," Peter says, and the two of them chuckle again.

Carlsen's horse wanders about, trailing its reins, snuffling at the short grass.

Moving away from the barn, Carlsen takes the cigarette from behind his ear and lights it with the wooden match that he strikes with his thumbnail. Even the acrid stench of tobacco doesn't erase the fleshy smell of female.

"Whaddya figure stud fees?" Carlsen asks after a bit.

Peter's peering down at Shep with a kind of goofy look on his face that Shep can't read at all. This is agony, all the mystifying talk and no real work getting done while the reek of bitch heat smothers everything. Shep's going to die of wild excitement if something doesn't break here soon.

"Pick of the litter sound all right to you?" Peter asks.

"Yep," Carlsen says, drawing deeply on his smoke. "Only one thing though . . ."

"What's that?" Peter asks.

Carlsen exhales a stream of smoke and stares out across the fields. "Only that," he says clumsily, as though this is difficult for him, "if you choose a bitch . . ."

"Yes?"

"Well, I'd kinda appreciate it if you could see your way clear to naming her for, you know, your late wife."

Peter's startled, then touched by the request. "I'd like very much to do that," he says, "and thank you for proposing it."

"Sure thing." Carlsen stiffens his jaw against what had looked like a slight trembling. "Breed 'em here or my place you figure?"

"You feel okay leaving her here for a bit? Give 'em time together?" It's really silly how much Peter is sounding the same as Carlsen, but humans are like that.

"Yep. That'd be good. Never sure first time up the pump."

"Well, I'm not going anywhere the next little while," Peter says, "so whenever works for you."

"She's been bleedin' for a bit now and humping everything that moves, so she should be ready to suck the stick soon enough. I could fetch her over tomorrow morning, give her a week or so here."

They agree with a handshake and Carlsen swings lazily back up into the saddle. He dips his grizzled chin towards Peter then canters off down the driveway.

"Well, old man," Peter says, getting down on one knee and taking Shep's smooth head in his hands, each of them looking deep into the other's eyes, "seems like you got some excitement coming." Shep wriggles with still mystified anticipation. "But it's a mighty responsibility entailed as well," Peter says, aware as he says it that old Carlsen's devotion to Cecilia is almost certainly why he's come up with this proposal to have Shep mate with one of his prized dams. "A mighty responsibility," Peter repeats.

Irene's gratified that she decided to travel alone to visit her mother. No sense dragging Phil along since he's made it perfectly clear that he has little interest in what has become for her a matter of singular and consuming significance. She can't get around it and she can't get past it, no matter what. How many times a day — dozens anyway — her head's wandering around in the same old story, replaying incidents, reworking grievances. She's been sleeping badly over it; her appetite has dwindled; even the intricacies of their business — normally the grist of her days and the familial currency between herself and Phil — have shrivelled into petty annoyances. Frankly she couldn't care less whether those crappy new townhouses have double or triple glazing. Irene's off her game. Way off. In a way she hasn't really been since . . . yes, since the day darling dad abandoned herself and her mother. He's like a pair of miserable bookends, old Nigel, bracketing that long-ago crisis with this current version. Two episodes of the same story, she sees that now. It's a life story she adheres to: abandonment. Pathetic, really.

No, she can hardly believe that's the case. She's overwrought, missing perspective. Nevertheless, she's perfectly clear that what she's feeling now as she's driving to Shetterly is totally different, for example, from all the upset surrounding Crystal's failed marriage and failed parenting. Difficult as it has been to watch her daughter floundering, Irene's sense of herself is never shaken by Crystal's tribulations the way it is by this business with her father. Damn him! Bloody well damn him to hell and back for undermining her so thoroughly. To encourage her childish love that way, to deliberately establish himself as the bright centre of her unfolding universe, and then suddenly vanish, without explanation or so much as a fare-thee-well. What sort of sicko would treat a child like that? Or do the same to Ginger, for that matter. And, having demonstrated his worthlessness so incontestably all those years ago, how can he still dominate Irene's emotions this way? No one could have been more zealous than she was in eradicating every last thread of him from her consciousness. The tender memories and the later bitter ones, the affections and bewilderments and hatreds and hurts. She'd long ago taken the whole smelly package out to a psychic dumpster and tossed it. Except now here it is again, as raw and unresolved as ever.

She maybe wouldn't feel whiplashed so badly if her father had showed up as a broken man, maybe a bankrupt or a drunk. A tragic character finally victimized by his weaknesses and arrogant self-interest. To discover him at her doorstep, contrite and ashamed, in need of her loving kindness — that wouldn't have hurt so much. She might have pitied him then, might even have taken him in, who knows, brought him back from the darkness. She's momentarily consoled by this largeness of heart that might have been. Forgiveness is not beyond her. The charity that's spoken of at church on Sunday, that's the kind of thing Irene can relate to.

But of course he didn't return as a supplicant, did he? He didn't return at all — she was the one who tracked *him* down, not the other way around. He hasn't come to her, and certainly not looking for anything. It's she that has gone seeking whatever it is she wants, needs from him. She's the broken one here.

Then to find him sitting in high splendour at that upscale establishment! The look on his face — what was it? — serenity, detachment, smugness even? Not someone in need of anything. The furthest thing from it. She saw it all in a glance. Before a word was even spoken. Then the polite but meaningless chitchat, all of it saying clearly that whether or not she existed didn't matter. He was detached from her entirely. No balm of loving forgiveness required, thank you. But *she* was not detached from him at all. Fool that she was, she needed him. Or something from him. But what?

She hasn't spoken with Peter about any of this. He never knew Nigel, of course, and by the time her brother was born, with Nigel just gone, the last thing Irene could handle was an emotional attachment to this newborn nuisance. By choice she played as little part in his childhood as she could get away with, a bit of babysitting when necessary, and fake enthusiasm over his birthdays. By the time Peter started school, she'd already graduated high school. Over the years their lives went off in widely divergent directions, so that even Cecilia's death, and the baby's, dreadful though it was, touched Irene only glancingly. She's not proud of that side of herself, but she can exonerate herself by blaming Nigel. In her present upset she realizes that, along with everything else, Nigel deprived her of a brother's love. Deprivation without reservation, that's her father's sick patrimony.

Ginger's her only hope in this. Surely her mother feels much the same, because Nigel really deserted Ginger, not herself. Irene was just collateral damage. But somehow Ginger seems to have put it in place, gotten beyond it, in a way that Irene hasn't. Zooming along the highway now, Irene feels the force of a familiar regret, that she closed herself off from her mother at the very time Ginger had needed her most. Selfishly, it seemed she couldn't properly erase Nigel from her mind without also placing Ginger at a distance. Having done so, Irene had never found a way back into the affection mothers and daughters should share. Plus, Ginger didn't exactly help matters either with her radical pretensions and weirdo associates. Irene got herself away from Stone House right after high school, and thereafter returned for visits as seldom as possible. She simply couldn't stand encountering the steady stream of know-it-alls, having to listen to their lefty twaddle, their patronizing responses to whatever she might say.

Yes, for a while there, when Crystal was a newborn, it seemed that things might improve. Irene's heart melted with that elfin baby at her breast. She felt such a softening and loosening within herself as she held the infant in her arms. Infatuated with her tiny, perfect daughter, Irene as nursing mother became everything she normally wasn't, her days spent in a kind of hazy bliss. And there's no way you could have asked for a better grannie than Ginger. With the newborn as a mutual source of joy, Irene felt she could relate to her mum with an openness and affection she hadn't known for years. But, eventually the gulf between them gradually reopened, leaving the two of them once again stranded on separate shores.

Only a few minutes more and she'll be in Shetterly. In the cold comforts of Stone House. Where Ginger will know.

Chrissie decides she won't say anything to Ginger or Sarina about her plan. For one thing, they probably wouldn't go along with it, being as they're both kinda ethical and like that, which doesn't really cut it when you're dealing with a scumbag like Illinger. So she kicks it into gear on her own.

She and Chazz are sitting on a park bench down by the river. The sunny afternoon has brought lots of people out, meaning she's totally safe being here, even though what she's fixing to do isn't safe at all. Knowing exactly what dazzles Chazz she's fixed herself up, tight jeans and a shimmering blouse like what Sarina might wear. She could almost believe that she and Chazz were back to how they used to be, crazy in love, tripping together in the sunshine.

"So I'll be leaving for college in a coupla weeks," Chazz is telling her, all smooth and cool. He's wearing a Hugo Boss sport coat and linen pants, and she realizes that this is the real him, his father's son, not the grunge rocker she fell for. She can tell from his attitude that Chazz thinks she's really trying to get back together with him, but unfortunately he can't promise anything because there's gonna be so many babes on campus with the hots for him. Schlurg.

"Sweet," she says. "Now, Chazz, there's just one little thing we need to figure out, you and me."

"Uh-huh," he says, trying for the ultra chill look. Trouble Chazz is having here is that his previous bad boy musician act doesn't fit with his current preppy appearance, so he's coming across as a kinda twisted dick.

"About that DVD," Chrissie says. She's told herself beforehand how she needs to be in order to do this. Calm at all costs. No anger or recrimination, none of that aggressive crap. Bend Chazz to her will, but bend him gently.

"Shit, Chrissie, you're not bringing that up again? I mean I thought all of that was behind us. Like move on, you know." She can sense the fear in Chazz's tone. "Let me tell you the whole story," he says. "Y'know I only did that ignorant film thing in the first place because I needed some cash right away. I had debts with people you don't want to have debts with, you know what I mean?"

"Already."

"Okay, so I made a few bucks and paid off the sharks and thought that was that, right? End of story."

"But?"

"But after you left I kinda woke up and realized what the fuck I'd done. Like if that film ever got released, sooner or later the old man's gonna find out and I'm gonna get fuckin' crucified, right."

"Go on." Mostly Chrissie's wondering how could she ever have been so turned on to someone this stupid.

"So I came clean with the old man. Told him everything. He went through the fuckin' roof; I've never seen him so angry. Normally with him none of that shows, but he was righteously pissed."

"I bet." Chazz has conveniently forgotten that Chrissie was like majorly pissed at him too.

"Anyways," Chazz says, "after he calmed down the old man went to the producers and bought them off. He wouldn't tell me what it cost him, but the whole thing is dead, disappeared. Never to be seen by anyone, because they hadn't figured out the distribution thing yet. And I am like so under the old man's thumb I feel like a fuckin' insect pinned to a board."

"So you'll be a well-educated insect anyway," Chrissie says. "But you didn't mention to your dad that I have a copy?"

"No, I didn't."

Again the depth of his dumbness amazes Chrissie. "Well, I hate to pee on your parade," she says, "but here's how it is, Chazz. I want you to tell your father about how I've got it, and how it's going to be all over the internet and TV and everything . . . unless he drops out of the mayor thing." Chrissie gulps after saying it, aware she's just tossed a live grenade into the park of genteel Sunday strollers.

"Aw, Chrissie, gimme a fuckin' break, will ya," Chazz says, slapping his hand on the bench. "I'm just gettin' my shit together here and this is gonna blow everything for me. I've told you I'm sorry about what went down between us, and how I miss you and all like that. Don't break my balls on this, Chrissie, please!"

She feels for Chazz, she really does, for what a child he is, for how it was between them when it was fine. "Nothing personal here, Chazz," Chrissie says. "I just don't want your old man elected mayor, and he's gonna be unless you change his mind."

"I can't change his mind! You don't know him, Chrissie, not like I do. No matter what, he doesn't lose. Ever. Even something like this, he'll twist it around somehow so that he comes out on top, and I'll pay the price, maybe you too. I'm telling you, he's not someone you want to fuck with."

"But I don't have to though, do I?" She wonders if maybe she will though, if this will come back around and slap her down again. Maybe, but that's okay too; she's done being afraid of snarling dogs.

Just then a tiny girl, hardly able to walk, but holding a string with floating balloon, stands in front of them and stares. They stare back at her, silenced by her simplicity. After a few moments an older girl runs over and pulls the toddler away.

"Chrissie, he'll cut you into little pieces and throw you out for the pigs to eat," Chazz says fiercely. A note of desperation now. "Take my word for it."

Chrissie's so calm and focused she's amazing herself. Partly she knows she's drawing strength from Ginger and Sarina, that she's somehow safe with those two women nearby. "I was thinking three days, Chazz. If your dad hasn't withdrawn by then, Johnny Cocker and Tamara Twot and, most importantly, *you* will be on like every screen from here to Uzbekistan. How many hits, you figure? Gotta be viral."

Chazz is frantic, but fumbling words.

"That's all I have to say," Chrissie tells him, standing up. She gives him a smile that's actually real. Poor Barney. "Been real nice, Chazz."

But as she turns to walk away, Chazz calls her back. "Sit down, Chrissie, please." A pleading child.

She hesitates then sits on the edge of the bench, as though only for a moment.

"There's something else," Chazz says.

"Like?"

You can see Chazz is all torn to pieces about whether or not he should say what he wants to say but doesn't. She's actually feeling bad for the poor schmuck. He's really not the total dicksmoke she's been seeing him as. More like someone trapped inside something he doesn't understand. A frightened innocent behind the swagger.

"Chazz?"

"What if," he says, looking down, hesitating, "what if I was to give you some information that would force my dad to quit the race."

"Like what?"

"Like dynamite. Nothing to do with the flick. Something way bigger."

"How'm I supposed to know?"

"We make the deal. You bring me the disk, don't make any copies, and you swear never to mention it to anyone ever and I give you certain information that will like instantly blow my father's campaign outta the water."

"Go on," Chrissie says, trying to figure what Chazz is up to.

"Here's the kicker: this thing, it's not something that can be traced to either you or me," Chazz says. "Firewalled in every fucking way. So after it blows, we're both in the clear, and we each get what we want, no strings attached. How about it?"

Chrissie's got to compute this. She doesn't trust Chazz any more than his dad. He could be setting her up some way. Punishing her. But she can see he's desperate. Like a trapped rat. Plus, you gotta admit, the whole thing with the pornie flick is really crackerfucking. Might not even make a dent on Illinger, just screw everything up for Chazz, and she's not as harsh on Chazz as she was. It's true that Illinger can twist almost anything to his own advantage and Chazz seems firm that what he's got is solid. She's dying to know what it is, but he's not giving her any more than she's giving him. So it comes down to trust. Chrissie doesn't trust hardly anyone on principle, why should she? And now she's supposed to trust Chazz, who's like untrustworthy in triplicate.

She gazes for a moment at the swallows swooping and gliding above the river's silver while she riffles through her options. She can always make a copy of the disk for back-up and still use it if Chazz's big secret is a nothing. If it's as good as he says, she'll destroy the second disk and everyone's a winner. Except Illinger. Ha.

"Okay, Chazz," she says, "so we have to trust each other on this, right?"

"Absolutely," Chazz says, as if honour was encoded in his DNA.

"Okay," Chrissie says, "I'm down. Deal on. We meet back here tomorrow, same time, you give me what you've got and I hand the disk over."

"Cool," Chazz says, "you won't be disappointed, Chrissie." As though Chazz were incapable of arousing disappointment.

"Right," Chrissie says.

Vaughn Krippen's telephone voice is as deep and smooth as fine single malt. You're inclined to believe whatever he says simply because his timbre's pitch perfect. Avuncular and self-assured. A lawyer and old family friend who's looked after Ginger's affairs forever and more recently Peter's too, Vaughn's filling Peter in on the latest developments around the Congregation of the Great Convergence.

"From what we're hearing," Vaughn says, "it would appear that all of those arrested and charged face a high likelihood of conviction. The FBI's got a swimming pool full of wiretap evidence, plus the hard drives and a growing number of victim statements. It looks very much like a slam dunk."

"Sounds promising," Peter says, pacing in his kitchen, smiling to himself at the thought of cosmopolitan Vaughn banging down a slam dunk.

"We understand some of the small fry are considering plea bargains in exchange for testifying against the main players," Vaughn continues. "Plus, I hear there are further arrests and additional charges imminent. Hard to imagine the breadth of corruption, but there it is."

"Pretty shocking, I agree," Peter says. "I'm seeing news reports that the church is liquidating assets, selling off properties and so forth."

"Quite so," Vaughn says. "They're facing massive legal bills just on the criminal charges, not to mention victim compensation claims that are sure to follow. These fallen angels are going to be in and out of courtrooms for years, if not decades."

Slam dunks and fallen angels — old Vaughn's getting way outside the barrister-at-law box this morning. Peter chuckles to himself.

"I wouldn't be at all surprised to see a bankruptcy filing in the very near future," Vaughn says.

"And that's not confined to the States?" Peter asks, glancing out to the front porch where Shep looks to be getting agitated over something.

"Apparently not. The Congregation does have a separate district in Canada, governed by its own board of directors, but ultimately all assets and liabilities are within the purview of the church headquarters in Atlanta."

"So what about Stone House, then?" Peter's trying to be a realist despite his growing optimism that the Congregation's disgrace may result in Ginger's home being salvaged from the moral wreckage.

"Too soon to know for sure," Vaughn says with sensible caution. "As you're fully aware, the property is held in trust for as long as your mother's alive, so I don't believe it can be considered an asset subject to liquidation like other church properties. Plus, your grandparents' will contained quite precise legal restrictions specifying that the property be used exclusively for church-related activities, something plainly not possible if the church were to be dissolved as now seems rather likely."

"Is there anything we should be doing at the moment?" Peter asks, remembering how he used to chafe back in his business days when you had to sit on the sidelines like a third-stringer while the legal beagles ran their arcane games.

"We should be getting an oar in the water, no question about that," Vaughn says, "but to be perfectly frank, I'm not entirely certain how to proceed, the circumstances being so atypical. We may need to initiate proceedings of our own to have your grandparents' will quashed and your mother recognized as rightful owner." Vaughn pauses for a moment, calculating. Again Peter's distracted by Shep's agitation.

"Tell you what," Vaughn says, "I've got an old friend — we were in law school together — who now sits on the superior court of justice in bankruptcy and insolvency. I'll give her a call, maybe go for a collegial drink, see if she can't provide us a bit of a heads-up."

"Sounds good," Peter says, thinking it also sounds like the beginning of an interminable legal wrangle.

"I believe there's reason for optimism," Vaughn says. "As appalling as it is, certainly for the victims primarily, this scandal may prove most useful in the end with respect to having Stone House remain in the family. I imagine your mother will be hugely relieved."

"I feel the same way," Peter says. "If things turn out. Should I fill her in or would you rather talk with her yourself?"

"No, no, by all means you pass on what I've told you, with my warmest regards to your mother. I'll let you know if I glean anything from the lofty heights of the superior court."

"Thanks, Vaughn," Peter says. As the line goes dead, Peter exhales deeply, perhaps only just now glimpsing how oppressive it's been having the potential loss of Stone House always lodged somewhere in the back corners of consciousness. Not for his own sake but his mum's. And maybe Irene and Crystal and Isha. Who knows. That place with Ginger in it, anachronistic and absurd as it may be, nevertheless is the only real hub the family has, and the prospect of reclaiming it at last has Peter now vaguely elated.

Peter's barely put down the phone when Carlsen's battered pickup comes clattering along the driveway kicking up a rooster tail of dust. Obviously Shep's agitation was from detecting the scent of his approaching mate. He's already up on his haunches, a fidgety lion of

Judah. By the time the old Chevy truck rattles to a halt in front of the house, Shep's emitting a weird kind of keening sound and vibrating as though there's an electric current running through him. Peter flops down on a porch chair alongside Shep, the fingertips of his left hand gently touching the dog's skull. Old Carlsen climbs out of the truck and grunts a greeting to Peter. Belle's sitting upright on the front seat, nervous and alert.

Peter remains in his chair, holding Shep against great urges. Like holding a canoe against white water. "Morning," Peter greets Carlsen. "Beautiful day again."

"Yep," Carlsen says, casually surveying the yard where several Rhode Island Reds are scratching in the grass. He's dressed the same as always, ancient coveralls and battered Stetson, but today, for Shep at least, the man's usually compelling scent is lost amid the sublimely streaming fragrance of Belle. Gaze riveted on the delectable Belle, penis swelling, toenails scratching the porch boards, Shep's swept towards Elysian Fields. The smell of her is everywhere.

"Well, I reckon she's good and ready," Carlsen says. "Her discharge's gone from red to pink. Put a finger into her this morning and she damn near pulled it off my hand, she's that ready for it. I reckon her eggs will ripen over the next few days or so."

"Sounds good," Peter says, resisting the temptation to say more.

"Yep. Well, we better let 'em have at it or stud here's gonna have a royal case of blue balls."

Peter grins, wondering whether Carlsen would be talking this way if it was Cecilia here rather than himself. Under Cecilia's civilizing influence Carlsen had shown an unsuspected gentlemanliness in his dealings with her — chivalrousness was how Cecilia described it — that instantly vanished with her death. In the three years since, until yesterday he has never once mentioned her name or alluded to her presence here.

"All right," Peter says to Shep, who's just about in orbit, "let's see some courtly behaviour from you." With a flick of his fingers he releases Shep who instantly bounds down the steps to the truck.

Taking his sweet time, Carlsen saunters around to the driver's side, opens the door and calls Belle out. After a moment's hesitation, Belle leaps from the truck, an eager little beauty, sleek and nubile. Shep approaches her not entirely in the courtly fashion Peter had suggested, tail raised high and gleaming penis protuberant. An orgy of sniffing and rubbing erupts. Belle's got her tail in the air too, held off to one side, flagging for her beau. Shep mounts her almost straight away while she stands willingly for him. He thrusts and thrusts with every ounce of who he is, eyes glassed over, mouth open, tongue lolling in unspeakable desire. Belle appears more detached, almost businesslike beneath him and in no time at all it's over. Shep drops off her, his mighty passion sated for the moment. They nuzzle and sniff some more, but the thing is done, at least for now. Glancing back up at Peter, Shep looks almost sheepish.

"Well," Carlsen grunts, "it's a start anyways."

"Care for a coffee?" Peter asks him.

"No thanks." Carlsen declines with a wave of his hand. "Gotta keep movin'. Like that black feller said, no tellin' what shit's gainin' on ya."

Peter grins again at the mauling of old Satchel's quip and at the sex-struck dogs and the sweet remembering of Cecilia.

III

The Drive

Sixteen

Ginger and Irene are hugging each other in a way they haven't really hugged for years. Not saying anything just yet. Impossible to delineate what portion of this is sorrow or regret or affection. Ginger knows it doesn't matter. Her daughter and herself. She can't remember the last time she felt so delighted to see Irene. Something's been released at last, you can feel it in this loving hug; rather than merely experiencing her daughter's visit, Ginger's prepared to savour whatever revelations it might offer.

After Irene's freshened up from the trip and changed into comfortable slacks and blouse, the two of them sit together in the kitchen nook sipping tea. Skipping quickly across a few preliminaries, mostly news about Crystal and Isha (and even here the tone is less censorious than usual), Irene again gets into the visit with Nigel and the tumult it's caused her since.

"I can't seem to get rid of it, Mum," she says. "It's like some weird addiction. I banish it from my mind and within minutes, it's back again. *He's* back again. Over and over. I wake up in the middle of the night and there he is. I swear I'll never look down my nose at an addict again."

Ginger chuckles. "Yes, I've had my share of Nigel moments too since we spoke," she says. "There's something rather surreal about it really, having him restored as an actual living person rather than a memory."

"How is it for you, Mum? I mean, are you still obsessed by him like I am?"

Ginger's more preoccupied at the moment over what a different version of her daughter she's seeing. Not so demonstrably the controller, on top of everything, cemented up in certitude. Her edges blurred now into someone unsure, tentative, vulnerable. More loveable for sure. It wasn't just Irene's temperament that calcified after her father's leaving; her physical being did too. Within a few years the supple and graceful girl had become blockish and stiff. Never obese, but no longer nimble and elegant as she'd been. Tightened up. Perhaps that would have happened anyway, more genetics than adversity, perhaps not. But the change in temperament and in body seemed to go hand-in-hand. By the time she was sixteen, the uncanny resemblances between herself and her uncle Frank had disappeared entirely.

"No, I wouldn't say obsessed," Ginger answers with a smile. She sips her tea. "He comes and he goes. I get angry at him and I love him and I forget about him for a whole long while. Your father was a charismatic character, as I'm sure you remember, so it's not surprising that his glitter is hard to forget, even after all these years. And certainly your discovery has brought him out of the shadows again. Oh, yes, I find myself talking to him sometimes, as though he's still here."

"What do you say to him?"

"Ha ha, dreadful things mostly. What a fool he was, a weakling, a coward. Very high-class name-calling, you see."

"Not that you loved him?"

"Oh yes, that too," Ginger says. "And how much *you* loved him too."

"I didn't just love him, I adored him."

"Yes, I know. And it's hard to admit, isn't it, that he was undeserving of our love, certainly unworthy of a child's adoration. It tempts you into thinking that perhaps all love is folly. That the cynics are the ones who have it right, and the romantics are delusional."

Irene is fidgeting with her wedding ring, twisting it as though she wants to remove it but can't. "Mum, I've never loved anyone as much as him, not Phil, not Crystal. I know it's not right, but it's true." She leaves unsaid Not You.

"You were a child, darling, an impressionable child, and he gave you the best of who he was, which was a lot. You weren't deluded in loving him. You have to remember it wasn't just you who was infatuated — I was, God knows, and others too — but he shone his brilliance on you more than on anyone."

"Not more than you?"

"Well," Ginger says, smiling again, almost coy, "perhaps at the beginning my experience was similar. I wasn't much more than a child myself at the time. Certainly an innocent."

"And he wasn't?"

"Well, he was older, for one thing, and vastly more experienced, but you know, in a strange way he *was* an innocent. Under all the polished pirouettes he was immensely sensitive and really quite vulnerable."

"I think of him as hard and cold."

"Oh, no, he wasn't either. I understand how you can feel that way, but he was not a hard, cold person, not at all."

"But his leaving?"

"Yes, I know, it seemed ruthless and heartless at the time."

"It was ruthless and heartless!" Irene exclaims heatedly.

"I thought so too, in all the hurt of it, in seeing how dreadfully it wounded you. My heart broke for you, darling, and I berated myself for being incapable of making it better for you."

"You couldn't have anyway, Mum. I wouldn't have wanted you to try."

"I know, darling, and I did try in my own ineffectual way, but still it weighed on me dreadfully."

"Plus, you had a newborn baby on your hands."

"Yes, yes, all sorts of valid excuses, no doubt. I only wish there'd been that tenderness between us that you see in mothers and daughters. I miss that we never had that. Or that we lost it so early."

"I know," Irene says, suddenly near to tears. "I didn't have that as a daughter with you and I didn't really have it as a mother with Crystal either, except when she was a newborn. And I blame him. Not myself, not you. Him."

"Well, dear," Ginger says, "I'm sure the last thing you need at this late date is a sermon from me on letting go of blame. Certainly your father is fully deserving of all the blame we can muster, but over the years I've come to view him a bit differently, at least in glimpses."

"How? How could you possibly see it differently? He abandoned us, Mum, deserted us."

"Oh, now you're going to get me angry with him all over again," Ginger says with a chuckle.

Irene stands up and goes over to the counter to get herself a Kleenex, wipes her eyes then sits back down.

Ginger smiles softly. "I'm convinced the truth of the matter is he had a piece missing," she says.

"What do you mean by that?"

"I was too young and inexperienced to recognize it at the time, but there were all kinds of clues that in hindsight seem so obvious."

"Like what?"

"Well, for example, I should have been forewarned by the way he dealt with his own family. He'd cut them off completely, as though they'd ceased to exist for him."

"Same way he cut us off," Irene says, reaching for the teapot and refilling their cups.

"Yes, that's what I mean. There was some abnormality, some deep deficiency, in him. I don't pretend to know what caused it or what might have been done about it. Trouble was, he seemed so brilliantly accomplished, that you had no reason to suspect this other side of him. So when it finally manifested itself, you thought: how shocking, how grotesque. But I don't believe it sprang from maliciousness of any sort. Self-absorption perhaps, but not maliciousness. He just suffered from a profound deficiency, the way some people are deficient in iron or insulin or whatever. So, kick him around as much as I might at times, I really don't blame him in the end."

"Oh, Mum!" Irene reaches out and takes Ginger's hand in her own. "It's not easy, you know, being the daughter of a saint."

"No, no, no," Ginger protests, laughing, "I'm no saint. We'd have to look to *my* mother for classic saintliness. I don't have the piety for it, or the patience."

The two of them say nothing for a moment, gently holding hands. Ginger realizes she must give Irene at least one piece of the puzzle that's been missing all these years. One of two, for now anyway. What is it she fears: her daughter's anger? Her disapproval? Disappointment?

"Darling," she says, still holding Irene's hand in her own, "there's something I never told you about what happened back in those days."

"What do you mean?"

"I mean I behaved rather badly, rather foolishly, for a little bit and my misbehaviour may have been a part of why your father left us."

Irene tries not to look shocked. "Oh, Mum, I don't think I want to hear this."

"And I'm certainly not eager to confess it," Ginger admits, smiling, "but it's best that you know. You should have known from the outset. But . . ."

"Tell me then."

"You remember I'd been taking courses at Carlyle at the time."

"Yes, of course."

"Well, the truth of the matter is, I became rather attached to another student that I met there."

"A man?"

"Yes, a lovely young man." And he was too, Ginger remembers now. Gary. She has no idea what became of him.

"Mother!"

"Yes, I know it sounds shocking."

"Well, it does." Irene withdraws her hand, ostensibly to get the Kleenex from her pocket, but really to brace herself. "Mother, you took a lover?"

"No, I wouldn't go that far," Ginger says.

"How far would you go?" Irene's censorious streak is back in action.

"Not very far, really. Some rather intimate conversations. A tender hug every so often, some indiscreet kissing."

"Don't tell me: Dad found out."

"He never said so. Never gave the slightest indication that he did. I broke it off before it could get truly serious. And then I got pregnant with Peter."

"But not from this fellow?" You can see Irene's appalled by the possibility.

"No, no," Ginger says, "I never slept with him, tempted though I may have been."

"But why would you even be tempted? When you were happily married to Dad?"

"Not so happily, really. A coolness had developed between your father and me, a distancing. That had gone on for years, especially as you got older and he put so much of his energy into you."

"Surely you weren't jealous over that, were you? Mother, say you weren't."

"No. No, I was lonely, I suppose, in need of tenderness that I was no longer getting from him."

Irene sits slumped in her chair, her face fallen.

"So," Ginger continues, "I have no idea what if anything your father knew. But after he bolted so suddenly, I wondered if that was why. The worst case scenario: that he imagined the child I was carrying wasn't his."

"Oh, Mother!"

"And of course I couldn't locate him anywhere. To try to clear the air. I could live with his leaving, I supposed, but not if he'd left over something that wasn't even real. And all the hurt it caused you. Peter not having a father. No, I was in a torment of guilt and remorse and frustration. But there was nothing I could do about any of it. So you see my alleged saintliness is a bit overstated to say the least. For the longest time I blamed myself for what happened, and that helped temper my anger towards your father."

There's more she must tell her daughter, Ginger knows, and more to ask, but not just yet. The door has been opened and the rest will follow as it should.

The two women smile at each other and sip their tea in silence for a while. Ginger's heart is floating like dandelion seeds.

"Speaking of guilt and remorse," Ginger eventually asks, "have you had a chance to talk with Peter about our favourite Congregation?"

"No," Irene says, "we've been playing telephone tag the last few days. What's up?"

"Peter's been consulting with Vaughn Krippen — you remember my lawyer — and he believes the church will almost certainly declare bankruptcy, meaning there's a better than even chance that we can get Stone House back."

"Wow!" Irene says. "That's terrific news, Mum."

"Certainly is. But how peculiar, don't you think, that you end up finding your long-lost father while your brother calls to say we may well get Stone House back. It's quite dizzying, really, all these sudden flashbacks to the past."

"I know. I feel really spinny with it all. Like everything's sort of unreal. Speaking of unreal meanwhile, how's the election coming along?" Irene asks. "Any chance of beating Illinger, do you think?"

"Oh, I'm afraid it remains a very long shot," Ginger says. "Our candidate Sarina really is superb and everyone's working full tilt, including Peter and my old friend Garth, but the odds are rather badly stacked against us."

"Well, I do hope . . ."

Just then there's a commotion at the back door and in bursts Chrissie with a wild and excited expression. "Oh!" she exclaims, realizing Ginger's got company. "Sorry."

"Not at all, Chrissie," Ginger says, "come in and meet my daughter. Irene, this is Chrissie, my new . . . what are you my new, Chrissie?"

"Um," Chrissie says, rolling her eyes and putting an index finger to her chin, as though she's thinking hard. "How about devotee?" she says with nervous laughter.

Irene appears bewildered by the sudden appearance of this offbeat-looking girl.

"Yes, devotee will do nicely," Ginger agrees, gesturing for Chrissie to come over. "Chrissie, this is my daughter Irene."

"Hiya," Chrissie says, holding out her hand and giving Irene's hand a brief shake.

"Pleased to meet you," Irene says, stuffing down her usual judgementalness about her mother's odd associates.

"Hey, look, I don't want to interrupt," Chrissie says. Ginger can see the girl's bursting with some news or other.

"Irene's staying over for the night," Ginger says. "Will you be here for supper, Chrissie?"

"Um, actually, no," Chrissie says, "I was thinking of going, ah, up to the farm."

"Really?" Ginger asks, suspecting this plan's just been concocted on the spot.

"Yea, I have to do some things with Peter."

"Are you going to cycle all that way? This late?"

"Sure. No probs."

"You could borrow the car if you'd rather. I'm not needing it."

"What, and help destroy the biosphere?" Chrissie says with a cheeky wink.

"*Touché*," Ginger replies with a laugh. "Say, could you take a few things up for Peter? Just a small package."

"Absolutely," Chrissie says, "it's what devotees are for."

Ginger could kiss the kid, though Irene's at a loss.

Chrissie disappears upstairs while Ginger fusses at the kitchen counter wrapping a small kit of baked goods.

"How *is* Peter?" Irene asks her. "As I say, I haven't really talked to him for ages."

"You know, I think he's finally getting over that tragedy," Ginger says. "Of course he'll never fully get over it, any more than I will, any more than you or I have gotten over you-know-who. But there's a spark in him now like there hasn't been. The election has him energized and he's loving being back at the farm again, and that's a really positive development."

"This girl?" Irene asks tilting her head towards upstairs.

"Oh, no. Nothing like that," Ginger says. "At least, I should think not." Although Ginger has wondered. The girl's certainly become attached to Peter; and these young women nowadays wear their sexuality so casually, nothing like the petticoats and primness of Ginger's own youth. Ah, yes, but what about Ginger's scandalous liaison with her professor? By Chrissie's age, Ginger was already a less than honourably married mother, and Irene here a babe in her arms. Behold the smooth and subtle convolutions of prevailing morality.

"Ah, here she comes," Ginger says.

Chrissie bounds down the big staircase and back into the kitchen, wearing her black lycra bodysuit, a brilliant magenta shawl from Sarina tied around her waist, a rucksack on her shoulder. Ginger gives her the care package and a quick hug.

"You won't be cycling back tonight, I can't imagine?" Ginger asks.

"Probably not," Chrissie says. "Nice to meet you," she says to Irene, "maybe see you later."

"Yes," Irene says, "nice to meet you too."

With Chrissie's freshness gone out of the room like a breeze died down, the women are back to their knotty considerations. "I sense you want to go see the old miscreant again, do you?" Ginger asks.

"I'd hardly say *want*," Irene answers with a grim smile, "but I feel I must."

"Yes," Ginger says, "I think you must, and so, unhappily, must I."

"Oh, no, Mum," Irene protests, "it's really not necessary."

"I'm afraid it is, dear," Ginger says. "Not for the same reasons as yourself, perhaps, but necessary nevertheless." She's not even clear what her reasons might be, perhaps only that she can't let this Big Theme in her life drift away into ragged nothingness. In truth, Nigel has not left her, even after all these years, and she can't pretend he has, or that he no longer matters to her. Had he not come back this way, had her life come to a close with no further connection to him, well, all right, that would have been what it was. She'd be at peace at least with his memory. But with the actual him again near at hand, and the whole unfinished business resurrected, inescapably she must take the opportunity to bring her dealings with him to a suitable close. She wonders to herself whether this wasn't Nigel's plan all along, to approach just close enough in his last days, that she and Irene would be inevitably drawn to him so that their disjointed saga might end with a decorous conclusion. Yes, that would be just like Nigel, the reckless aesthete's final turn.

She and Irene decide that the two of them will journey together to Strathmere Lodge in a couple of weeks and see what old Nigel has to say for himself.

⇢⇠

Shep's sprawled on the front porch, snoozing in balmy late afternoon sunshine, with Belle alongside him doing the same, the two of them sated after a day of sustained mating. Shep's away in an unfamiliar dreamland, one he's never visited before, rich in the deep red smells of Belle, when he's awakened by the familiar whirring purr of Chrissie's bicycle. He opens one eye.

"Whoa!" Chrissie calls, gliding in, then dismounting smoothly. "Two for the price of one!"

Shep flops his tail perfunctorily but doesn't jump up as he normally would. Instantly alert, Belle stares suspiciously at Chrissie as though she might be a black cat with evil intentions.

"Hi Chrissie," Peter hails her from behind the screen door, "behold our dog-tired lovers."

"Really?" Chrissie laughs.

"Mighty copulations throughout the daylight hours," Peter says, stepping out onto the porch. He's looking sort of rumpled himself. Both dogs stare at him beseechingly.

"Awesome," Chrissie says.

"Truly was," Peter says, "I only wish you'd showed up earlier, although it might have been a touch too raunchy for you."

Chrissie's come around to actually thinking it's sweet what a cornball Peter can be at times.

Shep, however, suspects that his amorous adventures may becoming the subject of ridicule and flops his head back down on the porch floor as though by way of rebuke. Belle continues staring at Chrissie.

"Who's she?" Chrissie asks.

"That's our lovely Belle," Peter explains, "one of old man Carlsen's dams."

"She's beautiful," Chrissie says.

"Sure is," Peter agrees, "but *hot*? Phew!" He waves a comic fan hand in front of his face.

"Right on!" Chrissie gives bewildered Belle a thumbs-up.

"Come on in," Peter says, holding the screen door open for her. They head into the big farmhouse kitchen where Peter's been concocting supper. "I got your message," he says, "sounded pretty urgent. What's up?"

"Yea, I hope it's cool, showing up like this, you know." Chrissie perches on a stool by the counter where Peter's got his salad greens in a colander, alongside a cucumber and a bowl of cherry tomatoes. "But your mum's got your sister visiting and they had like stuff to talk about that I don't think they needed me hearing."

"Quite so," Peter says, approaching his salad fixing like a maestro his piano. "Big clan clatter," he says. "Seems my father, who's been AWOL since I was in utero, has unexpectedly reentered the scene."

"Yea, Ginger told me," Chrissie says. "Talk about a flash from the past."

Peter precisely slices half the cucumber and slides the slices into a ceramic salad bowl. "My sister's taken it quite hard. She knew my father, of course, which I never did."

"It was her who found where he was, right?"

"Yes, she went so far as to visit him without saying a word to Ginger or me. Classic Irene. Control issues, you know what I mean?"

"Yea."

"Apparently the whole thing's made her really upset."

"But not you?" Chrissie cocks her head in a sideways parody of local TV's Rebecca Kleep.

"No. Why get upset about someone you never knew." Peter's slicing the golden cherry tomatoes in half and tossing them into the bowl with more panache than required. "He could have been an anonymous sperm bank donor for all I knew or cared."

Just like me, Chrissie thinks, but doesn't say. Instead she says, "Ginger thinks you're kinda like him in a lot of ways."

"Pah! Sons and mothers." Peter dismisses the notion. He knows Ginger sees a resemblance, but, to be honest, he dislikes any consideration of fatherhood, because it invariably brings up his own foundering. He says more seriously, "What happened with Cecilia and the baby . . . that was so bloody horrendous almost everything else, any of these sudden emotional squalls, seems pretty paltry by comparison."

"I guess." Chrissie can hardly bear to think about Cecilia and the baby dying that way. It's the saddest thing she knows of and makes her own weird trips growing up way less harsh than she'd thought back then. Whenever Peter mentions it, she kinda wants to hug him.

"I don't mean to diminish other people's feelings or experiences," he carries on, while adjusting the flame under a pan of tomato sauce, "it's just that having lived through what I did, I'm way less likely to get bowled over by almost anything."

"Sounds like enlightenment to me, man," Chrissie says in faux-hippie mimicry, trying to lighten the mood.

"Yea right," Peter says disparagingly, but appreciating Chrissie's clumsy attempt to move on. "More like scar tissue build-up than enlightenment," he says. "You good with salad and pasta, cheese, no meat balls?"

"Love it," Chrissie says, "plus your mum sent a bag of goodies."

"Yum. Sweet relief from my Spartan cuisine."

Peter pours a glass of red wine for each of them and guides Chrissie to a comfy old armchair in the living room. "So," he says, "we've got Shep and Belle engaged in red hot sex, my mother and sister deep into family dysfunction and you bursting at the seams with Big News. Do tell."

Chrissie takes a sip of her wine. She knows it's sorta weird that she's brought her story to Peter, but Ginger was tied up with her daughter and Sarina was out of town on some conference thing. It was either Peter or Garth, so here she is. Plus, well.

"You'll never believe it," she says, "but I just found out that Larry Illinger's been getting secret payments from the company that wants to build that garbage burner."

Peter stares at her for a moment, unable to quite assimilate what she's just told him. "Wow!" he says finally. "That *is* hot. How could you possibly have found that out?"

Chrissie gives him a run-down on the whole thing with Chazz. She still can't get her head around it herself. When she met with Chazz again back at the park, she was expecting something typically half-assed from him and was prepped to tell him that his Big Secret wasn't big enough. Then he lays this on, proof positive that his old man is on the take. Chazz even gave her photocopies of two cheques payable to a numbered company that his old man controls. Told her he'd planned to use the evidence himself against his father if push ever came to shove, but now they were needed to save his hide, so here they were.

"Ah, good old family values," Peter says. "Didn't it occur to this boy that his dad would know he was the leak?"

"That's exactly what I thought," Chrissie says, "but Chazz maintains he's like totally firewalled. Said there was all kinds of possible sources, and like absolutely no shortage of people who'd take a shot at Illinger if they could. Chazz figured he wouldn't be suspected because there'd be no reason for him to do it after his great reconciliation with his dad."

"Hmm. Prodigal sons should always be prime suspects," Peter says sipping his wine. "You have the photocopies with you?"

"Yep." Chrissie retrieves them from her backpack by the door and hands them over to Peter.

He switches on a lamp and examines the papers closely.

"It seemed so crazy, at first I thought maybe it was a set-up," Chrissie says. "You know, like a double-agent thing. Where we expose Illinger, only it isn't true and he comes off looking like the innocent martyr and Sarina's the scheming liar."

"Pretty good Hollywood plot for sure," Peter says, "except he's so far ahead in everyone's opinion, he hardly needs to be risking a dumb stunt like that."

"Yea, I know. I couldn't figure dick. That's why I wanted to check it with you, see what you think."

"So nobody else knows?"

"Chazz and me and you, that's it."

"Most interesting," Peter says. "Well, these cheques look authentic enough to me. We'd want to have an expert examine them, of course, and check out this numbered company, but if it is what it looks like, we've got a bombshell here. Three hundred thousand bucks under the counter. Wow."

"But what I don't get," Chrissie says, "is why would Illinger go for that? I mean, it's not like he needs the cash. Chazz wouldn't talk about it, but on the bike ride out here I flashed on the idea that maybe having to buy out Chazz's scumbag film-makers cost Illinger plenty and he needed cash fast."

"Quite possible," Peter says.

"The whole thing just seems mega stupid."

"What can I say? Money does funny things to people, especially to rich people."

"Like you, you mean?" Chrissie can't resist.

"Of course not," Peter says, "I get my kicks out of watching copulating dogs. Speaking of which, we should feed those two spent lovers after the strenuous day they've had. Following which we can properly celebrate what may prove to be the beginning of the end for our multi-million dollar burning barrel, not to mention friend Illinger's political career."

"Cool," Chrissie says, feeling relieved she's finally told her story to *someone*. She hadn't realized how wound-up she'd gotten just carrying the stuff inside her head. Now she feels like she just took off a super-heavy backpack and can relax all she wants.

While Peter's rattling in the pantry with the dog food, Chrissie gazes contentedly around the cozy old house. Strangely, despite her citified cynicism, she's come to feel more at home out here on the farm than anyplace else. What was it Ginger said in that first dumb interview Chrissie did with her? — something about bucolic dreams and pastoral fantasies. Who'd have guessed from that day to this. For her the farm's become a choice place and, yes, she has to admit it, Peter's a pretty cool dude. Plus, he's been really kind to her, paying her generously for helping out around Stone House and watching out for his mother since he's been back at the farm.

After dinner and a copious amount of fine wine, the two of them flop down on the living room couch together, giggling over something silly. Perhaps released by the imminent thrill of taking Illinger down, along with the mighty mating of Belle and Shep, there's a spirit of recklessness roaming the place.

"You good with me crashing on the couch tonight?" Chrissie asks.

"Wouldn't hear of it," Peter says. "But I'm unfit to drive you home and you're at least equally unfit to cycle that far."

"Could if I had to," Chrissie says defiantly.

"Unquestionably true," Peter concedes. "Fortunately you don't have to because there's a spare bedroom in the back, and I do mean spare."

"I'm good with spare," Chrissie says, as though she was royalty doing a bit of slumming for a lark.

"I'll bet you are," Peter says, suddenly more serious. Gazing at Chrissie through a haze of wine-soaked tenderness, he recognizes he's come to care for the girl in a way that's new to him. It's not like meeting Cecilia in the book shop that first time, not anything like it, but it is something. "You've been through some consequential shit in your time, haven't you?" he asks her.

The question startles Chrissie. She's not into self-pity at all. She didn't even fully realize what an absolute sewer she'd been living in as a kid until she got away from it. Then it was on to the next thing and the next. Same with Illinger and Harding; she'd just push through it. Angry? Oh, yeah, she could get fuckin' livid at the shit those kind of assholes would run on her. But it was always Fuck You! never Poor Little Me.

"Sorta," she says to Peter. He's looking at her in a kinda mushy way that makes her think of that first time she met him at Stone House. How weird he was. Since then he's been a different guy entirely. Someone she's come to enjoy hanging out with. Plus, the whole connection with Ginger, whom she loves. And Shep, of course. It's not safety they provide, she doesn't need safety. It's something else, something bigger.

"But it seems like you survived it all, whatever it was, amazingly," he says.

"I guess I kinda grew thick skin really early on," she says, "like your scar tissue."

"I think you're wonderfully gutsy," he tells her. "Like with this thing with — who is he? — Chazz. That takes some sass to pull a thing like that off."

"Yeah, sad ass Chazz. We had some times, me and him. Kids' stuff, though, you know? Gotta move on sometime." Truth is, she's feeling kinda slushy over Chazz just now. Like he really delivered on this thing with his dad. Big time. And he wasn't just covering his own ass, which was part of it. No, it was like a gift he was giving her, a farewell thing, kinda saying let's split as friends. She was stroked by that.

A long pause. Candlelight guttering from the dining table. The old farmhouse resting easy in the cool of the evening. "May I tell you something," Peter asks, "something I've never told anyone else?

"Yeah," she says, "go for it." She sorta hopes he isn't going to say how he's turned on to her, and she also kinda hopes he is. For sure she's finding herself more and more drawn to him. Which is weird. He's so not Chazz or even Sol. He's almost old enough to be her father, for one thing, and straight as a spoke. But there's something there between them, something she doesn't really know about. The two of them connect in a way she's never experienced before. She knows it's not just gratitude, the way it was with Sol, or horniness like with Chazz. It's got both of those in it, but other stuff too. Deeper stuff. She's somehow more herself around him. She's like that with Ginger too, but Ginger's sort of a saint, not an equal, even though she doesn't think so. For example, Chrissie would never tell Ginger about the secret language inside her head, how vicious she can be towards other people. It would be like telling homophobic jokes to the Pope. But she's told Peter about it, all the brutal terms she's got for Illinger and Harding and the rest. Peter laughed his head off and kept egging her on to say more. Bottom line: she knows she can trust him, absolutely, and trust is, as they say, one of her issues.

"I've told you already about how my wife Cecilia and our baby daughter were killed in a car crash," Peter begins.

"I think about it lots," Chrissie says. "It's like the saddest story I know."

"More than sad for me," Peter says, looking away, wondering whether he should.

"Tell me," she says, taking one of his hands in hers.

Peter stares ahead, seeing that concrete abutment hurtling towards him.

"I killed them," he says, almost a whisper.

She lets the words settle, like water birds alighting on a pond. One of the dogs out on the porch sighs in its sleep.

"I don't really think that could be true," she says at last.

"Not deliberately, of course," he says, "but through my negligence, my careless inattention."

"Tell me what happened," she says, drawing close, holding his hand against her.

So he does. He recounts the whole sordid story the way he's told it to himself a thousand times but never to another person. Even in the telling he can feel raw blocks of guilt and shame dislodging. He and the girl sit there together for a long time afterwards not saying anything.

⁂

Ginger can't quite believe what she's hearing as Chrissie explains how she's got a game-changer by the tail. Sarina looks completely bewildered, which is not something you imagine her ever being. The three of them are sitting in the Stone House library warmed by the glow of a brisk fire burning in the fireplace. Cold rain is sluicing down outdoors. Hundreds of eminent authors on the shelves, their own stories already immortal, listen in expectantly.

Chrissie tells the whole story, from the stupid porn movie and her getting fired to Chazz coming up with proof that his old man's on the take. Unbelievable really, but true. And Peter's confirmed that the cheques and numbered companies are for real.

"Of course it has to be an absolute secret," Chrissie tells them, "like where it came from and everything; Chazz can't be tied to it in any way." She'd debated whether to tell them the whole truth, but could see no way around it. She's kinda amazed with herself, how much she's trusting people in all of this, being as she's always had gut distrust as her default setting.

"Yes, of course," Ginger agrees, "we have to protect the boy at all costs. Having Larry as a father is punishment enough for anyone." The excitement she's feeling has all sorts of energies in it. A realistic chance to seriously impair the old boy's network that has abused the town for far too long. Her instincts about Chrissie proven in spades. Joy for Sarina. The need to proceed judiciously. And, unexpectedly, regret that Larry Illinger has exposed himself so recklessly. Ginger would far rather that Sarina wins the election on the strength of her vision rather than by their mugging her opponent.

"I agree completely," Sarina says, after Ginger's voiced her concern about shaming Illinger. "It smacks of what we've seen too much of lately, especially from some of the grey eminences in high places."

Chrissie's tripped up by this talk. Nothing like that had occurred to her. She'd discovered Illinger's vulnerability and thought it was a no-brainer that they just hammer the fucker as hard as they could. Sure, the porn flick scheme was maybe a bit of a stretch, more like a sleazy character assassination attempt, but not this.

"Yeah," she says, "but what he did was illegal. Forget the election, it's like a criminal act. There's poor people going to jail for shoplifting a loaf of bread to feed their kids, and this guy's gonna get away with hundreds of thousands? No way."

"I don't think it's a question of ignoring what he's done," Sarina tells her. "I'm not sure that his accepting the money is technically illegal, as it certainly would be if he was already mayor, but it does appear to be a breach of the public trust. No question he must be held to account. I think what Ginger's saying is that we don't want to be acting out of vindictiveness. Seeking revenge."

"I sorta do," Chrissie says.

Ginger laughs gently. "Ah, Chrissie," she says, "that's what I love about you."

"What's that?" Chrissie asks, thinking maybe the worst.

"Your audacity," Ginger says.

"Audacity?" Chrissie knows the word but doesn't connect it with herself.

"Yes, indeed," Ginger says. "Moxie, as we used to call it. Chutzpah.

Spunk. First class shit disturbing. It's how things get changed for the better, and you've got a real nose for it."

Chrissie thinks she's mostly got a nose for retaliation, payback, but that seems kinda shabby when you're talking to these two, so she just smiles at Ginger.

"So," Ginger says, "I think we're agreed we have an obligation to bring this matter to light. Sarina?"

"Yes," Sarina says, "but I'd still prefer it not be a humiliation game. We don't need any name-calling or finger-pointing. Certainly no gloating. Just let the facts speak for themselves."

"But how?" Chrissie says.

They bend their heads to strategizing and come up with a plan that's as clean and sharp as a surgeon's scalpel. Sarina takes on filling Garth in, though Chazz won't be mentioned. Chrissie will let Peter know what they've decided.

Before she leaves, Sarina gives Chrissie a big loving hug. "You're one swank grrrl, Chrissie," she says, "thank you for this."

Chrissie's kinda lovestruck being in her idol's arms.

After Sarina's gone, Chrissie remembers to ask Ginger how things went with her daughter.

"Remarkably well," Ginger tells her. "We've never been close, Irene and I, not as adults anyway, but something seemed changed on this visit, I think. I hope. She needs to go see her father again, and I'm intrigued enough to go have a look at him too, so we've made plans to visit him in a couple of weeks."

"You're going to go visit your old husband?"

"My ex," Ginger says with a smile. "Yes, I'll see what's become of him after half a century."

"Wow! That's what I call a separation."

Irene chuckles at the kid's irreverence. "It's more important for Irene in certain ways," Ginger says, "but talking with her now, I came to a clearer sense of how important it is for me too. It's one of those situations where there's a butterfly effect still rippling around in the family all these years later. My granddaughter, Irene's daughter, never met her grandfather and knows nothing about him at all, but his legacy's mixed up in her life whether she knows it or not. And even her young daughter's life."

"Yeah, Peter told me that you're a great-grandmother," Chrissie says. "Just about blew my mind."

"That's me," Ginger says, shaking her head. "Don't ask me how it happened."

"I wish I'd had a grandmother like you," Chrissie says, meaning it.

"Thanks, honey, and you would have made a marvellous granddaughter, believe me, but I haven't been much of a grandmother to Irene's daughter and an even worse great-grandmother to little Isha."

"I can't believe it," Chrissie says.

"Me neither," Ginger says with a rueful grin. "But there it is, one more victim of tragic circumstance. Anyway, we'll see how it goes on the trip with Irene. I've got a bit of a plan in my mind for the whole family. You never know, things might come out all right in the end."

"Yeah, I sure hope so," Chrissie says. "Like with Sarina, eh?"

"Oh, isn't it marvellous!" Ginger responds, clapping her hands. "Just between you and me, I'm thrilled to bits that Larry Illinger's finally going to get his comeuppance. Irene will be tickled too — she went to high school with Larry and disliked him as much then as the rest of us have for all these years in between. Still, I'm glad that Sarina is taking the approach she is. Taking the high road."

"Yeah, I just wanted to screw him to the wall for what he did to me, and even what he did to Chazz. But I see what you and Sarina mean."

"It's one of the tougher bits," Ginger says, "proceeding with integrity when every instinct's urging you to hatred and revenge."

"I guess. I can sorta see it when someone's old and wise like you, but Sarina seems to get it and she's hardly over thirty."

"Yes, she does," Ginger says. "A most remarkable young woman to be sure."

"I really like her," Chrissie says, "but I realized today that I don't know anything about her. She doesn't have a husband or kids, does she?"

"No she doesn't," Ginger says, "though I confess to harbouring a great compulsion to get her and Peter together. Of course I never say a word to either of them about it. At my age romantic scheming is entirely unseemly. And I'm not at all sure she's farm wife material."

Chrissie feels a freakish sort of spasm, thinking of Sarina, whom she loves, being with Peter who, yes, admit it, she loves. She pushes it aside for the moment. "I don't know if she's even into men," Chrissie says. "It's impossible to tell with her."

"Yes, it is," Ginger agrees. "Funny, we talk about everything under the sun, but not that. But this much we know: thanks to you, she's now well on her way to becoming one hell of a mayor."

"Yeah."

"Oh, and there's one other thing, Chrissie, if you don't mind my asking."

"What's that?"

"Well, you see, all of this commotion around Irene's father, how much she suffered from his disappearance . . ."

"Go on."

"It's none of my business, of course, but it did get me thinking all over again about the sorrow of being left, the unfairness of not knowing."

Chrissie sees right away where this is going. "You mean about my mum?" she asks.

"Yes."

"I don't want her to know where I am; I want nothing to do with her. Ever."

"I understand," Ginger says. "And I don't blame you in the least."

"But?"

"Well, from the little you've told me, I have the sense your mother's perhaps very troubled, but not malicious in any way. More ill than hurtful. Would you agree?"

Chrissie's kind of squirming, knowing Ginger's right, but not wanting to look back. Wanting the past to be past. "I guess so," she admits.

"It's just that a mother's love for her child runs dreadfully deep. To have a child disappear and not know . . ."

"I did send her a card," Chrissie says, sounding way more defensive than she wants to. "So she knows I wasn't murdered or anything . . ."

"Yes, and that's good. I don't want to press you, Chrissie," Ginger says, smiling. "It's just you may wish to put yourself in her shoes for a minute or two. Try and feel what it's like to be her, to not know whether your child is safe and happy."

"She doesn't care!" Chrissie blurts, suddenly close to tears.

"Possibly not," Ginger says softly. "Possibly not. But even if that's true, you've nothing to lose by considering her with compassion rather than anger or indifference. But chances are she does, dear, in her own perhaps tormented way, chances are she does."

Seventeen

Nigel's disappointed that the afternoon has turned filthy with a keen wind and spitting rain. He'd rather have had the meeting outdoors where things are more readily vented, but now he will have to receive them — his former wife and their two children — in a parlour at Strathmere. A nuisance, really, the whole business, but necessary somehow, one supposes. Even Menzies seems to feel the event might be salutary, although she was not at all convinced that Sophia's earlier visit had served any great purpose. Certainly it had stirred things up for Nigel, compelling him to revisit events and emotions he'd held in abeyance for going on half a century. Remarkable really how everything's telescoping down to singular moments, particles of time compressed in the same way diamonds are formed. Nigel's momentarily pleased with his metaphor.

But really, what's he supposed to say to these three who'll be arriving shortly. Sorry? Forgive me? What exactly is their purpose for crowding in at this late hour? Sophia didn't appear to have any clear objective on her previous visit and it's unlikely she's discovered one in the interim. For the life of him he could not connect that stocky and unimaginative lady with the charming girl he'd once loved. Nevertheless, in the days following her visit, he had found himself remembering facets of those early times together and something of the feelings he'd had for his young daughter. Memories that had lain dormant for decades became startlingly fresh for him. Descending to the level of cliché, he thought of the eggs or seeds of certain desert species that can lie waiting for many years before conditions are just right to trigger their emergence. God help us all.

But why Sophia would care to repeat the exercise he has no idea. And her brother. Somebody Nigel has never laid eyes on and wouldn't recognize if he passed him on the street. Ginger must be at the heart of this stirring. And what is he feeling now towards her, his former wife? That he did her wrong? Certainly. That she deserved better than him? Unquestionably. That things might have been better for everyone if he'd stayed in place? Well, no, here the certitude drops away. Would they have been better served with him still in the picture, would they really?

The marriage had been a bit of a debacle from the outset. He had badly muddled his feelings for Frankie Flynn with romantic delusions concerning that dear boy's sister. An easy enough mistake to make, of course, and not his alone either; nevertheless, a wiser man would have sensed the danger. Then to have little Sophia emerge as she did, so reminiscent of Frankie it was disquieting. At times he was convinced that the girl was a reincarnation of sorts. Her smile, her laughter, the sly way she'd glance at him sometimes. Absolutely uncanny. Yes, eventually there came to be a certain aspect of intoxication that he found both alluring and frightening. He did not trust himself. Of course he couldn't speak with Ginger about it; Frankie's shadow had already done sufficient damage to their marriage. He could not, would not seek professional help. His vanity forbad it. So he came to despise himself. His choices had been asinine from the outset and had led to a predicament that was intolerable. It could not hold. Something was bound to break, perhaps catastrophically. And so he must flee, simply get away and change his life course entirely. Which he had done. Clumsily. Hurtfully. Irrevocably.

After the break, his better self had known that he owed it to Ginger, and to Sophia, to contact them and offer some sort of explanation. But, try as he might, he could not. He simply couldn't find whatever words were required. No doubt some portion of his reticence was embarrassment, as well as cowardice, and some part the urgent need to place it out of mind forever. Once he'd put some distance between them, he became convinced the choice he had made was the right one. He was the better for it and so were they.

Now here they are again, Ginger and Sophia and the boy, trundling into his final days with all the dust and clatter of decades. Hurry up, please, it's time.

Dear Menzies ushers the three of them into the parlour where he sits waiting, then discreetly withdraws, closing the parlour door behind her. Nigel smiles warmly at his visitors, attempting to conceal his dismay. Sophia is as she was. The young fellow, Peter he thinks, at least in appearance a near copy of himself years ago. And Ginger. Outstanding still, as she was when first they met. She's got a quizzical grin on her face, as though this moment, which by rights should have at least a blush of poignancy about it, is really a bit of an amusement.

"Well, Nigel, you old reprobate," she says to him straight off, "we've tracked you down at last then."

"I suppose you have, yes," he says, somewhat disconcerted by her breezy tone. He has remained seated.

"You've seen Sophia, who's now Irene, not long ago," Ginger says, "and this, of course, is your son, Peter."

Peter steps forward and offers his hand. They shake hands and it's Nigel's impulse to hold his son's hand for a few extra moments. An admirable looking fellow with an appealingly gentle demeanour. Neither speaks.

Nigel's uncertain what he should do with Ginger, whether a handshake, a formal kiss, an attempted hug. Instead he says, "Do please sit down everyone."

Unhappily the three parlour chairs they seat themselves in are arranged in such a way that all three face him, as though this were an inquisition in the making. "I feel immensely awkward, really," he says to them.

"And so you should, Nigel," Ginger says, but without rancour. "As a husband and father you've been an unmitigated flop and so a bit of awkwardness on your part is entirely in order."

"Yes, I know," he responds weakly. "But . . ."

"However," Ginger interrupts him, "Irene and Peter and I have agreed that we shall let bygones be bygones, haven't we, darlings?" Peter and Irene murmur assent, Peter's perhaps a bit more full-bodied than Irene's. "We shall take the higher road," Ginger carries on good-naturedly, "perhaps even the path of enlightenment."

"Oh, my dear," Nigel says.

"Now don't start in with endearments at this late date," Ginger chides him, "it might smudge your enduring legacy."

My God, she's exceptional, Nigel's thinking. She must be closing in on eighty already and yet her life force seems as strong as when she was a girl, indeed stronger in some ways, certainly more self-assured. She's giving every indication that they're not here seeking retribution or demanding that he try to justify what is unjustifiable. He feels a wash of relief come over him. But how extraordinary that they have chosen not to berate him with grievances. He knows for a fact that, were the circumstances reversed, he would be sour with bitterness and animosity. Well, let's be honest, he wouldn't have initiated contact at all, would he? No, in a similar state of affairs, he'd be refining his grudges in solitude.

As though having read his mind, Ginger looks at him appraisingly for a moment.

"Do you remember," she says, "how on that dreadful day you abandoned us, you told me we'd thank you for it in the end?"

"I don't remember that," he confesses contritely. "Given the circumstances, it seems like a fatuous remark to have made, even for me."

"Dreadfully fatuous," Ginger agrees. "Asinine, in fact. And yet, you know, there was an element of truth to it."

"Surely not," Nigel says, discomfited.

Sophia, sitting alongside her mother, seems perturbed by the turn things are taking. Peter's observing it all with what looks like amused curiosity.

"Of course I couldn't see it at the time," Ginger continues, "or for a long while after. But in hindsight I've come to recognize that your leaving was a moment of emancipation for me."

"Indeed?" Nigel's startled by this notion.

"Unquestionably," Ginger says. "As much of a mess as you made of things, Nigel, your leaving wasn't all about loss. I truly found myself only after you'd gone, and I'm not at all sure I ever would have, had you remained."

With no idea how possibly to respond to this, he glances away from them all for a moment. But there's nowhere for his gaze to settle in the starkly formal parlour.

"Don't get me wrong," Ginger continues, "I fully appreciate how much you gave me in those early days. And what a marvellous father you were to Sophia. You opened so many doors for me, and I dread to think what might have become of me if it weren't for you."

Still Nigel can say nothing.

"But the remaining doors, those I needed to open for myself, and I don't know that I would have done so had we stayed together."

He nods in acknowledgement. She's right about this, he suspects. But the fault wasn't his alone, surely. It was so different back in those days, the expectations of the male and the female. He was supposed to be strong and assertive, a pillar of strength, all the things he really wasn't. She was supposed to be docile and dependent, things she certainly wasn't. He knew better even back then, of course he did, and so did she, but whether how they acted corresponded with what they knew . . .

"And of course," Ginger adds jauntily, "you gave me two wonderful children who've been the joy of my life." She glances lovingly towards Peter and Sophia. "And you know, Nigel," she carries on, "I'm genuinely sorry, for *you*, that you never got to share in their growing up."

"Yes," Nigel says, almost a whisper. He can't look at his children for the moment. Peter and Irene glance awkwardly about, and then for a moment share an understanding look between them.

There is something that Nigel knows he must say. He pauses for a moment, his old lips trembling. "Peter," he begins, looking directly at his son, "I'm sorry that I was never there for you as a father. And, yes, your mother's right, I regret that for my own sake as much as for yours. The times we might have shared."

Peter smiles back at him and nods in acknowledgement.

"Sophia," Nigel says at last, looking at his daughter. As she peers back at him he sees in her a glimpse of the girl she was. The girl he loved. "My dear," he continues, "I fear it was you that I hurt most of all by my regrettable behaviour."

Irene looks away, her face misshapen by sorrow.

"I'm more sorry than I can possibly convey to you, my dear, and I ask your forgiveness, I beg your forgiveness."

Irene plainly can't speak, can't even look in his direction. Ginger reaches across and takes one of Irene's hands in her own. On the other side, Peter does the same. The three of them sit there for a while, heads lowered, hands joined, silent except for Irene's gentle sobbing.

Sitting there, watching them, Nigel's feeling something very close to humility, which provides a surprisingly refreshing kind of sweetness. He feels unaccountably close to these three strangers from his past, more intimately bonded to them than to anyone else in his life.

Eventually, the overcast moves off and they're restored to themselves. Nigel and Ginger get to recalling old stories about the romance of their courtship, their honeymoon in England (a bowdlerized version, of course) and Sophia's birth. Even she, Irene, becomes enlivened remembering their adventures together when she was a child. All the memories teeter towards the dreadful break and yet the question at the heart of everything — *Why*? —is not asked. It is as though each of the four now recognizes there is nothing more to be wrung from it. A dreadful mistake, a culmination of mistakes made long ago that cannot be reversed. Better a few moments of loving forgiveness while there is still time. Forgiveness is everything.

As Nigel begins to tire and his visitors are preparing to leave, Ginger surprises him again by asking if he would be inclined to travel to Stone House for the family gathering at Christmas. To meet his grandchild and great-granddaughter. The offer brings him close to the tears he's been staunching throughout.

"I'm not sure," he says. "Of course I would love to. But the travel . . . I'm not sure. But thank you so much for the invitation. I'm touched by it, Ginger, truly I am. I would hope I can manage it. I'll certainly let you know."

Ginger then approaches him, takes his hands in hers and raises him slowly from his chair. She enfolds him gently in her arms so that his old heart flutters with love as it hasn't for so long. "Oh, my dear," he says, clasping her tenderly to him with the little strength he has left, "oh, my dear."

Chrissie and Shep have been left in charge of the farm while Peter's away. Not too onerous a burden this time of year, not like lambing season or spring planting or apple harvest, but still. Chrissie has come to flat out love the farm and she cycles over from Stone House as often as possible to spend time there with Peter and Shep. Which is weird because she's like a one hundred percent city person. She never even thought about where food came from or what animals actually do. All those times back in Scarberia when she'd make scrambled eggs for her whacked-out mom and herself — who knew how amazing it was to go into a hen house and gather from straw nests newly laid eggs still warm from the hen? Or to wander around a vegetable garden picking fresh strawberries maybe or a pod from the pea vines, which you'd slit open and pop a row of sweet fresh peas into your mouth. Yow. She's even taken over the veggie patch at Stone House since Peter's moved back to the farm. Of course she doesn't have a clue, but old Ginger fills her in on what's what. So now they've got tomatoes and cucumbers coming out their ears and just like a ton of beans and beets and carrots and everything.

From out of nowhere Chrissie's got her hands so deep into the earth they could start sprouting roots.

A rainstorm blew through earlier in the day and Chrissie's been out surveying the damage with Shep. A few things blown down here and there, but not too bad. Peter really knows what he's doing, though he always says his wife was the true farmer and he's just a paint-by-number copy artist. Pretty amazing guy really. Like hugely accomplished but no swagger at all. Maybe it's her imagination, but it seems to her as though Peter's lightened up a couple more notches since that night he confessed his guilt over the car crash. That was a very intense night, and not just about the accident either. There they were, the two of them sort of schnockered and blubbering away in each other's arms. It would have been so easy just to have a good fuck and get it over with. But they didn't. Not with his wife's spirit so close. It would have been like a sacrilege or something. So instead she went chastely off to the spare bedroom and slept like a baby. Next morning they both looked kinda sheepish, which Shep the paramour seemed to think was really funny.

She and Shep wander through the apple orchard under glistening fruits, then over to the barn where they enter its cool darkness. High up among the wooden rafters, barn swallows are swooping in and out and there's a soft cooing sound from unseen pigeons. Chrissie sprawls on a bed of straw in a corner and Shep nestles down alongside her, his head snuggled against her chest. She strokes the silky hair on his neck. What a beautiful creature he is. Smart. Loyal. Loving. She hugs the dog to herself and he responds with whimpers of pleasure.

As happens more and more these days, Chrissie feels a kind of joy stirring in her, sort of like the high she feels when she's totally in the zone on her bike, but with more added. There's a kind of peace moving in on her, something completely new and different. Part of it has to do with the farm for sure. And Peter. And Ginger. Shep whimpers again, and she says to him, "Yes, and you too, you're a jumbo part of it, aren't you?" Shep snuffles over the belated acknowledgement.

But it's true, he is. She feels the dog has discovered some core part of her and is methodically working it to the surface, the same way he'd fetch a stray sheep back down to the flock. Weird thing is Chrissie can't figure out how it's happening, just that it is. It started, she knows, with the day that Shep gave her the notebook and she broke down bawling. Then moving into Stone House, and what that's been like, getting to really know Ginger and being totally wired on Sarina's election campaign. And and and. The whole thing's better than any drug she ever took.

And, yes, she's been thinking about her mum, ever since that talk with Ginger. Even behind all the drugs and shit, it's probably true that her mum misses her on some level and worries about her. Chrissie's decided that she'll write a letter telling her mum she's fine, that she misses her and loves her. Not totally true, but what the fuck. And maybe not the beginning of any reconciliation — Chrissie's not sure she even wants that — but at least some sort of gesture towards her troubled mum. It feels like the right thing to do. Peter's agreed he'll mail it for her next time he's in the city, so she won't be traceable.

Listening to the gentle murmurings of the pigeons, lying here with Shep in her arms, she is, she realizes, also awaiting Peter's return.

⸺

The collapse of Larry Illinger occurred with stunning swiftness and remarkable ease. The election campaign had been proceeding along much the same lines as evident at the all-candidates meeting, with Sarina superlative at every turn, articulate and passionate, while Larry Illinger deftly consolidated his frontrunner position.

The campaign had inspired a crazy dreamer's zeal in Sarina's supporters. Ginger more or less stood calmly at the helm of the frenzied energy. Chrissie proved a genius at effective news releases and wildfire social networking. Even Peter got into the swing of things with his amazing computer skills. And Garth was as steady and meticulous as an atomic clock. Dozens of others pitched in as well with telephoning, fundraising, knocking on doors and all the rest. Together they were garnering far more support than anyone had anticipated and the talk around town was that the mayoralty contest, surprisingly, was turning into a real horse race. But even with the gap substantially narrowing, Illinger still looked to hold the upper hand.

Rather than incite a public brawl by exposing Illinger's clandestine dealings with the incinerator operatives — which had been Chrissie's original instinct — the decision was taken to proceed with stealth in order to better protect Chrissie and, ultimately, Chazz. Ginger's lawyer, Vaughn Krippen, undertook to contact an old friend now working in the upper echelons of the Attorney General's Department. Shortly thereafter, a senior adviser to the Attorney General paid an unannounced private visit for the purpose of reminding candidate Illinger that the receipt of undocumented emoluments by a private citizen was an altogether different matter from a similar transaction involving an elected official receiving funds from a corporation that stood to benefit substantially from decisions taken by that official.

The following morning, *The Shetterly Standard* carried a discreet front page announcement that Larry was, with regret and with great appreciation to his many supporters, announcing his withdrawal from the mayoralty race "for personal reasons." Although speculation as to what really triggered this dramatic about-face ran rampant around town, no further explanation was forthcoming and ex-candidate Illinger vanished from public view. Rumour had it that Larry, accompanied by his wife and son, had embarked on a Caribbean cruise in order to "get away from it all."

Following Illinger's startling withdrawal, the only other remaining candidate, Paul Vosher, also withdrew to throw his support behind Sarina. What support? the cynics wondered. (These same cynics had speculated for weeks that, over the course of the campaign, Vosher had become hopelessly besotted with Sarina.)

After such a tumultuous week, this evening there's a discreet gathering at Stone House to celebrate the incredible turn of events. The five co-conspirators — Ginger, Peter, Chrissie, Sarina and Garth — are clustered at one end of the enormous oval table in the dining room.

A champagne cork pops loudly and bubbly comes pouring up over Garth's hand. Everyone whoops as if they've never heard or seen such a thing before.

"A toast! A toast!" Peter calls once the flutes are brimming.

"Ginger, if you would, please," Garth intones assuredly, an arm extended towards Ginger. The others hush and turn to Ginger, their faces charged with reckless joy.

"Well," Ginger begins, beaming like an April sunrise, "isn't this too brilliant for words." She's wearing one of her retro-hippie tie-dye long dresses, and could reasonably be mistaken for Mother Earth's eccentric sister. Like everyone else, she's still riding high from the adrenalin rush of the last few days, the urgent phone calls and text messages, the growing sense of excitement that something really big was breaking. The turbulence had lifted her to a level of energetic stimulation she'd almost come to accept was a thing of the past.

"Oh, I tell you," Ginger says, with a sudden but not unfamiliar upwelling of tenderness towards them all, "this whole thing has done my old heart no end of good."

She glances fondly at this small group of friends, remembering similar celebrations for former campaigns — the women's shelter, the food bank, riverfront conservation lands, the recycling facility — each more of a struggle than it should have been, forever having to push against vested interests and dead brain inertia. Some causes lost, some won, and always the bracing camaraderie of fellow dreamers. Most of them gone now, her old comrades, replaced by younger faces, different ideas. But, she knows, the same underlying vision of true community.

"I still can hardly believe it," she says. "Only a few weeks back, I wouldn't have bet a bent loonie on our chances of pulling this one off." Nods and knowing grins all round. "It seemed like no matter how hard we worked, no matter how much finer a choice Sarina was in every way, we were going to get Larry Illinger as our next mayor and that dreadful incinerator would be a done deal. I can't say I felt despair, but I certainly wasn't feeling hopeful either."

"Well, you had us fooled," Peter interjects, "with all your true believer upbeat chatter."

"Yes, dear, but there are times when a touch of artifice is excusable, ends justifying means as they do. And then this splendid reversal!" She opens her arms as though she's dividing the Red Sea for everyone to walk across.

Sitting beside Ginger, Chrissie's got the goofiest grin on her face.

"I don't know that I've ever seen an episode quite like this one," Ginger continues, "and we've seen a lot of crazy episodes over the decades, right, Garth?"

"I've tried to keep the craziness to a minimum myself," Garth replies with a straight face, "but it's been a challenge with you along."

There's a palpable warm current of affection running between the two aging rabble-rousers. Perhaps they're both thinking that this might very well be their final campaign together.

"So," Ginger says, "I do believe it's time that we raise our glasses to Shetterly's next mayor-by-acclamation, her worship — and we do — Sarina Chand!"

They all stand up and raise their flutes. "To Sarina!" they exclaim in unison.

Sarina bows demurely to Ginger, then to Chrissie as well. A glob forms in Chrissie's throat and there's a warm mist rising behind her eyes.

Everyone but Sarina sits down again. Sarina tells them that as a relative newcomer she's humbled by the selfless work for the community done by so many over the years and especially at this critical juncture. Even in sandals, jeans and T-shirt, Sarina seems to embody impossible elegance. She thanks Garth particularly for his tireless efforts in assembling information on the proposed incinerator. "Because of Garth," she says, "we all know vastly more about this troublesome technology — tactfully she breezes across the reality that, other than Garth and possibly herself, no one can begin to comprehend the technical labyrinth of Garth's research — and I believe we can make a decision on it, and on preferred alternatives, informed by the very latest impartially generated data. Thank you so much, Garth."

Garth blushes like a schoolboy, able to glance only in brief flickers towards Sarina's affectionate attention. He strokes his goatee, clears his throat as though about to say something profound, but says nothing, instead nodding bashfully towards Sarina.

"And, of course," Sarina continues, "what can we say about the one person without whom none of this might have happened." Sarina pauses dramatically for a moment, then turns to Chrissie beside her and takes her hand. Chrissie's dying inside. With spilling-over affection for Sarina as well as Ginger and Peter and even old Garth. With batshit joy at what has happened, not so much Illinger's humiliation — well, maybe a bit — as Sarina's triumph. For other things she can't even identify. All of it beating like wild birds in her chest.

"It's not overstating things at all," Sarina continues, still holding Chrissie's hand in her own, "to acknowledge that this extraordinary woman has changed the fate of our town." Chrissie's cringing, like people are staring at her while she's back sleeping in the laundromat or something, only there's this amazing current she can feel pouring all through her from the firm clasp of Sarina's hand.

"We realize it's not something that can be spoken about outside this small circle," Sarina says, "but we four know it's largely Chrissie's courage and integrity that has prevented a dismal thing from happening here, a mistake that would have dragged a lot of other mistakes along behind it, degrading our community into something unrecognizable from what it is today."

Chrissie's so choked up she can't bear to look anywhere. Her? Changing the whole history of the town? What's in this champagne anyway? Plus, she's really not the Joan of Arc that Sarina's making her out to be. I mean, wanting to use a porn movie to humiliate someone, even an asshole like Illinger, isn't exactly a Gandhi-type tactic. Really Chrissie was more into spite than selflessness, at least at the beginning. But, yea, she did learn a ton of stuff, mostly from Ginger and Sarina, hard stuff about compassion and forgiveness. She's still not sure how much of it she buys, but what the hell.

Meanwhile, Sarina's on a roll. "Chrissie's fearlessness has set us instead on a new and better course," Sarina says, her tone kind of tender and sassy at the same time, "and for that we should be hugely grateful. Thank you, Chrissie."

The four of them raise their flutes again and drink to Chrissie. Then Sarina enfolds Chrissie in a tender embrace. Pressed against her, Chrissie can smell a rich scent of spices and blossoms. She holds onto Sarina for several life cycles, tears trickling down her cheeks, surrounded by joyful tumult.

Ginger gazes fondly at the two younger women, then says, "Well, we've had our share of victories over the years, and more than our share of disappointments too. But tonight's a good night for Shetterly, and I think for the future as well. With all this endless dreadful news of climate instability and refugees by the thousands fleeing impossible places, the bigotry and narcissism and selfishness of people who ought to know better, it's easy enough to surrender to despair, to imagine any effort is futile because the damage is already irreparable and the consequences inescapable. I remember once very early in life feeling just that way. I was only a child when word arrived at this very house that my brother Frankie had been killed in the final days of the Second World War. At that point, and for a long time afterwards, everything seemed to me more bleak and hopeless than I ever could have imagined." Here Ginger risks a glance at Peter and, marvellously, he smiles and nods to her.

"The point is," Ginger continues, "that despair begets despair just as hope begets hope. Only a naif would imagine that this is the best of all possible worlds, with so much injustice and suffering evident. But it would be even more misguided to ignore how much of beauty and goodness and compassion still moves among us. And the greatest mistake of all would be to embrace a belief that nothing can change for the better, that all effort is futile."

The others nod in agreement, even Chrissie.

"Tonight," Ginger continues, "we celebrate one tiny victory in an immense struggle. Peanuts perhaps. Possibly as insignificant as the pessimists would suggest. But we know there are other victories being celebrated all over the planet at this very moment. People like ourselves doing their little bit. Even amid the carnage and cruelty, the best of who we are refuses to submit. I've lived for eighty years, as I never tire of reminding you. The killing of my brother, the accidental death of Peter's wife and their baby, these are my personal small portion of the world's abiding sorrows. Sorrows that all the evidence indicates are going to worsen before conditions improve again. Or maybe don't. We all know that the human story represents less than an eye-blink in the unfolding of the universe. Nevertheless, it *is* our story and we do all get to add a few scribbles to it. For us tonight's a perfect couplet perhaps. Tiny, of course. Possibly irrelevant in the greater scheme of things. That we can't know. What we do know is that we're better people and our community a better place because you cared. Perhaps that's all we can ask of ourselves and each other. That we care. That we love one another, as I think we five feel this delicious affection for one another right now."

⟡

A bright autumn morning some days later, Ginger can tell by the ring tone of the phone that it's sour news coming, as though there's a call display for sorrow.

"Hello, Mother," Irene says in a muffled voice.

"Good morning, dear," Ginger says, "what is it?" She's instinctively thinking *problem*, likely involving Crystal or Isha.

"Dad," Irene says.

"Yes?" Ginger asks, knowing immediately.

"They called last night," Irene says, "that Menzies woman. It was quite late and I didn't want to disturb you."

"Yes," Ginger says again. Through the kitchen window she watches a scurry of squirrels industriously harvesting nuts and seeds from the trees.

"She said he passed away quietly in his sleep last night."

"Ah, yes, good. I'm glad it was a gentle death."

"Me too," Irene says. Ginger can't tell if her daughter is sobbing.

"Well, I'm sorry he's gone, even though he was gone for so long," Ginger says. The news hasn't entirely sunk in yet, as the news of death sometimes doesn't, as if it were an unfamiliar object she's holding in her hand, attempting to discover its purpose. Nigel dead after all this time.

"I just wish we'd gotten to spend more time with him," Irene says, a taste of bewilderment in her tone.

"Would it really have made any difference, do you think?" Ginger doesn't know that it would. Except that out of nowhere she's now picturing Holly Martins at the end of *The Third Man*, alone in the dark as Anna Schmidt walks coolly past him and away into the night. She's reasonably certain that Nigel must have died a lonely man, and that the visit from Irene and herself and Peter had, if anything, only underlined his aloneness. But maybe not. Quietly in his sleep. Yes, that would be Nigel.

"It was death that brought us together in the first place, you know," Ginger says. "I'm sure I've told you a hundred times."

"I don't think so, Mum," Irene says. "Tell me." As a child Irene had overheard occasional references to Uncle Frankie, his tragic loss in the war, but the topic was only ever lightly touched upon then dropped. After her father had abandoned them, she had no interest in any story in which he played a part.

Ginger recognizes that even a time-worn story is important for Irene just now. "Your father and my brother Frankie became friends during the war," she says, smiling to herself at what unscarred innocents they were, herself a child, her gallant soldier brother, and his elegant friend whom she'd come to love. "While he was in France," she tells her daughter, "Frankie wrote to Nigel back in England, and that was the last any of us heard from him; he was killed a day or two later."

"I remember you and Dad talking about it," Irene says.

"As chance would have it, some years after, Nigel was one of my professors at college and when he learned who I was, he showed me the letter. It was Frankie's death really that brought us together."

"I don't believe you've ever told me that part of the story," Irene says.

"There must be lots I haven't told you," Ginger admits, "among the many casualties of our peculiar marriage."

"Why did it fail, Mum? Was it just that man friend of yours you told me about? What really happened?"

It's a question Ginger tumbled around in her mind for years, then gradually less and less, and eventually more by way of habit than productive questioning. But initially, with Irene a sullen teen and Peter a babe in arms, she was wracked with it constantly. She'd spent more than a dozen years with Nigel in what had seemed to her a more or less reasonable accommodation. Not perfect, certainly, not the romantic confection she'd imagined back in those swooning days when they were courting. But what marriage is? None of her girlfriends from college had fared much better than she, except perhaps Dorothy who'd married a dashing ethnobotanist with whom she'd enjoyed a life of invigorating exploration in unimagined places. Little Dot and Indiana Jones — it was too perfect. But for others, certainly for poor Patsy and Diane, a variation on her own story: Poof! He's gone. Maybe they at least got an explanation.

That's what was maddening about Nigel, Mr. Word-for-every-occasion. That when it really mattered he had absolutely nothing to say for himself. A promise that he'll be back shortly to talk it all through, a promise never kept. A promise that he'll write an explanatory letter to his devastated daughter, not kept either. Starting and ending on broken promises. After that, just days, then weeks, then months of waiting. She knew he wasn't dead because the child support arrived regular as clockwork. Nothing else. Never a birthday or Christmas gift for the kids, nothing like that. She fought the whole time against self-pity and made sure the children never caught her weeping, though she did her fair share of it. And against guilt, too, the persistent nagging that it was somehow her fault, that she'd driven him off, become indifferent to him, selfishly stopped giving him the support she knew he required. That she could have and should have been a better wife.

But mostly she'd come over time to realize that Nigel was disloyal to himself at least as much as to them. That he had walked out on himself. Whether from disgust or shame or boredom or just what she could only speculate. Perhaps he'd simply wearied of being always on stage centre. Perhaps he couldn't live another minute with the artifice he knew himself to be. Perhaps *ad infinitum*. Oh, yes, she spent a disgusting amount of time doing battle with Nigel's ghost, trying to get one up on him, shamelessly wanting his unhappiness. Then, after how many years, he was truly gone. So was her anger, most of it. No longer an issue. She got on with who she was, not the waiting-for-Nigel shadow she'd been for too long. She wasn't going to spend the rest of her life under the malignant influence of his not being in it. She got back to being Ginger Flynn and felt the better for it. Eventually she could laugh about it all, poke fun in her mind at the flimsy caricature she named Flighty Nigel.

Except for the price her daughter had paid and continued to pay. Right up until now.

"Mum?" Irene's waiting on the line.

"Sorry, dear, I was drifting."

"Did he ever tell you why he left us?"

"Not really, no. There wasn't another woman," Ginger says, "he did tell me that, and I think truthfully."

Irene waits. "You know, Mum, I've always felt that I was to blame somehow, that it was something to do with me that caused him to leave."

"Yes, I sensed all along that you felt so," Ginger says, "and it broke my heart not to be able to convince you otherwise." So long ago now. She doesn't really want to go back there, but she will for her daughter's sake. What really did he say before leaving?

In the silence Ginger decides to take a risk. "Darling, I've never asked you this before, and I'm not sure I should now," she says tentatively.

"What is it?"

"Did your father ever . . . touch you or behave with you in an inappropriate manner?"

"Mother!" Irene is shocked at the suggestion.

"Think carefully, dear." Ginger herself must tread carefully too. "You were so close, the two of you, I did use to wonder if a possible explanation for your father's leaving was that he was finding himself improperly attracted to you and felt he needed to remove himself before some real harm was done."

"Oh, Mum, I don't think so, really I don't. I mean, we'd hug and stuff, but nothing sexual, I'm sure not. I'd remember that."

"So you never felt in any way violated by him?"

"Only by his leaving; that was a complete violation."

"Yes, yes. Well, I'm relieved to hear that the other wasn't an element. I've sometimes wondered, but been rather afraid to ask." Ginger remembers that in fact she did try to talk with her daughter about this very thing, but each time Irene flew into such a rage, she dropped it. Such things were not spoken of back then.

"Afraid? Of me?"

"Yes dear, we all are."

"Really?" Irene ponders this, as though, peculiarly, it has never occurred to her. She sets it aside for the moment. "Is there any other possible explanation for his leaving?"

"Oh," Ginger really doesn't want to say.

"Mum?"

"Back before I met your father, he and my brother had been very close." Ginger pauses, testing out her words carefully.

"Are you saying . . ."

"Yes. Yes I am. It too was not something mentioned openly in those days. Not beyond Cambridge anyway. But from the bit Nigel did disclose, it was obvious he felt your uncle Frankie was the love of his life. I'm more or less convinced that he took up with me as a surrogate of sorts, a stand-in for my brother."

"Oh, Mother, this sounds rather far-fetched, doesn't it?" Irene's bumping up against boundaries again. As she must. "I mean, surely you'd know, being together that long."

Ginger hesitates, then finally says, "I suppose I did know, darling. Almost from the start I knew. So did he. We never spoke of it, that's the confounded thing. And over time it no longer seemed to matter. It became one of those uncomfortable subtexts that can be glossed over with no real damage done. Or so you think. Until something snaps. Then you're left to wonder what element, if any, it might have played in the snapping."

"You suppose he might have left you, left us, for a man? Is that what you're saying?" A sharpness now in Irene's voice.

"Oh, I shouldn't think so. No. If it had been something as cut-and-dried as that Nigel would have said so. No, with your father it would have to be something much more convoluted and esoteric. For a while I did think he might have been diagnosed with some dreadful condition, an incurable cancer or something, that he wished to spare us from. But that obviously proved not to be the case. No, I think perhaps he was beset by some inner torment that he simply couldn't talk about. I did take to wondering whether he might himself have been abused as a child. Some sort of trauma must have caused him to blot out his parents so completely."

"Same way he blotted us out, you mean?" Irene asks.

"Yes. And you know, I think he'd even blotted out Frankie's memory after the war, the person he loved most in the world, and it was me who happened to revive it for him."

"It's hard to believe, isn't it," Irene asks, "that he could be so brilliant and so screwy at the same time."

"Yes, dear, it is. As I mentioned when we visited him, for myself I feel in the long run that I've benefitted immensely from being out from under your father's shadow. It's a particular kind of tyranny people like him, the gifted but flawed, exercise over others. Not deliberately, perhaps, or even consciously. But it's a cold shadow they cast over those too close to them."

"I never felt that," Irene says, "before he'd left, I mean."

"No, you wouldn't have," Ginger agrees. "You were in his light, not his shadow. But his leaving was part of his shadow-self." Ginger doesn't add that Irene's been under that shadow ever since, whereas she herself has not. She knew it best, that she had strengthened after his leaving in a way she wouldn't have if he'd stayed when Cecilia and the baby were killed. She was strong enough to pick up the sorrow of that tragedy and carry it, for Peter as well as herself, while Irene avoided the whole thing, sequestered herself from her brother's grief the same way Nigel would have done. She suddenly remembers that conversation with Nigel, back in his "digs" when they were discussing Orwell and historical revisionism. How Nigel had surprised her with his contention that we all revise our own stories in hindsight. How did he put it? — *Editing out the bits we're too ashamed of, shading events in memory so they're no longer quite what they were, even outright self-deception where required.*

Yes. She won't say this to Irene. But yes.

"Do you think he would have come to Stone House for Christmas?" Irene asks.

"I really don't know, dear. In hindsight I realized I shouldn't have invited him without first discussing it with you and Peter. But it seemed the thing to do at the moment."

"I was shocked when you did," Irene admits. "But afterwards I thought it was very smart to do. I even started looking forward to his being there, as if there would have been some sort of completion. I don't know. I'm sorry now it's not going to happen."

"Me too," Ginger says. "Did you speak with Miss Menzies about funeral arrangements?"

"Apparently he left very clear instructions that he wanted no kind of funeral or memorial service. A simple cremation, nothing more. No obituary in the papers."

"I see." Nigel's final disappearance.

"The Menzies woman said he'd left a will, a modest estate, was how she put it. She's obviously seen it already, maybe she helped draw it up for all we know."

"I hardly think so, dear."

"Well, surprise, surprise, he's left everything to that Strathmere Lodge *because of the comfort and care he enjoyed here in his final years*," Irene mimics Miss Menzies.

"Not all that unusual," Ginger says, "I may do the same myself when I get old."

"Oh, Mother! It's not what you do when you've got a wife and kids you could leave it to. I fully intend to find out how much is involved — of course, Menzies wouldn't tell me — and whether there's a reasonable chance of contesting it."

"Perhaps give it a day or two, dear, it might entail more anguish than it's worth."

"I know, I know, and they may have sucked him dry already. But, if not, at least some of it should end up going to Crystal and Isha."

Ginger doesn't want to say that Isha meant nothing to Nigel. Nor did Crystal. He likely didn't know of their existence, his granddaughter and great-granddaughter. The Tolpuddle Martyrs would have meant more to him. What his feelings in the end were towards Irene, the daughter he'd once cherished, or indeed towards herself, we'll never know. And that's his ultimate betrayal, that denial of connection. It's the bottom of the well of abandonment. Fighting over a few coins in the mud won't make any of that better.

⊱⊰

So there he's gone at last. Nigel on the night train. After being lost for so long, is this any greater loss. O, Death, where is thy victory? What thoughts did he have in those final hours, I wonder, or had he wandered already into dark caverns of shadows where words and thoughts disassemble. A man gifted with words, though not a man of his word. The Word was made flesh. I knew I loved him that day he told me about himself and Frankie. My gorgeous brother. And this man his lover. Both dead now, and where's the difference. I'm sure I spent time, back in those early days, wondering if all his love his only love was for men. But I truly don't remember ever thinking that he could not love a woman. Not love me. Not love anyone, perhaps, even Frankie. He may not have known himself back then. There's none so blind. Fools for love. Why do fools. Of course I should have known. So should he. Even after taking a wrong turning, we might have made it right somehow. But what was the wrong. We longed for beautiful communions, but loss was already in the longing. Frankie gone long ago, then Mother and Father, then sweet Cecilia and little Cagey, and now Nigel at last. My own death approaching like a new moon, silent and beguiling. O, Death, where is thy sting? Not a part of life at all, but perhaps as beautiful in its own way. Old John Muir it was, wandering his beloved mountains, contemplating the joyous inseparable unity of death and life. All divine harmony. Time to say goodbye to Nigel.

It's a mark of his deep regard for both Ginger and Peter that Vaughn Krippen has come to Stone House for a meeting. Irene is here as well, having arrived last evening, plainly still mourning the father she despised for so long. She's even decided, she announced at dinner last night, that she's changing her name back to Sophia. "I looked at Irene and all I could see was ire," she told Ginger and Chrissie. "Call me a flighty fool if you want," she said, "but I think Sophia fits me better now."

Vaughn's recently returned for the Christmas holidays from his winter home in Costa Rica and is unseasonably tanned. His long silver hair gives him what Ginger calls his leonine look. The four of them are sitting in wingback chairs in the library with a brisk fire burning in the fireplace, Peter having delivered a truckload of seasoned maple from the farm. Visible through one of the mullioned windows, Chrissie's out on the frosty lawn, tossing a Frisbee for Shep to catch and retrieve.

Dressed in a very smart business suit, sipping occasionally from a glass of single malt whisky, Vaughn's been talking for a good half-hour, summarizing the legal goings-on around the Congregation of the Great Convergence. He sprinkles his narrative of the churchly implosion with a dizzying cast of characters including the Superior Court of Justice in Bankruptcy and Insolvency, the Official Receiver with the Office of the Superintendent of Bankruptcy, various liquidation officials, the Trustee in Bankruptcy, an order from the Court of Queen's Bench under the Companies' Creditors Arrangement Act (known as the CCAA) and the court-appointed monitor in the CCAA process.

Everyone's smiling politely at Vaughn, trying to disguise the fact that none of them has much of a clue what he's talking about. Eventually it's made clear to the group that the Congregation has been effectively terminated and is being, in Vaughn's words, "systematically dismantled even as we speak." In his lawyerly way he seems to be deliberately teasing out the saga so as not to reveal the principal item of interest — the disposition of Stone House — until an ultimate climax to his narrative has been duly reached.

Finally Ginger looks him squarely in the eye and says, "Vaughn, as fascinating as we're all finding these legal complexities to be, and as much as we appreciate your scrupulous attention to detail, you know that we're hanging on every word awaiting something of substance about the one pressing item you seem determined not to mention."

Vaughn's smile is a masterpiece of impossibly white teeth and glinting blue eyes.

"My dear," he admits, "forgive me, you're quite right. But who could resist such a delicious opportunity?"

"We won't be toyed with, counsellor," Ginger says, laughing. "Now out with it!"

Vaughn smiles even more broadly than before. Just then a log collapses into the fire with an eruption of sparks.

"Yes, indeed," Vaughn says, "I'm delighted to be able to tell you that the best of all possible outcomes is within our grasp. Not today or tomorrow, but following a somewhat tedious series of legal formalities, Stone House will eventually be returned to Ginger's sole and exclusive ownership."

There's a detectable collective sigh.

"So you're telling us, are you, Vaughn, that it's a done deal?" Ginger asks. She's feeling a girlish exhilaration at what she thinks she's hearing.

"I's to dot and T's to cross," Vaughn says, "nothing more than that, I can assure you. The place is yours and yours alone."

Peter lets out a whoop of celebration and the mood of juridical solemnity quickly dissolves into excited chatter and congratulations. Even Sophia is swept up in the giddiness. Vaughn is heaped with accolades for his masterful handling of the case, although he assures them it was nothing a competent law student couldn't have done, but stops short of acknowledging most of the legwork was in fact accomplished by diligent functionaries at his law firm while he tanned himself beneath the Costa Rican sun.

Ginger's thrilled to bits. Not for herself so much. But for the possibilities that can now open up after she's gone. She's thought about this lots, what the house and grounds could eventually become, but never with great conviction so long as the Congregation still stood to acquire the property once she left it. But now. Now she can really set to serious scheming. She vaguely envisions the place serving the public good in some fashion. Maybe affordable housing or an environmental centre or a school for disadvantaged kids, who knows. She'll have to think it over. Perhaps set up some kind of trust fund or foundation. Sarina and Garth will help, she knows, Peter of course and maybe Chrissie too. She hopes so. Sophia may have other ideas of her own, and it will take some finesse to ensure that whatever's decided does not exclude her daughter or invite future conflict. In any event, Ginger's reasonably sure some good will come of having the place back in the family's hands, and that probability makes her old soul immensely happy.

⊁⊰

When Peter arrives at Stone House for Christmas dinner, he's got Shep with him and a suspicious looking bundle tucked under his coat. Greeting him at the door, Chrissie guesses right away what it is, mostly because Shep's looking so pleased with himself. Sure enough, it's a tiny pup with absurdly oversized paws and ears.

"Omygod!" Chrissie exclaims, reaching out to touch the little tyke. "It's like *so* adorable."

"Ridiculously so," Peter says, passing the pup over so he can take off his coat. Chrissie holds the furball in both hands, lifting it to her face for mutual sniffing while the little dog yelps scratchily.

"A female, as you can tell," Peter says.

"How long have you had her?"

"Couple of days. Old Carlsen likes to keep them with their mother for at least ten weeks."

"Oh, she's a beauty," Chrissie says, kissing the pup on its head then putting her down on the floor. The pup scrambles over to Shep and tries to entice him into a game of bluff and scuttle.

"Have you named her yet?" Chrissie asks.

"Not exactly," Peter admits. "I'm in a bit of a pickle about it."

"How so?"

"Well, you see, back when old Carlsen and I were discussing having Shep and Belle mate, he requested that if I chose a female as pick of the litter — and who wouldn't? — I'd name her Cecilia."

"Oh!" Chrissie gasps as though shocked.

"Peculiar as he is, the old guy was strangely attached to my wife, and very helpful with her training Shep, wasn't he, sport?"

Shep looks up from licking the pup but is not quite his usual attentive self.

"Anyway," Peter continues, "I felt I couldn't refuse his request. I could have dodged the issue by selecting a male, I suppose, but this little beauty captured my heart the moment I set eyes on her."

"Kinda like Cecilia," Chrissie says with a grin.

"Precisely. So I had no choice but to take her, and Carlsen lost no time in reminding me of his initial request."

"But?" Chrissie asks.

"Well, I have to admit I'm not a big fan of giving human names to dogs. Maybe Belle and Bess, that type of name, fits okay, especially for a sheepdog. But Cecilia? With all that emotional baggage. I don't know. I'm not at all comfortable with it."

"I can see what you're saying," Chrissie agrees.

"But I did promise old Carlsen."

"Yeah." Chrissie ponders for a bit, pursing her lips in thought. "What if you were to call her Lia?"

Peter considers only briefly. "Now that is a *really* smart suggestion," he says. "Lia. I like it. I really like it."

"Let's see if she does," Chrissie says, bending down and calling to the pup that instantly races over to Chrissie's outstretched hand.

"I think she relates to it!" Chrissie says smiling at Peter.

"And to you, too, I daresay. Speaking of which, how would you feel about taking the tyke on?"

"Me?"

"Certainly. She'll need some mothering for a while at least and neither of us is really up to the task, are we, sport?" Peter addresses Shep.

Shep focuses on his firstborn, pretending not to have heard Peter.

"Oh, Peter, that is so wicked awesome," Chrissie gushes. "Thank you, thank you." She can feel herself beginning to get misty and disguises the tears by giving Peter the hugest hug.

"Merry Christmas, Chrissie," Peter says, holding her close, the way he did that night she helped absolve him of his sin. Inescapably he's remembering the day he first brought Shep home for Cecilia, a pup like this one, his wife's delight just like this girl's. He's not such a fool as to underestimate the significance of what he's doing. This is more than a simple gift. How much more he's not entirely sure. And where it might lead he's not certain either. But he does know that he's opening himself to possibilities, just as he had with Cecilia, but never since, and that those possibilities, as before, can include death and pain and crippling remorse, just as they can transcendent happiness. He'll take his chances, he supposes.

"Merry Christmas," Chrissie echoes, also through damp clouds of remembering. Everything. She lingers in the man's warm embrace.

"What's all this then?" Ginger asks, emerging from the kitchen armed with a spatula and wearing a ridiculous Rudolph the Red-nosed Reindeer apron. "Hugging and puppies, you'd think it was Christmas Day or something. I swear to God, despite my best lefty efforts, this whole family's devolving into a sentimental Hallmark greeting card. Oh, but, isn't that little tyke divine!"

"I was just explaining to Chrissie," Peter says, "how this pup needs a good mum."

"Just as you did, you mean?" Ginger asks.

"Still do," Peter says enfolding her in a gentle hug. "Merry Christmas, Mother."

"Merry Christmas, darling," Ginger says, loving the warm tenderness of him, her son, and the strength of him too, strength restored at last. Sophia will be arriving shortly, with Phil and Crystal and Isha. Ginger's tribe. She wishes Sarina was here as well today, but she's gone to spend the holidays with her mum. Garth's away with family too.

Ginger's especially thrilled to have her granddaughter and great-granddaughter coming, as she sees so little of them. She's also hoping that their visit could be an opening that might just possibly lead to having Crystal and Isha spend next summer here. They could surely benefit by getting away from the toxic scene they've been stuck in since the divorce. Ginger knows that having Chrissie here will help a lot with Isha. And the pup's darling enough to demolish the girl's unpleasant cynicism.

"So this is the mighty offspring of Shep is it?" Ginger asks, pointing her spatula at the little pup cavorting on the floor.

"We've just named her Lia," Chrissie says. "What do you think?"

"I think that's a fine name," Ginger says, "a very fine name indeed." She walks across to give Shep due congratulations. *Finally* noticed, Shep wiggles with pleasure and pride. Chrissie kneels to give him a loving hug as well.

"Can you imagine a better dad than Shep?" Chrissie asks, looking up, and actually none of them can.

ABOUT THE AUTHOR

Des Kennedy is a novelist, essayist and veteran back-to-the-lander. The author of nine previous books, in both fiction and non-fiction, he has been three times nominated for the Stephen Leacock Memorial Medal for Humour. He's contributed many articles on environmental issues, gardening and rural living to a wide variety of publications in Canada and the United States, and has been featured on numerous regional and national television and radio programs. Des is a celebrated speaker, known for his passion and irreverent wit, and has been active for many years in environmental and social justice issues. He and his partner Sandy live a conserver lifestyle in their hand-built house surrounded by gardens and woodlands on Denman Island, B.C. [PHOTO: BOOMER JERRITT]

MARQUIS
Québec, Canada